W9-BBP-126

Borzoi Books IN *Political Science*

EDITED BY *V. O. Key, Jr.,* HARVARD UNIVERSITY

ADMINISTRATION *by Albert Lepawsky* 1949

A GRAMMAR OF AMERICAN POLITICS
by Wilfred E. Binkley and Malcolm C. Moos 1949
(REVISED AND ENLARGED EDITION 1952)

PUBLIC ADMINISTRATION *by Herbert A. Simon, Donald W. Smithburg, and Victor A. Thompson* 1950

THE ADMINISTRATION OF AMERICAN FOREIGN AFFAIRS *by James L. McCamy* 1950

PUBLIC AND REPUBLIC *by Alfred de Grazia* 1951

THE GOVERNMENTAL PROCESS *by David B. Truman* 1951

ELEMENTS OF POLITICAL SCIENCE
by Alfred de Grazia 1952

PUBLISHED IN NEW YORK BY

Alfred A. Knopf

The

ELEMENTS

of

POLITICAL

SCIENCE

ALFRED DE GRAZIA

The
ELEMENTS
of
POLITICAL
SCIENCE

NEW YORK: ALFRED A. KNOPF

1952

L. C. catalog card number: 51–11105

THIS IS A BORZOI BOOK
PUBLISHED BY ALFRED A. KNOPF, INC.

Copyright 1952 by Alfred A. Knopf, Inc. All rights reserved. No part of this book in excess of five hundred words may be reproduced in any form without permission in writing from the publisher, except by a reviewer who may quote brief passages and reproduce not more than three illustrations in a review to be printed in a magazine or newspaper. Manufactured in the United States of America. Published simultaneously in Canada by McClelland & Stewart Limited.

FIRST EDITION

To

MY FATHER AND MOTHER

INTRODUCTION

M Y AIM in this book is to introduce the student who has had no previous training in political science to its proper elements, in their most useful order, and with appropriate emphasis. The book is designed to be a first glimpse of a field of vast importance and universal interest, a glimpse, it is hoped, that will stimulate not only a general interest in the ever fresh problems of political science but also a special interest, among a fair number of students, in political science as a gateway to a thorough liberal education. From this book, the beginning student should be able to move easily into more concentrated studies in courses concerning political parties, American government, comparative government, international relations, and other special fields of political science.

The best books of political science are broad in scope, logical, and well grounded in the facts of political life. Like Plato and Aristotle, recent respected political scientists regard the field of politics as covering the most important problems of community living. The study of the form these important problems take is political science, and the study of political science, like the other sciences, rests on facts. Today we have increasingly accurate means of gathering and analyzing facts. Field surveys, sample polling, and intricate systems of punch-card tabulation and analysis are several of the techniques for studying human behavior that annually increase our reliable knowledge and make possible a better political science than had our predecessors. If we accept the good life as defined by great moral philosophers like Aquinas, Spinoza, or Jefferson, we have readier ways than they had of demonstrating how such a good life may be achieved. There are exciting possibilities in the future of political science, and it is hoped that this book will help to reveal them.

The work is divided into four parts. The first describes how scientists study political subjects, what those subjects are, and how the ordinary person can think correctly about politics. It then focuses on the state and on authority as the central concerns of political science.

The second part introduces the reader to some of the basic elements of political behavior: leadership, political groupings, public opinion, representation, party organization, and the use of economic, psychological, and coercive pressures in politics—all of which occur very generally, on all levels of government, in all political institutions, and in the pursuit of all kinds of goals.

The third part of the work discusses the common and specialized structures of government within which much of political behavior occurs. These structures are laws, constitutions, legislatures, executives, administrative agencies, and courts. It then takes up the study of the levels of political organization—local, national, and international. Enough of the main facts about key political institutions are given to enable the student to comprehend how the basic elements of political behavior operate within, influence, and are influenced by such institutions.

The last part of the work is in a large sense the continued study of the problems of Part I, now clarified in the light of our knowledge of political behavior and institutions. It discusses how men strive to realize their major goals by political action that is calculated to bring specific results. It inquires into the main branches of democratic thought and the moral and scientific obstacles to the realization of democracy. Finally, it investigates the nature of public policy and considers how policy affects private rights, and how it may be made more rational and productive of liberty.

Several years ago, when I began to write this introduction to political science, I scarcely appreciated how difficult the task would be. As my work progressed, however, I realized more fully the handicaps under which political scientists labor. Textbooks in political science are not simply a matter of will and patient competence. If they were, we would be easily supplied. Unfortunately, although political scientists are no less well trained, clear thinking, or logical than the natural scientists, their subject matter, as I have attempted to show in this book, presents special difficulties from which the natural sciences are exempt. In addition to the indefinite nature of social facts themselves, many of which lack any identity whatsoever save our calling them by a name (for instance, "social class," a "leader"), one encounters in human affairs a profusion of elusive values (for instance, "freedom of opportunity," "effective leadership") that cause no end of theoretical and practical difficulty.

Furthermore, beyond this intrinsic difficulty, which political science shares with the other social sciences, lies another, peculiar to political science: the problem of reducing to logic, order, and principles the greatest movements, motives, and institutions of mankind. Aristotle was the first but certainly not the last of scientists to be struck by the vast scope of political science. Nevertheless, since man has created the state, some science must study it, and the great tradition in political science has never quailed before the seemingly unfathomable mysteries of man's most complex creations. Political scientists have always undertaken to say what can be said, to draw those principles and findings that can be drawn from the behavior of men with reference to the most important problems of their community.

The complexity of human behavior and especially of politics, however, prohibits any final statement of the elements of political science. Many points must be made in preliminary form, as invitations to further study. And if some of the readers of this book should at some future time develop these preliminary forms into more substantial principles, then a major objective of the book will have been realized.

Over four centuries ago, Francis Bacon wrote that "the unassisted hand and the understanding left to itself possess but little power. Effects are produced by the means of instruments and helps, which the understanding requires no less than the hand." Thus the student's understanding of a book of this sort receives a crucial test when he is asked to apply what he has learned to specific problems. "Nature is only subdued by submission," declares Bacon. If theory without practice is dangerous in physics and biology, it is doubly so in political science, where it is also more common.

To encourage, therefore, the more active study of political science, I have placed at the end of each chapter a series of questions and problems pertaining to its contents. I believe that a student will appreciate more fully what political scientists do and know, if he is made to apply himself regularly to the solution of one or more of those problems. John Stuart Mill, though well aware, from his personal experience, of the defects of precocity, wrote in his *Autobiography* that the mind of youth is capable of much more than is usually exacted of it—nay, even willing for more. Given clarity, realism, and meaning in his materials, the student will assimilate them with surprising ease.

I should like to view this book as a co-operative venture. In a broad sense it already is that, for I owe much to many men and women. I should express my appreciation particularly to Professor V. O. Key of Harvard University, whose wise counseling and skillful editorial advice have contributed much to its substance. I am indebted also to Professor William Anderson of the University of Minnesota, Professor Leland Goodrich of Columbia University, and Mr. Ismar Baruch, Chief, Personnel Classification Division, United States Civil Service Commission: all gave generous assistance at various stages of the work. I should be grateful to receive criticisms of the book from colleagues everywhere, both as to its utility in the classroom and as to its statements of theory and fact.

ALFRED DE GRAZIA

West Barrington, Rhode Island

CONTENTS

PART III: *GOVERNMENTAL ORGANIZATION*

PART IV: *DEMOCRACY AND POLICY*

FIGURES & TABLES

I

SCOPE AND METHOD

T HINKING about politics may be done well or badly. Proper thinking is by no means something we acquire naturally, and thinking about political affairs is one of the most complicated of mental operations. The first steps, as the first chapter outlines them, require that one know how to define the issues and questions of politics, that one have some idea of the standards requisite for testing truth, and that one be able to do some creative thinking, whether or not one intends to translate thought into action.

The paramount subject of politics is the state, that center of decision for so many questions that affect one's life. What are "states"? How do they get the respect that they must have to survive? How do they influence and command human behavior? And, since some states behave quite differently towards their peoples than others do, what are their various forms and functions?

Once acquainted with the methods and scope of political science, one is prepared to study political behavior. There, leaders and followers, publics and parties, pressure groups and military forces move in unending contention for values, for those imagined future conditions that men desire and strive for.

1

THINKING ABOUT POLITICS

MANY people have only a vague idea of what is meant by the term "political science." Often they confuse it with political economy, which is economics; or they conceive it to be the discussion of current events, although there is no more reason for a political scientist to know offhand the present situation in the Near East than for a professor of physical mechanics to be able to describe the pilings of any bridge in North Carolina. They often believe that political science is civic ethics, that is, a system of moral exhortations that tell students what is good and bad about the political conduct of various persons and groups.

Political science is fundamentally none of these things. It is scientific method applied to political events. Like any other science, it is an attempt to reduce, by ever-broader statements, the facts with which it deals to a number of clear, precise, descriptive principles. Of course, in a science called political, these facts and principles are political. A principle of political science might be: "Third parties have a difficult time getting on the ballot in most states"; or "The system of filling committee chairmanships by seniority in the Congress operates on the whole to the advantage of the conservative Southern faction of the Democratic Party when that party is in the majority."

The Science and Art of Politics

POLITICS IS AN ART

However confused some people may be about political science, they seem to have clear-cut and dogmatic ideas about politics. To many voters, politics is a racket, a game, or a disgrace; but to those they elect to office, who are "in politics," it may be a noble

profession. Such epithets, however, can only express emotional reactions, not the realities of politics. Practical politics actually resolves
itself into the adjustments of human relations. It calls for a practical
skill that distinguishes one man from another—an art. Long training,
even if only self-training or experience, elevates one man above
another, and when training and aptitude increase a skill, we have
conditions that are typical of an art, whether it be bad or good, plain
or fancy art. A few men seem to be born to the political art.

Science presents the principles; the corresponding art applies them.
So, in theory, should the political scientist provide the principles for
the political artist—the politician, the administrator, the active citizen.
It would be false, however, to conceal the fact that the co-ordination
between the scientist and the politician, in practice, is slight.

This situation is by no means peculiar to political science. Knowing
the principles of anatomical mechanics hardly helps one walk better,
and he who trys consciously to operate by them may well fall on his
face. On the other hand, without a science of anatomy and engineering, artificial limbs could not be employed successfully. Even in those
areas where science and art are indispensable to one another, co-
ordination cannot be perfect. The engineer learns mechanics in school
and even takes courses in the art of bridge building, that is, "applied"
courses; but he does not learn how to build *the* bridge of real life. *The*
bridge is unique; it is his individual solution of a special bridging
problem—a problem of scientific principle, aesthetic principle, climate,
public opinion, and perhaps even politics.

POLITICS AND COMMON SENSE

Certainly, to the neutral observer and to the artist of
politics the political world seems so confused and complex that most
of the descriptions of it over the last two thousand years appear to be
monstrous oversimplifications, completely useless as guides for political practice. Everything seems to be done according to homely sayings
that people have acquired during their individual life experiences or by
reason of some complex "feeling" for the particular situation that
cannot be broken down into a statement of scientific principle or taught
to others. When one asks a politician whether there are principles of
political science that underlie his activities, he snorts in derision or else
emits several heavy dogmas that he would never in his right mind
pursue implacably: "Never offend anybody;" "Always vote for appropriations and against taxes;" "Be loyal;" or "God is on the side with
the most votes." When one turns to the diaries, lives, memoirs, and
accounts in political literature, one must, if one is reasonable, perceive
that the precious advice of Boss Plunkitt of Tammany Hall might in-

spire, but would badly serve, the budding politician in rural Nebraska, that the finesse of the diplomat, Talleyrand, reconciles poorly with the bumptious tactics of Huey Long, one-time boss of Louisiana.

It is true that powerful men have a weakness for citing other great men as their mentors: Napoleon cited Alexander; Mussolini, Caesar; Lenin, Marx; Mao Tse-Tung of Communist China, George Washington; and many American leaders, Jefferson. But the alleged "educators" are often discovered after the fact, when the new leader needs justification. The "model" often is fitted into the ego of the new man—a cloak he wears, a role he plays, a symbol of what he would like to be. The new men are not getting science from the old, but are getting propaganda. For the settled areas of science, and this is true of parts of political science, the founders, such as Newton, may, as men, give inspiration, but as contributors their work in mingled with and lost in the general body of scientific principles in their fields.

SCIENCE NO SUBSTITUTE FOR EXPERIENCE

In short, it would be false and vainglorious to declare that political science can provide its disciples with scientific tools that will give them a great advantage over uninitiates in practical politics. Political science cannot make a politician out of a scientist any more than physiology can make an athlete out of a physiotherapist. Nor can it make up to any great extent for the wealth of experience and the insights that the "practical" politician, administrator, or citizen brings to bear on individual political problems. Except in rare cases, such as that of Woodrow Wilson, a political scientist does not possess an aptitude for politics, and it is noteworthy that, although some of Wilson's political success was traceable to his excellent scientific preparation, his major political failures were an outgrowth of a temperament that was more congenial to scientific discovery than to politics.

SCIENCE MAY BE MISLEADING

Furthermore, political science is not always accurate in describing the political process. It is all too easy for one fresh from the textbooks to scoff at the "irrationalities" of politicians, who seem to be like the fabled bird that flies forward with its head turned backwards. The political novice tends to be cynical, like the playwright, Alexandre Dumas the Younger, who, when urged by an admirer to write about politics, replied: "Comedies about comedies don't go."

Often the supposed "irrationalities" turn out to be elements of the problem at hand that a more perfect political science would have taken account of in its body of principles. For example, when a group of students views the sessions of any of the world's important assemblies, it most frequently sees a scattering of members acting in a leisurely manner. The students often conclude on the basis of a "principle" they have been taught in class ("Laws are made in assemblies after debate on the merits of the bill") that the members are not living up to their responsibilities. The member will tell them privately, however, that if he attended all the meetings of this term of the assembly, he would not be around for the next. He has learned quickly that his job has many "angles," and the purely formal function of attending sessions and launching debates must take its proper place.

We have said that politics is the art, political science the science, and that the art has not had great help from the scientific principles. Still, one should not underestimate political science. There are many useful things that can be said about the ways in which men of different viewpoints and different standards of right and wrong behave in the political process. The chapters that follow will describe some of the materials of political science and their relationships. Their aim is to make general statements about politics that will be meaningful either to those who contemplate the political process or to those who are active in it.

In addition to these principles of political science, there is a science of political inquiry that this book aims to describe. As Karl Pearson has written: "The man who classifies facts of any kind whatsoever, who sees their mutual relation and describes their sequences, is applying the scientific method and is a man of science. The facts may belong to the past history of mankind, to the social statistics of our great cities, to the atmosphere of the most distant stars, to the digestive organs of a worm, or to the life of a scarcely visible bacillus. It is not the facts themselves which make science, but the method in which they are dealt with." *

What Is "Political"?

POLITICAL SCIENCE AND OTHER SOCIAL SCIENCES ARE MINGLED

Political science, as one of the social sciences that deal with human relations, is a member of a rather quarrelsome family. Psychology, sociology, anthropology, economics, history, and human geography are the other members. Each of these, like political science itself, is not very sure of its place in the family or its future as a science.

---

* *The Grammar of Science* (London: Adam and Charles Black, 1900), p. 12. Reprinted with the permission of The Macmillan Company, New York.

None has a private room, and each has a habit of wearing the others' party dresses.

For example, a psychologist will sometimes interpret international relations of the most complex sort on some theory of "reward and punishment" or "the aggressive instinct." An anthropologist will show that we can have peace, because he has found some primitive tribes that seem not to have war. An economist can be heard saying now and then that if we were to restore a world-wide free movement of goods and persons, the causes of war would vanish. And sociologists here and there raise their voices to state that war is essentially a struggle between "we" and "they," the "ingroup" and the "outgroup," who are jealous of their respective gods and customs, or that war is a struggle for social prestige. Not a few geographers seem all too certain that the control of strategic routes and raw materials is at the root of warfare. Not to be outdone, some historians have been prone to see war as the logical outcome of dynastic disputes, personal ambitions, or some combination of unique factors that are not capable of being fitted into a pattern for purposes of explanation.

The political scientist who studies war draws on his knowledge of one or more of the sister sciences. The best studies of war to this day, in fact, have been skillful combinations of the insights and evidence afforded by all of the social sciences. Each science reveals some facet that the other cannot. One may ask: Must a political scientist who studies war be skilled in all of the social sciences? The answer is, at the present time, yes. Since political science has chosen to study war as a whole, in its total meaning as human behavior, it cannot escape the obligation to bring to the subject all the contributions of the social sciences and to risk the danger of amateurishness in any one of them.

The same broad demands are made of political science in other problem areas. The political scientist is called on to be expert on matters concerning the state, for example. Again, he must be, as he has often been in the past, a jurist in speaking of the constitution and the laws, a sociologist in speaking of political institutions, a psychologist in describing public opinion and propaganda on public issues, a historian in describing governmental changes, and an economist in talking of fiscal policy, budgetary matters, and social legislation. If he is to study municipal government, he would do well to read that classic on city government, Aristotle's *Politics*, and see there how a great scientist treated the psychological, economic, sociological, and other elements in the operation of the city-state.

MOST POLITICAL SCIENTISTS ARE SUBJECT-AREA SPECIALISTS

Given this necessity for making use of materials of all the social sciences, the field of political science is usually defined by sub-

ject-area, in history and today. The prevailing broad divisions in
America are shown in Figure 1. Governmental institutions and the
major areas of life that government influences are the foci of attention;
a re-examination of the table of contents of this book will show that
most chapters refer to subject-areas. The reason why most political

FIGURE 1

THE FOUNDATIONS AND FIELDS OF POLITICAL SCIENCE *
(as practiced generally in American Universities)

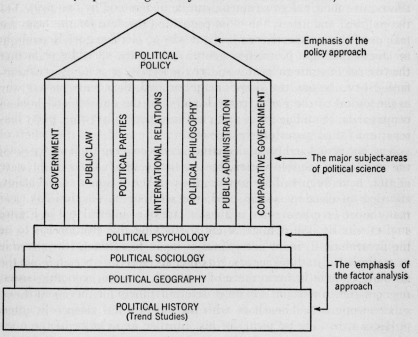

* Political theory is germane to all aspects of the diagram. All subjects cited relate to
all other subjects in many ways.

scientists are specialists in a certain area of government or politics is
that continuous, intensive study of one area of human involvement may
often produce better results than a one-sided application to a wide
range of situations of a "law" or "principle" obtained elsewhere from
a raw and crude science. For example, today it is probable that a
political scientist who is a specialist on *legislatures* can answer more
of the questions we ask about the principles of legislation than can
a political scientist who is an expert on the *psychology of group behavior*,
although, as we shall point out later, both men can give different and
yet useful answers, and the two in co-operation can be of even greater
use.

At this stage of political science, specialization by subject can work well. Given talent, a man concentrating on one certain area of behavior, such as political parties or public law, can come to understand it well. He can achieve a sympathetic relationship with the characters and events he studies. He can see the parts in relation to the whole without losing sight of the whole. If he is outstanding, he can bring to bear on his own area of specialization the new techniques and discoveries of the other social sciences.

Considerable doubt exists as to whether any complex situation in politics, such as war, elections, legislation, administration of public affairs, or municipal government, can be understood by one man. Yet the political scientist is the most probable candidate for the task. To take one instance, can anyone find out why an election goes Republican or Democratic in a particular county? Among the variables or factors that we can imagine to be at work are the following: sex, age, religion, nationality, income, the kind of neighborhood, the county history, the organization of the party, party leadership, the amount and kind of propaganda, the influence of past elections, party platforms, party history, individual histories, the personality of candidates, the beliefs of voters, the actual and presumed issues, press coverage and viewpoints, the number of eligible voters, the extent to which voters who were eligible actually turned out to vote, the number of names on the ballot, the type of election system used, the weather on election day, and many more (see how some of these factors are interrelated in Figure 11). Obviously, the political scientist studying this election has to be highly trained in many disciplines if he is to estimate the possible operation of all of these factors. No other social scientist can tell him the absolute or relative importance of sex, age, religion, economic issues, organization, and so on. He must determine them for this election and other elections by himself or with the aid of a few close colleagues.

He can, in fact, by virtue of his intimate knowledge of these influences as they function in this whole situation that he studies, give members of the other social sciences instruction regarding their own fields. The sociologist who studies race differences, for example, can learn something from studies of voting behavior. The political scientist's preoccupation with one problem of behavior may even produce more useful principles than would be produced if other social scientists were separately to apply the principles and methods of their disciplines to his field of interest. If so, we cannot expect to learn from the economist how money influenced the vote, or from the psychologists how age influenced it, or from sociologists how social class affiliations influenced it. The political scientist must be aware of what the economists, psychologists, and sociologists have said about these influences; but perhaps only he can assign to these factors their proper influence, for only he has considered them as they operate together in the election process.

EMPHASIS ON SUBJECT-AREAS CRITICIZED

There has been a great deal of criticism of the customary orientation of political science to subject-areas. Other social scientists sometimes greet with protests writings by political scientists on war, the state, the political party, or leadership. They claim, for example, that only an economist can talk of the economic causes of war, the sociologist of the cultural causes of war, or the psychologist of the tensions that cause war. However, such criticism, to be justified, must show that the political scientist used, for example, bad psychological techniques, uninformed estimates of psychological findings, and over-generalizations from psychological materials. The individual political scientist must defend his work in these respects.

But his harassment does not end here. For quite the opposite reason, political scientists who have taken a broad view of their subject have sometimes been reproached from within the profession of political science itself. He who discussed how the law was made ran some risk when he talked of the informal elements that enter into legislation. At one time he would have encountered real opposition to including in his description "extraneous" matters such as the influence of lobbies on lawmakers, the rule of legislative bodies by key committees, or the domination of legislatures by party bosses. Sociologists like Ostrogorski, Michels, and Bentley, and social psychologists like Sighele, Le Bon, and Wallas helped political scientists like Wilson, Bryce, Merriam, and Beard to force a treatment of these realistic questions so that many other political scientists could deal with them without incurring the distrust of their colleagues.

A certain amount of cautious sniffing and headshaking still occurs whenever a political scientist takes broadly the subject-area pretensions of political science and tries to describe the whole of the problem on which he is concentrating. As soon as a student moves about in the bibliography of political science in America and western Europe he will detect a strong legalistic air, persisting from the recent past, when political science was public law rather narrowly conceived. As such, public law concerned itself principally with the formal procedures a political system required in such situations as filing and running for office, being a party official, becoming an elector, introducing a bill, drafting a bill, judging its constitutionality, and following it through the continuous court redefinitions of its precise applications to particular cases. On the whole, however, today's political scientists are the better received the more materials and viewpoints they bring to bear on their subject.

Although a great many political scientists are experts on given subjects, a few have urged upon their colleagues a scope of study other than subject-area specialization. Two alternative points of view deserve mention. Each differs from the substantive area definition. Each attempts to make political science assume a more logical position in relation to other social sciences and a more advantageous position for undertaking the solution of political problems. One is the "policy science" approach. The other is the "factor specialization" approach.

POLICY SCIENCE

Exponents of the "policy science" approach (well known among them are Harold D. Lasswell and James K. Pollock) would share the problems of political science with other social sciences. Since it is difficult for one man to bring all the rapidly multiplying techniques and findings of the social sciences to bear on the solution of a particular political problem, they consider a form of interdisciplinary co-operation necessary. Wherever the community must have informed "policy," the social sciences are to co-operate. Thus, the political scientist would not venture to give sole judgment on a law governing the press, but would be one of a committee of economists, psychologists, sociologists, and ethical scientists who would contribute the findings of their respective disciplines to a complete description of the state of the press and the consequences of the proposed legislation. Under the guidance, preferably of practicing experts on the "possible," that is, representatives of the public or statesmen, these findings would form the basis for social action. The specific contribution of the political scientist would be in the design of the co-operative study and in the knowledge he possesses of how policies are made. Examples of the use of this co-operative technique have been such enterprises as the Committee on Freedom of the Press, the National Resources Planning Board, the Commission on Organization of the Executive Branch of the Government, and (to indicate how highly controversial this approach may be) the various four-year, five-year and other plans of collectivist economies abroad.

FACTOR SPECIALIZATION

The approach we term factor specialization would make of political science an analytic science. If we let economics analyze the "price-value" factor in human relations and motivations, sociology the "honor-value" or "prestige" factor, geography the "physical" factor, and psychology the "psycho-physical" origins of the various factors, political science would study the "power" factor. Just as economics often studies the conditions of the maximization of profit, political science would study the conditions of the maximization of power. Power we would define roughly as the control over the disposition of valued things—public offices, material goods, honors, and so on. The man who submerged all other values to the single-minded pursuit of the power to make decisions and to tell other people in a society how to act would be the pure "political man."

Factor specialization would differ from the usual approach to the field of political science in that it would be more limited and would depend greatly on the other social sciences to provide the missing elements needed for a complete analysis of any problem. For example, a political scientist would lean upon the economist, the sociologist, and others in treating of the administration of roads, schools, and other activities of government.

However, many political activities are not "power" activities; some, but never all, have to do with power. Exclusive preoccupation with one factor like "power," in the absence of ability to measure that element exactly, may thus produce a lopsided description of the event studied.

Neither of the two approaches just described can be ignored. If they operate at present on a precarious footing, they may be expected to become stronger as time goes on and the science of politics develops. Meanwhile both views help discourage more conventional political scientists from producing shapeless descriptions of transitory situations. The "policy" scientists point out the important problems, the need for co-operation in the social sciences, and the principles common to the processes by which political decisions are made. The "factor" scientists, by emphasizing the study of the central components of the political process, advance the development of dynamic principles of political behavior.

WHAT EVENTS FORM THE DATA OF POLITICS?

The three views jointly contribute to a proper construction of the field of political science, which at the present time can be said to discuss three classes of phenomena: politics, the politically relevant, and the politically conditioned. "Politics" or "political" includes the events that happen around the decision-making centers of government. Who makes the most important decisions locally, nationally, and internationally? What are the decisions, and what is their effect? What are the procedures, formal and informal, by which they are made?

The "politically relevant" encompasses those general and specific social events that are not directly political, but that have effects of political importance: the political beliefs of certain religious movements like Mohammedanism, the political effects of business cycles, the relative amounts of compulsory and free elements in the training of children in a society, the productivity of labor and machinery in a political jurisdiction, the effects of monopoly upon control of the nation, the rate of social and technological change, or the curricula of universities and the political influences operating on students.

The "politically conditioned" denotes those events that in large part follow from political decisions or are associated with political behavior. Typical are the effects of legislation. However, in so far as the effects of a particular law are the concern of the special field to which it pertains, political scientists lose interest. They are too busy observing those laws that affect behavior that is either political or closely relevant to politics. Thus, they customarily observe closely the effects of laws regulating lobbies, labor unions, and political parties, leaving the effects of child labor legislation, grain and money market regulation, or crop control legislation to sociologists and economists.

There are other kinds of politically conditioned events: the effects of state activities on religion—for instance the antireligious behavior of the Communist parties in eastern Europe after World War II; the effects of government ownership upon work motivation and capitalistic initiative; the use of political power to obtain personal revenge or make a fortune; or the way in which economic, educational, and social institutions bend to follow the direction of political events. These influences of politics are implied in verbal expressions. For example a stock broker says: "The President must become optimistic about business if economic conditions are not to get worse"; an educator says: "How can we teach students to be good when politics are so corrupt"; a Negro leader states: "Race relations will never be what they were before the war because so many Negroes fought and died for freedom."

The sphere of what is political, politically relevant, and politically determined is not fixed. It shifts with the times and the interests of men in what may be obtained through the apparatus of the state. In early Virginia, the vestry was a unit of religion and government together. It later lost political character and finally even political relevance. Certain mountain ranges like the Alps or the Pyrenees gain or lose political relevance as the nations around them move in different political directions. The education of the young is sometimes, as in ancient Sparta or Nazi Germany, directly managed by political leaders for their own ends; sometimes, as in the United States, it is politically relevant and politically conditioned.

Various scientific theories and discoveries have added new dimensions to the relevant and the conditioned. Marx's theory that the state was dominated by the class that owned the instruments of economic production, when adopted by some political scientists, made the study of the control of factories "political" and tended to make the study of the machinery of the state "relevant," but not central.

Freud's examination of the "unconscious" factor in human conduct, coupled with his theory that strong feelings of guilt may produce aggressive behavior, led to some important contributions to the study of nonrational behavior in politics. Thus today, when a political scientist studies certain destructive political characters in action, he may look as deeply as possible into their personal history. He may find evidence, for instance, that they were held to impossible standards of conduct as children and blamed for many unaccountable situations, until in desperation they sought relief from their anxieties by casting their feelings of guilt elsewhere and finding political opponents to blame and punish.

The Political Scientist at Work

THE GENERAL METHODS OF POLITICAL SCIENCE

Political science cannot be said to have any coherent and indisputable body of methods and techniques, partly because of the great depth and scope of its interests, partly because of the little success thus far achieved in measurement as the natural sciences know it. The political scientist ordinarily approaches some portion of the materials of politics that interests him, observes what is going on from as close a vantage point as possible, reads and listens to what others say about it, and forms a theory as to the key influences at work and how they interact with each other. Guided then by his theory or hypothesis, he goes deeper into the evidence, confirming, changing, or disproving his theory, depending upon what he finds.

Political scientists differ temperamentally and intellectually, and the results of their work very often express these differences. Four general approaches can be observed. One political scientist may present careful descriptions; he may provide a detailed and exact mirror of the events he is observing. Another may have a talent for analysis; he may isolate the influences at work in a situation and their essential relation to the events he is studying. A third scholar may prefer to work by comparison; if he is blessed with an acute ability to discriminate the characteristics of two similar events or institutions, he may be able to show as no one else can what distinguishes one event from another, and account for the different behavior of the human beings in each (see, for example, Figure 50). A fourth student may proceed by the genetic or historical method; his chief interest is then in trends over a period of time. Given an event to explain, such as the defeat of a candidate in a single election, he will immediately proceed to examine the sequence of events of which this is the latest. There are probably profound psychological reasons why different scientists emphasize one method over another in the discovery of truths. But little is known about how individual differences among scientists are transformed into different ways of studying the same events.

A glance at some studies in the field of American politics will illustrate these striking differences in approach. For instance, J. T. Salter's *Boss Rule* is a vivid description of the routine of the local politician. H. F. Gosnell's *Machine Politics: Chicago Model* shows how variables like income, religion, nationality, past party affiliation, and newspaper reading habits can be isolated and employed statistically to explain election results. The erudite work of Herman Finer on *The Theory and Practice of Modern Government* contrasts the cabinet systems and other institutions of the Western countries and relates their different effects to their different organization. In Harold Zink's *City Bosses in the United States* and H. D. Lasswell's *Psychopathology and Politics* two very different techniques of personal history are used to reveal how the lives of politicians influence the course of American politics. And W. E. Binkley's *American Political Parties: Their Natural History*, a broader history, shows how much of the present behavior of the parties in America rises out of past events and political crises.

No method is used alone. Each of the works above, and every other work, is colored by more than one way of explaining political reality. In Plato's *Republic* analysis and comparison (especially by detailed analogies) go hand in hand. Aristotle's *Politics* is much more descriptive, although he develops in a modern form some of the current concepts used in analyzing governments (such as the influence of the wealthier classes on politics). The other great works of political theory have also employed combinations of the four methods in order to ensure the validity and increase the persuasiveness of their findings.

THE TECHNIQUES OF POLITICAL SCIENCE

The methods just described are general; they represent basic and universal patterns of thought; they underlie what we may call the techniques of political science. By techniques are meant those many neat and precise ways by which the investigation of facts may be carried on in pursuance of the general methodology of the research worker. Although political science needs far more techniques than it presently possesses, their number is still too great to allow mention of more than a few.

The ability to work quickly and skillfully with documentary materials is of course of first importance. Yearbooks, encyclopedias, periodical files, law books, statutes, legislative records, and personal documents like diaries (see Figure 18) and letters are commonly used.

They contain an abundance of evidence on many points of great interest in all subject-areas of political science. Research workers studying the movements of public opinion preceding World War II found in the newspapers, periodicals, and documents that had preceded World War I certain trends that provided useful comparisons and theories to test. The voting records of a succession of Congresses as contained in the *Congressional Record* and journals afforded some researchers, for example, the chance to trace the extent to which the party leaders maintained or failed to maintain adherence of party members to the party line. Congressional hearings, which are often recorded, are mines of information on numerous subjects (see Figure 34).

Direct observation includes all those accounts that men make of events immediately perceived. The events may be recorded in systematic or haphazard fashion, using occasional notes or one's memory. Or they may be recorded by one of the new techniques. Wire recordings of interviews and movies of events have been used to gather materials for subsequent political study. The "participant observer," one who belongs to a group or movement in order to study it, is a favorite role of political scientists. For often they cannot otherwise get close enough to the center of events.

The "questionnaire" is used widely in studies of the political attitudes of a selected group and (to a lesser extent) of the political behavior of larger numbers of persons. Carefully drafted in advance, the same question may be presented to many individuals, and their answers may be tabulated and analyzed according to rigid standards (see Figure 2). Where the activities, attitudes and responses of a *large* number of people are to be found, a "sample" is made. If we have some foreknowledge of the characteristics of an entire group (for instance, the distribution of its members according to age, sex, residence or income), a small fraction of the total number *is selected in proper proportions* to stand for the whole. Where foreknowledge is slight or likely to mislead, a "random" sample may still be obtained. A random sample is taken by giving to all things or persons in the universe of data studied an equal chance of being selected. Sampling has come to be quite an intricate technique, mastered only by specialists who must be called on by the ordinary political scientist for assistance when he believes the technique might be useful.

The most extensive development of sampling and questionnaire techniques has grown out of the polling of public opinion. Often the polls are designed to prepare data for all four general methods of political science (see Figure 3). For example, a poll based on a sample of the population will give an accurate *description* of how people feel about a particular issue of current interest. The same poll may present data by states so that one area may be *compared* with another. It may break down its findings by income levels, or age groups, or sex and

FIGURE 2

THE QUESTIONNAIRE

Page 1 of a five-page mail questionnaire sent to county welfare-board secretaries, assessor supervisors, highway engineers, county agents, sheriffs and school superintendents in the course of a large-scale study of intergovernmental relations in the near Northwest.

RESEARCH IN INTERGOVERNMENTAL RELATIONS *

You and Your County Position:

(1) How chosen: elected _____ or appointed _____.

(2) Under civil service? Yes _____ No _____.

(3) Number of years in present position _____.

(4) Other public positions held (including other governmental units):
Position: _____ Government Unit: _____ No. of yrs. held: _____
_____ _____ _____

(5) Sex: Female _____ Male _____.

(6) Age _____.

(7) Number of years resident in county _____.

(8) If a part time official, what is your private occupation? _____

(9) Education (check one): 8th grade or less _____; attended high school _____, attended business school _____; attended college _____.

(10) Formal training beyond high school; if any (check one or more if applicable):

_____ accounting   _____ law   _____ public health
_____ agriculture   _____ law enforcement   _____ social work
_____ education   _____ medicine   _____ other: _____
_____ engineering   _____ public administration   _____

(11) Have you ever held a political party office (precinct or ward chairman, county committee, etc.)? Yes _____ No _____.

County Government:

1. Standing Committees: In administering your department, are county board standing committees of considerable _____, moderate _____, or little _____ influence? No standing committees _____. (check one)

3. Budget: Has any one officer the right to revise the budget requests of your department before they go to the county board? Yes _____ No _____. If so, who? _____

4. Over-all Control: a. *In actual practice,* is the amount of overall control the county board exercises over your department: large _____, medium _____, small _____, none _____.
b. *Should* overall control of your department by the county board be greater _____, less _____, same as now _____.
c. *In actual practice,* is the amount of overall control the auditor (or clerk) exercises over your department: large _____, medium _____, small _____, none _____.
d. *Should* overall control of your department by the auditor (or clerk) be greater _____, less _____, same as now _____.

5. Total number of subordinate employees in department, full time _____, part-time _____.

* Source: William Anderson and Edward Weidner of the University of Minnesota.

thus allow the behavior of the component parts of the population to be *analyzed* in relation to one another. Finally, the same poll, taken at several points in time, will afford opportunity to discern *historical* trends and perhaps to foresee the future.

Political science makes increasing use of statistics also, especially in the analysis of government finance and in the compilation of voting

FIGURE 3

RELATION BETWEEN ISOLATIONIST ATTITUDES AND INFORMATION LEVEL *

An example of sample survey materials allowing one to draw descriptive, comparative, analytic, and historical inferences with relative ease.

Has U. S. gone too far in concerning itself with problems in other parts of the world?	Scale of information possessed by respondents on foreign affairs (Oct. 1948)					Percentage of total population		
	LOW 0	1	2	3	HIGH 4, 5 & 6	Oct. 1948	Apr. 1947	Dec. 1946
Agree	40%	31%	31%	22%	22%	32%	33%	32%
Undecided	21	11	7	6	2	12	16	16
Disagree	35	54	60	69	76	53	49	50
Not ascertained	4	4	2	3	0	3	2	2
	100%	100%	100%	100%	100%	100%	100%	100%
Number of cases	196	157	121	85	45			

* Source: Survey Research Center: *Attitudes toward United States–Russian Relations* (University of Michigan, Dec., 1948), pp. 5, 70.

figures. Public opinion and propaganda studies are next in frequency of employment of statistical techniques, but one may expect to encounter rather simple statistics even in studies of Supreme Court opinions or legislation. As yet, however, no total subject of political science has been quantitatively presented in statistical or other exact language.

PROBLEMS OF LANGUAGE

Ideally, once the results of research by these and other techniques have been formulated in a large number of general statements about politics, these statements should all be phrased in a few exact words or symbols and fitted into an ever-diminishing number of even more general statements. Our knowledge of politics should be systematized, just as are the facts one knows about Lassie, about Collies, about dogs, about mammals, and about all animals.

However, although some political scientists are systematic, political science itself is not. The writers remain individualistic. To each systematizer his own system. They are like the blind men hired by the Chinese Emperor to describe an elephant; one felt a huge foot and described the animal as a tree, another felt the trunk and described the animal as a snake, and so on, with results scarcely helpful to the Emperor. Similarly, books on the state by brilliant scholars fail to talk about the same things in the same language and with the same purposes in mind. What is true of the concept "state" is true of many other concepts describing important political problems, such as "liberty," "authority," "representation," "power," "law," "public opinion," and "social welfare." We hardly need add "democracy," "fascism," and "communism." Political sects, far more than scholars, make a cult of language and tend to confuse further the language of science (see Figure 4). In order to understand many of the best writers on these concepts, one must know all about them, their troubles, the age in which they lived, and the meanings they give to these words in relation to all the other words they use; even so, one often cannot be satisfied.

FIGURE 4

COMMUNIST TERMINOLOGY

Simple *content analysis* reveals obvious ideological connections between communist propagandists in America and the Moscow party line by comparison of the Frequency of Use of Key Political Terms *

Moscow News 6 Issues

August 2, 1938; September 5, 1938; October 3, 1938;
November 7, 1938; December 5, 1938; January 2, 1939.

Bourgeois	61
Class	92
Class struggle	97
Collectivism	56
Collective and state farms	378
Commissariat	187
Comrade	78
Soviets (councils)	270
Diversionism	25
Exploitation	54
Five-Year Plan, plan	217
Lenin, Leninist	243
Masses	146
The Party (Communist)	172
Proletariat	45
Red Army	162
Revolution	217
Socialist construction and/or reconstruction	62
Socialist competition	29
Socialist labor	23
Socialist revolution	34
Stakhanovism	165
Stalin, Stalinist	280
The task	62
The people	1136
Toilers	35
Workers	633

The Communist jargon on the left is used constantly by the *Moscow News*, as shown by the figures on the right of the line. Under such conditions, the question was raised whether the publisher of this American paper ought not to have registered as a foreign agent.

* Reprinted with permission from H. D. Lasswell, Nathan Leites, and Associates: *Language of Politics: Studies in Quantitative Semantics* (New York: George W. Stewart, Publisher, Inc., 1949), p. 227.

Thus, to find a systematic political science, one must know the various systems thoroughly—there are not many, for all men are not Aristotles or Platos—and select that which provides the shortest course and the most usable body of principles; but this task is long and arduous and brings a student to middle age. One may build a "solipsistic" system of one's own, that is, a system that communicates rules and principles with meaning only to oneself, like a painting that is understood only by its creator. However, since no great science has sprung from the experience of a single man, but rather from the experiments and controlled observations of generations, the chances of such a personal science being of considerable immediate use to the man or his disciples will be small. *Scientific findings must be communicable. The language of science must be as precise, clear, and standardized as possible.*

Creative Thinking and Acting in Politics

A PRESCRIPTION FOR SOLVING POLITICAL PROBLEMS

Let us now suppose that two men, one a political scientist, the other a person active in practical politics, were to pool their intellectual and practical experience in working out a single prescription for creative thinking and action in politics. They wish to describe how a person, both enlightened and energetic, can effectively think about and deal with a real political problem. Their combined efforts would give the scientific and moral man who is pursuing a goal this prescription:

1. *He must not allow his values or desires to obscure the facts.*
2. *He must compare his values with the values of other individuals and groups.*
3. *He must examine the institutions of society that affect his desires and the desires of others.*
4. *He must take into account the unexpected and accidental behavior of others.*
5. *He must devise a strategy for achieving his goals.*
6. *He must decide on the extent to which he must revise his goals.*

DISSOCIATING FACTS AND DESIRES

Let us try to explain a little more clearly each of these six steps to competent political thinking.

Preventing one's desires from obscuring the facts is more difficult than it seems. Suppose, for example, that the city government is spending a great deal more money than it is taking in through taxation; this deficit is a fact. If the city cannot sell bonds and no one wants to decrease the spending, then it is also a fact that increased taxation is the only remedy. A citizen may not like to pay more taxes, but he can see that what he likes or does not like cannot change the necessity for them. So far so good.

But suppose the question of the tax is turned into a question of tax policy; he is called on to vote for either a sales tax on retail purchases or a progressive income-tax. The sales tax, which is paid on food, hits hardest the lower-income groups, who spend a large part of their income on food. The progressive income-tax hits hardest the upper-income groups, who pay a higher tax rate the higher their income goes. The man in question belongs to a higher-income bracket; his wishes, let us say, thus impel him to prefer the sales tax. He hears a slogan to the effect that the income-tax destroys the initiative of the "more productive elements" of society. Without bothering to weigh the evidence or look further into the matter, he uses this slogan to justify his support of the sales tax. Lacking the ability to examine his motives, he uses his own desires to produce a "mythical" state of reality. He does not investigate the real state of affairs. He is satisfied to take spurious evidence, asking of it only that it be on "his side." He rejects all facts that conflict with his desires. It is difficult for most of us to do otherwise.

RECOGNIZING DIFFERENCES

The second principle of political thinking is to compare one's own values with those of others. "One man's meat is another man's poison." The values of other people are facts like any others, although it may be difficult to discover and adjust to them. For instance, suppose a man votes Republican, his wife Democratic; each knows the other's position and avoids political argument in the home—an easy and simple adjustment to the conflict. But both believe society is divided into classes: the "upper class," to which they believe they belong, and the "lower class." Within their respective parties, they thus prefer to vote for men of high income, high education, and "good family." Since their favorite candidates are often defeated, they ascribe these defeats to a supposed political "machine" that conspires against "good" candidates. Both fail to realize that large numbers of people make no distinction between an upper and a lower class and prefer other candidates for other reasons. This inability to see that the rest of society has different values leads the couple to venture false, or at least unproven, explanations for the defeat of their men.

Another, rather complex, example was provided by Prime Minister Chamberlain of England in 1938. He valued the continuation of peace more than anything else. He believed that any concession should be made to preserve peace and that it was possible to make peace worthwhile to Hitler as well. This view turned out to be mistaken. Hitler did not desire peace so strongly; he accepted all the concessions that Chamberlain offered and demanded more. If Chamberlain had not believed that even Hitler shared his basic aversion to war, he might have foreseen more clearly the results of his policy of appeasement.

One may properly ask, of course, how much other people's values are worth in relation to one's own. By what standard shall we judge the values of others? This question is extremely controversial, and no answer can be given here, if anywhere. The standard itself is a value. He who regards other people's needs and desires as deserving as much consideration as his own will adjust his desires to what he knows of those of others. He will decide what he would like to see happen; he will find out what the other people concerned would like to see happen; he will then compromise between his "selfish" and "altruistic" desires and thus develop a new value position.

Take for example a man who dislikes war, who refuses to take part in any military preparation and becomes a conscientious objector. He realizes that the values of nearly all other persons are opposed to his, but he believes that there is no other means of avoiding conflict. He is then like Samson, who was willing to bring the temple crashing down on himself in order to destroy the Philistines. Take another man who also dislikes war, who also believes that it will not solve any problems. He believes, however, that it is up to the authorities to make such decisions; that is, he prefers to accept a group solution to any problem. He therefore accepts the duties imposed upon him by law. Each of these men knows his own values and the values of others, but each regards differently the value of compromising with the group. The man who compromises in such matters is, of course, far more common than the man who balks.

Such open conflict among one's values is common in political life. When a union member, for example, is told by his union leaders to strike and by his governmental leaders to stay on the job, he must choose between conflicting loyalties. Of course, most men decide without being aware of any problem, but correct political thinking requires that they be conscious of these conflicts.

KNOWING INSTITUTIONAL OBSTACLES

Getting one's values straight prepares one for the third step: to become acquainted with the institutions that affect one way or another the events important to one's desires. Let us suppose that a man is extremely interested in making as many political decisions as possible in conjunction with his neighbors. He wants a hand in deciding whether streets in his town should be curved or straight, whether the town should own or purchase electric power, whether the voting age should be eighteen or twenty-one, whether private schools should be supported by public funds or not, what tax rates should be levied, whether the constable should be elected or appointed by the mayor, and a host of other questions that have increasingly become the concern of more remote levels of government. Such a man must fight a number of institutions that have multiplied in modern times. Federal and state constitutions have long ago laid great barriers to the realization of most of his desires. The incumbents of federal, state, and even county offices are not inclined to sympathize with his desires, and the forces of entrenched interests (a loose term for institutional barriers) are opposed to him. A number of private and public pressure groups—another kind of institution—oppose his demands because they are afraid of what he might do with his powers once he possessed them. Even the United Nations looks forward eagerly to the day when it may enforce a bill of rights for the whole world and prevent this man from discretionary acts that would violate the civil rights of his neighbors. He must take into account all these institutions and attitudes in estimating his chances of putting his "home rule" plan into effect.

Our man may be told his ideal is impracticable but that he can participate instead in choosing and controlling the authorities who govern him from afar. It is argued that in return for the surrender of his immediate controls, he can exercise indirect control. But indirect control is not what he wants. He wants to help make decisions. So long as he continues to value this power despite the march of events, he must become a pessimist. The most he can hope for is to keep the freedom of action he still possesses.

Most men, of course, adapt themselves and accept necessity. Their values change under the impact of institutions and events; their children often do not even notice that there has been a conflict of values with events and that a change has occurred. Their values are the new ones, not those of their parents. History had hardly begun when in ancient Chaldea, a legend was inscribed:

> *We are fallen upon evil times,*
> *And the world has waxed very old and wicked,*
> *Politics are very corrupt,*
> *The sons of the people are not*
> *So righteous as their parents were.*

THE CALCULATED RISK

One must not only take into account institutional obstacles, one must allow for accidents—the result of imperfect knowledge or uncontrollable events. Imperfect knowledge often hampers the analysis of the institutional obstacles. For instance, the Russians are not very eager to tell Americans about their atomic bombs. Since the Russians' policy depends somewhat on their supply of bombs, any judgment about it becomes risky—a judgment about *probabilities*.

The uncontrollable event is typified by the weather. No political strategy can prevent storms or bring thaw. The wreck of the Spanish Armada on the English coast in 1588 made Englishmen bless the stormy Channel weather for many a year. The first winter offensive of the Germans against Moscow in 1940 literally froze in its tracks in the worst winter in many years. Crop failures have dashed the calculated expectations of many politicians, brought on terrible pogroms against minority groups, and sent tribes on the warpath. Some of the political process, we may conclude, is placed irrevocably in the hands of fortune. The ability of individuals to guide it is limited.

Some social scientists believe, with reason, that over the centuries these accidents are erased by the movements of general social forces, and they may well be right. But the individual political thinker or actor can be sure that his lifetime will see many of them and that they will inevitably alter his calculations.

In providing for these accidents, men must take what we call a calculated risk. Thus Mussolini took a calculated risk when he decided that if he invaded Ethiopia the League of Nations would *probably* not bring completely effective sanctions to bear against him. Hitler thought that England and France would *probably* not aid Poland if he attacked her in 1939. Churchill thought the Germans *probably* would not invade England in late 1940 and therefore sent more troops and arms to the North African theater. Roosevelt thought Hitler would *probably* not declare war if the United States provided England with a number of destroyers. Often, of course, such decisions prove to be mistakes. The North Koreans did not estimate that the United States would use military intervention to prevent their conquest of South Korea in 1950.

There are only two ways to cope with the double threat in the calculated risk; reduce the area of ignorance by constant scientific inquiry and prepare a detour for the unforeseen. An example of the prepared detour is the Vice-President of the United States, whose principal function is to replace the President if the President dies. Both ignorance and accident have been provided for in an American foreign policy that builds bigger atomic bombs while working for a stronger world government.

DEVISING POLITICAL STRATEGY

Having done what he can to analyze the present and foresee the future, the political thinker must lay his special strategy for reaching his goal. For this he must be familiar with the techniques of politics. He must be a practical man, not a dreamer. He cannot win with words alone, though he must use propaganda. He cannot win with amiable companions who have no political skills. He must realize that ends are not achieved without proper means. He must also realize that many ends are so utopian and remote that they cannot be reached; one cannot have Heaven on earth. One of the great contributions that a close study of politics brings to its disciples is the realization of the absolute necessity for proper means—proper skills, organization, and hard work.

CONTINUAL REVISIONS OF GOALS

In fact, to come to our last rule for competent political thinking, the very heart of politics seems to lie in this problem of selecting practicable goals and in modifying them as necessary from day to day. For the political artist is only one among a host of others, all with their own goals, and the game becomes one of pushing a bit here, giving a bit there, trading an advance in one direction for a retreat in another direction, often standing stock still and perhaps wondering whether progress will ever be resumed.

One may wonder whether any sensitive person can survive these six steps, whether a cynical mind, a strong back, and an iron stomach are not really the requirements for success. We can only answer that the political man must not only have clear goals, but he must want to reach them. He must prefer fighting for them to forgetting about them. He must prefer struggle to a detached contemplation of events. He must prefer justice, even if getting it brings indigestion.

Fortunately, also, one man need not perform all the difficult tasks just described. The division of labor operates in politics as elsewhere. There are specialists in thinking, in organizing, in planning, in speaking, in writing, in legislating, and in many other things. They join together in the political process. Success often falls to the movement that forms the best combination of ideas and action. When we have given sufficient attention to the various operations of the political process in Part II, and when we have examined the political institutions that channel political behavior in Part III, we will return, in the last two chapters, to a discussion of the goals of democracy and the various plans for their achievement.

Questions and Problems

1. Find the term "political economy" in an encyclopedia and compare and contrast its concerns with those of political science. Why are there two terms, political economy and economics, for a single general field?

2. Make four statements of general facts about politics that appear to you to be scientific, that is, true statements. (Use as clear and precise language as possible.)

3. From your own experience and from what you have learned from your family, friends, and newspapers, explain in three hundred words or less why a career in politics is often thought not to be respectable in America.

4. The practitioners of political science are politicians, administrators, and active citizens. List from your own knowledge (or by scanning this book) ten particular offices held by persons in each of these three categories. Examples are: the President of the United States, the Director of the Federal Bureau of Investigation, the President of the Minnesota League of Women Voters.

5. In what ways do you think the science of medicine is like political science? The art of medicine like the art of politics?

6. If a friend were to say to you: "It is useless to study political science if you want to go into practical politics," what would you reply by way of agreement or disagreement?

7. What courses listed in your college catalogue would you advise a younger friend to take if he desired to be a political scientist specializing in municipal administration? State briefly why he ought to take each course.

8. Describe the difficulties, dangers, and advantages of dividing political science into "subject-areas."

9. The chapter at one point describes some of the factors that one would have to study in explaining the way a county votes. Take the problem of deciding why a certain wealthy man has become a socialist. List as many influences as you can imagine might be working to produce such an unusual combination of wealth and radicalism.

10. Why is it insufficient to regard political science as the study of public law? What other parts of the political process need to be studied?

11. Apart from the examples given in the chapter, list six events that may be classified today in America as "political," six that may be called "politically relevant," and six that may be called "politically conditioned." (Hint: use a newspaper or magazine to aid your memory.)

12. Find the terms, "description," "analysis," "comparison," "history," and "genesis" in *Webster's New International Dictionary* or *The New Oxford Dictionary of the English Language*. Use the new ideas thus gained to write a lengthier definition of each method of attacking political problems that was discussed in this chapter.

13. List ten sources of documentary materials on political science by their specific titles (such as *The United States Government Manual*).

14. How does the F.B.I. use the techniques of direct observation in its investigations and preparation of cases? Answer from previous reading or read articles listed in the *Reader's Guide*.

15. Prepare for your classmates a brief questionnaire of ten well-chosen questions that will discover "The class opinion on making a high-school diploma a requirement for the right to vote."

16. Why are the words used in political and social science so often treacherous and ambiguous?

17. Suppose you want to defeat Joe Smith and thus be elected town dog-

catcher. How would the six steps in correct political thought apply to your problem?

18. Write down your attitude on the question: "Shall women as well as men be mobilized for war?" Then write down what you consider to be the attitudes of most other people. What is the degree and intensity of the difference as you see it? How would you predict that the question would be decided by the government? What difference would the government decision make in your own attitude and behavior?

19. Take this statement as true for the moment: "Since political science does not yet know how to measure all possible factors and probable accidents in any certain case, any political decision is a 'calculated risk.'" Give one example, if you can, of a decision that has been or could be made by government officials of any kind that would not be a "calculated risk." If you cannot, give an example of a decision that appears to you to involve very little risk.

Longer Study and Research
Problems Suitable for Term Papers

1. Ask any twenty fellow-students or people at large to list the five political problems they consider as the most important to solve. Compile the results, and write an essay describing them, analyzing them to see whether they fit into the scope of political science as set forth in this chapter, and, if they fit, how they fit.

2. Clip the editorials of any daily newspaper for two weeks. Then analyze them according to: the number of preferences (that is, values) and factual statements they contain; the kind of method used in each sentence of factual reasoning; and the special techniques, if any, that have been used in producing the evidence, apart from logic. Report your findings and your conclusions as to whether or not a clear line of thinking was followed generally.

3. Ask any ten fellow-students or people at large to give you a written brief definition of four of the following terms: democracy, fascism, communism, liberty, representation, intelligence, public opinion, majority, social class, Democrat, and Republican. Compare their answers, and write a thousand word report on similarities and differences in defining each word. Include your judgment as to what might be done to make communication clearer.

4. Read one of the following works, and describe the methods and techniques they use.

John Gunther: *Inside U. S. A.*
Alexis de Tocqueville: *Democracy in America*, Vol. I
Robert and Helen Lynd: *Middletown*
Delisle Burns: *Political Ideals*
Harold Zink: *City Bosses in the United States*
Robert Brady: *Business as a System of Power*
George B. de Huzar: *Practical Applications of Democracy*

Niccolò Machiavelli: *The Prince*
Aristotle: *Politics*
Plato: *The Republic*
C. E. Merriam and H. F. Gosnell: *Non-Voting*
William C. McLeod: *The Origin and History of Politics*

2

THE STATE AND AUTHORITY

THE MAJOR concern of political scientists is the study of the state —a subject that often seems to be infinitely complex. The state today is a rambling organization of human relations that affects a good part of the activities in which man is normally engaged; its functions and officers change constantly. Matters that once did not concern the state are now state functions; even the disposal of garbage, to take a humble example, was once purely a private matter. Furthermore, the state has its analogue in certain organizations such as colonies, armies, political parties, churches, labor unions, trade associations, and families. These often act like states, they may be organized like states, and they may even become states. A thorough study of the state is thus the study of a wide variety of human action, past and present.

Defining the State and Sovereignty

THE STATE—TERRITORY, POPULATION, GOVERNMENT, INDEPENDENCE

The state is an independent organization of land and people. It has a territory, which may be as small as Andorra or as large as China. Second, it has a population, which may vary greatly in size and in degree of homogeneity. The people may or may not be of the same race, religion, ancestry, or occupational habits, and may not even speak the same language; nevertheless, belonging to the state usually develops enough likemindedness and like interests in a population to differentiate it from the population of outside states. In addition, this population located within a territory is organized: it possesses *specialized governing officials who operate in the name of the land and its people.*

These officials we call the government. They carry out whatever may be the operations of the state at the moment; they may collect taxes, administer justice, or declare the law to the people at large. For the most part these men operate free from dictation from beyond their territory. That is to say, the state as here defined is an independent organization.

These several characteristics of the state—a territory, a people, a government, and independence—in combination distinguish well enough for our purposes the state from other forms of social organization, such as the political party, the church, or the family. However, in studying past ages, we sometimes have difficulty in finding social organizations that meet these requirements. The term "state" as we describe it here is most useful in discussing the ninety-odd entities that exist today, rather than for describing the whole medieval and ancient world.

The ancient Greeks and early Romans, for instance, thought of the political community as the city-state, as a close community, like Athens or Sparta (or like a small city in America today), where the citizens shared common ancestors and common interests from day to day. They felt they had nothing in common with the strange collection of peoples and cities that formed the Persian Empire. On the other hand, in many periods of the past and in some areas of the world today, the state is no more than a wandering tribe with no fixed territory. Yet such tribes had and have a homogeneous population, specialized hereditary chieftains, and independence of their neighbors. The German tribes that overran the late Roman Empire, the Huns who invaded medieval Europe, and the Moslems who swept over North Africa and southern Europe in the Middle Ages were organized in this fashion. At other times and among other peoples are found organizations that number only a few members of a single family, that are led by a dominant or oldest member, and that have no fixed territory. Also somewhat different from the state as defined are the feudal regimes that flourished in the Middle Ages in Europe and that exist in countries like Burma today. Such a state is a patrimony of a family; the land and its inhabitants belong as a kind of property to the barons or kings. The state is then a huge family holding-company, as was the empire of the "marrying Hapsburgs" before World War I.

NO "LAW" OF STATE EVOLUTION

It would be convenient if one could say that our modern state has been the goal of political evolution or is a stage in the evolution towards some ideal state. A number of writers have tried to apply a "law of evolution" to states; first, they have suggested, came the family, then the clan, then the tribe, then the city-state and the empire, and finally the complex, highly organized modern state. But most political scientists now think this theory is a gross caricature of history. Some states may have come up this road, but others have not, and still others have gone in the opposite direction. Many tribes have never developed into settled states; their members go on gathering nuts and berries, or fishing, without ever finding a necessity for a full-fledged state. On the other hand, complex states have been reduced to simple ones; the Roman Empire in the West, for example, broke down into many small principalities. Such a theory, furthermore, is not without dangerous consequences; it gives some state-worshippers a comfortable feeling of being in step with a natural law.

The evidence concerning the evolution of states might better be put this way: When a number of influences—new inventions, an infusion of different culture or ideas into its composition, or a peculiar kind of governmental organization—combine, a society transforms its state organization and may well bring change to its neighbors. The Huns light horse cavalry proved effective in transforming a tribe into a crude empire and reducing more complex states, which had "evolved" beyond the loose imperial form of government, into simple dependencies. A new commercial and trading class in the American colonies raised up a new nation with some novel state institutions (an elective president, a written constitution, and so on).

MYTH OF THE SOCIAL COMPACT

If the idea that states evolve rigidly according to some law is in large part false, so also is the idea that all states were originally formed by a compact among their inhabitants. From the sixteenth to the eighteenth centuries, political theorists were fond of reciting that men, because they wanted to co-operate, once upon a time gathered together and set up a state. This state was legalized by a "social compact" or "contract," to which the inhabitants promised to adhere. This theory is largely myth. All evidence indicates that as long as man has been man, he has known authority in some form.

In the centuries when the social contract theory was popular, it provided the intellectual basis for social revolutions; the "old regimes" were supposed to have violated the original compacts, and new governments were to be established, based on new compacts. But the fact that men of action once firmly believed in the social contract does not alter its mythical character. Revolutions require new beliefs. When men were revolting against kings, they expressed their belief that kings were wrong by declaring that the people were right—that only the people should set up governments, and that they should upset them, too, when governments become despotic. These revolutionaries believed that if the people were to contract among themselves to set up a government, this popular agreement would be a genuine social contract. The doctrine of the social compact was in reality a pledge of faith in the right of the people to rule and in the necessity of making a clear agreement between the people and their officers. It marked the beginning of the modern age of written constitutions; to some extent it was expressed in the American Constitution and all the state constitutions. But it was not a true explanation of the origins of the state.

SOVEREIGNTY

Another common word in the vocabulary of political writing since the sixteenth century has been "sovereignty." It has caused endless trouble because it has been given several different meanings. It was put forth by Jean Bodin, a supporter of monarchy during the times when the kings were trying to get more power from the nobles and clergy. Somewhere, he wrote, there must be a final right to make laws over men; this repository of right must be the state. "Sovereignty" is the "absolute and perpetual power of the republic," he declared. It is indivisible and inalienable, and is entrusted to the rulers. With a great deal of clever legal language, Bodin tied together absolute right and absolute power. The monarch had the right to do whatever he thought proper; the subjects had the duty to submit. What could be more acceptable to the chiefs of state than this formula?

But the formula fell into other hands. A competing theory of "sovereignty of the people" arose. What the king could do, so could the people. The absolute and perpetual power of sovereignty belonged to the people, wrote a growing body of democrats. They had merely delegated it to the king.

Impartial political scientists call down a plague on the logic of both houses. They can see that, as ordinarily used, this word "sovereignty" is really a slogan, a war cry. It acts as a legal spell to justify what power the people or the king *have* or *would like* to have. The word has acquired a magic that causes many to accept power from whoever claims sovereignty.

It is important, therefore, that we use this word, which is still necessary in political discussion, in a careful manner. The meaning we shall employ is the following: *Sovereignty is the claim to the power to make final decisions affecting a state when that claim is authorized by the existing legitimate order.* Sovereignty is a claim to power, not the actual exercise of power. Power is the ability to make decisions influencing the behavior of men. And sovereignty can exist without full exercise of the power claimed. As we shall see, those who hold sovereignty may be feeble rulers; or they may be reluctant to make many of the laws that they are entitled to make. Sovereignty has to do with final decisions. Human conflicts very often can be resolved only by an authority from which neither party believes he has the right to appeal. Men are forever looking for "the court of last resort." That "court" is the sovereign.

Nevertheless, sovereignty may be consigned, not to one, but to several offices or individuals. Thus, a federal state (the United States, for example) usually distributes the claims to the power to make final decisions among local bodies and the central government. Each unit is entitled to claim the right of final decision for certain matters within its jurisdiction. Even bodies such as churches, industries, and individuals are considered by the laws of some states (such as the United States) to have a legitimate claim to make certain kinds of final decisions. Furthermore, especially today, the distribution of sovereignty is changing. Laws transfer legitimate claims to power from one group to another or from local groups to the central government. *Thus sovereignty can be differently located and differently distributed in different states.*

LEGITIMACY

Sovereignty, we have said, is a claim that is authorized by the existing legitimate order. Of what does this authorization consist? What is the legitimate order? Legitimacy itself is the *lawful* condition or quality of an act or person. When a whole range of behavior is legitimate, it may be called a legitimate order. The laws of a state usually are clear enough about what actions are legitimate. There is always some disagreement, of course, over new problems, but the resulting conflict is usually not sufficient to destroy the prevailing fundamental authorities—courts, legislatures—and the belief of the overwhelming majority of people in the existing order and process of government.

When the overwhelming majority of people regard the existing order as unlawful, or when there is a basic dispute among powerful political groups over what is right or wrong, lawful or unlawful, we have what we may call the absence of legitimacy. Legitimacy is being contested. Without it, there is no sovereign, only various groups that may be seeking to establish their sovereignty.

The recent history of China provides an illustration. As World War II ended, the Kuomintang government of Chiang Kai-shek was the sovereign government of China. Its claim to make final decisions affecting China was authorized as legitimate over the larger part of the country, but a generation of civil war had reduced the chance of any government's establishing a claim to power that *all* Chinese would accept as legal. The uncertainty and insecurity induced by past revolutions and wars weakened any claim to final power. Furthermore, the power of the government itself, which might have contributed to a growth in the belief in the legitimacy of the Chiang government, was enfeebled by war and maladministration. Most important of all, in the northern parts of the country the Chinese communists were competing for sovereignty. Under Mao Tse-tung, they claimed the power to make final decisions for all of China, and in northern China, at least, that claim was regarded as legitimate by the laws and, apparently, by the people.

Mao's conquest of the whole of mainland China from Chiang destroyed Chiang's already weak legitimacy and sovereignty, but it did not create a new legitimacy and sovereignty, as we have defined these terms, even though Mao's regime may have had in fact huge powers, effectively administered. Given an interval of time and the successful employment of various devices to gain general acceptance within China and to set a new pattern of laws and beliefs, Mao's government may *then* come to be regarded as legitimate and sovereign.

THE THREE TYPES OF LEGITIMACY

Among states there are different kinds of legitimacy, which we might compare to different kinds of marriage. Most marriages today are legally consummated; a set of relationships governing the positions of husband and wife is declared by law as legitimate. However, a man and woman who have lived long enough together as husband and wife, even if they have not gone through the legal ceremony, are considered to be legimately married; their's is a "common-law" marriage. Then there is the illicit romance. If passionate enough, completely mutual, and powerful enough to overcome all convention, even this relationship is regarded as somehow legitimate in the sense that "Heaven meant them for one another." Nevertheless, save among certain small religious sects, *legal* marriage is the norm; the other two relationships are not accorded full legitimate status.

There are three similar kinds of legitimacy that determine the existence of sovereignty and thus, by necessary implication, the legitimacy of acts of authority: rational legitimacy, traditional legitimacy, and charismatic legitimacy. In different times and places, and in different amounts at the same time and place, people regard a claim to power and an act of power as *right* and *legitimate* for different reasons. So sovereignty, a court judgment, a police order, or a tax law is regarded as *right* in proportion as it satisfies the current character of legitimacy.

Rational legitimacy is the accord of a people with all claims and acts that are clearly defined as to meaning and objective and that are governed by respect for legal regulations. Acts must observe constitutional and legal procedures. The strong belief of Americans that ours is "a government of laws, and not of men" and the constant effort to get rid of personal, incongruous elements in government indicate that rational legitimacy is the strongest form of legitimacy in America. Indeed, Americans frequently set up a written constitution before they will act even in voluntary association together. Where rational legitimacy is strong, hereditary nobility is laughed at, and "reason and efficiency" are demanded of every institution, official, and act.

Even in a society whose belief in rational legitimacy is fairly weak, some activities may be organized according to the principles of rational legitimacy. Business enterprises throughout history have tended to be organized in a "rational" fashion with a hierarchy of offices, rules and regulations, and the selection of officers according to their technical qualifications for the job. Long-established armies and long-established government bureaucracies also develop this "rational" character, and all claims to office and all acts performed in them must be "according to the rules" before the other members of the organization consider them legitimate. A society in which the prevailing beliefs of governors and governed demand the extension of such methods of organization to all activities is a society ruled by rational legitimacy.

Traditional legitimacy is accord with claims and acts of rulers because these rulers have *"always"* made these claims and committed these acts. "The king's desire is law" because the king (the most common type of traditional ruler) is descended from the established Hohenstaufen or Bourbon or Savoy line, and the officers of the state owe him personal allegiance. Rights that are transmitted from generation to generation are sacrosanct. When traditional legitimacy is very strong, as in feudal times, the whole of the state is administered as a family affair. When it is weak, as it has been in America, each generation wants to make all decisions for itself. Jefferson, who believed in the "insurrection of science, talents and courage against rank and birth, which have fallen into contempt," also wanted each generation to write its own constitution.

Still, no state is without certain beliefs in the rightness of the traditional. There is a sanctity to certain "nonrational" customary laws in America; for example, the attempt of a presidential elector to vote for whomsoever he pleases is regarded as illegitimate, although the Constitution gives him this "right." "Old families," venerable constitutions, and other "old" things are respected over new, quite apart from the question of their legality. Naturally, rational and traditional claims often conflict; sometimes both are challenged.

The third form of legitimacy, charismatic legitimacy, is rarely found in a pure form. "Charisma" distinguishes those persons or acts that are deemed to be right because possessed of "the touch of grace"; certain persons and events are supposed to be miraculous and possessed of a special mission in, or significance to, society. All ordinary persons must toe the line of prescribed rational or traditional behavior, but the claims and acts of special individuals are sometimes considered legitimate because they seem to be "God-given." In a period of great confusion and change, a state may acquire a truly charismatic leader who asks no acknowledgment of his authority save the immediate recognition on the part of his followers that he, and he alone, has a divine mission to save the country or the world. To varying degrees, such have been men like Alexander the Great, Oliver Cromwell, Napoleon, Mussolini, Hitler, Washington, Franklin D. Roosevelt, Mahatma Gandhi, and Winston Churchill. As citizens, we must pass judgment on these men, but as political scientists, we are interested instead in a certain kind of legitimacy they all express—a legitimacy that comes from the belief of people that the men are endowed with superhuman powers, that they have a divinely appointed mission, and that their word is law. In the charismatic, popular movements that follow such men, the word of the leader is all the authority needed— traditions and rational procedures go by the board.

As charismatic movements grow older, they may take on more and more legitimacy from rational and traditional sources, either because of or despite the efforts of the leaders. Napoleon had himself crowned Emperor of the French, even though the French people had accepted him as a charismatic leader. Hitler, though he sought revolution and preached violence, nevertheless insisted on holding office. Each step in the violent career of the Nazi movement was justified by the stamp of legality; charisma was not enough. Not even the Communist Party, sworn enemy of Hitler, could be destroyed until Hitler passed a series of enactments "legalizing" his conduct.

LEGITIMACY IS OFTEN MIXED

All three types of legitimacy are frequently mingled. The administrative branch of the English government, for instance, is an intricate compound of the traditional and the rational. Offices with queer-sounding titles that mark their ancient origins in a personal relationship to the king more recently have been given regular duties, pay, and a place in the chain of command in the administrative hierarchy. On the other hand, the office of the king of England acquires a certain charismatic quality by virtue of its awesome character. People often expect superhuman qualities and deeds of high officers. In fact, one may say of all legitimate authority that a halo of charisma surrounds it.

The controversy over a third term for the President of the United States provides another kind of example. The President holds a powerful, legally created position that was provided with a rational set of functions, but no constitutional clause covered his standing for re-election more than once. A century and a half of tradition, however, faced Franklin Roosevelt when he decided to run for a third term in 1940. In a debate that followed, all three kinds of legitimacy became issues. True to American habit, the main battle was fought over the legal and constitutional question "What does the law say," though there was little "law" on the subject. Another struggle was waged over the "illegitimacy" of violating tradition. A third issue was the charismatic character of the President himself; some people felt that "only F. D. R. should be allowed to run again," or that "only Roosevelt could save the country."

LEGITIMACY AND DISORDER

Each form of legitimacy is most powerfully at work when people will not even consider changing to an alternative form. The Roman Republic was so deeply committed to rational legitimacy that it could not tolerate a traditional king, although it was not so immune to charisma. Legitimacy is less powerfully at work when its major forms contend openly against one another. Then revolutions may break out. For instance, in America in 1776, in France in 1789, and in England in 1832 (The Great Reform of Representation) switches were made from traditional to rational legitimacy. Such revolutions may shed much blood; at the least they cause psychological distress to a great many people.

Most disastrous to stability is the situation in which no claim to legitimacy is honored, in which neither laws, nor traditions, nor men are respected. Such, according to Guglielmo Ferrero, the late historian, is the situation today. The twentieth century, he wrote, inherited from the nineteenth century no principle of legitimacy. The result is constant change, a continual fight for boundless power, an insecurity of all ruling classes that leads them to take ruthless measures. There are no signs that people believe in either dynasties or elective officers. Messianic leaders have appeared, but sad experiences with such leaders have produced an even greater reluctance to accord them legitimacy. We have come to the point where we ask, not what kind of legitimacy "ought to exist," but whether any kind of legitimate order will be stoutly defended by people and officers.

The Instruments of Authority

LEGITIMACY ABETS POWER

Legitimacy is not only a fundamental characteristic of government, it is a powerful weapon. People often believe what legitimate authority tells them to believe, and act accordingly. They stop buying silk, they pay more taxes, they hate their enemies more cordially, when told to do so. Legitimacy gives an important magic to acts of state.

There are three other weapons by which governments typically carry out their policies: education (or propaganda); force (or violence); and economic measures (or economic manipulation). When people think these methods are used legitimately, they call them education, force, or economic measures; when they think such methods are used unfairly or illegally, they call them propaganda, violence, or economic manipulation.

POLITICAL EDUCATION AND PROPAGANDA

Political education and propaganda are attempts to build support for policy by using psychological techniques. The government constantly instructs its citizens, young and old, how to decide the merits of various issues, how to behave as citizens, how to protect their health, how to treat foreigners, and how to treat one another. The line between government education and propaganda is often hard to draw. When a policy being discussed is generally accepted, the government "educates"; when the policy is controversial, the government "propagandizes." What is in one context propaganda in another may be education. Take, for example, some of the films and reports put out by the government during the New Deal. One dealt with soil conservation by showing how farmers individually could do much to prevent soil erosion. It was accepted universally as legitimate educational material. Another film showed how soil erosion could be prevented by large dams owned and operated by the government. But government ownership was a controversial question, and the New Deal was attacked for using public funds for political propaganda. Instructions to the electorate on how, when, and where to vote provide another example. Such education is universally recognized as a legitimate undertaking of the state. However, when James I inserted in election writs containing such instructions a good deal of "educational" advice on behalf of his favorite candidates, this practice was frowned upon even under the loose system of election administration of his time; in America today, it would be regarded as a gross misuse of a state-controlled educational weapon.

When there exist sharp differences of opinion among the people or in the government, no use of government education goes uncriticized. A plea for better relations between white and colored citizens, though quite in line with all constitutional principle and with the beliefs of the greater part of the American people, is regarded in parts of the United States as an illegitimate intrusion on private rights. Important segments of public opinion in our country have been so suspicious of government propaganda that only in recent years has the government been able even to report fully on its normal performance of established duties.

FORCE AND VIOLENCE

Force is a basic weapon of the government; it is physical compulsion exercised by legitimate authority. Violence is unauthorized force. Some great political writers have called force the single essential characteristic of all states. All institutions and groups can propagandize, or spend funds, or even order their members to do certain things, but with one exception, only the state through its government can ordinarily employ physical coercion to make people behave in a certain way. In practically all communities force, it is true, may be also used by the heads of families towards family members, over whom they are considered to have legitimate authority. Otherwise, its use is usually allowed only to specified agents of the state, such as police, sheriffs, and soldiers.

The great public anxiety that is aroused whenever private individuals or groups make use of unauthorized force (that is, of violence) attests to the strength of the idea that the state alone should employ physical coercion. Although acts of vigilantes, acts of private revenge, duelling, and like behavior are not considered completely evil, they are frowned upon and in the long run repressed by most societies today. At most, there is a certain restricted area for unorganized, nongovernmental action.

When the customs are changing, the line between force and violence tends to be confused. When Aaron Burr killed Alexander Hamilton in a pistol duel, the participants and many other persons regarded this resort to force as legitimate. But a larger body of people considered his action a violent disregard of lawful procedure for settling disputes. The times and customs were changing, and he was one of those trapped between contradictory attitudes. His political influence diminished, and his friends decreased in number.

As we have already pointed out, in states where the conception of legitimacy is changing or legitimacy is absent the use of physical coercion increases, and here, too, the line between force and violence becomes difficult to draw. What the followers of Hitler, infatuated by his charisma, thought was legitimate force, a great many other Germans and non-Germans were convinced was illegal violence; or, significantly, they could not make up their minds where and to what extent it was right to use physical coercion at all.

Many societies dislike force even as a government weapon and prefer to use education and economic policy to regulate human affairs, reserving force for use only as a last resort. Others accept force as the most preferred way of making people conform to public policy. Herbert Spencer, in fact, divided all societies into "militant" and "industrial" types, according to the predominant way in which they get things done.

The United States today, for instance, is at least internally an "industrial society." The authorities in America try to convince and persuade persons, or to make it worth their while to conform to the government's policy. An elaborate court system is provided to give complete hearings to protesting parties before the coercive machinery of the state is called into play. The abrupt command, backed by the police, is disliked by the public and discouraged by the laws. The Agricultural Adjustment Administration (A.A.A.), for example, gets farmers to reduce plantings by asking their consent and by paying them not to plant crops. The Soil Conservation Service tries to educate farmers not to exhaust their soil by overuse. The agencies in the administrative branch of the government, which in other countries act freely as the executors of policy, in the United States must make their decisions in many cases with as great care and as much consultation as ordinarily occurs in the judicial branch of the government.

Even in its international relations, the United States has tried to implement its policies with loans, gifts, and technical assistance to potentially allied countries, rather than with its overwhelming military force. The Marshall Plan (the Economic Co-operation Administration) was created as a form of economic warfare against bolshevism. Nevertheless, America maintains strong armaments, not trusting to economic means of propaganda alone, and subscribing thereby to Clausewitz's dictum: "War is not merely a political act but a real political instrument, a continuation of political intercourse, a carrying out of the same by other means."

The Fascist movement in certain European and Asiatic countries, especially in Italy, Germany and Japan, sought to "recapture" for force its place as the supremely good political weapon, a place that the laws and public opinion of most Western societies had relegated to the "dark ages." Whereas Western thought constantly demanded further restrictions on the use of even legitimate force in the treatment of criminals, rearing of children, and the regulation of internal affairs, the Fascist movement demanded the re-establishment of force as a proper weapon of internal authority. In fact, it went far beyond and applauded "force for force's sake." In our terms, of course, when force is used for its own sake, it becomes violence and is illegitimate; it is no longer a weapon of, but a threat to, legitimate authority.

ECONOMIC MEASURES AND MANIPULATION

As an alternative to force, the government may employ various economic measures, which, taken together, constitute a broad power to compel conformance to government goals. The most common measure is taxation. Manipulation of the currency is another; regulation of the disposal of property by inheritance, gift, sale, or exportation is a third. Still others are the regulation of business enterprise and the ownership or management of productive enterprises, techniques aimed at realizing, among other goals, a higher standard of living for lower income groups.

Like education and force, such measures are not always clearly legitimate. They may have drastic effects and still be acceptable; for instance, colored oleomargarine may be taxed out of existence. But measures must not clash with the ideal expectations of society. For example, government officials must not disregard long practice or legal procedures in order to increase their personal fortunes; no matter how widespread such corruption, it is never regarded as entirely right and proper. Machiavelli wrote in *The Prince* that heads of states had to commit many crimes, such as the illegal seizure of property; but he still recognized that all acts of the "Prince" could be classified as moral or immoral. He merely insisted that power and goodness (or legitimacy) were very often incompatible, and that when they conflicted, goodness had to be sacrificed to power.

When in violation of stated public "policy" or general public sentiment, a private group uses its wealth to injure individuals or other groups, it is not exercising legitimate authority; it is using economic manipulation, tolerated more in some societies than in others. Vague or precise rules of the game dictate the amount of economic manipulation that can be used by private individuals and groups in the political process. For example, English election law limits the number of vehicles a political party may use to transport voters to the polls. American state law often restricts campaign expenditures used to employ or persuade individuals directly and allows only indirect use of money. Thus a man may be sent a hundred propaganda tracts by a candidate, but may not be given the equivalent in money in order to influence his vote. Organizations may pay lobbyists to influence legislators, but may not pay legislators to vote a certain way.

In thinking of economic measures and their relation to political authority, we may visualize the whole economic structure of the community—the ways in which men make a living, the control they have over their economic behavior, and the ways in which goods are distributed among them—as a map that is constantly being revised by the government. Sometimes the revisions come slowly, sometimes rapidly. Sometimes the government consciously directs the changes. At other times it may perform acts that cause unforeseen economic change; for example, the religious persecutions of the French Huguenots, who were skilled artisans, drove them from France to Prussia, England, Holland, and America, hurting the economy of France and aiding those of her rivals. Sometimes the government may be a mere cartographer, not causing change, but registering giant economic transformations, such as the Industrial Revolution, that alter the social and political map.

POLITICAL INSTRUMENTS ARE COMMONLY EMPLOYED TOGETHER

These three principal methods used by the government to carry out its policies—the psychological, coercive, and economic—are hardly ever used separately. American aircraft carriers in the Mediterranean, although instruments of violence, are also effective propaganda. Education on the conservation of the soil effectively guides agricultural production, an economic goal. Force applied to reduce labor-management violence educates the contestants to accept the supreme authoritative position occupied by the state. Just as we can look for a combination of the three main kinds of legitimacy in any given political event, so can we look for a combination of the three main methods of obtaining conformity to goals. The political authority of government, of the officials of the state, typically represents a concentration of legal, traditional, and charismatic legitimacy founded in the law and in acceptance by the governed; it acts through education, force, and economic measures. When legitimacy is disputed, the acts of those in authority may be deemed propaganda, violence, or economic manipulation.

The Classification of Governmental Forms

CLASSIFICATION BY FORMS OF LEGITIMACY

Given the essential character of the state and of government, we are now prepared to ask ourselves whether there is any pattern by which governments, and hence states, are organized. We may, of course, classify governments according to their underlying principle or combination of principles of authority: the legal, traditional, and charismatic, each of which has tremendous impact on their organization. For example, a government that chooses its officials by elections or open competitive examination can hardly be called charismatic or traditional in form; it is legal and "rational."

THE CLASSICAL DIVISION

There are, however, four other useful ways of classifying forms of government. First there is the classical division of all governments into three forms—monarchy, oligarchy, and democracy. Monarchy is government by the one, oligarchy by the few, and democracy by the many. Each form may be good or bad, depending on how power is exercised. Plato, for example, held in his *Republic* that there was a natural succession of forms of government. An *aristocracy* (his ideal Republic) that abuses its power develops into a *timocracy*, which, through greed, develops into an *oligarchy* (both are governments of the few), which in turn is overthrown by the *democracy* of the people, which through excesses becomes an *anarchy* (a lawless government) from which only the *tyranny* of one man can come. The tyranny in turn is overthrown, and the cycle begins again. Aristotle accepted this classification but thought there was no necessity for any one form to succeed another. Many succeeding political scientists followed the Greek theory, among them Polybius, Machiavelli, Campanella, and Spinoza. In fact, it is the "schoolboy's" classification; we learn it first of all.

ELITE AND MASS

The most systematic attack on the Greek classification of governments came from Gaetano Mosca, who advanced instead his own theory of the "elite." His predecessors were found among thinkers like Burke and Taine, and his followers have included twentieth century political scientists like Pareto, Michels, and Burnham. Forms of government, wrote Mosca, are often mere camouflages for the real rulers of a state. Whatever the form, be it monarchical, aristocratic, or democratic, there is always one political ruling group or "elite" that holds power in its own hands. The mass of people has little voice in politics. States are always ruled by the few; they are all oligarchies of some kind.

DEGREE OF CENTRALIZATION

A third system classifies governments as federal (or feudal) or unitary according to their degree of centralization. Federal and feudal states divide up the power of making important decisions among local and central authorities. A "confederation" generally refers to a weak federation in which the central authority has few powers. Unitary states, by contrast, give the right of decision on all important political matters to the national government. Such power may or may not be delegated to local authorities. If it is delegated, then the state is called a decentralized rather than a centralized unitary state. In the early nineteenth century, England exemplified the first, France the second.

An empire is harder to classify. Its central government holds sovereignty and power over countries of dissimilar nationality or culture. Generally, since all important decisions tend to be made by the imperial government, the empire has a unitary character; but many important cultural and social events and customs are determined by the colonies, which have, therefore, a considerable amount of decentralized autonomy. Indeed, certain components of the so-called British Empire are quite in a position to make very important political decisions by themselves; Canada and the other Dominions of the British Commonwealth of Nations are really independent affiliated nations nowadays. But other possessions of the British Empire are ruled directly by the central government in England as colonies, protectorates, or military bases.

FORMS OF INTEGRATION

A final system classifies states and governments according to their degree of integration, that is, the degree to which the apparatus of the state ties together all the activities of the political community.

One index of integration is the amount of government control of and contact with the various political groups of the society. There are, for example, "one-party states," (Fascist Italy or the Soviet Union), in which the government and party are closely intertwined, and, by contrast, "two-party states" (the United States) and "multiparty states" (France), in which the parties are quite distinct from the government.

Another index is found in the relationship of the government to the economy. In the *laissez-faire* state, for instance, there is little integration of government and economy. Economic practices such as investment and profit making are left to private persons and groups; the state does not plan or control them to a large extent. In a feudal state, on the other hand, community activities of all kinds, social and economic, are more closely tied into the political system. Each class— the clergy, the nobility, the administrative bureaucracy, and the commoners—is entitled to certain social, economic, and political privileges and must perform corresponding duties; there is no one law for all men, nor do all have the right to participate to the same extent, or in the same way, in social, economic, or political affairs.

A third level of integration is found in the corporate state, as essayed in Italy, Germany, and Portugal. All vocational groups are absorbed into the government. Fishermen, manufacturers of machinery, farmers, and other occupations are organized separately into councils to which the government adds representatives. Each council is given certain limited powers of government in its area of the economy. A final level of integration is found in socialism, as exhibited in England under the Labour party and in the Soviet Union. The governments own a large share of the resources and wealth-producing machinery of their countries.

We need scarcely add that in the same nation one may find several different kinds of integration at work at the same time. Unlike Russia, for example, England has a liberal two-party system to offset its socialism. In the *laissez-faire* United States, the states give medical associations rights of representation on boards that examine candidates for licenses to practice medicine, and the state governments carry out the policies of these doctor-dominated boards: moreover, the federal government and many states own and operate various public utilities and own huge tracts of land.

The Limits of State Activity

EXTENT OF GOVERNMENT REGULATION

We have now defined the character of the state, discussed the legitimacy of governments and of their methods of inducing conformity, and classified governments (and in effect, states) by their basic organization. But we have not answered the question: What are the limits of governmental activity? We know that it is difficult to think of any activity, however remote, that has not at one time or another been regulated or performed by the government. Governments have taken upon themselves the tasks of regulating the morality, the property, and the civil and political activities of persons and groups. The censorship of movies, the fixing of prices, the banning of political clubs, and the protection of civil liberties by courts are only several instances of governmental intervention in human affairs.

Certain terms have been used to classify the forms of government intervention, but they are not precise. The *"laissez-faire"* state is supposed to intervene in human activities only to protect property and persons from criminal attack. The "positive" state or the "welfare" state is supposed to regulate or manage some of the major industries and regulates most of the important economic and social activities. The "totalitarian" state is supposed to dominate and regulate all behavior.

These terms are not very useful. They are full of emotional meaning, good for inciting political action, but poor for building a political science. Rather than discuss the forms they supposedly describe, we shall try to understand in what major ways government intervention varies with social conditions. For the problem of analyzing such intervention—the problem of defining the "limits" of governmental activity—is one of showing what basic factors increase or decrease the tendency of political authority to interfere in each of the several areas of moral, economic, and political behavior.

HOW FUNCTIONS DEVELOP

An Inventory of Governmental Activities in the United States, prepared by Carl H. Chatters and Marjorie Leonard Hoover in 1947, listed almost four hundred services performed by American units of government. The table on page 50 (Figure 5) shows what these functions are. Federal, state, county, and city governments often carry on the same general kind of service. "Nearly all major activities of government are performed by some unit of government at all three levels, federal, state, and local." There has been a striking growth in the formal assumption of responsibilities by government, especially in the last fifty years.

One cannot, however, on the basis of this one index assert that government is swallowing up society. The new functions of government are often thrust upon it. Take, for example, the growth in America of two early government responsibilities, road tending and fire protection. The early nineteenth-century American communities placed on all citizens the responsibility for work on the roads and for the fighting of fires. These functions were performed in a completely decentralized fashion. For the sake of an efficient division of labor, however, men gradually substituted taxes for labor and professionalism for universal participation. A man could make more money and pay more taxes if he pursued his own vocation and joined with everyone else in hiring road workers and firemen.

Furthermore, basic social change can make the expansion of governmental functions unavoidable. In America the movement of women from the home into outside work, for instance, has indirectly caused a striking increase in government assistance to children and the family. These women have greatly increased national productivity, but they have left in the home a vacuum that the government has been charged with filling. Thus the schools teach children home economics, personal hygiene, and "family living"; social workers are hired to help problem children who have "working mothers." Many other examples may be found to illustrate our point—that the expansion of government functions is only in small part the result of an abstract belief in government interference; more often it has been the unexpected result of division of labor and specialization of activity.

As we shall point out in the last chapter, the profound consequences of some of these piecemeal, unplanned changes are often not realized. Their moral effects are great but are often too deeply buried to be uncovered in time for effective remedy. When our grandmother took a job, neither she nor the governing officials thought that she was demanding (1) a longer school day, (2) more public assistance for child welfare, (3) new labor laws, (4) the right of women to vote, (5) a lower birth rate, (6) increased taxes for vocational education, and other changes that her action indirectly influenced, including shorter skirts and fewer ruffles so that she could move more easily around desks and machinery. Most of the government's new activities have been caused indirectly by such individual actions of masses of people who have been responding to uncontrolled social forces. The few who have foreseen the future have been quite helpless to forestall the great initial changes. A changing culture cannot be thrown from high speed into reverse.

Thus one must always go below appearances to measure state activity. Functions of the state accrue when many people are aware of a problem. However, this awareness sometimes comes easily and at other times with difficulty. People can readily see, for instance, a severe scarcity of housing in wartime and may demand prompt governmental action. But a scarcity of housing owing to slow shifts of population, technological incompetence, or conspiracy between labor and capital, is perceived with less ease; opponents of public housing then are more able to blame proposals for change on some "whimsical" or "fanatic" idea that government should "do things for people."

On the other hand, new state activities may be so "obviously useful" that their indirect consequences are utterly ignored. In the nineteenth century, the various states and the federal government were so anxious to have railroads built quickly that they granted vast territories and many special privileges to private groups who gained in several cases a stranglehold on the politics and economy of the states.

If one surveys the Athenian commonwealth, the Roman government under Augustus, the medieval French and English feudal monarchies, or the sweeping changes introduced by the Labour government of England after 1945, he comes to realize that governmental activities are always numerous, but that at times some of them are not recognized as governmental. For example, governmental functions are often so incorporated into the individual's personality and his culture that he scarcely perceives them as functions. Thus the feudal serf worked for the state a good part of the time, but in ways that he scarcely realized; he was merely following customs he had learned from his ancestors. Or again, certain public functions are often unrecognized because they are carried on by nongovernmental subgroups, rather than by the formal organization of government. For example, mediation of disputes among private parties, which in the United States is regarded as a duty of government, was in the medieval Italian states often left to university professors of law.

LIMITS OF GOVERNMENTAL ACTIVITY

The limits of governmental intervention within a given society depend on several basic factors. The organization of the state and the efficiency of its officials is one; permanent, trained administrators are well adapted to organize human beings for getting things done. The emotional statement of a one-time United States Chamber of Commerce official gives striking support to this generalization: "The best public servant is the worse one," he declared. "A thoroughly first-rate man in public service is corrosive. He eats holes in our liberties. The better he is and the longer he stays, the greater is the danger."

Second is the degree of complexity of the division of labor in a society. If the society is complex, that is, highly "civilized," a great deal of government intervention may occur easily. New, specialized jobs grow out of old, generalized tasks, and the government takes over a certain number of the new jobs.

Third is the ideology of the people. How firmly are they committed to working as a collective group or as individuals? An Italian writer once remarked to the author that he perceived "a basic difference" between Americans and Germans in the behavior of their soldiers on leave. When the German soldiers visited Naples from the front, they would descend from their trucks, lock arms, and march down the street singing *lieder*. The American soldiers would disperse alone or in pairs on their private business. The lesson of this little story about cultural differences seems to be borne out by anthropological surveys. Margaret Mead, in summarizing studies of primitive peoples who occupy similar cultural levels of civilization, finds three basic forms of community life. Certain societies are fundamentally competitive in their politics, economics, and mating customs; others are individualistic; still others are highly co-operative and integrated. Most members of each culture see the world, including the political world, through the eyes of their cultures.

The limits of governmental intervention are thus determined by impersonal social and economic forces: the organization of the state, the complexity of the economy and society, and the cultural ideology of the people; but the actual amount of intervention will be partially determined by the kind of leadership in a society. The men in power can reduce or increase state intervention; their personalities will help to determine what methods—for instance, force or education—are likely to be used in new intervention and how effective those methods will be. We must therefore turn next to the study of leadership: of how men control the state and thus influence social change.

FIGURE 5

THE CHATTERS-HOOVER INVENTORY OF GOVERNMENTAL ACTIVITIES IN THE UNITED STATES *

ACTIVITY	GOVERNMENTAL UNITS				
	F.	S.	CO.	CITY	SD.
I *Overhead Activities*					
A. Passage of Law and Ordinances	x	x	x	x	x
B. Administration of Law and Justice	x	x	x	x	
C. Registration of Voters			x	x	
D. Conduct of Elections		x	x	x	
E. Community Planning and Zoning	x	x	x	x	
II *Protection to Persons and Property*					
A. National Defense					
1. Armed forces	x	x			
2. Naval forces	x	x			
3. Air forces	x				
4. Construction and maintenance of military, naval, air bases	x				
5. Training of members of armed forces	x	x			
6. Civilian defense	x	x	x	x	
7. Coast guard	x				
8. Control of aliens and alien property	x				
9. War material production	x				
B. Police Protection and Law Enforcement					
1. Records and statistics					
a. General and criminal records	x	x	x	x	
b. Identification records	x	x	x	x	

Key to columnar headings: F.—Federal Government; S.—State Governments; Co.—Counties; City includes boroughs, towns, and villages; SD.—Special purpose districts, including school districts.

* Reproduced with the permission of the Municipal Finance Officers Association.

Inventory of Governmental Activities (continued)

ACTIVITY	GOVERNMENTAL UNITS				
	F.	S.	CO.	CITY	SD.

II *Protection to Persons and Property (cont'd)*

	F.	S.	CO.	CITY	SD.
c. Collection of crime statistics	X	X		X	
2. Detention and custody of prisoners	X	X	X	X	
3. Police communications	X	X	X	X	X
4. Crime control					
a. Prevention of crime	X	X	X	X	X
b. Investigation of crimes	X	X	X	X	X
5. Vice and morals control					
a. Regulation and prohibition of prostitution	X	X	X	X	
b. Liquor control	X	X	X	X	
c. Narcotic control	X	X	X	X	
d. Regulating dance halls, poolrooms, etc.			X	X	
e. Regulating exhibition of motion pictures and censoring of books and magazines		X		X	
f. Supervising athletic contests		X		X	
g. Supervision of racing		X			
6. Traffic control					
a. Engineering and research	X	X	X	X	
b. Highway patrols		X	X	X	
c. Establishing and maintaining traffic signals		X	X	X	
d. Motor vehicle inspection and regulation		X		X	
e. Conducting drivers' examination		X	X	X	
7. Control of international borders					
a. Patrol of border	X	X	X	X	
b. Immigration stations	X				
c. Guarding against smuggling	X				
8. Fish and game protection	X	X	X		
C. Fire Protection and Fire Fighting					
1. Fire alarm and communication systems				X	
2. Fire prevention					
a. Education for fire prevention		X		X	
b. Inspection of arson cases		X		X	
c. Hazard inspections		X		X	
3. Hydrant and water service				X	
4. Fire fighting force		X	X	X	
5. Rescue and emergency service				X	
6. Preventing and fighting forest fires	X	X	X		
D. Protective Inspections					
1. Building inspection		X		X	
2. Plumbing inspection		X		X	
3. Electrical inspection		X		X	
4. Gas inspection		X		X	
5. Boiler inspection		X		X	
6. Elevator inspection				X	
7. Weight and measures inspection	X	X	X	X	
8. Mining inspection	X	X			
9. Smoke inspection				X	
E. Regulation of Business and Industry					
1. Prevention or elimination of monopolies or trusts	X	X			
2. Regulation of competitive practice	X	X			

INVENTORY OF GOVERNMENTAL ACTIVITIES (CONTINUED)

ACTIVITY	GOVERNMENTAL UNITS				
	F.	S.	CO.	CITY	SD.

II *Protection to Persons and Property (cont'd)*

ACTIVITY	F.	S.	CO.	CITY	SD.
3. Banks and banking					
a. Granting bank charters	x	x			
b. Conducting bank examinations	x	x			
4. Credit institutions		x			
5. Securities					
a. Regulation of sale	x	x			
b. Regulating security exchanges	x				
c. Licensing security dealers	x	x			
6. Insurance					
a. Establishment of insurance rates		x			
b. Inspection of financial status		x			
c. Granting right to do business		x			
d. Licensing of insurance agents		x			
7. Transportation					
a. Railroads	x	x			
b. Interurban railroads	x	x			
c. Street railways		x		x	
d. Motor bus and truck companies	x	x		x	
e. Water carriers	x	x			
f. Air carriers	x	x			
8. Transmission and sale of electricity and gas	x	x		x	
9. Communications					
a. Telephone, telegraph, cable companies	x	x		x	
b. Radio broadcasting	x	x			
10. Petroleum industry	x	x			
11. Employment bureaus—private		x		x	
12. Agriculture					
a. Inspecting and regulating warehouses		x			
b. Regulating commodity exchanges and futures	x				
c. Regulating and inspecting commission merchants		x			
F. Insurance of Life, Money, and Property					
1. Insurance of bank deposits	x				
2. Insurance of public moneys		x			
3. Crop insurance	x	x	x		
4. War risk insurance	x				
5. Life insurance for members of armed forces	x				
G. Other Protection Activities					
1. Navigational					
a. Coast guard	x				
b. Establishing and improving aids to navigation	x				
c. Lighthouse services	x				
d. Astronomical observations	x				
e. Hydrographic and hydrologic surveys	x				
f. Collection and dissemination of navigational information	x				
g. Ship experimental and developmental work	x				
h. Shipping regulations	x				
i. Prescribing use of navigable streams	x				

INVENTORY OF GOVERNMENTAL ACTIVITIES (CONTINUED)

ACTIVITY	GOVERNMENTAL UNITS				
	F.	S.	CO.	CITY	SD.

II *Protection to Persons and Property (cont'd)*

	F.	S.	CO.	CITY	SD.
2. Weather information	x				
3. Time observation	x				
4. Coinage and regulation of money	x				
5. Granting copyrights, patents, and trademarks	x				
6. Establishment and administration of standards					
a. Legal weights and measures	x	x		x	
b. Establishing commercial standards	x	x			
c. Commodity testing for compliance with standards	x	x			
7. Examination for licensed occupations	x	x	x	x	
8. Foreign trade					
a. Determining and supervising ports of entry	x				
b. Conducting inspection	x				
9. Coroner—morgue services			x	x	
10. Indian services	x	x			
H. Protection of Industrial Workers					
1. Compiling and publishing labor statistics	x	x			
2. Investigation of industrial conditions	x	x			
3. Regulation of hours and wages	x	x			
4. Prescribing and inspecting working conditions for women and children	x	x			
5. Administration of Workmen's Compensation Insurance		x			
6. Conciliation and mediation of labor disputes	x	x			
7. Industrial hygiene		x			

III *Highway Construction and Maintenance*

	F.	S.	CO.	CITY	SD.
A. Research, Planning and Promotion of Highways	x	x	x	x	x
B. Roads, Highways, and Streets					
1. "Primary" roads—state and federal	$	x			
2. County trunk highways		x	x		
3. County local highways			x		x
4. City streets				x	
C. Other Highway Facilities and Service					
1. Bridges	$	x	x	x	x
2. Viaduct and grade separations	$	x	x	x	
3. Grade crossing elimination	$	x	x	x	
4. Sidewalks			x	x	
D. Snow Removal		x	x	x	
E. Street and Highway Lighting		x	x	x	

IV *Development and Conservation of Natural Resources*

	F.	S.	CO.	CITY	SD.
A. Agriculture					
1. Agricultural research	x	x			
2. Dissemination of information					
a. Library services	x				
b. Extension services	$	x	x		
c. Broadcasts, bulletins, etc.	x	x			
d. Fairs and exhibits		x	x		

INVENTORY OF GOVERNMENTAL ACTIVITIES (CONTINUED)

ACTIVITY	GOVERNMENTAL UNITS				
	F.	S.	CO.	CITY	SD.

IV *Development and Conservation of Natural Resources (cont'd)*

	F.	S.	CO.	CITY	SD.
3. Animal husbandry					
a. Experimentation	x	x			
b. Disease eradication	x	x	x		
c. Inspection and quarantine	x	x	x		
4. Plant husbandry					
a. Experimental crops and farms	x	x			
b. Disease eradication	x	x	x		
c. Insect-plant control projects	x	x			
d. Quarantine services	x	x	x		
e. Seeds					
(1) Improvements and regulation	x				
(2) Certification of seed		x			
5. Farm real estate and production credit loans	x	x			
6. Marketing services and control					
a. Compilation of statistics	x	x			
b. Market reports	x	x			
c. Establishing standards for agricultural products	x	x			
d. Marketing agreements	x	x			
7. Advisory services					
a. Agricultural advisory services	x	x	x		
b. Farm and home management advisory services	x	x	x		
8. Price maintenance and subsidization					
a. Purchase, storage and resale of commodities	x				
b. Loans on commodities	x				
c. Parity payments	x				
d. Export subsidies	x				
9. Production adjustment payments	x				
10. Nutrition programs	x				
11. Farm youth activities		x	x		
B. Land Conservation and Utilization					
1. Research	x	x			
2. Soil conservation and erosion projects	x	x	x		x
3. Soil conservation practice payments	$				
4. Retirement of sub-marginal land	x	x			
5. Reclamation projects	x	x			x
C. Water Conservation and Utilization					
1. Research	x	x			
2. Control of water rights	x	x			x
3. Drainage			x		x
4. Irrigation projects	x				x
5. Flood control and prevention					
a. Surveys	x	x			
b. Dams, reforestation, and reservoirs	x	x			x
c. Inspections	x	x			
d. Flood forecasting	x	x			
e. Levees and protective structures	x	x	x	x	x
6. Lake and stream improvements	x	x	x		
7. Improvement of rivers, harbors, and waterways	x			x	x
8. Navigational canals	x	x			

INVENTORY OF GOVERNMENTAL ACTIVITIES (CONTINUED)

ACTIVITY	GOVERNMENTAL UNITS				
	F.	S.	CO.	CITY	SD.

IV *Development and Conservation of Natural Resources (cont'd)*

D. Forest Conservation and Utilization

	F.	S.	CO.	CITY	SD.
1. Forest and range research	X				
2. Forest product utilization	X				
3. Reforestation	X	X	X	X	
4. Timber salvage and control	X	X	X	X	

E. Wildlife Conservation and Restoration

	F.	S.	CO.	CITY	SD.
1. Research	X	X			
2. Providing game and bird refuges and restoration measures	X	X			
3. Predatory animal control	X	X	X		
4. Enforcement of game laws	X	X	X		

F. Fish Conservation

	F.	S.	CO.	CITY	SD.
1. Research	X	X			
2. Marketing services					
a. Collecting statistics	X				
b. Furnishing market reports	X				
3. Fish hatcheries and restocking	X	X			
4. Enforcement of fishing laws	X	X	X		

G. Petroleum

	F.	S.	CO.	CITY	SD.
1. Production control	X	X			
2. Regulating leases	X	X			

H. Mineral Conservation

	F.	S.	CO.	CITY	SD.
1. Geological surveys	X	X			
2. Establishing land classifications	X				
3. Regulating coal production	X				

V *Sanitation and Waste Removal*

	F.	S.	CO.	CITY	SD.
A. Research		X		X	X
B. Sewers and Sewage Disposal Facilities			X	X	X
C. Street Sanitation				X	
D. Waste Collection and Disposal Services				X	
E. Preventing Stream and Lake Pollution	X	X			
F. Other					
1. Noxious weed control		X	X	X	X
2. Comfort stations			X	X	

VI *Health*

	F.	S.	CO.	CITY	SD.
A. Research	X	X	X	X	
B. Collection of Vital Statistics	X	X	X	X	
C. Laboratories	X	X	X	X	
D. Serum and Vaccine Production		X			
E. Regulation and Inspection					
1. Milk and dairy products					
a. Dairy farm inspection				X	
b. Cattle inspection	X	X		X	
c. Inspection of milk depots and plants				X	
d. Ice cream plant inspection				X	
2. Meat Products					
a. Inspection of abattoirs, markets, and locker plants		X		X	
b. Ownership and operation of abattoirs and markets				X	

INVENTORY OF GOVERNMENTAL ACTIVITIES (CONTINUED)

ACTIVITY	GOVERNMENTAL UNITS				
	F.	S.	CO.	CITY	SD.
VI *Health (cont'd)*					
c. Meat inspection at packing plants	x				
3. Other foods					
a. Inspection of food stores and markets				x	
b. Enforcing pure food laws	x	x			
c. Examination of food handlers		x		x	
d. Grain inspection	x	x			
e. Establishing standards	x	x			
4. Drugs	x	x		x	
5. Establishing standards for biological products	x				
6. Establishing standards for cosmetic and therapeutic devices	x	x			
7. Inspecting eating and lodging places		x	x	x	
8. Inspecting camps and hotels		x			
9. Sanitary inspections					
a. Water supply		x		x	
b. Sewage disposal		x		x	
c. Places of labor		x			
d. Housing				x	
e. Extermination of insects and rodents				x	
f. Public bathing places		x		x	
g. Barber shops and beauty parlors				x	
F. Control of Epidemic Diseases					
1. Plague control	x	x			
2. Quarantine services	x	x	x	x	
3. Vaccinations and immunizations			x	x	
4. Disinfection of buildings			x	x	
G. Control of Communicable Diseases					
1. Tuberculosis	$	x	x	x	
2. Venereal diseases	$	x	x	x	
H. Prevention of Other Diseases					
1. Malignant	x	x		x	
2. Infantile paralysis	x	x			
3. Malaria	x	x	x		
4. Mosquito control	x	x	x	x	x
I. Maternal and Child Health Services					
1. Pre-natal clinics				x	
2. Licensing of maternity homes and hospitals		x		x	
3. Pre-school clinics				x	
4. Inspection of nurseries and boarding homes		x		x	
5. Medical and dental services		x	x	x	x
6. Nursing services			x	x	x
7. Nutrition programs	$	x			x
J. Crippled Children Services					
1. Clinic service	$	x	x	x	
2. Hospital care	$	x	x	x	
3. Nursing and therapeutical services	$	x	x	x	
K. Nursing Services and Training	$	x	x	x	
L. Dental Clinics			x	x	
M. Health Centers and General Clinics		x	x	x	
N. Industrial Hygiene		x			

INVENTORY OF GOVERNMENTAL ACTIVITIES (CONTINUED)

ACTIVITY	GOVERNMENTAL UNITS				
	F.	S.	CO.	CITY	SD.
VII *Hospital*					
A. General Hospitals	X	X	X	X	
B. Special Hospitals					
1. Tuberculosis		X	X	X	
2. Nervous—mental—feeble-minded and epileptic		X	X	X	
3. Cancer		X	X	X	
4. Leprosy	X				
5. Orthopedic		X			
6. Maternity			X	X	
C. Veterans' Hospitals	X	X			
VIII *Public Assistance and Social Services*					
A. Services to Children					
1. Institutions for children		X	X	X	
2. Aid to dependent children	$	X	X	X	
3. Foster home placement		X	X	X	
4. Adoption investigation		X	X	X	
B. Services to Veterans					
1. Soldiers' home	X	X			
2. Veterans' aid	X	X	X	X	
3. Veterans' credit facilities	X	X			
4. Veterans' reemployment	X	X			
C. Services to Other Special Groups					
1. Old age assistance	$	X	X	X	
2. Aid to the blind	$	X	X	X	
3. Training centers for the blind		X			
4. Training centers for the deaf and dumb		X			
D. General Services					
1. Legal aid				X	
2. General institutions for adults		X	X	X	
3. General assistance		X	X	X	
4. Medical care		X	X	X	
5. Vocational rehabilitation	X	X	X	X	X
E. Licensing of Private Instituions		X		X	
F. Disaster Relief	X	X	X	X	
IX *Corrections*					
A. Probation and Parole	X	X	X	X	
B. Correctional Institutions					
1. Penitentiaries	X	X			
2. Reformatories	X	X			
3. Jails			X	X	
4. Prison camps and farms		X	X	X	
5. Juvenile training schools		X	X	X	
6. Detention homes			X	X	
C. Prison Industries	X	X	X	X	
X *Social Insurance*					
A. Old Age and Survivors Insurance	X				
B. Unemployment Compensation		X			
C. Placement Services	X	X			

INVENTORY OF GOVERNMENTAL ACTIVITIES (CONTINUED)

ACTIVITY	GOVERNMENTAL UNITS				
	F.	S.	CO.	CITY	SD.
XI *Housing and Home Ownership*					
A. Low Rent Housing	X		X	X	X
B. Slum Clearance Projects	X		X	X	X
C. War Housing	X		X	X	X
D. Housing Advisory Services	X	X			
E. Loans to Encourage Public Housing	X				
F. Promotion of Home Construction Through Guarantee of Loans and Accounts	X				
G. Purchase of Mortgages	X				
XII *Educational Activities*					
A. Research in Educational Problems	X	X	X	X	X
B. Compiling Statistics on Education	X	X	X	X	X
C. Supervision Over Textbooks		X			
D. Certification of Teachers		X	X		
E. In-Service Training for Teachers					
1. Summer school sessions		X	X		
2. Conferences		X	X		
3. School visitations		X			
F. Technical Advisory Services	X	X			
G. Pupil Personnel Services					
1. Census		X	X	X	X
2. Attendance and truancy		X	X	X	X
3. Guidance services		X	X	X	X
4. Rating services		X			
5. Nurse services			X	X	X
6. Lunches	$	$	X	X	X
H. Kindergartens and Preschools			X	X	X
I. Elementary Schools			X	X	X
J. Secondary schools					
1. Vocational education	$	X	X	X	X
2. Evening classes			X	X	X
3. Correspondence and extension courses			X	X	X
4. General education			X	X	X
K. Junior Colleges		X	X	X	X
L. Teachers' Colleges		X	X	X	
M. Colleges and Universities					
1. Agriculture and mechanical art colleges	$	X			
2. Art and sciences		X		X	
3. Engineering and technical		X		X	
4. Professional		X		X	
5. Correspondence, extension, and continuation	$	X		X	
N. Education of Special Groups					
1. Handicapped					
a. Training and instruction for blind and defective eyesight		X	X	X	X
b. Training and instruction for deaf and dumb		X	X	X	X
c. Fresh air classes			X	X	X
d. Bedside instructions			X	X	X
e. Crippled	$	X		X	X
2. Adult Education					
a. Civic instruction			X	X	X

INVENTORY OF GOVETNMENTAL ACTIVITIES (CONTINUED)

ACTIVITY	GOVERNMENTAL UNITS				
	F.	S.	CO.	CITY	SD.

ACTIVITY	F.	S.	CO.	CITY	SD.
XII *Educational Activities (cont'd)*					
b. Conducting forums	X			X	
3. Specially gifted children			X	X	X
4. Mentally deficient children		X	X	X	X
O. Transportation of School Children		$	X	X	X
XIII *Library Facilities*					
A. General Libraries	X	X	X	X	X
B. Extension and Traveling Libraries		X	X		
C. Rural Libraries		X	X		
D. Special Facilities					
1. Books for blind	$	X			
2. Special collections	X	X		X	
E. Historical Commission	X	X		X	
XIV *Public Recreation and Cultural Facilities*					
A. Cultural—Scientific Recreation					
1. Art galleries	X			X	
2. Museums	X	X		X	
3. Botanical gardens and conservatories	X			X	
4. Arboreta	X			X	
5. Planetaria				X	
6. Zoos	X			X	
7. Aquaria				X	
8. Music and drama				X	
B. Organized Recreation					
1. Outdoor activities					
a. Playgrounds and playfields				X	
b. Golf				X	
c. Swimming pools				X	
d. Beaches		X		X	
e. Camps	X	X		X	
f. Winter sports		X		X	
g. Supervised park activities	X	X		X	
2. Indoor activities and recreation buildings				X	
C. Parks					
1. Forests	X	X	X	X	X
2. Parks	X	X	X	X	X
3. Parkways and boulevards	X	X	X	X	
4. Nurseries	X	X	X	X	
5. Monuments and historical sites	X	X		X	
D. Special Recreational Facilities					
1. Auditoriums				X	
2. Stadiums				X	
3. Auto and trailer camps		X		X	
4. Camp sites and buildings	X	X		X	
5. Recreation piers				X	
6. Yacht harbors				X	
7. Refectories				X	
XV *Public Service Enterprises*					
A. Post Office	X				
B. Railroads				X	

INVENTORY OF GOVERNMENTAL ACTIVITIES (CONTINUED)

ACTIVITY	GOVERNMENTAL UNITS				
	F.	S.	CO.	CITY	SD.

	F.	S.	CO.	CITY	SD.
XV Public Service Enterprises (cont'd)					
C. Street Railways				x	
D. Bus Lines				x	
E. Electric Power Plant	x			x	x
F. Water Works Plants				x	x
G. Gas Plants				x	
H. Liquor Monopolies		x			
I. Liquor Stores		x	x	x	
J. Airports		x	x	x	
K. Ferries		x	x	x	
L. Terminals (bus and trains)				x	
M. Markets and Warehouses				x	x
N. Grain Elevators		x		x	
O. Abattoirs				x	
P. Cemeteries and Crematories				x	
Q. Broadcasting Stations		x		x	
R. Telephone Systems				x	
S. Ports and Harbors				x	x
T. Rural Electrifications	x				x
U. Multiple Purpose Enterprise (T.V.A., Bonneville, Grand Coulee, Central Valley)	x				
V. Canals and Waterways	x	x			
W. Toll Roads and Toll Bridges		x	x	x	x

Questions and Problems

1. What features in each of the following organizations are comparable to the four elementary features of the state: Canada; Illinois; Hong Kong; the Hitler Brown Shirts; the American navy; the Congress of Industrial Organizations; the United Automobile Workers; the American Medical Association; the Episcopalian Church; the Roman Catholic Church; the National Association of Manufacturers; the Democratic Party; and, finally, your own family structure.

2. Name two states whose inhabitants have different languages; name two states that encompass principally the territory of one city; name one state where the tribal pattern of constantly changing residence is still very noticeable; name one state for the most part still organized along feudal nes; nam e three states whose existence is in question because it is difficult to decide whether they are or are not independent. Explain your answers.

3. Why must one by careful in describing the origins of the modern state?

4. Why is the theory of the social contract useful to people who want to change their form of government or increase their control over their government?

5. Taking each of the organizations listed in question 1 (above), analyze whether they possess "sovereignty" as we defined it.

6. Write precisely what you remember about what you felt, what your family felt, and what other people felt when Franklin D. Roosevelt died suddenly. Reason from your experiences what kinds of legitimacy his living acts might have possessed.

7. Describe from your own experience with the acts of legitimate authority how true it is to say that "people often believe what legitimate authority tells them to believe, and act accordingly."

8. When the word "government" is used as an active noun ("The government educates its citizens"), we are in danger of falling into a logical and scientific fallacy, that of giving life to an inanimate collective concept. How would you advise someone less clever than yourself to avoid this fallacy in using this word and others like it ("state," "liberty," "democracy," the "army," the "corporation," and so on)?

9. The same danger, comments John Dewey, is to be encountered in the word "individual." Discuss.

10. Give two examples each of political education and political propaganda from current events or from your own experience, and tell why you classify them as such.

11. Give two examples each of political force and political violence from current events or your own experience, and tell why you classify them as such.

12. Give two examples each of governmental economic measures and governmental economic manipulation from current events or your own experience, and tell why you classify them as such.

13. Find in newspapers, magazines, or elsewhere a fairly detailed account of the use of education by the government and show how force and economic measures are somehow also present.

14. Do the same for force with reference to education and economic policy.

15. Do the same for economic policy with reference to education and force.

16. Write an essay of six hundred words or less comparing Mosca's "elite theory" of government with the classical threefold division. Which theory do you believe is truer? Are both useful?

17. Distinguish between "centralization" and "integration." What are their opposites? (For more material, consult a dictionary, an encyclopedia, and the chapter on administration in this book.)

18. List ten functions that are performed today by some part of the government but that at one time in the past were performed only by individuals or private groups. Name ten functions that are performed both by some part of the government and by some private groups.

Longer Study and Research
Problems Suitable for Term Papers

1. Read Carl Van Doren: *The Great Rehearsal* (1948), and Thomas Hodgkin: *Charles The Great* (1897). Write a general review of both books; describe separately and then compare the different problems that faced the medieval king and the framers of the Constitution, respectively, in uniting diverse groups of people into one country.

2. Prepare a report on these three books: Franz Kafka: *The Castle* (or Aldous Huxley: *Brave New World*, or Leon Trotsky: *Stalin*); A. Hassell: *Louis XIV*; and Harold Lamb: *Genghis Khan* (or Ulrich Wilcken: *Alexander the Great*). Describe to what extent the governments or leaders discussed in each work conform to a pattern of legitimacy—rational, traditional, or charismatic—as these patterns are presented in this chapter.

3. Go through a file of newspapers or periodicals covering a six-month period. List and describe briefly all examples of actions taken by public officers, and classify them as education, force, economic measures, or expressions of legitimacy. If you can perceive in the evidence you have gathered any subpattern or subclassification, bring out your discovery in your report.

4. Make an inventory of governmental activities performed by your state, county, township, and local government; you may also add a category for functions performed by special districts.

II

POLITICAL BEHAVIOR

No HARD and fast distinctions separate political behavior, studied in this section, from governmental organization, studied in the section to follow. Generally speaking, however, political behavior consists of (1) a particular *area* of political activity and (2) *kinds* of political actions that are *common* to all politics.

Political behavior is an area of political activity—the activity that occurs outside the formal and legal organizations of government. The chapters of this section discuss a progression of concerns: first comes the political activity of large and vague groupings like the community and public; then comes that of tighter groups —the electorate, election constituencies, political parties, pressure groups, and conflict groups. Political behavior in this sense is the behavior of individuals and groups outside the government who are striving to influence or take possession of the government. The section ends as we reach the special organized activities of the state, as exemplified by legislative and administrative institutions.

Political behavior is political activity common to all politics. Certain principles of political science apply both to political behavior and governmental organizations. We find, for instance, that lawyers, soldiers, and professors maintain characteristic habits both in the contest for power and later in the offices of government; or that a person's attitudes will remain in many respects the same be he a voter or a congressman; or that leadership in the Department of Agriculture has a number of qualities in common with leadership in a club or political party. Principles such as these, which are common to politics as a whole, are traditionally and conveniently treated as part of the study of political behavior.

3

LEADERS AND FOLLOWERS

LEADERSHIP is a fitting topic with which to begin the study of political behavior. It is a relationship that pervades every association among men. Even Robinson Crusoe became a leader when he took into his life his good man Friday. In the most simple associations and in the most complex ones, leaders exert some directing influence, the nature and extent of which must be known if we are to understand how men get along together. To explain why people choose or follow one kind of behavior rather than another—why they go to war or remain at peace, vote Democratic or Republican, or do a job poorly or well—introduces a search for guiding influences. The study of leadership is therefore most important to political science.

A political leader may be identified as any occupant of an established political position or as any person, in or out of such a position, whose political activity has more influence upon a group's behavior than has the activity of the average member.

How are leaders created? In studying this problem, the political scientist must ask a series of further questions. Are leaders heroes of exceptional powers or pawns of social forces? Have they physical or mental traits in common? Do they develop like abilities through their experience in such typical political activities as organizing, bargaining, or fighting? Does membership in certain social classes increase or decrease a man's chances of becoming a leader? Is it the nature of all great organizations to be led by an active group that tends to monopolize leadership?

In raising these questions we must remember that there are many roles for leaders to play—leaders may be party organizers, legislators, judges, executives, diplomats, or soldiers—and we must ask how leadership is molded by the functional demands of each situation. Finally, in order to explain the inadequacies of our answers to all of the foregoing questions, we advance the theory that leadership cannot be fully understood before we examine the reciprocal relationships between the leader and his followers and the relationships of his group with the other groups that operate in the same environment and context.

The discussion of these successive questions provides the structure of this chapter. Taken together, the various answers, in so far as there are any, help one to understand leadership both as an isolated concept and as an integral part of political behavior and political organizations.

The Leader: Hero or Pawn?

THE "GREAT MAN" THEORY OF HISTORY

Two famous writers have presented us with opposite theories about the influence of leaders. Thomas Carlyle wrote most passionately: "Universal History, the history of what man has accomplished in this world, is at bottom the History of the Great Men who have worked here." Heroes teach us right and wrong, he said; heroes give us great inventions and discoveries. It is the great few who transform society; the multitude follows them. Modern democracy, he believed, has produced millions of fools who vote, other men who go to Parliament and palaver, and, inevitably, the few who act.

TOLSTOI'S INFINITESIMAL ELEMENTS

By contrast, Count Leo Tolstoi asserted that there is no greater fool than he who thinks he makes history and believes others when they assure him he does. Not even a leader like Napoleon Bonaparte, according to Tolstoi, has any part in determining the course of history. Napoleon was the tool of vast social forces beyond his control. "Studying the laws of history," Tolstoi declared, "we must absolutely change the objects of our observation, leaving kings, ministers, and generals out of the account, and select for study the homogenous, infinitesimal elements that regulate the masses."

Both Carlyle and Tolstoi are representative of long rosters of illustrious writers. Those who share Carlyle's view of the role played by men of genius tend also to be aristocratic in political viewpoint. Among the most enthusiastic have been men who believed that they themselves were to be among the great of history and that their indomitable wills could overcome all obstacles—Hitler and Mussolini, for example.

By contrast, those who have agreed with Tolstoi have often been socialists. For socialism, as Marx taught it, was a triumph of the masses over the few, and of irresistible historical tendencies over individual effort—socialism being the irresistible tendency of the modern age. Tolstoi's less specific determinism has also received support from most social and natural scientists, who have hoped that by applying the theory of determinism to all events they may explain history far better than can the biographers of greatness.

LEADERS ARE BOTH UNIQUE AND TYPICAL

Like many other puzzling problems in political science, the conflict between these rival theories dwindles in importance if we ask an appropriate methodological question: Why are we interested in the argument? What do we want to know? First, we want to discover the consequences of the acts of particular men; second, we want to explain the interaction of social forces—economic wants, nationalism, religious beliefs, and so on. If we are to understand the first problem, the peculiar combination of qualities that particular men undeniably possess become objects of serious attention. Men are the actors of politics; some men are more active than others; and the shape and direction of their activities earn them leadership, great or minor. If we are interested in the second problem, the interaction of social forces, the leaders become nameless carriers of influence, instruments of the environment, helpless products of their times. We then select abstractions such as the idea of freedom, or social movements such as the industrial revolution, or indeed any social force in which we are interested, and assess its contribution to the power of the leader. We see the leader as *caused*, like all things. He becomes an instrument.

Both kinds of information are valuable. Let us take the study of Napoleon as an example. Clearly he was the product of forces outside his own will. He owed his being to his parents, and was conditioned by his family life. He was, we are told, deeply influenced by his inferiority to the upper-class group at his military school. He was certainly deeply affected by the French Revolution. At the same time, *only* he had his *particular* parents, was born at that *certain* time, had that *peculiar* relationship to his fellow students at military school, and had many other *distinct* experiences *all to himself*.

It would seem, then, that Napoleon—a unique character—encountered various deterministic social forces throughout his life. Thus one may study him, like any other event, in his uniqueness, or, also like any other event, as a statistic. But one cannot say that *only his uniqueness* or *only social forces at work upon him* are of importance. We must understand both in order to understand Napoleon.

GREAT AND MINOR LEADERS CAN BE STUDIED TOGETHER

What is true of the "great" leaders is true of the minor. No grand principle distinguishes one from the other in political science. A psychological "halo"—to be treated later—surrounds the "great" leader and seems to distinguish him from others. But there is no more reason for thinking a different principle is at work than for thinking that the sound that bursts an eardrum is different in kind from the sound that brings pleasing harmonies to the ear or even from the sound that is not heard at all.

The Psychology of Leadership

TRAITS OF LEADERS

A common method of investigating the "principles" that explain leadership has been to seek among leaders of all kinds some uniform traits that distinguish them from their followers. Are leaders taller than the average, heavier, more intelligent, more studious, more loyal, more dependable, or more active? We may present an interesting example of a study that seeks to find traits distinguishing leaders from followers.

In 1950, Dr. John B. McConaughy reported a study of eighteen members of the South Carolina General Assembly. The politicians took standard tests that had been used throughout the country. The results, writes Professor McConaughy, indicate that the political leaders were decidedly less neurotic than the general male population; that they were more self-sufficient; that they were decidedly more extroverted; but that they were only slightly more dominant. Furthermore, "they are, to a large degree, more self-confident than the average person and have fewer feelings of inferiority; and . . . they are less irritable and tense than the average person." Finally, they appeared not to have "fascist ideas" and to be not much more conservative than the average South Carolinian. Many more studies of this character must be made, however, before one is entitled to generalize about politicians as a group. And, since there are many differences in the degree of power possessed among politicians, it is possible that this group typifies the "subelite," rather than the most dominant group within the community, state, or nation.

Less definite conclusions were reached by Dr. Ralph M. Stogdill, who surveyed 124 studies of leadership and found only a small amount of agreement concerning the traits of most leaders. He reports that over fifteen studies provided evidence that leaders were more intelligent than the average of their group, more studious, more dependable, more active and sociable and from a higher social and economic class. Ten or more of the studies indicated that leaders had unusual persistence and initiative, knew how to get things done, were co-operative, and possessed self-confidence, insight, popularity, adaptability, and verbal facility. There seemed to be vague indications in a number of studies that leaders topped their group average in such characteristics as age, height, weight, physique, appearance, and dominance. But the outstanding fact, as Dr. Stogdill discovered, is quite plain: It is at present impossible to say that any single trait distinguishes most leaders from followers in *all* groups taken together. Political situations vary so greatly that they require very different types of leaders at different times and places.

MOTIVATION OF LEADERS

Dissatisfied with the search for isolated *traits* that distinguish leaders, some modern political psychologists have suggested that we must study in greater depth the psychological motivation of leaders in order to explain how they developed. For instance, Napoleon was short; perhaps he compensated by furious energy for what is commonly considered a defect in would-be leaders.

One of the most outstanding of these political psychologists, Harold D. Lasswell, suggests that the most dynamic type of political leader compensates for personal inadequacies. If an individual feels deprived, consciously or not, of characteristics or possessions that he is trained by his environment to regard as valuable—good looks, family affection, money, social respect, a certain upper-class occupation, an education—his feelings of deprivation create a high tension that seeks outlets. There are many outlets, but those men destined to become politically active choose power or prestige as a compensation. Since power has always to be justified in terms of the public good, they repress their private motives and acquire a set of beliefs truly political —a notion of the "public interest." They may or may not in fact serve the public interest in the light of history, but the spark to their interest in public activity comes from tensions originally private. Of course, the intense motivation of such a man only partly explains his power; he must also acquire political skills—military, organizational or demagogic.

This type of exceptionally forceful leader, however, includes only a fraction of all those who satisfy our definition of a leader. Many political leaders "fall" into office; they may be born to it; they may get office with little effort because of family connections. Others may serve in high political posts simply because of technical skills; such, for instance, are many army leaders, undersecretaries and bureau chiefs of government departments. These men may have special character- istics typical of those who do their kind of work, but they would not be men of "pure power" such as we have just described. Most political leaders are subject to a variety of motives; they may wish to earn money, acquire leisure, help their careers, defeat personal enemies, and so on. Taking all political leaders into consideration, those who are compensating for intense feelings of deprivation are an important but unknown fraction of the total number.

CHARISMATIC LEADERS

This man of "pure power" is one of the types that some- times provides us with a special kind of political leader, the charismatic leader, who gains dictatorial powers during periods of widespread social distress. He seeks to incite as large a mass of people as possible. Unstable times, the twentieth century, for instance, provide him an immense audience that, to another age or land, seems unbelievably suggestible and stupid.

Max Weber first defined the nature of charisma. Charisma is the quality that enables one man, without measurable traits far exceeding those of his followers, without coming from any ruling group or hold- ing any office, to exercise surpassing magnetism and to gather a tre- mendous following. Charisma is "nonrational," nontraditional, and nonbureaucratic.

> It is a certain quality of an individual personality by virtue of which he is set apart from ordinary men and treated as endowed with supernatural, superhuman, or at least specifically exceptional powers or qualities. These are such as are not accessible to the ordinary person, but are regarded as of divine origin or as exemplary, and on the basis of them the individ- ual concerned is treated as a leader. . . .
>
> Pure charisma is specifically foreign to economic considerations. Whenever it appears, it constitutes a "call" in the most emphatic sense of the word, a "mission" or a "spiritual duty." *

Charismatic leadership, evidenced in a man originally by some re- markable or "miraculous" accomplishments, can be maintained only by the continuous demonstration of those abilities—prophecy, heroism, striking successes—or by a "routinizing of charisma." Charisma be- comes institutionalized or routinized when the initial contempt of a charismatic leader and his followers for organization, positions, money,

* Quoted, with permission, from Max Weber: *The Theory of Social and Economic Organization*, translated by A. M. Henderson and Talcott Parsons (New York: Oxford University Press, 1947), pp. 358-9, 362.

and laws diminishes in fact, if not in theory, and regularized ways of achieving the sinews of permanence, such as bureaucracies and taxation, are established.

Inasmuch as a charismatic leader challenges the existing political leadership, the offices of the state, and many of the existing laws, he cannot be expected to gain support from the *status quo* for his mission, be he conservative or radical in relation to the ideas of the existing political leaders. He therefore prospers on mass support and only belatedly receives adherents from among the established leaders. Such was the experience of men like the Gracchi of ancient Rome, Cola de Rienzi of medieval Rome, Savonarola of Renaissance Florence, St. Francis, Cromwell of the English Commonwealth, Robespierre of Revolutionary France, Napoleon I, Mussolini of Fascist Italy, Gandhi of India, and Hitler of Nazi Germany.

DANGERS OF OVEREXTENDING THE ANALYSIS OF CHARISMA

Caution is necessary, for charisma may be used to explain too much. Max Weber was careful to state that charisma is often mixed with the traditional kinds of authority, and that charismatic leaders, for all their contempt of rules and regulations, frequently utilized existing channels of ascent. Despite his messianic pretensions, for example, Hitler revered "legality" and sought to cloak many of his most radical acts in the garments of the pre-existing law and political order. Jawaharlal Nehru, leader of India after Gandhi, is, by his own words, of uncertain character; though at one moment rational, skeptical, and impatient of the adulation he receives as a "miracle man," he is at another swept into telling himself: "I drew these tides of men into my hands and wrote my will across the sky in stars."

Furthermore, essentially noncharismatic offices may acquire charismatic occupants. For example, thousands of Americans stood in the rain to pay their last respects to the cortege of Abraham Lincoln. Obviously, the meaning of Lincoln to his followers transcended the meaning of his office. He was much more than the President.

Besides, purely charismatic leaders cannot arise anywhere at any time. Charisma, which convinces followers of the leader's miraculous gifts, depends on the followers' receptivity. The mission of the leader must have psychological meaning to the follower. The French Revolution had to precede Napoleon, the Versailles Treaty and the depression, Hitler. Sebastian de Grazia has gathered a variety of evidence on the permanent, lurking, immanent, and transcendent character of charisma in his book on the *Political Community*. Both in tranquility and crisis, he writes, religious and political rulers fulfill a role identical in significant respects with that of the parents and attendants of infancy and childhood. In crisis we find exclamations such as the following about Hitler from the pen of Peter Drucker:

> It was not Hitler who made himself a demi-god; it was the masses who pushed him on this pedestal. For only a demon, a superman and magician who can never err and who is always right can resolve the contradiction between the need for a miracle and the impossibility of producing one. Only unquestioning belief in the Führer can give the security of conviction which the masses crave in order to be spared from despair. . . . Hitler must be right because otherwise nothing is.*

According to De Grazia, charisma is more often present in subdued form. The death of a ruler may reveal that he had charisma for many of his subjects. Thus when George V of England died, a psychoanalyst, Dr. W. R. D. Fairbairn, reported that one patient dreamed that he had shot a man resembling his father, another was exceedingly depressed by memories of his father's death, and a third dreamed that her own father was dead. All three showed aggravated nervous symptoms. Even for the week of crisis before the abdication of Edward VIII in 1936, Professor De Grazia reports signs of public turmoil. "An increase in absenteeism and a spectacular fall in trade were apparent. People seemed to have left off buying, going to the theaters, or attending meetings."

De Grazia has also made a study of how thirty patients under psychoanalysis behaved when Franklin D. Roosevelt died in 1945. The findings are not surprising to those who recall the event, but they are rendered impressive by the objective nature of the materials.

> All persons expressed great initial incredulity that the event had actually occurred and some related the unusual measures they had taken to verify the news. Once belief was definite, all persons felt for a time that "the world" had changed. Absence of direction in the environment was a dominant fear. "What will we do?" Another remark was, "What is there to live for now?" Or, "Now we're all alone." The environment was pictured as potentially hostile. "Who will save us now?" Or, "Who's going to save the world? Everything's stopped."
>
> All persons reported abdominally-located sensations and most of them had gastric disturbances. At the news, they said, their stomach knotted or tensed, or their stomach seemed to drop, or they had a sinking feeling. The gastric disturbances were mainly of a diarrhoetic character.†

Indeed, leadership in the larger political community seems to have a simmering charisma about it at all times. Rulers, no matter how they have acquired their positions, are expected to produce results in excess

* Quoted, with permission, from Peter Drucker: "The End of Economic Man," *Harper's Magazine*, Vol. CLXXVIII (1939), p. 562.

† Quoted, with permission, from Sebastian de Grazia: "A Note on the Psychological Position of the Chief Executive," *Psychiatry*, Vol. VIII (1945) p. 268.

of those expected of normal men. On occasion, grave crises produce leaders whose primary rather than secondary character is charismatic. They stand or fall by their performance unless, before their skill or luck runs out, they are able to routinize or consolidate their positions.

The General Skills of Political Leaders

SKILL IN USING THE INSTRUMENTS OF AUTHORITY

The statement of what we know about the traits of leaders, the psychological development of leaders, and the special case of the *charismatic* leaders (a small minority of all leaders), gives us some idea of the general psychology of leadership. We may now inquire whether there are certain persistent political activities that demand certain leadership skills.

We have said that the instruments of authority are education and propaganda, force and violence, and economic measures and economic manipulation, depending upon whether or not acts are considered legitimate. Political leadership (whatever may be true of other kinds of leadership) in part depends upon skill in working with these instruments of authority. Priests, teachers, lawyers, orators, writers, and journalists; policemen and soldiers; the organizers, the managers, the "bosses," and the mechanical and human engineers; these are the people that become political leaders.

OCCUPATIONS OF POLITICIANS

Different cultural and political patterns tend to produce different kinds of leaders. In the United States the military man must "civilianize" himself before he can acquire political power in local or national politics, whereas in Nicaragua or China, for instance, he can move directly from the army into politics. The largest number of American politicans are lawyers. A study of twelve American state senates and thirteen lower chambers from 1925 to 1935 showed that 28 per cent of all members were lawyers. Another count in 1937, this time of all state legislatures, revealed eighteen hundred lawyers in the total of seventy-five hundred legislators. A study of five successive national congresses found the percentage of lawyers in the Senate to vary between 61 and 76 and in the House to vary between 56 and 65. No other occupation, save, in the more rural states, that of farming, competes seriously with the law. The inference we may draw is that American political conditions favor lawyers as politicians, and that the particular

political requirements with which lawyers are equipped are the ability
to bargain among diverse groups and interests, the freedom to engage
in politics while earning money at the law, skill in handling people, and
facility in dealing with the legal procedures so prominent in the American apparatus of government.

Yet in early colonial times, in Massachusetts and nearby places,
theological status gave political preference. Religious leaders like John
Winthrop, John Cotton, and Roger Williams were politicians. In certain Southern colonies, on the other hand, the owners of large planta-
tions were active in politics. Nor ought we to forget that the American
Revolution was led in good part by businessmen and merchants. Even
today a background as businessman or military leader may help a
particular candidate.

Furthermore, European political leaders are not preponderantly
lawyers. Down to 1945, England produced a leadership of birth and
wealth. Of 306 cabinet ministers from 1801 to 1924, 213 lived off accumulated wealth and only 93 had to earn their own living; since 1945
a high proportion of British leaders have depended upon financial support and jobs supplied by trades unions. French and Italian legislatures
have possessed more teachers and intellectuals than other national
legislatures; the Third French Republic was sometimes referred to as
the "Government of Professors." The German Reichstag before Hitler
had some lawyers and a noticeable number of representatives of special
economic interests such as trades unions and landholders, together
with a considerable number of professional civil servants. In the Soviet
Union, an increasing number of Communist party leaders have come
from the managerial group—those who control and operate the state-
owned factories, farms and transportation system. The bona fide factory worker is becoming a scarce person in official circles. In India
intellectuals and businessmen, most of them from high castes, rule the
masses, whereas in Japan's postwar House of Representatives, business
owners and executives are prominent, and bureaucrats, educators, and
farmers fall considerably behind. Militarists have abounded in Chinese
politics of the last century, but early modern China saw the domination
of politics by the *literati*, a group of scholarly civil servants. On the
whole, only American legislatures may be said to be lawyer-dominated.
Other legislatures have had more representatives from a larger number
of occupations.

IMPORTANT POLITICAL SKILLS

This information about the background and training of political leaders suggests that certain skills give their possessors perennial or recurrent advantages in the struggle for political power. Cere-

monial and rhetorical skills, soldierliness, and organizing ability have always characterized the office holders and office seekers of societies everywhere. Furthermore, particular environments seem each to favor particular skills. Pareto called Prussia of a half century ago the habitat of the lions, Paris of the foxes. Prussians were prone to gain political advantage by force, the French elite by guile.

Revolutions accelerate changes in the skills demanded of politicians, but they do not transform them. The Nazis weakened the grip of the bureaucrats and *Junkers*, but did not destroy them; indeed, they worked out an uneasy co-operation with them. In America, the New Deal replaced conservative lawyers with liberal ones. Fascism, although claiming to destroy political bargains and "deals," replaced the politicians of democratic Italy with the untitled "fixers" of despotic Italy. The Italian political milieu had not changed overnight because of the Fascist revolution.

Although different cultures tend to favor different skills, no one of the general political skills is ever quite absent. The modern state, especially, is based on a complex division of labor, in government as elsewhere. Military skills, for instance, have always had a place in politics, though the success of military men in making the *most important* decisions may go up and down sharply. Similarly, educators and journalists succeed in maintaining, even in the most anti-intellectual of political environments, a share of political power disproportionate to their numbers in the population as a whole. Whatever the form of society or its temporary condition, someone must educate and justify it, administer it, and fight for it. To the specialists in these tasks goes some return in the way of power.

Social Class and Political Mobility

SOCIAL CLASS AND POLITICAL SKILL

In addition to possessing useful political skills the successful leader often belongs to the proper social class. In all societies of which we have knowledge, at least a slight boost on the ladder to political leadership comes from belonging to that group in the society that is held in highest respect. Very often there is a close connection between the possession of, or the right to learn, political skills and membership in the group of highest respect. Thus in the England of the last century, top administrative posts—that is, the offices that demanded skill in handling men and procedures in the systematic execution of legislative policy—were occupied by members of the more fortunate social classes. A study by Harold Laski showed that the British foreign office was staffed in its higher posts almost exclusively by men of high birth and expensive education.

On the other hand—and this example shows why skill may be analyzed separately from class—the administrators of the *ancien régime* in France before the French Revolution were not members of the aristocracy. In fact, their skills, by helping to make the aristocracy useless, contributed to the revolutionary abolition of aristocratic privilege.

SOCIAL CLASS DEFINED

A social class is a group of persons with similar chances in life of gaining recognized goals—education, property, honors, leisure, and political office. An upper class person is one who belongs to a social group highly privileged in its chances. Societies range from rigid caste societies—where all the scarce and desirable values obtainable on earth are rationed at birth to the persons of different classes and cannot be much modified in the struggles of life—to the almost classless society in which men move readily up and down in the class scale according to their abilities and the accidents of life.

CASTE SYSTEMS

The contrast between a caste society and a relatively classless society is very striking and of course produces two contrasting kinds of politics. One caste society about which we know a fair amount is that of India. There, in the census of 1901, twenty-three hundred castes and subcastes were reported, and no Indian was entirely outside the system. Each caste was an exclusive and hereditary group with its own governing organization. Its members generally pursued a common occupation, celebrated their own festivals, and disciplined offending members through the caste council. Members of one caste could not marry into another caste, eat food prepared by a lower caste, or dine with anyone but their caste fellows. The whole caste system was supported by Hinduism, and caste obligations were decided by the Hindu priests—the Brahmin caste. The leaders of the caste system were hereditary: the princely castes, the Brahmin caste, and the conciliar leaders within each caste. However, the present rulers of India dislike the caste system, and it is crumbling perceptibly.

Twentieth century American society is, in many respects, the extreme opposite of the Indian caste society. Yet even in America one tenth of the people is divided from the other nine tenths by racial barriers that are, in fact, caste lines, even though lacking the religious and legal sanctions so prominent in the Indian caste system. In practice, the essentials of a caste system—bars against intermarriage and social intercourse—operate to segregate whites and Negroes. Whatever the legal theory, the Negro is effectively restrained from political leadership over whites in most parts of the country, though there are numerous exceptions.

SOCIAL MOBILITY IN THE UNITED STATES

Nevertheless, with the striking and important exception of the Negro-white caste system, the significance of social class as a factor in political leadership in America is slight. In this respect, America is much like most countries of Europe today, although before the two world wars it could be said that the United States was much closer to a classless society than were the countries of Europe. The present similarity of America and Europe in this respect is due both to a certain increase of class stratification in the United States and to a decline of such stratification in Europe as a result of wars, reforms, and violent economic fluctuations.

What categories of life chances can we find in America today that indicate the existence here of social classes? And if we find such categories, how do they affect an individual's chances of becoming a political leader—ignoring for the moment the effect of individual traits, skills, and other factors upon the chances of attaining political leadership?

Two of the most important attempts to ascertain whether and to what extent social classes exist in America are found in the work of the social anthropologist Lloyd Warner, and in that of the social psychologist Richard Centers. Dr. Warner, after making a number of intensive studies of small Eastern and Midwestern cities, came to the conclusion that six "social classes" could be said to exist in America: the upper-upper, lower-upper, upper-middle, lower-middle, upper-lower, and lower-lower. By ascertaining the kind of occupation pursued by a person, the source of a person's income, the type of house inhabited by the person, and the kind of neighborhood in which his dwelling was situated, one could assign to the person a composite index that would place him in one of the six classes. The observer could then make certain predictions about the probable behavior of such a person on the basis of the known behavior of persons on the same level or on different class levels.

According to Dr. Warner and his associates, the composite index of status characteristics just described tells in most cases what groups of people a person associates with, what general possibilities such a person has of obtaining wealth, excellent marriage arrangements, and social honors, and—most important for us—the Warner studies confirm the fact that political influence does not always depend upon office. In America, as in western European civilizations, it is often divorced from office. Those who actually hold political office may have economic and social characteristics quite different from the people who have the most political influence. There exists in a certain sense a "behind the scenes" government that is closer to "class" government than a study confined to the characteristics of the elected and appointive office holders would give one to believe. For example, John Gunther in his book *Inside U.S.A.* concluded that the United States is essentially "run by the propertied class."

Richard Centers, in his study *The Psychology of Social Classes*, pursued the search for classes in American life by means of opinion polls. He found that when a representative sample of the American population were asked to identify themselves as upper, middle, working, or lower class, the results were: 3 per cent, upper; 43 per cent, middle; 51 per cent, working; 1 per cent, lower; and 1 per cent, "don't know"; 1 per cent did not believe in classes. When asked what was most important in determining the class to which a person belongs, these people answered: 47.4 per cent, the person's beliefs and attitudes; 29.4 per cent, the person's education; 20.1 per cent, the person's family; 17.1 per cent, the person's money; 5.6 per cent, other reasons; and 9.1 per cent, "don't know." Dr. Centers believes that this last tabulation, showing that "beliefs and attitudes" ranked highest in determining why people assigned a person to a particular class, is significant as showing class *consciousness* to be the most important unifying element of a class.

What do studies of the kind just cited reveal about an individual's chances of becoming a political leader? They show that many Americans have a vague belief that social and economic classes exist. They show that a person of wealth, skilled occupation, good home, and respected family can ordinarily exercise more political influence, if he wishes to, than can persons of lower standing. But more than this can hardly be concluded from the existing studies of class in America. The American population is still very mobile, socially and physically. Men move up and down the social, economic, and political ladder with bewildering and sometimes distressing rapidity. They move in space, from city to city and state to state, more than the men of any other society in history. This rapid turnover in life-chances or class-chances means that "class" in the United States tends to change in each generation; that is, it tends to become what has usually been termed "freedom of opportunity." Up to the present time at least, the road to political leadership has been more dependent upon individual opportunities or chances for political mobility than upon fixed, graded, and handicapped starting positions.

INFLUENCES UPON POLITICAL MOBILITY

One need only compare the powerful influences working for political mobility in the United States with the feeble influences working toward class stability to see why it is that the American political scene as a whole, despite little islands of class dominance, gives a profound impression of classlessness. Intermarriage, for instance, between men and women of different social and economic groups, a frequent event in America, extends the chances for general and political success to a new group of relatives. Successful politicians may marry into wealthy families and acquire new political resources. Historians often emphasize how Emperor Napoleon Bonaparte, of fairly humble origins, married off his relatives into the royal families of Europe; but they find nothing remarkable in such behavior in America where it occurs so frequently.

The financial power that brings political influence, and *vice versa*, the business opportunities that open up for those who have political training or power, also create political and social mobility. Poor but bright lawyers move from government employment into the employ of wealthy corporations. Privately accumulated wealth helps win political influence through campaign contributions, contracts, and the purchase of the private-time services of politicians. Political leaders of immigrant groups move through politics into contracting, thence to real estate, thence to community activities such as the Community Chest drive. Sometimes this change occurs in one generation, sometimes in two or more.

The growth of new functions in government increases political mobility by raising clerks to prominence in political policy-making. Poorly paid bookkeepers in government offices rose to executive positions when the federal government moved into the field of social security insurance. Shifts in economic chances give a lift to many more people. Land on the frontier doubles and trebles in value as the country fills up. Fortunes and political power go to the first landholders, provided that they cling to their possessions—such opportunities present themselves in places as widely separated as Manhattan Island and California. As the financial and banking systems come to be regulated and dominated by the government, administrative officers shift readily from positions of power to positions of wealth and *vice versa*.

The rise of new types of organizations produces new types of political leaders. When John Gunther came to name sixty-four men "who run America," he named labor leaders among them, remarking that their emergence was a recent phenomenon in American politics. Whereas, for example, the automobile workers were scarcely organized twenty years ago, today they are tightly organized, and the

President of the United Automobile Workers, Walter Reuther, is a powerful political leader. Another new kind of political leader in twentieth century America has been created by the voluntary association for lobbying and agitating—for example, the trade associations and the reform groups such as the League of Women Voters. Because the membership is voluntary and usually not very active, the executive secretaries of such associations have come to wield a good deal of influence in politics.

Certain genetic considerations also operate constantly to increase mobility. The families whose indices fall into Dr. Warner's upper and middle classes have fewer children than those with lower class indices. Thus, especially in periods when the number of political positions is increasing, politics, no matter how strong the class system, must draw a large proportion of its leaders from the lower social and economic levels.

Finally, the easy availability of educational opportunities, which makes parental sacrifice for the young remunerative within one generation, is a great influence. It is not too difficult to help one's sons to obtain a legal education, for example. Of the vast number of lawyers in American legislatures and politics generally, a considerable number are using politics to make connections with clients-to-be, to enhance their prestige—in short, to attain success more quickly than they could in private legal practice. An American farm boy faces a social and political structure offering him chances for a wide variety of adult careers. Social mobility is so great that an individual can rise as far in one generation as a European family traditionally could in several. America's constitutions, laws, education, and ideology tend to speed the individual upward. He has chances for education in state universities, chances to move freely in space, and chances to enter politics. That the vast majority of men do not follow these routes is due to choice and circumstances. A horny-handed farmer or mechanic in his forties, it is true, is an implausible prospect for political leadership in competition with others who have specialized in acquiring political skills; but by his time of life it is unlikely that he would wish to compete. The fact that most men count themselves out of the race does not mean that the race is not open to most. It would be useless to define "class influence" as any and every influence and habit in a man's life that inclines him *not* to seek advancement in money, skill, respect, and political power, or that prevents him from attaining such things.

The conclusion one reaches, after surveying both the influences making for class stratification of chances and the influences making for classlessness, or social and political mobility, is that the groupings of Americans according to occupation, income, education, kind of house, and respectability are mainly "statistical" categories rather than social entities; that is, they are categories of *individuals*, who occupy *acquired*, *tenuous* ratings on scales of occupation, wealth, housing, education, and respect. When we move into the study of men who are active in politics we find even less indication that the present position or office of a politician could have been predicted on the basis of the life-chances foreseen for him at birth.

SOCIAL MOBILITY IN EUROPE

To a lesser extent, this same mobility exists in twentieth-century Europe. There, of course, limited resources, a more inflexible tradition, and remnants of aristocracy slow down social and political circulation, so that a man's political behavior and political prospects can be predicted to a considerable extent once his family history is known. But wars, revolutions, economic changes, and political reforms (such as the extension of the vote to the whole people) have profoundly modified the class character of politics, changing "class" from its ancient meaning of "those who possess special birthrights" to something more like "a convenient statistical category for classifying the population."

A number of writers, including Roberto Michels, T. S. Eliot, and Ortega y Gasset, have challenged the belief that increasingly rapid class mobility improves the quality of leadership. They assert that self-made men are likely to be poor rulers. Michels declares, for example, that the new men of power lack the respect for culture, the humaneness, and the relaxed sense of security that are possessed by men who achieve power without undergoing dehumanizing tensions and conflict. We should bear these criticisms in mind when evaluating the consequences of rapid political mobility as against a slowly changing ruling class.

THE POLITISTS

As we have learned from the foregoing discussion, a man's social class may not be the most important influence upon his chances of attaining political leadership. Nevertheless, with or without a strong class system, there is to be found in every community, large or small, and in every organization, large or small (save the most minute), a group of individuals, howsoever selected, who constitute the active political element. This element, constituting always a small fraction of the total community or organization, has been called by some writers the "elite," by others the "oligarchy," by some "the ruling class," and by others, especially in America, the "active citizenry." We shall call this group the politists, that is, those who differ from the rest of the population in that they are particularly occupied with the political process—with varying success, out of varying motives, and in different ways.*

If rank and privilege are strongly entrenched in a society, such influence will, of course, be manifest in the character of the politists. In England, until very recently, the aristocracy and upper middle class of company owners and merchants were the most powerful group among the politists. In Germany, even after the Empire was replaced by a republic following World War I, the Prussian junkers and the high career officers of the bureaucracy were among the most influential policy makers. In America, certain genuine class influences can aid political careers in a few places—certain districts, for example, in New York, Maryland, Virginia, or Massachusetts, where old, wealthy families maintain their political activity. But with or without such class influences, a group composed of politically active persons may be said to exist everywhere.

THE "IRON LAW OF OLIGARCHY"

Just as the politists are not to be confused with a ruling social-class, so they are not to be confused with an oligarchy, with rule by the few. The politists *may be* a certain social class, or they *may be* an oligarchy, but this is not necessarily so. Perhaps the best description of how the politists can evolve into an oligarchy in most large groups, no matter how classless in theory and origins, is that presented by Roberto Michels in his book *Political Parties*. From the study of a wide variety of European political parties he concludes that in all organizations, no matter how democratically conceived and organized, there arises a trend towards actual domination and rule by a few. He writes: "The appearance of oligarchical phenomena in the very bosom of revolutionary parties (workers, socialists, social democrats, communists) is a conclusive proof of the existence of immanent oligarchical tendencies in every kind of human organization which strives for the attainment of definite ends." Case after case shows how organizational leadership develops out of the complexity of work, how leaders become specialized and managerial, how well-trained leaders, recruited from intellectuals as well as from workers, take over union leadership, party administration, the party news organs, and the party's represen-

---

* The term "politist" has been used but rarely. It means one versed in polity, one who is particularly occupied with the affairs of the political community. This writer introduces the term of necessity, to fill a gap in the terminology of political science. Pareto, for example, would have avoided many difficulties if he had constructed a second term to avoid using "elite" ambiguously as (1) those with the highest index of any given trait, (2) those psychologically and socially fitted to govern a society. Dr. Gabriel Almond and Dr. Paul Lazarsfeld have been experimenting with the utility of the concept "opinion leader," which certainly would be included in the term "politist."

tation in parliament. Leadership becomes technical and indispensable. It is reinforced by routine, extended experience, acquisition of parliamentary skills, and the renown that accrues to actual leaders.

Sidney and Beatrice Webb pointed out the same tendency toward professional leadership in the history of British trades unions in the nineteenth century, but they furnished a somewhat different interpretation. British trades unions started as direct democracies, using the town-meeting form of government and emphasizing direct participation of all members in all union matters. Tardily and incompletely, the workers adopted representative institutions.

> The workman has been slow to recognize the special function of the representative in a democracy. In the early constitutional ideals of trades-unionism the representative finds . . . absolutely no place. The committeemen elected by rotation of office or the delegate deputed to take part in a revision of rules was habitually regarded only as a vehicle by which "the voices" could be mechanically conveyed. His task required, therefore, no special qualifications beyond intelligence to comprehend his instructions and a spirit of obedience in carrying them out.*

Power, the Webbs found, leaked into the hands of executive secretaries. Elected leaders become more specialized and powerful in the process of controlling the secretaries. Finally expert and trained leadership was demanded. The disagreement in evidence and findings between Michels and the Webbs is negligible. Their interpretations differ in that Michels speaks of the observed trends as "inevitable," whereas, the Webbs speak of them as "rational adjustments" of the workers themselves.

The trend, here observed in trades unions, exists in all large organizations that are not subject to constant check. Most detailed studies of group structure and leadership, from infant play-groups to national legislative bodies, reveal tendencies towards the crystallization of a leading group of individuals from the politists. Traditions, habits, expertness, prestige, and the possession of chances to stay in office combine to convert politists into oligarchs.

POLITISTS NOT A HOMOGENEOUS GROUP

The politics of a large nation, when they are not dominated by a single social class or oligarchy or by a single party (in which the "iron law of oligarchy" holds sway), show a great deal of flux and change. The politists are not a uniform group, a single elite, but are a mixture of leaders from many different organizations and associations. A brief table of the American political occupations will show how heterogeneous are the origins of the people who have something to say

* Sidney and Beatrice Webb: "Representative Institutions in Trade Union Democracy," *Political Science Quarterly*, Vol. XI (1896), pp. 655–6.

about political decisions in this country. There are several large categories of individuals who find themselves in government. They may be listed as follows:

I. OCCUPATIONS OF THE POLITICAL FORUM

    a. National elective offices (President, senators, etc.)

    b. State elective offices (governor, state legislators, etc.)

    c. County and township elective offices (county board member, etc.)

    d. City and town elective offices (mayor, town clerk, etc.)

    e. National party offices, elective or appointed (national chairman of the Republican Party, etc.)

    f. State party offices, elective or appointed (member of the state central committee of the Illinois Republican Party, etc.)

    g. Local party offices, elected or appointed (chairman of the county central committee of the Democratic Party, etc.)

    h. National appointive offices (department heads, ambassadors, various committees, commissions, etc.)

    i. State appointive offices (liquor control board, state commerce commissions, department heads, etc.)

    j. Local appointive offices (chief of police, commissioner of streets and sewers, civil service commissioners, etc.)

    k. Precinct captains or committeemen, holding minor state and local government jobs and paid from public funds for part-time party work.

II. PUBLIC CAREERS IN POLITICAL ADMINISTRATION

    a. National foreign service offices (ministers, consuls, clerks, etc.)

    b. National civil service offices (clerk in Bureau of Mines of Department of the Interior, personnel officer in Department of Justice, national forest ranger, etc.)

    c. The armed forces (general, pilot, infantryman, etc.)

    d. State civil service offices (engineer in highway department, warden of state penitentiary, etc.)

    e. Local civil service offices (principal of high school, sewers engineer, etc.)

    f. International organization offices (translator in Secretariat of the United Nations, statistical clerk in the World Labor Organization, consultant to United Nations Educational, Scientific, and Cultural Organization, etc.)

III. THE PRIVATE (I.E. NOT DIRECTLY GOVERNMENTAL) CAREER VOCATIONS IN POLITICS

    a. Executive secretaries and other offices of national, state, and local civic organizations (League of Women Voters, Taxpayers' League, Parent-Teacher Association, etc.)

    b. Executive secretaries, research positions, and other offices in philanthropic and political study foundations (Russell Sage Foundation, Brookings Institution, Ford Foundation, etc.)

    c. Interest group offices (research worker for the American Medical Association, labor economist for the International Ladies Garment Workers Union, director of political action for a union, etc.)

    d. Research, consultant and advisory positions (Public Administration Service, consultant on political and industrial problems for industrial concerns and other private associations, etc.)

    e. Journalists, lecturers, commentators, and writers on political affairs.

    f. Educational positions, administrative and teaching positions in the political science areas in secondary schools, junior colleges, and universities.

    g. Special interest representatives before policy-making governmental bodies (lobbyists for Farm Bureau Federation, American Manufacturers Association, Congress of Industrial Organizations, etc.)

IV. AVOCATIONS IN POLITICS

    a. Appointments on special political affairs ("dollar-a-year" men, investigating commissions, national and state jurors, advisory committees, etc.)

    b. Membership of specialized associations with public-private membership (public health associations, associations of social workers, American Political Science Association, American Psychological Association, etc.)

    c. Reformers and other part-time politically active persons and groups, ordinarily activated only by the existence of a special combination of political conditions (Committee to Defend America by Aiding the Allies, independent citizens' committees to defeat the political machine, Audubon League, fourth-ward committee to save the old water tower, etc.)

    d. Officials of labor unions and large corporations, with their public relations staffs; trade associations officers; church leaders; and other socio-economic group officers.

    e. Political lawyers, political real estate and insurance brokers, and others specializing in political-private arrangements.

    f. Contractors, sellers, and buyers for governmental services and goods.

SIZE OF THE POLITIST GROUP

    A few of the people concerned with government may well have escaped our classification: no doubt there are a number of politi-

cally trained ditch-diggers and bartenders, as well as industrial ty-
coons and Hollywood screen writers. For two facts stand out even in a
preliminary listing of political occupations in America and in most
Western or Westernized nations: governmental activity is widely
distributed throughout the population; and in consequence, individuals
move readily into and out of the politist group and up and down the
various levels of the political hierarchy. America was for a long time
not typical of the western European nations. But since the beginning
of the twentieth century, with the advent of socialist and labor parties
and with the succession of internal and foreign crises, the class of
politically active individuals has become as large proportionally in
many other nations as it is in America.

The number of American politists has never been accurately measured. Both De Tocqueville and Bryce in their famous commentaries on
the American system of government remarked at the astonishing
number of politically active citizens. Lord Bryce estimated at about
200,000 the "persons whose chief occupation and livelihood lies in
politics." This was in 1891, and his definition included roughly the
members of our Class I (above) with a considerable number from our
Class II who were at that time political appointees. In contrast, Bryce
estimated the politically active class in England, then at the height of
her prestige and influence in the world, at about 3,500. De Tocqueville, writing some fifty years earlier, had ventured no numerical
account, probably because all America seemed to him to be political.

> No sooner do you set foot upon American ground than you are stunned
> by a kind of tumult; a confused clamor is heard on every side, and a thou-
> sand simultaneous voices demand the satisfaction of their social wants.
> Everything is in motion around you; here the people of one quarter of a
> town are met to decide upon the building of a church; there the election
> of a representative is going on; a little farther, the delegates of a district
> are hastening to the town in order to consult upon some local improve-
> ments; in another place, the laborers of a village quit their plows to
> deliberate upon the project of a road or a public school. Meetings are
> called for the sole purpose of declaring their disapprobation of the con-
> duct of the government; while in other assemblies citizens salute the
> authorities of the day as the fathers of their country.*

AMERICAN POLITISTS

Fifty years after Bryce, and a hundred after De Tocqueville,
the population had increased enormously, the machine age had concentrated half the population in large cities, and the governments of

* Quoted with permission from Alexis de Tocqueville: *Democracy in America*, The
Henry Reeve Text, as revised by Francis Bowen, now further corrected and edited with
introduction, editorial notes, and bibliographies by Phillips Bradley (New York: Alfred A.
Knopf, Inc., 1946), Vol. I, pp. 249–50.

nation, state, and locality had increased their scope and function. In 1949, Merriam and Gosnell estimated the total of party workers over the whole nation at 800,000 in normal times and as many as 1,500,000 in an exciting campaign. Probably no more than 300,000 of these are regularly engaged in politics unless they hold, or hope to hold, office. But to these "grass roots" workers, mostly of our Class I, k (above), must be added the elective office-holders, usually several apiece from the some 155,000 units of government estimated by the Census Bureau to be operating in 1942. Of these, let us say, there are 500,000—a conservative figure. Then, from some 1,529,000 school teachers and school employees must be added perhaps 250,000 who are active in politics, civic activities, and reform groups. Perhaps 250,000 of the 638,000 appointive state administrators are important either by virtue of their office duties or because they are political workers as well as state employees. There are 1,622,000 local government employees of whom perhaps 1,000,000 are politists by virtue of their duties and political interests or because of their civic and political activities beyond the demands of their formal duties. Of the 2,000,000 employees of the federal civil service, no more than 30,000 can be reckoned as "activists." And of the 3,000,000 individuals of the armed forces, perhaps only 5,000 exert political influence beyond their immediate tasks. All the foregoing would be classified by us in Classes I and II. There may be about 15,000 persons in Class III, and perhaps some 75,000 persons in Class IV. Therefore, the total number of people, very roughly calculated, whose occupations concern the governments of the United States lies in the neighborhood of 9,879,000 persons. The number of these who are unusually active in political affairs is roughly 2,425,000 persons.

These 2,425,000 are the persons, then, who during a good portion of their adult, productive years are preoccupied with politics more than most people. Beyond them lie millions of persons occupied with government and many millions more whose interest in politics is intellectual and passive; they may vote, read the political columns of the newspapers, talk occasionally about their opinions with friends, and have some taste of political activity at long intervals. But the bulk of law sponsorship, political decision-making, and the other tasks of the political process remains with these 2,425,000 out of the 9,879,000; they form only about 1/62 of the total population and the whole 150,000,000 depend to a considerable extent for their fortunes and misfortunes upon the leadership of this group.

A study by Drs. J. L. Woodward and Elmo Roper, published in December, 1950, approaches our problem differently. They polled a representative sample of the adult population of the United States on six types of political activity and scored the responses as shown in Figure 6.

FIGURE 6

THE POLITICAL ACTIVITY OF AMERICANS *

A. *Scoring System for Political Activity Index*

	% OF TOTAL SAMPLE QUALIFYING	SCORE POINTS CREDITED	TOTAL POSSIBLE SCORE FOR CHANNEL
Voting			
Once or more in last four years	75	1 ⎫	
Three times or more	47	1 ⎬	3
Five times or more	21	1 ⎭	
Discussing Public Issues with Others			
Discusses frequently and takes an equal share in the conversation	21	1 ⎫	
Discusses frequently and usually tries to convince others he is right	6	1 ⎬	2
Belonging to Organizations That Take Stands on Public Issues			
Belongs to one or more such organizations	31	1 ⎫	
Belongs to two or more	7	1 ⎬	2
Written or Talked to Congressman or Other Public Official to Give Own Opinion on a Public Issue			
One or more times in the past year	13	1 ⎫	
Two or more times in the past year	7	1 ⎬	2
Worked for Election of a Political Candidate in Last Four Years	11	2	2
Contributed Money to a Party or Candidate in Last Four Years	7	1	1
TOTAL POSSIBLE SCORE			12

The scores made by the sample were as follows:

B. *Distribution of Political Activity Scores*

SCORE OF RESPONDENT	% OF TOTAL SAMPLE WHO MAKE THE SCORE	CUMULATIVE PER CENT
12	0.1%	0.1%
11	0.3	0.4
10	0.7	1.1 Very Active
9	1.2	2.3 (10.3%)
8	1.6	3.9
7	2.4	6.3
6	4.0	10.3
5	6.5	16.8 Active
4	10.3	27.1 (16.8%)
3	15.6	42.7 Inactive
2	19.0	61.7 (34.6%)
1	19.1	80.8 Very Inactive
0	19.2	100.0 (38.3%)
	100.0	

* Reprinted with permission of the *American Political Science Review* from Julian L. Woodward and Elmo Roper: "Political Activity of American Citizens," *American Political Science Review*, Vol. XLIV (1950), pp. 872, 874, 876.

It will be noted that, even though the authors generously classify as "very active" a person who scores as little as six points out of a possible twelve, only *10.3 per cent of the adult population* achieved this classification. This would be about ten out of every one hundred American adults. And if the minimum score for this classification were raised (justifiably, we think) to nine points out of twelve, only two out of every hundred adult Americans would qualify as "very active" politically. Our own politist ratio of one in sixty-two, if applied only to adults instead of the whole population, would come to about the same figure, that is, something like two politists for every one hundred adults. Research is badly needed on this whole question and can readily supply a more valid and reliable estimate of the number of politists in the population. These preliminary estimates, however, are probably not so greatly in error as to be useless for our purposes.

SOVIET POLITISTS

Unfortunately, if we wish to compare the number of politists in America with their number abroad, we cannot expect much help from sample surveys, and must rely principally on the guesses of skilled observers. This is especially true of the Soviet Union, where freely operating opinion pollers are unthinkable.

We can make some estimate of the size of the Soviet politist group, using official figures modified by our own judgments. Figure 7 shows such a computation. It seems to indicate that the Soviet politists outnumber the American in proportion to population by about two to one; that is, the ratio of politists to population in the Soviet Union is one to twenty-three and the ratio of governmentally occupied to population is one to thirteen.

The comparison invites two contrasting questions: Why is the Soviet politist ratio so small and why is it so large? Russia's politists are more numerous than America's probably because of the intense effort of the Bolshevists to agitate and activate the nation. The citizens are given every kind of inducement to be obediently active. On the other hand, the Russian politist class is small, considering that Russia is presented to the world and widely regarded as the nation where government embraces everything. As implying universal *control*, this view is accurate. As implying universal *participation*, it is not; Russia's politists are a small part of the population. The great mass of people are still not active.

Although this large group of politically inclined persons that we call the politists—a group that we find in every state—has no sharp form or character, it does provide the milieu from which the more prominent and influential leaders arise. Obviously, not all of these

Figure 7

The Politists among the Governmentally Occupied in the Soviet Union *

GOVERNMENTALLY OCCUPIED CATEGORIES [1]	NUMBER
Intelligentsia [1]	9,591,000
Armed Forces	2,600,000
Communist Party (excluding CP members among the intelligentsia and in the army)	1,257,000
TOTAL	13,448,600

POLITISTS AMONG GOVERNMENTALLY OCCUPIED CATEGORIES [2]	NUMBER
Heads of enterprises, institutions, workshops, state farms, collective farms, etc.	1,441,000
Agronomists and scientific workers [3]	80,000
Teachers	969,000
Cultural-educational workers (journalists, librarians, club directors, etc.)	297,000
Economists and statisticians	822,000
Bookkeepers, accountants	1,617,000
Judicial-procuratorial workers (judges, procurators, investigators, etc.)	46,000
TOTAL	5,272,000

	NUMBER
Less Communist Party members of this group	1,845,200
REMAINDER	3,426,800
Deputies of Soviets (excluding CP members and members of above group)	1,796,173
Members of the Communist Party [4]	2,600,000
TOTAL	7,822,973

Population: 181,000,000
Ratio of Politists to Population: 1 to 23
Ratio of Governmentally Occupied to Population: 1 to 13

[1] Term used in the Soviet Union to include all trained personnel, almost all of whom hold government jobs.
[2] Categories of intelligentsia conforming most nearly to our definition of politist.
[3] The scientific workers include professors and college instructors. Agronomists in the Soviet Union are considered politists since they are politically active in the machine tractor stations both in deciding vital matters in regard to the collective and state farms and in checking on the execution of the party line.
[4] Note that in 1949, the membership of the Communist Party had risen to 6,000,000.
* Source: Materials contained in Julian Towster: *Political Power in the USSR 1917–1947* (New York: Oxford University Press, 1948), and Barrington Moore: *Soviet Politics: The Dilemma of Power* (Cambridge: Harvard University Press, 1950).

2,500,000 persons in America are equal in influence. They all are leaders in a sense, but few are powerful leaders. Many acquire their "political" roles through skills not very different from the skills a person not employed by the government might possess. Obviously, too, a great number of these millions are political foot soldiers, even if they are party workers. They work, obey, and receive modest emoluments—honor, favors, money, and perhaps the excitement of the "game" of politics. The top ranks of the politists, who set the pace for the rest to follow, may number no more than a few hundred in each state of the Union and perhaps no more than 2,500 at Washington, D. C.

Special Functional Conditions of Leadership

PARTY LEADERS

Membership in these top ranks requires, besides the traits, general skills, and the class background sometimes needed, the ability to perform specialized functions—to play the role of elected executive, legislator, member of the Department of Agriculture; to influence legislation, lead reform groups, manage a political campaign, and so forth. Thus, in discussing the traits required of party leaders, Merriam and Gosnell wrote:

> Broadly speaking, the common qualities of great party leaders have been: (1) Unusual sensitiveness to the strength and direction of social and industrial tendencies with reference to their party and political bearings. (2) Acute and quick perception of possible courses of community conduct with prompt action accordingly. (3) Facility in group combination and compromise—political diplomacy in ideas, policies, and spoils. (4) Facility in personal contacts with widely varying types of men. (5) Facility in dramatic expression of the sentiment or interest of large groups of voters, usually with voice or pen—fusing a logical formula, an economic interest, a social habit or predisposition, in a personality. (6) Courage, not unlike that of the military commander, whose best laid plans require a dash of luck for their successful completion.*

LEGISLATIVE LEADERS

Leadership in the halls of legislatures requires, besides these qualities, an ability to select and give priority to the proper issues, to introduce issues in the most acceptable form, to dramatize them, to bargain for support, to gather a following among the members of the legislature, to seize the appropriate moment with the proper formula and the best procedures, and to force through a decision. The legislator must know when to reformulate his issue or withdraw it; he must be able to shift tactics skillfully and be able to fight off crippling amendments; he must use his connections, contacts, privileges, and tangible resources to support his efforts.

* Quoted, with permission, from Charles A. Merriam and Harold F. Gosnell: *The American Party System* (3rd ed., New York: The Macmillan Company, 1940), p. 126.

EXECUTIVE LEADERS

There are special requirements, also, for executive leaders; Chester Barnard, in an article on "The Nature of Leadership," suggests several. The activities of executive chiefs are in general "the determination of objectives; the manipulation of means; the control of the instrumentality of action; and the stimulation of co-ordinated action." For these, five basic qualities are demanded. In order of importance they are: vitality and endurance, decisiveness, persuasiveness, responsibility, and intellectual capacity.

MILITARY LEADERS

In discussing military leadership, Napoleon Bonaparte noted: "It is exceptional or difficult to find all the qualities of a great general combined in one man. What is most desirable and distinguishes the exceptional man, is the balance of intelligence and ability with character or courage." Furthermore, "the effect of discussions, making a show of talent, and calling councils of war will be what the effect of these things has been in every age: they will end in the adoption of the most pusillanimous or (if the expression be preferred) the most prudent measures, which in war are almost uniformly the worst that can be adopted; true wisdom, so far as a general is concerned, consists in energetic determination." These words, of course, are rather vague adages of a great leader. They are mere common sense comments on rather intricate matters.

PERSONAL LEADERSHIP VERSUS OFFICIAL ROLE

In discussing the requirements for leadership in an institution like the legislature or the army, we must keep in mind the distinction between personal leadership and the leadership of office. In completely informal groups and situations—that is, those where external law and office rules do not govern rigidly his activities—the leader's so-called personal qualities count for a great deal. In formal groups, on the other hand—those set up and governed from the outside, or organized in a special way by a preceding generation of members— the leader's personal qualities count less and the status of his office more. Thus the fiery stump orator may be contrasted with the Supreme Court Justice.

Hence, each type of leadership in politics—executive, legislative, judicial, military, and so on—has its peculiar requirements. Success in one situation does not imply equal ability for success in the others; sometimes, in fact, it may imply quite the opposite. A successful legislator may prove to be an unsuccessful governor. A conscientious reformer may prove to be a bad politician. A good soldier may make a ludicrous President. Even if political science were to prepare ideal "job analyses" for all political offices, the accidents and fortunes of politics are such that those who hold or aspire to political office will, as often as not, lack a good part of the qualities called for. Political scientists, like ordinary mortals, are often struck by great disparities between the assumed demands of a position of political leadership and the character of the leaders who successively occupy it.

The Total Analysis of Leadership

THE PROBLEM OF NUMEROUS CONTRADICTORY LEADER TYPES

How does it happen that such great differences of character are apparent in the men who hold the same office? How does it happen, for example, that a reticent, cautious, conservative man like Calvin Coolidge can hold the same office as an extroverted, daring, tradition-breaking man like Franklin D. Roosevelt? Or—to put the question on a lower level, showing thereby the universal nature of this problem of leadership—how does it happen that a fussy, petty bureau chief may be succeeded by a flamboyant, impatient chief who appears for all the world to be a politician fresh from the campaign stump? Or, on still another level, why are there genial, baby-kissing city bosses, and taciturn, shy bosses, both of whom may come from the same community? Does not this incessant chain of contradictions deny the essential thesis of the study of leadership: that there is a pattern of leadership? Does it not deny the assertions of this chapter *in toto?* We have, it is true, been extremely cautious in asserting that there are universal physical and mental traits of leaders; and we have been careful to show that only most general statements can be made about the extent to which certain political skills bring political leadership. We have declared that certain kinds of class structures promote certain kinds of leaders who have the qualities favored by the class structure, but we were also careful to point out that describing the class conditions of a community could still not adequately explain the rise of individual leaders, especially when those leaders are "outsiders" as were Edmund Burke, Napoleon Bonaparte, Adolf Hitler, or Disraeli.

LEADERSHIP PART OF AN INTRAGROUP RELATIONSHIP

We can present, however, a theory of leadership to explain the great diversities in the qualities of different kinds of leaders. This theory holds that we cannot adequately explain leadership through trait, skill, class, or functional analysis—individually or all together—because leadership is a relationship to a particular political group situation that is itself determined by all related group situations. Ralph Waldo Emerson wrote of leaders: "They satisfy expectation and fall into place. What is good is effective, generative; makes for itself room, food and allies."

Leadership cannot be understood by studying merely individuals, or a single group, or even the general conditions affecting all related groups. One must study all three at the same time. For the leader operates somewhat like a communications control-system. He is a set of acts and signals that are prearranged by his personal history and that communicate to his group and related groups. A study of only one part of this communication system *cannot help* but result in the disconcerting number of contradictions and exceptions that have up to now characterized the study of leadership.

We shall give simplified examples of each of these three kinds of study in order to show by contrast the advantages of our theory of leadership. First we illustrate the study of the individual leader. Let us construct three simple listings for three leaders, Bacchus, Apollo, and Hercules. All hold, so far as we can see, *identical positions*, and are having equal success, but they have markedly different qualities. It is

BACCHUS	APOLLO	HERCULES
① GENIAL	② WISE	③ STRONG
2 *some wisdom*	— *no friends*	— *unwise*
— *weak*	3 *some strength*	5 *good organizer*
4 *some money*	— *poor*	④ *wealthy*

very difficult to make any generalization about the qualities necessary for leadership in this position, even though the situation is simplified to the point where only four traits are given each man. Such inconclusiveness is what has vitiated study after study based on comparisons of individual leaders. The hope of drawing general conclusions from such studies—except about positions requiring the most specialized kinds of abilities, such as knowledge of Latin—is vain.

If we now make a diagram to include the leader's group, we have, according to our theory, the following kind of picture, provided that the groups perform identical functions with equal external results.

FIGURE 8

LEADERS AND FOLLOWERS WITHIN A GROUP

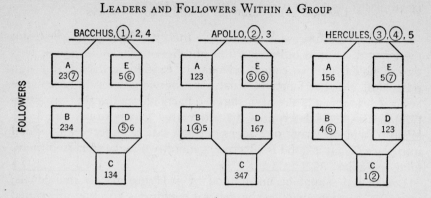

There are now three groups, composed of six members each. Bacchus, Apollo, and Hercules are viewed *with their followers*. Each follower has certain qualities, and it will be seen that in every case the followers provide what the leader lacks. Thus, Bacchus is genial, but weak; three of his followers have some strength. Bacchus is possessed of some wisdom; that wisdom is supplemented by that of two followers who also have some wisdom. The same balance exists in the groups of which Apollo and Hercules are the leaders. We see that each group produces the qualities needed to equal the cumulative balance possessed by the other two groups, and even adds new qualities (6 and 7).

Leadership, therefore, is a function of the group and cannot be understood by merely studying the leader. Leaders who occupy identical positions will seem to possess inexplicably diverse qualities when they are studied in isolation from their followers. Thus, according to our theory, an attempt to find uniformities in the traits of American Presidents would be doomed to failure unless it also studied the "men around the President." A satisfactory comparative study of wartime leadership in America, England, and Germany would have to include not only Roosevelt, Churchill, and Hitler, but also Hull, Hopkins, Marshall, Morgenthau, and Byrnes, as against Attlee, Eden, and Bevin, as against Goering, Goebbels, Himmler, and Schacht, in order to observe how the collective qualities in each group add up.

At the same time, this method detracts nothing from the importance of the leaders. It leaves the admirer of great leaders free to marvel at the unusual combination of qualities that great leaders commonly possess, enabling them to bring several critically necessary qualities to a situation to which their best lieutenants bring only one or two.

But our theory will not permit us to confine our study to the leader and his own particular group. The following two diagrams illustrate what happens if we do. In each case two groups sum up the parties acting in a given situation with reference to goal X.

FIGURE 9

LEADERS AND FOLLOWERS IN AND AMONG GROUPS

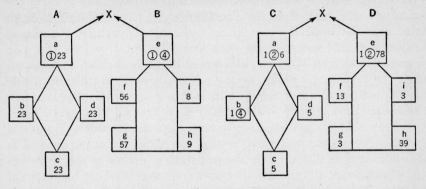

It will be noticed that the qualities possessed by the *leaders* in the comparable groups A and C are not identical. That is to be expected from what has been said above. But in addition, if one adds up the qualities possessed by the comparable *groups* A and C, *these too* do not add up to the same sum. The process of adding leadership qualities has *passed over the single group boundary.* We must examine the sum of qualities possessed by A together with B, and by C together with D, and only then do we see that the cumulative leadership qualities are the same in the two double groups. These qualities, however, are so distributed that neither the study of individuals nor the study of single groups can explain the diversity of the leaders.

What our theory asserts here is not startling, in the light of the history of institutions. *The theory is that the supply of qualities of leadership appropriate to a given situation may be a function of more than one group.* A classic example of this theory is found in Polybius' discussion of the separation of powers in his history of the Roman Republic. He wrote that Rome had become great largely because of its balanced constitution, which contained elements of monarchy (the consuls), aristocracy (the Senate), and the people (assemblies of plebs). Governance in accordance with the best interests of the nation was guaranteed by a combination of the strengths of the three branches of government: weak consuls could be buttressed by strong Senates, harsh Senates modified by popular protest. A study of consular leadership alone, ignoring the Senate and plebs, would show a puzzling succession of men of very different traits and backgrounds.

Similarly, in regard to the United States, a study of the Presidents alone, or of the Presidents with their cabinets and kitchen cabinets, will not reveal any intelligible pattern of presidential leadership qualities. To the study of the President's group must be added the study of the other leadership groups of the United States that influence the decisions of the President. Within these groups we should study the top men, their immediate cliques, and their relation to their followers. We should have to add up their leadership qualities, add to them the qualities that come from the President's group, and determine from that sum the leadership equilibrium of such a structure. We should expect this final sum to be the same for equivalent situations. One may constantly expect, however, differences in the leadership qualities of, say, the President's group, or any other subgroup, at different times.

The empirical work required in studying any leadership situation by the method implied in this theory is, of course, very great. Some may say that we are shutting out an elephant in order to admit a whale. To this the reply may be that difficulties are never avoided in science. It is as difficult to make painstaking studies of foolish things as of important things. Another answer is that the best biographical studies do proceed in the manner we have outlined. Sandburg's biography of Abraham Lincoln is an example. Seeming contradictions in the behavior of the leader can be resolved often only by unraveling a difficult knot of circumstances that contains ultimately all the contending influences in a given situation.

Finally, we may argue that we claim no certainty in our studies of leadership. Absolute certainty, so far as the future can be foreseen, is not going to be achieved by social science. Problems concerning leadership will remain indefinitely a puzzle to political science; the conceptions and materials of this chapter can only add some understanding and clarify the important features of the picture presented by politics. Certain "mysterious" phenomena, such as the charismatic leader, can be made to seem not so awesome and incredible. It is not impossible that some knowledge of such leadership, even if not total knowledge, will increase the possibility of braking, modifying, or otherwise controlling the circumstances under which leadership operates.

The same possibility of clarification, understanding, and control exists in the materials that are next to be studied. Public opinion, the community, and the majority—the related subjects of the next chapter —seem, like leadership, somewhat mysterious. The words themselves suggest a vast fog of shapeless forms and indistinguishable forces, an atmospheric setting for countless political disasters. Yet these subjects, too, are not impervious to correct thinking and objective study.

Questions and Problems

1. Compare and contrast leadership theories of the Carlyle group and the Tolstoi group. How can political science regard both approaches as acceptable?

2. Note the two parts of the definition of leadership. Why are both parts considered necessary? What differences can generally be expected to distinguish formal office-holding leaders from informal, nonofficial leaders?

3. List across the top of a sheet of paper the traits mentioned by the Stogdill study as *possibly possessed* by most leaders. List down the left hand side the names of ten persons in your graduating class in high school or prep school who you think were leaders. Indicate for each person whether he possessed each trait to a greater degree than the average graduating student.

4. Searching your memory of the leaders in your former classes, ball clubs, associations, scout troops, and all other groups with which you might have been familiar, find and describe as many leaders as you can who were apparently compensating for some feeling of inferiority by greater leadership activity.

5. Write the names of the ten greatest men who ever lived, in your opinion. Taking them one by one, decide whether each is a charismatic leader and say why in each case.

6. Classify the examples of occupations given in this chapter, plus all other occupations you can think of, on a scale from 1 to 20 according to the extent to which their skills are useful in rising to important positions of power today in America. Do the same for any other country at any period of time (e.g. ancient Athens, medieval Italy, Tudor England, revolutionary America, Soviet Russia today).

7. Ask five people who have lived in your community for some time to list the five men who are most powerful politically. Make a composite list, and discover the main occupational skills of each person listed. Does the result contradict or support the statements of this book?

8. Describe the essential differences between a caste society and a quasi-classless society. From your own experience and knowledge, tell why it is difficult to state dogmatically that Negro-white relationships in America are a caste relationship.

9. Can you distinguish Warner's six classes in the community with which you are most familiar? Were there fewer classes? Were there no stable criteria of class, so far as you can see?

10. How do you explain the book's statement that "there exists in a certain sense a 'behind the scenes' government that is closer to 'class' government than study confined to the characteristics of the elected and appointive office-holders would give one to believe"? Why is this "government" more classlike than the legal government?

11. Summarize the dynamic factors working for political mobility and against class advantages in the United States. Add other examples known to you from reading or personal acquaintance if you can.

12. Comment on the statement "self-made men are likely to be poor rulers," giving your viewpoint and such evidence as you possess on the negative or affirmative side of the question.

13. Distinguish among: the "politists," "social classes," and "oligarchy." Do you think it true to say that the "politists" will always be a fraction of the total population. Why?

14. It was estimated that there are perhaps no more than 20,000 top influential leaders in the United States. Allot what you think would be the

appropriate number of this 20,000 to each category in the table of American political tasks, granting that in some categories there may be no representation among the top 20,000 of the land.

15. Distinguish between special functional skills and general political skills. Why can a leader possessed of a general political skill fail in a special functional situation? Give an actual or hypothetical example.

16. Assume three leaders named Joseph, Clarence, and Paul, holding identical positions and blessed with equal success. In terms of qualities, on a "+, 0, −" scale they rank: in energy, Joseph +, Clarence 0, Paul +; in good looks, Joseph 0, Clarence +, Paul +; in education, Joseph +, Clarence 0, Paul 0; in the special functional skill of oratory, Joseph 0, Clarence +, and Paul +. Show (1) why it is almost impossible to explain their equal position and success by trait similarities, (2) how this frustrating problem can be solved theoretically by looking at each leader's entourage of six members and adding up all their various qualities.

17. Using the same example as above, together with your development of the problem, show now how the analysis of the leader's group alone may be inadequate to explain the results of the group activity unless there be taken into account a co-ordinate and supplementary group or groups.

18. Using the definition of a political leader given in this book, make a list of all persons who qualify as political leaders as judged by their description in a week's file of daily newspapers available to you. State information provided on the psychology, general skills, social class, functional skills, and relationship to followers of each leader. Where might you turn for further information to supplement your file on each one of the persons described?

19. The term "leader" is common in everyday conversation. Relate what you can of the common fallacies on the subject of leadership that appear to be refuted by the materials of this chapter. (Suggestion: Remember that exaggeration, too, is a form of fallacy.)

20. Determine who are the leaders whose acts are given most prominence in each of three of the following periodicals during the same week. How do you account for differences in emphasis? Would you say that the importance of a leader is entirely a matter of opinion? Explain your answer. The periodicals are: *Time, U. S. News and World Report, Nation, New Republic, America, The New York Times Sunday Review of the News of the Week, Newsweek, Life.*

Longer Study and Research
Problems Suitable for Term Papers

1. Using an outline summary of the contents of this chapter for reference, read one of the following works, and whenever you find evidence or theories pertinent to some point of the outline, insert them in the appropriate place or places in the outline. The final paper should take the form of a heavily documented outline.

Max Nomad: *Rebels and Renegades*
Harold Zink: *City Bosses in the United States*
Harold F. Gosnell: *Boss Platt and His New York Machine*

J. T. Salter: *The American Politician*
Saul Padover: *John L. Lewis*
W. L. Riordan: *Plunkitt of Tammany Hall*
Sidney Hook: *The Hero in History*
You may substitute any other suitable, recognized biographical work.

2. Take as your subject of study any local or national council, commission, legislature, or legislative committee, numbering over ten persons. Prepare a chart of the birthplaces, education, age at first election (or appointment) to public office, total time in office, national origin, and religious affiliations of all members. What conclusions can be drawn from this data, or what does the data suggest about the kind of leadership in the group being studied? (Often this information is difficult to obtain; find what you can. Sometimes you may be lucky enough to find additional items of a biographical character to add to the indices recommended for the chart here.)

3. Select any two persons from your local community who qualify as politists. Arrange an interview with each one and ask him about his training, his interests in political matters (in both broad and narrow senses), the way in which he arrived at his present formal or informal position. Supplement this information with whatever printed information may be available about these people and with the comments of other people who may know them. Seek to shed light on the factors in leadership that are presented in this chapter. Write a frank paper, but keep all identities confidential, and merely designate the persons by symbols (A, B, etc.), rather than by name. Political scientists, like medical practitioners, must exercise great discretion in handling the knowledge they possess. This discretion applies especially to data obtained directly from the subjects. Remember that political scientists are *not* collectors of juicy gossip.

4. Read Richard Centers' *Psychology of Social Classes*. Prepare for your class a questionnaire asking the same questions as he does; make enough copies for everyone (or 50 at a maximum). Administer the questionnaire to the class and tabulate the results as Dr. Centers does. Do your results agree with his? Are there discrepancies? Do you think these occur because college students are not typical of the population, or are there other reasons that you are aware of?

4

THE COMMUNITY AND SPECIAL INTERESTS

POLITICAL leaders supply much of the dynamism that operates and changes political institutions. But leaders by no means act in isolation; they are themselves mirrors of the people in many ways, and their actions are modified at every step of the political process by the energy, reactions and demands of the less active and less authoritative citizenry.

If we reconsider the conditions from which leaders emerge, we can see how utterly important it is to know something about people as a whole. Leaders may emerge because they possess unusual psychological and physical traits—often acquired from the culture rather than inherited. Leaders may emerge from certain occupations, certain social classes, certain power-commanding environments (public offices), and from fulfilling certain balancing roles in and among their various groups. As we attempted to explain more and more of the conditions that produced leaders, we came to see that the people themselves must be taken into account, and we are now compelled to seek other concepts that can cope with the people as a whole.

This chapter is devoted to concepts for studying the political behavior of the people as a whole. It seeks to explore the general social foundations of politics and of the politists. Therefore it treats several large and diffuse social groupings: the community and public, less general interests of an economic or other social character, public opinion, and the majority. Later chapters will discuss the more tightly structured political groupings—electoral constituencies, political parties, and pressure groups. Both kinds of groupings are the bases upon which the politists rest and function.

If men were all alike and society were static, how easy our analysis would be! We could define the several major concepts of this chapter as follows and little would be left to explain. We would say that the state (territory, population, officers, independence) is the same as the community. The people of the community are the *public;* the political beliefs shared by everyone in the community are *consensus;* the opinions they hold are *public opinion;* and *public opinion* is divisible into a *majority* and minority opinion.

All of these statements are often true, but more often are not true enough. In order to use the several concepts more exactly and with greater realism, we must define them more carefully and—more important—use them carefully. For the state is not always the community, and the community does not always have consensus, and several communities and publics may be found among the same people, and the several publics do not always have public opinions, and there may be several public opinions in the same public, and, finally, a majority is not always to be discovered.

The redefinition of these concepts is therefore in order.

A community exists to the extent that a people is knit together by mutual intercourse and mutual belief. Hence *a community is defined as a people who have many habitual relations or communications with one another*. To find the community, one observes the relations and communications among a population and judges that they are so many and all-embracing as to give the people a culture or character.

A public exists to the extent to which the people of a community have political relations with one another. Hence *the public is defined as the political part of the community, that is, the people with respect to their political relations and communications*.

A consensus exists when the people almost universally agree upon a basic set of beliefs about right and wrong in politics and about the organization of the state. Hence, *consensus is defined as a basic agreement of the public upon the general method of organizing and conducting the political process*.

Public opinion exists whenever members of the public are divided over the proper solution of an issue that is relevant to the state. Hence, *public opinion is defined as a belief held by a number of people regarding a political issue*.

If more than half of any given group are in agreement upon an issue, they are what we call a majority. Thus initially we see that consensus implies a heavy majority of the community agreeing upon a *number* of *interrelated basic issues*. We also see that many majorities may exist without there being a consensus. Thus one majority can agree that Smith is a better politician than Jones, another majority, that high tariffs are better than low.

Thus far, we have only set the frame for understanding these concepts. The concepts will become clearer and more useful as we examine them in detail and with respect to one another.

The Political Community and Consensus

THE STATE AND COMMUNITY CONTRASTED

First of all, a state may not be a single community. Take the case of England, Scotland, and Southern Ireland in the nineteenth century. All three were united in the same state. They constituted a population inclosed within a territory, governed by public officers (the government) not subject to higher authority. Yet to some extent Scotland and certainly Southern Ireland contained peoples apart from the English in many important respects, including dialect, customs, and religion. The differences among the three included many important political differences, less marked in Scotland than in Ireland. Hence three general publics existed. Not the least of the differences that made Ireland and England different communities and publics was the presence of a consensus in England with respect to English political government and politics and the absence of the same consensus in Ireland with respect to English rule over Ireland. Thence came the great dissatisfaction in Ireland, the attempted revolts, and the demands for Irish independence. The legitimacy of English rule was stoutly contested. Yet on particular political issues that came up from time to time, there can be little doubt that segments of Irish and English opinion coalesced and agreed. And there may have been occasions when a majority of Irishmen and Englishmen agreed on some political viewpoint or principle.

OVERLAPPING COMMUNITIES

The community differs from other social groups in that it embraces all the physical and psychological connections among people necessary to give a person an over-all way of life. For example, being born and raised in Shanghai or Peiping usually suffices to make a man or woman Chinese. He is a member of Chinese culture and shares many customs and beliefs with his fellow Chinese. Being a carpenter or farmer influences a great deal of one's life, customs, and outlook, but not nearly so much as membership in the greater community. The first affiliation is to a community, the second to a social group, perhaps occupational. A man ordinarily can change his occupation without becoming a different kind of person, but hardly his community.

Where do we place individuals whose lives are complicated by universal claims and attachments stemming from more than one source? What happens to a South Carolinian who feels the claims of two community systems, regional and national; to an Italian who has dedicated himself to the priesthood of the Catholic Church? We can only say that such men belong to two communities, each with all-embracing cultures that he must hope will never make conflicting demands upon his loyalties.

THE COMMUNITY A NETWORK OF COMMUNICATIONS

By the community, therefore, we mean a people who maintain a considerable number of habitual relations or communications. The community includes such important relationships among people as their co-operation and competition, their mutual dependence, the interconnections among their special group affiliations, and their shared beliefs and impulses. A community may be visualized as a giant spider web. The outer limit of the community is that area under observation where the number of communications diminishes in extent to a tiny amount and in duration to temporary and sporadic contacts. Thus, the United States and Soviet Russia form different communities. In one sense there is no inner limit to the community; that is, all relations contribute to determining the nature of the community. But where those communications are intensified according to some special criteria —such as religion, occupation, or (especially) locality—we see social groups; and when such a special group (the locality is most frequently met with) affects markedly most aspects of the lives of many people, it too may be called a community.

GREAT AND LOCAL COMMUNITIES FORMED BY PHYSICAL INTERDEPENDENCE

The study of a great community reveals patterns of relationships among the community members. Modern American society, for example, can be described physically as a community in which over 150,000,000 people depend upon one another through an exceedingly complex division of labor that clothes Californians in New England's textiles and feeds New Englanders with California fruit. People across the continent read the same news, compete with each other in business, fight the same wars together, and travel to each other's resorts and schools. Yet local communities persist in abundance, for a great number of one's social relations are made locally. Two hundred years ago, the separate colonial communities were of even greater importance to their respective members because the American colonists had not nearly so much to do with one another as Americans today.

The political scientist must not overestimate certain types of connections in the network of the community. For example, it was often stated before the last two wars that the existence of certain international agencies, such as the International Postal Union, meant that a community of nations existed. However, the mere fact that nations communicated with each other did not mean that they were in ideological agreement. Ideological ties are among the most meaningful of community ties, but because they are intangible and hard to measure, they are often ignored.

HOW A COMMUNITY ENFORCES CONFORMITY

Out of the myriad human contacts in the community there evolve various modes of thought and moral beliefs. A community teaches its members to do things in certain ways through its mores, customs, folkways, and fashions. Not all of these patterns of behavior are given equal significance by the community, and their strength may best be judged by the penalties for nonconformance. While a man will only receive frowns for not wearing a tie on certain occasions, he will be treated very harshly for betraying his country, killing his children, or walking the streets naked. Sociologists, anthropologists, and psychologists have collected much material on the way the community regulates the conduct of its members.

THE COMMUNITY SANCTIONS

The community can command conformity and obedience from most of its members, be they humble or great, without using formal procedures. Most persons follow community rules without the intervention of laws, courts, police, or discipline. One need only name the community sanctions in order to prove that most men are made acutely aware of their existence at one time or another in their lives. The first sanction is habit. Most men never know much of what is "wrong" because they encounter little but what is "right." Their habits, the repeated performance of certain social obligations in learned ways, tend to exclude the learning of other ways of doing them.

But the fear of isolation and frustration also impels men to conform. To act in uncommon ways usually means that one acts alone and is prevented from gaining valued responses. To most men, especially in political activities, which are social to begin with, such a condition is not pleasant. They would rather conform than lose the companionship of their fellows and the respect and rewards of the community. Jobs, appointments, election, privileges, and other tokens of social esteem can be denied an offender by general community consent. Thus, custom imposes its own sanctions without invoking the formal, legal sanctions of the criminal law—the compulsion of force.

In rare instances, an allegedly flagrant violation of community mores is met by mob violence, vigilantism, political assassination, and other sporadic manifestations of disapproval. Such "crowd" behavior, however, should never be considered by the political analyst even as *prima facie* evidence that a "community spirit" has been thoroughly aroused. Too many "spontaneous" crowds of protest, vengeance, and "righteousness" have been found by historians to be aroused, organized, led, and manipulated by a few directing agitators towards goals having little to do with the members of the crowd themselves. As we shall see in the concluding section of this chapter, the community is too diffuse a grouping to act directly in the political process. It must always be transformed by other groups before it can effect its desires.

THE PUBLIC IS THE POLITICAL COMMUNITY

The public consists of the people's *political* relationships in a community—the politically specialized part of all the communications that exist among community members. Essentially, as we shall see shortly, this specialized part is what we commonly call public affairs, and those people some part of whose relationships to the community concerns public affairs have opinions the special sum of which constitutes public opinion. When some people are entirely excluded from political affairs by law and tradition, as has happened in many states, they are not to be considered part of the public.

THE VARIETY OF PUBLICS

There are as many publics as there are communities. The number of both is not fixed for all time by an immutable law. As both terms have been defined, the key criteria for distinguishing one community and public from another are the scope, number, duration, and intensity of their human bonds. Certainly the Athenians were a community to themselves, separate from the Spartans and the Corinthians. Their attachments to the great Greek cultural community were not so numerous and strong as their local attachments. The big nation-state of today would not be a meaningful community to most ancient Greeks. Many people predict that the modern nation, as the most important community, is to be replaced by a community of mankind.

Furthermore, some men may acquire stronger over-all loyalties to their unions, localities, or states than to the nation as a whole; they may possess less relations with the great community. For them there exist two communities and two publics, perhaps even more. Political scientists therefore must describe, enumerate, compare, and analyze all the human contacts in each situation that they study in order to determine whether there are one or more communities present.

RELATION OF COMMUNITY BELIEFS TO PUBLIC AFFAIRS

Enough has been said to demonstrate that a community and its public are closely related. What happens to the basic customs of a community must transform the nature of a public. Changes in characteristic social sanctions mean changes in political sanctions. If a community rejects the use of force, public opinion will evidence this feeling. If community standards place a high value on material things, politics will be generally materialistic.

We must always be aware that politics operates within such a framework of community custom with its penalties for deviation. The preparation, enactment, and administration of laws are only the baldest points of contact between community beliefs and habits and the political process. Few men are so naive as to insist that the law could command and the community would knuckle down. To the innocent query: "What is the limit of the power of the English Parliament if it is supreme?" Leslie Stephen gave the sensible answer: *

It is, of course, omnipotent in the sense that it can make whatever laws it pleases, inasmuch as a law means any rule which has been made by the legislature. But from the scientific point of view, the power of the legislature is, of course, strictly limited. It is limited, so to speak, from within and from without; from within, because the legislature is a product of a certain social condition, and determined by whatever determines the society; and from without, because the power of imposing laws is dependent upon the instinct of subordination, which is itself limited. If the legislature decided that all blue-eyed babies should be murdered, the preservation of blue-eyed babies would be illegal, but legislators must go mad before they could pass such a law, and subjects be idiotic before they could submit to it.

Even apparently "lawless" politicians, who by-pass or violate established formal procedures for making political decisions, are acting either in accord with the tacit understanding of the community or at least are not flagrantly disregarding the limits of toleration set by the community.

* Quoted with permission from *The Science of Ethics* (2nd ed., New York: G. P. Putnam's Sons, 1907), p. 137.

CHANGING ATTITUDES TOWARDS POLITICAL INSTRUMENTS

Different communities and the same community at different times vary in the sort of conduct they expect and demand from politicians. It is apparent in reading about the Roman-Carthaginian wars, the Spanish-American War, the Texan war of liberation, and the Korean War of 1950 that the parties operated according to widely differing standards of humaneness. Notions of "chivalry" and "humaneness" varied widely in the different conflicts.

Other examples of changing standards that affect both the community as a whole and politics specifically may be cited. The English penal law of the seventeenth century would not be tolerated in England today. Chronic corruption was accepted by the people of certain modern American localities like New York City until relatively recently. Today, propaganda is used much more extensively as a political technique than it was in medieval cities; the "re-education" of criminals is a common form of "punishment"; and "laws of war" are generally able to give some protection to belligerents. The power of the English King to appoint his choice for Prime Minister has given way to the power of the victorious party to dictate the choice. Community belief has so changed in this respect that an independent appointment would be received with horror and anger. Similarly, the power of popularly chosen Electors to name the President of the United States has been transmuted into a delegated function of electing the man the electorate voted for. Although violations of this tradition have occurred, the culpable Electors have been subjected to considerable popular resentment.

Community Problems and Consensus

CONFLICTING LOYALTIES HARM CONSENSUS

Since a community is intimately associated with its public, disorders of the community are quickly communicated to public affairs and become political problems that affect the state. A rutted, broken road, for example, may incite discontent, may lead the discontented community to engage in public controversy, and may finally bring a political reaction against the government.

The community problem usually regarded as gravest of all is of a different order. It results from overlapping community identifications. As we have suggested previously, a person may feel himself part of two communities—one local, the other national, or perhaps less frequently, one a social class and the other a local or national community. In modern Western society, the national community is a strong contender for one's total affiliations, but one's social class in a European country, or one's locality or occupation in America, may claim an equal or greater loyalty. If the two loyalties conflict, the individual becomes disloyal to one or the other, or withdraws from the conflict by becoming apathetic towards both. Both disloyalty and apathy produce personal anxiety. What is more, they produce anxiety in others who are affected by the behavior and attitudes of the individual in question. A kind of rootlessness and rulelessness grows and spreads. Consensus is weakened. Yet there is no neat method by which such individual dilemmas may be solved, the anxieties reduced, and consensus fostered.

HOW COHESIVE IS THE MODERN GREAT COMMUNITY?

Practically all writers on the subject of the community and the public have asserted that the vast technical changes of modern times complicate the individual's role in the great community. Science, technology, rapid physical communications, movements of population, and many other factors have built a physical community in which many men feel ill at ease. Physically, they may be more comfortable than their ancestors; psychologically, they often feel little sympathy with the larger community. Furthermore, they lack any effective control over their environment. Great economic, physical, and political changes take place, vastly important political decisions are made, and they can only applaud or condemn or escape. Their work life is transformed, their cities grow like weeds, they are automatically made members of a "United Nations."

To make their lot even more difficult this loss of active power has come at a time when men everywhere have learned to demand democratic practices. Men are supposed to be active in decision making at a time when the decisions to be made concern matters completely beyond the ken of individuals. Americans, for example, are told from childhood that they should control government policy; but how can they conceivably control the delicate, shifty, secret maneuvers of the so-called cold war? Englishmen are told that a socialist government is a people's government, rather than the government of a few. Yet how can the British worker actively participate in the intricate plans of the socialist government or in the decisions of the government to co-operate or not to co-operate in the Schuman Plan to integrate western European industrial facilities?

To tell the citizens of various countries today that they are responsible for events in their new enlarged communities and that they must participate in molding the direction of those events may be flattering to their beliefs about democracy, but such directives have also proved terribly embarrassing to many people and to their governments as well. For in trying to exercise the controls to which they are entitled by the beliefs of the times, people make impossible demands of their governments. The governments themselves, in reconciling their decisions with democratic theories, trip and stumble in trying to keep in line with the shifting, jerking moods of the various groupings of the people.

Seeming solutions of the problems of democratic leadership often are suggested. For instance, officials are sometimes tempted to transform the theory of political democracy into a theory of social engineering; that is, many officials feel that the only way to escape from the intolerable fickleness of popular pressures is to control those pressures by propaganda. The people are assured that they are being consulted, that their wishes are being followed, and that popular controls are real controls.

Unless such a policy is carried out with ruthless efficiency, as it appears to be done in Russia today, it tends to make many people more suspicious of the intentions of their rulers. They feel that control is being stripped from them by unscrupulous politicians. They turn to "sincere" men, ones who, they believe, voice truly the needs and aspirations of the masses. They are willing to confide their active interests to such men to rid themselves of the "plague of self-interested politicians" who are supposed to exist.

The danger of another kind of dictatorship appears at this stage of community anxiety. The charismatic leader finds the political environment in which he may prosper. The Mussolinis and the Hitlers appear to many people, not as destroyers of democracy, but as the only true democrats, the restorers or builders of the new great community in which such people can recapture their sense of control or understanding of events.

The despair over controls felt by many citizens of modern democracy has not gone unnoticed among political writers. We can name Walter Bagehot, Émile Durkheim, Gaetano Mosca, Max Weber, Roberto Michels, Ortega y Gasset, T. S. Eliot, Elton Mayo, and John Dewey as writers who have concerned themselves with the tensions of modern great communities and with the political consequences for democracy that such tensions possess. In general their argument parallels William James's theory that individual self-esteem is the ratio of success to pretensions: when one wants much more than he can possibly get he is miserable. So the people of modern societies, clamoring for the immediate direction of their vast and complex governments, may well lose faith in the institutions of representative democracy and thus contribute to democracy's ruin.

CONSENSUS AS AGREEMENT ON BASIC PRINCIPLES

Such a loss of faith would mean that there was no longer a community consensus, that the vast majority no longer agreed with the body of basic principles that originally held them together. According to Walter Bagehot, consensus is the essential feature of a well-organized community; a country cannot be happily governed unless the people are generally agreed as to what is right and wrong in politics. When governmental or social institutions are not in harmony with consensus, or where there is no consensus, a society is in for a bad time. The people are apathetic or frightened into desperate measures to establish some new order of community relationships.

DEWEY'S "HEALTHY" COMMUNITY AS CONSENSUS

By contrast, according to John Dewey, the healthy community would be one in which the individual is neither boss over others nor bullied by others. The individual would feel that he controlled the destiny of the community in co-operation with the other members, all sharing similar aspirations and responsibilities—an adaptation of Jefferson's idea of local community self-rule. Dewey's ideal community is

> a society in which the ever-expanding and intricately ramifying consequences of associated activities shall be known in the full sense of that word, so that an organized, articulate Public comes into being. The highest and most difficult kind of inquiry and a subtle, delicate, vivid and responsive art of communication must take possession of the physical machinery of transmission and circulation and breathe life into it. When the machine age has thus perfected its machinery, it will be a means of life and not its despotic master. Democracy will come into its own, for democracy is a name for a life of free and enriching communion.*

But Dewey's formula is most difficult to apply to the great community. The self-governing and tightly knit localities of Jefferson's day are gone.

REQUIREMENTS OF COMMUNITY INTEGRATION

The modern age can derive inspiration from the past, but it requires a host of new techniques and beliefs if it is to achieve the nec-

* Quoted with permission from *The Public and Its Problems* (Chicago: Gateway Books, ed. 1946), p. 184.

essary minimum of integration. Often its subgroups are so unrelated, separate, and mutually hostile that politics operate solely by means of temporary compromises, expedients, and stopgaps, while group conflicts are emphasized and total community sentiment means little. Often there is such widespread apathy in the community, so little attention to public affairs, so little active communication among the members that the government becomes disconnected from the public and works to impede rather than to encourage the development of consensus.

Nothing less than a wholesale transformation of individual viewpoints can make the community recognize and appreciate the bonds that unite them solidly, and bring them into accord on fundamental issues. They would have to agree on matters most important to political behavior—on what constitutes legitimacy, on basic religious matters, on the extent to which individuals should be competitive or cooperative, on the use or nonuse of violence and propaganda, on the main opportunities an individual should be allowed in his lifetime, on the limits of public restraint and private indulgence. These items of agreement would form the consensus of the political community. They would not be seriously challenged, and change would be gradual.

Although rudiments of these common beliefs are present in some great national communities, they are scarcely even visible in relation to the world as a whole. Several national and many local societies have a profound consensus whereas others have an abbreviated consensus. Most leaders of contemporary national or local governments can hardly feel that their power rests upon an unshakeable foundation of unquestioned popular belief.

Separatism and Voting Behavior

SUBCOMMUNITY AFFILIATIONS (SEPARATISM)

The last section affirmed that community ties and sentiments, based on both physical and psychological bonds, exist and influence political behavior. For example, everyone living in a community is usually required to be loyal to it, be it a tribe, city, or nation. When, as often happens, a person belongs to more than one community and public, his deep loyalties must be divided among his plural communities. Usually there is no grave conflict; a man can be quite loyal to his city and the nation at the same time.

A man is more than a citizen of a community, however. He is most often also a member of special separate groupings within the community. He possesses special interests that drive him to act differently in politics from the way he would act if he tried only to consider his all-embracing community obligations. Besides owing great services to his communities, a man is likely to behave "selfishly" on behalf of other groupings into which he may fall, voluntarily or involuntarily. He is likely to possess a special occupation, income, religion, and attachment to locality that mark him off from other members of his community and cause his political behavior and attitudes to be different from theirs.

In addition, he may belong to organized groups that correspond to his special interests—a church, a club, a fraternity, a trade union, a manufacturers' association, or the like. As a member of such a group he becomes active in politics in a manner that is quite different in effect from the manner in which the totally unaffiliated person is active. Perhaps 50 per cent of all Americans belong to one or more

FIGURE 10

A PERSON'S AFFILIATIONS

As an individual, one may have a combination of personal and political motives directed at increasing the power, wealth, respect, health, education, and so on of himself and of those men, few or many, with whom he identifies himself. His identifications are often shown by his affiliations and he accomplishes his goals through them.

TYPE OF AFFILIATION	A PERSON WITH SIMPLE INVOLVEMENTS	A PERSON WITH COMPLEX INVOLVEMENT
I. Family (*all-embracing*)	Ia Only tied to immediate family	Ib Many relatives tightly bound together
II. Community (*all-embracing*)	IIa National community is exclusive	IIb May be heavily involved in national community, home city, and religion (or trade union)
III. Behavioral Grouping (*partial*)	IIIa Possesses a religion, an occupation, and a neighborhood—each influencing his voting behavior and political attitudes	IIIb Possesses a religion, occupation, neighborhood, nationalistic leanings towards second country, and investments in business other than his own occupation.
IV. Association or Group (*partial*)	IVa Belongs to a church	IVb Belongs to a church, a political party, social club, trade union, civil defense organization, foreign affairs study group (or other similar groups)

Social separatism emerges from IIb, IIIa, IIIb, IVa and IVb in most cases. Conflict among one's affiliations is not always present, but frequently results from contrary directives of two affiliations. For instance, a worker who tries to be a Catholic and a Communist at the same time undergoes great emotional stress that may be reflected in apathy and apparent withdrawal from political concerns.

such associations, although the extent of such participation abroad is much less.

These three types of belonging—the community, the separatist grouping, and the organized group—complicate a person's political behavior. Figure 10 serves to show how involved a person's connections may be.

We must conclude that a political theory that speaks only of the *community* of interests is inadequate. Political theory must also study the *separatism* of interests in order later to show how the various interests become organized in the political process and obtain a favorable place in the structure of the government.

The several social sciences offer us various routes by which we may investigate the special interests of individuals. Social philosophy, economics, anthropology, psychology, sociology, and special fields such as industrial relations and public administration are all deeply concerned with problems that arise from conflicting and co-operative groups and have their own ways of solving such problems. Political science has a traditional way of addressing such problems too; it pursues the study of the community and separatist interests of men through the study of voting behavior in order later to understand the nature of representation, political parties, pressure groups, and the institutions of government. We shall follow the route of political science, emphasizing, because of the introductory nature of this work, only the major concerns of political scientists.

Voting behavior is a common subject of political study. Among the human differences that express themselves in different ways of casting ballots are traditions, localisms, economic motivations, religious beliefs, nationalities, races, and sex. We will discuss them in turn.

TRADITION

One of the most striking facts in the field of voting behavior is the tendency of people to support repeatedly the same parties.*

* Tradition, economic and religious interest, and other factors that determine voting behavior are studied in various ways. We may describe one technique often used to determine the economic or social significance of a particular candidate, party, or issue and to ascertain whether or not voters sharing certain socio-economic qualities share preferences for such candidates, party, or issue. The logic and procedure are as follows:
1. *Hypothesis:* Candidates of a given religious affiliation are supported disproportionately by members of their affiliation.
   We would then expect, for example, that a Catholic candidate would receive a greater proportion of votes from the Catholic members of his constituency than he would receive from the Protestant members.
2. *Method:* We compare the behavior of Protestant and Catholic voters, similar in all respects except religious affiliation, with reference to the candidacy of Mr. Smith, a known Catholic running against a Protestant.
3. *Techniques:* Possible ones are many—participant observation, interviews using multiple-choice questionnaires with a large cross-section of the voting population, depth

Changes in conditions, in rival candidates, or in party platforms do not seem to change the attachment of many people to their favorite party. This phenomenon has been often seen to perpetuate itself through generations; many men vote as did their grandfathers (see figure 11). Only about one quarter of the American voting population regard themselves as independent of party affiliation, according to several surveys. Professional men, businessmen, white collar workers, and skilled workers tend to be more "independent" according to the *party* criterion of independence.

PSYCHOLOGICAL TRADITION

"Traditional voting," however, is difficult to define and hence difficult to study. There are, in fact, two useful meanings of the term. First, voting may be called traditional when a study of the motivation of a voter reveals that he identified himself with ancestral behavior in preference to other interests he may have in casting his ballot.

For example, if a certain congressional district is composed mainly of dairy farmers who vote time after time for a party that tries to ban the sale of oleomargarine, they are not *traditional voters* in this sense because economic motives might be assumed to be more important here than any identification with their forebears. If, however, the party switches to support the sale of oleomargarine on equal terms with

---

interviews with a smaller sample of voters, or an analysis of the voting figures after the election. We shall use the last technique in the balance of the illustration.

4. The votes of the two candidates are assembled and tabulated according to the smallest units for which tallies are available. (Let us say wards.) These are converted into percentages.

5. A poll is discovered that gives the religious affiliation of the population of each ward in percentages. (Since people are often reluctant to reveal their religious affiliations, we must make sure that the information is reliable. We must also make sure that the sample was accurately drawn from a cross-section of the population.)

6. A table is prepared showing the percentage of Catholics for each ward and the percentage of votes for Mr. Smith. A mere glance shows that where the ward population is heavily Catholic Mr. Smith's vote was heavy and *vice versa*.

7. If there are many wards and figures that are not absolutely clear, we calculate the simple coefficient of correlation between votes for Mr. Smith and percentage of Catholics. (This is done according to a generally available formula. It allows one to handle two large contrasting sets of data. It brings out any tendency of the two sets of data to be associated with each other. or dissociated from each other.) We find it to be .78, definitely significant.

8. We cannot say that Catholicism *caused* the heavy Smith vote, nor can we say immediately that other factors might not be at work. For example, we may find several exceptional wards that are heavily Catholic but somewhat anti-Smith. Further study reveals that those wards are composed of wealthy people for the most part. So we surmise that economic level *as well as* religious affiliation played a part in determining the sources of Mr. Smith's support. On the whole, however, we are reasonably satisfied that the hypothesis has some element of truth to it.

This is one of the principal techniques of studying voting behavior (see Figure 12 and the discussion surrounding it). New techniques are constantly being sought for and discovered, refined and retested. From the various studies that actually have been made, we can make some statements about the five major forces that operate in the voting process.

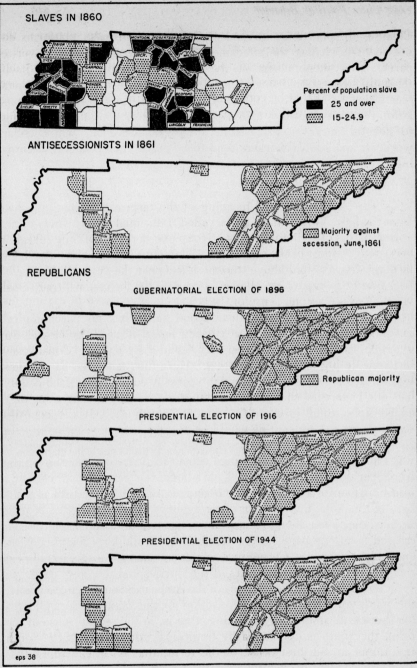

FIGURE 11: A CENTURY OF TRADITIONAL VOTING *

Note how the Tennessee counties that had fewer slaves in 1860 tended on the whole to oppose secession from the Union in 1861, and subsequently tended to vote Republican in the elections of 1896, 1916, 1944, and on other occasions as well.

* V. O. Key, Jr.: *Southern Politics in State and Nation* (New York: Alfred A. Knopf, Inc., 1950), p. 77.

butter and the congressional district still continues its support at the polls, then we may suspect that certain traditional influences are at work. Traditional voting in this sense implies that all conceivable current reasons for a person to support a party, candidate, or issue are disregarded and that he continues his support of the party because he feels identified with his own past conduct or with the habits of his forebears.

STATISTICAL TRADITION

A second useful meaning of the term can be distinguished from the first. Voting may also be called traditional when a study of the voting habits of an individual or a group over a period of time reveals a persistent support of the same party. Thus, in the example of the dairy farming district cited above, the mere fact that the voting behavior of the district is repetitive allows us to call the behavior "traditional voting" in the second sense of the term.

"Traditional voting" in this second sense has no psychological meaning, but it is an analytically useful *index* of trends employed, for example, by Ralph and Mildred Fletcher in their article: "Consistency in Party Voting from 1896 to 1932." Here they tabulated party votes by counties for the various election years. Assuming that each county had one chance to change party affiliation at the next election, they added up a total of 26,151 "chances to change." If the counties switched 26,151 times, this would be 100 per cent nonconsistency. In fact, nonconsistency was observed in only 29.2 per cent of the cases. It was found that 591 counties voted consistently for one party over the whole period. They thus would have a nonconsistency of 0 per cent or a traditionalism of 100 per cent. Of course, as with all statistical problems of this kind, the behavior of each county might register no change as a whole, even though many nonconsistent individuals may have crossed from one party to the other. Gosnell similarly found consistency very strong in Chicago voting even during the great political changes of the depression years of the thirties and the New Deal.

Now let us take the example of the American South. On the whole, the South votes in election after election for the Democratic candidates for President. Statistically speaking, that is, in the second sense of the term, the South is dominated by traditional voting. But is the South traditional in our first sense of the term, that is, in the sense that Southerners identify themselves with ancestral behavior in preference to other interests in casting their ballots? The answer here too is "yes," but "yes" only in part. Many Southerners are still "fighting the Civil War" or following their grandfathers' advice. Many others, however, who do not care for their ancestors' behavior, have current reasons for voting Democratic. They vote Democratic because they can get what they want *via* the Democratic Party; they do not need nor care to establish another party. Such men as these are traditional in the statistical sense, not in the psychological sense.

Frequently, men speak of traditional voting in the psychological sense as being "irrational." They say, for example, that those Southerners who vote Democratic, even though they agree far more with the national policies of the Republican Party than with those of the Democratic Party, are "irrational." One can define "rational" as he pleases, of course; but objective political science cannot say that identification with one's ancestors is morally inferior to favoring some kind of economic self-betterment. It is not for political science to tell a man that he ought to prefer wealth to honor or a tariff to his father's habits. Objectively we can only say that a person or a group that wants mutually contradictory values—for example, *both* Republican policies *and* agreement with ancestral behavior—is going to have a conflict of conscience and will act differently than other people in certain ways.

LOCALISM

Localism is as universal as traditionalism in affecting people's political behavior. By localism is meant a strong sentiment favoring one's neighborhood, town, city, or regional interests over the broader geographical community. In many cases localism is so strong a force that the only community a man belongs to is a local one. In most cases, however, localism is a partial bias, a separatist emotion, rather than a total community involvement. In Chapter Six, we shall mention the strong local character of American party politics. When we discuss legislatures in Chapter Ten, we shall again mention the play of local interests in the behavior of representatives. In Chapter Fourteen, on local institutions, we shall treat at some length the limited horizons that politics has for many people. And in the chapter on federalism, local interests such as states' rights come into play. Thus, localism affects much political behavior and many political institutions. For the moment, to indicate its pervasiveness as a motive is enough. Many studies of election returns or of opinion polls discover that localism is a potent contributor to political behavior and attitudes.

ECONOMIC FORCES

Men often act politically according to their occupation and income level. The most extreme proponent of economic motivation was Karl Marx. He would say the voter acts according to his relation to the means of production. An "exploited worker" votes for revolutionary candidates; an owner of a business votes for a "capitalist." Voting figures, being records of real happenings, show no such pure behavior. Rather economic motives are tied up with all the others that influence the way a vote is cast, and they are often subordinate to ideological, political, and social forces. What studies of voting behavior do show, and polls of opinion in general corroborate, is that there does exist a measurable tendency for people in like economic circumstances to vote alike on economic issues.

Sometimes we may find a poor man backing candidates who use slogans that appeal to the economic interests of the poor, and a rich man supporting a candidate using opposite slogans. Sometimes there is no apparent economic factor, but the rich men cast their votes differently from the poor men. The first event gives some support to the Marxian hypothesis. The second, however, shows no strong motive of economic class-interest in political affairs at all. We are merely using an economic index to show political differences between social groups. Very often only an economic index may be available, and when we find a positive correlation, we have the illusion that only the *economic* force separating the two groups is being measured.

Here is an example of how the use of an economic index may give an exaggerated impression of the strength of economic motivation: Let us suppose that a certain Englishman is a faithful supporter of the policies of the established Church of England. Let us suppose that he votes for a candidate who also supports this church. It is likely that the economic views of both the voter and the candidate will also for the most part coincide. Therefore, if we use a set of economic views as an index, and apply it to the two men, they will be seen to be alike in their views. However, this does *not* mean that these views are *economically determined* or *economically self-interested*. It only means that the economic *index* is associated with *whatever does determine* their behavior. The economic viewpoint is the only thing that is being measured, and *not* the total personality and its motivations.

Let us turn to Figure 12, which is an elaborate correlation matrix showing the degree of connection among a number of indices (variables) based on areas. Any two indices that are not strongly associated in the same areas have numbers close to 0. Any two indices that tend to be found in different areas of the city will have a negative number (for example, −.8). Any two indices that are found associated in the same areas will have a positive number (for example, .8). *But no index is the sole determinant of a person's position on political matters.* For example, the fact that the Roosevelt vote of 1932 has a high correlation of .76 with Unemployment (an index based on the amount of heavy unemployment in the various areas) does not mean that all the unemployed voted for Roosevelt or that all the people in areas

FIGURE 12

A STATISTICAL PRESENTATION OF POLITICAL RELATIONSHIPS

CORRELATION MATRIX: INTERCORRELATIONS OF VARIABLES RELATED TO VOTING BEHAVIOR IN CHICAGO, 1930–36

	SMITH (a)	LEWIS (b)	ROOSEVELT 1932 (c)	IGOE (n)	ROOSEVELT 1936 (v)	WOMEN (d)	PARTY VOTING (e)	BOND ISSUE (f)	WET VOTE (g)	INTEREST IN VOTING (h)	FOREIGN BIRTH (i)	CATHOLIC ORIGINS (j)	MEDIAN RENTAL (k)	HOME-OWNERS (l)	UNEMPLOYMENT (m)	MOBILITY (s)	DOUBLING-UP (t)	EDUCATION (u)
Smith (a)		.78	.94	.91	.88	-.57	.79	.46	.68	.35	.64	.78	-.62	-.15	.69	-.31	-.18	-.62
Lewis (b)	.78		.84	.80	.81	-.55	.62	.17	.64	.21	.60	.57	-.53	.03	.57	-.33	-.10	-.63
Roosevelt, 1932 (c)	.94	.84		.96	.96	-.66	.84	.40	.65	.27	.73	.78	-.68	-.05	.76	-.35	-.11	-.73
Igoe (n)	.91	.80	.96		.94	-.66	.84	.44	.61	.27	.71	.76	-.64	-.05	.72	-.36	-.06	-.70
Roosevelt, 1936 (v)	.88	.81	.96	.94		-.61	.81	.39	.61	.26	.81	.78	-.68	.07	.75	-.34	-.03	-.75
Women (d)	-.57	-.55	-.66	-.66	-.61		-.68	-.37	-.49	-.21	-.51	-.54	.58	-.07	-.68	.42	.14	.65
Party voting (e)	.79	.62	.84	.84	.81	-.68		.42	.47	.48	.66	.75	-.76	.08	.81	-.51	-.01	-.81
Bond issue (f)	.46	.17	.40	.44	.39	-.37	.42		.58	.08	.14	.20	-.12	-.57	.25	.20	-.02	-.05
Wet vote (g)	.68	.64	.65	.61	.61	-.49	.47	.58		.17	.34	.34	-.27	-.38	.37	.02	-.29	-.30
Interest in voting (h)	.35	.21	.27	.27	.26	-.21	.48	.08	.17		.32	.32	-.43	.18	.32	-.49	.16	-.44
Foreign birth (i)	.64	.60	.73	.71	.81	-.51	.66	.14	.34	.32		.72	-.66	.16	.70	-.48	.14	-.74
Catholic origins (j)	.78	.57	.78	.76	.78	-.54	.75	.20	.34	.32	.72		-.74	.15	.78	-.52	-.17	-.73
Median rental (k)	-.62	-.53	-.68	-.64	-.68	.58	-.76	-.12	-.27	-.43	-.66	-.74		-.25	-.80	.62	.01	.88
Home-owners (l)	-.15	.03	-.05	-.05	.07	-.07	.08	-.57	-.38	.18	.16	.15	-.25		.25	-.72	.40	-.36
Unemployment (m)	.69	.57	.76	.72	.75	-.68	.81	.25	.37	.32	.70	.78	-.80	.25		-.58	.01	-.84
Mobility (s)	-.31	-.33	-.35	-.36	-.34	.42	-.51	.20	.02	-.49	-.48	-.52	.62	-.72	-.58		-.19	.68
Doubling-up (t)	-.18	-.10	-.11	-.06	-.03	.14	-.01	-.02	-.29	.16	.14	-.17	.01	.40	.01	-.19		.14
Education (u)	-.62	-.63	-.73	-.70	-.75	.65	-.81	-.05	-.30	-.44	-.74	-.73	.88	-.36	-.84	.68	.14	

An explanation of this involved chart need not be complete for the purposes of this book. It is offered to illustrate how the study of voting behavior selects certain indices like education, the vote for a candidate, and Catholic origins, as found in governmental statistics, and how it tries to discover whether areas high in one index are high or low in the other indices. The table is read like a chart of mileage between cities. For example, the areas where the Lewis, Roosevelt, and Igoe votes were high are also areas where the Al Smith vote was high, as evidenced by the correlations of .78; .94; .91. Since all are Democrats, this is expected. Why they vary somewhat requires much more intensive analysis. Source: Harold F. Gosnell: *Machine Politics: Chicago Model* (Chicago: The University of Chicago Press, 1937), p. 109. Copyright 1937 by the University of Chicago and reproduced with their permission and that of the author.

of high unemployment voted for Roosevelt. Nor does the obviously strong Roosevelt support in these areas mean that the people therein or the unemployed therein were thinking of the interests of the working class. The correlation is to be construed primarily as an indication that if one is looking for the sources of Roosevelt's support, he should examine the many factors that have to do with unemployment and the whole life of the poorer communities. If one does not realize that the "unemployment-Roosevelt vote" correlation is only an indicator, a pointer, he is likely to be misled into all sorts of fallacies about "popular mandates," "rising of the masses," "the effects of Roosevelt's program of reforms," and so on.

At bottom, we find that the remarkably complicated studies of electoral behavior made during the last twenty-five years measure largely the tendency of voters in the same economic group to be characterized by the same voting movements. It is risky to say more. The tendency is moderately widespread among people at a particular economic level, and certain studies in America indicate a slight tendency towards an increase in this economic cohesion of voters. Even if this last is a true trend, the possible explanation may be that economic issues are more frequently campaign issues than they used to be, and the voters must therefore vote a little more in accordance with economic criteria. For a voter can choose only among the limited alternatives offered him on the ballot.

IN EUROPE, SOCIAL GROUPINGS MORE MEANINGFUL

In Europe, the tendency for people of one social category to vote differently from those in other categories is more distinct than in America. Giving the vote to the poorer classes brought notable changes in the growth of new political parties and the composition of the political class. For example, after the Act of 1918 had given the vote to all adult English males, the Labour Party advanced to power rapidly; and before that, the Reform Act of 1832 had increased notably the representation of the merchants and manufacturers in the House of Commons. The abolition of the three-class Prussian representation system after World War I brought an immediate change in the party composition of the *Landtag* in favor of the liberal-socialist parties of the left. All other countries saw an intensification of political groupings of voters according to economic features they shared in common. The workers became strongly organized into leftist parties.

RELIGIOUS INFLUENCES ON VOTING BEHAVIOR

The effect of religion upon voting behavior, like the effect of economic conditions, is often indirect. If one examines the programs of religious parties of Europe, one finds many nonreligious appeals, especially conservative economic appeals. Obviously, therefore, religion and economic measures are tied together. In America, we find no religious parties, but we find religion at work in politics, nevertheless. We find Democratic sentiment more common among Catholics and Jews, but again indices of economic conditions, urban residence, national origin, and so on overlap with the religious index.

An analysis of four opinion polls of a sample of the American population in 1945 and 1946 presents the American pattern of religious influence in voting. It agrees substantially with other studies. We give the rank order of the religious denominations on three questions. The questions were:

(1) "Would you agree that everybody would be happier, more secure and more prosperous if working people were given more power and

FIGURE 13

RELATION OF RELIGIOUS PREFERENCES TO POLITICAL ATTITUDES *

| | RANK ORDER OF RELIGIOUS GROUPINGS | | |
RELIGIOUS GROUP	*In Desiring More Power for Workers*	*In Giving High Importance to Guaranteed Security*	*% in Group That Voted for Roosevelt*
Baptist	2	4	4
Catholic	4	1	2
Undesignated Protestants	6	6	7
Protestant (smaller bodies)	5	5	5
No Preference	3	2	3
Christian	7	11	6
Lutheran	9	7	9
Methodist	8	8	8
Jewish	1	3	1
Episcopal	11	9	10
Presbyterian	10	10	11
Congregational	12	12	12

* Central Department of Research and Education: *Information Service*, Vol. 27, no. 20, part 2 (May 15, 1948). National Council of the Churches of Christ in the United States of America, New York, New York. See also, Wesley and Beverly Allinsmith: "Religious Affiliation and Politico-Economic Attitude," *The Public Opinion Quarterly*, Vol. 12 (1948), p. 377.

Note than an economic factor is obviously operating here. Most of the named religious groupings hold rankings corresponding to the average income status of their members. Thus, the average Congregationalist is somewhat better off than the average Baptist or Catholic and the "conservatism" of the Congregationalists is partially explainable by that fact. On the other hand, this study and others (such as a forthcoming study of a New York town) show that Jewish and Catholic views and affiliations are not completely explained when the economic factor is taken into account. Cultural and religious influences seem to be operating also.

influence in government, or would you say we would all be better off if the working people had no more power than they have now?"

(2) "Which of these statements do you most agree with?

   (a) The most important job for government is to make certain that there are good opportunities for each person to get ahead on his own.

   (b) The most important job for the government is to guarantee every person a decent and steady job and standard of living."

(3) Voted for Roosevelt, Dewey, or Didn't Vote in 1944.

Figure 13 presents the results of the survey.

Other studies also find consistently that Catholicism is related positively to Democratic affiliation. The anti-Catholicism of segments of American opinion was manifested during the 1928 election, when Alfred E. Smith, a Catholic, ran for the Presidency on the Democratic ticket and lost the support of several Southern states previously staunchly Democratic. Smith, however, also favored repeal of the prohibition amendment, and the South was strongly against its repeal. Furthermore, Gosnell pointed out that if Smith had run in 1932, he would have been elected on economic grounds despite his religious affiliations. Religious affiliations, like economic ones, become more important in voting behavior whenever religious issues are raised in the campaign (as they were in the election of 1928).

NATIONALITY AND RACE

Just as with religious and economic motivation, the most extreme examples of voting motivated by nationality or racial differences occur when the differences become political issues. European democratic politics have seen many a case of electoral differences over nationality. The Austro-Hungarian Empire, Czechoslovakia, Spain, Italy, and England have all had experience with electoral movements that arose from the demands of constituent nationalities. Canada faces similar difficulties with its voters of British and French origin.

These experiences make all the more remarkable the ability of the American political system to repress overt divisions along lines of national origins. Differences are known to exist—between "Cajuns" and hill folk in Louisiana, old immigrants and new immigrants in the North, Irish elements against Polish elements in several Northern cities, and so on. But no compact organization of voters on the basis of nationality persists for any length of time. Typically, in country and city, national blocs dwindle with each added year of settlement in America, until finally they cannot be manipulated at all as cohesive and integrated electoral forces.

Persons of groups that have settled recently in America—the Irish, Poles, Italians, Czechs, and other groups—tend to be Democratic more often than do persons of groups that have settled less recently—English, Scotch-Irish, Irish, Scandinavians, and others. The latter tend to be Republicans. There are, however, notable exceptions, and nationality here again is perhaps mostly a reinforcing influence on other economic, social, and historical factors. The Negroes in the United States, originally heavily Republican, have, during the period of the New Deal, become about equally Democratic and Republican outside the South. This change, in fact, has been one of the most significant to emerge in the area of voting behavior in the last fifty years.

SEX

We might imagine that the women, having achieved the vote at a late date, might differ from men in their subsequent use of it. On the whole, this is not so. There exist only small differences between the political affiliations of women and of men, and these differences have little to do with when the vote was achieved. Rather they seem to relate to more basic differences in the upbringing of men and of women. Studies by Tingsten and others in Europe and America indicate that women tend to vote somewhat more for conservative and religious center parties than do men and are less inclined toward extreme reaction or radicalism. They incline, at least in Britain and America, to support pacifist ideas more than men. And they tend to be more rigid on moral issues, supporting more strongly movements such as that for the prohibition of the sale of alcoholic beverages.

Public Opinion

RELATIONS WITH COMMUNITY AND PUBLIC

We have already declared, in studying communities and personal interests, that people gain opinions from their various affiliations. If two communities and publics overlap one another, engaging the affiliations of some of the same people, or of different people living side by side, we should still have public opinion about issues of concern to one or both publics. In fact, these differences in degree and kind of affiliations are a common source of disputed opinions. For instance, some American states' rightists wish to recapture for their state communities certain powers from the national government and find their opinions opposed by nationalists who have no sympathy for the state as a community. And when we consider also that individuals belonging to the same public may belong to different subgroups—religious, national, professional, neighborhood—we can perceive another important source of contested opinions. For instance, South Carolina states' rightists owning textile mills may oppose the C.I.O., whereas South Carolina states' rightists working in such mills may favor a union.

PUBLIC OPINION NOT CONSENSUS

We may ask now about the nature of public opinion and look into its several dimensions. Public opinion is not to be confused with consensus. Consensus is not present in every community or public; it requires a high cohesiveness that such groupings may not possess. Consensus may not be present in a public wherein public opinion is abundantly displayed.

Conversely, when consensus does exist, those beliefs that compose it are beyond dispute and hence beyond the scope of public opinion. The English monarchy is favored as part of the English consensus; it is too important and agreeable to most Englishmen to be debated in the forum of public opinion. Hence it is most useful to think of consensus as the unquestioned moral principles about politics and government that may be held by a public. By contrast, public opinion may be perceived as arising over any controversy, whether or not the controversy is framed within an existing consensus or develops in the absence of any consensus at all. Without proving finally here that a great consensus exists in the United States, we can say that one belief that would form part of such a consensus is that the President must be elected. Whether Truman or Taft or Eisenhower or someone else should be elected is a matter of public opinion.

DEFINITION OF PUBLIC OPINION

If these relationships between public opinion and other concepts are clear, there need be little difficulty with the precise definition of public opinion. Public opinion is *a belief* held by a *number of people* regarding a *political issue*. By a belief is meant a delineated, definable feeling about the rightness or wrongness of a projected course of action. By a number of people is meant all those holding to one or more of the projected resolutions of the belief. By a political issue is meant any problem for the solution of which people turn to the government.

SIX DIMENSIONS OF PUBLIC OPINION

Public opinion has no real existence apart from the people who form it. It is a concept, a way of referring to parts of people's psychological activities, useful for analytic and statistical purposes and for predicting behavior. Once posited, we can give its dimensions and show how to assess or measure it. The important dimensions are as follows:

1. The number of alternative opinions that exist on an issue.
2. The distribution of social groups according to their adherence to one or more of the alternatives.
3. The intensity with which the beliefs are held.
4. The number of people adhering to the various alternative opinions.
5. The degree of organization of and critical political controls held by the opinion groups.
6. The rate of opinion change over time periods.

Once these data are collected on a particular issue, we have a reliable basis for analyzing and predicting the behavior of the public on that issue.

THE NUMBER OF VARIANT BELIEFS

Let us take a hypothetical case to illustrate how it is possible to analyze and speak and think more exactly about public opinion. Given political issue X, we find five major subcategories of beliefs regarding X. Let these be called A, B, C, D, and E. The relationship of the subcategories to X may be diagrammed as in Figure 14.

FIGURE 14

VARIANT BELIEFS ON AN ISSUE

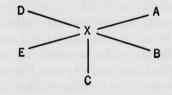

EXAMPLES:

(1) G. C. Thompson, in *Public Opinion and Lord Beaconsfield, 1875–1880* (2 vols., 1886), gives us a splendid account of the relations of

English opinion and political leadership on the issue of British policy towards Turkey and Russia over a five-year period, ending in the electoral defeat of the ministry of Lord Beaconsfield (Disraeli). Mr. Thompson describes four major variants of belief on the issue: supporters of Turkey and haters of Russia; advocates of isolation and avoidance of war; believers in international order and legalism; and advocates of anti-Turkism and emancipation of Christians from the Turks. These major views dominated opinion over several years.

(2) Morton Grodzins, in *Americans Betrayed* (1949), presents a remarkable full-scale study of the evacuation of persons of Japanese ancestry from the West coast of the United States in the months following the Japanese attack on Pearl Harbor, with particular reference to the opinions and pressures shaping the policy. The major beliefs regarding the issue were: advocacy of evacuation and stringent control of all persons of Japanese race to prevent treason; advocacy of the same with respect to Japanese aliens; and advocacy of individual treatment of all persons on the basis of specific violations of the law.

COMMENT: Both authors point to much rationalization. Thus some English supported emancipation of Christians in order that English control over Egypt might be obtained. Some Americans supported evacuation to prevent treason because they disliked the Japanese as a race and as economic competitors in California. In short, there are always layers upon layers of subbeliefs. It is incorrect to believe that a poll of two sides to an issue provides a full description of subbeliefs on the issue.

POSITION OF SOCIAL GROUPS ON THE ISSUE

If we examine the persons holding to the subcategories of belief, we find that many of the people holding, for example, to variant A will belong to certain social groups, those holding to D to other social groups. Figure 15 adds these social groupings (indicated by arabic numerals) to the diagram as given in Figure 14.

EXAMPLES:

(1) Thompson's analysis shows that English opinion on the Near East was reflected in associational activity. The character of English government and society at the time resulted in a loose pattern of social groupings with reference to the subbeliefs. The main groups were in Parliament, with the Conservatives under Beaconsfield and the Liberals under Gladstone. In the Foreign Office "the right of Public Opinion to be sovereign was most explicitly challenged." Outside the government, we note the role of the press, petitions of occupational groups, many letters, a variety of meetings of organized and informal groups, the participation of Catholic and Jewish viewpoints along

FIGURE 15

SOCIAL GROUPINGS IN RELATION TO VARIANT BELIEFS

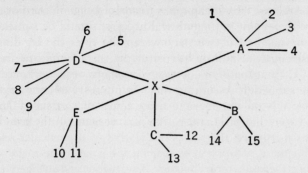

with those of the Anglican clergy, and even the presence of spokesmen for foreign nations like Russia, Turkey, Germany, and Hungary. The social groupings, we note, are not formal save in a few instances.

(2) Grodzins' analysis of American opinion on the evacuation of Japanese shows greater formal group participation. Here, too, we have government opinion—that of the War Department, the Department of Justice, and Congress—that must be differentiated from outside opinion. However, since this issue is internal and local political influence potent in America, we find the West coast Congressmen as a group veering towards the evacuation and carrying along the whole Congress, and we observe how active are the state and local politicians. Outside the government the American Legion, Lions clubs, vegetable growers, and chambers of commerce are working hard to achieve evacuation. Contrariwise, the Civil Liberties Union, the League for Industrial Democracy, the Japanese American Citizens League, and other groups fought evacuation or at least tried to confine it to "enemy aliens" alone. Writes Grodzins: "Not all organizations, by any means, were calling for evacuation. But opposition groups were far outnumbered and almost unpublicized."

COMMENT: It is impossible to determine the exact extent to which opinion is formed by groups and policy is made by groups (see Chapter Seven). Issues of the nineteenth century did not seem to be surrounded by group activity as do contemporary issues, especially in America. The precise position of a single group is difficult to ascertain also. Thus the Liberal Party of Gladstone never had a precise position. Nor could the Western Growers Protective Association, which urged evacuation, be pinned down to one subbelief. All that we learned about leadership in Chapter Three and that we shall learn about pressure groups in Chapter Seven should warn us against taking any group as a unanimous mass of opinion.

INTENSITY OF CONVICTION

　　　An issue may mean more to some people than to others, and this fact, so important in the political process, should be somehow considered. To visualize it, we may widen the lines in our diagram to represent strength of pull or intensity; the thicker the line from X to the subbelief, the greater the average intensity of belief held by those holding the subbelief. Assuming that the intensity of conviction of the members of A is on the average three times that of the holders of B and C and twice that of D and E, the new version of the lines of belief would be as in Figure 16.

FIGURE 16

THE AVERAGE INTENSITY OF CONVICTION AMONG HOLDERS OF SUBBELIEFS

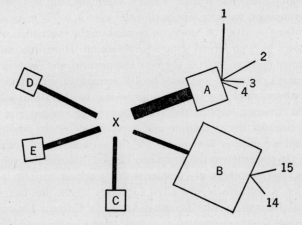

EXAMPLES:

　　(1) Thompson's study reveals much about the intensity of opinion on the Eastern question indirectly. The common usage implying intensity is a statement of consequence, to wit: "If belief A is followed, we will do Y (Y being vote against you, agitate more strongly, lose faith in England, decline to co-operate, stop reading your newspapers, never pay you honor, or inflict other sanctions within our command). In addition, Thompson speaks variously of "serious misgivings," "extraordinary manifestations of opinion," "the Crusading Spirit," a "certain hostility" or a "universal hostility," "dread," "panic," "the fever" that "had long been rising," and other expressions of greater or lesser emotion.

　　(2) Grodzins is more conscious of the need to assess intensity closely. He counts the number of favorable and unfavorable editorials, letters

to the editors and to public officials, and space given to stories about resident Japanese. He calculates the news space devoted to demands for evacuation and otherwise tries to indicate precisely the lengths to which people will go in supporting their opinions. He also takes care to describe how terrible was the fear among some people for the safety of the Pacific coast. He uses crime records to indicate the extent of vigilantism against Japanese, and reports speeches that make allegations about "hysterical people taking matters into their own hands."

COMMENT: Grodzins' less florid style, his greater awareness of the problem of intensity of opinion, and his use of new techniques of opinion research enable one to judge better the intensity of the opinions he is studying. And, judging well the intensity of opinion is highly important in predicting the reactions that follow a decision favoring one opinion. One heated critic can often hurt a politician more than ten luke-warm friends can help him.

NUMBERS OF ADHERENTS TO A BELIEF

The intensity of conviction may be countered to some extent by the number of adherents to each subbelief category. Let us say that A has twice as many adherents as C, D, and E but only half as many as B. We have shown these relationships in size by rectangles in Figure 16.

EXAMPLES:

(1) Thompson attempts only briefly to analyze election returns as an indication of the support given Disraeli's policies. He judges or leaves the reader to judge the extent of popular support for any viewpoint by reporting countless news articles, meetings, Parliamentary votes, and individual opinions of participants and observers. He as much as admits that there was needed "some machinery beyond mere guesswork for ascertaining how far Public Opinion responds." He is in the position of an experienced night watchman at the zoo who tries from the outside to judge the sources, sides, and number of participants in a pandemonium coming from the monkey house.

(2) Even though his techniques for studying the flow of communications are superior to those used by Thompson, Grodzins is up against the same problems. He judges the number of adherents to a belief from meetings, from letters to the press and to officials, and from the guesses of the press, public officials, and journalists. But he can find only one, poorly conducted, "honest" poll, and that disagrees sharply with a high official's declaration that "the American citizens of California, with hardly a dissenting voice say that the Japanese, both alien and American-born, must go."

COMMENT: Constant, careful polling is the best way to judge the extent of support of an opinion among the public. Pressure groups and politicians tend to claim excessive support for their opinions. Often followers back the views of their leaders in official actions but do so with reservations or reluctance.

ORGANIZATION AND CRITICAL CONTROLS

Finally, the social groups (1 to 15), involved in the opinion configuration, do not all have the same degree of efficiency in organization or the same amount of critical political controls (that is, number of offices held, wealth, social prestige, propaganda media). Let us assume that they could be rated as follows on a scale of 1 to 5:

	EFFICIENCY OF ORGANIZATION	COMMAND OF CRITICAL POLITICAL CONTROLS
1	5	5
2	3	5
3	1	4
4	1	2
5	2	1
6	4	1
7	3	2
8	3	2
9	3	1
10	2	1
11	2	2
12	5	5
13	4	5
14	4	2
15	1	4

In Figure 16 we have given equal length to each point on the 1 to 5 scale. Thus, for example, group 1 is drawn twice as long as group 3, since it equals $5 + 5$, whereas group 3 equals $1 + 4$. Our operation here distorts reality, for we cannot measure organizations so neatly. Nevertheless, even such rough evaluations of the potential political energy of the groups involved in a particular issue may aid our insight.

EXAMPLES:

(1) Conclusions about the strength and strategy of the groups involved in the Eastern question depend upon indirect evidence on the character of the participants. Outside the government, one gets the impression of formlessness—committees are formed, and later dissolved; few are

continuous and staffed by professionals. These loose groups are judged by the "big shots" in them. Thus the first meeting to support the rebels against Turkish rule was described by the *Times* as "not a crowded one and which certainly could not boast the presence of any distinguished person." Also "it was said that the Queen was significantly displaying marks of favour towards Lord Beaconsfield."

(2) Grodzins makes sharp comparisons between the organizations advocating and those opposing evacuation, showing the preponderance of wealth, staff, and connections of the former. He shows in a number of instances how the leaders of organizations brought pressure to bear upon the press, public officers, and the opposition, and how the leaders of like-minded organizations co-operated to increase their collective force. He emphasizes the secure political and economic positions held in the community by advocates of evacuation.

COMMENT: The subjects of efficiency of organization and command of critical political controls are at the juncture of the study of public opinion and the study of parties and pressure groups, treated elsewhere in this book. We note, however, that organizations are the means by which public opinion gears into public policies. At this point, informal behavior is becoming transformed into formal behavior. Well located and organized groups can direct terrific pressures of opinion—backed by an array of inducements and sanctions—towards a person making a public policy.

PATTERNS OF PUBLIC OPINION ARE UNSTABLE

But our charts are static; real opinion is often in flux. If we suppose the lines leading from X to ABCDE in Figure 14 to be directional lines indicating how much in opposition the alternative beliefs are, we can say that at this one point in time A and B, although powerful and mutually opposing, have more in common than they have with C, D, and E. In fact, C appears as if it might be "on the fence" or torn between both constellations, AB and DE. Shifts and changes by C could spell a crisis for either AB or DE. Since AB and DE are almost diametrically opposed on the issue, can we say that "consensus" is broken? No, we cannot, because the primary indicator of consensus is the intensity dimensions of AB and DE, plus the compromising strength of C—the "crucial center" from one point of view. If X were a proposal to close taverns on Sunday, or a money appropriation bill, without hidden meaning, opposite positions would not be intense enough to threaten consensus. But if X were a proposal to declare illegal all trades unions or to confiscate all industrial establishments employing over 1,000 workers, or a declaration of war, then "consensus" would be in some danger of being destroyed, and our intensity scale would have to reflect it.

EXAMPLES:

(1) In the works of Thompson and Grodzins, cited above, the instability of opinion becomes quite clear. Other studies by Gabriel Almond, Hadley Cantril, George Gallup, Robert Merton, and Angus Campbell reveal similar fluctuations. Thompson, for example, discovered an Incubation Period, an Atrocity Period, a Period of Reconciliation of people and government, a Conference Period, a Parliamentary Period, a Period of Conditional Neutrality and of Armed Neutrality. He speaks of gatherings, the tone of which in 1876 was "full of self-confidence" and in 1878 was "downcast and distrustful, distrustful of its own backing in the country, and daunted by the forces with which it had to contend."

(2) Grodzins shows in a chart the progress of front-page newspaper attention to resident Japanese, ranging from 1,000 picas in the period December 8–14, 1941 to almost nothing between January 5–25, 1942, to 9,000 picas in the period January 26—February 1.

COMMENT: It hardly needs saying that one of the most exasperating problems in studying public opinion is the failure of opinion to "stand still long enough to be photographed." If we think of public opinion as being only a man's voting record, we fall into grave misconceptions. A man may vote Republican all his life and have many thousands of opinions.

Having considered the main factors in the public opinion surrounding issue X—namely, subbeliefs or alternative solutions of A; the location of social groups related to the subbelief alternatives; the intensity of conviction and the number of adherents to each subbelief alternative; the degree of organization and number of critical controls possessed by the social groups involved in each alternative, and the fluctuations of opinions over a period of time—we can make a fair guess as to who may win out in the battle of opinion.

The astute politician often judges public opinion according to these several dimensions, though he may not be aware of it. And it is safe to say that any politician—in the United States or in Russia, in elective or in appointive office—who is totally unaware of just one of these dimensions will get into trouble from time to time. One must emphatically dismiss as childish and useless the notion that public opinion is like a self-renewing and massive electric charge that strikes all issues, showing eager leaders exactly what is wanted and what to do.

The Majority

MAJORITIES AS SIMPLE OPINIONS

The majority, as we previously defined it, is the agreement of more than half of any given group upon an issue. If a majority occurred whenever an issue arose, the analysis of public opinion would be enormously simplified. We should merely have to substitute Figure 17 for our bothersome opinion analysis diagrammed in Figure 16. For then there would be only a majority and a minority opinion and presumably the public would be so simple as not to include the many groups that contribute to the complexity of opinions. Only a most primitive and cohesive society might approach such a condition. In our own society only small discussion or committee groups might possess such a simple division of opinion.

THE MAJORITY AS A WAY OF RESOLVING ISSUES

On the other hand, the majority principle is used frequently to decide questions at issue. This should not be taken to mean that the public opinion on the question exhibits a majority. Not at all. Public opinion may be vastly complex, with nothing like a majority discernible and with many power groups tugging at the issue from all sides. But some way is needed to stop the tug-of-war in order to get on with *some* policy and to attend to other matters. The issue must be resolved. Hence, the majority principle is frequently used to resolve issues. Very often, when one examines the reasons behind a majority agreement, be it a majority vote for the Presidency or a congressional majority vote on a bill, he finds that many different and even conflicting opinions contributed to the majority. The majority was simply the technique for creating a decision when the decision had to be made.

FIGURE 17

PUBLIC OPINION, ASSUMING A SIMPLE MAJORITY

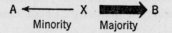

In this manner the majority is used as an expedient. As Prime Minister Gladstone of Great Britain once described it: "Decision by majorities is as much an expedient as lighting by gas. In adopting it as a rule, we are not realizing perfection, but bowing to an imperfection. It has the great merit of avoiding, and that by a test perfectly definite, the last resort to violence; and of making force itself the servant instead of the master of authority." Or, as Professor Charles Heinberg asserted: "The majority principle is simply a convenient rule of law, and contains no inherent ethical validity."

Thus we find that the majority principle frequently is used in organizations and governments that are not committed to any general belief in the rightness or wrongness of the majority. The Spartans, not great believers in majority rule, used the principle; some medieval German kings were elected by majority vote of the important vassals; and most corporate bodies use it as a way of getting things done. We must grant that it is convenient and simple to take the desire of 51 per cent as conclusive and decisive, especially when heated matters are not being decided, and when many petty decisions need to be made by people who are agreed on more basic things.

EMPLOYMENT OF OTHER PRINCIPLES OF RESOLVING ISSUES

Other principles besides that of the majority may also be employed to resolve issues. Courts and executive officers make many decisions. An assembly may require that issues be decided by unanimity, plurality, majority of members in attendance, majority of members constituting the total assembly, or by two-thirds rule. The unanimity rule, often regarded as ludicrous and unworkable, has worked under circumstances where it is conceded that no one need agree with the group, or where the pressures for the voters or members of an assembly to conform to the group are great and a method of counting is not required. The English House of Lords and other medieval assemblies of the nobles and high clergy worked on the principle of unanimity. In some of the earliest gatherings of the House of Commons, certain members refused to acquiesce in decisions of the body and returned to their constituencies. Medieval kings of Poland were elected by a unanimous vote of the princes of the electoral body. John Calhoun, in the American Senate before the Civil War, argued, with considerable support, that decisions of the federal government affecting the basic nature of the Union could not be made by a mere majority but required a "concurrent majority" of all "parties" (states) to the Union.

Furthermore, in pursuance of more general principles that conflict with the majority principle, such as the principle of checks and balances, a two-thirds or some other high ratio vote may be required of an assembly on certain issues. Treaties prepared by the President of the United States and foreign nations must gain the approval of two thirds of the Senate to be binding and constitutional. The veto is given the executive in practically all American governments; some extraordinary number of votes are required of the assembly if it wishes to override his action. The number is most frequently, as it is in the national government, two thirds.

BEYOND OPINION AND EXPEDIENCY

Thus, a majority may denote (rarely) the condition of opinion and frequently may be used as a principle or technique to foreclose an issue. But beyond its possible status as an opinion or as an expedient, the majority is often a key symbol in a great many political disputes that reaches back a number of centuries. As an agitational symbol, the "majority" is not at all a clear condition or technique. It is a term holding numberless meanings, yearnings, threats, terrors, and promises. It is really in such a complete· state of semantic decomposition that the most we can do with it is to extract two general meanings from this third level of usage and describe generally their historical career.

1. On the third or *ethical* level of its meaning, the majority may be a profound belief in the rightness of using the majority principle for deciding issues whenever possible, rather than any other principle. The majority is then not opinion or expediency; it is part of a consensus. Most Americans hold to this meaning of majority as part of their consensus. This may be called *majority rule*.

This belief in majority rule, so widespread in America, values highly majority opinions and the use of the majority principle for resolving issues. It tends to demand both, but where the first cannot be found, it still insists upon the second. Often people who believe in majority rule erroneously believe that majority opinions always exist, and their thinking suffers sadly as a result. They fail to realize that they have two lines of defense and can fall back from one to the other. A brief history of the belief in majority rule will show its complications and variations.

MEDIEVAL THEORY OF THE MAJORITY

Early modern western European political theorists, most of them jurists, inherited the majority principle from the practice followed in corporations under the law of the late Roman Empire. In the early modern period close relations still existed between the Catholic Church and the late feudal states, and when the clergy began to employ the majority principle as a means of resolving disputed questions in certain orders and convocations, men in what we now consider the secular, political sphere surmised that the principle might also be useful to them. However, medieval theorists did not allow the majority clear sailing. Marsiglio of Padua, for example, referred, not to the "larger part," but to the "prevailing part" as the voice of the community. That is to say, power, eminence, and worth were to be valued along with numbers. But at least he *mentioned numbers*. That was his concession to the majority principle, and a radical one it was in those days.

It is noteworthy that most medieval political theorists and their predecessors thought that the values of the community ought to be the objectives of the state. The law was "declared custom." For example, the forerunner of the modern jury was a group of neighbors, a sample of the community, convoked to declare what the common law of the community was in order to inform the King's courts. Both medieval and modern theorists seem to agree that the majority will is at minimum the *passive will* of the people that sets the boundaries within which the laws are to be made. The majority will, in this sense, is what modern theory calls consensus.

IS THE MAJORITY OMNICOMPETENT?

A more modern variety of the belief in majority rule declares that the majority is omnicompetent. It is right and can do what it wills. There is a great reluctance to condemn it on any grounds, and the community is supposed to acquiesce gladly in the majority verdict. This is the extreme democratic notion and is found in the more unguarded utterances of Jefferson, the aggressive politics of Jackson, and beneath the devious subtleties of Karl Marx. Jeremy Bentham, in his exuberant desire for a grand rational principle of legislation, was captured by the majority principle and demanded that the greatest number be the judge of what would bring happiness to the greatest number.

MAJORITY AS COURT OF LAST RESORT

Variations of this idea of the omnipotence of the majority shade off into the idea that the majority ought to be the court of last resort on basic matters affecting a society, and the idea that the majority ought to have some voice in the selection of officers. John Locke, in the second part of his work *Of Civil Government*, declared that the rights of liberty, property, and revolution must not be taken from the total community. Otherwise, he felt that the legislative body might operate according to its majority will. Modern writers, Lindsay, for example, justify the majority idea with the slogan "only the wearer knows when the shoe pinches." This is a watered-down version of the Locke theory and gives the majority a sort of veto on the actions of government. On the other hand, Edmund Burke would not concede that basic rights were reserved to the people. He would permit the electorate only a modest voice in the selection of representatives.

All these beliefs may be grouped into the first of our two basic attitudes towards the majority, that the majority must be understood and followed. Inherent in these ideas is the attitude that the majority has a sense, a reason, a voice or a capacity for specific activity. The Leveller movement in seventeenth-century England, many leaders of the American and French revolutions, and the greater number of political leaders of the nineteenth century took this attitude.

2. Also on the third or ethical level of its meaning, the majority may be considered to be bad and harmful if allowed to rule. This is *anti-majoritarianism*. It holds that the majority must either be ignored or coerced. Its history too may be sketched.

The belief that the majority should have nothing to say is an absolutistic, monarchical notion and is also an aristocractic notion that persists to the present time. Examples of this fear of the majority and the hope that it can be politically ignored are found in the writings of Europeans like Émile Faguet, in his book *The Cult of Incompetence*, and Ortega y Gasset, in his book *Revolt of the Masses*. John Adams, James Fenimore Cooper, and Henry Adams were early American exponents of this belief. Among those who argued that the majority cannot rule are writers such as Roberto Michels, Max Weber, Gaetano Mosca, and Vilfredo Pareto —they say the majority is nonrational, cannot act of its own accord, and is generally manipulated through propaganda and violence.

A related view, which does not dislike the idea of majority rule necessarily, asserts however that a majority never exists. Of course, they mean by this that opinion analysis rarely reveals a majority.

Perhaps one of the most complete attempts to banish the majority principle is the complete gild, syndicalist, or corporate-state idea. This idea would have the state governed by organized occupational groups; men would be represented according to occupation rather than according to geographical districts (see Chapters Five and Seven). Each occupation would be autonomous, not governed by central rule or majority rule from above. Gabriele d'Annunzio, fiery poet, passionate novelist, and the dictator of Fiume after World War I, drew up in 1919 a blueprint for the perfect corporate state that influenced the Fascist idea. He modeled his gilds after the nine muses of the ancient Greeks. Nine great corporations were to be named for them—a corporation of salaried workers, technical and administrative employees, commercial employees, all employers, civil servants, professions (2), consumers' co-operatives, and seafarers. The tenth muse of the Greeks was nameless. And so d'Annunzio declared that there would be a tenth nameless corporation that would gather up the loose ends that evaded the other corporations. It was, he said, to direct the mysterious forces inherent in a people in labor and ascendancy. The meaning of the nameless muse and of d'Annunzio's exotic language is startling—that is that the life of the total community could not be neatly divided. There was a sentiment somewhere, an interest that could not be categorized. That interest, we infer, would be the community interest that could never be syllogized out of existence. Perhaps such is the elusive "majority" of Marsiglio, Jefferson, and the others.

At its least, the majority idea adds flexibility to one's view of the structure of society. William James once said that no relationship between two objects or between a person and the outside world ever includes everything or dominates over everything. There is always the word "and" trailing off after every descriptive sentence. So it is with the tenth muse, that gathers no specialized craft, but rather the echoes of the total concept of society.

THE MAJORITY IS MORE THAN OPINION OR MERE EXPEDIENT

It is apparent that the adherents of the theories just described see some problem connected with the idea of the majority that goes beyond the mere examination of opinions or the use of the majority principle for getting things done. There is some ethical quality in the idea that appears to some as a great good, to others as a menace. No amount of technical definition can diminish the force that the majority idea has generated. Revolutions have been fought and rivers of blood shed over the principle. Public opinion polls and intensive studies of the dynamics of small groups and of the attitudes of students and of voters have all indicated the strength of the belief, in America at least, that majority agreement is and ought to be the test of truth on matters of opinion, and that the denial of the right of "majority" rule is blasphemy.

We see, therefore, in the great struggles of centuries between majority rule and antimajoritarianism a struggle to elevate or depress the degree to which the community is allowed to become a public and to which the public is allowed to make laws. The political community, say the advocates of majority rule, has its customary sanctions, but it needs a new will and way. The community has the only instruments that it can and should justly employ, respond the antimajoritarians. The contest shows no signs of ending. The belief that a community of men, a public, may somehow generate devices for forming and executing decisions persists strongly. And the obstacles before it—mechanical and human—seem insurmountable. The story of representation and elections, and of parties and pressure groups—now to be treated in order—accents our conclusion that the great social groupings are like the ocean surfs: they may gradually wear away the beaches, but in the immediate reckoning they exhaust their force on the many rocks of organized interest that surround public policy.

Questions and Problems

1. List the past and present affiliations of your father. Rank them in order of the importance he attaches to them. Do the same for your affiliations. Are the differences explainable by differences in age solely? Or are they reflections of changes that have taken place? Explain your results.

2. Ask ten members of the class to furnish you with their own answers to question 1 (above). Tabulate the affiliations you discover. What are the differences among parents, among offspring, and between parents and offspring? What conclusions may be drawn without extensive further study?

3. List as many important "relations, connections, and communications" as you can think of that make up the national community to which you belong. (Examples would be language, telephone, geographical contiguity.)

4. Referring to Chapter Two, is the belief in rational legitimacy an element making for community? Explain your answer in 150 words.

5. Distinguish among: the community, the public, the electorate, and the majority. If the chapter provides insufficient distinctions, use the *Encyclopaedia of the Social Sciences* for more material.

6. Consult an unabridged dictionary, the *Encyclopaedia of the Social Sciences*, or another general reference work for statements regarding the terms: social group, economic determinism, profession, public, customs, and sanctions. Describe each in a single paragraph.

7. From a legal point of view, the American Constitution would not have prevented the United States from destroying the governments and property of Germany, Italy, and Japan and selling the populations into slavery to pay off the national debt. The Greeks, Romans, and many other peoples paid for their wars and prevented future wars in this way. Explain America's conduct, with reference to the Leslie Stephen quotation.

8. How do you account for the shift in public attitudes away from violence as a political weapon to propaganda?

9. What are the sanctions of the community? Describe them, adding examples from your own knowledge, if that is possible.

10. What does the chapter state are the probable political results of the tendency for the community to become more complicated in its inner workings and the tendency for the whole people to demand control over the community? Do you agree with the ideas presented? Why?

11. Describe what is meant by "consensus"? To what extent do you think consensus exists in the United States and the world as a whole today?

12. List the main influences that seem to affect the way a person votes. Which do you think is the most important, and why do you think so?

13. In political science, one must always mistrust statistical relationships that seem simple and clear. In the table on religion and political beliefs,

given in the chapter, what other elements may be entering into the picture to influence the results (although such elements are not mentioned)?

14. Write an interpretation of the factors influencing the following election, using the evidence gathered and presented below.

For the state senate: JOHN ZALINSKI   23,900
HAROLD BAUER   19,200
JAMES MUELLER   12,500

Zalinski, having a plurality, is elected. A survey of the senatorial district shows the following facts:

	FOR ZALINSKI	FOR BAUER	FOR MUELLER	% CATH-OLIC	% LU-THERAN	% BAP-TIST
County A	3,000	9,200	3,200	12	62	13
County B	1,500	1,200	6,100	14	22	20
County C	4,200	3,800	1,000	21	17	25
City I	7,300	2,500	1,200	35	20	18
City II	7,900	2,500	1,000	46	32	11

	% FOREIGN-BORN	% COMPLETED HIGH SCHOOL	% UNION MEMBERS	% VOTED FOR FDR IN 1944
A	14	72	3	40
B	6	61	11	39
C	19	65	14	44
I	28	60	28	52
II	32	52	33	64

	% VOTERS VOTING STRAIGHT TICKETS	% FAVORING AID TO EUROPE
A	48	45
B	72	36
C	57	53
I	52	57
II	70	52

(Advice: State your conclusions cautiously. You have here only a small part of the information that is needed for a complete analysis.)

15. List ten examples of current political issues. In addition, considering the issue with which you are most familiar (use the newspaper if you wish), give a general idea of the condition of public opinion on the issue, using the six dimensions of opinion described in the chapter.

16. Describe the two main moral positions towards the majority. With which one do you agree most? Why?

17. List ten questions from your experience, knowledge, or imagination, that you believe *ought* not to be decided by majority decisions of whatever group is concerned. Why do you think they *ought* not be so decided? Could others disagree with you on permissible grounds? (Possible examples would

be: the prohibition of drinking alcoholic beverages; the declaration of war; the construction of public works.)

18. What are some of the ways of deciding matters on any level of decision—national, state, local, international, family, club, union, and so on—other than by majority decision?

Longer Study and Research
Problems Suitable for Term Papers

1. Write an autobiographical sketch of about ten pages on some incident in your life when a group to which you belonged exercised one or more informal sanctions to bring a member of the group (perhaps yourself) into line with group behavior or attitudes. Be as detailed and precise as possible on how all the participants felt and how the sanction worked or did not work.

2. Taking your present community, or one of your past communities about which you remember a good deal, describe in about ten pages the evidences you have seen both of political apathy and of political excitement. Emphasize what you think to have been the consequences of both kinds of events. Use newspapers or other written accounts if they are available.

3. Select a current political issue; using the dimensions of opinion described in the chapter, and the evidence provided by newspapers, magazines, various statements of experts, and so on, prepare a report of ten pages on the state of public opinion concerning the issue. Use a diagram to picture the condition if the evidence warrants it.

4. (a) Select any one of the biographical works listed in the questions or bibliographical note to Chapter Three and write a ten-page paper on the attitudes of the subject or subjects of the book towards community opinion and the principle of the majority.

(b) Prepare a book review and report of about ten pages on one of the following works:

John Dewey: *The Public and Its Problems*
Hadley Cantril: *The Psychology of Social Movements*
Erich Fromm: *Escape from Freedom*
Leo Rosten: *The Washington Correspondents*
Gabriel Almond: *The American People and Foreign Policy*
Lindsay Rogers: *The Pollsters*
Ortega y Gasset: *The Revolt of the Masses*

5

REPRESENTATION AND
ELECTIONS

IN SEVERAL ways the preceding chapter on the public and personal interests forms an essential part of the study of representation and elections. The presence of numerous overlapping and often conflicting connections among men sets the stage for the struggle for representation. These interests will cause men to seek governmental forms benefiting their interests—be the interest so large as the safety of the community itself or so small as a tariff to keep out foreign-made shoelaces. Those community influences we have discussed—such as technological interdependence and national loyalties—and those separatist traditional, local, economic, religious, and other leanings we have described combine into dynamic movements to determine the forms of government. The more enduring and basic the interest, the more likely it is that men who share it will organize and wage political battle on its behalf. It is a grave error to think of representative government—or any other form of government—as a static organization, designed to give all conceivable desires equal weight in the determination of laws. In reality, representative government originated in a conflict of interests and is perpetually maintained and changed by the conflict of interests. This chapter will reveal such facts as they are discoverable in history and today. It will show how the numerous facets of men's political characters, described in the last chapter, cause men as individuals and in groups to promote representative and elective devices that help them achieve their ends.

Representative Government

Preparatory to sketching the career of representative government, let us define it and its companion term "representation." Representation is a relation between an official and citizen that exists whenever an action of the official accords with the desires of the citizen. Representative government is a government that makes great use of devices to ensure representation, such as the election of officials. The representative principle is built into the state; it is regularized, provided for as a normal procedure, and given certain important powers to work with.

ANCIENT REPRESENTATIVE GOVERNMENT

The origins of representative government are still somewhat unclear. Early Greek democracies were governed directly by the citizens, not by elected representatives who were authorized to pass laws. When these democracies formed leagues for religious or warlike purposes, their delegates operated under strict instructions. The Roman Republic passed into the Roman Empire without employing the principle of representation, and, so say a number of scholars, one of the reasons for the failure of the Republic lay in its inability to "invent" the principle. The Republic of Rome, built on the city-state, town-meeting pattern, had no mechanical way of representing the people of their far-flung possessions. Tenny Frank, however, in studying the semi-independent Macedonian republics set up by the Romans, has concluded with reservations that "the Macedonian state had a republican form of government that was not very different from that of more advanced republics today."

IMPORTANCE OF MIDDLE AGES TO REPRESENTATION

We do not know whether the Macedonian and other ancient experiments in representation were handed down into the Middle Ages. There is more evidence to show that a second Roman device persisted and had some influence on the development of representative government. This device was the corporation, a legal fiction whereby an organization could be created with an existence apart from that of its members and with powers to perform tasks in their name. Ecclesiastical bodies, such as the Dominican Order, were organized along corporate lines and in several important cases held assemblies attended by delegates of their scattered component groups.

By the beginning of the thirteenth century, this idea of the corporation was adapted to a growing secular, political pattern in western Europe. Kings were reaching out for power. They were trying to consolidate realms more extensive than the average principality. Towns were growing up and had much to gain from some form of monarchical stability, for trade prospered with wider markets and longer periods of peace. At the same time, the wealth and populations of towns could help the Kings subdue feudal competitors. Feudal ways of financing the King gradually disappeared because they were not as flexible or as generous as periodic consultations and contracts between the towns and the Kings.

In the English countryside, we find the King extending his influence through his itinerant judges, who would call up inquest juries to describe what the local law was. "Twelve men, therefore," wrote an early English historian, "were chosen to make known the provisions of their laws and customs, so far as they were able, omitting nothing and changing nothing by deception." Commenting on these events, Maude Clarke, in *Medieval Representation and Consent*, writes: "Thus between 1066 and 1226 the principle of representation was, by means of the inquest and jury, elaborated to such a point that the knights of the shire were brought to the frontiers of political responsibility."

Both the *untitled proprietors of the land* and the *town leaders*, therefore, came to have a certain role in relation to the King. Both were useful administratively. Both provided political support to kingly aspirations. Both were affected by the idea of consent in this new, nonfeudal situation; they felt that new practices that were not covered by the law ought to be settled by bargaining. The King was given what he wanted most of the time, but not without some bickering, protests, and refusals.

CONVOKING THE COMMONS

The high nobility and clergy of the late Middle Ages were already entrenched behind their privileges. In England the Magna Carta legalized their position. They were frequently consulted and already constituted an assembly. In the thirteenth century, however, the Kings called in the commons, that is, the representatives of the untitled landed interests and the commercial interests of the towns. Early in the century, parliaments of the three estates—nobles, clergy, and commons—were called in Spain, Sicily, and France. In 1265, Simon de Montfort called to the English Parliament for the first time the three estates of England. The exact method of selection in the beginning is in doubt. In 1295, the writ calling the Parliament prescribed elections. Members of these parliaments were strictly controlled by their home constituencies. The suffrage was limited, and the elections were conducted by a number of different methods in the various countries and localities. Within the parliaments, the landed interests far outnumbered and dominated the town representatives, but town membership grew gradually in numbers and power.

REPRESENTATIVE GOVERNMENT BY AN OLIGARCHY

There is some evidence that the idea of representative government was close to realization in the fourteenth and fifteenth centuries, even though representation was based on the estates, and not on the nation as a whole. Within this estates system the assemblies had considerable power and prestige. But everywhere the estates type of representative government declined as the Kings overpowered the nobles and reduced church influence. Only in England did the representative form of government survive, though weakened and pallid under the Tudors (1485–1603). Its tenacity and durability there prepared the way for important changes in the locus of power because the government at least provided a tolerant atmosphere for the growing influence of commerce and of the towns. Elsewhere those promoting the causes of the middle classes and of the "rights of man" could find no ladder of power up which they might climb. In England they could move, slowly, it is true, and not without great effort, into positions from which they could protect their interests. Finally in 1689 a combination of landed, commercial, and religious interests in England, represented in the House of Commons, determined that the ultimate legislative authority should be the Parliament, not the Crown.

However, this form of government, although it used representation, was an oligarchy, not a representative government as we define this term—direct control of the assembly by a large electorate. The controlling forces in the Commons of eighteenth-century England were the agents of a tiny group of wealthy and often titled men.

ADVENT OF MODERN REPRESENTATIVE GOVERNMENT

Modern representative government arose out of bitter disputes over the relation of the representative to his constituency. One group proclaimed that the representative is a free agent, attached only by the bonds of good will and remote influence to his constituents. The opposing group demanded that the representative should be elected, restrained, and tutored by his constituency. Since the first view conformed to the existing representative situation in England, its advocates might be expected also to be defenders of the *status quo*.

This is what in fact occurred. Edmund Burke, the foremost spokesman of the established system, declared in 1774 that "*mandates* issued, which the member [of Parliament] is bound blindly and implicitly to obey, to vote and to argue for, though contrary to the clearest conviction of his judgment and conscience; these are things utterly unknown to the laws of this land, and which arise from a fundamental mistake of the whole order and tenour of our constitution."

But Burke's order had not long to live. In the last part of the eighteenth century and in the early nineteenth century, growing opposition to "irresponsible" representatives induced Parliament finally, in 1832, to reorganize the whole electoral system of England, giving many more persons the vote and evening out the number of people who stood behind each member of Parliament. Exact obedience to instructions or mandates was not demanded by law, but the representatives became much more sensitive to sentiments of their constituents than their predecessors had been.

Meanwhile the English development was surpassed in America and France. In early nineteenth-century America, the vote was given to all white males, elections of most government officials were held at brief intervals, and, in some states, the constitutions even authorized the constituents to instruct their representatives (though in practice, this was almost impossible). The Jeffersonian ideal, the belief in "the people acting directly on all things concerning them," came to be held by millions. The egalitarianism that Burke thought dangerous became a cardinal belief of the peoples of America, England, and France. Declared Jefferson, "Equal representation is so fundamental a principle in a true republic that no prejudices can justify its violation."

MAJOR PROBLEMS OF REPRESENTATION AND ELECTIONS TODAY

The twentieth century, prolonging and developing the trend of the nineteenth century, brought representative government to most parts of the world. This triumph, however, has not simplified by much our problem of analyzing governmental institutions. Not only are there still many significant differences in the structures of the governments of the world, as seen in their constitutions and laws, but there are wide differences in practices to be found among governments whose structures superficially are quite similar. In this chapter, we shall have a good deal to say about certain of these differences. We shall answer the questions: Who has the right to vote? How many people exercise their right to cast ballots? How much power does the vote give to the electorate? How are the voters grouped, that is, apportioned, for the purposes of electing officers? How is the balloting for officials conducted and how are the ballots counted?

A discussion of these questions will take us a good distance toward understanding the different forms of government and political practices. But we shall have to devote a chapter apiece to political parties and pressure groups before we can adequately understand the forces working on systems of representation and elections.

Universal Suffrage

As has been shown above, much of the struggle for representation in government takes place through the fight for the vote in which different social groupings in society try to exercise disporportionate influence. Many think that every man, by virtue of being *homo sapiens*, ought to be allowed the vote, while others think the vote should go only to those who own land or some other form of personal wealth. Other claims have been advanced for and against women, minorities, the young, the noncitizens, the nonresident, and so on. Each new restriction and each abandonment of an old restriction shifts some amount of influence from some interests or values to others. We will observe this phenomenon now as we discuss the qualifications for the vote, as well as later on, when we discuss election systems and other representative arrangements.

Let us see what the situation of the electorate is today, and who must be considered when we speak of electoral behavior. *Generally speaking, all adults of all politically organized communities who are not affected by certain limiting disabilities have the right to vote in equal measure.* Some interesting exceptions to this generalization occur with respect to (1) property and taxes, (2) sex, (3) race, (4) education, (5) citizenship, (6) residence, and (7) age. Selected examples will show the things men wish to accomplish by suffrage restrictions. We will also need to discuss plural voting and compulsory voting.

PROPERTY AND TAX QUALIFICATIONS

In some countries the electorate is universal except for a few scattered property and tax restrictions. The poll tax in several of the Southern states of the United States is an example. Although the poll tax is usually only one or two dollars per year, many potential voters find other ways of spending their money more gratifying or forget to pay it before registration and election time. It then accumulates and twice as big a sum must be paid the next year. In many American localities, only property holders are allowed to vote on certain kinds of bond-issue proposals and other financial propositions.

SEX

All major countries now grant the vote to women. Generally, throughout the nineteenth century, liberals and radicals fought for women's suffrage on grounds of natural rights, equality, individualism, and socialist theory. But the parties of the left in the twentieth century have been cold towards women voting, believing (with some reason as we have seen) that the newly enfranchised women would vote more conservatively than the men as a whole.

NATIONALITY AND RACE

Before the wars and revolutions of the twentieth century, nations composed of more than one nationality, but dominated by only one, limited the vote mainly to the dominant nationality. This was true, for example, of the Austro-Hungarian Empire. The United States and the Union of South Africa, both composed of more than one national strain, discriminate against Negroes. In the United States, the legal theory forbids such restriction, but the tradition of slavery and civil strife has made the law a dead letter in a number of Southern localities.

Repeated opinions of the Supreme Court directed against overt or semiovert discrimination have failed to give the Negro impartial treatment at the polls. Intimidation, apathy, strict enforcement of literacy requirements for the suffrage against Negroes (but not against whites), refusal of the Democratic party to tolerate Negro members, and other nonlegal but nevertheless strong social pressures have effectively blocked a large percentage of the population of certain Southern states from voting. Yet in the Northern and Western states, Negroes vote freely, and even in the South they are voting in ever-increasing numbers.

In South Africa, the whites have prevented the more numerous Negro population from voting at all. In the Soviet Union, many races vote without hindrance. In Brazil, the Negroes and Indians, who are very numerous, have the vote, and so it is with a number of other Latin American and Caribbean countries. In Indonesia, Dutch and natives, of full or mixed Indonesian origin, have equal suffrage rights.

EDUCATION

Most countries have abolished educational requirements and even literacy tests for voting, although a few American states, Northern as well as Southern, have literacy requirements. To require more than literacy, that is, the ability merely to read and write on a low level, would introduce new political issues, for everywhere, people of means are more educated than the poor. The former can afford an education, and education itself promotes economic and social success. To require even a high school education in most countries would disfranchise large segments of the poorer classes and weaken the political parties of the poor. Therefore, no radical or liberal party can consent to an educational test, even if it seemed abstractly desirable. Furthermore, it would be extremely difficult to demonstrate any connection between education and "political intelligence"—in political disputes one side usually regards the other as politically unintelligent.

CITIZENSHIP

Citizenship has almost always been a prerequisite to the right of suffrage, from the Greek city states to modern times. Frontier or revolutionary nations provide a few exceptions. Foreigners voted and held office during the French Revolutionary Period and in the early days of the Soviet regime. Among frontier states, the United States (at one time), Argentina, Chile, and Australia have afforded examples of alien suffrage.

RESIDENCE

Many believe that, in order for a person to use the vote intelligently, he must have dwelt in the same locality for a certain length of time. Citizenship, of course, satisfies the basic need for some residence requirement. Conservatives have frequently expressed the opinion that longer residence requirements promote stability and responsibility in local and national government.

Ideological considerations aside, however, residence requirements of some minimal sort are necessary to allow time for registration lists to be prepared and checked. Otherwise "floaters" might wander from polling place to polling place on election day, voting at will. Each American state sets its own minimum residence; the period ranges from six months to two years. In addition, somewhat shorter periods of residence in the polling district itself are also required. In England only a three-month residence period is required.

ABSENTEE VOTING

A number of countries and states allow voters who are to be absent from their locality on election day to vote ahead of time or to vote by mail or proxy. When large standing armies or navies exist, how to arrange for their vote becomes a difficult problem. France before World War II denied the armed forces a vote for fear of military participation in politics. English and Soviet military forces have special arrangements to facilitate their voting. American soldiers, sailors, and airmen depend entirely on the laws of their home states.

DISCRIMINATION AGAINST CAPITAL CITIES

· A final and exceptional residence disqualification occurs in the District of Columbia. Residents of the American capital city are deprived of any right to vote except in so far as they retain residence in another state. The reason given is that being at the heart of the government the residents could exercise political influence beyond their numbers. The result is that, even though their number exceeds that of nine states, they cannot influence the vote at all (except those who continue to maintain residence outside the District). It is true, however, that the voting residents of Paris and London are reputed by some to rule the rest of their nations in their own interests. Still, in denying the voting right under any circumstances, the whole gamut of democratic theory must be opposed or answered. Positive evidence on both sides is available, but it is insufficient and vague.

AGE

In most countries, the age of acquiring the vote and the age of acquiring legal majority is the same—twenty-one years. A few nations require voters to be twenty-three to thirty years old. Others establish eighteen and twenty years as the voting age. The United States holds to twenty-one years with the exception of Georgia, where eighteen years is the voting age. France, Britain, and Italy maintain the twenty-one-year line. The Soviet Union and several of the new governments formed since 1945 have set eighteen as the voting age, and considerable opinion in the United States and elsewhere advocates the same age. The chief argument is that military and job responsibilities begin more often at the age of eighteen than at twenty-one.

Age requirements, like most other requirements, have indirect political consenquences. Younger people vote less conservatively than do older ones, according to studies of Swedish, Swiss, German, Danish, Dutch, and American elections. Opinion polls in America indicate the same trend; the youngest age groups tend more to favor the Democratic Party, whereas the oldest age groups tend to favor the Republicans.

PLURAL VOTING

Plural voting is the legal right to cast more than one vote in an election. A plural vote may be granted for a double residence, as formerly in England. Belgium had before World War II a law conferring an extra vote on the heads of families who possessed some wealth, education, or paid some taxes. In Prussia from 1849 to 1918, the total body of men over twenty-five were divided into three classes of voters, each class drawn to contain one third of the total taxes paid to the state. Each class could then elect one third of the members of the *Landtag* or parliament. As a result, about 6 per cent of the people, who paid one third of the taxes, elected one third of the representatives. In recent years there has been an attempt in France and Italy to give the head of a family more political power than single persons.

MISCELLANEOUS RESTRICTIONS

Scattered through the history of suffrage one finds other qualifications of the right to vote. Catholics were excluded in a number of Protestant countries until recent times. Jews received similar treatment in various countries: in England for a time, until 1923 in Rumania, in Germany before 1848 and during the Nazi period 1933–45, and so on. The Greek clergy were forbidden to vote before World War II. The Mexican Constitution of 1917 prevented the clergy from voting. The clergy in the Soviet Union were likewise disfranchised. English peers, possessed of their own personal "representation" in the House of Lords, cannot vote. Persons unfavorable to the existing regime are denied the vote in the Soviet Union, the Soviet bloc of nations generally, and in other countries where elections are used to give "applause" to a powerful ruling group. For a time, men who actively supported the Confederate States of America were disfranchised by the victorious Union Congress. Persons judged morally incompetent or criminal, and insane persons, are generally prevented from voting.

SUFFRAGE NEARLY UNIVERSAL

In general, we may conclude that the world's representative governments today give the vote to everyone. The remaining restrictions described above are not of great practical importance to the total picture. But we must not believe that the vote in itself guarantees that total power, even of an indirect sort, rests with the public. The vote is only one of the many devices used by representative governments. Universal suffrage means only that men can participate alike in the casting of ballots.

VOTING AND NONVOTING

Despite centuries of controversy over the right to vote, a large number of individuals will not vote unless driven to do so. The United States lags about a dozen points behind the countries of western Europe in the percentage of eligibles voting. In Soviet Union elections, where great official pressure is exerted to get out the vote, participation is close to 100 per cent. Something of a modern high in electoral participation in a free election occurred in republican Germany in 1933, when 88.7 per cent of the electorate voted. (This was also the German Republic's last free election before the Nazi repression.) One of the lowest records in a general election since World War I was the American presidential election of 1920, when somewhat less than half of the electorate participated. In American state and local elections, low participation is the general condition, especially in primaries.

Studies of nonvoters have given us a number of generalizations about why certain countries and certain groups within countries participate more heavily in elections. Under most circumstances, new voters vote less than those who have exercised the franchise for some time. This has been true of the working classes, the women, Negroes, and naturalized citizens of the United States. The factors at work are mainly timidity, remnants of social disapproval of the recent change, ignorance of the new procedures, and lack of interest in the new instrument of power. Larger proportions of educated individuals vote than of noneducated people, presumably because the schools of a nation stimulate interest in public affairs. More people of higher income vote regularly than do the people of lower income. Some element in this difference may arise from the feeling among higher-income earners that they have more at stake in government policy. A smaller proportion of young eligibles vote than do older eligibles except for the over-sixty age group, wherein participation declines somewhat. This may be due to a preoccupation of the young with getting a start in life and a feeling of incompetence at facing a new task.

All of these propositions must be used cautiously. For example, education, American birth, whiteness of skin, and higher income commonly are found together in the same groups in America. It is then a difficult statistical-analytic problem to assign the proper weight to each factor.

SITUATIONAL FACTORS AFFECTING PARTICIPATION

Various political and social conditions also seem to affect the amount of over-all participation in elections. Foreign or domestic crisis increases the percentage of participation. Individual excitement is expressed in the collective act of joining other citizens at the polls. The more important the elections seem to be to the voters, the greater the participation; that is, a presidential election or a British general parliamentary election will turn out more voters than local elections. Usually, elections of the top officers of the state draw out more voters than elections of lower-level officers.

The proportion of eligibles who vote in an election increases as the voters believe the race for office will be a close one. Participation is usually greater in elections the results of which definitely select the winner than in preliminary elections or primaries. Multiple-party systems draw greater participation than one- or two-party systems, perhaps because the range of choice is larger in the former systems, at least in the eyes of many voters who might not otherwise see any point in voting. Systems of proportional representation (see p. 165) increase participation.

Participation varies directly with the simplicity, intelligibility, and easy availability of the electoral machinery. "Get-out-the-vote" campaigns have a positive effect on participation if the campaign is adroit. A vigorous labor movement increases participation. The unions get out the working-class vote.

A tradition or habit of participation, formally or informally learned, tends to maintain a high level of participation. Finally, the general social evaluation of the vote as (a) precious, (b) useful in coping with the perceived political problems, and (c) authoritative affects the rate of participation. If voters are confident that an election will solve important problems, they will vote in larger numbers.

COMPULSORY VOTING

The experience of the few countries that have forced their citizens, by some mild but well-administered sanction, to vote shows that a greatly increased turnout results. A mere declaration of policy is not enough. In Australia, the adoption of a compulsory voting law in 1924 imposing a $10 fine on nonvoting brought an increase in participation from 59.4 per cent in 1922 to 91.4 per cent in 1925, 93.6 per cent in 1928, and 94.9 per cent in 1929. Belgium, Holland, Czechoslovakia, Spain, and the Argentine Republic also experimented with compulsory voting.

American opinion seems to shy away from the idea, although drives to "get out the vote" are part of every American election campaign. Professor Munro once declared the "slacker" vote was not worth getting. But that assumes a connection between intelligent voting and the act of voting that is hard to prove. In fact, in American elections, a light participation usually means a heavy proportion of machine-organized to "independent" votes. Several American colonies at one time required electoral participation. The voters of Massachusetts and the legislatures and conventions of several states have rejected compulsory voting laws in recent times.

In America, nonvoters are more common, though the difference is not striking, among the poorer, less-educated groupings. This means perhaps that compulsory voting would favor slightly the Democratic Party. In Europe, by contrast, the Conservative parties, not blessed with the natural organizations afforded left-wing parties based on trade unionism, have seen in compulsory voting a way of getting their supporters to the polls. Gosnell believes that compulsory voting would tend to lessen the power of political machines in American local elections. Primaries and many crucial general elections find only a small proportion of the potential voters coming out to choose mayors, aldermen, judges, sheriffs, and even state-wide officers. Only the presidential elections in America bring out two thirds or more of the voters regularly.

RESTRICTIONS ON THE MEANING AND POWER OF THE VOTE

How much the vote means depends in part upon how much legal authority is given the voters. Some of the devices that limit the powers of the voters are: (1) the existence of many nonelective offices, (2) constitutional limits to the events the electorate may influence, (3) bicameralism and other checks and balances on the free play of the electoral will, and (4) the principle of separation of powers to keep a popularly elected organ of government (for example, the House of Representatives) from dominating an appointed organ of government (the Supreme Court). Creating a "short ballot" for example, in the interest of "administrative efficiency," may give the electorate controls over a very few top officers but change and perhaps diminish their controls over a number of minor offices, previously elective. A constitution like that of the United States, which is hard to amend, prescribes freedom of the press, assembly, contract, religion, and other rights; the electorate is limited in the effects it may have on those rights. When one house of a bicameral assembly must pass on another's bill, the possibility of a check to the electorate is enhanced, especially when the terms of the offices of the members of one house are longer

than those in the other or staggered in such a way that the appearance
of a new, popularly chosen majority in one house often encounters an
incumbent opposing majority in the other. The American, British,
French, Italian, and other bicameral systems employ these checking
devices or have used them in the past.

HISTORICALLY, THE SUFFRAGE BROUGHT CHANGES

Despite these checks upon the electorate, the meaning of the
vote over a historical period is clear. The extension of the suffrage to
new groups has been associated with changes in the composition and
behavior of officials of the state. We may cite Negro advances within
Northern cities of the United States, the great impetus given the
Labour Party in England by the suffrage reform of 1918, and the
passionate opposition to the extension of the franchise to new groups
by the privileged classes wherever the issue arose. However, mere
multiplication of votes does not accomplish changes; new social strata
must be involved. The extension of the franchise to women was
followed by no recorded visible results in the United States, but it
seems to have given some strength to centrist and religious parties in
certain European countries. (However, even though it brought no
startling changes in the legislative sphere, we should not ignore the
profoundly democratic meaning of the franchise for women who were
working out adjustments to their changed situation in modern life.)

ELECTIONS CALL THE PUBLIC AND OFFICERS TO ATTENTION

Suffrage has a massive, general influence, rather than being
an intelligible source of specific decision, and it deserves respect as
such. The simple large fact that the vote can cause extensive movements of political personnel has been sufficient to give it a high value in
the minds of that personnel and consequently in the minds of the voters.
The behavior of officials is conditioned by a deep respect for it, and a
large body of myth surrounds its use. An election is like the morning
roll-call in the army; it brings all public officers to attention, and,
though it must discipline the "good" ones, it also forces the "bad"
ones into line.

THE BALLOT

The kind of ballot used in an election is also of some importance to the representative system. Although a century ago most
elections were conducted viva voce, that is, by a verbal expression of

preference for a candidate before the polling officials, the secret ballot is almost universal today. Even in absolute regimes that exercise complete controls over the elective process to make certain the election of the regime's candidates, some kind of "secret" ballot may be used. Then outside pressures are counted on to force the election according to the regime's wishes. The secret ballot, when printed by the government, is known as the Australian ballot from its country of origin. Its use is practically universal today, although it was not long ago that each party printed its own list of candidates for the various offices or the voter wrote up his own choices.

The state today also regulates the way in which the names appear on the ballot and the way in which a voter has to mark his ballot. The so-called Indiana ballot and the European list system ballot have a major point in common. In both it is possible for a voter to make only one mark that automatically casts his vote for every candidate of the party for which the mark is made. This encourages "party regularity," that is, adherence to the party all the way down the line. In practice, the effects of the Indiana ballot are probably quite small because a voter who is determined to be independent may easily check candidates in more than one party. The "straight-ticket" voting fostered by the Indiana ballot is not encouraged by the Massachusetts ballot, which lists the candidates in office groups in the same column, according to whether they are running for President, Vice-President, congressman, mayor, or alderman, regardless of party affiliations. Then the voter must pick and choose; if he is a party regular, he must take the trouble to search out with his pencil the candidate for each office who represents his party.

ELECTION ADMINISTRATION

The administration of elections in most jurisdictions of the world is a technical operation, publicly operated and directed with no relationship to the parties. In the United States, however, the administration of elections is partly in public hands and partly in party hands. Three criteria are commonly used to determine the "efficiency" of systems of election administration. The "efficient" system allows the voters to participate with a minimum of personal inconvenience by providing them with convenient polling places, easy registration and identification procedures, and in some cases a legal holiday from work to cast their votes.

"Efficient" systems prevent frauds. The American system operates on the principle that by using officials of the major parties to conduct the polling, each will watch the other and fraud will be prevented.

The European, including the English, systems have nonpartisan state employees doing the work.

Systems are also "efficient" if they get the job of balloting done in the shortest possible time with the least expenditure of money. Here possible contradictions arise, however, between the different objectives. The convenience of the voter often means greater expense. Using untrained personnel as in many American jurisdictions also means greater expense. Furthermore, in order to avoid the intervention of "foreign" officers and jurisdictions, the American elective machinery is extremely decentralized.

Practically all other elective systems are extremely centralized, as in the cases of France, Italy, the U.S.S.R., and, to a lesser extent, England. In these countries the local polling places are manned and managed by persons responsible to distant authorities. Historical evidence shows that many local frauds have occurred in the American system of decentralized administration. On the other hand, in the German Republic a system that was efficient in terms of cost was converted rapidly into a perfect instrument of central control by a dominant party. However, only careful study and expert judgment can decide in any certain case whether the disadvantages of the one system are graver than those of the other.

AMERICAN AND SOVIET SYSTEMS COMPARED

A comparison of the American and the Soviet systems of election administration shows remarkable differences. The American is almost completely federal, while the Soviet system is directed in a stringent fashion from one Central Electoral Commission of the Soviet Union, which is appointed and instructed by the Central Executive Committee of the Soviet Union. The American states generally delegate practically the whole of the election operation to the counties, sometimes not even bothering to keep adequate records of all local elections, much to the despair of political scientists. The Central Electoral Commission of the Soviet Union, however, directs the activities of central electoral committees in each constituent republic, which in turn supervise the work of local electoral commissions in the villages and in the farm and factory soviets. The Communist Party is active at all stages of the Russian electoral process, although in most instances the elections are held without coercion and in secrecy at the polls. In America, the parties are active everywhere and have a legal responsibility in the conduct of elections that the Communist Party in Russia does not have. The Communist Party, standing allegedly outside the administration of elections, limits in advance all significant free choice of the voters at the polls.

The Use of Election Forms to Achieve Values

Although the suffrage is a highly important device to produce representation for the different social groupings of a community, other devices require attention as well. Such devices are subsumed under the general subjects of electoral constituencies and balloting methods.

THE CONSTRUCTION OF CONSTITUENCIES

A wide range of possibilities for intertwining and adjusting values and interests opens up in the field of constituency construction and in the balloting process. A constituency is the group legally charged with the election of an officer. Given the qualified voters and the officers to be elected, how are the voters to be apportioned and how are the ballots to be drawn? Both processes can be carried out in many ways. We shall discuss apportionment first.

Apportionment is the division of qualified electors into constituencies. Voters may be apportioned by governmental boundaries, territorial surveys, official bodies, functional divisions of the population, or by personal or "free" population alignments. A combination of two or more is often encountered.

APPORTIONMENT BY GOVERNMENTAL BOUNDARIES

Governmental boundaries always form the ultimate basis of the constituency. Thus the United States as a whole is the constituency for the election of the President and Vice-President, speaking realistically. Speaking legally, the constituency of the President and Vice-President is an official body known as the Electoral College composed of men elected by the people of each state. The American governors are all legally and in fact the representatives of governmental constituencies composed of the whole state. Some of the American state senates are elected from counties, which are governmental areas of some independent powers. The American Senate, formerly elected by the state legislatures, each of which chose two Senators, is now elected by the entire electorate of the individual states, and thus is based on governmental boundaries.

APPORTIONMENT BY TERRITORIAL SURVEY

Territorial surveys are the favorite method of constructing constituencies in modern times. "Artificial" areas are cut out of the map, and their populations serve as constituencies. The survey method is popular because it is the easiest way to conform to the demand that all men be treated alike, that each vote weigh as much as every other vote, and that no subgroup of the population (race or class, for example) should be differentiated from the others for the purposes of voting. This was a specific demand of the Levellers, direct democrats of 1647, who in their first "Agreement of the People" declared: "That the people of England being at this day very unequally distributed by Counties, Cities, and Burroughs, for the election of their Deputies in Parliament, ought to be more indifferently proportioned, according to the number of the inhabitants."

"Indifferently proportioned, according to the number of the inhabitants" has become the standard principle in most representative governments today. Most election districts tend to be drawn to enclose equal numbers of inhabitants (certain exceptions will be noted in this section).

OFFICIAL BODIES

Official bodies as the apportioned unit are of two general kinds, *ad hoc* and permanent. In a number of representative systems we find special bodies called together for the primary or sole purpose of electing another body. This is the object and function of the American Electoral College. Modeled on the American idea, which Condorcet so admired, was the French system of indirect elections of the Senate (now the Council of the Republic) by an electoral college composed of various officials and persons designated by town councils. Permanent official constituencies take many forms. The Speaker of the House of Representatives is elected by the members of the House, who thus constitute an official constituency. The French President is elected by the two chambers of the French parliament. The English Prime Minister is elected by the House of Commons, though nominally appointed by the King. The German city councils elect their burgermeisters, some American city councils elect the city managers, and so on.

FUNCTIONAL DIVISIONS

Relatively few regions construct their constituencies by functional divisions of the population. Under the Fascist regime in Italy there existed a weak legislative body known as the Chamber of Corporations, which was based on constituencies of major occupations. The American National Industrial Recovery Administration from 1933 to 1935 gave certain powers to groups composed of the representatives of the various firms in particular industries. Russian factories until 1936 returned members to the local soviets or councils, which in turn sent members to the higher councils. English university men used to have special representation in the House of Commons. The Irish and Portuguese legislatures are based partially on functional representation.

FREE APPORTIONMENT BY VOLUNTARY CONSTITUENCIES

A final way of dividing the population into constituencies is by allowing the *population to create its own constituencies* during the voting process; that is, the voters are told that they may vote for whomsoever they please among the candidates up for election, regardless of their place of residence, functional occupations, or other spatial or social characteristics. Of course, there is practically always some spatial limit to the electorate itself, such as national boundaries; a pure personal constituency does not exist. But within the larger boundaries, free choice is allowed. The mechanisms by which this is accomplished will be dealt with below (pp. 165 ff.). We need indicate here only the two basic requirements for free constituencies: more than one representative must be chosen, and a limited quota of votes must be enough to elect a candidate.

"ROTTEN BOROUGHS"

Two irregular but widespread phenomena occur and create a pattern of constituency population different from the results of the apportionments already mentioned. These are "rotten boroughs" and "gerrymandering." *Rotten boroughs* are historical accidents that give disproportionate weight to the votes of a thinly populated district in relation to a thickly populated one. Strictly speaking, a rotten borough is such only when the prevailing principle or belief about constituency construction is that it should be on the principle of equal populations. Thus the famous English rotten boroughs, which lasted for centuries, were originally boroughs of considerable population that declined to practically nothing while other towns of considerable size grew up as a result of the Industrial Revolution and other reasons. The declining centers kept the same representation, and the growing centers gained no new representation. To those who believed even remotely in some connection between representation and population, this situation appeared most unjust. The Reform Act of 1832 established the English representative system on the equal population principle of territorial constituencies. All subsequent legislation reinforced the idea.

Some American writers have quipped that the American Senate is the "worst rotten borough in the world." This statement is not accurate, because the Senate was never designed to be based on the principle of equal population; all states, large and small, were supposed to have equal representation in it. However, the United States has its full share of rotten boroughs in practically every state that has a considerable urban population. All states based their construction of constituencies in large part on the notion that the population of each should be the same. But the plan depends, for practical effect, on periodic reapportionments in order to adjust to population changes. As a consequence, rural regions must give up memberships in the legislatures if new memberships are to be given to the growing urban regions. This the rural representatives have been loath to do, and as a result, in states with large urban populations, such as New York, Illinois, Pennsylvania, and Minnesota, many more people are to be found in the districts of urban representatives than are to be found in those of rural representatives. In Illinois, reapportionment, supposedly mandatory each ten years according to the state constitution, was thirty years overdue in 1951. The largest district, according to a 1940 calculation, held 191.4 per cent more people than the average district, while the smallest held 54.7 per cent less than the average. In New York the situation is roughly the same; in Michigan it is a little less disparate.

GERRYMANDERING

Rotten boroughs are caused by a failure to reapport according to the population principle, but *gerrymandering* is a positive act of malapportionment. The first violates the principle that equal populations should have equal weight, but gerrymandering violates the territorial principle that the boundaries of districts be "indifferently proportioned," that is, geometrically drawn without reference to the characteristics of the population. For gerrymandering is a process by which the dominant party in a legislature draws the boundaries of electoral districts so as to augment its strength in the assembly. By observing past electoral behavior and thus ascertaining where the consistent majorities of its opponents' voters and its own voters live, the dominant party draws the district boundaries in such a fashion as to concentrate its opponents' votes in as few districts as possible and to spread dependable majorities of its own voters over as many districts as possible. Sometimes this results in obvious distortions on the map such as the famous one committed by the party of Governor Gerry of Massachusetts when it formed a constituency that looked like a salamander. A cartoonist perceived the resemblance and called the malapportionment a "gerrymander."

BALLOTING PROCESS: MAJORITY AND PLURALITY

The balloting process fulfills the process of the construction of constituencies that begins with apportionment. It is most convenient to group the types of balloting under systems of majority and plurality voting and systems of minority representation. Majority systems may be either expected as a matter of course or deliberately provided for. In countries having regularly only two parties running candidates for office, a majority is expected to elect its candidates and usually does. Where the presence of several parties or no parties at all means that there will be several candidates in the field contending for a single office, agitation arises for some system that will insure to the candidate elected a majority of votes. Where a third party or candidate musters a very small percentage of the total vote, say 5 per cent, and the victorious candidate wins by a plurality of 49 per cent to 46 per cent for his other competitor, the problem is not considered ordinarily to be serious. But where in similar cases the vote is regularly something like 36 per cent, 34 per cent, 30 per cent, then it is felt that steps should be taken to get the constituency's "real will," that is, to force a majority.

FORCING A MAJORITY EXPRESSION

There are many ways to force a majority from the constituency. Three general types of forced majorities may be described. The first is the *run-off election*. In a preliminary election, several candidates contend against one another. The two with the most votes run against each other in a final election. This is found in the American South and in some localities where candidates are not allowed to list their party affiliations on the ballot. The French *ballottage* system allowed all candidates to run again if they pleased, but generally only the two highest pleased to do so.

A second general type of forced majority is the *alternative vote*. The voter is authorized to rank his choices among the candidates, giving the number 1 to his first choice on the list, the number 2 to his second choice, and so on. In the first count all the first choices of each candidate are totaled. If one candidate has a majority of all the ballots cast, he is declared elected. If he has no majority, and no one else has, the candidate with the least number of first choices is eliminated and the second choices on his ballots are distributed among the candidates who have received them. This may well result in one of the top candidates completing his majority. If so, he is declared elected. If not, the same process is repeated with the choices of the second to the bottom candidate.

MINORITY REPRESENTATION THROUGH BALLOTING ARRANGEMENTS

Among the many systems of voting that give minorities representation, four may be presented briefly here. The simplest is the *limited vote*. Assuming that it is bad that a majority party should have all the voice of a district in the legislature inasmuch as it may have only won 51 per cent of the vote, a multimember district is created from which three or five representatives are to be elected instead of merely one. Then, where three representatives are to be elected, each voter is told that he may vote only for two candidates; or where five representatives are to be elected, he is told that he may only vote for three candidates. Thus a majority of the voters will under no circumstances be able to elect all three or all five members.

Notice that the essential feature of minority representation in this and the other systems to follow is the "voluntary constituency." And, as we stated above (p. 162), voluntary constituencies require more than one representative to be elected from the district and allow each candidate to be elected with a quota rather than a majority of votes.

Simply providing for more than one candidate to be elected from a district is not enough. For example, the *block system* of *election at large*, under which every voter votes to elect several men from a single constituency, invariably becomes a majority or plurality election. For under such a system, the voters, instead of making up personal constituencies by scattering their votes, quickly gather or are gathered by managers behind a slate of candidates for all three, four, or however many offices are to be filled. Then the group with the largest number of voters wins all of the offices. The only regular methods of creating constituencies that are personal and free in the sense of our limited requirements here are the systems of minority representation that require only a limited quota of votes for a candidate to be declared elected.

MINORITY REPRESENTATION: THE CUMULATIVE VOTE

A second type of minority representation is the *cumulative vote*. Three representatives are to be elected from each district. A voter is allowed to give three votes to one candidate, one and one-half votes to two, or one vote to all three, depending on whether he marks an "x" in the square of one, two, or three of the candidates in the race. Then the total points of each candidate are tallied, and the three highest are declared elected. Under this arrangement, a minority may instruct its adherents to mark only one "x" and that for their candidate. The majority party meanwhile is compelled to concentrate its strength on two candidates and, even if very strong, could hardly hope to give three times as many votes to each of three candidates as the nearest minority competitor could muster through his triple-strength supporters.

MINORITY REPRESENTATION: P.R. BY THE SINGLE TRANSFERABLE VOTE

A third type of minority representation is provided by the so-called Hare or Andrae system of proportional representation (PR) by the single transferable vote. Like all other systems of minority representation here described, a multimember district is required. The desired object of this system of proportional representation is to give each group in society a number of members in the legislature proportional to its numbers in the population.

For example, let us say that five representatives are to be elected. Let us suppose for the moment that each major social group has a political party representing it. Let us also suppose that the parties rank as follows: Party A has about 20,000 voters; Party B has 10,000; Party C has 10,000; Party D has 7,000; Party E has 5,000; and Party F has 3,000. Accepting the premise that it is good to have all major groupings in the population represented in the legislature in proportion to their voting strength in the population, we would probably agree then that Party A should have two members, Party B and Party C one member each, and Party D one member, although we wouldn't feel too unhappy if Party E, instead of Party D, were represented with one member. How would we go about forcing this result?

First of all, we decide that no vote should count for more than one candidate. Otherwise we would have the block system, which is a multimember district in which the voters vote for as many candidates as have to be elected: invariably the party with the majority or plurality of the votes sweeps all the offices. We accomplish this by having each voter designate his rank order of choices, one for his first choice, two for his second, three for his third, and so on.

We then would allow the voters to establish their personal constituencies. We would say that any candidate receiving over one fifth of the total vote cast ought to be elected, since there are five men to be elected from the district. We therefore set up a quota. The most common formula for arriving at a quota is the Droop quota used in the Hare system of proportional representation. The total vote cast is divided by one more than the number of representatives to be elected, and one is added to the quotient. The result is the number of votes required to elect a candidate. In our example we find that the total number of votes cast in the election is 55,000. The number of men to be elected is 5 (plus 1 is 6). And 55,000 divided by 6 is 9,166+. Add 1 to this figure and the final quota is 9,167. Therefore, any candidate that gets 9,167 votes is bound to be elected. For no matter how the vote is cast, *providing we insist that no voter's choice is to be counted for more than one candidate*, no more than five candidates can possibly get 9,167 votes.

Now we will show how the counting is done. We take a count of first choices and find the result is as follows:

Party A candidates		A1	8,000
		A2	8,000
		A3	4,000
Party B	"	B1	10,000
Party C	"	C1	9,167
Party D	"	D1	6,000
		D2	1,000
Party E	"	E1	5,000
Party F	"	F1	3,000

In this remarkable election, two candidates, B1 and C1, have already made their quotas, C1 on the head, B1 a little over. Next we take the surplus from B1, reaching into his barrel of 10,000 votes and extracting at random the difference between that number and 9,167. We examine the second choices on these 833 ballots and find they go to F1. We give them to F1, making his total 3,833. Lacking any more surpluses and still having to elect three more representatives, we eliminate the low man. This turns out to be D2. But, as we might expect, the second choices on the D2 ballots all go to D1, giving him 7,000, but electing nobody for the moment. We go to the new low man who happens to be F1 with 3,833 votes. We take the next available choice on all of these ballots and find that 3,000 go to D1, 833 to E1. D1, with 10,000, is declared elected, while E1 has now 5,833 votes. We distribute D1's surplus of 833 votes and find that they now go to E1, giving E1 6,666 votes. But it is too late to help him, for the next low man whose vote is to be dissolved is A3, and his 4,000 second choices go roughly 2,000 each to A1 and A2. Before they are even fully distributed, both these gentlemen are up to their quota and are declared elected. Their poll watchers have had some uncomfortable moments during the proceedings and probably have been regretting the lack of party intelligence and organization that put A3 in the field, but the results have finally come out as they should according to the party's strength. Party A elects two, B one, C one, and D one.

MINORITY REPRESENTATION: LIST SYSTEM OF P.R.

The fourth type of minority representation is the *list system*. It is a little less nerve-racking to the party managers than the single transferable vote system, for each party submits a list of its candidates and the voter, instead of wandering all over the ballot, simply designates the party of his choice. Then the quota needed to elect having been established roughly as in the Hare system, previously described, as many of the top names on the party list are declared elected as there are multiples of the quota in the total number of votes cast for the party list. In the example above, using the same quota, Party A with its 20,000 votes would again get two seats, Parties B and C would again get a seat each, but the results for Party D with 7,000 votes would be in doubt. To assign the fifth seat, following the Swiss system of list voting, we would give it to the party that would have the highest average vote per seat as a result of having it. Thus: A has 2 for 20,000; with 3 it would have an average of 6,666+. B has 1 for 10,000; with 2 it would have an average 5,000. C has 1 for 9,167; with 2 it would have an average of 4,583+. D with 0 for 7,000 would have 7,000 votes for its one seat, higher than any of the other averages, and would therefore receive the seat.

Generally, the majority or plurality types of balloting just discussed are found in North and South America and in England and its Dominions and are used in part in a number of European systems. The Hare system and other types of single transferable vote systems are found in scattered localities in the United States, the British Commonwealth, and the Scandinavian countries. The list system is popular in Europe but varies in details from country to country.

EFFECTS OF MAJORITY AND MINORITY SYSTEMS

If we ask what kinds of values the various elective systems introduce into representative government, we can make certain partially substantiated statements. The majority election provides a working majority of members of a parliament, sharing many common views on issues. If it does not do so, the lack of a majority reflects aimlessness rather than any bitter conflict of party blocs. The systems of proportional representation or minority representation, on the other hand, when they do not produce majorities, tend to produce crystallized party blocs in the legislatures. Ordinarily a representative under a majority system has to appease a great number of his constituents, whereas a representative sent to the legislature by a certain quota of constituents can rest easy so long as he appeases that quota and may be little concerned with sparing the feelings of the rest of the community. The list system of proportional representation, on the other hand, can certainly be said to encourage strong party discipline, especially where a party determines whether a man goes on its list and assigns him his priority of election position on the list.

Before the coming of the Labour Party to power in England, it was often said that the majority election kept issues of a burning sort out of politics. That, of course, can no longer be said. But one may say that only heated issues that concern almost half or more than half the population will emerge readily in a majority system, while in a system of proportional representation any quota of the population can send its torchbearer to the legislature. A one-ring circus then becomes a several-ring circus. The exhibition that follows may be somewhat more disquieting.

RECONVERSION OF ELECTIONS TO "TOWN MEETINGS"

It is scarcely necessary to say that no system of electing officers produces universal satisfaction. Often a great many members of the public feel that no representative can ever be relied on to represent them adequately. At certain times in the past, this feeling has been reflected in proposals for special procedures to "return the government to the people." Among the devices favored to accomplish this task are the initiative, the referendum, and the recall. The *initiative* is an arrangement of government whereby a given number of people may demand that a particular proposal be acted upon by the legislature or be referred to the electorate as a whole for a referendum. The *referendum* is an arrangement whereby an initiated proposal or a bill of the legislature may be submitted for approval and enactment into law by the total electorate. Sometimes the legislature may itself call a referendum on a bill. At other times, any bill of a certain kind must be referred to the electorate. The *recall* is a procedure for allowing a prescribed number of voters to demand a special election to be held for the purpose of retaining or dismissing an elected officer whose conduct is at issue.

Hints of all three devices are to be found in American colonial history but were submerged after the American Revolution. The device of the New England town meeting, coupled with Swiss devices of the late nineteenth century, attracted many Americans who were anxious over losing control of their officers. It is difficult to generalize about the results of the three devices in a number of American governments that adopted them before 1920. However, we can say that it has not been proven that the "people" as a whole find them useful to get things done in accordance with the majority will. V. O. Key and W. W. Crouch, for example, concluded from a painstaking study of the California experience that "the initiators of propositions have usually been pressure organizations representing interests—commercial, industrial, financial, religious, political—that have been unable to persuade the legislature to follow a particular line of action." Also, Gosnell and Schmidt concluded from a general survey of "Popular Lawmaking in the United States" that participation or voting interest on issues brought up through initiative or referendum devices was generally somewhat below the interest expressed in the elections of candidates. There was also some variation according to the type of legislation proposed. More voters turned out to vote on legislation concerning morals and education, less on issues of revenue and public welfare, least on technical matters concerning governmental organization. The Swiss history of popular legislation has proved similar. A comparison of "popular" legislation with laws made by the legislature shows no striking differences in scope, novelty, moral quality, or radical majoritarianism.

POLITICAL PARTIES AND THEIR REGULATION

Besides using many kinds of elections to gain representation, elements of the public have endeavored constantly to control the actions of political parties. If a single group of men dominated the major parties and the parties dominated the whole representative process, the universal suffrage and the many different representative devices would have small effect. Consequently, governments often force parties to admit members freely, to avoid corruption and bribery, and to allow representation to their rank and file. However, the subject of political parties is a large and important one, and we shall have to know much more about it. We ought now to turn, therefore, to the study of political parties, asking not only what they aim at and whom they represent, but also how they are formed, organized, and supported.

Questions and Problems

1. Give three instances in which ancient governments contributed devices of government approximating the principle of representation. Why should the medieval king look kindly upon methods of representing the commoners?

2. Why did the theory of Edmund Burke on relations between constituents and representatives prove congenial to the Parliamentary oligarchy? What ideas opposed it?

3. What are the limitations to the right to vote in the world today?

4. Write an essay of 200 words on the possible effects of a requirement that would permit only high school graduates the right to vote.

5. Residence requirements seem to be both technically expedient and widely demanded by community sentiment. What are the reasons for both types of motives?

6. What are the factors or conditions very often associated with a high participation in an election? With nonvoting?

7. List the criteria by which constituencies may be apportioned in a jurisdiction and give an example of each.

8. The present senate of a mythical legislature convenes with 5 Democrats and 4 Republicans. The Democrats have the power to control the redistricting of the state and decide to make their majority more secure in future elections. The constitution merely provides that "the State shall be apportioned into 9 senatorial districts of as equal populations as possible." Acting as the Devil's Advocate, gerrymander the districts to assure consistent Democratic majorities in the Senate. Do so by copying the accompanying map on another sheet of paper and marking with a double line the new boundaries.

There must be nine districts, each of which elects one representative. Each district (A, B, C, and so on) has two electoral precincts (A1, A2, B1, B2, and so on), shown on the map by dotted lines. The average percentage in each precinct that was Democratic in the 10 preceding elections is as follows:

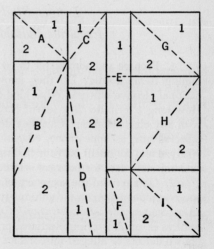

A1—51	A2—55
B1—49	B2—56
C1—52	C2—55
D1—48	D2—43
E1—50	E2—49
F1—45	F2—40
G1—49	G2—48
H1—58	H2—45
I1—60	I2—42

The population of each precinct is about 5,000; of each district about 10,000. These figures should remain the same.

9. Describe briefly the three general ways of forcing a majority instead of a mere plurality.

10. Describe the limited vote and the cumulative vote.

11. Using the Hare system of proportional representation with the Droop quota, perform the counting and declare the winners of an election (3 to be elected) in which the voters' ballots appear in the following manner:

CANDIDATE	A	B	C	D	E	F	G	H	I	J	K	L	M	N	O	P	Q	R	S	T	U
Jones	5	2	2	1	1	3	5	6	1	1	3	5	4	1	3	1	5	6	6	4	2
Smith	4	5	1	2	2	4	1	2	3	4	1	1	1	2	4	6	3	2	3	5	3
Brown	6	6	5	3	4	5	6	5	5	6	4	4	5	3	5	5	6	1	5	3	4
White	1	4	3	5	5	1	4	4	2	5	6	6	3	4	6	3	4	4	4	2	6
Grey	3	3	4	6	6	2	3	3	4	3	2	2	2	5	2	4	1	3	2	1	1
Black	2	1	6	4	3	6	2	1	6	2	5	3	6	6	1	2	2	5	1	6	5

12. Compare the results of the Hare and list systems of proportional representation with the single-member district majority system. List and describe briefly the controls that governments often exercise over the political parties indirectly by suffrage and election laws.

13. What is the general nature of and the purpose of the initiative, the referendum, and the recall?

Longer Study and Research Problems Suitable for Term Papers

1. Prepare and administer to 20 of your classmates a questionnaire containing items asking: Do they know the names of their local, state, and national elective officers? What kind of election is used to elect such officers? How long a term do they serve? Have they ever communicated in any form with any elected officer? Can they describe any characteristics of any of the officers, such as appearance, education, position on any issues, and so on? Analyze and comment on your findings. (Advice: a person's ignorance is just as admissible data for political science as his knowledge.)

2. Obtain from the secretary of your state, or from any written or oral sources, information on the administration of elections in your state, and write an account of the administration of elections. Besides giving the legal procedures in administering elections, present any information you may have on known defects or alleged misconduct under the system.

3. Every major election is preceded by many statements alleging what the voters will do; afterward many interpretations are made of their verdict. Select the latest election in your community—state or national—and compile from the newspaper files a list of such statements and predictions made before and after the election. Is it possible to agree with any of the statements on the basis of the election results? (Try to get as complete figures on the elections as possible; also, you may get help by asking experts like newspapermen, party workers, and so on.)

4. Read and report in ten pages on one of the following works, giving information on the method used by the author in arriving at his conclusions,

listing his conclusions, describing his proposals for changes (if any), and giving your opinion of the truth and usefulness of his conclusions and proposals:

Charles A. Beard: *The Economic Basis of Politics*
Mary P. Follett: *The New State*
D. C. Blaisdell: *Economic Power and Political Pressures*
Alfred de Grazia: *Public and Republic*
Frank Kent: *The Great Game of Politics*
V. O. Key, Jr.: *Southern Politics*
C. A. M. Ewing: *Congressional Elections*
Paul Lazarsfeld and others: *The People's Choice*
John Stuart Mill: *Representative Government*

6

THE POLITICAL PARTY

F ACTIONS, cliques, gangs, lobbies, and caucuses always accompany
political events. However, the condition called "party government" is a recent occurrence, with so many points of difference from
and developments beyond the above-mentioned organizations that it
deserves a distinctive place in the annals of politics. It would be
abusing the term "political party" if we applied it to every opinion
group among the politists of a society or if we regarded the major
social groups—such as labor, capital, farmers, and churches—as if
they were the same as political parties. Party government and its
chief feature, the political party, have a rather distinct habitat, a
peculiar mode of operation, and special characteristics of structure and
function. A glance through history may give us some idea of how the
modern political party has come about. Afterward we will define at
length the qualities of the party, its aims and organization, its variations from place to place, and its relationship to the government.

The History and Types of Parties

ANCIENT AND MEDIEVAL FACTIONALISM

In the Greek city-states, a kind of party politics that is
usually termed "factionalism" was common. Men formed themselves
into groups that stood for or against something. For example, they
favored aristocratic or democratic values, they were followers of
strong personalities such as Pericles or Philip of Macedon, or they
were for or against some such issue as war against the Persians or
alliance against Sparta. Romans, too, both under the Republic and
under the Empire, split into opposing groups of plebeians or eques-

trians, landed and landless, into the advocates of leniency for or annihilation of the Carthaginians, into the followers of Sulla or of Marius,
of Caesar or Pompey.

The Middle Ages were similar. The medieval Italian cities re-
sounded with the clamor of factional struggle in the piazzas and in the
narrow streets. The medieval Romans were no less susceptible to
appeals to democracy and equality from the lips of Cola di Rienzi than
were the Americans of nineteenth-century South America to the
republican slogans of Bolívar. Guelf and Ghibelline fought bitterly in
Dante's time, and the medieval citizen of Florence would probably
have had as difficult a time distinguishing issues from personalities,
church from state, sincerity from hypocrisy as the American citizen
who sits in judgment on the Democratic and Republican Parties on
election day.

The triumph of monarchy in most of Europe from the thirteenth
through the nineteenth centuries brought the factions off the streets
into the salons and courts of the Kings. The matters of sovereignty,
legality, succession, and legitimacy were settled in some places for long
periods of time, but the ancient pattern of conflict and compromise
continued among the interpreters of these concepts.

CHANGING TECHNIQUES OF FACTIONS

This history of partisanship and factionalism gives us the
impression that there is a lack of continuity and regularity about the
factional process, a lack of organization of the struggle, a lack of
agreement on the weapons to be used in the fights, all of which distinguish them in general from the modern phenomenon of the political
parties. Perhaps the agreement on the weapons to be used came first.
The long tenure of monarchs was partly responsible for this development, since the contending factions had to use the tactics of court
diplomacy. Rioting, assassinations, wholesale massacres, and direct
appeals to the populace went out of style for the most part. Flattery,
discussion, and maneuvering for place in the royal court, the armed
forces, and administration became the accepted techniques of factional
conflict.

BEGINNINGS OF ENGLISH PARTIES

In England, where party government began, the presence
of a legislative body of some consequence, the House of Commons,
allowed further scope for tactical "party" maneuvers. There was an

electorate to contend with. Men could even appeal from the Crown to the people or from the people to the Crown. The developing interests —among them the Puritans, the manufacturers, and the commercial companies—found a political structure in the courts, Commons, and Crown administration that was loose enough to give room for party maneuver. There was greater place for the bargaining, manipulating, and conspiratorial activities so important to party strategy. A half century of revolution had burned out the forces of fundamental conflict and left a rather dulled group of factional protagonists when the seventeenth century drew to a close.

One could barely distinguish between men who were known as Whigs and others who were known as Tories; yet everyone seemed to agree that these two parties existed, much like people in America who are hard put to tell specifically the distinction between Democrats and Republicans but who are positive that some difference exists. As Lecky described the difference, the Tory group was somewhat overcast with sentiments favorable to the Crown, the Anglican Church, and the landed interests, while the Whigs were just as slightly tinged with bias towards the House of Commons, religious independency, and the commercial interests.

Whatever the real state of affairs, it hardly corresponded to Edmund Burke's famous definition of a political party that he enunciated in the last quarter of the eighteenth century: "Party is a body of men united, for promoting by their joint endeavors the national interest, upon some particular principle in which they all agreed." Parliamentary politics in most of the parliamentary sessions in which Burke served could have better fitted his definition of a "cabal," a clique striving for positions and favors, united temporarily for those particular purposes on the principle of subservience to the King.

Yet the psychology of party was fixing itself on the minds of the English ruling class to such an extent that long before Burke, when William of Orange became King of England and wanted to appoint a Cabinet, he found considerable opposition to the idea of selecting men of both parties. He could not comprehend the difficulty at first. He felt that the best men should serve the "national interest" regardless of party and saw no incongruity in their serving it at the same time. His concession to the spirit of party was a lasting one, and coalition cabinets became an exceptional occurrence. The Whigs grew imperceptibly into the Liberals, the Tories into the Conservative, or Union, Party. Their identity and continuity were assured, even though their membership and leadership occasionally shifted, not to mention their policies. The ruling class of England was still small, and a few managers arranged the electioneering. Hardly any semblance of formal structure existed to mark the location and operation and identity of the parties. Yet English politists were agreed that the party that controlled a majority of the seats in the House of Commons ought to name the Prime Minister and Cabinet.

FIGURE 18

THE CAUCUS IN COLONIAL AMERICA *

---

144   DIARY.   [1763.

house officers, gentlemen of the army, the bar; retails prosody, writes upon money, Province sloop.[1]

Boston. February. This day learned that the Caucus Club meets, at certain times, in the garret of Tom Dawes, the Adjutant of the Boston Regiment. He has a large house, and he has a movable partition in his garret which he takes down, and the whole club meets in one room. There they smoke tobacco till you cannot see from one end of the garret to the other. There they drink flip, I suppose, and there they choose a moderator, who puts questions to the vote regularly; and selectmen, assessors, collectors, wardens, fire-wards, and representatives, are regularly chosen before they are chosen in the town. Uncle Fairfield, Story, Ruddock, Adams, Cooper, and a *rudis indigestaque moles* of others are members.[2] They send committees to wait on the merchant's club, and to propose and join in the choice of men and measures. Captain Cunningham says, they have often solicited him to go to those caucuses; they have assured him benefit in his business, &c.

[1] It is scarcely necessary to say that each of these points has a direct reference to some event in the life of Otis. The question raised as to the Governor's authority to fit out the Province sloop is spoken of by Tudor as "one of the preparatory causes of the Revolution." *Life of Otis,* p. 117.

[2] Gordon assigns a very early date for this practice. He says, "More than fifty years ago," (from 1774,) "Mr. Samuel Adams's father and twenty others, one or two from the north end of the town, where all the ship business is carried on, used to meet, make a caucus, and lay their plan for introducing certain persons into places of trust and power. When they had settled it, they separated, and used each their particular influence within his own circle. He and his friends would furnish themselves with ballots, including the names of the parties fixed upon, which they distributed on the days of election. By acting in concert, together with a careful and extensive distribution of ballots, they generally carried the elections to their own mind. In like manner it was, that Mr. Samuel Adams first became a representative for Boston." *History of the American Revolution,* vol. i. p. 365, note.

This is a page from John Adams's diary, illustrating the personal document as a source of political data and presenting a classic description of political management.

* *The Works of John Adams,* 10 vols., edited by Charles Francis Adams (Boston: Little, Brown and Company, 1850), Vol. II, p. 144.

MODERN PARTIES BEGIN IN AMERICA

It was in the United States that the *modern* political party came to fruition. There the factors of agreement on the weapons and continuity and regularity of party procedures and functions were joined with the factor of durable organization. This did not occur all at once. There was a great deal of preliminary skirmishing on the English model, and the Federalist Party, which held the most influential posts in politics, was of the English variety.

Colonial and Revolutionary Americans often disapproved of factionalism. Government was to be by gentlemen, who were presumably well-equipped to govern the nongentlemen. The caucus was the prevailing method of organizing political strength (see Figure 18). George Washington believed strongly that faction and parties were unnecessary evils. He even warned his youthful nephew against the dangers of participating in a current affairs discussion group. His attitude was shared not only by the most influential Federalists but also by many of the American intellectuals and well-to-do of the nineteenth century. New England, for example, which had furnished a most active political class from among its wealthiest and best educated citizens, lost the services of most of these men when the American party developed into its later mass-organized form. Alexander Hamilton was one of the few Federalist leaders who saw the future clearly and wished to engage the party in an organizing campaign at the grass roots, but his ideas found little support.

THE MASS PARTY OF JEFFERSON

Thomas Jefferson built the first great mass-democratic party of modern times. He gave the modern party its essential mode of operation—winning the active consent of the mass of voters. His Democratic-Republicans, using the techniques of the majority principle, grass-roots control over elected politicians, universal suffrage—in short, all the devices that the radical democratic idea contained—maintained a substantial monopoly of American politics until the Civil War. In the haste to credit Jefferson with the philosophy of the pure democrat, subsequent generations have failed to respect him as the master organizer. It was he who created the modern party by adding the factor of organization. Jobs, favors, a constant stream of letters, advice and exhortation, the encouragement of organization in the state and county and village, the consistent reiteration of slogans of self-government and egalitarianism—all came forth to convert a party of anti-Federalism into a continuing and durable structure. The Democratic-Republicans became the prototype of the political parties of the nineteenth and early twentieth centuries.

SIGNIFICANCE OF UNIVERSAL SUFFRAGE

The key change associated with the rapid development of the Jeffersonian type of political party was the gradual extension of the suffrage to all adults. As a great many people obtained the right to vote, the advantages of efficient party organization on a grand scale were maximized and inefficient organization heavily penalized. And only among an extensive electorate could the typical appeals of rationalism, individualism, egalitarianism and democracy that characterized party life in later times find their most appreciative audience.

Wherever universal suffrage was delayed, the political party in its most advanced democratic form was late in appearing. Europe and England were two generations behind the United States in gaining universal suffrage. Aristocratic residues in social and political life and limitations on the suffrage retarded the emerging pattern. During the nineteenth century, English parties were traditional and liberal. They contended over specific economic issues and benevolent reforms. They did not "trust the masses," as the Jeffersonians would put it, but rather trusted to enlightened leadership. The European parties tended to be still the mouthpieces of declining aristocracies, romantic exponents of heroic ideals, or revolutionary movements, uncertain whether to use party, cabalistic, or violent techniques to make their weight felt. Personal parties were common, dominated by striking individuals of oratorical and idealistic pre-eminence. When the working classes received the vote, the parties reflected the change and modeled themselves after the Jeffersonian pattern.

ADVENT OF CLASS PARTIES

However, the resemblance did not last long. By the end of the nineteenth century the socialist doctrine began to take hold of large parts of the lower economic groups, and party demands became utopian. Complete reforms of the social and political system became part of the propaganda baggage of many European parties. Jefferson had assembled his party before the industrial working class in America had developed into a sizable portion of the population, but the English and European working classes were ready to step into the new parties of universal suffrage with a full and drastic program. The European parties were of no mind to play politics for politics' sake. Their members felt the party ought to use its organization for far-reaching economic and political reform; it should not exist merely as a vehicle for jobs and favors; and when the Jeffersonian type of party system failed to produce something other than the behavior typical of the American parties, the Europeans were fast to contemn it.

From 1880 to the present time, although many dozens of European parties have possessed the structure of the Jeffersonian model, two aberrations persistently intruded to prevent their working along American lines. In the first place, despite their possessing all the paraphernalia of the American machine organization—political managers, professional politicians, elaborate hierarchical structures, and appeals to democracy and equality—the European parties could never build up the tremendous traditional, affiliated vote of the American parties. They constantly fluctuated in membership. Their supporters, discouraged by the ineptness of their parties to attain remote goals, tried other parties one after another. Most Americans learned over a long time to contemplate without shock the paradoxes and inconsistencies of the American party system. Many Europeans abandoned hope for their parties before they became accustomed to them.

In the second place, rabidly monopolistic parties appeared on the European scene, conceiving that the function of the political party was rather to drive out the other parties and establish the government on the one True Idea than to alternate at holding office with the other parties. The "one-party" idea, although strictly speaking quite contrary to the idea of party itself, was not uncommon to the continent or even to England, and it finally came to fruition in the Italian Fascist Party, the Russian Communist Party, the German Nazi Party, the Spanish Falangist Party, and several other groups. This kind of party, which develops into the only party of a one-party state, has a peculiar status of its own and scarcely can be called a party in the same sense as we apply that term to the parties of a multiparty state.

MAX WEBER ON PARTIES

Let us look more closely at the idea of the political party as it stood after World War I. As Max Weber described it, the political party was *a voluntary society of propaganda and agitation, seeking to acquire power in order to procure chances for its active militant adherents to realize objective aims, or personal advantages, or both.*

In other words, the party is composed of joiners; one is not born into it. It is a social group with the same pressures on its members to conform to the group that are found in all social groups of any considerable degree of organization. It is organized to conduct propaganda and agitation; thus it has a certain militancy and a goodly number of leaders who possess skills in orating, writing, bargaining, and organizing. It seeks to acquire power and therefore always is plagued by the problems of means and ends, for power can often be attained only by the "temporary" sacrifice of other values held by the party leaders and members. Often the values sacrificed are the very ones that are used to justify the existence of the party in the first place. For example, Michels, in his famous study *Political Parties*, quotes several socialist leaders, otherwise advocates of direct, egalitarian democracy, who denounced submitting issues to the action of the total membership of the party by referendum. They felt such action would cripple the party leadership, lead to vacillating party policies, and cause internal dissension.

Nevertheless, once attained, power can conceivably provide the party with increased chances to do things. Once it gains office, the authority of the state is behind its acts. It controls the state's resources—financial, mechanical, and human—although only to the extent that these resources have been entrusted to the part of the government that is generally agreed to be subject to capture by the party. In the United States, a victorious party in the national elections is limited initially in the fullness of its triumph by the federal system, the separation of powers, the system of checks and balances, and a written constitution. The American party, because of the consensus developed within the last generation, cannot transform the administrative offices of the nation to its purposes. It cannot eliminate the influence of the Supreme Court, though it may conceivably cripple it by adding party adherents to its membership.

The active miltant adherents of the party get most of the new chances brought by victory. The rank and file of the party have to be content with less. The mass of party members are completely passive and generally have to wait for the next election to register their opinions again. The party leaders distribute the chances: the offices, the favors, and the positions of authority and power. This may be done efficiently by a few men or, in such a party system as the American, in a haphazard, informal manner with much pushing and shoving and many mutual accusations of inadequate militancy among the aspirants.

The chances, now won and distributed, should enable the chance holders to realize their political objectives. But as everyone knows there is no assurance of this by the time that victory occurs. Considering the travail, the disasters, the means, and the obligations that have littered the career of the party marching towards power, it is too much to expect that at the end of it all, the conquerors will dispense only the pure milk and honey of altruism. We need not, however, change our definition of the party so as to say that the personal advantages necessarily outweigh objective aims in the minds of its adherents. That remains to be studied in the case of any particular party.

THE GUIDING THEMES OF PARTY LIFE

Within broad limits, political parties are established around some guiding theme. Members of a party, when called upon to explain their actions, will give reasons. They will say they are working for a leader, or for a cause, or for a class. The facts may disprove their stated motives, of course. It may turn out that a man who claims he is working for a cause is really working because he expects to get a good job in the government if his party wins. Still, perhaps the most useful classification of parties, as suggested by Bluntschli and Michels, may be one that is based on the preponderant motivation of the active members of a party.

Using such a criterion for classifying parties, we would arrive at six significant themes: *nationalism, political and moral issues, socio-economic class, charismatic or personal leadership, religion, and elitism.* Although it tends to condition much of the party's behavior, the guiding theme of a party does not exclude the presence of other themes—one may find individuals in every party whose guiding motives correspond to any one of the six themes. Thus, in the American Democratic Party, one finds enthusiasts for Puerto Rican independence, economic reforms, the working class, the charms of an F. D. R. or a Huey Long, the beliefs of the Catholic Church, and the permanent elimination of the Republican opposition. On the whole, however, one influence predominates and gives a certain character to a party.

NATIONALISTIC PARTIES

The principle on which nationalistic parties are based is the desire for independent statehood. A minority within a larger realm conducts a campaign for self-government. The former Irish Nationalist Party agitated against the British for a free and united Ireland, often openly and at other times in the shadow of police repression. The German Sudeten Party, in close co-operation with the German state, played a part in the sabotage of the Czechoslovak state; first demanding merely autonomy, it finally insisted upon and won separation from Czechoslovakia and incorporation in the Greater Reich by the Munich Pact of 1938. The Far East, after World War I, saw the birth of several nationalistic parties in the Philippines, Burma, Indo-China, Indonesia, India, and elsewhere.

The end of World War II found nationalistic parties in Southeast Asia ready to take control of independent governments. Partly by peaceable means and partly by violence, the transformation of former colonies into nation-states was accomplished. Perhaps the most notable of the nationalistic parties of Asia is the Congress Party of India. It developed under British rule, partly in defiance of the authorities, and when the British withdrew from India it constituted the only effective governing group. The Congress Party included all shades of opinion before the attainment of independence and, even afterwards, maintained a one-party domination of the government under the leadership of Gandhi and, after Gandhi's assassination, Jawaharlal Nehru. From a nationalistic party, it has evolved into a kind of giant holding company for all sorts of political and moral ideas short of communism. In 1951, however, opponents of Nehru broke away from the Congress Party to form the first opposition party.

The mandate of Palestine, before it became the state of Israel, presented a contrast to the Indian condition. The nationalistic parties that formed the provisional government when the British left Palestine had developed out of the British mandatory government's offices and from the co-operative-labor organizations, especially the Histadrut. Most of the members of the first cabinet held triple membership in the Jewish Agency Office, the Histadrut, and the Zionist movement; and they formed the leadership of the Mapai and Mapa parties. Several smaller parties soon took the field as well. Unlike several of the Asiatic countries, Israel's party system quickly took on the appearance of the multiparty system that prevailed in western Europe.

Parties Founded on Nonbasic Issues

PARTIES INSPIRED BY POLITICAL AND MORAL IDEAS

A second guiding theme of political parties may be a program of doctrines and principles. One variety is the constitutional party, which is based on a preference for a particular form of government. Examples of this kind would be the many monarchist, republican, and unitary (for example, Pan-Slavic, Pan-German, antiregional) parties of nineteenth-century Europe. The States' Rights Party that broke off from the American Democratic Party in the 1948 presidential elections would be another example. A second variety of the party of ideas would be the party that is organized on behalf of specific issues. Perhaps the classic model of this type was the British Liberal Party, which stood for free trade and other economic principles for over a century. Another example might be the French Radical Socialist Party, which has been neither radical nor socialist and has shifted its positions on issues many times within the century. The loose alignment of center and progressive parties in France after World War II, known as the Third Force, has the same general character. The Third Force is alleged to be neither right nor left, but down the "middle."

A third variety of the party of ideas would be the two-party system of the "ins" and the "outs," as it is found in the United States. One party operates as the government, and the other party acts as the critical opposition. We may do well to discuss at some length the American party system, with particular reference to four of its principal features: the two-party pattern, its decentralization, its political machines, and its heterogeneity.

THE AMERICAN TWO-PARTY SYSTEM

One notes throughout American history a tendency towards a two-party system. Over the last century, the Democratic and Republican Parties have dominated the national political arena, except for minor and transient trespasses by Populists and Progressives. For a few years before the Civil War, several parties contested for national pre-eminence, but before that time, we find that two parties also prevailed.

It is by no means clear what caused this bipartisanship; but there is no necessary connection between bipartisanship and democracy. Other countries that may be termed as democratic as America have had several parties—Switzerland and Norway, for example; and the two-party system has often occurred in nondemocratic forms of government. Eighteenth-century England, with its Whigs and Tories, could better be called an oligarchy than a democracy. And several South American republics that have shown an equal affinity for bullets and ballots have had only two parties.

We may also exclude the degree of complexity of a society as a factor explaining the development of a two-party system. Both rural America of the early nineteenth century and diversified America of the twentieth century seem to have favored the two-party system. Industrialized Germany has had several parties, whereas industrialized England has fostered two parties. Furthermore, industrialized Germany received warmly a one-party system under the Nazis, Soviet Russia a one-party system under the Communists, and agricultural India a liberal one-party system under the Congress Party.

Perhaps we are incorrect in seeking the origins of bipartisanship in such basic social factors as a democratic way of life or economic organization. We may do better if we seek the explanation of the two-party system in more limited structural and psychological conditions.

STRUCTURAL SUPPORTS OF TWO PARTIES

The structural or legal conditions are fairly clear. The prize office of American party politics is the Presidency. In order to capture the Presidency a party must capture a majority of the electoral votes or else face the difficult task, if no one gets a majority, of controlling a majority of the state delegations in the House of Representatives. This feat requires that the parties expand their ranks at any cost in order to solicit successfully the electoral vote of as many states as are necessary to obtain the majority.

Now this pressure to expand, in other party systems of the world, would be balked by the intensity of convictions of some groups of politicans. They would refuse to share the same roof with men of contrary principles. But in America, politics are so decentralized, the state parties are so independent and isolated, that uniting to elect the President does not throw politicans of contrary principles together forever and irrevocably. They can remain aloof from their brethren both in victory and in defeat. Thus the lure of the Presidency combines with the comfortable autonomy of the state party to establish a condition in which a majority and minority party are the most compatible arrangement of national politics.

In addition to this major legal condition there are other legal supports of the two-party system. The general employment of single-member districts in elections discourages any small party that has no hope of quickly achieving a majority or plurality of all the votes cast in the district. (Proportional representation would assure the small party of at least some representation in a legislature.) Furthermore, the two major parties have for generations piled one legal difficulty upon another to prevent minor parties from arising. In some states it is almost impossible for third parties to get a place on the ballot, and the participation of the two major parties by law in the administration of elections gives the parties ample opportunity to discourage dissident voters and opposition candidates. This second kind of legal hold possessed by the major parties can be broken in only one way—a faction of a major party must desert the main body and gain control of particular localities, as occurred in certain Southern states in 1948 when the States' Rights Democrats revolted against the Truman Democrats.

TWO-PARTY PSYCHOLOGY

Certain psychological influences, historically imparted, add their weight to the maintainence of the two-party system. The American colonists were familiar with the "ins" and "outs" system of old

England. To change it in the new republic would have required break-ing a habit. Moreover, a host of colonial governmental structures, too numerous and detailed to list, depended implicitly on the politics of the government party and the opposition. For example, old parlia-mentary rule-books could be adapted easily to colonial needs, whereas many new rules of procedure would have had to be devised for a multiparty system. Today, a hundred and fifty years of perpetuated customs have done their work—Americans are not likely to be per-suaded by proposals for a multiparty system.

Another psychological force, present in America from its beginning, also bolsters these customs. This is the popular belief in the majority. Call it the will of the people, or the mandate of the voters, or the general will, or something else; in essence, it is the satisfaction felt when most people seem to be behind a government and the sense of insecurity, even of shame, felt when a government has to operate without most people at least *seeming* to be behind it. Consequently, the programs of both the Democratic and Republican parties veer more towards each other than they veer apart. There are far more cases on record of Democrats and Republicans, or Democrats and Whigs, edging closer to one another on the same vaguely defined platform than there are cases of the Democrats and Republicans moving toward the programs of third parties. The major parties, leaders and followers alike, monopolize each other's attention.

Both the law and the psychology of the two-party system have been rationalized to the satisfaction of the great majority of people. The two-party system has been declared on countless occasions to be the most simple, the most workable, the most democratic, the most com-patible with American institutions of all party systems. Thus to the effect of the laws, of habit, and of the belief in the majority, must be added the effect of political education over several generations on the advantages of the two-party system.

DECENTRALIZATION OF AMERICAN PARTIES

We will now discuss the second notable feature of the American party system: its decentralization. This is of two types: a lack of power at the top of the national party to control the state and local branches of the party; and a lack of central direction or integra-tion of party efforts at the national, state, and (often) local levels. These two types of decentralization shape the general structure of the party. The accompanying internal phenomena are a lack of party discipline and a lack of party program.

HOW THE NATIONAL VOTE GOES

However, before analyzing these phenomena, we should summarize the distribution of party strength as it varies from election to election. As Figure 19 shows, the strength of the two major parties

FIGURE 19

THE POPULAR VOTE IN PRESIDENTIAL ELECTIONS SINCE 1912

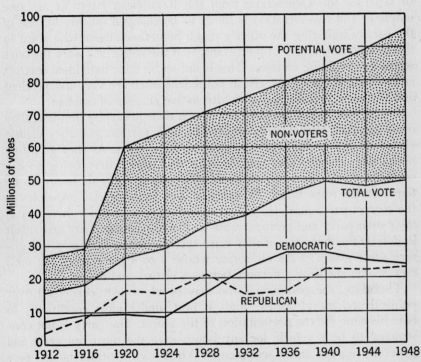

is distributed rather evenly over the population of the *nation as a whole*. In relation to the total popular vote, the parties are well matched. The gaining of a million or two million votes out of forty-eight millions may well spell the difference between victory and defeat in a national election.

This close national competition is the more remarkable when we see how unbalanced the parties are in the several states. The Republican Party hardly exists in most of the South. The Democrats usually carry the border states of Kentucky, Tennessee, West Virginia, Oklahoma, and Maryland by comfortable majorities. The Western states shift their alignment frequently. The Midwest, New England, and the East are solidly Republican in the rural areas and Democratic in the cities.

THE POLITICIAN AND ISSUES

This close competition has a reinforcing influence on the phenomena mentioned earlier, the lack of a party program and the lack of party discipline. Only the narrowest and vaguest of principles seem to separate the Democratic from the Republican Party at any one moment, and this situation is likely to be changed quickly by one of the parties imitating the other's stand. Sometimes those who point to this fact become angry at politicians, as if the politicians were the ones who were avoiding an issue. This is not so; in their individual conduct and private opinions, American politicians often are very independent and seriously preoccupied with alternative courses of conduct.

But, if such politicians want to convert their principles into law, they must combine with kindred spirits in both parties, and they cannot very well expect their party to espouse their issues. As they go into a political campaign, they must realize that, their party being so decentralized, all sorts of politicians disagreeing with them are to be found on the same ticket. To proclaim one set of precise principles as the correct party platform will arouse the anger of other members of their own party and perhaps cause a split within the party and result in defeat. Furthermore, if they raise specific issues, they may antagonize some group of the electorate whose 3 or 4 per cent of the total vote would spell the difference between victory and defeat.

Therefore, the politician—who may be vigorously concerned over political and moral issues—finds it best, under most conditions, to bide his time for the presentation of the issues. The party is not constructed to be a vehicle for any issues save the most universal and generally agreed upon sentiments. When such sentiments are perceived to exist, usually the managers of both parties are able to recognize that the issue may now safely be proclaimed.

If we conclude, then, that the party cannot afford to espouse specific principles "prematurely" without threatening its own internal disintegration and the dissolution of its popular following, we must ask how the party *does* go about keeping itself together. First of all, bowing to the inevitable, the party allows its individual members to espouse issues in their own districts. Thus we have the typical phenomenon of a politician apologizing to his constituents because his party did not support a particular bill that he had been arguing for, and promising them to continue his efforts. Fortunately for him, his opponent is likely to be getting no greater support from his party on similar problems. A Chicago Democrat will be elected on issues that a Mississippi Democrat shuns, and a Chicago Republican running for the State Senate will believe in different principles than a Republican State Senator from "downstate."

THE ORGANIZATION OF THE PARTY SYSTEM

But the program of the party in the American system is not as important for maintaining the party as is its organization, which is motivated mainly by friendship, favors, and patronage. The party must trust to a vague program of "glittering generalities" to attract some part of the electorate, and get down to the endless day-to-day task of building a huge number of individual connections.

The national organization of both parties is relatively primitive. The party that controls the Presidency has certain advantages. The President can surround himself with a certain number of loyal supporters in top positions of the government, and the various perquisites of his job allow him to do many more individual favors for important and influential people in the national community than the opposition party can do. But beyond his patronage of a few hundred appointments and a chance to help some thousands of individuals directly, the President runs into the feudal structure of American politics and is prevented from consolidating his position as the leader of an integrated and centralized party.

Apart from the Presidency, the "in" and the "out" party are in much the same loose condition of organization. Each has a national committee composed of party representatives from each of the states; its task is to tie together the forty-eight autonomous party domains in national campaigns and on national issues. In recent years, the committees have maintained a small permanent staff of organizers, publicity men, fund gatherers, and research clerks to keep the party's case before the people continuously. The committees perform also a liaison function between the President and the party in Washington and the state parties, or between the presidential nominee and the state parties.

CONGRESS HAS STRONG LOCAL INTERESTS

It is not easy to place the congressmen as a group in the party system. Senators and representatives are elected from different states and districts, and in that sense are *local* representatives. But the great majority of congressmen are local representatives in another sense also. They are the "delegates" of state party organizations.

They will co-operate sometimes with their national party leader, but will not go against their states' interests. Some congressmen are really administration supporters; they will go down the line for the President's program. Most of the latter come from districts that are closely contested in each election, such as a number of the metropolitan districts. In these areas, which are more closely tied to national interests than to local interests and where the independent vote is eagerly solicited by both parties, joining forces with the President is often more effective politics than following the views of the local politicians.

In general, however, the national Congress has a local character. Whereas in England, for example, one sometimes gets the impression that the members of Parliament are Londoners who deign to visit the provincials who elect them, in America one senses that the congressmen are provincials who deign to visit Washington. A congressman in Washington will have a retinue of people from "back home," and hundreds of constituents from his state or district will come to him from time to time with requests for information about and help in connection with the great agencies of the government. There is no strong national *party* spirit among these legislators. Just as, legally speaking, the national leaders cannot control the state parties, sociologically speaking, the national leaders for the most part cannot comprehend a truly national party. Whatever goods are parceled out by the national party are divided forty-eight ways or among the several states according to population. There is little thought, except when the President brings up the matter or when some money is to be given out by the national party, that the total resources of manpower, locally gathered money, and most appointments should be under central direction or devoted to victory in the crucial districts that determine which party shall gain control of Congress and the Presidency or reserved to insure the election of key leaders of the party.

INTEGRATED STATE ORGANIZATIONS POSSIBLE

Integrated national parties have never existed in America. Perhaps Mark Hanna came closest to organizing a truly national party for the Republicans in the nineties. But integrated state parties have existed under the leadership of certain men—for examples, we need think only of names like Huey Long in Louisiana, Vare in Pennsylvania, Horner in Illinois, or Dewey in New York. The state is the legal unit for purposes of general party-organization. State statutes govern the pattern of organization, and, once a powerful group can find a means of mutual co-operation among its members, it can operate on a statewide basis.

Two general kinds of state party-organizations in America are worth notice. One is the bureaucratic organization or the state party machine. The other is the personal faction. At one extreme, in states like Pennsylvania and Illinois, the parties are organized, integrated, and continuing bodies. At the other extreme, in states like Nevada and Louisiana, the parties are shifting, transient, and personally led combinations. The organized state party ordinarily has a semiprofessional governing group within the party itself. These people have a definite personal stake in the success of the party. The bulk of the members of the organization are officeholders, although as one moves to the top of the national and state parties, he finds that the leaders tend to have other occupations as well as political ones—they may be lawyers, businessmen, or manufacturers. Down at the grass roots, on the other hand, most of the faithful and persistent workers hold public jobs.

THE PARTY MACHINES

As often as not, however, the state party and its central executive committee do not control the cities. In a good number of the cities, one finds the political machine par excellence, the machine that foreign observers and many Americans exaggeratedly regard as typical of all American politics. The political machine of the city is a bureaucratic organization; it has a full complement of permanent and professional workers, a hierarchy much like that of a government bureau or an army division, and an elaborate system of rewards (including promotions), punishments, and activities. It is composed of managers and runners for office; the top leader may or may not be an elected official. Thus the chief or boss may be the mayor, as were Mayor Hague of Jersey City or Mayor Thompson of Chicago; or he may be a metropolitan county chairman of the party, as was County Chairman Arvey of Cook County in Illinois. The subchiefs may hold positions such as county sheriffs, party district leaders, ward committeemen, aldermen, or city attorneys.

THE PRECINCT CAPTAINS

The rank and file of the well-organized city machine is composed of the precinct captains or precinct committeemen, as they are sometimes called. A party will have hundreds of precinct captains to staff the many polling districts of the city. Without the precinct captains, an organization cannot move, and the man who controls the precinct captains controls the whole party system. A large number of precinct captains hold public office in return for their services. Others have no personal interest but are fascinated by the great game of politics. Still others have received some privilege or favor from their political leaders or have special business interests that they can protect by actively engaging in politics. Thus one finds tavern owners, rooming-house keepers, real-estate men, and lawyers holding posts as precinct captains to facilitate agreeable relationships with the various agencies of the local government.

Various surveys made in recent years show that precinct captains are the prime instrument for administering the party's *mediation function*. The precinct captains of a city like New York or San Francisco will perform thousands of individual favors, most of them quite legal, within a single year. A large proportion of these favors are interventions by the party on behalf of a person who is having some difficulty with one of the various governments. The party depends upon the captains strongly for maintaining a wide network of favorable connections among people of all kinds.

The nature of much of the party's work as a mediator between individuals and a sometimes adamant and threatening government is apparent when we look at some of the social developments that have occurred since the heyday of the city machines in the late nineteenth and early twentieth centuries. A new profession of social service has grown up and numbers many thousands of workers. Extensive social security measures have been enacted providing institutionalized services of many kinds—to the old and the young, to the unemployed, to widows, to the poor, and to the sick. The precinct captain, who used to be a general practitioner on problems of human relations, has been replaced or at least supplemented by specialists of all kinds, working under distant auspices and regularized laws. The city machine, it turns out, has fallen victim to the bureaucratization of social services and full employment.

HETEROGENEITY OF AMERICAN PARTIES

Both in the country as a whole and in most localities, each party contains all types of leaders and followers. At the core of the political party is a central group of active leaders, an inner circle that directs the whole group. Next, outside of this nucleus, comes a much larger outer circle of those who take a lively and practical interest in politics and are, one might say, the rank and file of party workers. Then comes a wider circle of those who are strongly partisan and can hardly be shaken from their party affiliations by any sort of issue or economic condition. After this group would come another circle composed of those who habitually follow a particular party, but who on occasion will stop short and vote for another party. These circles shade off into groups of voters who are largely independent of party affiliation and who move freely from one party to another, depending on their feelings at the particular time an election is held.

Many of the individuals in all of these circles are organized into a variety of groups—nationality groups, unions, trade associations, women's clubs, reform organizations, and the like. While some people operate in politics as individuals, many others—probably just as many —operate through the group or by representing the group to which they belong. The party is a mixed mass of persons who have traditions, tendencies, habits, or principles that make them Republicans, or Democrats, or sometimes insurgent members of third parties.

The party leader, or politician, in America, if he is more than local in influence listens to the electorate as the expert musician to a chord struck by a great symphony. He can hear it as one meaningful voice with a given tendency; but he also can hear the many individual voices. Sometimes, like the ordinary symphonic listener, he can hear only the whole chord and must guess at the parts. At other times, he can hear only the flutes or the timpani and has no perception of the total chord.

PARTY DIFFERENCES AS SEEN BY POLITICIANS

Whereas the unsophisticated observer of the two American parties sees no differences save in name, the expert politician perceives a number of rather fine distinctions among those on whose votes the Democrats and Republicans may depend strongly. He knows, for example, and political scientists have verified his experienced guesses, that north of the Mason-Dixon Line Republicanism tends to be more widespread among Protestants, the well-educated and the well-to-do. He knows that recent immigrants tend to vote for Democratic rather than Republican candidates. He knows that the press represents for the most part a Republican bias. He knows that organized labor is more strongly Democratic than unorganized labor. He knows that business interests, especially finance and manufacturing, are strongly Republican, but that liquor and entertainment interests are more inclined to be Democratic. Real estate groups, commonly divided among the parties locally, tend to support the Republican Party nationally. Yet so fine are most of these distinctions that a campaign can scarcely be based on them. The heterogeneity of the party following, like the heterogeneity of the party leadership, throws the individual politicians back on the reliable techniques of friendship, favors, and patronage.

Class and Charismatic Parties

CLASS PARTIES

Parties having class as a guiding theme include various socialist, labor, and agrarian parties that believe in a fundamental class conflict that can be resolved only by the victory of some major class-interest. The socialist parties everywhere fall into this category. A notably successful class party is the English Labour Party. It deserves our close attention. Three of its characteristics are especially important: its stout presentation of significant issues, its tight integration, and its strong leadership.

THE ENGLISH LABOUR PARTY

The English party system, like the American, contains two major parties. They are the Conservative, or Union, Party and the Labour Party. The Liberal Party, one of the two great English parties of the nineteenth century, no longer holds a firm grasp on a huge party following. It began to decline in the late nineteenth century, and is now only a minor influence in the party struggle for power. The Labour Party won its first decisive parliamentary majority and consequent mastery of the government in 1945, shortly after the end of the war in Europe.

STRIKING ISSUES RAISED

The Labour Party, unlike either of the two major American parties, is based on economic and social class-issues. Aside from the monarchy, which remains unchallenged in political campaigns, the whole structure of British economy and society is subject to controversy in politics. The Labour Party traces its origins to the growth of the labor unions and to the socialist theories of British intellectuals and labor leaders in the late nineteenth century. The party has always advocated socialization of the means of production and an equalization of individual opportunity for education, medical care, old-age security, legal justice, and private and public employment. Once its power over the Commons was achieved, it set to work immediately on its program and with little difficulty nationalized large and important elements of British industry such as the mines, transportation, gas, and electricity;

it also established national health-services for all, charging part of the costs to the government.

SOCIAL COMPOSITION OF LABOUR PARTY

The main influence on the Labour Party is the trade-union idea. It is, one might say, the premise from which only minor deviations in party activity are possible. This leads to conservative, reformist socialism, with the biases and habits of trade unionists predominant. It leads also to a strong pressure for immediately beneficial changes in the conditions of organized labor, especially in working conditions, hours of work, and rates of pay. Deviant pressures come from the intellectuals of the universities, professions, and the press, who are inclined to view socialism more broadly and internationally. The "marginal voter" assumes some importance too, for the success of the Labour Party in national elections depends to a vital extent on voters who have no immediate desire or pressure operating on them to follow the Labour Party. Fifty per cent of the total electorate, after all, may not be a permanent percentage; many "independents" are among them. They are responsible for the wide appeals put out to the British public in Labour Party propaganda and perform a function not unlike that performed by the independent voters in America, though the former are weaker and less effective.

PARTY INTEGRATION AND CENTRALIZATION ARE STRONG

The Labour Party is integrated and centralized. Members of the House of Commons and candidates for office are much more responsible to the leaders of the party for their party behavior than are most American legislators. The force of the party program is so great and the leadership of the party so securely in control that the individual member in the constituency is carried along, prodded, and disciplined. The personal ambitions of the individual party-member are rather well channeled along party lines. He may hope for advancement, but that depends on his maneuvering within the party framework. He may want more income, but that is not acquired easily and through outside connections, as it is in America. He looks to the party for immediate honors and must depend upon it to get ultimate recognition by the state as a whole. Therefore, in his politics the English politician gives the impression of being more earnest, hard-working, single-minded, public-welfare-conscious and informed on state affairs than the American legislator, who, so to speak, "scatters his shots" over a wide range of interests, occupations, groups, and private affairs.

What keeps the Labour Party candidates and members of Parliament in line? What explains the integration and centralization? To say that England is a small country and thus tends to allow easy centralization may be partly true, but still England has been until recent decades one of the most decentralized nations, politically and administratively, in the world. The centralization of the Labour Party can be traced back to the organization of the working class as a whole. Trades unions came and then came the trades unions' party. The already bureaucratically constructed unions influenced the party structure. Other parties in England and elsewhere, both from external and internal causes, have shared these characteristics of centralization and integration, but not nearly to the same extent as the Labour Party.

THE LABOUR PARTY CONFERENCE

A great part of the voters who vote for Labour candidates also belong to labor or co-operative organizations that themselves are forceful groups in politics through their resources, skilled leadership, and permanent dedication to public activity. The trades unions (ranging from the more to the less member-controlled) joined hands in England with groups of intellectuals and nonlaboring orators, writers and organizers; they also joined hands with certain co-operative societies (also more or less democratically organized) and with purely local political organizations (their members impelled by a wide variety of motivations) to produce a general organization that today constitutes the Labour Party Conference. It meets annually to prepare a program (already, however, drawn up to a large extent by the leadership of the party), to discuss party organization, and to elect the central National Executive Committee.

The National Executive Committee of twenty-five members, twelve of whom come directly from the trades unions, operates continuously. It is the heart of the organizing and active force of the Labour Party. It tends to control party policy. It controls the central headquarters of the party organization and helps greatly in the local campaigns. It must approve all Labour Party candidates, and it can expel dissident individuals or organizations.

THE PARLIAMENTARY LABOUR PARTY

The Parliamentary Labour Party is composed of the members of Parliament who have been elected on the Labour Party ticket.

When it commands a majority of the Parliament, its leaders are appointed to the Cabinet. The Prime Minister of England, though legally appointed by the King, is in fact the chief of the parliamentary majority party. Also, legally, the Prime Minister and his Cabinet are chosen by their victorious party colleagues in the Parliament. But the Labour members are already part of a large and integrated organization when they come to perform this public duty. Therefore it cannot be expected that the choice of these men is a popularity contest decided on the spur of the moment. They are well-known beforehand. Some modifications in the cabinet choices are perhaps made; some discussion and advice are heard. But the Labour Party moves inexorably as a permanent organization; the weight of the parliamentary party leaders is felt; the influence of the Executive Committee of the Labour Party Conference is strong; individual eccentricities may be viewed with indulgence, but they are not rewarded.

CHARISMATIC PARTIES

Charismatic parties are founded on the personal qualities of some great leader who may be himself the exponent of some class or nationality. But the party members do not bother with much of a program; they rely primarily on the leader to produce good through his personality. He has a mission in which they believe firmly. Thus between 1863 and 1875 in Germany the socialists under Lassalle were distinct from the other Marxists and followed wherever he led. In France before World War II the Blanquists, the Guesdists and the Juaresists subscribed to the deviations of their leaders from the central tendency of socialism.

In Italy, the party of Mussolini was a personal party. The Duce's charisma convinced the *Fascisti* that he could not fail, that his will ought to be followed blindly, and that no precision in program ought to bind him. He was free to do what he wished as the leader of the party. He was identified with Italy, with the party, and with the party membership. The whole arrangement rested on his personality, not on his program. So it was with Hitler and the National Socialists of Germany.

DE GAULLE AND FRANCE

A prominent charismatic party of the post-World War II period sprang up as the *Rassemblement du peuple Français* (or R.P.F.). This party was formed by General Charles de Gaulle in early 1947. It was called by James Burnham (the prophet of the "managerial revolution") the "first genuinely new political reality since Hitler." However, to the other parties in France it seemed to be the old phenomenon of the "man on horseback." The Communist Party of France referred to it as neo-Fascism, and to de Gaulle as the "mouthpiece of reaction," and a large number of the leaders of the "Third Force," the coalition of the older parties, regarded it as destructive of parliamentarism or even of democracy itself.

The new party or movement, for it was really a combination of both, came on the French political scene after General de Gaulle had emerged from a self-imposed retirement from the Presidency of the Republic. During his retirement he had planned and organized his new movement. Six months after the R.P.F. was organized, it took 33.1 per cent of the votes for municipal officers; this percentage would be greater if coalition votes joining an R.P.F. candidate with other party labels were counted. In the elections of June 1951, the R.P.F. obtained the biggest single bloc of seats in the National Assembly.

The R.P.F. derived a great part of its *raison d'être* from a belief in the personal qualities and mission of General de Gaulle. The belief of his followers was reinforced by the remarkable success he had had in leading a small group of resistance fighters against the Germans when the legitimate authorities of France had surrendered in 1940, thereby becoming recognized in the eyes of the non-French and French worlds as the symbol of France. The General's abstemious, religious, and mystic personality impressed many. He was intensely patriotic, held factionalism in horror, and believed in the future of France as spiritual and political leader of Europe.

WHEN A PARTY IS NO PARTY

One indication that the R.P.F. was charismatic lay in the denial by its leaders that it was a party. "We are not just one more party," exclaimed de Gaulle. The R.P.F. disdained to present an economic program to the nation. One of de Gaulle's closest advisers, the novelist André Malraux, declared: "What de Gaullism stands for, first of all, is the restoration of a structure and vigor to France. . . . We have declared that the party system in France, as it functions at the present time, is in no condition to take measures for the public welfare." Malraux further said: "We maintained from the beginning: 'We have no faith in programs, but only in objectives. Let us define our objectives one after another, reach them as fast as possible, and then go on to what follows. To put it another way, let's begin by doing what we say.' You can imagine how annoying this is to the program mongers."

A DECISIVE GOVERNMENT DEMANDED

De Gaulle himself advocated a thorough revision of the structure of the Fourth Republic to allow for greater permanency of leadership, the strengthening of the executive branch, and the exclusion of the Communist Party from any part in the government. In announcing the aims of the new movement, de Gaulle declared, "To move towards its right goals, the nation must be guided by a government that is coherent, orderly, capable of choosing and applying directly those measures imperatively required for the public safety. The present system, by which rigid and conflicting parties divide all powers, must be replaced by another wherein the executive power follows the country rather than the parties and where all insoluble conflict may be resolved by the people itself." Although careful at first to avoid an outright demand to outlaw the Communist Party, the idea of outlawry was undoubtedly implicit in his thinking.

R.P.F.'S THREAT TO THE COMMUNISTS

The appeal of this personal party, which utilized symbols of patriotism, unity, religion, family integrity, and camaraderie, was strong. Suffused with enthusiasm and ostensibly possessed of direction, it posed a threat to the other parties of the state that did not go unrecognized. The reaction of the older liberal parties and the Communist Party was intense and continuous. A personal or charismatic party is one type of non-Communist party that has been able to compete with the appeal of Marxian dogma and discipline. For under a "leader," as under a Duce or Fuhrer, individuals regarded by traditional "issue" or "class" politicians as wholly antagonistic or at least dissimilar seem to be able to group together in a powerful political combination. Thus, among the de Gaullists, one finds radical intellectuals, Catholic clerics, conservative businessmen, middle-class government workers and clerks, professional soldiers and ex-soldiers, opportunistic politicians, and generally some of the most active of the non-Communist youth. A heavy R.P.F. vote came from the rural areas and towns, from the Catholic and conservative portions of France, and from the middle-class urban residential areas.

Religious and Elite Parties

RELIGIOUS PARTIES

Examples of parties whose main theme is religion would be the early Belgian Catholic Party and the German Center Party. In general, the Democratic Christian Parties found under various names in Italy, France, Germany, Belgium, and elsewhere after World War II were strongly motivated by religious zeal and an antipathy towards atheistic communism. They seemed to be the most likely competitors of the charismatic (for example, de Gaulle's R.P.F.) and elite (Communist) parties of postwar Europe.

WHENCE COME THE NEW RELIGIOUS PARTIES?

One may ask: "How could a political sentiment that was rather weak in prewar times achieve such dominance after the war?" There are several reasons. For one thing, the bipolarization of the world into American and Soviet groups required that some party rise up and become a center of anti-Communist or non-Communist activity. For once, an external force appeared ready and willing to support such an idea. That was the United States, which gave encouragement, vast gifts of food and machinery, and treaties of alliance to the non-Communist parties of western Europe. This was a novel event. Never before had nondestructive parties been able to get democratic support on a large scale. The effect was evident in the increased courage, enthusiasm, and decisiveness with which the new parties went about their work.

Another reason for the rise of religious parties is that parties of the extreme right—that is, nationalist and totalitarian parties—were repudiated during the war both by the victorious nations and by the conquered or liberated peoples. Also, general changes had taken place in the economic and social life of Europe, making a rigid defense of the capitalistic *status quo* a practical impossibility in democratic politics. Progressive reforms had to be promised. Furthermore, both Catholic and Protestant religious groups felt increasingly fearful that if the Communists came to power, religion would be subjected to rigorous state control or eradication.

Corresponding to this feeling among churchmen and active religious adherents was an impression that spread widely among nonadherents. Social order and peace were deemed preferable to rationalistic insistence on the secular, materialistic aims of the nineteenth-century democratic movements. In other words, the idea of believing the state could do everything well and right declined in force and acceptance. There remained a mixture of conservatism, pessimism, and antimaterialism.

THE ITALIAN CHRISTIAN-DEMOCRATS

To illustrate our points about the religious parties, let us take the Christian-Democratic Party of Italy. This party began as one of a number of parties contending for power in the first postwar elections in Italy. An acceleration of the influence of the factors listed in the above paragraph, together with skillful leadership and improved organization, gave it victory in the highly important elections of April 1948. The Christian-Democrats, under Premier Alcide De Gasperi, won 53.3 per cent of the seats in the Chamber and 43 per cent of those in the Senate. The Communists and part of the Socialists united in a "Popular Democratic Front" and won 31.8 per cent of the Chamber and 31.7 per cent of the Senate. De Gasperi's strength was not great enough to govern comfortably, and he formed a coalition cabinet with progressive and conservative elements in it. Although his party lost some ground in elections held subsequently, he continued as Premier of a coalition government.

IMPELLING PARTY MOTIVATION

The Christian-Democratic Party is not based on issues— although it expounds issues and professes a program of reform; it is not a "class" party nor a charismatic party. It has neither dogma nor prophets. It is held together basically by a conviction that, since other absolute solutions to social problems—Fascist or Communist—are intolerable, there remains only a course of exploiting the "civilized virtues" of European liberal conservatism together with piecemeal reform. Guiseppe Glisenti, a Christian-Democrat, described in 1948 "the different psychological structure of the two political forces."

> On the one hand, the CD (*Christian-Democratic Party*), whose members, even though active and though they are propagandists, have a vision of the world that inclines them to seek the composing of human differences rather than a struggle for the undisputed victory of their own ideas; men who, the surer they are in their doctrine and the more apostolic in their life, the more they seek that pacification, that balance and that wisdom which excludes extremes in any action, even in the necessary struggle. On the other hand the PCI (*Partito Communista Italiano*), whose members, especially party workers—all the more so when they are "sincere"—are permeated with the conviction that they must overturn a mistaken world. They can accept no halfway stage, no truce and no intermediate position between the actual world and the world in which they believe. While for us there is a better world and a less good world, and in any case an improvable world, for them there is always an unacceptable world until the day of the perfect world.

The Catholic Church, while eschewing overt and official favoritism for the C.D., has openly avowed its hostility to the Communist Party and its collaborators and has urged *united* support of anticommunism.

In a multiparty country where the only unity might come from the strongest progressive party, that is, the C.D., this was tantamount to throwing the Church's weight on the side of the C.D. Consequently, the C.D. derived some strength from Catholic "Civic Assemblies" organized locally, and benefited from a wide network of local organizations of the *Azione Cattolica* (Catholic Action).

Because of the pulling and tugging of regional interests, always strong in Italy, the party cannot maintain a doctrinaire position. To retain its quasi-majority, it must organize locally and produce "machines," and we find this urge to organization strongly voiced in party circles as the condition for survival. Of the alternative bases for establishing machines—fanatic dogma (as with the Communist Party), patronage and favors, a long period of rule with honors and habit adding their forces, or auxiliary organizations—at present only the fourth is possible for the C.D. And, although the party is increasing its influence in labor unions, its real dependence here is on the hierarchy and membership of the Catholic Church. Meanwhile the Communist Party, with its class appeals, picks up readily a solid mass of support from the industrial workers and tenant farmers. It need only defend its position among these voters and perhaps extend it a little.

Temporarily, something much like a two-party system, with the Christian-Democrats dominating, came to a multiparty country. The permanence of this situation depended on the C.D.'s maintaining co-operative rather than dependent relations with the Church (for many of its supporters are suspicious of clerical politics), on the continued material and moral support of the United States, and on the wooing of secular organizations such as labor unions from the revolutionary or socialist fold.

PARTIES OF THE ELITE

Roberto Michels classified as elite parties the Fascist Party and the Soviet Communist Party. Elite parties, he wrote, defy the majority principle. They refuse to consider that they may remain forever a part of the nation rather than become the nation itself. They regard the idea of elections as abominable, but are fond of plebiscites. Yet, existing in an age when the idea prevails that the whole body of the people should be active in government, they oscillate between trying to represent the whole people and insisting on the special capacity and right of a few to rule.

THE SOVIET COMMUNIST PARTY

Like the former Italian Fascist Party, the former German National Socialist Party, and like the present Spanish Falange, the Communist Party in the Soviet Union established itself as the only

FIGURE 20

THE SOVIET GOVERNMENT AND THE COMMUNIST PARTY *

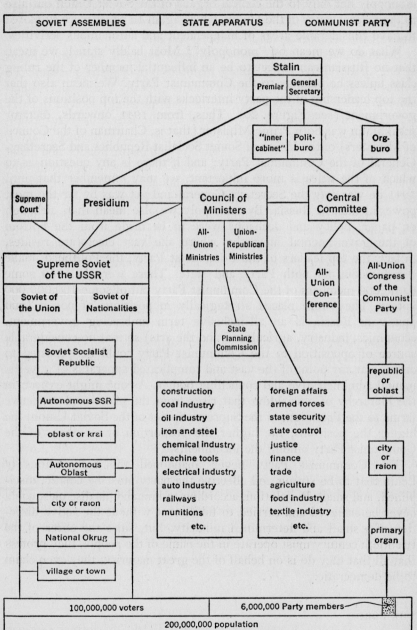

* Reproduced with permission from "The Government of the Soviet Union," Harper and Thompson, D. Van Nostrand Company, Inc., 1949.

party in a one-party state. It monopolized the controlling positions in government despite the fact that on paper at least the structure of the Soviet Union was democratic and representative. It extended its monopoly not only to the central organs of the Soviet Union but also to the federal states of the Union, which again on paper were supposed to have considerable areas of independent and autonomous activities.

What do we mean by "monopoly"? Most baldly stated, we mean that no Russian can expect to be an influential member of the ruling class unless he belongs to the Communist Party. We mean also that the top leadership of the party interlocks with the top positions of the government (see Figure 20). Thus, from 1941 onwards, dictator Josef Stalin was both Prime Minister (that is, Chairman of the Council of Ministers) of the Union of Soviet Socialist Republics and Secretary-General of the Communist Party; and if there is any question as to which of the titles is more important, we may remember that until 1941 he was *only* the Secretary-General and yet was by far the most powerful man in Russia. By monopoly we also mean that, although on paper, policy and decisions were to be made from the bottom of the governmental hierarchy where the vast electorate resides, in fact, the top leaders of the Communist Party, the Politburo, make the decisions for both Party and state. There were in 1949 some 6,000,000 members of the Communist Party out of some 100,000,000 voters. They were placed strategically in positions of power (and power in Russia is an all-inclusive term embracing government, economics, industry, agriculture, and the arts) so that no considerable source of opposition to the Communist Party could be expected to develop at any point of the vast and complicated apparatus of governmental administrative and counciling bodies. As one might expect, in the hierarchy of officialdom that rises from the plants and collective farms to the Presidium of the Supreme Soviet of the Soviet Union, the higher the positions, the higher the proportion of members of the Communist Party among the incumbents.

The Communist Party never abandoned the exhortations of Lenin that to be strong and effective the party must be fanatic, disciplined, and small. Revolution, according to him and his disciples, could never be achieved and carried to fulfillment without the active direction of a small and determined minority. But, since the elites of the twentieth century must operate in the name of the people, they profess that all that they do is on behalf of the great majority; they even claim to be democratic.

THE PURGE

A great contradiction therefore arises in their behavior. As the elite, the party is synonymous with the political or ruling class. For its *raison d'être* it looks to the masses. Caught in this trap, to use Michels's description of the phenomenon,

> the parties of the elite, turn by turn, swell their structures excessively up to the point of embracing nearly the whole nation and boast of their millions of political and syndical assessed members, and then suddenly contract their frames by expelling the excess, attempting to become again minority parties. . . . Between these two extreme limits, the one signalized by the indispensability of the authority of numbers, and the other fixed by the principle of homogeneity and of the strength which flows therefrom, the pendulum oscillates unceasingly.*

Thus we have the well-known purge of the elite parties of Italy, Germany and Russia. The party, subject to constant pressure from would-be joiners and from the feeling that it ought to contain a greater part of the people it directs and leads, enlarges its ranks. This enlargement slows down activity toward other objectives and, fearful of losing its missionary zeal, the party then cuts into its membership ruthlessly, declaring that the party principle must remain "pure" and that the deviants and the lazy must be eliminated. Sometimes the purge assumes an extreme form as a method of destroying internal opposition. Those in control accuse the opposition of treason and subversion of the party line and eliminate them in any way that is convenient, usually by violence, exile, or judicial condemnation.

The purge is characteristic of single-party systems where the elite is the party. In systems with two or more parties, rotation in office is the accepted means of changing leadership; most party officials come from the same social and economic strata, so that no drastic changes in the social order are brought on by electoral changes.

COMMUNIST PARTY MONOPOLIZES POLITICAL CHANCES

The functions of the Communist Party are, in line with the foregoing, to carry on the Bolshevist Revolution, to inspire and train the masses along Bolshevist principles and action, and to govern the land. Unlike the American and other parties, the Communist Party (in the Soviet Union and in its satellite countries) never has to act as the opposition; it denies that there is any need for an opposition party. Changes in policies occur as a result of the changed attitudes of the party leaders. The leaders may change the "line" or may allow a subject matter to be discussed in party circles. In the latter procedure, which the Russians like to call "democratic centralism," problems or issues are discussed freely within the party, although possible reac-

---

* Quoted with the permission of the *American Political Science Review* from Roberto Michels: "Some Reflections on the Sociological Character of Political Parties," *American Political Science Review*, Vol. XXI (1927), p. 772.

tions from above are watched for. At a point designated by the leadership, discussion is closed, and a decision is arrived at by whatever means the leadership deems desirable: by vote, party-group consensus, or leadership consensus. Once decreed, the decision cannot be challenged by the party membership or organs. It persists until the leadership decides to reopen the matter again.

SOCIAL COMPOSITION

The original ideal of the Communist Party was that it should be the instrument of the workers, and working class members were sought diligently. However, since the qualifications for party leadership (short of the stable top group) demand the same qualities of vigor, ruthlessness, dedication to duty, and organizational ability that are demanded of the people who manage industry and government, middle-party leadership and managerial leadership very often coincide. It is idle to conceive that the thousands of managers, directors, and officials who operate the government and industry are ruled by soviets composed of the factory workers who during most of the time work under them. And it is also idle to assume that the party members and leaders, who are directing the energies of the country, sit back in manual jobs, allowing or assigning nonparty members to the important and well-paying jobs in the management of industry, economy, and government.

This conclusion is inescapable from a deductive evaluation of the power structure of party and government, and from the inductive evaluation of the evidence on party membership, interlocking office-holding in party and government, and the social origins of party officials. The ruling class in both party and government is the same. The class of managers, directors, and officials runs the Soviet Union. Intellectuals are given honors and party positions, but they furnish adornment to the party, rather than leadership. Agricultural workers, even if they dwell on the collective or state farms, furnish relatively few members to the party. The armed forces contribute a much higher percentage of the total membership, and the ruling members of the party constantly strive to maintain party activity within the armed forces at a high level. Here, too, however, there has been an increasingly close identification of army leadership and party leadership. The time has passed when army officers might be checked by party political commissars; the ruling elements in the army have coalesced.

In sum, the Communist Party permeates the state and the economy. It is still a part of the whole; but it directs the whole, and it holds the formal titles, the legal positions, that are given to the chiefs of administration, industry, and the armed forces.

Oligarchic Influences and Party Trends

OLIGARCHICAL INFLUENCES IN PARTIES

Political parties, whatever may be their *raison d'être* are susceptible to certain conservative and oligarchic influences. Of course, in an age of universal suffrage, they must employ many democratic symbols and try the best they can to sound sincere. Each party invariably claims that it is the most democratic and has the welfare of the whole nation at heart.

> At election time, the *aristoi* candidates deign to descend from their mansions and to bestir themselves among the yokels in order to obtain the majority in their districts [writes Michels]. The majority parties also take care, in political elections, to address themselves not alone to their associates. In democracy everyone appeals to the people, to every one of the people, without discrimination. . . . A socialist who before the elections, and afterwards, has only a very narrow conception of what is meant by the working-class, loves, during the campaign, to stretch the theoretical extent of this class to the point of including capitalists, providing, of course, that they are not too refractory to accord to their employees, in such a case, some small wage increment.*

As Alexis de Tocqueville stated the point in his *Democracy in America* (1835): "Democratic republics extend the practice of currying favor with the many and introduce it into all classes."

Michels also describes how a party is transformed through success. Once its flush of youth has gone and its first appeals—backed by fiery intent—have echoed away into the distances, it begins to acquire a bureaucratic mien.

> From a means, organization becomes an end. To the institutions and qualities which at the outset were destined simply to ensure the good working of the party machine (subordination, the harmonious cooperation of individual members, hierarchical relationships, discretion, propriety of conduct), a greater importance comes ultimately to be attached than to the productivity of the machine. Henceforward the sole preoccupation is to avoid anything which may clog the machinery. Should the party be attacked, it will abandon valuable positions previously conquered, and will renounce ancient rights rather than reply to the enemy's offensive by methods which might 'compromise' its position. . . . We have now a finely conservative party which (since the effect survives the

*Quoted with the permission of the *American Political Science Review* from Roberto Michels: "Some Reflections on the Sociological Character of Political Parties," *American Political Science Review*, Vol. XXI (1927), pp. 762–3.

cause) continues to employ revolutionary terminology, but which in actual practice fulfills no other function than that of a constitutional opposition.*

But parties not only tend to grow bureaucratic and conservative as they grow older, they also become oligarchic. More and more of the important decisions are made by the leaders with ever more feeble, formal and informal communication with the party membership, and even less communication with the party's general following in the electorate. At the conclusion of his sociological study of the oligarchical tendencies of modern democracy, Michels summarizes his findings:

> Now, if we leave out of consideration the tendency of the leaders to organize themselves and to consolidate their interests, and if we leave also out of consideration the gratitude of the led towards their leaders, and the general immobility and passivity of the masses, we are led to conclude that the principal cause of oligarchy in the democratic parties is to be found in the technical indispensability of leadership.
>
> The process which has begun in consequence of the differentiation of functions in the party is completed by a complex of qualities which the leaders acquire through their detachment from the mass. At the outset, leaders arise *spontaneously*; their functions are *accessory* and *gratuitous*. Soon, however, they become *professional* leaders, and in this second stage of development they are *stable* and *irremovable*.
>
> It follows that the explanation of the oligarchical phenomenon which thus results is partly *psychological*; oligarchy derives, that is to say, from the psychical transformations which the leading personalities in the parties undergo in the course of their lives. But also, and still more, oligarchy depends upon what we may term the *psychology of organization itself*, that is to say, upon the tactical and technical necessities which result from the consolidation of every disciplined political aggregate. Reduced to its most concise expression, the fundamental sociological law of political parties (the term 'political' being here used in its most comprehensive significance) may be formulated in the following terms: "It is organization which gives birth to the dominion of the elected over the electors, of the mandataries over the mandators, of the delegates over the delegators. Who says organization, says oligarchy." *

If only we had figures on the duration of the oligarchic process that could be used to compare one kind of party with another, we might make greater use of Michels's concept. However, as matters stand, many differences distinguish one party from another, and we can only suggest a wary attitude towards sweeping statements about all parties. One party's rank and file may be more forceful than another's. We can

* Quoted with the permission of The Free Press from *Political Parties*, translated by Eden and Cedar Paul, 1915, reprinted 1949 (Glencoe, Ill.: The Free Press, 1949), pp. 373-4, 400-01.

assume that communications among leaders and followers—the Iron Law of Oligarchy notwithstanding—are stronger and more meaningful in one party than another. The conservative and oligarchical tendencies will always suffuse party organizations with their qualities and effects. But the strength and character of a party's guiding theme must pose varying resistance to these tendencies, and—much to the harm of our neat "laws"—the times, the events, the public, and the men will conspire intermittently to interrupt and destroy any smooth progression that the abstract law of oligarchy may picture.

TRENDS IN THE POLITICAL PARTY SYSTEM

We have now come to a point where we may make several observations about the trend of political parties generally in the contemporary world. Today parties and governments are on the whole much different from those of the eighteenth and nineteenth centuries. The main trends have been fourfold: The executive branch of the government has become more influential in directing, controlling, and organizing the party. The party machine-organization has grown stronger in relation to the party membership, rather than weaker. The relation of political parties to government has grown closer. And those parties that could count on the tangible support of auxiliary organizations such as labor unions have forged ahead of parties that rely simply on the support of the "independent" electorate. All of these trends are of increasing importance in contemporary politics.

EXECUTIVE BRANCH OBTAINING STRONGER CONTROL OF PARTIES

The development of the executive branch of government and the development of strong parties go together. We have seen that the Italian and German charismatic (and later elite) parties of Mussolini and Hitler were integrated and centralized, and that their advent to power meant the abrupt decline of the legislatures. Also we have seen that the Communist Party is controlled by its executive committees and that the Soviet government itself is mastered by the top executives who simultaneously occupy party and state positions. In France, we saw that de Gaulle directs his party without challenge and that his primary demand for the reform of French government is that the executive be strengthened. In England, the executive leadership of the party and the Prime Minister and Cabinet of the state have grown stronger in parallel lines, so that it is difficult to say which came first, the strong state executive or the strong party executive.

In either case, the fact is apparent that the party membership and the Commons have suffered equally in force and influence.

In Italy as in America, the situation is less clear. However, so far as Italy is concerned, politics based on colorful personalities is being overshadowed by party politics. People vote the party label increasingly. The executive is stronger under the new constitution than under the pre-World War I constitution. Although De Gasperi was not the strong *personal* figure that Crespi and Orlando were before World War I, still his position came to be as secure and dominating as were theirs. This might indicate that the executive leadership of the government is *per se*, that is, without regard to the personality of the incumbent, stronger today than it used to be.

UNITED STATES SYSTEM STILL RESISTS TREND

Now let us look at the picture in the United States. The American party system historically joined with the governmental structure in promoting legislative leadership. Federalism and the separation of powers have contributed to making the local party strong and the national party weak. Yet, as Leslie Lipson and Leonard D. White have shown in their studies of the governors and national administration respectively, the executive power has been generally expanding in both state and nation. It is true that the party has lagged behind; it is not as much subject to the executive as is the administrative machinery of government. Nevertheless, the governor is a stronger political party figure today in most states than he was fifty years ago, and even a strongly criticized President such as President Truman was able to command party support in achieving his renomination as candidate for President in 1948. Separate state elections and independent state officers, however, seem to provide a barrier to the national executive's assuming thorough control over the party. Even President Franklin Roosevelt could not impose his choice of candidates on the local parties and electorates, nor could he compel the co-operation of Democratic Party members in Congress. And the very fact that the state governors have become stronger as party leaders means that they have less motive for following in the wake of the national executive.

PARTY DIRECTORS' INCREASING CONTROL OVER MACHINERY

Of the parties we have described above, only the American parties would seem to be reluctant to participate in the tendency ob-

served by Roberto Michels in his study of political parties before
World War I. As we have seen, he found that in every party he studied,
the party organizations were increasing their controls at the expense
of the membership, a process that he regarded as inevitable. However,
in the American case one must distinguish between centralization and
integration. Resistance against centralization often occurs when the
lower levels themselves are undergoing a process of integration. Thus,
as the governor gains party power within the state, he is likely to
resist strongly the turning of such power over to the national party.
Similarly, the American scene has a multitude of tightly integrated
county machines that resist incorporation into the state machine. Let
us say, then, that there exists, if at all, only a slight tendency for
American parties to become centralized, if only because the American
machines local and state, are already integrated. The American machine actually became oligarchic before the parties of which Michels
spoke became oligarchic; the advocates of "better organization" in
Europe have referred wistfully to American party organization since
the nineteenth century.

PARTIES GROWING CLOSER TO THE GOVERNMENT

We also stated that the political parties seem to be drawing
into a closer relationship to the government. In the Soviet Union, of
course, the Communist Party runs through the government and economic system like a core of steel. But even elsewhere the victory of a
party means more and more change in the activities and personnel of
government. Party leaders are more and more often the same people
as the government leaders. The parties are increasingly controlled by
statutes in their activities and membership. Nevertheless, the idea that
opposition parties should be completely out of office is changing in
two different but related ways: First, in America and England, on
issues regarded as vital, a two-party or bipartisan policy is sometimes
adopted. This occurred in England during World War II, and of course
the opposition party in England has had at all times a stipulated duty
and office. The same policy of bipartisanship occurred in America during and after World War II when, on matters concerning foreign affairs, Republican leaders joined the Democratic Administration. Thus
the problem of a basic split in consensus, which many critics claimed
would destroy representative government based on the party system,
was attacked by stopgap, "emergency" measures. Second, as in France
and Italy, a combination of coalition and fundamental rejection of the
opposition is employed. The French and Italian governments have
pursued the policy of inviting in all parties but the extreme left and

right. The rejection of the Communists is to be considered a final and fundamental rejection—that is, a forced split in competing elites with the object of ultimately eliminating the extreme left. The R.P.F combined the coalition and rejection ideas in a remarkable way. It insisted that it was not a party and recruited its members from all parties, but rejected utterly the Communist Party not only because the C.P. was in opposition but because it was composed of "non-Frenchmen."

PARTIES MUST SEEK INCREASINGLY SOLID GROUP SUPPORT

The modern party cannot live on the votes of isolated individuals and affiliated volunteers. It needs a richer diet of support from outside organizations. The Communist Party of Russia, of course, feeds right from the state. It has no problem of sustenance. The English Labour Party relies on the mass strength of organized labor. The Italian Christian Democratic Party depends, with many doubts and self-interrogations, on the support of Catholic Church organizations. The Rally of the French People provides its members with the excitement of a cause, a movement, a crusade, and the ultimate promise of victory. In the event of victory, a different solution to the organizational problem would have to be found.

The American political party still depends ultimately on favors and jobs for the local machine-workers and supporters and on "idealistic" politists. A slight challenge to this condition comes from the political strength of organized labor, which inclines towards the Democratic Party. The unions can give state-wide officers and national candidates a kind of support in which union favors are exchanged for machine favors. A more serious challenge to the traditional condition of American parties is the spread of the merit system in the civil service, which gives jobs to the qualified for as long as they remain qualified. Deprived of this source of work and favors, the local party is somewhat in flux; it is more vulnerable to attack by insurgents, more friendly to the influence of volunteers, and more tempted to rely on the support of organized groups like labor.

Also, we should remember that pressure groups representing special interests, which we are to consider in the next chapter, have been developing concurrently with these several trends in party politics. One may almost perceive a race occurring between the assimilation of highly organized social and economic groups into the party system and the independent establishment of special interests as agencies of the state. Perhaps we may better judge the potential victor in this race and the consequences of its triumph when we have observed more closely the tendency of contemporary pressure politics.

Questions and Problems

1. Trace the history of political factionalism and distinguish between most factions and the modern political party.

2. Trace the modern development of the political party.

3. What is the meaning of each part of Max Weber's definition of the modern political party?

4. Write a summary of the history of political parties in the United States.

5. Compare the American major parties, the English Labour Party, the Rally of the French People, the Italian Christian Democratic Party, and the Communist Party of the U.S.S.R. in respect to the motivation and goals of the party leadership and following.

6. Compare the same parties (as above) with respect to their states of integration and centralization.

7. Compare the same parties with respect to the social composition of their membership.

8. Compare the same parties with reference to their relationship to the state.

9. Examine three issues each of *two* of the following magazines: *Time*, *Newsweek*, *New Republic*, *Nation*, *U. S. News and World Report*, *Life*, the Sunday *New York Times Weekly News Review*, *America*. Extract all items having to do with the magazine's opinion or various individuals' opinions on what are party issues. Point out any inconsistencies in the various views as to what a particular party stands for, and trace, as best you can, what seem to be the opposing views of American parties.

10. Basing your material on this chapter, on the section on voting behavior in the last chapter, and on any single one of the works on American parties cited in the note on bibliography to this chapter, write 300 words on the differences between the Democratic and Republican parties. If particular differences are only sectional in extent, not national, so specify in describing them.

11. With special reference to Chapter Nine of W. E. Binkley's *American Political Parties: Their Natural History*, describe the origins of the Republican Party.

12. How are the American major parties organized from bottom to top?

13. Referring back to Chapters Two through Five, are there any comments you might be able to make or any predictions you might deem possible with reference to De Gaulle's Rally of the French People, in addition to what was said in this chapter? State your predictions and comments in 150 words.

14. If you (as an American, Englishman, or Russian) wanted to have a bill to forbid the grazing of sheep on the same land for more than one year incorporated in a party's program, how would you go about obtaining the support of: the American Democratic Party, the English Labour Party, the Russian Communist Party?

15. Which of the five parties described in detail in this chapter do you think would be most resistant to Roberto Michels's Iron Law of Oligarchy? Why?

16. Supposing yourself to be a professional propagandist for any of the parties studied in this chapter, write a 300-word appeal designed to get new members in a city block for one of the parties.

17. Ask five persons outside of this class what the American Republican Party stands for, what the English Labour Party stands for, and what the Russian Communist Party stands for. (Be scrupulous in recording only what *they* say, and do not disregard obviously ignorant or flippant remarks.) Compare their answers with what you know of the parties from this chapter. Prepare a brief report on how far they agreed with the statements made in the chapter, and explain what may be the causes of the disagreement.

18. What particular examples can you find in the body of the chapter to confirm or deny the statements in the last section on Trends in the Political Party System?

Longer Study and Research
Problems Suitable for Term Papers

1. Write a ten page book report on one of the following works, presenting its principal points, its method of studying the materials it deals with, the major values held by the author, and your criticisms of the treatment in general:

J. D. Hicks: *The Agrarian Revolt*
Edward J. Flynn: *You're the Boss*
G. D. H. Cole: *A History of the Labour Party from 1914*
W. E. Binkley: *American Political Parties: Their Natural History*
Thomas Beer: *Hanna*
H. J. Desmond: *The Know Nothing Party*
John Chamberlain: *Farewell to Reform: The Rise, Life, and Decay of the Progressive Mind in America*
A. N. Holcombe: *The Middle Classes in American Politics*
Matthew Josephson: *The Politicos, 1865–1896*
John Gunther: *Behind the Iron Curtain*

2. Prepare a questionnaire on the basis of the main factors mentioned in this chapter as being important to an understanding of party dynamics: motivation and goals of the leadership, integration and centralization, social composition, and relationship to government. Select any two local persons who know about or are active in politics and interview them on the basis of your questionnaire. Describe how the evidence you have gathered adds to the material of the chapter. (Suggestion: Use half your time for preparing the questionnaire, one quarter for interviewing, and one quarter for analysis and reporting.)

3. Collect the results of the latest elections conducted in the United States, France, Great Britain, Italy, and Russia. On the basis of these results, together with any commentaries accompanying them, report on the present status of the parties dealt with in this chapter. (Suggestion: start with the

New York Times Index and the *International Index to Periodical Literature*,
latest issues, and move backwards in time.)

    4. Obtaining from the Secretary of State in your state, or the League of
Women Voters, or your library, or elsewhere, copies of the state election law
in full, outline the many ways in which the parties of your state are regulated
by state law.

7

PRESSURE GROUPS

C HAPTER Five presented the view that no arrangement of representation, no system of election, can be neutral. By any arrangement, some broad value or values, of a majority, of a local region, of an economic or of some other type of group, will be pushed a little deeper into the character of the government. Political parties are of especial relevance, since they have the stated goals of representing certain values and interests in the government that differ from the preferences of their opponents. This characteristic bent of political parties is manifested clearly in countries that have several parties. Parties in France, Italy, Germany, Belgium, and other lands are often small and vociferous on behalf of minority interests. In America, where the major parties differ over principles so broad and vague as to be sometimes impossible to discover, party statements often cloak the struggle of values and interests that continually agitate the internal life of the party.

PRESSURE GROUPS PART OF THE STRUGGLE OVER VALUES

The pressure group is on another level of the conflict of values with which politics is concerned. The pressure group in America commonly is called the lobby, and the image of the lobby that many Americans carry in their minds is not a flattering one. They visualize several well-paid, suave gentlemen who, knowing all there is to know about the inner workings of legislatures, use fair means or foul to induce legislators to raid the public treasury. In essence, however, the pressure group is simply any organized social group that seeks to influence the behavior of political officers without seeking formal control of the government. The lobby is one type of pressure group whose agents apply whatever influence they may command directly upon the legislators.

PRESSURE GROUPS IN DIFFERENT SOCIAL SYSTEMS

In modern society, pressure groups can be found among the numerous voluntary associations, such as labor unions, trades associations, and reform groups, that have some interest at stake in politics. However, essentially the same phenomenon as the modern pressure-group existed in other times when society was not so mobile and associations not so voluntary.

"Almost every interest in medieval society," writes Helen Cam, "almost every element in its make-up, has left its trace on the legislation of council and parliament." * She listed the principal sources of legislative activity as: "The directive or planning urge in the ruler, the need for clarifying and defining experience by the judicature, and the demand from the ruled for redress of grievances." This last source, "public" demand, meant, especially by the end of the fifteenth century, about what it means today, although the interests have changed somewhat. The medieval pressure-groups were the legal profession, the clergy, the nobility, the landowners, the sheriffs and bailiffs, the merchants, and the leaders of localities. Also, developing continuously as an influence on law making through the late medieval and early modern periods was the notion of the commonweal, often a mere pretense or rationalization and yet often truly advanced.

Modern pressure-groups have grown in close relation to the various party systems. When there are many parties, a number of such interest groups can be absorbed into the party system. Then the problem of pressure groups becomes almost inextricable from the general study of the political parties. In England, where one kind of two-party system exists, pressure groups play a role different from the role they play in America, where another kind of two-party system exists. In England, until recently, a small group drawn from the same social class had been able to represent dominant landed, religious, and commercial interests. Many members of Parliament incarnated the values that might have otherwise prompted strong and numerous pressure groups.

But in America, society has been for a long time relatively classless. The politician has been an individualist, footloose by comparison with his British counterpart, free to bargain and willing to deal with a variety of opposing groups. Furthermore, the American economy is tremendously diversified, the population exceedingly heterogeneous, and the political structure greatly decentralized and unintegrated. The formal structure of the government cannot reflect faithfully any large part of the interests, which must seek informal ways of influencing the government.

* "The Legislators of Medieval England," the Raleigh Lecture on History, read June 13, 1945, and published in the *Proceedings of The British Academy* (1945), 137–50.

An analysis of seventy parliamentary enactments of 1936–7 by Professor W. Ivor Jennings shows that private interests do inspire legislation but also reveals how orderly is the process by which the interests affect the British law. If we abstract, not without some loss of realism, the data furnished by Professor Jennings on the informal sources of law, we find that, of the 70 enactments, the sources of 9 lay in Cabinet policy, of 27 in the departments of the government, of 7 in a combination of departmental and pressure-group interests, of 5 in a combination of departmental and local authorities, of 3 in combinations of individual members and pressure groups, of 3 in pressure groups, of 2 in local authorities, of 2 in combinations of departments, pressure groups, and local authorities, and of 1 each in 10 different elements or combinations of elements.

Thus, if one may take 1936 as a usual year, one may conclude that local authorities and pressure groups are active in the British legislative process. Scrutiny of the many sources reveals, however, that English pressure groups and authorities operate more publicly and with more formality than do pressure groups in American legislatures. Furthermore, British interests appear to be tamed by Cabinet and department to an extent undreamed of in American legislatures. The external interests are operative, but in a consultative and organized fashion. The looseness, informality, and mystery of American lobbying is mainly absent.

THREE LEVELS OF ORGANIZATION OF PRESSURES

This chapter will distinguish degrees of organization in the pressure groups. Beginning with the sporadic attempts of individuals to influence the government, we shall move on to discuss the pressure group as it has developed in the United States, and we shall conclude by describing the cases in which pressure groups have been integrated into the government and made responsible for public duties. On each level of organization, we shall be concerned with appraising the social groups producing the pressure, the amount and the impact of such pressure, and the techniques of the groups.

Individual Influence in Politics

SELF-INTEREST IN POLITICS

Analysis of voting behavior shows that economic and social interests condition the way many people vote. Although we certainly *cannot* make the statement that most people are obviously motivated by their own immediate interests when they cast their vote, there does seem to be some relation between the way people vote and their economic and social levels. Many people vote the way they think will benefit most immediately their pockets or their particular religious, nationality, local, or racial groups. Furthermore, many voters are active in politics and seek their personal interests through the political party.

ANY INTERESTED INDIVIDUAL CAN EXERT MUCH INFLUENCE

We are concerned here with those politists who, without belonging to continuously organized groups, still exert pressure on the government over and above their party or voting activities. Among them would be individuals who seek favors of some sort from the government, ranging from an exception to a municipal zoning ordinance to the granting of a contract for a huge dam that the state or national government intends to construct. Among them also would be the individual advocates of "causes," ranging from the construction of a municipal swimming pool to the establishment of a national bird sanctuary.

The number of such persons, contrary to popular belief, is not infinite. The active public, we have pointed out, is not large. A single citizen, inspired by an intense selfish or altruistic purpose, can exert an influence greatly disproportionate to his numerical influence as one of 150,000,000 people. Most politicians who have had any considerable experience in public life can name specific individuals in their constituencies who are intensely interested in some aspect of politics and who persist in making their influence felt. For example, almost every politician who has had a hand in any legislation concerning the conservation or destruction of wild life will have heard from one active woman who has devoted much of her adult life to influencing public attitudes towards wild-life conservation.

Whatever the country, so few people pay attention to the workings of government that anyone who will spend a few hours a month on some subject of government over a long period of time can become a leader of opinion and action. This is true not only of party politics but also of activity in any one of the hundreds of areas in which the government is doing something—the control of floods in the Dakotas (or in China, for that matter), the habits of the Navaho Indians, the tax rate on personal property, the problems of sewage disposal in Chicago, or the construction of a superhighway.

"The wheel that squeaks, gets the grease." A mere handful of individuals, raising a clamor that cannot be stilled by constitutional

means, can embarrass, badger, and even control a politician, a party,
or an agency of government. Citizens who discover this fact for the
first time are as astonished as the small boy who enters a great cavern
and hears the resounding echo of his shouts. A few people are permanently unbalanced by the shock. They become experts on everything, and appear at every stage of the legislative process, as drunk
with power as ever a government official might be. Their entrance on
the scene of a meeting, hearing, or conference brings shudders to those
acquainted with them.

PRESSURES CAN BE GOOD OR BAD

Unfortunately, no formula can say which of these various
individual pressures that have been described are good and which bad.
Pressure in itself, obviously, is neither good nor bad. One can influence
the government to his own financial profit; but one can also influence
the government to relieve famine in India. This is as true of individuals
we are now discussing as of the social groups we shall discuss below.
The student must determine in his own mind the extent to which the
pressure of an individual or group is for an unjustified personal benefit
or for a justified larger cause.

If one has no settled standards for making such evaluations, he
ought to turn to some of the moral philosophers for help. Aristotle's
Ethics, Plato's *Republic*, Marcus Aurelius' *Meditations*, Augustine's
Confessions, Dante's *Divine Comedy*, and Spinoza's *Ethics* are only a
few of the older works that can help one to formulate his ethical position on general questions of politics. The problem is not an easy one,
and we shall touch on it again in the next to last chapter.

Nowhere is it more apparent than in the debate over pressure politics that most people consider their own ideas legitimate and true and
those of their opponents illegitimate and false. The mere fact that a
person advocates reforms on behalf of others does not argue in itself
for his goodness. Napoleon almost ruined France by policies that
sought glory for that country.

POLITICAL HISTORY IS COLORED BY UNENDING PERSONAL INTRIGUE

Perhaps we can say, however, that the nature of politics
over most of history has been such that the individuals one finds on
the political scene seem to be motivated most of the time by a desire
to benefit themselves. They are in the business of influencing politics

for "what they can get out of it." Applying only the simple index of
honesty about money, one rarely finds a society whose politicians are
not widely suspected of greed, and one also rarely finds a society in
which a person could not purchase disproportionate political influence.

USE OF MONEY TO INFLUENCE OFFICIALS AND PUBLIC

Money has been used often by officials or private individuals
to influence other officials. King George III spent so much money
buying seats in the House of Commons that his broker warned him of
approaching private bankruptcy. Benedict Arnold tried to sell out West
Point to the British for £10,000 during the Revolutionary War. Before the Reform Act of 1832, some members of the British House of
Commons would sell their vote for the going price of one guinea and
a free meal each day of the parliamentary session. Certain American
financiers made deal after deal with a notorious boss of Tammany Hall
under a kind of syndicate arrangement for their mutual profit. The
boss died in disgrace, but his partners lived respectable lives.

Money also has been used by individuals to influence the public. A
well-known mayor of a large American city, who is recorded historically as a reform mayor, had accumulated a fortune in public utilities
promotion by manipulations of questionable legality. Later he used
his wealth to achieve efficient and honest government, having spent
his money freely to become elected and to stay in office. The transformation of John D. Rockefeller is similar. A part of his fortune was
accumulated by collusions to raise the prices people had to pay for oil;
much of it was spent later in philanthropic enterprises benefiting the
public. The prominence of the public relations expert today goes back
to the success of Rockefeller's public relations adviser, who influenced
the industrialist and financier to clear his name with the public by
means of large-scale philanthropy.

Many different kinds of people—campaign managers, government
executives, diplomats, corporate businessmen, and speculative businessmen—have used money to accomplish their purposes. A Senate
committee investigation during Taft's administration discovered that
supporters of the candidate who won election to the United States
Senate from Illinois had contributed $235,000 to a "jack pot" for the
Illinois legislators. The "jack pot" was a pool of "contributions," one
sum for a favorable vote on utilities, another sum for a "correct" vote
on a tax bill, and so on for other purposes. At the end of the session,
the representatives that had voted "right" were given a share of the
loot.

THE USE OF OFFICE FOR PECUNIARY GAIN

No period of American history evidences quite the picture of purity the idealistic citizen dreams of. Certain periods of political history seem particularly venal and corrupt. Yet often the same periods show a lofty and religious dedication to public tasks on the part of some elements of the population. The Civil War and Reconstruction had this double character. Americans sacrificed careers, fortunes, and even their lives in the War and in the reform movements afterwards. Yet scandals were frequent during and after the War. Individuals speculated in stocks, bonds, and commodities on the basis of inside information they possessed as government officials. Others were partners to grafting and bribery. State and local as well as national government experienced investigations and disclosures that shocked the idealistic and seemingly confused the cynics. It was, said Henry Adams, an age of damaged reputations.

The prohibition period in America produced similar behavior. A large number of prohibition agents were fired or convicted of crimes during the "great experiment." Indeed, new cases of official profiteering are revealed each month in the country's newspapers. Often the transactions reported are shady rather than illegal. For example, the Chicago Downs Association, which runs harness racing in Cicero, Illinois, was shown in 1951 to have sold stock at $.10 a share to a number of politicians on whose good will the Association depended. The $.10 stock paid dividends of $1.75 a share in two years.

Some diplomats of all nations have promoted business enterprise for their own financial gain in the areas of the world to which they have gone. We are not speaking here of "dollar diplomacy," which is a legitimate, though disputed, policy of a government to help its nationals expand and protect their business enterprise abroad. We are speaking rather of the numerous ways in which diplomats and other public representatives have increased their private holdings with the help of their public office. A Roman provincial governor or general expected to return to Rome as a very wealthy man. Only rarely, as in the case of Verres, who was prosecuted successfully by Cicero for stripping Sicily of its wealth, did the law interfere with private gains.

Venetian and British naval officers and privateers were for centuries commissioned to take what they could find and to keep a part of it for themselves. No army of invasion or occupation, even today, moves into foreign territory without its complement of uniformed (or official civilian) speculators, promoters, and businessmen. Private trading and transportation companies often maintain little "diplomatic services" of their own. The British East India Company was notorious for its ability to influence politics wherever its stations were established. The families of Christian missionaries to Hawaii became active leaders of island politics and built great fortunes in business there. Certain airlines have policy-influencing organizations not only in their country of origin but wherever their planes alight.

SALE OF OFFICES

The great profits to be obtained from holding public office often have fostered the practice of selling offices to the highest bidder or at a fixed price. The sale of offices was nearly a universal practice in the seventeenth century in Europe and has been found throughout the world at various times. In the seventeenth century one might buy a governorship of Syria for 60,000 ducats from the Grand Vizier of the Ottoman Empire, any city office in Milan, a judgeship from Frederick III of Brandenburg, a clerkship of assize from an English sheriff, the office of sheriff in Mexico for 122,740 pesos, and a judgeship in the High Court of Paris for 18,000 livres. Profits from office salaries, fees, and graft made the investments good ones; but in many countries, notably France and Spain, the prices of offices soared also because of the social prestige accruing to the holder of official position. The practice harms the efficiency of an administrative machine and prevents control over it. It is prevalent under aristocratic governments that have a large bureaucracy, but the American spoils system is somewhat like the sale of office. Thus a wealthy man who gives liberally to the national party that wins an election may hope for an ambassador's post and the prestige that goes with it. Instances of more direct payments are not lacking. Congressional hearings in 1951 disclosed that federal offices in Mississippi were being sold, and a Rhode Island grand jury in the same year indicted several Woonsocket officials for selling city jobs.

SOLICITATION OF MONEY FOR POLITICAL USE

Individual corporate businessmen become factors in politics, willing or not. On the eve of Nazi triumph in Germany, twenty German industrialists were called to an "important" conference. There they were introduced by Hjalmar Schacht to Adolf Hitler. They listened to a passionate harangue against communism and were dunned for 3,000,000 reichsmark. Not a few American businessmen have been on the "sucker list" of Gerald K. Smith and other extremists, just as not a few professional men and humanitarians have been on the lists of leftist agitators. Some of them are induced to pay the piper even if they are unwilling to dance the tune.

USE OF MONEY

What do they all want—these millions of people who since the beginning of recorded history have used money to get something extra out of politics? Their motives and values are as complex and numerous as are those of the leaders, the mass of voters, and the party members that we have discussed in the four preceding chapters. Some seek power for its own sake, as did Julius Caesar when he distributed his wealth among the Roman citizens. Others seek wealth by converting a smaller amount of wealth into power and then cashing in on the conversion, as did Cameron. Others seek social respect as did Rockefeller in his old age and Boss Croker of Tammany, who spent his graft in easy retirement as a country squire and breeder of race horses in Ireland. Many seek protection from imminent peril; among this kind would be those who bribed or bought their way out of the ranks of the Revolutionary and Civil War armies, and the shopkeepers and tavern owners who have paid sums of money to officials to remain in business in eighteenth-century France, pre-Revolutionary America, twentieth-century United States, and elsewhere.

Some pay directly to obtain "efficiency" in government, because if they rely on the law and administration alone, they cannot get their due. They must pay for a pension that is theirs by right, a license that they are qualified to receive, a paper that they are entitled to possess, a damage settlement they deserve, a prompt administrative action that never should have been delayed. Some find sport in the game of influencing politics; they like to be on the "inside" or "in the know." But, of course, a great many of these people who attempt to influence government have identified themselves with the cause of others. For example, they may feel uncomfortable when they perceive suffering around them or even across the world, or they may worry about the discomfort of the next generation should it be saddled with a huge public debt.

DIFFICULTY OF DISTINGUISHING BETWEEN INDIVIDUAL AND GROUP PRESSURES

It is sometimes difficult to dertermine whether a particular attempt to influence politics is the act of an individual *qua* individual or *qua* public official or group member. One would find it hard to decide, for example, whether a good part of Thomas Jefferson's huge correspondence was private or public; his private letters often discuss and take a position on public matters. Public office even seems to deprive a man of his right to a private character. Edward VIII of England found that he could not be both King of England and husband of Mrs. Simpson. Secretary of State Acheson met with hostility when he attempted to draw a line between his "private" friendship for Alger Hiss and his official conduct towards a convicted perjuror.

Such problems arise because in the process of influencing politics, individuals move in and out of pressure groups. They act as individuals; they act also as group representatives. A common question asked by legislators of witnesses in hearings before a committee is: "Do you come in a private capacity or do you claim to represent some group?" Sometimes a person leads several lives. The German millionaire, Stinnes, was a member of the *Reichstag*, a contributor to parties, an owner of influential newspapers, and the controller of large traction interests in the Ruhr Valley with political influence. He was thus a representative being pressured by himself as the agent of himself.

Sometimes even the advocates of a similar point of view are divided. They are not sufficiently organized to know whether they are representing only themselves or others. Is there a single "business lobby," or are there many business lobbies, or are there many individual businessmen who are expressing their views? Only a careful analysis of the facts of a single case can tell whether the opinion being expressed and the pressure being exerted is that of one individual, of several individuals, or of a continuously organized group. Obviously, the attitude that the official, the press, the public, and all other interested parties will take towards the expression or activity will be influenced by the result of such an analysis. Laws regulating lobbies have sometimes stumbled over this distinction between individual and group pressures, finding it hard to draw in legal language. Lone individuals attempt to masquerade as representatives of large groups; representatives of large groups attempt to evade regulation and acquire an air of neutrality by parading as individuals. (However, suspicion can be carried too far; writers who are prone to scent garbage in a rose garden will find in every individual's attempt to influence government a tightly organized and corrupt conspiracy.)

ORIGINS OF PRESSURE GROUPS

Usually pressure groups originate in the felt needs and shared sympathies of individuals concerned with some subject of politics. Wild-flower lovers form leagues to protect wild flowers; haters of drunkenness gather to form temperance unions or antisaloon leagues. The telltale mark of the true lobby is the lobbyist, the professional hireling of the interested group. He is working year in and year out to influence legislation. His presence is continuously felt. No difficulty in distinguishing special cases can conceal the important special effects of this kind of pressure.

The Lobby and Pressure Groups

The heavy impact of the lobby was felt for the first time in America before the Civil War. In 1857, a noted economist, Henry C. Carey, wrote to President Buchanan that the legislation of the country had fallen into the hands of the shipping and railroad interests. Ten years before, he wrote, one would have been thought a false prophet if he had predicted "that there would have arisen a 'third house of Congress'— composed of lobby members and embracing men who had filled almost the highest legislative and executive offices—abundantly supplied, to use the words of Colonel Benton, 'with the means required for concili-ating members and combining interests,' and thus securing the passage of almost any bill, the applicants were willing, sufficiently liberally, to pay."

PRIMITIVE LOBBYING TECHNIQUES

The techniques first used by American lobbyists were, as Carey indicates, quite crude. The primary ones were bribery, sharing the profits of new ventures, personal supplication, and lavish entertain-ment. The results were startling. Never had so many been bought for so little. Huge tracts of land, vast natural resources, precious public rights were dispensed to special interests. The popular clamor against lobbies became frightening at times, but it was of doubtful effect. Actually political scientists scarcely understand what caused the gradual transition from the crude methods and wholesale plunder of two generations ago to the more genteel techniques and more accep-table objectives of the pressure groups today. It may have been popular anger that played the major role in tempering the old type of lobbying, or it may have been the very multiplication of lobbies that produced better-behaved pressure groups.

During the last decades of the nineteenth century, in any event, and concurrently with the popular movements against political corruption, there came on the scene the opposition lobbies. Where there had been only lumbermen's lobbies, there were now conservation lobbies. Where there had been only railroad lobbies, there were now farmers' lobbies. Where there had been only public utility lobbies, there were now public ownership lobbies. School lobbies arose to contest economy lobbies. Labor lobbies entered the arena against industrial lobbies. Elected representatives who had lost their equilibrium as the result of one force moved about now in a more stable balance of forces.

TRANSFORMATION OF LOBBIES

Furthermore, the techniques and objectives of the lobbies had to change. The lobby—that is, the group directly influencing lawmakers—grew into the pressure group, a broader social organization that made direct lobbying only a part of its total operations. Less money was spent on buying votes and more on persuading representatives. Crude demands had to be fashioned (and changed somewhat in the process) into the "legitimate" requests of interests whose "well-being was important to the country as a whole."

Public relations became an object of much concern to the leaders of pressure groups. The public was informed by all means possible of the "reasonableness" of a group's needs, and attempts were made to convince the representatives that the cause of a particular lobby was just by the weight of logic, information, and press comment. Furthermore, the pressure groups had to acquire constituencies. Their voice was more effective when it was known that they spoke on behalf of thousands of organized citizens. Representatives listened and attended more carefully to particular interests if they knew such interests carried large numbers of votes on election day.

By such means and in such ways did the lobbies transform themselves into the pressure groups that are to be found today. They are highly organized; they claim large membership lists; they have agents who are skilled in persuasion and public relations; they insist that their purposes are consonant with the public welfare. Figure 21 shows the bare structure of a modern, important pressure group, the National Association of Real Estate Boards.

Business, labor, farm, and "reform" pressure groups are found in all modern nations where social groups are free to combine, to govern themselves, and to exert pressure on political affairs. Where several religious groups exist, we find religious pressures. Where several nationalities are present, we find nationality pressures. Where there are notable social and economic differences between one part of a country and another, we find local pressure groups. An estimate of the United States Office of Domestic Commerce in 1950 found 150 national labor groups and 40,000 to 50,000 local labor organizations; 150 national agricultural organizations and 14,000 to 15,000 local ones; and over 3,000 national business groups and some 20,000 local ones.

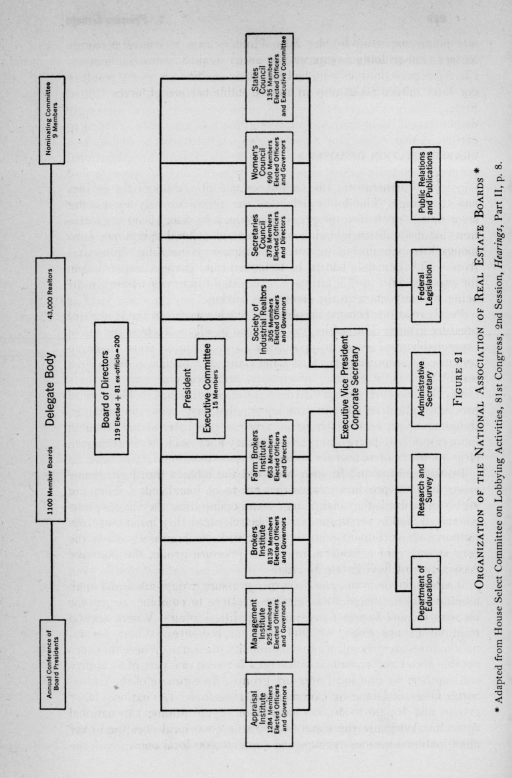

FIGURE 21

ORGANIZATION OF THE NATIONAL ASSOCIATION OF REAL ESTATE BOARDS *

* Adapted from House Select Committee on Lobbying Activities, 81st Congress, 2nd Session, *Hearings*, Part II, p. 8.

NUMBER OF LOBBIES LARGE TODAY

The total number of lobbying pressure groups in the United States, where the pressure group phenomenon is most strikingly demonstrated, is unknown. One reason for this ignorance, alluded to earlier, is that a lobby or a pressure group is difficult to define. Is a university that, in trying to get large appropriations for educational purposes, sends its skilled administrative and faculty personnel before legislative committees to be considered a lobby? Most state universities have such "lobbies," but they are rarely, if ever, registered under state or federal lobbying acts. Other state and federal agencies also have lobbies, and they, too, are not registered. Are newspaper publishers who attempt to influence legislators to be called lobbyists? Apparently they, too, escape most registration laws. Another reason for our ignorance is that lobbies are not required to register in almost half the states and in most cities and counties; yet there are local as well as national lobbies. Furthermore, a lobby in one state is not defined as a lobby in another, so that one has no reliable standard of comparison. And if one took lobbying in its broader pressure-group sense, *every organized group with political interests* would come under the term.

No one, however, would dispute the statement that the number of pressure groups maintaining lobbyists amounts to several thousands, including about eighteen-hundred organizations actively engaged in influencing legislative and administrative opinion in Washington (Figure 22), a hundred or so in the more populous states, and an unknown number in the fifty largest cities. The amount of money spent for lobbying in Washington alone each year is at a minimum six million dollars and at a maximum, depending on whether one counts all public relations expenditures as lobbying, well over ten million dollars. This amount, if multiplied by four, exceeds easily the total spent by the national political parties on national campaigns over each four year period. In the states, though our information is even less accurate, the lobbies perhaps spend annually more than the state and local political parties do. The total expenditures in the country for all influencing of opinion with an eye to legislative policy would be even more staggering.

THE CHIEF NATIONAL LOBBIES AND GROUPINGS

What are the top lobbies in the government? A list of the chief lobbies active in Washington would, without doubt, include the

FIGURE 22

PRESSURE GROUPS IN WASHINGTON

Estimated total number and the number registered during the 80th Congress, 1947–8, classified by type.*

REGISTRATIONS DURING THE 80TH CONG., CLASSIFIED BY TYPE OF ORGANIZATION

Type of organization	Estimated number of organizations in Washington	Registered under Lobbying Law 1947	Registered under Lobbying Law 1948	Not registered either year	Committee appearances [1] (Total)	Committee appearances of organizations not registered
Agriculture	51	31	26	12	9	1
Business: general	78	29	39	29	15	9
Citizen organizations:						
Civil and Political	115	53	57	39	16	8
Economic	38	9	7	25	6	5
Education	34	7	10	24	6	5
Financial	49	24	22	20	10	6
Food and beverage	96	44	48	30	5	3
Health	28	3	6	20	2	2
International	58	10	14	37	6	4
Labor:						
Government employees	30	21	18	7	1	1
Private	104	54	49	35	28	12
Lumber and forest products	30	10	7	18	1	....
Official (governmental)	113	8	14	96	12	65
Oil, gas, and metal products	107	46	57	28	16	10
Power and communications	41	22	23	5	3	2
Printing and publishing	34	6	8	24	22	19
Professional	117	14	12	103	44	2
Real estate: building and construction	45	14	12	28	5	5
Religious	42	10	10	26	12	9
Tax groups	42	23	30	2	2	1
Textiles and apparel	34	15	12	19	17	15
Trade groups: miscellaneous [2]	129	56	61	39	20	14
Transportation:						
Air	17	5	10	4	2	1
Highways	34	8	14	19	7	5
Rail	96	60	57	23	32	17
Water	30	12	20	8	7	4
Veterans and military	53	21	22	23	6	3
Welfare	28	16	15	8	0	0
Women's organizations	30	14	13	14	20	11
Individuals [3]	107	22	31	59	60	59
Total	1,810	667	724	824	392	298

[1] Limited to Senate and House Judiciary Committees only.

[2] These are specialized groups, as contrasted with general over-all groups included in "Business: general."

[3] Single individuals, operating alone, and probably in most cases not required to register under the terms of the law.

* Source: The Library of Congress Legislative Reference Service, *Administration of the Lobby Registration Provision of the Legislative Reorganization Act of 1946* (Washington: United States Government Printing Office, 1950), p. 6.

Committee for Constitutional Government, National Association of
Manufacturers, Chamber of Commerce of the United States, National
Association of Electric Companies, American Federation of Labor
(A.F. of L.), Congress of Industrial Organizations (C.I.O.), railway
brotherhoods (several unions), American Farm Bureau Federation,
National Grange, National Farmers Union, American Medical
Association, American Legion, Veterans of Foreign Wars, American
Veterans Committee, National Council of Churches of Christ in Amer-
ica, General Federation of Women's Clubs, League of Women Voters,
and the Townsend National Recovery Plan.

It may be observed that the list of lobbies breaks rather easily into
the categories of business, labor, farmer, church, and reform, with the
exception of the veterans' lobbies. The Townsend National Recovery
Plan lobby is typical of a large group of lobbies, not listed here, the
objectives of which are reforms of many kinds—humanitarian, financial,
prohibitive, or educational. The predominance of business, labor, and
farm interests is significant. Beyond doubt it is these three parts of
modern society that have found the traditional representative system
unresponsive to their needs. To find business and labor pressure-
groups is not surprising; businessmen and workers are urban phenomena, and form minorities even in the cities.

To find farm pressure-groups is more surprising, for, as we pointed
out in our discussion of representation, farmers are overrepresented
in almost all American legislatures (if we take the position that equal
populations should send equal numbers of representatives to the
legislatures). However, the farmers nationally are a minority group,
and they find pressure politics as useful in gaining their own ends, as do
other minority groups. There are other reasons for the farmers having
a national lobby. They are isolated; under ordinary conditions they do
not find it easy to organize for political activity. Their incomes are
middle or lower class; they cannot bring immediate financial pressure
to bear on opposing politicians. Only by belonging to a large organization, permanently administered, and supplied by small dues from
thousands of farmers, can they acquire effective spokesmen for their
immediate interests.

BUSINESS INTERESTS ARE NOT UNIFIED INTERNALLY

None of the groups mentioned, however,—business, labor,
farmers, or any other large segment of the population—is organized as
a unit. For example, we cannot speak of "business" as a pressure
group; there are many pressure groups based on business interests.
There exist organizations of industrialists, exporters, shippers, railroads, fruit growers, fashion designers; national, New England,

Western, and Southern manufacturing interests; small businessmen, stock brokers, and a number of other business groups. It is true that several threads of common interest unite most of them. They incline towards conservatism; they do not favor high taxes on corporations or personal income; they tend to dislike government regulations of any large part of the economy; they oppose active support of labor unions by the government. But they differ and even conflict in many ways. Manufacturers' lobbies may oppose the shippers' and railroads' demand for higher freight rates. The manufacturers of fashionable textiles may join with certain industrial interests to favor high tariffs and find opposition from exporters and maritime interests. New England manufacturers may support legislation to increase wages throughout the nation in order to fight off the threat posed to New England industry by low wages in the South. The coal industry will sit by while the oil industry tries to fight off government controls; and the oil industry hardly protests when the government forces the coal industry to pay higher wages to the coal miners.

CERTAIN CENTRALIZED TENDENCIES EXIST

Yet certain tendencies towards the centralization of business policies have been apparent for a half-century, beginning with the founding of the National Association of Manufacturers and the growth of the United States Chamber of Commerce. Whatever agreement may be present among most of the interests of American business seems to find its way into the policies of these national pressure-groups. No one, however, should make the mistake of believing that the policies of these agencies reflect the deliberations of many thousands of their members. As in most trade associations and pressure organizations, a small group of members lead and speak on behalf of the whole membership, and even on behalf of the whole area of the economy or of the whole country. But one would be foolish to believe, and no Congressman or official does believe, that the National Home and Property Owners' Foundation, for example, is fully supported by and acts in accord with the desires of the millions of American home and property owners throughout the country. Nevertheless, a genuine point of view is being expressed by the Foundation; it represents a solid bloc of opinion and power. The legislator may take it, or leave it, or, even better, evaluate it along with the other interests of his constituents.

EUROPEAN BUSINESS PRESSURE

In Europe, business pressures evolved in somewhat the same way as they did in America. As we shall see in the third section

of this chapter, European industry has in certain crucial cases moved
out of pressure politics into the government itself. But, as in America,
the business interests of Europe have fought amongst themselves.
There has not been one line of policy; there have been many. As
Roberto Michels wrote during the twenties:

> Homogeneity is wanting in the businessman type, even when for defen-
> sive or offensive reasons of foreign or internal politics the various types
> sometimes become allies to the point of forming an apparently compact
> elite. Such occasional apparent compactness does not prevent there being
> in the bosoms of the elites traces (visible to the naked eye of anybody
> whose glance is not dimmed by arch-socialist or arch-middle class preju-
> dices) of strongly different types of economic elites, such as the great
> professional and patrimonial rentiers, the great industrial and landed
> interests, the great bankers and the great speculators, the great exporters
> and the great importers.*

CLEAVAGES AMONG UNIONS

Nor is the working force of American cities united as a
pressure group. There are wide cleavages in personalities and policies
between the American Federation of Labor and the Congress of
Industrial Organization. The spokesmen on behalf of both groups,
when they testify before congressional committees and speak privately
to legislators, claim to represent, respectively, six million and five
million workers. Both great combinations of unions agree on several
major policies. They favor government intervention on matters of
wages and hours in the poorest sections of the economy. They seek
legislation that makes it easier for them to increase their membership
and fight opposition from business management. But they disagree on
other important issues. The C.I.O. tends to favor more governmental
ownership of basic industries and resources than does the A.F. of L.
The C.I.O. tends to take positions on issues concerning foreign affairs
and fiscal policy that the A.F. of L. regards as beyond the appropriate
sphere of labor pressure-group influence.

The differences and conflicts in the labor movement are compounded
when we examine the structure of the two great aggregations of
unions. In some localities, the A.F. of L. unions are allied with C.I.O.
unions. In other places, the A.F. of L. unions may be joined with the
Republican Party while the C.I.O. unions pledge their support to
Democrats. Moreover, in many places, each individual local union
may endorse individual political candidates and need not adhere to

* Quoted with the permission of the University of Minnesota Press from Roberto
Michels: *First Lecture in Political Sociology*, translated with an introduction by Alfred de
Grazia (Minneapolis: University of Minnesota Press, 1949), p. 120.

any general unified program of political action. Some unions are politically energetic; some are apathetic; some are almost parts of the local political organization of a major party; others endorse men from both parties. Both individual unions and state organizations of unions may be active at the same time in the halls of the same state legislature, one proposing policies different from those of the other.

About a million and a half wage earners are organized in unions other than the C.I.O. and A.F. of L.—the railway brotherhoods or some other, "independent," union. The unions may all agree on certain national policies concerning wages, hours, high corporate taxes, and government labor legislation; but they move just as often along their own paths, asking always for particular attention to their special needs.

Finally we should mention that there are some sixty-two million employed persons in the United States. The overwhelming majority of workers in factories, farms, and offices are not organized by occupation in any fashion. They are affected by, but do not participate in, the pressure-group process, not even in the remote sense that a cinder-snapper participates in the decisions made by Philip Murray of the C.I.O.

AMERICAN LABOR LESS ACTIVE IN POLITICS THAN EUROPEAN

On the whole, American labor unions are less active politically than the European unions. Collective bargaining is the chief justification of American unionism, which tends to stay within the bounds of the traditional economic definition of unions as monopolistic sellers of labor engaged in maximizing the wage bill of an industry. In France, Italy, Germany, Belgium, and Britain, the labor unions strive for the greater glories of politics, often, like the British Labour Party, affiliating directly with political parties.

Most European unions strongly advocate the nationalization of basic industries by the government, while American unions often are neutral or split over government ownership of basic industries. The American unions place much more reliance on pressure-group politics than do the European unions. This is partly because European labor is more politically bent, partly because the multiparty system allows labor unions to dominate certain parties, and partly because European labor has often faced a class-dominated political elite that was implacably opposed to the interests of workers.

MAJOR FARM ORGANIZATIONS

Farmers, unlike union workers, may belong to several organizations at the same time. An Ohio farmer, for example, may belong to a dairy association, a live stock association, and one or more general associations. Most of the organized farmers of America fall into three large general associations. The offices of these organizations conduct vigorous lobbies in the national capital, in almost all state capitals, and in many local communities. The three major farm organizations are the Farm Bureau Federation, the National Grange, and the Farmers Union. The Farm Bureau Federation is the largest and most influential of the three. Its policies favor government assistance to farmers by means of loans, crop controls to prevent "overproduction," and a variety of technical assistance. The Grange was once a great force for government regulation of the industries and interests that served and often "enslaved" the farmers, but it has evolved into the most conservative of the three groups. The Farmers Union is the most radical of the three and proposes more than the Farm Bureau Federation in the way of government protection for farmers, public ownership of utilities, transport, and storage facilities, and co-operation with consumer and labor groups against the policies of business interests.

In Europe and England, the policies of the farmers' associations tend to resemble those of the Farmers Union. They are staunch advocates of agricultural and other co-operatives as a means by which producers and buyers may control the mark-up of prices on the things they need. They are friendly to the socialist labor movement, and they are active on behalf of government aid to rural development of electric power, housing, transportation, and education. Often they urge the requisitioning of large estates and their fragmentation into small farms for the benefit of landless tenant farmers.

VETERANS ORGANIZATIONS

The business, labor, and farmer pressure-groups mentioned are the major elements in the total pressure-group picture. But other groups are important. Veterans groups, for example, are very powerful. The American Legion is known to influence legislation not only on matters directly affecting veterans—problems concerning pensions, health, and bonuses for war service—but also on matters of social and economic policy. Its leadership agrees on the whole with the philosophy of government expressed by the National Association of Manufacturers and the United States Chamber of Commerce. The American Veterans Committee (A.V.C.), on the other hand, is, though much smaller, quite active on behalf of the main policy line of the Farmers Union and the labor groups.

REFORM LOBBIES

It is much less easy to describe the myriad "reform" groups that inhabit the legislative corridors. Some of them, like the League of

Women Voters, are old, trusted, and skilled representatives of opinion on problems affecting governmental structure and efficiency of government, as well as on matters affecting the legal and political status of women. Others, although adhering to a noble general purpose, propose schemes the principal effect of which is to frighten legislators into voting for measures more likely to achieve the noble purpose without disaster to the economy. An example would be the Townsend Plan, which advocates generous pensions to the aged.

TECHNIQUES OF MODERN LOBBIES

Here and there during the discussion, we have mentioned several of the methods by which pressure groups have operated. In describing the ways in which individuals have made themselves effective in politics, we mentioned that merely "being around" the places where political events are occurring produces influence over a period of time. Calling, writing, and "buttonholing" representatives and administrators is effective when done by individuals simply because, even in a democratic society, few people do such things. To these techniques we added the materialistic weapons of the individual and of the primitive lobby—the speculative collusion, the bribe, lavish gifts and entertainment, and solicitation in an atmosphere of intimidation.

We then mentioned the techniques of the modern lobbies proper. Information is provided legislators to aid them in voting "right" on an issue. The pressure group hires skilled and professional lobbyists. It reformulates its special needs into a program of legislation that allegedly will benefit a large part of society and the best interests of the nation. It conducts vigorous recruiting campaigns to get as many members as possible; this is done to impress legislators or administrators with the wide popular demand for the lobbyist's program. It tries to activate this largely passive membership as much as possible, exhorting them at the proper time to exert individual pressures on their representatives. Several pressure groups have gone into the "publishing business" as a way of avoiding both the stigma of the word "lobby" and the regulations imposed upon lobbies as legally defined. For example, the Committee for Constitutional Government, a strong opponent of governmental intervention in economic life, announced in 1944 that in seven years it had sent out 82,000,000 pieces of literature, 10,000 transcriptions for radio programs, 350,000 telegrams, and many thousands of news releases, all, of course, favoring its point of view. Some 700,000 copies of one book alone were distributed nationally by the Committee in 1949 and 1950.

SPECIAL BUSINESS TECHNIQUES

In addition, each major type of lobby employs techniques of persuasion and influence appropriate to its particular kind of strength. Business groups, as has been indicated, do not typically operate in close-knit organizations. The peak cartels and the top trade associations may on critical occasion band together for a time, but they have always been a minority influence, even when popular myth regards them as ruling the government. Sporadic clusters of businessmen pay to influence politics. Thus, about twenty wealthy men gave a few thousand dollars apiece to Truman's campaign in 1948 and helped him to raise about a million dollars besides. In the localities, businessmen are much more likely to spend money for direct political returns. Notable among such persons are real-estate men and businessmen who are dependent to some extent on government contracts or good will—contractors, lawyers, automobile dealers, insurance agents, and utilities executives.

Although there is some evidence that in Germany, France, and Italy, the leaders of large industrial aggregates have organized their personnel and equipment directly for political warfare, for the most part, the huge material and manpower resources under the command of the industrial managers have been employed, if at all, only for passive resistance. The Boston merchants in 1769 used nonimportation agreements against English goods to force the revocation of import duties. They punished their unco-operative fellow-merchants by boycotting them, by proclaiming them enemies of their country in town meetings, by stoning and smearing their houses, and even by beatings. When modern American industrialists, bankers, and realtors have on exceptional occasions resisted government intervention, they have done so by instituting interminable legal controversies and by slowing up co-operation, rather than by covert conspiracy.

Finally, we ought to add, in speaking of the techniques of business pressure groups, that businessmen and their allies from the press, the legal profession, and finance have commonly made their influence felt on government by doubling their jobs; that is, possessed of more personal resources and freedom of movement than other occupational interests, they have been able to accept appointive positions in many offices of the government.

FAVORITE LABOR PRESSURE TACTICS

Labor pressure-groups operate through their organizations more than do businessmen. They can, of course, call on the rock bottom methods of exerting economic, social, and political pressures—the strike and the boycott of products the manufacturers of which are considered hostile to labor, and there have been a number of industry-wide strikes, partly political in purpose; but there has never been a general strike of all union labor throughout the nation, for American labor has never been sufficiently organized or politically motivated to carry out a general strike.

A general strike has never yet been purely economic in nature. It has always been a means of exerting direct political pressure to destroy an opposing political alignment or defeat a threat to the interests of labor. Belgium, England, France, Italy, and other lands have had general strikes during this century. The Belgian strike of 1893, which had to do with a demand for the extension of suffrage to all workers, was notably successful. In most other cases, internal difficulties in the strike movement and vociferous public reaction to the complete cessation of productive and service activities strengthened the hand of the opposition power.

For two generations in Europe and England and for the last generation in America, labor unions have used their organization and man-power for direct intervention in politics. Since personal persuasion is one of the most effective of campaign techniques, the group that can activate its membership during political campaigns and between campaigns will add considerably to its strength in politics. The rise of the English Labour Party to its present position is due in great measure to the ability of the labor leaders to call on their rank and file for the interminable but vital chores of bell-ringing, pamphlet distribution, and getting out the favorable vote.

Where the same techniques have been applied in America, the political influence of unions has been enlarged. For example, the unionized janitors of Chicago supply a valuable service to their favored candidates by seeing that campaign literature is placed at the doorstep of each occupant of apartments and hotels and by disposing of the material of the opposition as trash. On a much larger scale, the "independent" organization known as the C.I.O. Political Action Committee (P.A.C.) has been able to use the manpower of C.I.O. unions throughout the country for political campaigning of all types and for exerting pressure on representatives. A related Citizens P.A.C. is organized separately from the unions themselves because the Hatch Act forbids labor unions and corporations to make expenditures in campaigns in which federal officers are being chosen.

FARM INFLUENCE ABETTED BY CLOSE RELATIONSHIPS TO GOVERNMENT

Farm pressure-groups use the techniques common to all pressure groups, but they especially benefit from the organized efforts of co-operatives and dual office-holding. Agricultural producers' co-operatives parallel the efforts of the large farm pressure-groups in organizing support among their membership for favored candidates and measures. Consumers' co-operatives are able to draw in many nonfarm citizens in a program of legislation and activity common to farmers and farm sympathizers alike. The national Department of Agriculture and many state agricultural agencies abound with officials who have been or are also active members and officers of the Farm Bureau Federation and other agricultural pressure and welfare organizations. Hundreds of county agents, for example, are in constant touch with the farmers of their counties. The agents are paid from federal, state, and county funds. A considerable proportion of them are also active in one or more of the farmers' organizations that are, of course, private in character. The combination of affiliations tends to make the government agencies more responsive to farm group-pressures.

Since the American government has generally intervened to force farm prices up rather than down, American farm politics have not experienced the turmoil of farmer-government strife that Europe and Asia have known. Direct action by American farmers occurred sporadically during several of the American economic depressions; it usually took the form of resistance to foreclosures on farms and of damage to railroad property and grain storage facilities. Abroad, farm strikes are more common. In the Soviet Union, for instance, when the government in January 1930 announced the aim of complete collectivization of farms within three years and the "liquidation" of the kulaks (the rich peasants), the peasants killed their animals. The situation was so serious in its consequences—it reduced milk and meat products and fertilizer as well as leather goods and other secondary products—that Stalin's famous speech "Dizzy with Success" called a halt to the government's policy on March 30, 1930. Faced with a scarcity of flour and meats, governments have often fixed maximum prices, and farmers have refused to send their products to market. Thus, in Italy in 1943, while bread sold in the black markets of Palermo for 70 lire a kilo, in Enna, some miles in the interior, it could be had for 5 lire a kilo; strenuous efforts were necessary to get enough flour into the capital city to meet a barely adequate bread ration for the population.

ORGANIZED PRESSURES INEVITABLE TODAY

Several conclusions should be emphasized as we close this section on the lobby. The United States has had a century of experience with lobbies; during this period it has become apparent that the lobbies cannot be destroyed, that they are very difficult to regulate, and that very likely the peculiar conditions of American politics make the vast number and intense activity of lobbies an invariable factor in American government, at least in the predictable future. The techniques of lobbies have changed over the last century. The role of organization has increased relative to the role of cash spending in the technique of lobbying. As Pendleton Herring wrote some twenty years ago: "The minority groups arose to obtain from the government legislative action that they could not get through the political parties." He termed the lobby "part of the American system of representation."

POPULAR FALLACIES REGARDING LOBBIES

Whether we speak of European politics or of American politics, we should point out that the lobbies are not as tightly organized as many people believe. Firstly, hardly ever does one lobby, stemming from one pressure group, gather together all the people who are eligible to be its constituents; all major groups of the population are represented by several pressure groups and lobbies that often fight among themselves. Secondly, pressure groups are often so constructed internally, being the rather disconnected offshoots of more integrated occupational groups, that they do not command the obedience, activity, or even passive agreement of any considerable number of their members. Finally, the influence of pressure groups and lobbies tends to be underestimated in some quarters and overestimated in others.

On the one hand, for example, a study by Lawrence H. Chamberlain of the *major* federal legislation of the last sixty years indicates that congressional lobbyists could conceivably claim sole credit for no more than 10 per cent of the laws. His study, however, neglects *minor* legislation (in which pressure groups are especially interested). Furthermore, state legislatures are more vulnerable to lobbying than is Congress. Also his figures do not cover dead bills; and the highest achievement of a lobby, often, is to kill an unfavorable bill or even to delay its passage. Admittedly, it is hard to measure the influence of pressure groups; this would be true even if one could observe every one of their actions. Still, given the fact that lobbies exist on both sides of almost every issue, it is a rare event indeed that a bill, backed by a single lobby and introduced surreptitiously by some friend of the lobbyists, ends as an enactment of Congress, except in drastically amended form.

On the other hand, many politicians and agency chiefs are perhaps more impressed by the strength of lobbies than they need be. They often take seriously lobbies that could not muster popular opposition to the representatives. It is just as hard for the representative to analyze correctly the strength of lobbies as it is for the political scientist, and the ordinary legislature does not provide him with the scientific help that is necessary to measure lobbying strength.

Finally, preparatory to taking up the matter at length in the next section, it may be stated here that the pressure groups in modern society have, in a number of crucial cases, moved into close working co-operation with the government. They have taken on public responsibilities and have been entrusted with official duties.

Legal Representation of Interests

INTEREST GROUPS' QUASI-OFFICIAL FUNCTIONS

There are some indications that pressure politics, as we know them today, may be undergoing changes of a basic kind. The interest group in a number of different areas of American government is being vested with functions of a quasi-official nature. To understand the fragments of evidence that lead us to this conclusion, we must venture abroad to countries where interest groups have had different roles to play.

ROLE OF ESTATES IN MEDIEVAL TIMES

In the Middle Ages, society in the countries from which America has drawn much of its culture—England, France, Holland, Italy, Spain, and Germany—was divided into several classes based on modes of living. The nobility, the clergy, the yeomen, the merchants, and the artisans—although they all formed part of society—were assumed each to play a separate special role in society and to have certain duties and privileges in connection with their status and occupation. Each grouping had some elements of self-government; there was no single body of law covering all individuals for all purposes.

THE GILDS

Merchants and artisans were organized into gilds that were formed in each type of occupation. The gilds often had power to determine for all members the conditions of work, the wages, the obligations of membership, the quality of production, and the price of articles sold. Elections were held to determine the leadership of the gilds, although in many gilds, only the richest and oldest members held real power. In some cases, the gilds held political power over and beyond their economic power. For example, the English gilds sometimes controlled the choice of their local representatives to the early House of Commons.

REVOLUTIONS DESTROYED ESTATES AND GILD SYSTEMS

The economic and technological revolution in commerce, agriculture, and industry destroyed the basis for the gild organization in the cities, but the gilds often were able to hold out for generations, adhering to their ancient regulations and to restrictive practices that had once held real meaning. Adam Smith's great book *The Wealth of Nations* (1776) is to be understood as a reformer's attempt to break the antiquated barriers that the gilds, with the help of the government, maintained against the more productive techniques of the Industrial and Commercial revolutions. The radical movement in late eighteenth-century England, the American Revolution, and the French Revolution were struggles that had as one of their purposes the relief of the new middle classes—technically equipped to produce and exchange more goods than the old middle classes—from the restrictions of the old society.

In the French Revolution this fact was more clearly realized than elsewhere, and a specific law was promulgated in 1790 declaring that all combinations of merchants or workers of any kind were prohibited. An English act of 1799 was similar. The age of individualism in economic affairs therefore dates from the beginning of the nineteenth century. The economy was to be separate from politics, and all economic arrangements were to be based on individual contracts, drawn without reference to any political or gild interference.

RESULTS OF PURE INDIVIDUALISM

From this period of theoretically pure individualism (no form of behavior is ever absolute and pure in politics, law or no law) several important modern social movements grew, nourished by the problems of *laissez-faire* individualism. Despite legal hostility and popular distrust, a number of monopolies were able to emerge. In the same unfriendly atmosphere, combinations of laboring men formed to attack some of the more brutal consequences of the new factory system in the industrialized portions of western Europe, England, and America. In 1848, Karl Marx and Friedrich Engels published the *Communist Manifesto*, which exhorted the laboring classes of the world to revolt against those who were alleged to control the means of production and the state. In order to do this, of course, individualism had to be destroyed and the workers had to unite in one great class movement.

COMMUNISM AND SYNDICALISM

In several countries, the new socialists interpreted Marxism to require the organization of a political party that might in time destroy the other political parties and conquer the state. In other countries, however, especially in Italy, France, and Spain, the new socialists were syndicalists. They believed that the workers might take over the industry in which they worked and run it themselves, guided in a mild sort of way by some central planning committee of workers. This idea was not entirely dissimilar from the medieval gild idea, with the important exception that the tools and buildings were now to be owned by the workers' union rather than by individual masters.

In England, syndicalism was called gild socialism. Both theories proposed worker control and ownership of their factories; both had strong decentralizing tendencies. It is significant that even many Marxist communist parties have urged that economic and political control be decentralized by industry and by factory. However, soon after achieving power, they abandoned this ideal, for they found it threatened their ability to control the economy and state from the center.

MODERN UNIONS AND GILDS COMPARED

In one way, then, socialism has been favorable to the autonomy of local production. But we have also mentioned that certain combinations of working men were formed that were not socialist. Such was the traditional trade union movement, much as we know it in America today. Here it is represented to the highest degree by some of the craft unions of the American Federation of Labor. The policies of such unions have resembled the policies of the medieval gilds. Steam fitters, for example, are skilled workers; this means that employers are not able at a moment's notice to find substitutes for striking steamfitters. By controlling the admission of new union-members, by obtaining contracts with employers that provide for the employment of union members only, such a union can gain considerable power over the area of life where steam fitting is essential. The union can then raise the qualifications of members, provide insurance and other fraternal benefits to its members, and give its members a kind of occupational "home," an *esprit de corps* that means much to human beings, especially in the modern world where most of men's attachments are transient and impersonal.

That is one side of the union's behavior. But there is the fact that in localities where steam fitters are abundant, young men who would rather pursue that trade than anything else had better look for something else. Furthermore, if someone devises new techniques that would cause the unemployment of steam fitters but would also save the consumer's money, he would undoubtedly encounter severe opposition. Much of the power amassed by such a union will be turned against the innovations of the Industrial Revolution (which, it is sometimes necessary to state, is still going on). Furthermore, the steam fitters are likely to possess a high evaluation of their own skill and importance and thus are likely to demand and receive as much for their services as they can get.

Since World War I, numerous trades in America—barbers, plumbers, bricklayers, carpenters, machinists, and many others—have in many parts of the country achieved a position something like that of the steam fitters. The politicians of today are in much the same position as the medieval kings with respect to such trades; the unions are not assaulted because they are compact and can convert readily to political warfare; usually, politicians co-operate with them and accept their accomplishments as beyond change, emphasizing publicly the positive features of such unionism.

PROFESSIONAL INTEREST REPRESENTATION

Certain professions, in particular medicine and the law, have moved faster than the crafts unions in acquiring the power to regulate and discipline their own members. Medical associations and bar associations in most American states set the training for students, the moral qualifications required of them, the ethics of their practice, and the conditions under which they may be suspended from practice. The governments have tended to give some power to the professions over their own affairs. By implication, power over their "own affairs" has tended sometimes to be power to determine what constitutes the "public interest" concerning medicine and law.

THE NEW PATTERN OF INDUSTRIAL INSTITUTIONS

A third reaction to the age of individualism, mentioned above, has been monopoly capitalism. Or, to put it more accurately, there have been several important deviations in practice from the pure theory of competition. Only one of these deviations is monopoly as the popular mind visualizes it—that is, a situation in which the total production of an essential commodity is controlled as to its amount and as to its price by a single owner or corporation. Another deviation that has come to be more typical of modern Western economies is oligopoly, a situation in which several huge firms control the bulk of the productive resources of an industry and set a pattern of leadership in working conditions, output, styles, and pricing that is followed by the small independent producers. A third deviation has been the trade association, an organization of the owners and managers of business enterprise in a particular field dedicated to the attainment of labor, market, production, and price policies on which the leading firms or a majority of members can agree. A final deviation from the theory of individualism of the early nineteenth century has been the separation of ownership of corporate wealth from management. As the stock issues of large corporations have been distributed among hundreds of people, as the financial affairs of large corporations have become more complex, as the privileges of the owners of stock have been reduced to hardly more than the right to receive dividends, the managers or top executives of the large corporations in many cases have become the real rulers of corporate property.

These industrial deviations have been of great importance to economic theory and practice. Their significance to politics is more relevant here and is worth describing. The managers have come to have a more personal stake in the careers of their enterprises than have the owners. To many owners, income alone is at issue in all the doings of their corporations; to the managers, not only income (for the top managers usually draw large salaries and also own stock) is at stake but also power and prestige. To them, the battle for control of all major decisions affecting their enterprises involves their opinion as to what is right for production and efficiency, and their internal and external prestige as the directors of the destiny of enterprises legally entrusted to them, and also their influence in determining external political policies affecting their concerns. As the government has turned more and more to the regulations of economic activities that had once been "industry-governed" or anarchic, the top managerial posts have required new skills—political skills that go beyond the technical abilities required in the management of large-scale enterprise. Public relations, institutional advertising, labor negotiations, community activities, and political pressure have come to consume a larger proportion of the time of top management. Scarcely a large corporation exists today that does not need constant and expert counseling on relations with governmental agencies, administrative and political.

In Germany, Italy, France, Japan, and England the growth of partial monopolies over many basic industries and the development of influential trade associations have gone hand in hand. Cartels have often been formed by oligopolies to ration out products under agreed-upon prices to maximize profits. There are many evidences that, in addition to economic agreements participated in by the leaders of the cartels and the trade associations, political pressure has been exercised on behalf of the policies of big business.

CORPORATISM

The Italian Fascist government was the first modern government to attempt a synthesis of these modern industrial tendencies with elements of the practices and theories of socialism and trade unionism. "Corporatism" was the name given the new structure of government. The major productive areas of the Italian economy, such as the maritime industry, agriculture, textile, industries, and others, were organized into "corporations" with power, at least on paper, to determine the working conditions, pay rates, production quotas, and other matters concerning the area. The various corporations were members of a Chamber of Corporations that planned and directed the major part of the economy. The system was practiced too little to draw conclusions about its results. But one notes with interest that it originated from very different sources: (1) the gild and craft-union idea that supports pluralism and all the advantages to be gained when workers in an industry have a good deal to say about how it is run (this idea, incidentally, received important backing by the Catholic Church); (2) the syndicalist and gild socialist variety of socialism that received mass backing in several European countries; (3) the obvious tendency of big businesses in modern life to act in concert in political and economic affairs.

FUNCTIONAL REPRESENTATION

Other countries also experimented with functional representation. Democratic Germany experimented with an Economic Council, composed of the representatives of management and labor. The council advised the government on economic and fiscal policy and on the regulation of industry. Functional representation was also debated in France, England, and Japan, and in several smaller countries. But none of these experiments or projects was seriously tried, because deep class antagonisms existed in politics and because the traditional governmental structure and government leaders resisted the development of new and competing political institutions. Leaders of industry and commerce feared to trust their interests to politicians; a good part of the public was deeply suspicious of big business; and the politicians, themselves, had too great an investment in the *status quo* of politics to risk their personal fortunes in novel schemes.

Nevertheless, European governments are still fumbling for a political formula that will allow for a closer integration of economics and politics without offending irredeemably the spokesmen of labor or management. The Schuman Plan of 1950, proposing the integration of western European heavy industrial production under a combined public-private international agency that would have considerable economic and political power, demonstrated that integrated pluralism along functional lines was far from dead as a goal of political theory.

U. S. A. INHOSPITABLE TO FUNCTIONAL REPRESENTATION

In the United States, formal interest-representation developed in scattered areas of national life, often unnoticed. It has not developed from conscious theory, but from grasping at particular solutions for particular problems. We mentioned that a number of craft unions and professions have powers over their members and over the contribution of their occupation to the great society. This is more than pressure-group politics. Such groups are little governments; by virtue of occupational competence, the group leaders are given special responsibilities with reference to public affairs. Thus, the state medical associations determine what are the legitimate tasks of doctors and the Missouri Bar Association nominates state supreme court justices. Associations of security dealers are required by the federal government to place certain requirements on their members and also to punish offending members. The farmers who raise certain regulated crops conduct elections to determine whether they wish to control the production of such crops. If two thirds of them so vote, a plan for the specified crop controls is put into effect in each county under the supervision of the Department of Agriculture, and all farmers are required to conform to the policy.

The famous National Industrial Recovery Administration (N.I.R.A.) (1933–5) allowed each industry to prepare a code of regulations governing the working conditions, ethics, and production policies of all the firms within the industry. The codes, upon being approved by the President, were executed by the officers of the N.I.R.A. The N.I.R.A. marked the high-water mark of functional representation and integrated pluralism in America. Leading opinion at the end of the experiment believed that the nation was moving into the "corporate state" too rapidly. But since then, many administrative agencies of the national government and of some state governments have been authorized by law to form boards composed of representatives of the industries regulated by the agencies, to consult with such boards on administrative policy, and to use such boards to assist in the execution of government policy. During World War II there were created over 750 Industry Advisory committees in the war establishments alone. Each committee gave representation to small, medium, and large companies, to the geographical sections of the industry, to the product specialty components of the industry, and to the members and non-members of the industry's trade associations.

SIGNIFICANCE OF DEPRESSION AND WAR EXPERIMENTS

These arrangements differed significantly from pressure politics of the older, traditional, lobby type. They introduced definite, structural relationships between special interests and the government. Although the N.I.R.A. was abandoned in the thirties and practically all of the Industry Advisory committees were dissolved at the end of the war, a large number of interests remain represented in the various subdivisions of normal, peacetime agencies. Pressure groups have moved far from their origins in the buttonholing of legislators in the lobbies of the legislative chambers. The state of the future, it can be predicted, will have more, not less, techniques for gaining technical assistance, administrative help, and legislative inspiration from the multitude of special economic, social, and religious groups that exist in modern society.

The involved and complicated processes of political influence in the modern state cannot be much simplified or easily controlled. Men have built, mostly without conscious thought, an incredibly complex institutional structure. A highly productive society and an intricate pattern of influence are closely related. If one collapses, the other also falls. It is impossible to destroy the pattern of influence without causing a great decrease in productivity. To destroy productivity in order to rid society of the influence that producers wield would seem idiotic to almost every one. We conclude, then, that the adjustment of influence is a problem that requires serious scientific attention, and that the alternatives to such an adjustment are primitivism or open conflict. As Charner Perry has written:

In the later stages of social development more and more understanding of the functioning of institutions is needed. As individuals, groups, and the factors of existence become more and more interdependent and delicately organized, there is increasing danger that the malfunctioning of some part, or the operation of some factor not considered, or a lack of proper adjustment among institutions will produce a serious or even disastrous breakdown.*

Such breakdowns, however calamitous, have not been infrequent in human communities. Now that we possess some understanding of the political dynamics that establish peaceful equilibrium, we will examine the origins of such breakdowns and two of their consequences: civil conflict and war.

* Quoted with the permission of the American Political Science Review from Charner Perry: "The Semantics of Political Science," *American Political Science Review*, Vol. XLIV (1950), p. 394.

Questions and Problems

1. Under what conditions does a nation tend to have many pressure groups?

2. How does a pressure group differ from a political party?

3. How do individuals become influential through personal political pressure, without using money?

4. How has money been used by individuals in pressure politics?

5. What are the motives of sporadic individual pressures in politics?

6. Describe the development and transformation of the American lobby.

7. Why is it difficult to regulate lobbies?

8. Using your own criteria of right and wrong, how would you go about distinguishing between a "good" lobby and a "bad" lobby?

9. Classify and give examples of the chief kinds of lobbies in the United States.

10. Describe the variety of and the techniques of business lobbies.

11. Describe the variety of and the technique of labor lobbies.

12. Describe the variety of and the techniques of farm lobbies.

13. Are there any important groups in society that seem not to possess lobbies? What are they, and why is this so? (Or if the answer is no, why do you think some groups have stronger lobbies than others?)

14. Go through a week's file of the *New York Times* or two weeks of a local newspaper, and list all stories that originate from or have to do with lobbies.

15. Ask five friends to list the four chief lobbies in the state and the four chief lobbies in Washington. Explain any lack of agreement on the most important lobbies and any lack of clarity about particular lobbies.

16. Describe briefly the history of functional representation before 1800.

17. From what sources has modern legal interest representation developed? Describe them.

18. What was "corporatism"? Is anything in American experience comparable to it?

Longer Study Questions and Problems
Suitable for Term Papers

1. Read David Loth: *Public Plunder* (1938), which is concerned principally with individual economic manipulations, and Belle Zeller: *Pressure Politics in New York* (1937), which is concerned primarily with group pressures. Compare the differences between individual and group techniques; compare the results in each case to the community at large. What conclusions can you draw that would help someone who has only the vaguest idea of pressure politics?

2. Read among, and write a report of fifteen pages on, the numerous documents and records of hearings published by the Select Committee of the

United States House of Representatives to Investigate Lobbying Activities (81st Congress, 2nd Session, 1950). Conduct your research so as to answer the question: "Did the Committee do a fair and thorough job?"

3. Investigate via the library the operations of one of the following bodies that utilizes or utilized functional representation: the medieval town councils, the Italian Chamber of Corporations, the modern Irish Senate, the Portuguese parliament of today, or the German Republic's Economic Council. Write a description of its legal structure, its operations, and its practical effects.

4. Report on the lobbying law of a state (preferably your own) in twenty pages, giving its provisions, the circumstances under which it came about, its effectiveness, the criticisms voiced against it, and the proposals that have been made to change it.

8

CIVIL CONFLICT AND WAR

WHILE economic and psychological means can resolve many
political disagreements, the use of physical coercion for the
same purposes has never been remote from human experience. An
adequate introduction to the political process must admit this fact and
relate the uses of force and violence to the struggle for values. First,
we will determine the difference between force and violence when they
are used as instruments of the government. Next, we will examine the
motives for using physical means of coercion, rather than economic or
psychological ones. We will then analyze the ways in which physical
coercion is organized and employed—revolutions and wars, for example. Finally, we will ask whether coercion ever produces the results
expected of it in governing human beings.

Force and Violence

WHEN IS COERCION LEGITIMATE?

An intelligent appraisal of civil conflict and war requires
some knowledge of force and violence in politics. Our chapter on the
state and authority declared that force was the legitimate use of physical coercion and that violence was the illegitimate use of physical
coercion. If a government is held to be legitimate by its people, its
use of force is approved, with whatever reservations the people may
have about the usefulness or lack of usefulness and the adequacy or
inadequacy of force. Thus, although the people of a state may agree
that the government is entitled to use force against a riot of strikers,
they may well prefer that the government prevent such outbreaks by
establishing a more sound economic policy or by persuading the clashing parties to accept some peaceful settlement. Furthermore, a people

rarely holds to a single principle of legitimacy. Thus many Americans applauded the personal leadership of Colonel "Teddy" Roosevelt in the Spanish-American War; whatever "Teddy" did was all right. However, many other Americans deplored the nation's "descent" from legality into "violence." These Americans would have preferred to arbitrate the Spanish-American dispute.

VIOLENT CONFLICTS AMONG ORGANS OF STATE

We must also consider this fact: Even when its legitimacy is unquestioned by the people, the government—composed as it is of a number of different organs—may develop internal conflicts. The people then may have to side with one element of the government against another, with each part of the government claiming legality, reason, and legitimacy. The people are united in expecting a government that acts according to legal rules; but when one branch of the government is in open conflict with another branch, either or both may resort to violence in order to prove its own *legality*.

America has had some close escapes from violent conflict among governing organs and some unfortunate explosions. President Jackson arbitrarily removed the deposits of the United States Treasury from the United States Bank, even though the Supreme Court had declared that the bank was constitutional and might be the financial agency of the federal government. Jackson disputed the Supreme Court's interpretation of the Constitution and used the executive forces of the government to carry out his theory of the Constitution. Again, during his term of office, Jackson disagreed with the State of South Carolina on the question whether a state might refuse to obey a law of Congress. Partly in response to his threat of force, South Carolina accepted an "honorable compromise."

The most disastrous experience of the United States with conflicting interpretations of legal legitimacy came with the Civil War. Calhoun's interpretation of the federal union held that the states reserved the legal right to disagree with the decisions of the majority in Congress and of the President. Both Southerners and Northerners professed their attachment to legality, constitutionalism, and the lawful union. Both sides resorted to coercion to uphold the "correct and legitimate" legal order.

We must therefore warn the unwary student that the theory of legitimacy is only simple at first glance. We must remember that in the same society, more than one principle of legitimacy may be held by the people or by a single person; force is only one of the instruments of legitimate authority, and other instruments, like education and economic policy, may be preferred by the people or by the rulers; and finally, different branches of the same government may use physical coercion as well as other instruments of power to foist their policies on each other. Such are the main relationships between legitimate authority and force and violence.

PHYSICAL COERCION DEFINED

Force and violence both involve physical coercion. Physical coercion is the direction of human activities (a) by commands that are accompanied by sanctions of a bodily kind or by the threat of bodily sanctions, and (b) by the unexplained but deliberate infliction of damage to persons—in every case associated with a minimum of symbolic, verbal, and economic tactics.

Why do we require such an involved definition of physical coercion? There is a reason for each element of the definition.

We want to include physical arrest, detention of the person, the physical restraint of children, physical self-defense, the dispersing of a riot, and other cases of manhandling human beings. We also want to include not only such things as the Communist invasion of Southern Korea but also the American actions in resisting the invasion by force.

The threat of bodily sanctions is usually enough to accomplish obedience to commands. The presence of a police force, of an army, of a fleet, and of a court system inhibits disobedience. Most enactments state what conduct is legal and what is forbidden; they also state the consequences of violations of the law.

Sometimes physical coercion occurs as the unexplained but deliberate infliction of damage to persons. By "unexplained" we mean that it is superfluous, or not justified, or not rationalized, or not preceded by command. The application of coercion may be beyond the intention of the law. Further than that, it may be inflicted for its own sake, without reference to any command. The former is more common; there is no more reason to believe that men can always mete out the exactly justifiable amount of punishment in a situation where force is deemed necessary than to believe that men can always levy the exact amount of taxes needed or distribute the exact number of food coupons required. It is as true of coercive means as of any other means of influencing human behavior that the unforeseen consequences of purposive action sometimes far exceed the predicted consequences. "It was a mistake to arm the rabble," thought many an unhorsed knight in the late Middle Ages. Admiral Perry did not awaken sleepy Japan so that it might arm, in the style of the West, to attack the United States a century later.

POLITICS COMPOUNDED OF COERCION AND OTHER MEANS

Physical coercion exists in its clearest form when it is not accompanied by a great deal of ceremonial justification, logical argumentation, and employment of economic tactics. We stress this "pure" form of coercion only in order to emphasize the fact that coercion is rarely seen in this form in the world of political events. "Pure" coercion is naked force or naked violence. It is a command that is stripped down to the mere indication of direction desired, accompanied by the flourishes of the weapons of force and violence. Almost every political event is a compound of physical coercion with psychological and economic weapons. Thus, on the same day in 1950 that the United States ordered its planes into action against North Korean Communist armies, it issued a statement of its moral principles, recounted its attempts to keep peace, asked the Soviet government to put pressure on the North Koreans to withdraw from the South, and announced that it acted with the moral, psychological, and material support of the United Nations. At the same time it declared that it would supply arms

FIGURE 23

THE TECHNIQUE OF CONTENT ANALYSIS ILLUSTRATED
(*as used by government prosecutors in a sedition trial against the publisher of* The Galilean) *
"The Galilean" (December 22, 1941—March 2, 1942)

STATEMENTS IN "THE GALILEAN" CONSISTENT WITH AND CONTRADICTORY TO NAZI PROPAGANDA THEMES

	CON- SISTENT	CONTRA- DICTORY
1. The United States is internally corrupt	279	26
2. The foreign policies of the United States are morally unjustifiable	39	0
3. The President of the United States is reprehensible	70	0
4. Great Britain is internally corrupt	28	0
5. The foreign policies of Great Britain are morally unjustifiable	23	0
6. Prime Minister Churchill is reprehensible	16	0
7. Nazi Germany is just and virtuous	12	2
8. The foreign policies of Japan are morally justifiable	15	5
9. Nazi Germany is powerful	19	2
10. Japan is powerful	79	2
11. The United States is weak	317	5
12. Great Britain is weak	113	3
13. The United Nations are disunited	29	0
14. The United States and the world are menaced by: a. Communists	43	0
b. Jews	112	0
c. Plutocrats	1	0
Total	1195	45

* Reprinted with permission from H. D. Lasswell, Nathan Leites, and Associates: *Language of Politics: Studies in Quantitative Semantics* (New York: George W. Stewart, Publisher, Inc., 1949), p. 227.

and other goods to protect Formosa and French Indo-China. Also note, in Figure 23, how "fifth column" propaganda is used domestically to aid the war aims of an enemy power.

A remarkable proof of the intimate relation of physical coercion to propaganda is afforded by a study of German civilians who had suffered bombing attacks. The United States Strategic Bombing Survey found that one out of three civilian Germans indicated that his morale was more affected by bombing than by any other single factor including the successive defeats at the front. That the morale factor *is* separable from the physical coercion factor is implicit in this statement by the Survey: "The maximum *morale* effects of dropping a given tonnage of bombs on Germany would have been attained by lighter raids as widely distributed as possible, rather than by concentrated heavy bombing in limited areas." In other words, psychological effects might well be the primary motive for the use of coercion under certain conditions.

CHILDHOOD TRAINING IN COERCION

How we interpret physical coercion depends largely on how it was used and interpreted in our childhood training. How a person's father used physical coercion in the family gives most men some ideas on how force should be and should not be used in politics. How the child's playmates, with their varying family backgrounds, used coercion and interpreted coercion will help provide the framework within which the adult will employ and interpret coercion. This is an age-old discovery of political science. It is startling how many people today profess not to believe it.

The Spartans knew the principle and applied it in the training of their young; the Romans knew it and also applied it rigorously to get the kind of attitudes and practices with respect to force and violence in later life that they wanted. The Fascists, Nazis, and Communists reoriented their educational systems, once they achieved power, so as to insert a new respect for force in the minds of their children. The psychiatrists of today know how a child may be trained to use and accept varying systems of physical coercion. (Several of them have commented on the large number of battle neuroses among American troops that might be traced back to childhood training. Many American children, especially in the middle income and higher educational groups, have been taught to abhor physical compulsion of any kind. They were not taught to abhor education, propaganda, economic measures, or economic manipulation. But, of course, expertness in these instruments does not suffice to win battles.)

The Objectives of Physical Coercion

THE AIMS OF FORCE AND VIOLENCE

Force and violence may be chosen as the effective means of achieving economic objectives—markets, control of factories, the "wealth of the Orient," and so on. They may be used to establish the honor and respect "due" to a group in order to wipe off a "disgraceful" defeat of the past, for example. They may often be the means of self-defense, of insuring the safety of one's position, of protecting one's "rights." They are often used to gain power, that is, the right to make important decisions that govern a community. They sometimes have as their end the satisfaction of an urge to destruction—vandalism, sadism, the relief of deep and undefined hatreds that have no evident rational connection with the objects of the coercion.

MOTIVES OF COERCION USUALLY PLURAL

In many, perhaps nearly all, cases of coercion, the agents have more than one objective. Thus the Italian campaign in Ethiopia in 1936 was prompted by several motives, among them the desire to exploit the mineral and agricultural resources of the country, the desire to avenge a massacre of Italian troops some fifty years earlier, and the desire to increase the power position of Italy relative to England in East Africa. One of Mussolini's sons, an aviator, lived to regret his rash description of the beauty and pleasure of seeing his bombs dropping on hapless tribesmen—a way of expressing destructive urges common in the literature of war. It is safe to say that wherever more than a handful of men engage in violence, one will find a plethora of motives, varying in kind and intensity.

COERCION FOR ECONOMIC ENDS

The use of coercion for economic ends is ancient. As we mentioned earlier, some of the most illustrious investigators into the origins of the state assert that the state originated in conquest for reasons of economic benefits—spoils, food, and land. It was said of the Romans that they never learned the true meaning of trade; they conquered, carried back to Rome the captured wealth, and thereafter levied tribute; they treated their imperial provinces like beehives, extracting the honey upon occasion but rarely contributing to the honey-making process. Also, the booty extracted by medieval warriors —in spite of the fact that they fought for honor and prestige as no men have fought since—makes the economic reparations that modern· nations demand of the vanquished (perhaps the Soviet Union should be excepted) seem comparatively small.

In the domestic life of several nations, the Jews have been massacred or violently evicted at various intervals to provide bankrupt governing groups and pirateering political factions with accumulated wealth. A number of Nazis emerged as millionaires from the violent persecution of the Jews. The ownership of the loot was "legalized" by selling it for a pittance to preferred buyers. Similar scenes were enacted in the early modern period, when the Jews were expelled from Spain, and during the Middle Ages in various countries. Not to be outdone, the French monarchy destroyed the Protestant Huguenot movement in France, in part out of religious fanaticism, but also in part out of covetousness. Else why were the Huguenots not allowed to carry their property with them, and why were so many royal henchmen suddenly enriched? The destruction of the Catholic Church in England was also accompanied by large-scale looting and confiscation of property. This kind of event is so common in history as to require no elaboration here. We may mention finally that among the most vociferous spokesmen for the imprisonment and exile of the Japanese-Americans of California were individuals who stood to gain by the elimination of Japanese competition in agriculture and by the forced sale of Japanese-owned property.

One need not subscribe to Lenin's theory (that monopoly capitalism, having exhausted its domestic markets, turns to imperialism for profits) to perceive that there was a strong economic motive operating in every century of European imperialism. Drake, Raleigh, and the court of Elizabeth had never heard of Communist theory, but they perceived opportunities for wealth on the Seven Seas that little England could never have afforded them; centuries later, workmen in the drab factories of the Industrial Revolution who *had* heard of the communist ideology acted to seize factories by violence (for example, France, 1871), and their pulses beat quicker when they thought that now there would be more to divide amongst themselves. When the Americans and British liberated Southern Italy in 1943, the landlords were flabbergasted to hear from many of their tenants that the age of rents had gone: what better purpose could be assumed for the invasionary violence than to make farm owners of farm tenants? When the Communist North Koreans captured Seoul, stocks of goods were thrown to the people and a radical redistribution of land occurred.

PRESTIGE, HONOR, AND "FACE"

Acts of coercion made with the intention of restoring prestige or honor, gaining respect, or maintaining "face," are numerous. Indeed, one can marvel at the common idea that the age of chivalry is gone. True, in ancient and medieval times, men did not feel the need to conceal the fact that they were fighting on the grounds of honor. It was taken for granted as a legitimate motive for war or personal combat. Leonidas and his Spartans fought at Thermopylae for the honor of their city while their Greek allies retreated. Long before that time, Greeks had fought amongst themselves at Troy——over the fate of a woman named Helen, according to Homer.

We shall never know to what degree clannish pride entered into the cause of the fabled Trojan War. Nor shall we ever know the exact extent to which the Germans of Hitler's Germany condoned the resort to international violence in order to avenge their humiliating defeat in World War I. Nor shall we know, for that matter, how many of the hundreds of thousands of Frenchmen who went to death at Verdun went the more willingly because they remembered the crushing defeat of their armies in the Franco-Prussian War of 1870. Memoirs, eye-witness accounts, and historical researches tell us that honor and "face" were involved. Personal experience tells us that Americans had the same motives when the Japanese struck at Pearl Harbor in 1941 and when the North Koreans invaded South Korea. The Japanese, Chinese, and other Orientals are reputed by Westerners to value "face" above every other value; but Westeners, though prone to justify coercion on economic, "rational," or other grounds, including self-defense, undoubtedly value honor to a considerable extent.

In most modern countries, recourse to coercion for the sake of honor is severely discouraged. Dueling has gone out of style, although American and European politicians once knew and practiced the custom. In eighteenth-century England, the London mob was a distinct influence on politics, a kind of measure of the temper of the people. It was, however, a most crude measure, not at all like the Gallup poll; the mob was destructive, not always active when it had good reason to be, but prone to activity when issues were personal and even trivial. It would not gather to declaim against the repressive penal law, or to demand support for popular revolutions in France; but it would rage through the streets in support of a demagogic mountebank like Wilkes, seeing in the opposition to seating him in the Commons the snubbing of a commoner gentleman's just ambitions.

CLASS WARFARE AND SOCIAL STATUS

The class war of modern European nations shows how complicated the problem of social prestige may be. Ranked against one another are the working classes who appeal to the universal principle of equality, and the middle classes who feel their social rank slipping. While many industrial workers are organizing, gaining higher pay and better working conditions, and claiming that the future belongs to them, many members of the middle class are finding clerical skills less rare and less valued than in the past. They are losing their financial advantage over manual workers and are finding promotion to positions of ownership or high income more difficult to achieve. The upper ranks of society also are directly threatened; the deference, the honor, the bows, the respectful address given their status for centuries hang at issue in the class struggle. The upper and middle ranks have joined frequently against the workers; the aristocracy and the upper middle classes could never have held out in all of Europe from Napoleon to Hitler if they had not gained support from the middle classes, who wanted to go up, but never wanted to go down, even if to go down meant to join in the "inevitable" triumph of the proletariat. The use of violence by one class against another, then, is more easily understood when one appreciates the threat that an aggressive working class poses to the classes above it.

COERCION FOR SAFETY AND PROTECTION

The use of coercion for self-defense and protection is authorized by all major legal systems of the world. In cases of international violence, the plea of "self-defense" frequently is used to justify all kinds of aggression, but it need not be dismissed as a real motive for that reason. The poor showing of Spain in the Spanish-American War and the weak defense of Poland against Germany in 1939 are pathetic instances of self-defense, mixed, no doubt, with motives of honor and prestige. The Germans in 1945 had exhausted practically all motives other than safety; many of them, weighing the relative severities of Anglo-American and Russian occupation, hoped to forestall the Russians in the East until the Allies in the West might move in.

POWER AS AN AIM OF COERCION

Power is another general objective for which coercion is employed. Obviously, the attainment of economic ends by force or violence will often increase the power of the victorious party; so also will the attainment of greater prestige through the use of force or violence. But control of the apparatus of the government can be in itself a goal of coercion. A violent strike for a closed shop (economic value) is not as clearly a striving for power as is a violent general strike to bring on the collapse of the existing government. Hannibal, Caesar,

Alexander, and Napoleon seemed to want nothing more than the utter defeat of their enemies. Lasswell quotes Genghis Khan, the Mongol conqueror as declaring "a man's highest job in life is to break his enemies, to drive them before him, to take from them all the things that have been theirs." Other values enter the attitude of violence, but the power drive may be foremost in intensity.

The clearest employment of coercion on behalf of the maintenance or the attainment of power is one where, with the consent of both the users and the subjects of coercion, force is used to maintain order, punish crimes, and discourage subversion of the government. Coercion is employed because it is the rational instrument to use in a given case; it is quicker, readier, more adapted to the situation, and more lasting in its consequences than education or economic policy. This is the principle for the use of coercion with which most people would agree.

Other uses of coercion to attain power abound, however, and many of them would not be agreeable to most of the people most of the time. Political assassinations preparatory to seizing power, palace revolutions, "kidnapping" ballot boxes to prevent free elections, dispersal of all assemblages believed to be in the political opposition, intimidation of political opponents—these, too, are violent acts that aim at the achievement or retention of power.

DESTRUCTIVENESS AS A ROOT OF COERCION

Finally, destructiveness must be mentioned as a general objective of coercion. Destructiveness is used here to mean all motives that have no instrumental connection with the persons who are the recipients of violence. The man who is nagged by his wife and thereupon beats his dog would fall into this category. His motive in beating the dog is to relieve the tensions and anxieties caused by his wife's hostile actions. This "irrational" character of destructiveness should not lead one to think destructiveness is insignificant in politics. Men who have seen atrocities inflicted on helpless enemies in war by exhausted and maddened soldiers or who have seen race riots flare up among men who had never seen each other before that moment, can testify to the strength of destructive impulses in human beings. Even children perceive that certain other children and adults "have a chip on their shoulder."

PSYCHOANALYTIC THEORY OF DESTRUCTIVENESS

Perhaps the most prominent theory used in modern psychology to explain destructiveness is that derived from the psychology of Sigmund Freud. The theory is built on the interaction of six concepts: guilt, frustration, displacement, projection, rationalization, and aggression.

A large number of people in our society are trained as children to feel personally responsible and very uncomfortable whenever they violate any moral principle they have been taught. Whenever anything goes wrong, they believe that they themselves are to blame. The burden of this guilt makes them miserable whenever the environment does not provide them with a minimum of the things they need—affection, security, material things.

In addition, modern Western civilization abounds in frustrations. A frustration is simply the foiled attempt of a person to get something he wants. Continual frustration seems to mark modern Western society more than many others. An American of 150 years ago could exercise greater control over his environment than can the American of today. Still, today or 150 years ago, civilization demands many restraints, and considerable frustration is an unavoidable accompaniment of civilization.

The human being cannot dissipate frustrations automatically. He can, however, shove them off onto something else, in his mind or in the outside world. This is displacement. When a man is fired, he is prevented by long training and by law from beating his employer. The man will be tense and anxious about the event, and if he is encumbered by many more major and minor restraints and frustrations, he may seize upon outlets for his tensions. He is, fortunately for them, also to some extent prevented from "taking it out" on members of his family. He may possibly get away with kicking the dog.

Among the objects of the world onto which tensions are pushed or affects are displaced are both primary and secondary objects. Thus when a father punishes his boy, the child often represses the hostility he feels at the "unjust" punishment. If he displaces his hostility onto his teacher, that is a primary object; if onto authority in general, that is a secondary object.

Projection is a well-nigh universal occurrence. One imputes to others motives he himself possesses. People who know or believe themselves to be cheaters tend to regard other people as cheaters. Projection stands ready to help displacement. When it is inexpedient to release hostility against frustrating objects, the hostility is repressed and often seeks displacements on secondary objects. Projection affords a motive for the particular displacement. First the subject feels hostile; he imagines then that the other fellow feels hostile. The subject then justifies his feeling of hostility towards the other fellow on the ground of self-defense. Projected hostilities arising out of displacement constitute destructiveness.

Rationalization gives a socially accepted veneer to the destructiveness; usually some slight, insubstantial act of the target-person or group is magnified out of proportion, and, since proof is a very difficult thing in social affairs, most people do not realize that rationalization is occurring—often because they, too, are undergoing the same process. Finally, aggression occurs as a result of these destructive motives along with any other motives present in the situation. The aggression may be expressed verbally, or by depriving someone of something that person holds dear, or by injuring physically another person—the last being perhaps the most satisfying type of release to the aggressor.

Guilt is one of the frequent companions of displacement and projection: the subject acts "wrongly" by being destructive; he feels guilty; he cannot bear more guilt than he already possesses without extreme discomfort. He therefore projects the guilt onto the objects of his destructiveness. The object is now not only hostile but also wrong, that is, guilty. It is all very convenient to some sick souls who have been brought up badly and to not a few normal adults whose personal situations happen to be very difficult and tense.

OTHER THEORIES OF DESTRUCTIVENESS

There are theories of destructiveness other than the Freudian theory sketched roughly above. Ian Suttie, for example, traces destructiveness to the original shock of the infant being born, modern psychology assuming quite rightly that the mother is not the only person involved in the pains of childbirth. The initial birth-trauma, that of being separated from the mother, sets up an anxiety of a general and massive character that can only be allayed by affection and security. Frustrated love, then, causes destructiveness, whether it is directed against parents, friends, or nations. Sebastian de Grazia has expanded Suttie's analysis into a general theory of social co-operation, in which the tensions that abet wars rise from the fear of the destruction of one's revered symbols and in which the satisfaction of closer fraternity with one's own kind is often sought at the expense of outsiders. It will be some time before any single theory will win the minds of scientists. At present, each theory suggests the deep and hidden nature of human motives that somehow work their way through infancy, childhood and adulthood into the behavior of people in politics (see Figure 24). It is perhaps unnecessary to warn against the quick acceptance of any one theory—especially since these psychological problems are formidable enough to baffle even expert psychiatrists.

FIGURE 24

THE USE OF THE PSYCHOLOGICAL INTERVIEW
THE GENETIC ASPECTS OF MACK'S AUTHORITARIAN PERSONALITY *

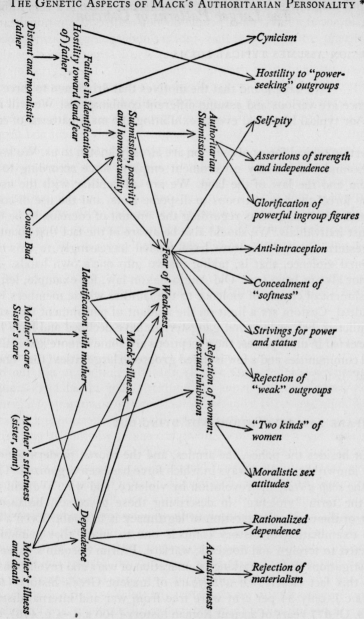

Here is illustrated the use of psychological interviews into intimate life history to find explanations of adult political attitudes. Although the case of Mack cannot be understood by this diagram, the diagram shows us what some psychologists are looking for in the way of connections between childhood (bottom) and adult beliefs (top).

* Reproduced with permission from T. W. Adorno, Else Frenkel-Brunswik, Daniel J. Levinson, and R. Nevitt Sanford: *The Authoritarian Personality* (New York: Harper and Brothers, 1950), p. 801.

The Larger Patterns of Coercion

COERCION ASSUMES TYPICAL FORMS

We have found that the motives that drive men to force and violence are various and assume different combinations. We will now look for typical historical events exhibiting the main patterns of coercion.

Certain typical forms of coercion are already known to us. We know, for example, that every government employs force according to the custom and the law of the land. We are all familiar with the use of police force, the use of troops to disperse riots, and the use of courts to hand down judgments regarding the amount of coercion to be used against individuals. We should also be aware of the fact that countries of western European culture have tended increasingly to frown on personal violence, that is, taking justice into one's own hands. This has not always been true. Old Anglo-Saxon law, for example, left the punishment of crimes of violence to the families whose members were assaulted. Custom set a limit on the amount of punishment that could be inflicted. Brigandage and gangsterism have declined and have been suppressed in most places; the exceptions are some remote and isolated rural communities and a few isolated groups in large cities (the "underworld").

WARFARE AND REVOLUTIONS NOT DYING OUT

But besides the police, the armies, and the courts, modern societies have known three other ways in which force has been organized. These are the *coup d'état*, the revolution by violence, and war. We will now use the term "violence" in describing these processes, because, in most of the cases, the question of legitimacy is in doubt. Even a cursory examination of history compels one to admit that mankind is addicted to foreign and domestic warfare. Pitirim Sorokin's extensive investigations and painstaking enumeration of wars and revolutions reveal this fact clearly. Of 375 years of ancient Greek history (500–126 B.C.), only 34 per cent were free from war and internal disturbances. Of 877 years of ancient Roman history (400 B.C.–A.D. 476), only 46 per cent were free from wars and disturbances. England in the period from 656 to 1933 suffered 162 violent disturbances; in 875 years (1051–1925), England had, according to Sorokin's estimates, 493 years (56 per cent) of war.

These and many other figures caused Sorokin to conclude that wars and revolutions have neither increased or decreased through history. There are merely unexplained fluctuations in violence from time to time. Furthermore, regarding the character of revolutions, every country has had mad and bloody revolutions; the "terror" was not unique to the French Revolution of 1789. There seem to be about three times as many civil wars (that is, severe internal disturbances) as international wars, according to Quincy Wright's figures on 278 conflicts from 1480–1941. Since 1941, every year has seen more war. From 1941–5, the whole world, with isolated exceptions (Sweden, Switzerland and very few others), was at war. The years 1946–50 saw civil war in China and Korea, revolution in Indonesia, and guerrilla warfare in scattered parts of the Orient including Burma, Malaya, Indochina, and the Philippines. India suffered mass murders among Hindus and Moslems in 1947 and 1948. Successful *coups d'état* occurred in Venezuela and Brazil in 1945, Haiti and Bolivia in 1946, Nicaragua and Ecuador in 1947, Costa Rica, Paraguay, Peru, Venezuela and El Salvador in 1948 and Paraguay in 1949. In fact, 43 successful *coups d'état* or revolutions marked the period from 1930–49 in South America. The Near East and eastern Europe have had even more hectic careers during the last several years.

THE SCIENTIFIC STUDY OF PRINCIPLES OF VIOLENCE

There have been many attempts to discover what general scientific laws govern the processes of *coup d'état*, revolutions, and war, but regrettably few principles have emerged. For instance, Dr. Quincy Wright studied warfare in all times and all places about which information is available, and yet, after ten years, could not feel free to state the exact conditions under which wars occur, the exact components in the strength of a nation, the exact conditions under which the laws of war will be observed, nor could he answer several other vital questions concerning this universal form of violence. The same criticisms may be voiced about Curzio Malaparte's study of *coups d'état* and of Aristotle's or Mosca's or Pettee's studies of revolutions.

Yet much progress has been made in the study of these events during the last generation. Groups and individuals from the sciences of politics, psychology, and sociology have made many intensive partial studies that enable us to feel much more sure of our ground when discussing the violent behavior of groups than we ever were before. While there is no agreement about many of the factors entering into intranational and international violence, science can answer certain kinds of questions and make the whole area one of partial light rather than complete shadow.

These problems are similar in many respects to problems that social science has already solved in studying public opinion. An extensive and intensive examination of attitudes and behavior allows a highly probable prediction to be made about who will win a particular election. Predicting such events as attempts at the violent seizure of power, revolutionary attempts, or wars rests on many of the same observations, methods, and techniques. The main difference is *not* that the number of factors at work in the case of an election campaign are less numerous or less complex than those at work in the dynamic and violent events we are considering here; the main difference lies in the fact that the factors at work in the coming of a war, a revolution, or a seizure of power are dangerous to work with. *Indirect* indices must be devised that have a high correlation with the factors to be predicted. Premier Stalin cannot be asked by a casual interviewer: "Do you plan to go to war in ninety days?" "What will you do if the United States and her Allies mass troops in Germany?" Rather one must make elaborate studies of all Stalin's habits, speeches, gestures, journeys, conferences, communications, and so on in order to arrive at a predictive index; that is, there must be a careful interpretation, based on the various social sciences, of all deviations from regularities of behavior on the part of the subject to determine whether an unusual act is in the offing, what kind of an unusual act it is, and whether the act seems about to take place this month, in two months, or six months from now. One also would have to analyze thoroughly all evidence bearing on the Premier's character. From this analysis a theory of his cognitive structure must be built up. That is, how does he view events? What does he continually see as important features of events?

The objection may be raised that leaders are not prone to give away their hands by their behavior, especially as a crucial situation approaches, because they know they are being observed closely by potential enemies. In reply, it may be said that leaders are human and can conceal only part of their behavior if they are to conduct themselves as leaders. They still must communicate with their publics, their subordinates; they still must give orders whose effects are often visible.

Furthermore, any increase in cover-up measures may be significant. Psychoanalysts often get their first clue that a patient is approaching the revelation of important experiences in his life and even a clue to the nature of the experience by the patient's anxious diversionary and secretive behavior. An apocryphal story of the exaggerated action of a hospitalized mental patient illustrates this point. Realizing that one of the reasons he was hospitalized was his insistence that the earth was flat, he decided to behave normally upon escape. He ventured forth, accosting everyone he met with the words: "The world is round." Soon thereafter, he found himself back in the hospital.

The close scrutiny of a leader, of course, is only one of the numerous facets of the situation that must be studied, but enough has been said to indicate that there are resemblances between this twin problem of predicting elections and predicting international violence and the twin problem of building uranium atomic bombs and building hydrogen atomic bombs. Success in solving one problem leads one to conceive of the way in which the other might be solved, even though no absolute assurance is forthcoming and even though many new special techniques would have to be devised.

Another fact is worth noting in the kind of prediction that we are discussing here. Predictions of this order may well be possible even if the underlying causes of wars and revolutions are not known. Pollsters do not have to know why people vote the way they do in order to predict how they vote, any more than astronomers have to know how the heavens were created in measuring the speed of the stars.

The present book is not a laboratory manual; it is not a study in the application of specific techniques to the solution of particular problems. We must therefore rest content here with a general summary of the most important factors operating in *coups d'état*, revolutions, and wars, with some comment on the way the factors affect each other.

PATTERNS OF THE COUP D'ÉTAT

The *coup d'état* (stroke of state) designates the acts of violence accomplished in a short period of time in a direct attempt to seize a government. The *coup d'état* is *part of all revolutions* and *exists also in a form sufficient in itself* to take over the government. It is the violent seizure of the apparatus of the state by revolutionaries who overturn the existing governing group and substitute their own personnel. Certain elements characterize a *coup d'état* that is sufficient in itself to overthrow the existing government. The government to be overthrown must be weak domestically, like the Czarist government of Russia in 1917 or the Kerensky government of Russia two years later. Perhaps the chief component in the weakness of authority is the loss of support from the population. Riddled with incompetence, with personal quarrels, and bereft of the capacity for quick decision and vigorous action, the ruling group cannot turn to the population for supporters, and must succumb to the rising group.

Machiavelli was one of the earliest writers to observe that republics are hard to overthrow. The ranks of the rulers in a republic extend downward in considerable depth; a simple changing of places or the annihilation of a small top group has only a momentary effect. The great republics of history die hard, and rarely by simple *coups*. *Coups d'état* abound wherever politics are managed by a tiny proportion of the people—for example, in absolute monarchies or in states with meaningless republican forms. They were everyday occurrences in early medieval times in Europe, in different periods of the Near East ancient empires, in China for centuries past, and in the South American republics of the nineteenth and twentieth centuries.

Where the government is not palsied, or where it might gain some popular support, the *coup d'état* requires for its success the connivance of members of the government—especially in the armed forces—or a source of strength in the population at large sufficient to counterbalance the armed forces that are expected to defend the existing regime. Most commentators believe that Mussolini's "March on Rome" in 1922 would have been thwarted if the King simply had brandished the legitimate authority of the Crown on behalf of the democratic state. His failure to do so was taken as tacit consent for the change. But, of course, "ifs" do not make history. The fact is that Italy was ripe for the *coup* because, among other things, it had a weak monarchy that had never been educated to the democratic regime. The Fascists had the advantage not only of this passivity of the existing regime but also of the active support of elements in the army, the police, and industry.

In contrast, the Nazis in Germany were able to seize power in 1932 in a democracy that had considerable strength. Aside from considerable street-fighting between Nazi gangs and various Socialist and Communist opponents, the transition of the Nazis to power was cloaked in legal forms. Hitler's party obtained a large vote, and Hindenburg was finally influenced (some compare his behavior to that of the Italian King) to appoint Hitler Chancellor. A series of extraordinary decrees placed Nazis in key positions in the government; the violence that had been confined mainly to the street invaded the government itself. Opposition politicians were killed, deposed, or intimidated. Mock elections were held in which the Nazis gained a large majority of votes. Hitler pursued the new popular "mandate" to its extremes, purging the government of opposition, both actual and potential. No sufficient force was left to oppose the ruthless progress of the Nazi Revolution. But again, Hitler's *coup* found passivity at the top (that is, low morale), sympathetic minds in the bureaucracy, and help from extremists in the army.

CHARACTER OF REVOLUTIONARIES

Let us examine the composition of the revolutionary group. The *coup d'état* is carried out by a small number of active revolutionaries, who, while they may have some respect for legal forms, are determined to carry their ends by any means. Invariably some violence is involved. The leadership must possess the skills needed in the critical hours; the most important are the skills of agitation, violence, and administration. In proportion as the *coup* is carried out in a society that is complex and democratic in sentiment, the top leaders must be political and agitational. Oratory, flamboyancy, acute judgment of the timing of the stroke, and decisiveness are much in demand. The conditions of modern society demand that oratorical skills be supplemented by their kindred propagandistic skills. The press must be won over by force, fraud, or persuasion in the early days of the revolt.

The revolting group, wittingly or not, often seizes the sacred symbols of the existing regime. The French rebels of 1789 took possession of the person of the King, a lucky stroke that brought over crowds of Frenchmen despite their knowledge that the King was a virtual prisoner. The President of a republic serves the same purpose in some South American revolutions. When other rebels in history have seized the Capitol, the official seals, the high tribunal of justice, or the temples of the gods, they have gained the same symbolic advantage over the threatened regime.

The group leadership must have an aptitude both for violence and administration. Usually this means army traitors, ex-army officers, or workers trained in the use of arms. The police force, the key military garrisons, and the key government buildings must be taken over quickly and any opposition found there must be crushed. The administrative skills are needed to manage the treasury, the crucial offices of the government, and the vital physical communications that connect the center of the revolt with the rest of the country—railroads, trucks, radio stations, telephone systems, and utilities. The influx of adherents to the new regime must be quickly mobilized and committed to favorable action to give a firm foundation to the government.

REVOLUTION IS A MORE FUNDAMENTAL CHANGE

A *coup d'état* is often only the inauguration of a revolution. A revolution is more fundamental in meaning to a society. It is a forcible and rapid transformation that alters the basic structure of power and the distribution of benefits in a society.

There is no doubt that behind every revolution lies some motive for the redistribution of some value, material or ideal (like prestige). But before such a redistribution of values is actively desired by a considerable part of the population, profound changes must take place. A period of gestation must occur, sometimes, as with the great French Revolution of 1789, lasting for a century before erupting into swift change. Allegiances must weaken, and the existing principle of legitimacy must deteriorate (from traditional to rational in the case of the French Revolution; from rational to charismatic in the case of the Nazi Revolution).

AN ORGANIZED FORCE LIES BEHIND REVOLUTIONS

The new forces of revolution cannot succeed without visible, organized, and permanent interests. For instance, the Great Revolution in England in the mid-seventeenth century was essentially a revolt by the parliamentary party, partially dominated by religious dissenters and by the new capitalistic wealthy and middle classes, against the powerful monarch and his coterie of nobles. The parliamentary forces won a definite victory that lasted for a long time, despite a partially successful reaction towards the end of the century. The victorious movement possessed tangible strength and cohesion; it combined strong religious and economic interests.

A second revolutionary movement, it is not often enough realized, existed within the parliamentary party. This was the Leveller movement, composed principally of soldiers and company grade officers of the parliamentary army. The Levellers wished to extend the revolution by sweeping economic and social reforms. They hoped for complete equality of rights and privileges. But the Levellers were citizen-soldiers: once the main revolution was consummated they might be demobilized at any time; meanwhile they were under martial law and were not associated with any strong economic or social groups outside the army. Since they were hostile to landlords and merchants, they were opposed by the parliamentary party; since they were republican, the royalists hated them; since there were no masses of factory workers, they could not get organized strength from that quarter; and since the gentry held the small farmers and farm tenants in economic thrall, no support could come from the country. The Leveller movement therefore failed almost completely in its program, although its ideas lived on to inspire the American and French Revolutions over a century later.

GROUP MOTIVES NECESSARY FOR REVOLUTION

These interesting facts lead one to conclude that individual motives are not enough; if revolutions are to be successful, there must be some basic interest that ties men together and makes them ready to stand shoulder to shoulder over a considerable period of time and through great sacrifices. This basic interest or interests must be shared, not just by a handful of men, but by a much larger group; and, since a frustrated interest among a large body of men is a formidable thing, it is no wonder that a revolution may shake society to its foundations.

CLASS REVOLUTIONS

One of the interests that seem to inspire at various times in history a prolonged and intensive loyalty of many men is *class* interest. Class interest, as we defined it in Chapter III, refers to the interest of a social group that shares semifixed chances of obtaining certain important benefits and that is conscious of the differences in life chances. If we now add to these elements a widespread feeling of injustice about the present distribution of chances, we have marked off one of the basic group of factors leading to revolution. Aristotle surveyed a large amount of data that he collected from the many ancient city-states and concluded that most revolutions are fought to gain equality or to create inequalities where equality existed. He subscribed to a kind of class theory; a state that does not satisfactorily adjust the relations between classes faces the danger of revolution. The poor are repelled by inequality of the rich and seek to destroy them, or the few are repelled by the equality of a democracy and seek to destroy it. There seems much truth in Aristotle's conclusions.

Examples of revolutions in which one socio-economic class was pitted against another would be the great French Revolution, the American Revolution, and the Spanish Civil War (1936–9). One must be careful, of course, to specify exactly what part of a revolution can be attributed to class conflict. Many planters of the American South were revolutionaries despite the fact that their commercial interests were not so sharply in conflict with those of England as were the New Englanders' interests. The French Revolution went through several phases and was colored throughout by the directing influence of the urban middle-class. Yet many radical egalitarians assisted the Revolution, and even a few aristocrats collaborated. Furthermore, in both America and France, a good part of the urban middle-class clung to traditional loyalties to the king.

In Spain in 1936, a Popular Front composed of Republicans, Socialists, Syndicalists, and Communists won a general election and instituted sweeping social changes, including the redistribution of land, the reduction of the influence and property of the Catholic Church, and other socialist measures. A group of monarchists and conservatives revolted in Morocco, incited army insurrections in Spain, and established headquarters in Spain. For three years a bloody war raged until Franco's rebels triumphed. Italy and Germany sent men and supplies to help the rebels, while Russia sent supplies and advisors to the elected government. About 750,000 lives were lost, Spain suffered enormous damage, and a complete change in the political equilibrium resulted. The power of workers' movements in Spain was indefinitely crippled.

NATIONALITIES AND CIVIL STRIFE

Nationality is another interest that has often produced violent domestic struggle. Wars of independence pit one group in the population that is distinctive by language, culture, or attitudes against the dominant, governing group. An example would be, again, the American Revolution where, over a period of a century and a half, thirteen British colonies had developed their own peculiar customs, beliefs, and economic problems. Following specific injuries, such as the attempts to enforce the Stamp Act and various navigation laws, important sections of the population revolted and, after several years of warfare, won formal independence.

The American pattern of revolt is paralleled in ancient Latium (unsuccessful revolt of various Latin cities against Roman hegemony, 340–338 B.C.); in Spanish America (an unsuccessful phase, 1809–16, and a successful phase, 1816–25, that freed the continent of South America and southern North America); and in the Dutch East Indies (1946–50, leading to the founding of the Republic of Indonesia). One might mention many more—for instance, the numerous Irish rebellions against England, or the numerous risings of the nationalities of the Austro-Hungarian Empire.

REGIONAL AND RELIGIOUS CONFLICTS

In addition to assuming the character of class wars and wars of independence, revolutions may take on a regional or religious guise. By regional revolutions is meant the many rural or urban insurrections that have dotted the pages of history. Notable among them are the forays of tribesmen into the glittering "Babylons" of ancient and medieval times and even twentieth-century China. A sense of general unity exists among the parties, and no class interests are espoused by the rebels, but fighting can be a habit, and when life becomes dull in the hills, an invasion of the cities on the plain can furnish exciting diversion and afford much booty. As Mosca remarks: "In France, Spain, and Italy, there are a few cities in which it is relatively easy to lead masses to the barricades. That is one of the many effects of habit and tradition. Once a population has exchanged shots with a constituted government and overthrown it, it will feel, for a generation at least, that it can make a new try any time with favorable results." *

Revolutions sometimes have religious aims, but it is often hard to distinguish the religious factor from the other factors at work in the struggle. The English Glorious Revolution of the seventeenth century

---

* Quoted with the permission of McGraw Hill Book Co. from Gaetano Mosca, *The Ruling Class*, translated by Hannah D. Kahn and edited by Arthur Livingston (New York: McGraw Hill Book Co., 1939), p. 220.

is perhaps one of the clearest cases on record of division between an established church and dissenters in a revolution. Yet we have already mentioned it as an example of class warfare. The confusion of influences is thus apparent. The religious doctrines of Luther were prominent in the rebellion of German principalities from the Holy Roman Empire at the beginning of modern times. Often international and internecine struggles occur together and religious differences may underlie the whole conflict. The Albigensian Crusade (1208–1312) was proclaimed by Innocent III against heretics of southern France, but it also occasioned a power struggle among the French barons.

WHAT FORCES CAUSE REVOLUTION TODAY

One may only guess what the future holds for religious, regional, and independence movements in the world. Independence is demanded ever more forcefully by the colonial peoples of Asia and Africa. Recent history would indicate that religious and regional interests will not assume a leading role in the present century, although they may have some influence on foreign policy. In domestic affairs, although they may act as political forces of a pressure type, they have lost their will and capacity for organizing revolutions. Modern nations have so developed their internal ruling apparatus—armies, police, and bureaucracy—that class warfare and institutional elite struggles are the remaining sources of serious internal conflict. By institutional elite struggles we mean such occurrences as the futile revolt against Hitler in 1944, which was backed by some military and political leaders who had been members of the ruling group.

The reason why class struggle may still threaten a modern government is that the very division of labor and complex organization from which the government derives its extensive controls over a country are built on a potential opposing force—the industrial and communication workers. As the workers are organized in the Western world, their influence can be diminished in three ways: by destruction, in which event the whole nation is weakened terribly; by a complete reorganization of their loyalties and affiliations within a short time, in which event we have counterrevolution that brings the same consequences as other revolutions (like the Fascist revolutions in Italy, in Germany, and in Spain); or by a progressive adjustment of loyalties and affiliations over a long period of time.

RELATIONS BETWEEN REVOLUTION AND WAR

From *coups* and revolutions, we may turn our attention now to international violence. International warfare is prompted by the same underlying motives for violence that stand behind revolutions. Also, several of the patterns of revolution are repeated in international warfare. Thus, class conflict and religious conflict sometimes repeat themselves in international affairs. The spreading of the middle-class, liberal movement from France to other parts of Europe in the nineteenth century shows the transformation of a domestic problem of revolution into an international one. Napoleon's invasions were the final international culmination of warfare that originated in the civil war of the French Revolution, when a revolutionary army was organized to fight the monarchical supporters. Ultimately the class warfare of France became the international warfare of the Napoleonic period. The Christian Crusades against the Mohammedans were meant to destroy the kingdoms of the unbelievers and introduce the rule of the true God. American intervention abroad has been motivated partly by the desire to extend the benefits of American practices and ideals to other lands. One should not underestimate the eagerness of people to fight for the "good" of other people. In both world wars, millions of Americans pursued a war policy for ideological reasons.

THE ELEMENTS OF NATIONALISM

The most common form of international warfare in modern times, however, has been based on nationalism, and we should examine this idea in order to understand the pattern of modern international violence. Nationalism combines love of country and suspiciousness of foreigners. Love of country comes from shared values, and suspiciousness of foreigners comes from the belief that foreigners do not share such values in the same strength. The first shared value is the love of familiar places—the neighborhood, the land, the homes, the valleys, and the mountains, all of the surroundings that one loves because they have been "part of oneself" from infancy. To the love of place is commonly added the presence of or the feeling of shared racial ancestry. This feeling is hardly ever one of purity of race, but is most often a feeling of "difference from" the race of somebody else. Every nation that has been inflamed by a claim to superior race has been a racial mixture. Its logic has taken a peculiar form, something like this: Whatever my kind of mongrelism may be, it must be better than yours. It is not even remotely possible at the present time for biology or socio-biology (eugenics) to establish more than bone, color, and physiognomic differences among the average persons of various races and subraces. What these differences tell us about "superiority" is six of one and a half-dozen of the other.

To understand the "racial" basis of nationalism, one need only think how people who speak alike, dress alike, and act alike also "look" alike. This fact has been noticed of couples who have been married a long time. By taking each other's speech forms, manners, gestures, postures, tastes and other peculiarities, they get to look like brother and sister to other people. National haircuts, costumes, mustache styles, and other externals make different nationalities seem racially more distinct than they are.

Very often identity of language is a third shared value of national groups. People who understand each other feel akin. A direct communication of thought and culture becomes possible. Yet the Swiss speak three different languages—German, French, and Italian. Many other nations have geographical regions that speak different dialects—France, Italy, and Russia, to name three. And England and America speak almost the same language but have distinct feelings of nationality, as do Spain and Spanish America.

Religion sometimes plays a part in the establishment of a national identity. Witness the turmoil the people of Pakistan underwent to separate themselves from the Hindus of greater India in 1947 and 1948. The Thirty Years War of the seventeenth century was motivated in some part by the mutual hostility of Catholic and Protestant countries. Furthermore, a sense of historical continuity and shared destiny can often be a uniting factor. Every national group has its William Tells, its George Washingtons, and its sense of a future in which it will be widely respected because of its accomplishments in war or peace. Most people feel that, just as they judge other individuals by the group from which they come, they themselves will be subject to "guilt by association." Thus they link their fate with the fate of their nationality.

The elements in nationalism just mentioned—place, race, language, religion, and myth—may be joined to a host of historical, shared experiences to produce a common culture. A shared culture, in the last analysis, is what patriots possess; they are ready to stand together and against outsiders because they have lived through and bear the cuts of countless discrete happenings, each one of which marks the possessors as kindred souls. They are partially isolated from the outsiders by their upbringing and by the triumphs and disasters that were contained within the boundaries of their lands. Americans stick together not only because they share a high standard of living, have the same government, and like movies and chewing gum but also because they know the same gangsters, have the same racial problems, and have lived through the great depression of the thirties.

THE DYNAMIC CHARACTER OF NATIONALISM

That the factors referred to are a powerful combination is beyond doubt. They have successfully resisted international developments of all kinds, cultural, economic and political. The wonders of Hellenic civilization never broke down the barriers among the Greek city-states, nor have the great writers, musicians, and scientists of the Western world softened by much the animosities of nations. The dependence of nations on foreign trade for part of their standard of living, the foreign entanglements of international finance and business, and the international postal, telegraph and other arrangements have been feeble barriers to international conflict. And the cries of socialism and communism for a union of all the workers of the world were stifled in the throats of the workers themselves as soon as a crisis involving their individual nation arose. Nor has religion had a greater effect. The ancient Persians had Greek allies of different religion who fought Athens and Sparta in the Greek-Persian wars. Catholic Italians united with Lutheran, Catholic, and nonreligious Germans in the beginning of World War II against Catholic France. Catholic France fought Catholic Austro-Hungary in World War I on the side of Greek Orthodox Russia, which held in bondage Catholic Poland.

Considerable mutual communication, then, seems to bind the people of a nation and to separate them from all other national groups. Geographical, racial, linguistic, religious, mythical, and cultural identity make up a good part of the compound that seals people together. An increase in intercommunication would have to be prolonged, extensive, and intensive in order to decrease the feelings of separate identity among nations. This would be a most difficult task, even if it were deemed desirable.

The relative hopelessness of this objective has led many writers to suggest that only certain crucial modifications in the present condition of nationalities can prevent war. Many have suggested, for example, that some power greater than the individual nations should prevent them from making war. It also has been suggested that permanent peace cannot now be assured, but that correct national policies can cut down the number and diminish the violence of wars. These suggestions, in so far as they find their way into the foreign policy of nations and into the international organization of states, are treated in a later chapter.

THE CAUSES OF WAR SUMMARIZED

A war, then, is a condition that exists when members of one state commit organized acts of violence against those of another state with the approval of their government. The *causes of war* go back to the *motives behind force and violence*—economic gain, prestige, security, power, and sheer destructiveness. They may *assume the character that revolutions take*—for example, of international class or ideological warfare, of religion, and especially of nationality. National differences, with the suspiciousness engendered by them, are a primary condition of conflict.

CLOSE RELATION OF WAR POLICY TO PEACE POLICY

To some extent, certainly, the nation that succeeds in war is the one that maintains a successful foreign policy in peace. Strong and dependable alliances with friendly nations are as much a preparation for war as is the accumulation of munitions and the training of soldiers. What these agreements mean in peace and what they mean in war are twin problems for the men who draft treaties. The Marshall Plan to restore western European economies after World War II was a combination of altruism, economic policy, and defense against possible Russian aggression. Billions of dollars were gambled on the calculation that Europe could fend off Soviet imperialism by being economically strong. The alternative gamble, that American military power alone could accomplish the same thing, was rejected. In critical times such as the twentieth century, the distinction between peace policy and war policy becomes difficult to maintain. It is hard to believe that before World War II, the State Department and the military establishment saw very little of each other, so closely are they associated today.

THE PRECIPITATION OF WARS

The timing of warfare is another important factor in military success. The events that *begin* wars are not usually the *causes* of war. The assassination of the Austrian Archduke by Serbian nationalists did not cause World War I. It was only a tiny factor among many large factors; it precipitated the war crisis that fed on an accumulation of international rivalries and tensions—militarism, extreme nationalism, German-French rivalry in Europe and Africa, Austro-Russian rivalry in eastern Europe, Anglo-German competition, Italo-Austrian boundary difficulties, clashing imperialisms in Africa, and so on.

Many of the greatest wars were not started by nations "bent upon war." In World War I, it appears that the leaders of the principal nations, propelled by their own characters and by the forces operating on them domestically, blundered their way into the war. They involved themselves so deeply that they could not pull out. There is even evidence to indicate that Hitler, as confident as he was of Germany's strength, thought to the very last moment that England and France would not go to war over his proposed attack on Poland in 1939. Whether he would have changed his mind if he had known the truth is another question.

Control over the precipitating cause of a war is impossible in one sense. No one guided the hand of the Serbian assassins, and many wars have started after such spontaneous incidents. The only control that can be exercised over a precipitating incident is to create the incident. One advance in the technique of modern warfare has been just this. By deliberately provoking border clashes, hostile riots, and deeds of individual violence, aggressive nations have been able to point to incidents justifying their intervention on a large scale. In order to pacify domestic qualms of conscience and to appease or at least confuse world opinion, no nation today attacks another without crying that it has been attacked first.

Despotic governments have the advantage in this condition of contemporary international politics. They can measure their actions more carefully, time them more accurately, and conceal both the incident and their own preparations for its follow-up more easily than can republican governments. There seems no reason yet to doubt the common belief that the advantage of the first strike in war goes to the dictatorial governments. This meant less in former times than it does in these days of mechanized warfare and the blitzkrieg. The battles of the Lowlands, France, Russia, the Philippines, and Singapore in World War II, and of Korea in 1950, demonstrate the proposition. Only new defensive weapons of a high order of effectiveness can whittle down this advantage of the initial attack.

FACTORS IN THE ABILITY TO WIN WARS

A nation's alliances and the events precipitating war, therefore, are two elements of importance in determining the ability to win wars. The other important elements are geography, natural resources, population, morale, industrial capacity, and military preparedness. Geography is beyond men's control. England can congratulate itself on having the English Channel between itself and the continent of Europe, but it had nothing to do with the Channel's being there. Similarly, Italy's importance is enhanced by its strategic position in the Mediterranean Sea so long as naval warfare and sea shipments are necessary. Germany is strategically located for wars in which land armies are of paramount importance. For world warfare, with planes, rockets, and long-distance strikes, the Soviet Union is ideally situated. It can move out in all directions over a huge area stretching from from Japan to western Europe. An opponent wishing to amass powerful striking forces against it must select a very few points on the U.S.S.R.'s perimeter and must supply them from great distances. Meanwhile the initiative must go to the Soviet armies, which are capable at the same time of launching attacks into unprepared areas and breaking up incipient enemy concentrations.

Natural resources undeniably separate those nations that can be important military powers today from those that cannot. The world's resources of iron, coal, oil, rubber, tin, and other vital metals and ores are unqualifiedly available to the United States if they lie in the Western hemisphere or Africa, to the Soviet Union if they lie in the Asiatic belt surrounding the Soviet Union, and at stake in war if they lie in the southern fringe of Asia, the Near East, or in western Europe. Each of the two large areas controlled by the two great powers is rich enough in raw materials to support a prolonged war for control of Europe, Africa, and Asia. The outcome of a world war between the two great powers, therefore, will depend on some factor other than an imbalance of natural resources like that partially responsible for the outcome of the last two world wars.

Under certain conditions, the size of population will be a crucial factor. Rarely have wars been lost because of insufficient manpower. The men may be untrained, or unmobilized, or unwilling, but there are usually enough of them. The number of soldiers available is only important when the strategy of the war is one of attrition of manpower —that is to say, the side that is willing to sacrifice large numbers of men in return for roughly commensurate losses by the enemy will have an advantage, provided that it can maintain the willingness to sacrifice so many men and that the enemy's willingness to make such sacrifices decreases. Human life does not have the same value for all people. The Russians and Chinese can take heavy losses of life without questioning the reasons for the losses as intensely as do the peoples of western European civilization. The ancient tradition of warfare is to use machines to support men; the American psychology attempts to use men to support machines. America therefore seeks to avoid to the last moment a war of manpower attrition.

How far America can go in using machines rather than men in a war depends not only on undisturbed industrial production and a minimum loss of equipment but also on the geographical conditions under which the war is fought. The loss of life relative to the enemy's loss of life will be small if the war can be kept mobile and huge armies do not become locked at close quarters for a long period of time, for it is the crowding of armies that causes great loss of life. The greatest tactical value of atomic bombs may well be that they may be used to prevent heavy concentrations of infantry and thus may throw open the field to quick maneuvers, fast strikes, highly skilled staff work and intricate physical communications. That the United States (if it keeps its Allies, especially) is suited to this kind of warfare is beyond question.

The industrial capacity of the United States at present far exceeds that of any nation or alliance and can only be roughly equaled by the junction of western European industry with the Soviet bloc. Since the eighteenth century, industrial efficiency and productivity have become primary factors in military importance. The weapons of war have become increasingly expensive. Artillery pieces are more complex, infantry arms are almost completely automatic, ammunition is expended at a rapid rate, aircraft have become larger, and a host of new weapons have been devised that depend upon fine automatic calculators and sensitive electronic devices. Modern warfare makes constant and monopolistic demands on every erg of machine energy in the nation.

THE BROAD MEANING OF PREPAREDNESS

We may take military preparedness broadly to cover all the factors mentioned above. Some time ago Colonel Mayer of the French army wrote a book on military leadership in which he stressed that the initial conditions for effective discipline were a "friendly press," a military spirit in education of the young, and a co-operative government, economy, and working population. It is of little use to say that this opinion exhibits rank militarism, incipient Fascism, or Russian slavery. A favorable orientation towards the violence of war must be part of military preparedness, and where it is not present, it must be compensated for in other respects or very quickly indoctrinated into a people. Betrand de Jouvenal wrote in his book *Power* that international conflict is a furious competitive struggle in which no nation can avoid taking the antihumanitarian measures adopted by its opponents. If one nation musters its population in a totalitarian fashion, its competitor is compelled to follow suit. For example, universal conscription, once introduced in France, spread quickly through Europe. Full industrial mobilization, once its effectiveness for war was demonstrated by Germany, was decreed in England, partially carried out in America, and will probably occur in every country of the world today, the moment war breaks out. Italian and German bombing of civilian centers in the Spanish Civil War was the prelude for the German devastation of Rotterdam and London, and for the havoc wreaked on the German cities by British and American air forces.

Military preparedness in the stricter sense couples traditional exercises with new ideas. The old patterns of preparation must be gone through: Men must be taught to take care of themselves under the unusual conditions of battle and bivouac; supplies must be inventoried and distributed with efficiency; marksmanship, intelligence, leadership, and other military subjects must be taught; and so on. In addition, each war introduces its surprises. It is never quite like the last war. New formations, procedures, and tactics are forever being devised or dredged up from the long history of warfare. Like all human innovations—television, for example—the inventive period has to be succeeded by the adaptive period. When to decide on a new kind of jet-propelled plane, when to substitute a bazooka for the small arms of a rifleman, when to decrease the size of aircraft carriers, and many similar questions are of continual concern to military and civilian experts in this age of rapid technological change. Military preparedness under these conditions also requires wisdom in making "change-over decisions."

The Effects and Limits of Physical Coercion

THE OUTRIGHT REJECTION OF COERCION

The application of force and violence undeniably changes the behavior of people. The simple statement becomes a complex problem, however, when one tries to relate the *effects* of the application of force or violence to the *motives* of those who use them and to the *welfare* of those on whom they are applied. One school of thought throughout history, especially throughout the history of Christianity, contends that violence never succeeds. "Love thy neighbor" and "turn the other cheek" express sentiments older than Christianity itself and presuppose that under all conditions pacifism is the true path to the highest values of this world and the Hereafter.

NONVIOLENCE AND CIVIL DISOBEDIENCE

Complete pacifism characterized Gandhi's movement to unseat British authority in India. Making strength out of weakness, the followers of Gandhi, while refusing to co-operate with the British, carefully abstained from violence. In turn, the British, hampered in their efforts to administer the country and watched suspiciously by the humanitarians of the world, had not the will to repress ruthlessly the Hindu freedom movement. After World War II, the English left India with mixed regrets and relief.

The rarity of such nonviolent, non-co-operative movements is evidence of the great difficulty encountered in organizing them and of the success of organized force as an instrument of the state. Nevertheless, non-co-operation is found to some extent in every society. Farmers who refuse to produce, merchants who avoid taxes, workers who slow down their productivity, and soldiers who avoid battle are practicing Gandhi-ism on a small scale or on a less conscious level. Such non-co-operation relates to concepts previously discussed in this book—the strength of the beliefs in legitimacy, the condition of consensus, and the skills of leadership.

With few exceptions, notably among the Quakers, Christian churches have never taken the extreme position of Gandhi towards physical coercion. They have been willing to tolerate and even to encourage the use of force and violence as means to an end, provided that the end is an estimable one. Other people, like Aldous Huxley in his essay on *Ends and Means*, maintain that, even assuming that violence is justifiable in theory as a means, violence in practice never succeeds in attaining its ends. Violence is by nature, Huxley declares, incompetent to attain good ends.

As political scientists we cannot pass judgment on which of man's ends are good ones and which are less good. However, we can say which ones are more practicable, provided they are described accurately and precisely enough to discuss them intelligently. And we can say which goals (again, if they are precisely described) are inconsistent with each other. We can also determine by studies what are the values that men hold. On the pros and cons of pacifism we can say that the evidence of the existence of rewards in an afterlife for nonresistance in this life is not the kind that science can deal with. While we can assure religious pacifists that they will be dealt with roughly on earth (something they know very well anyway), we cannot tell them what will happen to them after death. Similarly, we cannot say to the nonpacifist religions that God smiles or frowns upon the methods they use in carrying out their holy objectives.

COERCION, LIKE OTHER POLITICAL WEAPONS, IS LIMITED

We can say something more, however, about Huxley's proposition that force or violence never succeeds. Men in various times and places have been able to achieve their goals and values to as great an extent by force and violence as by education, propaganda, economic policy, and economic manipulation. There is nothing inherent in coercion as a method that is not inherent in any other method of achieving ends, beyond the forms and patterns its application takes. Though force has been used when education might have sufficed, education has been used where only force could suffice; and contrariwise, though economic policy has sought to do what only force could do, force has often been a poor substitute for economic planning. To quote examples on which most people will agree, while it is true that force corrupted religious inquisitioners, it is likewise true that economic policy destroyed the souls of factory workers and that education (in our special sense of legitimate indoctrination) impeded enlightenment.

When we turn to the nonlegitimate instruments of authority, instances on which most people will agree are even more abundant. The brutal father is equaled by the miserly or the superstitious father in his effects upon the character of his children. The savagery of the police state is equaled by the calloused, inhuman bleeding of its inhabitants by a profiteering government and the spiritual deception and manipulation of its people by the thought-control state.

COERCION SOMETIMES SUCCEEDS

To maintain that force and violence never succeed takes either a completely unhistorical view of history or a set of standards never possessed by more than a few men. Americans who believe that the American Revolution had a good end must either accept the goodness of the violence employed or else maintain that independence could have been achieved otherwise than by violence. If they take up the latter proposition, they would have to maintain it for a great number of the events in history in the face of overwhelming evidence to the contrary. They would have to explain how Carthage could have been subjected to Greek civilization by economic policy (the Carthaginians were eminent traders) or by education (the Carthaginians were hostile to Greek ideas); how Mexico could have released Texas by its own free will; how the Bolshevists could have been invited to collectivize all of Russia at the invitation of the existing liberal, capitalist regime; and how Hitler could have been bought off or talked out of his designs on the democratic, peaceful world.

FORCE AND VIOLENCE OFTEN IN DISREPUTE

The criteria for the use of violence, like the criteria for economic or psychological policy, must be adapted to the special case. If one is in favor of a particular end, he must decide on the means. If he is against the objective, no means will be good. In deciding on the means, he must take into account the relative merits of the means at hand. Force and violence have several limitations, like other means. They are not at present in favor as means in certain parts of the world and among certain groups in the population that, like Aldous Huxley, refuse to regard them as means at all. Consequently, force and violence are most often supposed to be used "as a last resort," that is, after economic and psychological techniques have been employed without success. This may be called a *mores* or cultural limitation on the use of physical coercion. We also should point out that when people do not want it, do not understand it, and do not obey it, physical coercion is a dangerous and poor instrument of government.

COERCION OFTEN WASTEFUL AND CRUDE

Force and violence are often wasteful. This is a consideration of *expediency*. If the Ostrogoths can be bribed not to invade the

Roman Empire, costly campaigns are saved and the tottering old Empire preserved for the time being. If the Russians can be freed from the "encirclement complex" by being allowed to share Germany and control eastern Europe, then a terrible war might be averted. If, of course, these economic and psychological policies do not work, physical coercion may be the next policy employed.

Force and violence are also inexpedient very often because they do not necessarily teach or influence the subjects to act exactly as those who inflict the coercion wish. Force cannot teach children mathematics, nor can it even be used to teach soldiers how to use force. Nor can force accomplish the delicate effects of a highly complicated income-tax schedule in bringing about a redistribution of wealth, activities, and incentives. The income-tax laws of modern capitalist countries are literal marvels of instrumental policy. With only sighs and quivers from the population, effects are achieved that would have bloodied every street in medieval England. The history of lands and times when physical coercion diminished relative to education and economics is the story of politics that has learned more ingenious and sophisticated ways to accomplish its purposes.

Questions and Problems

1. Define physical coercion. Distinguish between force and violence. Give two examples of each from the materials of this chapter.

2. Describe the main relationships between legitimate authority and the use of physical coercion.

3. Describe how the meaning of coercion is acquired in life. What effects does this training have on attitudes towards coercion in politics?

4. Give two examples, from outside sources, of events involving the use of force or violence that are accompanied also by economic and psychological acts.

5. Outline the main points of the Freudian theory of destructiveness. Does the existence of destructiveness as a motive for coercion stand and fall by the acceptability of Freud's theory?

6. Define and give examples of the various objectives of physical coercion.

7. List the reports on coercion found in one week of a daily newspaper. Classify them by objectives as best you can (suggest hypotheses if the evidence is not available), remembering that an individual's simple act can have several motives and a group's actions is bound to have various motives. If there is more than one motive, determine which one seems to be predominant.

8. Using examples from the chapter (enlarge them by reference to encyclopedia articles on them if they are insufficiently detailed), show how motives for coercion are often rationalized rather than true.

9. Select a fellow student who is fond of athletics, one who is active in military reserves, and one who is active in nonathletic spheres and interview them regarding "what they get out of" their pursuits. Write a commentary on the results of your interviews as they concern this chapter's theories of coercion.

10. Consult an encyclopedia (or other sources) for material on any example of a *coup d'état* that is cited in the chapter, and write an account of it (600 words), fitting it into the framework of analysis given in this chapter.

11. Give as many suggestions as you can of how one would go about investigating the possibility that a prospective strike will become violent. (Put yourself in the position of a political scientist who is appointed by the mayor or governor to indicate danger points in a situation.)

12. Consult an encyclopedia (or other source) for an account of any revolution mentioned in this chapter and write an account of it (600 words) using the framework of analysis provided in this chapter.

13. To what extent might political science contribute to an understanding of warfare?

14. Distinguish in 300 words between a revolution and a *coup d'état*, as these terms are used in this work.

15. What are the requirements in most cases for a successful revolution (including its *coup d'état*)?

16. Describe the various group interests underlying revolutions, and give examples of each. Show how several interests may operate simultaneously in a particular revolution.

17. Comparing what was said about political class in the United States in Chapter III with what was said about class revolutions in Chapter VIII, what would you say are the barriers to class conflict in the United States?

18. Define nationalism, describe the factors contributing to it, and give an example of each factor.

19. Describe the main factors for success in war.

20. How does force as a means tend to become force as an end? What are the effects and limits of physical coercion?

Longer Study Questions and Problems
Suitable for Term Papers

1. Read one of the book-length works cited in the bibliography, and using this chapter or other sources, explain (1) why coercion was resorted to in one of the main decisions described and (2) whether the resort to coercion was decided upon after weighing the advantages of various other instruments of political struggle (15 pages). (Note: Do not be content with events and thoughts immediately before the decision, but place the decision in the major setting to which it belongs.)

2. Prepare a report of 20 pages intended for the Department of State, describing the *utility* of, and the *procedure that might be used* in, a government research agency for studying international tensions, approaching war crises, and the success or failure of a diplomatic policy.

3. Write a paper of 20 pages on the effects on crime rates of physical punishment as contrasted with re-education and mental therapy.

4. Using government statistics (for example, *Historical Statistics of the United States, 1789–1945*), works in labor economics, and such commentaries as Robert R. Brooks: *When Labor Organizes* (1937), write a paper of 20 pages on the rise and decline of labor violence in the United States. (Analyze the reasons for labor violence, the possible causes of fluctuations in amounts, and the trend possibly being established.)

III

GOVERNMENTAL ORGANIZATION

THOSE who have been attracted by the dramatic and often perplexing conflicts of political behavior need not feel that political organization will prove less interesting. The ingenious and stupid, striving and apathetic human beings that lend variety and color to political behavior will, it is true, now be bound by a stricter application of rules and formalities. But, as anyone knows, the emotions at the root of a slanted remark at high tea may scarcely differ from those in an exchange of remarks by fishwives. And we will not be content with a description of the superficial procedures of government. The study of political organization is most profitable and entertaining when one searches beneath the surface of procedures for the basic motives behind and the important patterns of political structures.

In the several chapters to follow, we can see that the mixture of procedures and behavior in political organizations present remarkable problems. We would be hard put to find other principles of politics as important as those that are derived from the struggle to establish a rule of law to be described in the next chapter. Moving farther along, we will depict the momentous struggle between legislators and executives for political supremacy. And we will ask in subsequent chapters: What motivates and directs those millions of public servants who staff the bureaucracies of the world? What enables a court system to give a man "his day in court"? What is left for the "home town" to decide if Washington is to acquire every power of importance? Can a world union be accomplished in an age of hostile states?

Such questions pertaining to political organization are as close to everyday problems as the materials of political behavior. A story is told of a lecturer who surmised that the earth would burn out in ten billion years. "How many?" asked a man in the audience. "Ten billion," replied the lecturer. "Oh," said the man, with obvious relief, "I thought you said ten *million.*" Obviously we are not asking that one be as emotionally attuned to infinity as this man. A spark of interest in something beyond today and earlier than yesterday is enough to illuminate for one the significance of the birth, growth, change, and decline of the massive governmental organizations that form the subjects of this section.

9

LAW AND CONSTITUTIONALISM

THE SUBJECT of law and constitutionalism is broader in scope than that of the court system of a state. Accordingly, the treatment of the legal order will introduce the entire subject of political organization, while the study of courts will take its place in the sequence of chapters on more specialized political institutions. The breadth of the subject of law and constitutionalism results from the place law holds in society. We shall shortly define the term law, but meanwhile we may visualize its role in society if we remember that every culture has a system of orderly and continuous procedures enveloping its political institutions and regulating the behavior of the members of the community. Men can *expect* certain *acts* because they are *lawfully* required of individuals. The legal role of political institutions and the legal relationships among them make up the constitution of the society. The culture determines the state of the laws and the constitution, and, in turn, the laws and constitution—because the men who work with them acquire various interests and habits—influence the culture to some extent.

Our discussion of the legal and constitutional order is divided into three parts. In the first section, we discuss the relation of law to custom and to ethics, define law, and present various ways of classifying it. The second section depicts the growth of modern constitutions and explains how constitutions change. The third and final section, taking the concept of constitutionalism in its deepest meaning, tries to explain the social forces that support or disturb the constitutional order.

The Analysis of Law

THREE WAYS OF STUDYING LAW

There are three principal ways of studying law and the legal order. One is to study them as the habits or customs of a community. Another way is to study law and the legal order from the standpoint of some system of ethics that would allow us to decide that one law is good and another bad. A third way is to regard law and the legal order as a specialized part of the political community; as such, they envelop the political institutions of the community and take as their special province the enforcement of prescribed relationships among the officers of the institutions and between the officers and the members of the community. This third method of analysis is regarded as most useful for this kind of book and is followed generally. However a brief discussion of law as custom and law as ethical principles will help one understand several important problems of law.

LAW AS CUSTOM

If we study the sources of law thoroughly, we realize that all human communities have definite beliefs regarding the rightness or wrongness of various acts. All communities, large or small, simple or with a complex division of labor, reward and punish the behavior of their members. Courts, sheriffs, administrative officers, and armies are present in most communities. Yet, with or without such specialized officers, rewards and punishments occur. Chapter Four mentioned the ties that bind a community, and the sanctions of ostracism and frustration that follow acts opposed to the customs of the community.

However complex and numerous the rules of a society may be, a considerable part of them will be obeyed without the intervention of special machinery. For men, from infancy onwards, are trained to follow the rules and to do "right" by parents and teachers who themselves have learned the rules the same way as they now impart them. These regular ways in which men learn to behave, with or without formal political officers to proclaim and enforce the "right" behavior, may be called the conventional order. Following Max Weber, "a system of order will be called *convention* so far as its validity is externally guaranteed by the probability that deviation from it within a given social group will result in a relatively general and practically significant reaction of disapproval."

When we speak of the law, therefore, we ought not to forget the conventional order that joins with the law to make up the general social order. General notions of what is legitimate and illegitimate in politics, of what is right and wrong, of how citizens and officials ought to conduct themselves—all of this kind of moral principle, while it is often spelled out in law, is nevertheless based on the conventional order.

In accepting these points, however, one need not believe some enthusiasts who claim that the community is the source of all law.

Many anthropologists and some writers on jurisprudence, especially from among the schools of sociological jurisprudence and conservative historicism, have overemphasized the role of custom in creating and enforcing law. They see the political process as a rubber stamp for the conventional order. They reason that law almost always has a base in custom, in what the community believes is right, and that a pure declaration or command will have little or no effect. Law to them has the medieval meaning subscribed to officially by the medieval kings and barons, who believed law could only be the declaration of the already established behavior patterns of the community.

This view is too exclusive for us. The infinitely complex and changing world of human relations produces ever new situations and consequently ever new law. A new law is declared in order to meet a novel situation, and being declared, is enforced, and being enforced, creates a new condition to which the community adjusts. The law may be determined by the past, but it may be "new," nevertheless, and it can in turn determine to some extent the future.

LAW AS ETHICAL PRINCIPLES

A second way of studying the law is to establish for oneself a system of ethical principles, a set of beliefs about what is good and bad, and to evaluate the statutes of various countries according to those beliefs. Usually a writer who adopts this procedure terms the statutes he likes "lawful" and those he does not like "unlawful." This is no crime, of course, but it is often uneconomical, scientifically speaking, and also causes difficulties of communication. For we have to learn not only a set of facts but also the set of preferences and prejudices of the writer in order to understand what is being said. Furthermore, writers of this kind often discuss values that they themselves have not defined. They neglect to tell us what they mean by "good," "just," "reasonable," and other terms denoting values. They only delude themselves if they think that everyone agrees on the meaning of such words.

Those who use evaluative definitions of the law can find agreement to their definitions only among those who share their ideas on what "justice" and "good conduct" are. For example, St. Thomas Aquinas defined law as "an ordinance of reason, for the common good, made and promulgated by him who has the care of the community." Notice the words "reason" and "good"; they signal that there lies behind them a system of values that must be accepted or understood before the meaning of the definition can become clear. For otherwise, people who think they are using the term "law" as Aquinas defines it will in fact have various different and often incompatible notions about what is good and bad, law or not law.

We could use the definition of Aquinas only by explaining his system of values. This would require a lengthy treatise on morals. Unfortunately, there are many writers who use words like "good" or "reasonable," but unlike Aquinas have never defined or systematized anywhere the meaning of those words. They will cite an action, call it lawful or unlawful, and leave one to accept uncritically their dogma or to lapse into bewilderment. Thus, if a man believes Gandhi a just person and defines law as "the principles of justice," then we are likely to be trapped into accepting whatever Gandhi did as just and lawful and what his opponents did as unjust and unlawful. We shall then either be fooled or bewildered unless we see the verbal trick being played.

LEGAL RELATIVISM VERSUS "NATURAL LAW"

Another kind of difficulty, related to the difficulty of treating the law as moral precepts with which we agree or disagree, appears when writers speak of natural law. "Laws of nature" (the "law of gravity," for example), say some, need no sanctions or compulsion apart from their internal compulsion or inevitability. Are not human laws the same? Two possible answers may be given, but we adhere to the second for the purposes of this book.

The first answer would be "yes"; the morals of mankind, if plumbed to their depths, *may* reveal universal agreement as to what is good and lawful. This universal agreement may be regarded as the basic or "natural" law; it causes men to tend toward similar "good" behavior everywhere. What is "true" is also "good." This is the view of the "natural law" school of jurisprudence. We do not use this approach because there is insufficient evidence to prove that there are universally held ethical ideas of law in man's nature.

The second answer would be "no"; it is more useful to recognize that there exist different systems of ethics and ethical directives among human communities. This is the view of men like Roscoe Pound of the school of "sociological jurisprudence." We can make scientific statements about the ethical directives of each community and the manner in which adherence to directives by the members of the community is systematically compelled. However, faced with strong and widespread disagreement among men as to what is right and wrong, we could never say that what everybody regards as law is the same, and consequently could never agree that there is only a single body of laws that is at the same time universally agreed to and universally right.

Temporarily, at least, we believe that more can be found out about the legal customs of people by taking a relativist viewpoint. Thus, following our own notions, we find a law in one country that may require a free press and another law in a second that may prohibit a free press. Both are laws, even though we think one good and the other bad. By putting our prejudices aside, we can study both laws objectively.

LAW DEFINED

Reserving as separate issues, then, the interpretation of law as custom and the ethical meanings that might be given the term, we may define law as *the ethical directives in a community, deviations from which are met usually by measures to compel conformity or by punishment, applied by public officers.* This is essentially the definition employed by Max Weber.

THE QUALITIES OF LAW EXPLAINED

A discussion of the elements of the definition of law is now in order. The words "ethical directives" denote that there is always stated or implied in a law that something is good, that the behavior described is better than the behavior prohibited. The "thou shalt" and "it is forbidden to" discriminate "good" from "bad" conduct.

The term "community" has been previously defined as the people with respect to their interrelations. The law exists with respect to such a community; but what of the multitude of laws that affect only a part of the community? Examples would be laws governing hours of work, or business contracts, or railroads. Such laws may be included in our definition since they cover all the members of the community who may engage themselves in the network of relationships covered by the law. Thus a man need not sell liquor, but he must have a license if he wishes to sell liquor.

"Deviations" mean *not doing* what the law tells one to do or *doing* what the law tells one *not* to do. The term "usually" is introduced into the definition in order to convey the fact that the machinery of justice need not be invariably effective for law to exist. A great many laws are successfully violated at least once.

The salient point of our definition, the point that differentiates law from the conventional order and gives to law its important place in the study of the state, is in the phrases that deal with enforcement. Deviations are met usually by "measures to compel conformity or by punishment, applied by public officers." While customs are enforced by scorn, ostracism, and like sanctions, deviations from the law spur into action men who hold office to enforce the law. If all men are to register for military service, public officers round up the reluctant and procrastinating few and compel them to register. Anyone who continues to avoid registering is charged with deliberately violating the law and is subjected to trial and, if found guilty, to punishment. If fire prevention and safety precautions are to be taken by all theater and hotel owners, inspectors visit the premises to ensure compliance with the law. Offenders may be ordered to conform, warned of possible criminal actions, and, if unheeding, subjected to indictment, trial, and punishment.

LAWS CLASSIFIED BY FORMAL AUTHORSHIP

Who make the laws of a society? The law in American society, under our given definition, may be classified according to its formal origins as *common law*, *judge-made law*, or *legislation*. Most other modern societies depend for their laws on legislation and judge-made law. Law may also be created by the political constituency, the body of citizens, in which event it may be called *popular law*.

THE COMMON LAW

The common law, the important body of law found in English-influenced legal systems, is the findings, declaration, and enforcement of the customs of the country by a court, together with the modifications introduced into these findings by changes in community, judicial, legislative, and executive opinion, but especially in judicial opinion. The forty-eight American court systems follow interpretations of the common law different from those that prevail in English courts. The "common law" of Illinois, for example, is not the same as the "common law" of England. In a number of cases, the statutes of the various countries and states have adopted, modified, or repealed common law principles.

JUDGE-MADE LAW

Judge-made law is frequently confused or identified with the common law. However, all judges, whether they are interpreting the common law or the most formal kind of enactment, make law in a more or less subtle fashion. They do so by interpreting the meaning of abstract words in a large number of particular cases, as when they decide in particular cases to include or exclude certain kinds of persons or actions from the coverage of the law. Over a period of time, there accrues a judge-made slant in the law. The extreme version of this process is found when judges are allowed to pass on the question of

whether a legislative enactment conforms to a constitution. Such is
the case in the American state and national governments, where it is
called the power of "judicial review."

LEGISLATION

Legislation is the formally structured process that is given
a monopoly or at least a quasi-monopoly of the designing and promul-
gation of new, positive law. Thus legislation may be made by a legislature alone, an executive officer alone, or by a combination of both.
Where the executive is confined entirely to administrative tasks or
honorary tasks—examples being some of the early American state
governors, the English King, and the type of weak presidency found
in several European countries—the legislature has a quasi-monopoly
over legislation. Where the legislature is entirely absent (as in the
France of Louis XIV), weak from external causes (as in the England
of Elizabeth), or weak from internal causes (as in the German Republic just before Hitler), the executive branch of the government, be
it a kingship or republic, designs and influences the design of, and
sometimes even promulgates, the positive law.

At other times, the legislative function is divided among the legislature, the executive, and even the judiciary. The legislature may be
entitled to design and propose laws, but the executive may be allowed
to reject them. This process characterizes the contemporary American
national and state systems in their formal structures. Their informal
or actual structures may give the executives, because of their powerful
political position and other factors, even more power to propose and
amend the laws.

POPULAR LAW

The law that is created directly by the body of citizens can
only exist when there is an active belief in popular sovereignty. City-
states and other small, compact communities have of course a technical
advantage in implementing such beliefs, for there the qualified and
active people can assemble conveniently to discuss and approve laws.
In a larger society, the initiative and referendum, by which the electorate proposes and passes on laws, may exist as examples of the
popular law-making process.

OTHER CLASSIFICATIONS ARE USEFUL

The classification just given of the kinds of law is primarily
a formal classification. It calls attention to the formal organizations
that process, approve, and promulgate ethical directives. It tends to

slight the relative strength of the influences that play on the lawmaking process—community leaders, pressure groups, and other influences that are not formally required to operate in order to have a particular event called a law.

Other classifications, both informal and formal, could focus on other criteria. For example, laws could be classified according to the group in the community that has most to say in the making of law—the business interests, the military, the majority of the people, the party leaders, the representatives assembled in the legislature. Or we could classify laws by the number of people they affect—all the people, the electorate, the people of a region, the armed forces, a certain business group, labor, and so on; or by the sanctions attached to them: capital punishment, prison terms, restraints, withholding of benefits, ostracism, publicity, disapproval, and so on; or by the parties entitled to contest one another: nation *versus* state, nation *versus* corporate bodies, nation *versus* individuals, state *versus* state, corporation *versus* corporation, individual *versus* individual, and so on.

Furthermore, laws may be classified according to the type of judicial procedure that is required to determine cases that arise, such as criminal procedure, civil procedure, procedure in equity, or administrative procedure; or according to the kinds of cases: crimes, torts, contract disagreements, and so on; or according to the kinds of courts that have jurisdiction over cases involving the law—international courts, arbitral commissions, national courts (arranged according to whether they have original jurisdiction over a case or whether they take cases on appeal, by appellate jurisdiction), state courts, municipal courts, special courts such as tax courts and traffic courts, and so on. All these classifications may be useful for particular purposes.

Development of Constitutions

CONSTITUTION DEFINED

Constitutional law is the important body of law that allocates to the agencies of government their part in the making and administration of law. It takes, so to speak, our forms of law and gives them a general relationship to each other. It describes broadly the spheres of operation of the citizenry, the common law (if present in the society), the judge-made law, and legislation.

Bouvier, in his legal dictionary, defines a constitution as "the fundamental law of a state, directing the principles upon which the government is founded, and regulating the exercise of the sovereign powers, directing to what bodies or persons those powers shall be confided and the manner of their exercise."

ORIGIN OF THE TERM

Americans, and many people of nations influenced by the American idea of a constitution, tend to think of a constitution as a written document, drafted at some convention of the citizens or of the representatives of the political community. It is therefore necessary to point out that a constitution may be unwritten and yet serve the same general function as a written constitution. The Romans had the word "constitutio" that pertained to the collected orders of the Emperor. In medieval England, the same word was used to describe the more important enactments and promulgations. In the course of time, it came to refer only to the more fundamental statutes of the realm, and finally to a body of basic statutes, common law principles, and customary law corresponding rather closely to the definition of constitution given by Bouvier.

LEVELLER CRITICISMS OF THE ENGLISH CONSTITUTION

The American colonists were familiar with the unwritten English constitution and with the radical criticisms of the unwritten constitution by the Levellers of the midseventeenth century. The Levellers possessed three ideas that are the key to the historical understanding of modern constitutionalism of the American and French variety. They believed that the members of a community, in order to put *definite checks* on the government, had the *unquestionable right* to *contract with one another* to establish a frame of government. They therefore wrote several "Agreements of the People" and other documents that they wished to establish as the constitution of the English republic.

Oliver Cromwell, although he believed in the idea of constitutions, found the Leveller proposals too radical for his tastes. In 1654, he declared that every government ought to be founded on an unchanging standard. He actually accepted Lambert's "Instrument of Government" and swore to support it. He later accepted a new "Humble Petition and Advice" as his model of government. But he soon found constitutional documents an inconvenience for his dictatorship and ignored them in practice. The history of written constitutions switches thereafter to America.

EARLY CONSTITUTIONAL IDEAS IN AMERICA

The idea of the written basic law begins very early in American history and gains strength from the Leveller beliefs in popular sovereignty, natural rights, and, especially, the social contract. Though the first colonists in Massachusetts and in Virginia did not favor some of the Leveller ideas, they did agree with the radicals that new societies and governments were formed by a contract among the citizens.

Some of the colonists professed to see in the colonial charters granted by the Crown a kind of social compact and fundamental law. Yet the use of such charters could be traced to the charters of the medieval merchant gilds and even to the corporation of ancient Rome. Perhaps more closely resembling the ideal of the compact were the ordinances that the London Company in 1621 sent to Virginia, and that prescribed the structure of the colonial government.

Some historians believe that the Pilgrim Compact was a more important step in the development of constitutions than the charters or corporate orders. Signed on the Mayflower in 1620 by the 41 men of the Plymouth Colony, the Compact was an agreement of a fundamental nature on the manner of governing the colony. Certain other writers credit the colony of Connecticut with the first constitution. There, in 1639, the towns of Windsor, Weathersfield, and Hartford became associated in a body politic under an instrument that they entitled "The Fundamental Orders." This was undoubtedly the first independent formulation on paper of a democratic plan of government in America, but it was not a final document or a wholly legal document, for the men of Connecticut soon thereafter asked the Crown for a charter.

Another share of the credit for inventing the constitution has gone to the Puritans' use of the agreement or covenant in founding churches. Governor Winthrop of Massachusetts Bay spoke of "the covenant between God and men in the moral law and the political covenants and constitutions among men themselves." He added that "it is of the nature of every society to be knit together by some covenant either expressed or implied."

In all these cases, it is apparent that the belief in the social contract was at work. The conviction was running strong in many places that men, who were solitary individuals by nature, might come together and compact a form of government, and, indeed, that all governments were originally based on such compacts even though the records of them might have been lost. Whatever the relative strength of the influences—the Roman Law, the English examples, the social contract idea, the colonial charters, or the church covenants—the colonists began very early to codify important political practices. The final result was an embodiment of the fundamental law in one comprehensive document, a form of expression that differed from the disconnected, fragmentary elements of the fundamental laws of England.

CONSTITUTIONS OF THE REVOLUTIONARY PERIOD

In the period before the American Revolution, then, the idea of a constitution as a necessary and written fundamental document was in the air, and many colonists looked forward to the time when they might write their own constitutions without depending on the royal charters or on a scattering of customs, usages, and statutes. The great event that opened the modern constitutional period came in May of 1776, when the Continental Congress recommended "to the respective Assemblies and Conventions of the United Colonies, where no government sufficient to the exigencies of their affairs has been hitherto established, to adopt such government as shall, in the opinion of the representatives of the people, best conduce to the happiness and safety of their constituents in particular, and America in general." Thus the states were invited to draft their own constitutions, and shortly thereafter came the famous Declaration of Independence approved by all of them.

In a few of the original states, the constitutions were framed at first by ordinary legislative bodies that had been convened for legislative purposes rather than solely for the purpose of drafting a basic law. But ever since then, it has been the practice to call special conventions of constitutional bodies for drawing up fundamental documents. The greater part of the original states and some that came along later worked on the theory that these conventions were themselves the embodiment of the people and that their acts needed no ratification by popular vote. As the nineteenth century wore on and popular movements became stronger, the general practice developed of referring draft constitutions to the electorate for final approval.

However, the federal Constitution came too early to be subjected to the full force of the popular ratification movement. The drafters of the new Constitution did not wish to submit the document to the scrutiny of state legislatures, because some states were controlled by antinationalists. They therefore suggested it be debated and voted on by conventions called for the special purpose and formed of delegates chosen by the existing electorates of the states. They expected, with good reason, that they might influence the special conventions more than the legislatures. They also wished to be able to say that the Constitution rested on the approval of the whole people, rather than simply on the votes of the state legislators. Only by a narrow margin did the new Constitution triumph, and that margin might not have been achieved if the Constitution had been submitted to popular vote or to the state legislatures.

POLITICAL OPPONENTS STAND AGREED ON CONSTITUTIONS

Whatever the fate of particular constitutions, the idea of having *some* constitution became ineradicable in America. One of the reasons that constitutionalism has remained so important in American life has been the fact that two major branches of American thought—the moderate or Madisonian democrats and the extreme or Jeffersonian democrats—have been able to agree among themselves that constitutionalism was a good thing. They have agreed that there should be a basic document stating rights and privileges with relation to the govermnent and defining the operations of the state.

However, the reasoning by which each group arrived at this idea is different. A constitution is desired so that the powers of government should be limited by a fundamental law. Yet there are two ways of looking at this fundamental law. One view holds that the government has to be restrained on behalf of the individual. Power has been perverted so frequently that the liberties of the individual require protection by fundamental statutes. The Levellers, and other extreme democrats, were constitutionalists in this sense. They thought that they might limit executive and legislative authority in order to foster the free will of the mass of people.

On the other hand, constitutions were demanded by conservatives as well, for fundamental statutes, as laws created by the past, limit the present and future generations. John Adams, James Madison, and a long succession of Supreme Court justices emphasized this viewpoint; in contrast, Jefferson would have preferred to set a limit to the duration of any particular constitution.

AMENDMENT

These attitudes towards change—resistance and advocacy—are reflected in differing attitudes towards the amending process. While the founders of the American federation made the Constitution difficult to amend, Jefferson believed that the Constitution ought not to burden the present generation with the legal conceptions of the past. Patrick Henry, the famous Virginia patriot and orator, attacked the Constitution when it was before the state convention for ratification, declaring that it was aristocratic in nature. Its amendment procedure, he insisted, would allow one twentieth of the people to block constitutional change, no matter how desperately the change was desired by.the rest of the people.

As the views of Jefferson and Henry grew in popularity and influence, later constitutions reflected them. A difficult amending process characterized more frequently the first state constitutions and the federal Constitution than the constitutions that followed. Actually, several of the later ones provided that the people be consulted periodically for the purpose of suggesting amendments. Others provided for amendments through a simple majority vote of a legislature followed by ratification by a majority of citizens voting in a special election. As a result of a movement in the late nineteenth and early twentieth century, thirteen states today provide a constitutional initiative whereby the voters may bring up proposals to amend the constitution and have the proposals acted upon in various ways.

Constitutional change in most states has occurred more frequently than in the Federal Union. About two thirds of the states have had more than one constitution; some of the remaining third that have had only one are recent to the Union, like Arizona. The average number of amendments to the various state constitutions considerably exceed the 22 amendments to the federal Constitution. However, a number of states have found amendments difficult to obtain. Some states once had, or now have, complicated amending clauses in their constitutions. Furthermore, in several states these clauses have been strictly interpreted by conservative courts. Also, in some states the overrepresentation in proportion to population of the rural areas in the state legislatures has often blocked urban demands for constitutional changes.

THE LENGTH OF CONSTITUTIONS

The length of constitutions has grown ever since the first ones were adopted by governments in the Revolutionary Period. The early ones confined themselves principally to stating general propositions about the organic law, but soon both old and new states began to insert what seemed to be ordinary laws in their constitutions. One state would specify the salaries of various officials, another would define fishing and hunting privileges, while still another would prescribe the procedures of elections in great detail. On the whole, the newer the constitution that a state possesses, the greater its length and attention to matters of detail.

Although textbook writers tend to condemn lengthy constitutions that provide much detail on small matters, a great many Americans have felt that the more detail the better. In 1845, a radical democrat, Hurlbut, praised the tendency of constitutions to challenge the authority of rulers. Human rights, he felt, received service of value from written limitations on government. Many details should be set forth, and "every year of a nation's experience will enlarge its specifications of abuses which ought to be carefully named and provided against." Here again is substantiation of the theory that constitutionalism has had great force in America because it could at the same time be a restraint on the popular will of the moment and a way of restraining the officers of a government from doing any number of unpalatable things. Which of these two ideas was responsible for the adoption of a particular constitution can only be told by examining its contents.

CONSTITUTIONS AND AMERICAN LEGALISM

The American Constitution, the state constitutions, the statutes passed in consequence of them, and the attendant debates have given to American politics and government a legal cast that has often surprised foreign observers. When a change of any kind is proposed in the laws, a great deal of attention is paid to its degree of accord with the basic constitutions, down to the slightest meaning of the last word.

In 1950, even after two decades of great changes in the meaning of many important phrases in the constitution, constitutional interpretation precedes legislative discussion. Thus, in hearings before the House Select Committee on Lobbying Activities during 1950, the Committee had difficulty in reconciling the details of a projected clause regulating lobbyists with the first amendment to the Constitution that guarantees various individual liberties. When Congressman Albert asked Dr. W. Brooke Graves about a possible contradiction between a proposed detail and the first amendment, Dr. Graves could only answer that the question "has been raised in this case that has been before the Court for, I think, more than a year now. There has been no decision on that. It would be very helpful to us if the Court would dispose of that case."

Constitutionalism in America, that is to say, has grown into a philosophy of change. Change must be rationalized legally as well as morally and socially. Unless an action accords with the constitutions, even though the action be thought good in itself, it is regarded or obeyed by many with hostility or shame.

GROUP STAKES IN THE CONSTITUTION

The strong psychological position of the Constitution is reinforced by the direct protection which it affords to many important interests. The Constitution is vehemently brandished both by those who speak for rapid and radical change and by those who wish to prevent all change. The courts may in the same session forbid police to break up radical political meetings and forbid administrative agencies to sequester the papers of a rich corporation. No greater admirers of the national Constitution are to be found than those who are determined supporters of states' rights. The passage of time and the great economic and social successes of the United States have added the force of tradition of the belief in the rationality and legitimacy of this legal order.

CONSTITUTIONS CONTINUOUSLY TRANSFORMED

The national Constitution has been amended twenty-two times, and a great many more amendments have been proposed, but not adopted. As we have said, most states of America have had more than one constitution or have changed considerably their first one. In addition, in state and nation alike, great political changes have occurred without changes in the language of the Constitution. Political parties, so important to the politics of America, are nowhere mentioned in the national Constitution. The President, whose election was assigned by the Constitution to a college of electors, has come to be chosen by the voters directly, although not always by majority vote. The President has powers (over foreign affairs, especially) that were not given him by the Constitution, save perhaps by remote implication. The same thing is true of many of the most important functions of the national government such as the Social Security program, the grants-in-aid to the states, the Tennessee Valley Authority, and the Federal Reserve System.

But all of these changes are rationalized legally; social change in America must be worked into the single fabric of the Constitution. A course in Constitutional Law in an American university, if it is long enough, may cover every aspect of government on the theory that all of it is deduced from the Constitution. In fact, for many years, political science in America was mainly just that, a long course in the "constitutionalization" of every feature of governmental activity. So masterful has been the legal rationalization, so great has been the reverence for constitutions that, despite the continual change in the practical meaning of the Constitution, the term itself has always conjured a firm image of a real thing to most people, changeless and weighty.

THE IMPORTANT CONSEQUENCES OF AN "UNCHANGEABLE" CONSTITUTION

Now it would be a grave error to dismiss the great respect for constitutions as "a mere psychological state." It is one of the great constellations of attitudes into which human activity is organized. Science can describe and analyze it but is not permitted to dismiss or depreciate it. Its dismissal or depreciation is purely a political affair—to be left to people attached to different values, to another tradition, to a magnetic leader, or even to cynicism.

It is, of course, natural for persons who believe in one set of values or in one kind of legitimacy, to view the beliefs of others as "irrational." For example, Americans frequently regard the monarchs of England and other countries as irrational, useless, and comical idols. Yet Americans revere constitutions of all kinds (every little club has one) in much the same way that the English revere their royal family. Americans rarely know what the practical effects of their constitutions are (if they have, indeed, ever read them); and they have, by interminable legal debates and thousands of legal commentaries, furnished amusement to generations of royal subjects abroad.

MEANINGLESS WRITTEN CONSTITUTIONS

Evidence of the essential psychological meaning of constitutionalism is afforded by certain meaningless constitutions. The fact that a constitution is written down does not mean that the people hold to it. The English are constitutionalists and therefore have a constitution, even though it is an unwritten one; certain other peoples have written constitutions, but are not constitutionalists. Such meaningless written constitutions are incongruous with the existing sentiments and social organization to which it was hoped they would apply.

How such constitutions came to be adopted is not difficult to explain historically. A number of South American republics, the republics that were founded in Central Europe after the first world war, the communist republics of Eastern Europe today, and the U.S.S.R. have or have had written constitutions. It is generally observed that these constitutions do not perform the same function as does the American Constitution. All of these constitutions were drafted by small groups of men at a point in history when the United States and France were apparently successful republics. The obvious symbol of their success was the constitution. The new constitutions, therefore, carefully imitated the structure and wording of the existing models. The written document, it was thought, would somehow magically produce all the happy conditions of the model countries. If, as sometimes happened, the national leaders realized the futility of constitutions, given their countries' history, they were still forced to accede to the clamor of public opinion for "something democratic like America has."

Recounting the successive failures of this approach to constitutionalism would be futile. A general respect for legality, for reason in public affairs, for popular consent and participation, and for certain dominant shared values of society must precede a written constitution. These conditions were barely present in America in 1787, and the American Constitution might easily have failed (as it did in 1860). The internal conditions existing today in most countries that have not had long experience with written basic documents are such that a written constitution can hold little meaning. Proclaiming a constitution where there is hardly a legal order is like trying to achieve happiness by assuring oneself that one is happy.

Yet constitutions are the fashion in the twentieth century. Ninety per cent of the world's nations have written constitutions. Communist dictatorships succeed other kinds of dictatorships and promptly draft new meaningless constitutions to replace the old meaningless ones. The several constitutions promulgated by the Republican, Nationalist, and Communist rulers of China since 1900 have had a negligible effect. The Constitution of the U.S.S.R. seems to lead a life of its own. It may be ventured, perhaps, that the repeated failure of this kind of sorcery will produce skepticism among masses of people, and that new revolutions will not for many years more be succeeded invariably by paper documents.

Constitutionalism

CONSTITUTIONALISM AND CONSENSUS

The preceding section has implied that one must search far beyond the language of a written document to explain the durability of certain constitutions. An *effective* constitution is part of a more basic legal order that may be called constitutionalism. The task of this section is to understand the qualities of a constitutional order.

Constitutionalism, to place it in the perspective of earlier chapters of this book, is the *legal or juridical expression of one type of consensus.* Consensus, as was stated in Chapter 4, is the shared and agreed-upon political beliefs of most members of the political community. Hence constitutionalism, as part of a consensus, is the "due process" facet of the belief system of a people.

By our definition, in order to have constitutionalism, we must have a consensus. When people cannot agree on any important political issues, they cannot agree on a constitutional order. On the other hand, we can have forms of consensus without having constitutionalism. The Germans subscribed for a time to the doctrines of Nazism to such an extent that a consensus may be said to have existed. But constitutionalism, as we shall treat of it, did not exist in Germany. Similarly, the people of the Soviet Union favor the beliefs of the existing regime, but their paper constitution cannot be said to be based on constitutionalism.

To make ourselves perfectly clear and to be fair to everyone, we should state that we mean by constitutionalism only one kind of juridical condition and the expression of only one kind of consensus. *Constitutionalism, then, is a legal order in which the ethical directives of the community are determinate and stable as a whole, and the measures taken to compel conformity with and punish deviations from the ethical directives do not depend upon the power of the deviant individual.* "One law for all men," and "government by laws, not men" are two common slogans that express the essential sentiment of constitutionalism.

RULE OF LAW DEFINED

This definition of constitutionalism is very close in meaning to the rule of law, as the English scholar, A. V. Dicey, defined it. The "rule of law" means that "no man is punishable or can be lawfully made to suffer in body or goods except for a distinct breach of law established in the ordinary legal manner before the ordinary Courts of the land." Furthermore, "every man, whatever be his rank or condition, is subject to the ordinary law of the realm and amenable to the jurisdiction of the ordinary tribunals."

JURIDICAL DEFENSE DEFINED

Constitutionalism is also close in meaning to the condition of juridical defense, as Gaetano Mosca described it. Juridical defense is the high discipline of the moral sense, brought about through social mechanisms, which prevent the uncontrolled aspirations of individuals from governing society. It is the condition of a government characterized by established and regular rules.

According to Mosca, various social arrangements can abet or destroy the condition of juridical defense. The political organization proper, he felt, is the most important object of study because it determines the relationships between officers and public, and among the branches of government. Within the political organization, he thought, juridical defense is destroyed if a single political force predominates and checks and balances are absent in the various branches of the government. Juridical defense cannot survive, he says, if the religious and the secular power are one and the same group, if wealth is concentrated in a few hands, if a huge army is maintained over any length of time, and if universal suffrage is used to select personnel for all important offices.

This bare recital of the institutions constituting juridical defense readily suggests the political theory of James Madison. The proceedings of the American Constitutional Convention of 1787—a century before Mosca essayed the conditions of juridical defense—and the great debate over the proposed Constitution had much to say about each of these problems. It is significant that a writer who drew his materials primarily from European experience and world history could agree on the essentials of a constitutional environment with a group of Americans who, while in the great European intellectual tradition, had specific and pressing problems to solve. One must admire the fine application of theory to practical conditions that characterizes the American Constitution.

FACTORS AFFECTING CONSTITUTIONALISM

Rather than adhere exclusively to the views of Dicey, Mosca, or Madison, we shall draw liberally from them and others in presenting the factors that foster or discourage constitutionalism in the political community. However, we shall use Mosca's categories because they are excellent for analytic purposes. The factors affecting constitutionalism, therefore, will be treated under the headings of the separation of powers, economic concentrations, church-state separation, standing armies, and universal suffrage.

SEPARATION OF POWERS

The theory of separation of powers (and its related theory of checks and balances) received its first formulation in Polybius' history of the Roman Republic, although Plato and Aristotle certainly had something like it in mind. More recently, Baron de Montesquieu, in his *Spirit of the laws* (1748), proposed the clear and permanent division of the executive, judicial, and legislative authority. The making of the law and the administration of the laws were to be assigned to different branches of the government. Such an arrangement, he believed, would not only increase the competence of each part to perform its assigned duties, but would also prevent any simple agency from monopolizing power and abusing its exercise. This separation of powers implies checks and balances, for each of the great powers— legislative, executive, or judicial—can block the free working of the other power. The power to make laws, for example, is the power to determine in large measure the substance of administration. The power to execute the laws is in turn the power to determine their substantial content.

In a brilliant stroke on behalf of constitutionalism, American theory put the theory of Montesquieu into effect. It gave the legislature, the executive, and the judiciary more precise spheres of operation than ever before or afterwards. Furthermore, not relying solely on the negative aspects of the separation of powers to prevent a monopoly of power by one branch, certain deliberate checks and balances were inserted in the political organization. Thus the President was given the veto power partly to protect him from domination by the Congress. The veto was widely regarded in the early days as intended principally to shield the executive.

The theory of the separation of powers has come under considerable attack in recent times. It has been stated that the American governmental branches, while admirably suited to self-defense, are poorly equipped for efficient and expeditious law-making. Antagonists of the American system have pointed with favor to the British parliamentary system. There the Cabinet and Parliament depend upon one another for survival, and the Prime Minister and Cabinet combine executive and legislative leadership. The Parliament may force the Cabinet to resign by voting against its bills, and the Cabinet controls the introduction of proposed legislation. They are so closely connected that they cannot remain for any length of time hostile to one another, as can the American Congress and President. Yet the British system seems to provide no less due process of law and juridical defense than the American, and in some ways it seems to provide more.

However, though much has been written on this controversy, the great complexity of the problem has prevented agreement among political scientists. In both countries a separation of powers does exist, but in different degrees and with somewhat different consequences. In neither country is there a monopoly of power by either the executive or legislature, and in both countries the judiciary is independent. Such variations on the theme of the separation of powers incline us to the view that this device is only one of several major elements in constitutionalism. Neither the British nor the American system can be said to provide the "optimum" balance of protection and efficiency. Too many factors of a historical and institutional nature interfere with a sharp distinction.

The separation of powers exhibits its meaning more clearly when one examines governments that make no pretense of employing the principle. In the Fascist states of yesterday and in Eastern Europe, in Asia, and in certain of the South American countries today, the ruling groups have explicitly denounced the separation of powers. The courts, the legislatures, and the executive branches descend in a single, authoritative monolith, directed, so far as events will allow, by a single set of wills. The very idea of a separation of powers is abhorrent, because it implies compromise, indirection, frustrations of power, and legalizing of conflict. If Lord Acton spoke the truth, that "all power tends to corrupt and absolute power corrupts absolutely," then a completely integrated governing group, possessed of many functions and united in force and direction, would indeed terrorize those who agree with Lord Acton on what constitutes corruption. Individuals, under such conditions, could not depend upon impartial and objective execution of the laws.

ECONOMIC CONCENTRATIONS

Whereas the separation of powers supports a constitutional order economic concentrations form a barrier to constitutionalism. Aristotle recognized the political importance of the form in which wealth is distributed. He emphasized that the concentration of wealth increased the possibilities of class warfare and proposed the middle class state as the most stable. James Madison clearly foresaw the political troubles that would arise from dividing society into a rich and a poor class. Yet neither the American nor any other constitution has established a formula to prevent the wealthy from becoming arbiters of justice. And since wealth is often a means to power, there is always the threat that such power may be used to alter the interpretation and administration of the law, and so destroy constitutionalism.

It is a moot question, not to be answered in a few words, whether constitutionalism suffers more from private concentrations of wealth or from government nationalization that consigns political and economic power to one and the same group of officials. Therefore we cannot say that a socialist or communist constitution, by proclaiming the nationalization of the means of production, solves the age-old problem of preventing great economic concentrations that crush the smaller interests and reduce individual choices to the mercy of administrative discretion. Here political policy may face an impossible decision, unless administrative planning can make giant strides. The technological revolution will not be halted merely because it creates political problems: concentrations mount steadily, and whoever controls the great industries will have awful political power.

CHURCH–STATE SEPARATIONS

An organized religion can, under certain circumstances, monopolize political power as much as can a plutocracy. It is then a barrier to constitutionalism. Until the twentieth century, most Europeans and Americans saw the politico-religious problem as one of freeing the state from the church. Thus the French and American revolutionaries, following various English and continental reformers of the seventeenth century, set up the liberal position of the nineteenth century. Constant religious struggles had brought intermittent chaos and costly wars to Europe and England. The leaders of the late eighteenth century and nineteenth century revolutionary and liberal movements in Europe and America became convinced that a political organization that was identified with a religious creed could rarely make rational changes. And it is true that theocratic states in which the same individuals are secular legislators and interpreters of religious dogma tend to determine all kinds of everyday matters by reference to some unchangeable religious dogma.

The American Constitution, in declaring that the Congress shall make no law respecting the establishment of any religion, provides the classic form of the doctrine of the separation of church and state. The American example is followed, in law or in fact, in every constitutional government; one should not be unduly impressed with the fact that certain countries, like England and Sweden, have state churches. Such churches do not actively participate in the political process. Nor should one feel that the principle of separation is not working because there are religious pressure groups. The principle need not be driven to its extreme to make sense.

Actually, the twentieth century, reversing the trend of centuries past, has introduced the problem of the state that pursues the church, swallows its tenets, and regurgitates them in secular form. Thus, the Eastern European communist governments, not satisfied with the separation principle, have taken control of the churches and use them as instruments of the regime. This action is simply an inverse abandonment of the principle, and consequently increases the totalitarian nature of the state. The church becomes a means of destroying political enemies of the regime. For instance, in certain Eastern European countries after World War II, the priests were compelled to reveal to political authorities the secrets of the confessional.

STANDING ARMIES

Another commonly encountered foe of constitutionalism is a large and uncontrolled standing army. The control of standing armies has been a live problem in the Western world ever since the legions of Rome turned on the Republic and then revolted periodically against the imperial government. The American Consitution sought to restrict the power of a standing army to destroy the constitutional order by providing that each state might raise and govern its own militia or national guard. It thus allayed the fears of many who wanted protection against future emergencies but felt that standing armies, if large and unchallenged, would threaten local liberties. The Constitution also sought to assure civilian control of the military by designating the chief executive as the commander-in-chief of the armed forces, and by delegating to Congress the power to declare war and to raise and equip an army. However, the American system, like every other system of civilian control that has been devised, is not immune to the possibility of military control. For juridical defense, in the case of this institution more than any other, is at the mercy of external events. Wars, even more than those massive industrial changes that concentrate a nation's wealth, threaten the defensive barriers of the constitutional state.

ROLE OF UNIVERSAL SUFFRAGE

Now we may turn to the final political factor that has been alleged to be destructive to constitutionalism—universal suffrage. Most modern constitutions, as was indicated in our study of electorates, provide nearly every adult with the vote. However, the leaders of the American Constitutional Convention and political theorists like James Kent, Mosca, Taine, Guizot, and Ortega would have preferred to limit the suffrage to men who hold some property. The American Constitution encourages, but does not demand explicitly, universal suffrage. Who is right and who is wrong depends upon our answer to three questions: Is universal suffrage absolutely destructive of constitutionalism? If not, is it harmful to constitutionalism? If so, what kind of suffrage should be substituted for universal suffrage, if constitutionalism is the objective most desired?

The answer to the first question, so far as it may be given, is as follows: Universal suffrage, absolutely construed and absolutely employed, is absolutely destructive of constitutionalism. That is to say, if all offices of the government are subjected to election by a universal electorate, if all the major decisions of the political community are centralized in the offices of the government, then the condition of the political organization will be highly unfavorable to legal stability and the rule of law.

But this situation is practically inconceivable. All known electorates, universal or not, have been limited, both internally and externally. Most voters are limited internally by a frame of mind that will never allow them to focus on particular objects with the intensity of desire that individual politicians may possess; they are ordinary people with ordinary apathies; in order to become absolutist or fanatic, they must first be regimented into an elitist or charismatic party; and this process invariably brings an oligarchic clique to the fore—like the Nazis or the communists—so that, if damage is done to the constitutional order, it can hardly be said to have been done by the universal electorate.

In fact, the critics of universal suffrage have succumbed to the same fallacy as their opponents. While they ridicule the idea that universal suffrage can attain democracy, they gullibly accept the idea that universal suffrage can get so strong as to destroy juridical defense. Universal suffrage has not turned out to be the instrument of sweeping change that either its advocates or opponents thought it would be. It causes great commotion, of course; some men move in and out of office rapidly. But this fact, if it means anything, is a positive step towards a rule of law since it tends to prevent the establishment of a permanent ruling group.

Political, economic, and social change have come most abruptly and drastically—that is, without the rule of law or juridical defense—in countries like Nazi Germany or Communist Russia, where universal suffrage was meaningless because no general issues were presented to the voters for decision. No one, we suppose, would take the totalitarian plebiscite to represent the normal operation of universal suffrage.

The normal functioning of universal suffrage, it would seem, almost requires a matured, half-solved issue. The issue must not split the population irrevocably. For example, an outstanding decision by universal suffrage was the vote of the Italian electorate to replace the monarchy by a republic. This followed World War II and the margin of victory was a modest one. The same government remained in office before and after the event. If such an issue had been put on the agenda of universal suffrage in the mid-nineteenth century, nothing less than a violent revolution would have occurred. That the issue was important, no one can deny. Seldom has a great community voted on the issue of monarchism *versus* republicanism. But one must also agree that the issue was mature, not revolutionary; conditions were ripe for a public decision, whether we agree with the verdict or not. Consequently, the decision was accepted peaceably.

Electorates are always limited externally too, by laws that restrict their rights to act. The national judiciary in America is appointed on indefinite tenure. The state governments have a number of powers that they may exercise independently of the national legislative authority. The Senate has six-year tenure, and never turns over by more than one third every two years. Governments of the British and French type also allow the electorate to make only limited and general decisions.

Electorates adjust over a period of time to the demands made upon them and to the limitations imposed upon them. It is impossible to prescribe exactly that condition of an electorate that is best reconciled with the condition of juridical defense. But one may observe, among certain past and present electorates in America, Britain, and Europe, a kind of mass "sensing" of the limits of what "ought to be asked for" and what "ought to be withheld from" popular decision. If we could describe more precisely this "sensing" process among peoples experienced or "fitted" for the exercise of suffrage, we might perceive more clearly how the process operates as an element in consensus. There is little doubt that the "sensing" of electoral functions in a manner consonant with juridical defense is an important facet of consensus, and, thence, a determinent of constitutionalism. The dependence of a constitutional order on the "sensing" ability of its people lends importance to the expression that "a people gets the kind of government it deserves."

What has been said of the internal and external limits of universal suffrage holds for restricted suffrage as well. The crux of the Mosca argument against universal suffrage seems to be this: universal suffrage enlarges the span of demands with which a government must contend. Instead of providing only a few with a means of stating their demands or feelings, it provides everyone with the means. This complicates the problem of distributing the goods of life. Internal conflicts increase. Thus universal suffrage, by bringing on internal conflict, reduces the conditions favorable to juridical defense. In short, if scarce prizes are being dispensed, better order can prevail if only a few are allowed to apply for the prizes.

This problem of competition for scarce values is discussed in the next to last chapter on democracy, but a word may be said about it here. The legislative and judicial processes of colonial America and eighteenth century England, both of which had a limited suffrage, were not more favorable and perhaps much less favorable to the condition of juridical defense than their counterparts today, when universal suffrage prevails. It seems that in both countries, universal suffrage, while associated with changing economic policies, has not destroyed or seriously harmed the general state of constitutionalism. When we add to this example the well known fact that oligarchies have undergone at least as many bloody crises and ruthless expropriations as democracies in proportion to their number, we must conclude that a limited class is apt to do as much damage to constitutionalism as an enlarged electorate. We would conclude, then, that not only is universal and absolute suffrage an impossibility, but also that a universal suffrage that is limited in power is inherently no more harmful to constitutionalism than is a restricted suffrage that is limited in power.

THE VARIOUS FACTORS OPERATE TOGETHER IN CONSTITUTIONALISM

No one of these various features of political organization, such as the separation of powers and the suffrage, *can carry the weight of constitutionalism by itself. Nor can any one of these features destroy constitutionalism by itself,* under conditions that actually occur, except perhaps, in the very long run, and then only if it has meanwhile rendered meaningless the operations of the other institutions supporting constitutionalism. In a constitutional order, the effective separation of powers, the wide distribution of wealth, the separation of church and state, civilian control of the military, and the universal electorate of limited power combine and buttress one another, establishing the condition of juridical defense and providing the basis for the rule of law. *Juridical defense* and the *rule of law* give a *written or determinate constitution* effective meaning. The three together establish the presence of constitutionalism. And they are all manifestations of the type of consensus that is a condition of democracy, to be described in Chapter 16.

At this point, these statements, though quite general, must satisfy us. But their meaning will be rendered more clear and will be corrected in part by our further investigation at closer range of the institutions of the legislature, the executive, and the courts.

Questions and Problems

1. What is the conventional order and what are its sanctions?

2. Define law and explain the terms of the definition.

3. Find the term law in an unabridged dictionary and list all of its meanings. Which is closest to the meaning given in this book?

4. Distinguish between the ethical usage of law and the usage employed in this book.

5. What is meant by "natural law"? (Supplement your facts from the *Encyclopedia of Social Sciences* or Bouvier's law dictionary.)

6. Classify laws by formal origin and elaborate the meaning of each part of the classification.

7. Present four alternative classifications of laws. For instructing political scientists, what classification do you think would be next most important to amplify after the classification by formal origins? Why?

8. Obtain a copy of the constitution of your student body, club or fraternity. Compare it with the American Federal Constitution. What are the important similarities (350 words)?

9. Define "constitution" and describe the origins of written constitutions.

10. Explain how both moderate and radical democrats could agree on the desirability of a written constitution.

11. Describe the characteristics of the American state constitutions, as they have developed.

12. How has the American federal constitution been transformed?

13. What is constitutionalism? Why is an effective constitution part of constitutionalism?

14. What are the significant elements in the social order which evidence the presence or absence of constitutionalism?

15. What is the significance of the separation of powers for constitutionalism (200 words, consult Chapter 2)?

16. How do economic organizations and religion enter into the question of constitutionalism?

17. Compare the constitution of your state with the federal Constitution. What imitation seems to have taken place? How do they differ?

18. What role does the suffrage play in determining whether constitutionalism exists in a society?

19. Show that a country that has a written constitution may not have contionalism, and that a country without a written constitution may have an effective constitution and constitutionalism.

Longer Study and Research
Problems Suitable for Term Papers

1. Write a summary history (10 pages) of your state constitution, describing its origins, its contents, its amendments, and present expert views about it.

2. Read and review in ten pages one of the following works:

C. H. McIlwain, *Constitutionalism and the Changing World* or *Constitutionalism, Ancient and Modern*

E. M. Burns, *James Madison, Philosopher of the Constitution*

Max Farrand, *The Making of the Constitution*

C. Van Doren, *The Great Rehearsal; The Story of the Making and Ratifying of the Constitution of the United States*

Don M. Wolfe, ed., *Leveller Manifestoes of the Puritan Revolution*

Hamilton, Madison, and Jay, *The Federalist*

W. Ivor Jennings, *The British Constitution*

Conyers Read, ed., *The Constitution Reconsidered*

3. Using as a source Amos J. Peaslee's *Constitutions of Nations*, compare the constitutions of the United States, Argentina, the Soviet Union and France. Which of these constitutions is most like the American? Which is least like the American? Do your findings agree with what you know about the presence of constitutionalism in these countries? Present your findings in a ten page essay.

4. Write an account of the amendments and the unwritten changes in the American Constitution, answering the question—Which of the two kinds of change has been most important in transforming the Constitution? (15 pages)

10

LEGISLATURES

AMERICAN legislatures are so powerful that most Americans identify lawmaking with elected assemblies. A moment's reflection, however, reminds us that government by legislatures is an intermittent rather than an invariable phenomenon of history. The eras of rule by legislatures can be recited in short order. The small city-states of ancient Greece and Italy were often governed by assemblies, composed sometimes of hereditary officers and sometimes of all the citizens. Assemblies of an advisory kind existed within provinces of the Roman Empire, in the Catholic church councils of the Medieval Period, and in the kingdoms of western Europe from the thirteenth to the sixteenth centuries. The medieval English Parliament, a bicameral body of nobles and clergy on the one hand and of elected town and country representatives on the other hand, is perhaps the most familiar case of such an assembly, inasmuch as it carried into modern times. And, of course, toward the end of the eighteenth century, a period of revolt began that established legislatures within two generations in most countries of Europe and America.

Government by Legislature

COMING OF THE AGE OF LEGISLATIVE SUPREMACY

The eighteenth century revolt had two consequences that allow us to term the nineteenth century the age of legislative supremacy: First, legislatures appeared on all sides. Second, they assumed a greater share of the lawmaking power. We may adopt therefore, as the standard of *government by legislature, the condition that exists when the bulk of important laws originate in law and in fact through the opera-*

tions of a selected group of officers of equal status, organized into a constitutional branch of the government.

LIMITS TO POWER OF LEGISLATURES ALWAYS PRESENT

We should emphasize that legislatures have existed without legislative supremacy, and legislative supremacy may exist without a monopoly of power by legislatures. Some form of council almost always seems to be present, even if it is only a cabinet of ministers to an absolute monarch. The English Parliament existed for centuries before it emerged, in the Revolution of 1689, as the supreme policy-determining institution of the realm. What is true of the past is sometimes true of the present and may be true of the future: legislatures, that is, may exist without real power.

Furthermore, legislatures have rarely possessed a monopoly of power. The last chapter on law revealed several formal organs that make law besides legislatures. The amount of power these organs have taken from legislatures has sometimes been great and sometimes small. The American Congress and state legislatures have been limited by written constitutions, even when the Presidency and the governorships were weak offices. They have always faced a court system highly esteemed by an influential public. And in Europe, over most of the nineteenth century, kings reigned, and they limited the power of legislatures. One can always visualize the position of legislatures, relative to other branches and institutions of government, as having moved upwards or downwards in their *average disposable power* (see Figure 30, below).

MAJOR FUNCTIONS OF LEGISLATURES

The power of the legislature (particularly during the age of legislative supremacy) has been expressed in the following major functions.

1.) Legislatures usually have the power to determine whether persons seeking admission to them have been duly qualified and elected.

2.) Legislatures usually have something to say about the general organization of the government—they define the functions of many executive offices, establish new agencies of government, give jurisdiction to courts, and initiate amendments to constitutions.

3.) Legislatures rule themselves. They set up regulations for their internal working, provide committees to investigate at length particular matters pertaining to old and proposed laws, and select their officers.

4.) Legislatures appoint or approve the appointment of many key officials of the government and usually have powers to force the removal of appointed officials for grave causes (by the impeachment, trial, and conviction process). They scrutinize the operations of executive agencies.

5.) Legislatures vote money. The first important power of the English House of Commons was the right to refuse and to grant funds to the king. Parliaments gained considerable respect from kings because of the wealth and the means for guarding that wealth possessed by the representatives of the lower houses, for example, the Commons. In modern times the tradition that the popular chamber should control the voting of new taxes and of new appropriations has persisted. In the American Congress and legislatures, bills for raising revenue usually must, according to the Constitution, originate in the House of Representatives and may be amended by—but not introduced in—the Senate.

6.) Finally, legislatures draft, debate, and pass bills. Sometimes, as in America, the executive has to sign all public bills or veto them. But in several European countries, bills become law if they are approved by the legislature.

BICAMERALISM

The prevailing structure of legislatures in recent times has been bicameral. Fifty-one nations—approximately sixty per cent of all nations—employed the bicameral system in 1950. Members of the "upper" chamber, examples of which are the many senates of the world and the British House of Lords, are selected ordinarily from narrower groups of the population than the "lower" chambers such as the American House of Representatives, the Italian Chamber of Deputies, and the British House of Commons. Only twenty-eight of the fifty-one nations having bicameral assemblies elect their upper houses in whole or in part by popular elections. Most upper houses are partially or wholly filled by indirect election through local legislatures (like the original American Senate), election by vocational bodies (the Irish Senate), election by regional councils (France), election by the lower house (Denmark), or appointment by the executive branch (England).

CONSERVATISM OF UPPER HOUSES

In effect, the nonpopular techniques of filling upper chambers meant that the more conservative, propertied elements would have greater strength in upper houses than in the lower ones. This was actually the reason for instituting bicameralism in the first place in most countries. It was contended by the more privileged and wealthier groups that a check was needed against possible hasty and demagogic laws of the lower chamber.

In judging this assertion, we must agree that the upper houses did come to represent the more solidly entrenched members of society while the lower houses more actively sought change. But we cannot assert that hastiness and demagoguery are the sole possessions of lower houses. Nor can we agree or disagree with the assertion that the upper houses possess the vice of obstinacy more than the lower houses possess the vice of rashness. Hastiness, demagoguery, and obstinacy are all terms best reserved for propaganda, not science. We cannot make any objective statements on this matter without studying the thousands of discrete enactments of the many legislatures (something no one has done).

DECLINE OF UPPER HOUSES

It is obvious, however, that the major political forces of the late nineteenth and early twentieth century played on the side of lower chambers. Upper houses lost power in three ways: they were often limited further in the powers they possessed for making laws or for obstructing the acts of the lower chambers; they were sometimes subjected to the same principle of election as the lower house; they were in several cases abolished.

The limitation of the power of upper chambers has occurred in most continental countries and in England. The House of Lords in England has been losing powers for centuries and now has lost the last shred of its formal ability to retard the acts of the House of Commons. The French Council of State is a weak body, simply expressive of the ideas of French parties and of French local governments, who elect its members. Its legal and actual powers are few. The careers of other continental upper houses show a similar relapse over the past two generations.

The election of upper houses on the same principles as the lower houses is common in America. Whereas, in the early years of the Union, the national and state senates were elected by restricted electorates—indirectly or by men of property—today there exist no differences between the qualifications for voting for senators and representatives. The same electors, practically all of the adult citizens, elect the members of both houses.

Upper houses have been abolished in the course of several revolutions. Under peaceful conditions, enough respect for special traditional interests is present and enough power is possessed by them to prevent a total exclusion of their influence. Thus the English Commonwealth Parliament abolished the House of Lords temporarily. The French revolutionaries abolished the Estates General, only to make way soon for bicameralism under the Directorate Constitution. The Russian Bolshevists established unicameralism on the ruins of Czarist and republican bicameralism, but later restored bicameralism.

EFFECTS OF REMAINING DIFFERENCES BETWEEN THE TWO CHAMBERS

Putting aside questions concerning the differential powers of the two chambers and the differential electorates for them, several other differences remain and produce behavioral consequences. These are differences in 1) the special qualifications a candidate to the two houses must possess; 2) the size of the chambers; 3) pay of members; 4) the tenure and turnover of membership; and 5) differences in geographical apportionment, especially in America.

SPECIAL QUALIFICATIONS FOR CANDIDACIES

The age of qualification for membership in upper houses averages several years more than for membership in the popular chamber. Traditionally this greater age has been held to account for the greater conservatism in upper houses. Such a conclusion is hard to demonstrate. What seems to be due to an age difference may be in fact the result of other factors. Thus, older men in a society of high mobility may be expected to have more possessions and to be somewhat more influenced by considerations of stability and fiscal conservatism than younger men. But there is always an adequate supply of old radicals for any system. British Labour Party politicians have been older on the average than British Conservative leaders, because it has taken longer to organize political power among the masses than to buy or inherit power. This fact would seem to indicate that age is a negligible cause of conservatism among political leaders.

In addition to age, the most common special qualifications demanded for membership in the various upper chambers of the world are the possession of property above a certain amount, membership in a learned profession, a title of nobility, and the prior achievement of official position or civic honors. Experience confirms the expectation that property and status requirements, if greater in the upper than in the lower house, will produce more resistance to change in the upper house than in the lower. The more property and status a man has, the greater is his investment in the *status quo*, and the greater is the likelihood that he will defend that status.

SIZE OF THE CHAMBERS

The influence of numbers upon the behavior of legislative assemblies is difficult to determine. The most widely accepted judgment is that the higher the number of legislators, the more prone is the body as a whole to be subjected to an oligarchy of leaders. The individual American Senator, it is pointed out, has more freedom in debate, more influence in committees, and more respect among the public than the individual Representative, because he is one out of 96 rather than one out of 435.

The American practice of making senates smaller than lower houses is the usual practice elsewhere as well. The tendency seems to be to enlarge the upper house beyond the number of the lower house only when its functions become purely ceremonial. The size of the lower houses varies greatly. The English House of Commons contains over 600 members, the American House of Representatives 435, and the American state houses from 35 in the case of Delaware to 399 in the case of New Hampshire. The largest legislature is the Supreme Soviet of the U.S.S.R., with about 1300 delegates, divided almost equally between its two chambers. The number of delegates does not, however, rise proportionately with the population of the country. Smaller countries have smaller ratios of representatives to constituency populations than do more populous countries.

PAY OF MEMBERS

In some countries, the number of which is diminishing, members of the upper houses are paid a token sum of money. Other upper houses do not compensate their members at all, while working upper houses that possess real power, like the American senates, have the same general salary levels as the lower houses. The salaries of popular representatives have generally been considered low, especially in view of the high expense that political activity involves. American state legislators are paid stipends ranging from $100 per year in New Hampshire to $5,000 per year in New York. The national representatives earn $12,500 plus an allowance of $2,500 for expenses. Members of the English House of Commons receive 1,000 pounds per annum.

The miserly character of most legislative emoluments has prompted a general belief that higher pay would produce "better" legislators and reduce corruption of politicians. More men would enter legislative election contests. Many petty temptations would disappear. And, no doubt, legislators would be happier human beings, a status they should not be denied more than any other groups of the population. But it is difficult to argue these points one way or the other. Men who earn so much that they regard legislative salaries as too small usually earn enough money to serve in legislatures at a loss, if they feel political activity is worthwhile. It is doubtful that the average annual income of state legislators from all sources is inferior to the general average of the population. Again, if one ranged the American states from 1 to 48 on the amount of salary they pay their legislators, and then ranged them according to the number of scandals in which their legislatures were involved, it is almost certain that no relationship would be observed to exist. However, even granting that the top salary of $5,000 per year is too small to reveal the difference between low and high paid men, one may still doubt that a crowd of able and honest men will join the rugged game of politics even if annual salaries were to be doubled. In any event, the character of democratic politics makes the granting of high pay unlikely.

TENURE AND TURNOVER OF MEMBERSHIP

The tenure of office in upper houses is generally longer than in lower houses. It ranges from three years to life; the average tenure is six years. Two years, three years, four years, and five years are the favored tenures for popular chambers, with the usual term four years. The American House of Representatives is elected each two years—a common term among the state legislatures, which, however, are elected annually in some cases. Short tenure of office, formerly so strongly demanded by radical democrats, proved to have technical consequences working against its widespread adoption. Hardly did men achieve office and organize a session of the assembly when they had to begin campaigning for the next election. Only those politicians coming from safe constituencies, where their majorities were regularly assured, could begin to know governmental affairs well. Consequently, the principle of short terms deduced from a theory of democracy, has given way to practical need. The tendency has been to lengthen terms.

A number of upper houses are renewed only partially in each general election while, as a rule, the lower houses turn over completely. For example, one-third of the American Senate is subject to election each two years, and one-eighth of the Swedish upper house is elected annually. Partial renewals, in contrast with wholesale renewals, have two consequences of importance. The partially renewed house is permanently organized and always has available many members who are skilled in conducting parliamentary business. Also, the partially re-

newed house reflects less of the transformation of opinion that may
occur from one election to the next. Thus the American Senate settles
down easily after each biennial election while the House has initially
a period of confusion. At a single election, the Senate cannot swing
from one party to another by huge majorities, as can the House, because its membership cannot be altered by more than one-third in each
biennial national election.

DIFFERENCES IN GEOGRAPHICAL APPORTIONMENT

As we mentioned earlier, upper chambers are often elected
by constituencies different from those of the popular chambers. Examples would be senates selected by vocational bodies, appointed by
executives, or elected by state legislatures. But even where both chambers are elected by the same people, say by universal suffrage, differences in the geographical apportionment of members may be present.
In the American national Senate each state has two popularly elected
senators regardless of population. Also, in a number of American
states, representation in the senate is apportioned by local jurisdictions
such as counties, giving a certain minimum representation to each
local area, while representation in the house is apportioned according
to districts of roughly equal population. The main result is the em-
phatic presence of rural voices even though the county or state is
heavily urban. This amplifying effect, together with the refusal of
many rural-dominated legislatures to increase the representation of
rapidly growing urban districts, helps to give American legislatures
their strong rural outlook and to explain the cramped incompetence
of American city governments in attending to some of their most
pressing problems.

Legislative Organization and Procedure

LEGISLATURES FOUNDED ON OPPOSING FORCES

Legislatures differ from most other human organizations
that are required to do work in that they are compelled by their own
"theory" to be composed of opposing forces. While most other organizations have internal factions, such divisions are visualized as non-
essential. For example, an administrative agency or a large corporation is not supposed to have internal factions. On the other hand,
legislative divisions, at least since the eighteenth century, are regarded
as the appropriate symbol of effective organization, paradoxical as
this may seem. This division within legislatures has been re-enforced

by the more recent advent of strong political parties that lay claim to unanimity among their members on certain matters—such as support of their programs.

"Divided unity" causes some grief to legislators and public alike. Unanimity in a legislature is suspect. Yet divisiveness in a legislature is looked upon sometimes as unpatriotic. Legislators must tread carefully the line between collusion and hopeless factionalism. Over a long period of time, a way of accomplishing this has been worked out (mostly unconsciously) and is revealed in a number of ways. A notable and clear method of coping with the paradox is to give all power to the majority of members in deciding a matter introduced as a bill but, at the same time, to give the opposition the status of a regular and respected part of government. This is the case in the House of Commons, where the Opposition is regarded, not as something to be ignored and discriminated against in every way possible, but as the possessor of an established position, with specified privileges in seating, debates, and committee memberships. American legislatures do not go so far as the English in institutionalizing the opposition, but only rarely do they attempt completely to exclude the minority membership from participation at any stage of the legislative process. Almost every legislative committee has several minority members. Formal leadership is consigned to the majority party through the Speaker of the House, the chairmen of the committees, and majorities in all committees. The minority party is deprived of equality with the majority party. That is a far cry from carrying out strictly an extreme view of the majority principle, requiring that the majority have absolute sway.

This relationship between opposing elements of the legislature is so rooted in a long historical development that its critical, delicate, and incongruous nature is not often enough realized. New legislatures often encounter difficulty in overcoming this essential paradox of legislatures. The degeneration of the short-lived democratic parliaments of east Europe after World War II reveals that, when suddenly and consciously advanced, the compromising demands of the legislative way of life are hard to grasp and to put into practice. The first thought of the new victorious parties of such legislatures is to rid themselves of all conceivable threat from opposing party members who remain in the assembly.

"ESPRIT DE CORPS" OF ASSEMBLIES

The legal concessions to the minority that characterize long-lived legislatures are accompanied by an informal organization of the legislature that scarcely is evident to outsiders. We refer here to what may be called the *esprit de corps* of legislatures. Like quarrelsome families, legislatures are torn by internal dissension but are held together by scarcely mentioned bonds. This may seem extraordinary to those who believe that "anything goes" in politics. But one may, after close scrutiny, prepare a rather lengthy list of things one legislator will *not* do to an opposing legislator. Some are prohibited by rule, others by unstated convention. Even violators of conventions are dealt with by informal means—ostracism, deprivation of expected perquisites like consultation in making appointments—rather than by formal action. Rarely will a legislature formally discipline an ill-behaved member. Apparently, legislators would rather undergo a lowering of public esteem for the whole body than institute a new principle for the punishment of offenders.

Pertinent to this kind of behavior is Garland Routt's observation that "in general, the *esprit de corps* displayed by legislative bodies, especially the smaller ones, is probably not rivaled by any other formally organized, self-governing body." Dr. Routt discovered that among Illinois legislators there was in some cases as much social communication among members of opposing political parties as among the members of the same party. Two other observers have made similar comments. Karl Abshegen said that the House of Commons resembled an exclusive and influential club while James Bryce wrote of the collective self-esteem of the American Senate. T. V. Smith noted that "the cloak rooms of Congress, and legislatures, are more important than committee rooms."

CLASH OF EGALITARIAN AND OLIGARCHIC PRINCIPLES IN LEGISLATURES

The necessary internal contradiction between unity and dissent that affects legislative institutions is supplemented by another contradiction just as important. The legislature is formed on the assumption that each member equals every other member. Theoretically, each member derives an equal amount of power from his constituency. On this basis each member has only one vote on all matters put before the whole assembly. But this egalitarianism, that finds force in the minds of most electors and receives deference in the formal rules of procedure, is opposed by the tendency in acting organizations towards leadership by a few men. Because legislatures are founded on the principle of the equal power of its members, they must avoid any appearance of hierarchy and oligarchy. No one challenges an executive officer because he gives orders to his subordinates, but a legislative officer is exceedingly vulnerable to such challenges.

On the other hand, the pressure of work is as great in the legislative branch of the government as in the executive branch. Bills must be processed, legislative time must be budgeted, many decisions must be made. All of this must be accomplished while satisfying internal and external critics that the equality of members is being preserved.

FORMAL LEGISLATIVE PROCEDURE AND INFORMAL PROCESS

The foremost consequence of this contradiction is the discrepancy between the formal legislative procedure and the informal

FIGURE 25
LEGISLATIVE PROCEDURE: AMERICAN TYPE
(*Highly abbreviated*)

HOUSE OF REPRESENTATIVES   SENATE

Bill introduced by member A
(in this case, a house member)

Bill is placed in the appropriate committee by the Speaker

It is assigned to appropriate committee by the Senate President

It is considered by the committee in private and public hearings, and is reported back with *pro* and *con* recommendations

It is subject to further hearings, approval or disapproval, and sent to the floor

It is debated by the whole membership

It is debated by the whole membership

It is voted on. If rejected, it dies. If passed, it goes to Senate.

It is voted on. If rejected, it dies. If approved, it goes to President for signature. If amended, it goes to a Conference Committee.

Conference Committee appointed with members chosen from each house by its presiding officer. It compromises the amendments, and returns bill to both houses.

House approves bill or rejects it, as a whole.

Senate approves bill or rejects it, as a whole.

Executive signs bill and it becomes law. Or he vetoes it and sends it back. It then may be passed over his veto, provided usually that a two-thirds majority so votes in each house.

legislative process. Let us picture first the formal legislative procedure in a bicameral assembly of the American type (where the executive is separate) and then the informal legislative process. The formal legislative procedure is diagrammed in Figure 25.

These are the main formal steps that must be taken before a bill becomes law in the United States; the same process is followed in a number of other countries. Often the same or a similar bill is introduced in both houses by two co-operating members at the same time. Such action expedites the bill by allowing it to be simultaneously considered in both chambers.

Few bills that are introduced by isolated individuals go through the legislative process with such facility. In most cases unless a bill is known to be powerfully backed it is marked for an early demise. In legislatures like the English, a bill that is powerfully backed is almost sure to get through, once it is set in motion. In American legislatures, where party lines are not held to so tightly, a bill favored by the leaders of the legislature will often get through several of the main barriers with ease but be blocked for a time at some point that cannot be controlled, like the unfriendly committee chairman of one of the houses, or the President or governor. Nevertheless, we can present a second diagram (Figure 26) this time of the informal legislative procedure, which is as true on the average as the first diagram.

FIGURE 26

INFORMAL LEGISLATIVE PROCEDURE: AMERICAN TYPE

HOUSE   SENATE

A bill is simultaneously introduced in both houses by the leaders of the majority party.
↓

The bill is sent to a friendly committee by the friendly speaker, and after establishing a case for it by controlled hearings, the committee chairman uses his influence to have it referred quickly and with approval to the floor.
↓

The bill is given a favored position for debate; debate is closed whenever seemly to do so; and the leadership musters support for early passage.
↓

Unforeseen amendments are handled by a conference committee, appointed as recommended by the friendly chairmen of the committees originally considering the bill.
↓

The bill is quickly passed by both houses.
↓

It goes to the executive for signature.

The first diagram portrays the legal "musts" of legislative procedure, the "right" of every member to introduce any bill and see it through into law, and the "rational" function of debate and hearings. The second diagram portrays the strong control a few old, skillful, and entrenched officers can wield over the legislature. They can co-ordinate both houses in a planned campaign on behalf of a favored bill and they can hamper the bill of an ordinary member by curtailing hearings and debate. Both diagrams can be true, and various combinations of both processes normally occur as the contradictory principles of egalitarianism and oligarchy interact in practice.

THE STRUGGLE FOR CONTROL OF OFFICES AND COMMITTEES

Extreme conflict between egalitarian and oligarchic tendencies in legislatures is most likely to occur over questions of control of the legislative business. Who decides what bills to consider and who has the power to delay or advance proposals are the crucial internal issues of legislatures. Each American chamber has from a dozen to several dozen committees. A committee is established for every important area of legislation and for considering questions of internal governance. The most important committees are those attending to the rules by which the legislature operates and to the activities on which most money is spent or the activities most important to the welfare of the community. Examples would be the committees on rules, appropriations, ways and means, foreign affairs, and atomic energy. Those congressmen who are elected to the key positions of Speaker of the House or Majority Floor Leader, or who are chairmen of the important committees, together with their close supporters, are each equipped with a legislative potential far exceeding that of the ordinary members of the House of Representatives.

The egalitarian principle prevails formally in the organization of a legislative body. The assembly elects its officers and elects its committees. The party that commands a majority determines the party affiliation of officers such as the presiding officer of the lower chamber and of the chairmen of committees. And, still speaking formally, each member of the majority party has an equal say with every other member. But important facts cannot be gainsaid. Some "equal" members are old in service, some are new; some are leaders of blocs of members, some are without followers or loyal associates; some have been holding important committee posts, others are without important appointment. Therefore, the members who remain from previous sessions, who lead blocs, and who have been in command of the legislative offices and committees before, direct the organization of each new session of a legislature and, beyond that, the substantive work of the legislature. The election of officers and committee chairmen is controlled by such members and the bulk of other legislators are consigned to the role of followers or critics of the dominant few.

Committee chairmen are formally elected in the American type of legislature. However, they usually are designated from among the entrenched group by the Speaker and "run" without opposition. The

Speaker in turn observes the principle of seniority; that is, he favors the candidate for a committee chairmanship who has had the longest tenure in the legislature among the "acceptable" aspirants for the post. It is naive to view this procedure from the standpoint of "efficiency." The seniority principle is not pursued simply because the legislators believe "erroneously" that experience is better than intelligence or that age imparts wisdom. The seniority principle is followed mainly because the seniors are pleased with themselves and see no sufficient reason for consigning their powers to others. In other words, seniority accompanies oligarchy and the revolts against the seniority principle that occasionally occur are mainly revolts of the dispossessed egalitarians against the entrenched oligarchs.

EXTERNAL INFLUENCES ENTERING THE LEGISLATIVE PROCESS

Thus far we have spoken only of the internal conditions of legislative organization and process. We will now describe the other factors that influence the operation of the legislature: the chief executive, administrative agencies, pressure groups, and public opinion. Again, the American type of legislative organization remains our model.

EXECUTIVE INFLUENCE

Observing the American elective executive at work in his legislative capacity, we find the following: the President or Governor influences his supporters in the legislature to introduce in the legislature a bill that reflects his policies. If his party is the majority party, and if the majority party leaders on the floor agree with his bill, then the second process diagrammed above takes place. If his party is the majority party but there is a split between, let us say, the President and the congressional leadership, then the President must muster an effective alliance among some other legislative leaders and his personal followers; a combination of the first and second processes results. If the President is faced by a Congress the majority of whose members are in the opposition party, he must resort to the first process, using friendly individuals to buck the oligarchy in getting fair treatment for his bill, and employing his own personal and official powers to assist this effort.

AGENCY PRESSURES

The influence of administrative agencies can be distinguished from the influence of the executive in studying the legislative process (1) whenever the appointive bureaucracy is unintegrated and has political connections with the legislature, and (2) whenever the bureaucracy is permanent and highly respected, and is joined to a weak political executive. The first is common in the American past but is less frequent today. The second is found in weakly controlled monarchies that have legislatures (for example, eighteenth-century England; the period of Louis Philippe in France) and in turbulent republics (for example, the Third and Fourth French Republics).

In the nineteenth century the ordinary department heads and bureau chiefs of American administrative agencies maintained autonomous relations with legislators. Many legislators had favorite agencies, whose growth they fostered, whose appropriations they ensured, and whose personnel they helped to select. Bills considered good or bad by the agency were sponsored or opposed by its friends in the legislature. Often the President or Governor, although called the "chief executive," had little knowledge or control of the growth and change of an agency. Recently, in America, the national executive has grown stronger, and agencies that flagrantly disregard the wishes of the "chief executive" concerning proposed legislation are punished by reprimand, or in extreme cases, by dismissal of the offending officers. However, although today the executive controls the agencies in general, certain agencies still have special "friends" in Congress who will defend them and who know more about the operations of the agency than the President's office itself. In state governments, the extremely autonomous agency still predominates, with striking exceptions such as New York State.

In the American examples just given, agency influence on legislation was strong because the appointive bureaucracy was unintegrated and agencies could use their political connections in the legislature. Agencies, however, can also strongly influence legislation if the bureaucracy is permanent and highly respected. In the Republics of France and Germany and in various other places at different times, the permanent bureaucracy had a firm grasp on the key offices short of the few elective offices and a secure position in the social class system. For these reasons the agencies often were able to initiate legislation that then went smoothly through the formal legislative process prescribed by law. We shall have something to say in the next chapter about the instability in position of the chief executive that promotes this kind of agency influence in lawmaking.

EFFECTS OF PRESSURE GROUPS

The role of pressure groups in legislation, it was said in Chapter Seven, is not as great as commonly believed. Nevertheless, where opposing pressures are weak, an integrated lobby can markedly influence particular legislation.

LEGISLATIVE BLOCS

Legislative bloc leaders, who can control a dozen or so legislators and especially when they control the committee pertinent to the issues in question, are the favorite instruments for initiating legislation on behalf of pressure groups. Here it must be remembered that very often the vote of a legislator is cast on an issue with several motives in mind. A common motive is to help someone else on a matter of "not too great" consequence in order to get his help in turn. Even a small bloc of legislators, united in support of a particular interest group, such as the producers of dairy products or the owners of silver mines, can find occasion when their position on another issue will gain them support on their favored issue. Therefore, it is because much legislative business is settled through compromise that special interests get the opportunity to make their ideas into laws. The small bloc and the strategic committee are the favored transformers of special interests into law.

PUBLIC OPINION

Finally, public opinion has its own peculiar way of influencing the legislative process. Ordinarily, public opinion is divided rather than unified, and mild rather than tempestuous. Bruce Barton estimated in 1939 that letters to Congress averaged over 100,000 each ordinary day. But letters are only one of the symptoms of the condition of opinion; others were mentioned when we dealt with public opinion (Chapter Four) and pressure groups (Chapter Seven). The regular mail constitutes a sort of ballast to the legislative process to which a continuous but relatively minor attention is paid.

When, on extraordinary occasions, the mail sharply increases, one can see heightened adjustive activity on the part of many representatives. When Congress in 1939 was considering lifting the embargo on shipment of arms abroad, over a million and a quarter pieces of mail arrived in a short time. According to Dwight Anderson, "an aroused public sentiment evidenced by an unprecedented volume of letters, telegrams, and petitions, actually defeated" the Supreme Court and executive reorganization measures that had been proposed by Franklin D. Roosevelt, and this happened at a time when Roosevelt's party nominally controlled 335 of the 435 members in the House of Representatives.

But we must be most careful not to credit aroused public opinion with a monopoly of pressure. The Chicago City Council once imposed a tax on movie admissions in the face of an avalanche of contrary petitions, amounting almost to a full instruction by electoral majorities in several wards. The councilmen were, however, desperate for funds. They judged that the hostility of the public would diminish in time, and they united in their mutual crisis and passed the tax in spite of public disapproval.

We should also realize that an outburst of opinion is rare, not at all available upon demand or upon necessity, and in itself contains no inherent wisdom other than the wisdom of both sides of the particular case at point.

THE FOREGOING ILLUSTRATED BY A CASE STUDY

In order now to fix in our minds what has been said thus far of the legislative process and to learn something more of the details of the activity, let us take one complicated piece of legislation and follow it from beginning to end, describing each influence as it comes to bear on the bills from which the final act emerged. Our illustration is drawn from Stephen Bailey's *Congress Makes a Law*, an excellent detailed study of the Employment Act of 1946. This act attempted by various means to forestall any period of heavy unemployment in the United States, such as occurred during the depression following 1929.

THE EMPLOYMENT ACT ORIGINATED IN MANY MOTIVES

The Employment Act of 1946 (see Figure 27) developed from the efforts of a number of politists. They had different motives; they often worked at cross-purposes; some of them spent three years on the specific problems of the first and succeeding bills. We cannot say that the bills arose from a general dislike of widespread unemployment; that is far too simple an explanation of the process. As soon as we examine the behavior of the men working for or against the different versions of one or another bill, we find many motives. Whatever their opinion of unemployment, some participants in the process were active because they were paid to be active, others were active because they were forced into action, or because they had personal likes or dislikes for people on one side of the issue, and so on.

THE MANY HISTORICAL ANTECEDENTS DIFFICULT TO ASSESS

Just as unknown and unmeasurable as the motives entering the contest by way of active participants were the historical antecedents

FIGURE 27

THE TITLE PAGE OF A PUBLIC LAW

(*The Employment Act of 1946*)

[PUBLIC LAW 304—79TH CONGRESS]
[CHAPTER 33—2D SESSION]
[S. 380]

AN ACT

To declare a national policy on employment, production, and purchasing power, and for other purposes.

Be it enacted by the Senate and House of Representatives of the United States of America in Congress assembled,

SHORT TITLE

SECTION 1. This Act may be cited as the "Employment Act of 1946".

DECLARATION OF POLICY

SEC. 2. The Congress hereby declares that it is the continuing policy and responsibility of the Federal Government to use all practicable means consistent with its needs and obligations and other essential considerations of national policy, with the assistance and cooperation of industry, agriculture, labor, and State and local governments, to coordinate and utilize all its plans, functions, and resources for the purpose of creating and maintaining, in a manner calculated to foster and promote free competitive enterprise and the general welfare, conditions under which there will be afforded useful employment opportunities, including self-employment, for those able, willing, and seeking to work, and to promote maximum employment, production, and purchasing power.

ECONOMIC REPORT OF THE PRESIDENT

SEC. 3. (a) The President shall transmit to the Congress within sixty days after the beginning of each regular session (commencing with the year 1947) an economic report (hereinafter called the "Economic Report") setting forth (1) the levels of employment, production, and purchasing power obtaining in the United States and such levels needed to carry out the policy declared in section 2; (2) current and foreseeable trends in the levels of employment, production, and purchasing power; (3) a review of the economic program of the Federal Government and a review of economic conditions affecting employment in the United States or any considerable portion thereof during the preceding year and of their effect upon employment, production, and purchasing power; and (4) a program for carrying out the policy declared in section 2, together with such recommendations for legislation as he may deem necessary or desirable.

(b) The President may transmit from time to time to the Congress reports supplementary to the Economic Report, each of which shall include such supplementary or revised recommendations as he may deem necessary or desirable to achieve the policy declared in section 2.

of the precise idea that entered the first bills proposing the Employment Act. Have not most men always agreed that heavy unemployment was an evil? Why were there not many previous laws and bills on the same subject? Why was this certain bill proposed at this moment? Professor Bailey suggests a number of factors that combined to make imminent and to shape the form of *some* bill to fight the depression phase of the business cycle.

First was the vivid memory of the Great Depression that started in 1929 in the United States and which was hardly ended when the heavy orders for armaments in 1940 and the induction of many men into the armed forces induced full employment. Second, there seemed to be general agreement that something "ought to be done" to plan against such widespread depressions. Other generations, on the whole, had accepted severe depressions as inevitable consequences of the business cycle that could not be controlled without seriously disturbing the free enterprise system as well as general political freedom. Now, many of the new generation of officials and politicans in Washington believed they could diagnose accurately the sources of such disturbances and could institute countertendencies that would relieve depressions, without disturbing the various political freedoms and the system of relatively free enterprise.

THE STRONG BELIEF IN GOVERNMENTAL COMPETENCE

At this point we will not evaluate the evidence on both sides of the question whether governmental intervention in economic matters is effective or desirable; we will discuss the general topic of planning in a later chapter. Here we should note that there developed a strong conviction that depressions could be competently controlled by the government. Many officials and politicans abandoned the *laissez-faire* theory that was derived from Adam Smith and that opposed governmental regulation, in favor of the theory of John Maynard Keynes that defended governmental regulation. Confidence in governmental regulation was also increased by the general belief that governmental planning had played an important part in the remarkable success of the war effort.

The new economic theory, incarnated in Keynes and some economists of the New Deal, found adherents in Washington not only among government officials but also among liberal politicians and pressure group leaders. It is not surprising, then, to learn that the sharpest and most influential idea of the whole movement for the key bill was first formed by men from the National Farmers Union (a private group), the National Planning Association (private), the

Fiscal Division of the Bureau of the Budget (public), and the National Resources Planning Board (public) in 1943.

As drafted by James Patton of the Farmers Union, the proposal for a bill had one generally acceptable notion: unemployment was bad. In addition, the proposal had several controversial notions: something could be done about the business cycle; the national government was the most effective instrument to do it; and a formula, as part of the law, should require the government to intervene with large expenditures for useful purposes whenever the amount of capital investment by private enterprise should decline below a certain figure. This proposal was well received by Senator James E. Murray, who promised to support it.

THE PRELIMINARY CONGRESSIONAL STRUGGLE

Meanwhile in Congress, the War Mobilization Sub-Committee of the Senate Military Affairs Committee (under Kilgore) held hearings in the spring of 1944 on problems of reconversion to peace, paying special attention to a bill proposed by Senator Kilgore (S.1823) to create an office in charge of planning an orderly reconversion.

Though lacking enthusiasm for state planning and concerned more with the immediate problems of mustering out millions of soldiers and resettling millions of war workers, the Senate and House each created a Special Committee on Postwar Economic Policy and Planning. Finally, Senator Murray's War Contracts Sub-Committee of the Senate Military Affairs Committee also became interested in the problem of postwar economic planning.

Between September 1943 and August 1944, to quote Dr. Bailey, "an almost unbelievably confusing struggle developed in the Senate for control of postwar legislation. Senators Kilgore, Murray, and George and their respective staffs spent most of late 1943 and early 1944 jockeying for position in the race to dominate reconversion policy. The three-cornered struggle was due partly to differences in philosophy, partly to Senatorial and staff jealousies."

During a phase in the struggle, Senator Murray was able to affix the Patton proposal to the Kilgore bill as an amendment. But that bill was defeated, and Senator George's reconversion and demobilization bill, which contained no peacetime planning and regulatory mechanisms, triumphed.

Congress adjourned. The next session reopened the matter of peacetime economic planning. Senator Murray now incorporated the central idea of his old amendment into a new proposal. The new scheme had been worked over carefully. Three men from the Bureau of the Budget, one from the Bureau of Labor Statistics, two from the Office of Price Administration, one from the Bureau of Agricultural Economics, one from the National Farmers Union, and two staff men from congressional committees shaped the proposal for the use of Murray. Succeeding private conferences brought in new people who helped to popularize and sloganize some of the technical language of the bill.

THE PRESS ENTERS THE SCENE

The first public print of the Murray proposal at the end of 1944 brought the influence of the press to play. Most newspapers alleged that the measure fostered "gradual collectivism" and were hostile to it. F. A. von Hayek's book, *The Road to Serfdom* (1944), gave intellectual support to many opponents of any positive plan for full employment. The public at large, despite the considerable press coverage and pressure group activity, did not become excited either by the proposal or by the bill that followed.

AGITATION FOR THE BILL

Civil servants and politicians interested in the proposal encouraged speeches favoring it and wrote encomiums of it for various newspapers throughout the country. Co-sponsors for the prospective bill were approached—a tactic not legally required, but definitely helpful. Senators Wagner, Elbert Thomas, and O'Mahoney agreed to co-operate with Murray in sponsoring it, but some concessions had to be made to O'Mahoney. Between January 8 and 22, 1945, the bill proposed by the subcommittee was revised seven times. The appeal of the bill was broadened and sections that might incite violent opposition were removed. The "liberals" who had supplied the initial push to the idea behind the Patton amendment were forced to give up several of their principles in order to gain conservative support in and out of Congress.

On January 22, 1945, the bill was introduced in the Senate by Murray as S.380. At the same time, he inserted propaganda for the bill in the Congressional Record. Senator Murray's staff, under the direction of Bertram Gross, prepared many reports and speeches on the measure for use by its supporters. Hundreds of opinion leaders in the country were canvassed in support of the bill. Suggestions were solicited from the same people. One fifth replied. Agencies of the federal government were asked to comment on the bill and the services of the Legislative Reference Division of the Budget Bureau were called upon. Murray's staff, writes Bailey, "rapidly increased the ferment of discussion on the full employment issue in and out of Washington and was able to provide the sponsors of the bill with intellectual ammunition and support."

USE OF FAVORABLE HEARINGS

The staff also scheduled and arranged hearings, seeking to mobilize external support on behalf of the bill. The "liberals" and labor lobbies that supported the bill were organized into a group to meet weekly and co-ordinate the pressure activities of their organization and membership. The support of "liberal" businessmen was consciously sought to offset the expected counterattack by "conservative" businessmen and legislators. The National Farmers Union and the Department of Agriculture joined forces in an "educational" campaign to offset the strength of the opposing American Farm Bureau Federation. The pressures of opposing veteran groups made the Veterans Administration inactive and noncommital. The Union for Democratic Action, in search of a *raison d'être* at the time, seized upon and actively supported the bill. The national labor organizations were rather cool, but not opposed. Local unions here and there helped actively.

Direct lobbying was heightened in intensity as final Senate action neared. The extraordinary efforts of the so-called "Lib-Lab Lobby" heightened the effect of the hearings before the subcommittee of the Banking and Currency Committee, where favorable views were selected and pointed up by the committee majority.

Still the full Banking and Currency Committee's subsequent consideration of the bill was marked by heated debate over several crucial amendments, and the bill could be said to have slipped through intact only by virtue of the favorable votes of two or three members. The first strong opposition to the bill was felt in the subcommittee and then in the committee.

The bill moved onto the floor, there to be heralded by several influential members who lauded the various aspects of the bill. In a full dress debate, the bill's sponsors fought off several amendments. The crucial Hickenlooper amendments, that would have cut into the positive statement of governmental responsibility for full employment contained in the committee's bill (already less strong than the "liberals" had originally intended it to be), lost by a large majority. In this vote about one-fifth of the Senators crossed party lines, depending on whether they were more or less "conservative" than their fellow party members. The final vote was 71–10 for the bill, a rather meaningless figure, for the significant vote already had been cast on the amendments.

FORMING OF OPPOSITION

The opposition lobbies had been slow to gather strength. But as the bill moved to the House, the National Association of Manufacturers, the United States Chamber of Commerce and its local affiliates, the Committee for Constitutional Government, and the American Farm Bureau Federation began to appear on the scene in the persons of their lobbyists. The legislators were spoken to and provided with long statements of the case against the bill; local memberships throughout the country were incited to protest against the bill to their representatives; and several well-known lobbyists (in exactly the same way as did their "liberal" counterparts) worked hand in glove with the committee of the House charged with considering the bill.

This committee, by a stroke of fate, was the Committee on Expenditures in the Executive Departments. Lacking guidance by the Speaker, the Parliamentarian of the House overlooked more important committees and more friendly committees in assigning the bill to committee. As it happened, the Democratic Chairman of the Committee, as well as the Republican members of the Committee, was hostile to the bill's chief provisions. Hearings on the bill were adverse rather than friendly now.

Meanwhile, Harry S. Truman had become President and had arranged a system whereby his policies would be promoted among congressmen by committees of his cabinet members. One of these committees kept an eye on full employment legislation, but special assistants, rather than cabinet officers, actually worked on congressional relations. In October of 1945 it became obvious that the House committee was going to damage the Senate bill seriously, and Truman was prevailed upon to speak personally to the three key Democrats on the House committee. The President was able only to extract a promise that some sort of bill, rather than simply an unfavorable report on the Senate bill, would be offered the House by the committee.

Various members of the President's high administration testified before the Committee on the bill. Chief of the Veterans Administration, General Bradley, was noncommittal towards it; Chief of the Office of War Mobilization and Reconversion Snyder was obviously unfriendly to the bill; and, of course, the President himself had not insisted on the strong version of the bill. Truman now appealed to public opinion in a radio address (October 30), apparently with little effect. However, his address irked the Committee members, for he had accused them of deliberately delaying the bill.

Finally, the hearings concluded, a drafting subcommittee was appointed which toned down to a murmur all promises of government responsibility in connection with full employment and left only the

provision for a weak economic planning body and for a moderate
public works program in economic emergencies. The "conservative"
Rules Committee of the House helped the hostile Expenditures
Committee by allowing only one day's debate for the bill and assigning
the time during that day to the Chairman of the Committee and the
minority leader of the Committee; these happened to be, as the Rules
Committee knew, two opponents of the Senate bill, Representatives
Manasco and Hoffman.

The "liberal" friends of the Senate bill in the House decided to fight
the new substitute for the Senate bill by demanding a vote on the
Senate version, thus forcing either a victory for the Senate bill or a clear
issue that might be used as material in the 1946 elections. Secretary of
the Treasury Vinson, who was directing the President's part of the
struggle, called on Secretary of Commerce Wallace to help influence
the reluctant "liberals" to vote for the bill as the House Expenditures
Committee had reworked it, and the pressure of both caused the "liberals" to subside. A final attempt by several House "liberals" to force a
vote on the Senate bill failed. And when they tried to have a roll-call
vote on the House bill, by which the members would have to put their
position on the record, the Speaker recognized only the Committee's
supporters. The final vote of 255–126 in favor of the House version
was relatively meaningless, since no vote was tallied on the crucial
issue of the Senate version versus the House version.

THE CONFERENCE COMMITTEE AND FINAL ENACTMENT

A conference committee was now in order. This was
selected from the membership of the two committees of the Senate and
the House that had first considered the bill. Truman, again prevailed
upon by supporters of the bill, stated in his January message to Congress that he preferred the Senate version to that of the House, and
wrote both the Senate and the House leaders of the conference committee to the same effect. But friction between two administrative
chiefs, Vinson and Snyder, prevented a memorandum from being dispatched in the name of the Truman Administration that would give
the exact way the White House thought the compromise between the
Senate and House might be attained. The bill was hardly modified
from the House version, and the Employment Act of 1946, as finally
passed by the two houses, and signed by the President, was a weak
version of the original idea of the Patton Amendment to the Kilgore
reconversion bill of 1944. The Act contained no strong commitment
by the government to take all "necessary" steps to eliminate business
depressions, nor did it create an organization competent for such a task.
Instead, the Act provided for a weak Council of Economic Advisers to

report to the President and Congress on the economic condition of the nation and for a Joint Committee of the Congress to consider such matters that the reports indicate require consideration and action.

EXPECTATIONS OF LEGISLATION MUST CONFORM TO LEGISLATIVE REALITIES

We shall not inquire whether the results of this vast and complicated activity, stretching over many months, were good or bad, nor how such results might be altered by alternative ways of organizing the American congressional and legislative procedure in general. Our purpose has been achieved if we now realize how intricate the legislative process is and how legal and informal influences interact throughout the duration of the process. This illustration is one of the many cases that led us to the conclusion, mentioned earlier, that knowledge of the formal procedures prescribed for the enactment of law in a legislature is only one step towards complete knowledge of how laws are made.

As we observed this law come into being, we saw that many formal and informal influences found their way into the legislative process. Many other laws are similarly influenced. So far, political science can only name these influences as they appear and cannot measure their strength accurately, or predict their timing. Also, we can tell what has happened in the past, but we cannot expect the same combination of events to reoccur. In any case, the judgment of experienced politicians (see Figure 28) can help appraise the legislative process and should be considered seriously.

THE BURDEN OF WORK IN A LEGISLATURE

We can appreciate the complexity of the legislative process even more if we recognize that the intricate activity surrounding the Employment Act was only a small part of the total activity of Congress during that time. Bailey reports that "during the first session of the Seventy-ninth Congress, which lasted from January 3 to December 21, 1945, the Senate passed 1,005 bills and resolutions, voted for 23 investigations of which nine were by special committees, handled 11,056 Presidential nominations, and filled up 5,960 pages of the Congressional Record with its proceedings." Matters of such importance as the death of Roosevelt, the organization of the United Nations, the end of the war, and the control of atomic energy competed for the attention of legislators. This situation is perhaps only slightly exaggerated over the normal. In contrast with nineteenth-century legisla-

tures that saw much debate and few laws, twentieth-century legislatures have too much to do and cannot wholeheartedly study particular
issues without slighting many other serious problems.

THE BRITISH CONTRAST

One cannot doubt, turning to the British type of legislature,
that it has an easier way of sweeping its business under the bed.
British members of Parliament are not on the average as beset by
immediate trifles and trivial legislation, because their government and
cabinet have more flexible constitutions. The cabinet, formed of the
majority leadership in the assembly in most cases, joins with the
permanent staffs of the departments and together they draft, propose,
and manage the career of most of the bills. Strong party discipline
restrains the legislative forays of individual members and blocs. Only a
few public enactments in each session originate from private members
rather than from the cabinet leaders. Prof. W. Ivor Jennings listed only
eleven out of seventy parliamentary enactments in the period 1936–7
as being introduced by individual members. Also, the committees of the
House of Commons are not little principalities like the American
committees, but tend rather to act as agencies of the Cabinet itself.

Despite the growth of the practice of delegating the power to make
very important decisions (quasi-legislation) to appointed officials in
America, American legislatures and courts are far less indulgent in
this respect than the British Parliament and courts. In England great
powers are turned over to appointive officials with little fear of the
consequences. It is, indeed, almost impossible to isolate the Commons
as an operating body from the Cabinet, so intimate is the connection
and so remote the idea of the formal separation of powers in England.

THE FRENCH PATTERN

There are, however, other countries besides the United
States, particularly France, in which the executive and legislature may
hold separate policies, conduct separate operations, and have clashing
encounters. In France, in great part because the National Assembly
serves a fixed term and is not subject to an immediate election if its
majority disagrees with the incumbent ministry, the legislature moves
along under its own regimen. The bills of individual members are
introduced with greater frequency and success than in Britain, and
individual members successfully solicit greater legislative attention to
local and bloc interests. As with the American legislatures, there is
little love lost between the French Parliament and ministry (executive).

FIGURE 28

WHAT INFLUENCES CONGRESS *

AN INTERVIEW WITH SAM RAYBURN

Speaker of the House of Representatives

EDITOR'S NOTE: *What Congress does is recorded at length, but what influences the action of Congress isn't as well known.*

To present an intimate view of how Congress operates and what the outside impact is on its legislative policies, the editors of U. S. News & World Report invited the Speaker of the House Sam Rayburn, to its conference rooms for an interview. The Speaker's position has been called the second most powerful in the country. Mr. Rayburn is perhaps the best qualified man to discuss the workings of Congress.

SAM RAYBURN *was born 68 years ago and elected to Congress 38 years ago. He has been re-elected every two years—never suffering a defeat.*

Schooling earned the hard way, a bit of teaching and six years in the Texas Legislature preceded his coming to Washington as Woodrow Wilson entered the White House. Only two men have been in Congress longer than Mr. Rayburn.

The Speaker, who is unmarried, has presided over the House of Representatives for eight years. During the Republican 80th Congress, he was Minority Leader.

• • • •

Q *The Congress and the White House don't always see eye to eye in what the objective is, do they?*

A Well, no two men that have got the good, common sense that I was talking about a while ago agree on everything. If they do agree on everything, one of them is doing all the thinking.

Q *The executive and legislature don't have to see alike? One shouldn't necessarily dominate the other?*

A I don't believe in any sort of domination.

Q *In Great Britain, they have a system of government where the executive makes a decision, or the party in caucus makes a decision, and then everybody has to go along, don't they?*

A Yes, they do that or they get thrown out.

Q *Do you think that system over there would work over here?*

A No.

Q *Why not?*

* Reprinted from *U. S. News & World Report,* an independent weekly magazine on national and international affairs, published at Washington. Copyright 1950 United States News Publishing Corporation. This selection is presented to show the use of a formal interview in obtaining knowledge of the legislative process from experienced legislators.

Figure 28

WHAT INFLUENCES CONGRESS—*Continued*

A It is too rigid. Our Congress is more independent, and our executive is independent, too, and their executive is not. We elect a President for a definite time, and we elect a Congress for a definite time. I think that is much more responsible.

Q *Why couldn't we have a responsible-ministry form of government here?*

A I feel that the people of the United States are the dominant power. They know that under the Constitution they are voting for a legislator for two years or for six years. I think they have the right to try him out for that length of time. And the party in power that would be overturned today might be the proper party to be in power tomorrow when a bigger issue is coming up. You cannot change Presidents all the time.

I don't like the system of splinter parties, either. We have not recognized more than two parties in the House of Representatives since the Civil War. When I came here in 1913, there were Teddy Roosevelt Progressives. But that party was not recognized. Members of the splinter parties in this country go to the party in the majority for assignment on committees.

Is Two-Year Term Enough?

Q *Do you think that two years is a long-enough term for a member of the House?*

A I have always felt that it ought to be four years. I don't know whether I think that as much now as I used to. A fellow hardly has a test in two years. He has a better test now than he used to have.

Q *How much influence do lobbyists have?*

A Well, now, it depends upon what you mean by lobbyists. People are called lobbyists, and, of course, the word "lobbyist" has a bad sound.

Some so-called lobbyists are men of outstanding ability, honest men who would tell you the truth and are helpful to committees. Now that kind of lobbyist is very helpful because he has studied one question for many years and maybe some of the members of the committee hadn't studied it at all. Members generally want to learn about it in order to have both sides honestly put forward so they can make a sane, sensible judgment.

Also there are lobbyists of the sort usually talked about, but they don't come to see me.

Q *You feel that different groups should get the chance to put their views to Congress?*

A Of course. And that will always be true. Some people who hire people to come here to Washington to represent them make mistakes in the type and character of man they get. But, as far as any of this so-called lobbyist influence in any pernicious way influencing members of Congress, that just doesn't exist, in my opinion.

•   •   •   •

At times one is led to suspect that the chief occupation of many deputies is to muster a majority to vote out a ministry by refusing its request for a law. At other times, one remarks the persistent, but encumbered, efforts of ministries to carry on a government without consulting or relying upon the Parliament that elected them. The Council of the Republic, the upper chamber of the French Parliament, can suggest amendments of bills coming to it from the Assembly, but cannot otherwise obstruct lower chamber proceedings.

THE SUPREME SOVIET OF THE U.S.S.R.

The Supreme Soviet and the other legislatures of the Soviet Union were originally supposed to have been more powerful than any existing legislatures, but, despite the theory, today have less collective power than any of their western European parallels. The legislature of the Soviet Union is called the Supreme Soviet of the U.S.S.R. (see Figure 20). It is bicameral, with one chamber elected by districts of equal population and the other by the soviet republics and regions that form the federal union. Each house has between 600 and 700 members and meets twice annually for about a week on the average. The work between sessions is done by a Presidium of 32 members. A third organ is termed the Council of Ministers. Legally the Supreme Soviet elects the Council of Ministers. But this election, like practically all matters on which the Supreme Soviet votes, is settled in advance. No opposition of a fundamental nature arises.

According to the Soviet Constitution of 1936, "The legislative power of the U.S.S.R. is exercised exclusively by the Supreme Soviet of the U.S.S.R." The Constitution explicitly limits legislation to the Supreme Soviet. Other organs such as the Presidium of the Supreme Soviet and the Council of Ministers are confined to issuing decrees, decisions and orders. Thus the Supreme Soviet legally has extremely broad areas within which it may legislate.

Formal legislative procedure follows a common pattern of other parliamentary governments. The Council of Ministers originates bills; commissions or committees consider them, and suggest revisions to them; the Supreme Soviet debates them and passes them into law. Although legally it alone may legislate, the Supreme Soviet in actuality is the source only of a small proportion of the laws. The Presidium of the Supreme Soviet issues decrees that are really laws. The Council of Ministers promulgates decisions and ordinances that cannot be separated in their legal effect from laws passed by the Supreme Soviet. As Julian Towster says, "whatever the present theoretical distinctions between law passed by the Supreme Soviet, decrees issued by the Presidium of the Supreme Soviet, and the 'decisions and ordinances' of the Council of Ministers, the scope and volume of its enactments make it abundantly clear that the Council of Ministers is the greatest producer of obligatory, state-enforced, activity-guiding norms in the Soviet system." Thus the Supreme Soviet, composed of deputies who must agree enthusiastically to the principles of the Party leadership, appears to be convened to voice approval of the government and its ruling Party and to affirm faith in them.

The duties of a deputy are to participate in the meetings of the Supreme Soviet and to work in its commissions, to maintain contact with the electors of his district through correspondence and visits, to receive petitioners, and to initiate action in local or central institutions for the solution of problems brought to his attention. He may address inquiries to the government or to a particular minister that must be answered within three days, and he is immune from arrest and prosecution and from legal responsibility without consent of the Supreme Soviet. Also, he receives free transportation by rail and water, and in addition to a daily allowance during sessions he receives a monthly sum for reimbursement of expenses in connection with his duties. That the life of a deputy is difficult may be surmised from Towster's description: "First, there was the difficulty of finding time to receive callers and answer correspondence while holding down a regular job in industry, agriculture, etc. Second, since most of the requests and petitions dealt with complaints against some official action or lack of such, there was the delicate job of prodding the relevant governmental agencies along without appearing to be stepping into their shoes. Finally, since the nature of the problems that a citizen could take up with his deputy was not clearly defined, many deputies found themselves overloaded with petitions of a purely personal nature, requests for jobs, etc." These facts incline one to believe that perhaps the Soviet slogan of mass participation in government is not the only explanation for the rapid turnover of personnel in the position of deputy to the Soviet.

The Critical Age of Legislatures

AGE OF LEGISLATIVE SUPREMACY OVER

Whatever the variations in power of the legislatures of various countries may be, it does seem that the age when legislatures were supreme, short as it was, is past. The seemingly impregnable power position that legislatures achieved a generation ago has been subjected to successful assault by new social forces. It is in order now to state what have been and continue to be the main sources of parliamentary strength and, then, what are the forces working to weaken legislatures.

DIFFICULTY OF DEFINING LOCAL INTERESTS

The principal features of legislative supremacy have been the power to determine the most important policies of a nation, the power to supervise and control the executive branch of the government, and the power to express local interests. The first and third of these powers have often worked at cross purposes. A wholehearted attachment to the demands of one's small constituency may impede the development of a policy that appeals to the nation. For the reflection of those interests that cling to geographic or occupational constituencies, the individual legislators are often well-fitted. And many people would admit that *some* attention ought always to be given to small parts of the society in order that the interests of a greater part of the society may not be ruthless and overbearing.

Yet the same conditions that guarantee such fidelity to local demands, that is, elections by district or occupation, cannot be expected to provide—save in a most homogeneous community—personnel who will seek always for a solution desired by, or directed at, the good of the largest number. Nor, furthermore, can such elections, with or without a party system, be expected to furnish representatives who can consistently ignore the interests of the constituency when they conflict with those of the greater community. Even Edmund Burke, for all his faithful past service and elegant statement of the case for independent judgment by representatives, was defeated by Bristol electors who sought more obedience and less reasoned conduct.

Scarcely a public law is passed by American legislatures without contest or amendment by strategically placed legislators on behalf of their single constituencies. The same is true in all countries where legislatures have not lost their essential power to make the law. However, it is not so true in England because the party system there is so strong as to defeat or seriously hamper candidates devoted eagerly to local interests and because the Cabinet is the initiator and manager of practically all important legislation.

WHY LOCALISM IS A SORE POINT TODAY

Historically speaking, the expressions of local interest afforded by legislatures of times past were not received with great hostility because the objects of legislation were fewer and different. From the eighteenth to the early twentieth centuries governments were not so active as they are today. There was more local self-government and the national government concentrated often only on taxation and foreign affairs. The burdens of taxation often rested equally on the constituencies of all members, and what was desirable to one member was often equally desirable to many other members. Foreign affairs also offered the possibility for greater agreement among territorial constituencies than do internal affairs. It was when the states took up the extensive ordering of internal interests by means of legislatures that local interests were called into play more frequently and violently.

Today, individual legislators fight desperately in national legislatures to obtain local concessions on matters that once never came within the province of national legislatures. For example, the early American states conducted many more programs of internal public works than did the national government. Today that situation is reversed, and every congressman is jealous at the thought that other congressmen may be getting more money, appointments, and contracts for their districts than he for his. This attitude overflows (by the "bloc" and "bargaining" methods discussed earlier) into legislation on completely extraneous matters. A vote for a United Nations bill may depend on whether or not the friends or foes of the bill had supported an individual congressman on some matter affecting his personal and local political interests.

DOES A NATIONAL INTEREST EXIST?

This issue of the conflict between local and national (or greater) interest is complicated by a grave problem that political science and philosophy have not solved: whether such a thing as knowledge of the national interest exists in such form as to enable us to discriminate between local and national interest. In extreme cases, we can make such a distinction: we can easily see that a legislator who will trade his every vote for some concession advantageous to part or all of his constituents has no conception of a national interest. But many of the most important situations perplex even the most conscientious scientist. For example, is a vote against universal military training in the national interest or in the local interest? The issue itself tells us nothing. A legislator may want UMT because the army will establish encampments on the poor land of his district or because he believes everyone should be prepared to defend his country. Contrariwise, a member may vote against UMT because he fears the vote of mothers in his district or because he believes UMT will defer the technical training of youth and provide no real military skills for war.

If the issues themselves are very bad indicators of their general or local nature, what remains? Two positions: (1) one may set up his own standards of general and local interests and apply it to the actions of legislators, or (2) one may set no standard save the one stated in the last paragraph. A legislator who by all signs consistently approves or disapproves all policies because of their effect on his constituency is defined as a local interest representative and is to be sharply distinguished from one who asks himself always "Is this good for the country?"

The second distinction, though crude, is clear enough to be useful in appraising legislators. (We cannot, of course, say that such men are *wise* legislators; wisdom is then to be judged by additional standards, once we have determined whether a legislator is "local" or "national.") If we apply this distinction to the legislative process in countries where other factors like parties or dictators do not blur the picture, we must conclude that legislatures are essentially particularistic bodies, only moderately interested in a national interest.

CERTAIN LEGISLATURES STILL FORMIDABLE IMPEDIMENTS TO EXECUTIVES

This tendency of legislatures, noted especially by adverse critics of the late nineteenth and the twentieth centuries, was an open invitation to the executive to return to power, this time as presidents and dictators rather than as kings. However, legislatures had acquired powers that were exceedingly difficult to excise, and they continue to wield them with gusto.

Legislatures of the American and French type, continue, through statutes, to set up, modify, and destroy various bureaus and offices. Also, through their committees and in debate, legislatures continue to investigate administrative operations and to question their propriety. By hearings, to which witnesses, no matter how reluctant, may be compelled to come, legislatures can acquire information on proposed laws and on current laws. And, finally, there remains that venerable first and very important prerogative of assemblies, the voting of funds for the conduct of the administration and courts.

A legislature that loses the power to tax and spend is no longer an important branch of government. In American legislatures, this power has been monopolized by the legislatures and jealously guarded. In fact, so intent on keeping this power have been the legislatures that the principle of equality of members was almost carried out in matters of money. That is, the amendments to American money bills embodied the local interests of so many legislators that there was a constant scandal over the ineptitude and inefficiency of legislative budgeting, taxing, and spending.

To counter this fiscal "anarchy" American governments, including the national government, began to reduce and exclude the number of occasions on which individual members of the legislature might express their local interests. At present, the executive in many American jurisdictions, like the executive abroad, has considerable power to plan taxes and expenditures and to spend money. But the legislatures still can impede seriously the whole administration simply by refusing to vote funds or taxes. In such cases, the executive is temporarily or permanently powerless. Nothing can function until the legislature changes its position, the executive gives in, a new election is held, or a revolution erupts.

DECLINE OF RESPECT FOR LEGISLATURES

The powers of legislation, supervision, investigation, taxation, and spending have not preserved the position of legislatures. A number of social changes produced a different attitude towards legislatures. The extension of suffrage to nearly every adult broke up the class solidarity of the earlier legislatures. Once the same group that ran society also ran the government. Now the politician is primarily dependent on friendships and on a massive constituency of unknown voters. Whether parliamentary government in the name of a restricted group in society is the only kind that can work is a matter for future political scientists to decide. We only can say that universal suffrage seems to have produced a situation in which the constituents approve the actions of their legislators but do not respect them.

RESIGNATION OF THE ACTIVE COMMERCIAL CLASSES

The middle class group of free farmers and merchants who elected the first powerful legislatures are now joined by servants, clerks, and workers. The merchants moved out of active politics, once they satisfied their demands for freedom of economic enterprise, and are presently in no mood to re-enter politics in competition with the professional lawyer and labor politician. We might note, for example, that, whereas American, French, or English merchants of the late eighteenth century would have leaped at the opportunity to force economy measures on a debt-ridden government, the private citizens' committee to support the economy proposals of the Hoover Commission in 1949 met a wall of indifference. The modern businessman, as was indicated in Chapters Three and Seven, tends to operate politically in the executive establishment, in an increasing number of cases.

CLASS POLITICS ARE ANTILEGISLATURE

The organization of social classes in Europe and England through labor and socialist parties cannot be considered as strengthening parliamentary government. To the contrary, executives were strengthened and parliaments weakened. The class parties themselves obviously aimed at a strong executive (if only they were supplying it) because their radical programs required a vigorous administration if they were to succeed. Their programs were also long-range ones that could not be reviewed *in toto* at each sitting of the legislature. Legislatures might therefore meet to consider only less important questions. On the other hand, when in parliament as minorities, many class parties were determined to hold their own lines tight, to resist "partial" solutions, and to impede the efforts of the legislature to run the government on a day-to-day basis.

NATIONALISM FAVORS THE EXECUTIVE

The growth of nationalism and its various consequences joined with the developing idea of a rational national interest to generate enthusiasm for conformity, for integration, and for a powerful executive to represent the nation. In times of war, the executive of every democracy has been strengthened, as much by the psychological "herding together" that occurs in crisis as by the clear efficiency of the executive for conducting war. In peacetime, in every democracy of this century, the national community has grown in people's affections to the detriment of the local community. In so far as local interests have set the tone of legislatures, the legislature has lost an important number of supporters among the politists.

Thus, today, legislatures face a moral crisis more than they do a technical crisis. There is a wide clamor for national unity and efficiency in every country; local interests, it is believed, may well be sacrificed to national interests. There is an extensive faith in planning and efficiency in government, matters usually accorded to the executive for action.

INDICES OF THE LEGISLATURE'S WEAKENING

The threat to legislatures from the executive occurs in such various forms as the increasing power of the independent elected executive of the American type; the strengthening of the English cabinet executive; the growth of a permanent bureaucracy entrusted with many powers; the consignment of more prestige and power to military leaders; the growing influence of party leaders over individual legislators as in England and Russia; and the appearance of the revolutionary executive, the charismatic, popular dictator who cannot tolerate the "ineffectuality," "selfish localisms," and eternal discussions of representative assemblies.

THE DEFENSE: ATTACK ON THE "NATIONAL INTEREST" IDEA

Several lines have been pursued in defense of legislatures, but so far none of them has been sufficient to guarantee the continued ascendancy of parliaments. One theory, already described, argues that often no national interest is to be found and that the legislature, representing local interests, is the best guarantee that contentment will prevail throughout the land. This conservative argument, which could be accepted at one time when government was not active and was giving more than it was taking away, suffers now under all the hardships of an age geared to national crisis and to the demand for sacrificing individual interest to the whole. It does no good to claim that the executive decisions are no more national than the actions of legislatures; the executive branch of the government is so organized as to give an astonishing impression of unity and direction. It is enough that the executive claims not to be divided in affiliations and to be wholly dedicated to a national viewpoint. Few legislators can claim that and survive.

ALLIANCES OF LEGISLATURES WITH GROUP INTERESTS

An alliance with powerful special interests is another line of defense against invasion of legislative power by the executive. By taking, with all their defects, the support of corporate and propertied interests, legislators individually and as groups can maintain strong positions. But such support is rarely inspiring. It is given in order to prevent national legislation that would regulate and burden business interests. It is not given in the name of abstract symbols and slogans that can win mass support.

CONTROLLING THE EXECUTIVE

Control of the executive or part of the executive is still another line of defense for legislative leaders. But the British House of Commons has lost most of its controls over the Prime Minister; the

American governors are freeing themselves from state legislatures; and the little administrative domains that individual legislators used to carve out amongst executive agencies are being appropriated by the executive in the name of efficiency. "Ultimate" controls like impeachment, withholding of funds, and wholesale elimination of governmental functions do exist. However, legislators rarely attempt to use these controls until it is too late for them to succeed.

LEGISLATURES MAY CLAIM ONLY A CRITICAL FUNCTION

Another defensive technique is for legislatures to abandon all claims to legislative supremacy, and to move back to a second line of defense—investigation and criticism. It was John Stuart Mill who, in the age of legislative supremacy, first launched an influential attack on the "overworking" of the legislative principle. Let there be a strong and permanent executive, he wrote, and confine the legislature to supervision, general (vague) policies, and criticism. And, in America, many writers have agreed substantially with Mill, notable among them Charles E. Merriam, who would consign large powers of planning, policy-making, and policy execution to the elected executive and his bureaucracy, leaving advice and exposure of malfunctioning to the legislature.

INCREASING THE MECHANICAL EFFICIENCY OF LEGISLATURES

A final approach to the difficulties of modern legislatures is well summarized in the study by the Council of State Governments, an organization supported by the State Governments, entitled *Our State Legislatures*. The study makes a number of recommendations that, if extensively adopted, would strengthen legislative bodies. Longer sessions and terms are suggested for state legislatures to allow men time to learn their jobs and time to act without fear of imminent election campaigns. Better statute-drafting is recommended, and more staff assistance for legislative committees and individual legislators is urged. Other suggestions are to reduce the number of committees; to regularize and publicize hearings; to limit the number of bills that may be introduced after the session is begun; and to restrict the numerous time-consuming private bills granting individuals pensions, damages, and other assistance.

CLEANER DESKS AND SCIENTIFIC PROCEDURES

The two major ideas here are to clear the legislative desks of trivia and confusion, and to sharpen the legislative "thinking" procedures. The legislature has a magnificent fact-finding apparatus in the hearing and committee processes. They provide opportunities for research into human behavior that are unsurpassed by the facilities of outside scientists and governmental executives. First, policy and science are joined closely together so that what is found out can be most relevant and most practical. Second, the legislature's powers are sufficient to command ordinarily inaccessible sources of information. Third, the viewpoints of a legislative committee are sufficiently diverse to prevent only one viewpoint from being investigated.

To tap these hitherto unused resources, legislators must educate themselves concerning the differences between social policy and social science in order to reassure themselves that science can study values and facts without commanding policy. Once this attitude is achieved, we might expect investment in legislative research to expand into many millions of dollars and hundreds of staff members. If we reflect that a professor who is surveying a complex social problem requires a staff of scientific assistants, it seems rather absurd that a legislator, whose needs are more crucial in the same kind of analysis and who requires dozens of analyses, should refuse to allow himself the continued services of a single social scientist.

Without exception, these various recommendations of the Council of State Governments could, conceivably, raise the prestige and power of legislatures. However, we do not know whether these or any other improvements could so streamline and change legislatures as to cause them effectively to resist the admittedly powerful influences already enumerated as weakening the position of modern legislatures. In the next chapter, in our discussion of the executive branch we will pursue farther the answer to this great question about the future of legislatures.

Questions and Problems

1. What is legislative supremacy and when has it occurred historically?
2. List the major functions of legislatures.
3. What usually has been the motive behind bicameralism and how has the motive been carried out in the structure of bicameral legislatures?
4. By what methods has the power of upper chambers been weakened?
5. What general statements can be made about the size of legislatures and the tenure of their members?
6. Discuss the problem of the payment of legislators.
7. In what way is the majority principle in legislatures adjusted to the presence of an opposition?
8. Describe the clash between the egalitarian and the oligarchic principles in legislative procedure.

9. Diagram the passage of a bill according to formal legislative procedure in America. ;

10. Explain how informal legislative processes alter the formal legislative procedure.

11. Describe the various external influences that enter into the legislative process.

12. Using the materials on the Employment Act, describe first the formal legislative procedure in passing the bill, and second the informal process, emphasizing the important influences opposing or supporting the bill.

13. In what ways is British legislative procedure more direct and more responsible than the American?

14. What is the organization, operating procedure, and importance of the Supreme Soviet in legislation?

15. Describe the causes of the decline in power and prestige of modern legislatures.

16. Is Congress or the President more representative of the "national interest" at this moment, as you define the national interest? (350 words)

17. How do legislatures align with group interests against the executive?

18. What is meant by the "critical" function of the legislature?

19. What have been the proposals for improving the efficiency of legislatures?

20. Discuss in 350 words the problem of impelling legislatures to employ scientific methods.

Longer Study and Research Problems
Suitable for Term Papers

1. Read and write a report of ten pages on one of the following works, with special attention to the problem of the decline in legislative power:

James Burnham: *The Mangerial Revolution*
James M. Burns: *Congress on Trial*
Stephen Kemp Bailey: *Congress Makes a Law*
G. B. Galloway: *Congress at the Crossroads*
T. V. Smith: *The Legislative Way of Life*
H. J. Laski: *Parliamentary Government in England*

2. Write an essay of fifteen pages on the major types of city councils in America, their powers, and their relationship to the mayors (see Chapter Fourteen).

3. Write a summary history of twenty pages on the British House of Commons from 1265 to the present time. (Use a standard constitutional history of England together with recent articles to bring the paper up to date.)

4. Search your library for a file of hearings by a committee of any legislature on any subject that may interest you. Take as your guide: "What is the committee looking for and how is it trying to find it?" Describe the techniques used, evaluate the intelligence of the participants, and give your opinion of the validity of the committee findings.

11

EXECUTIVES AND CHIEFS OF STATE

MILLIONS of Americans will recall that their first formal lesson in American government taught them that the people elect the legislatures, *the legislatures make the laws, the executives carry out the law,* and the judges interpret the law. The reason why Americans learn this sequence is that for two centuries American politicians and theorists have aimed at separating the powers of the government into several branches. But we have already been prepared by our previous chapters for another fact, less simple, but far more realistic: legislative powers fade into the executive powers, and the executive powers fade into administrative powers. This fact, perhaps not immediately apparent if we concentrate only on American institutions, becomes evident as soon as we observe the principal executives of other countries. For there, often, the same persons both make and execute the laws. In this chapter we shall examine this dual policy-making and policy-execution role of high executives. Furthermore, if we want to understand fully the differences between high executives, of whom there may be a number in a community, and the highest executive, the chief of state, we must extend our study to the peculiar political and psychological position of the chiefs of state and search the cultural settings from which they emerge. Such are the tasks of this chapter.

Functions of the Executive

EXECUTIVES AND ADMINISTRATORS DISTINGUISHED

Let us first describe the functions of important executives in the government. According to one common interpretation, an executive or administrator is one who carries out policies he did not determine. Given the goals to pursue, he sets out after them, be they the erection of a bridge, the winning of a war, or the delivery of the mails. However, we prefer to follow a recent American usage and distinguish between the executive and the administrator: *The executive is one who participates in the determination of the most important policies of an organization of any type, and who also sets the general course for carrying out such policies.* The administrator, on the other hand, is charged with less responsibility for making policies that determine the major actions of his organization and is given more responsibility for everyday results.

This distinction, although it is not precise, does allow us to visualize public officers as graded according to degrees of discretion. It allows us to focus our attention on that small group of officers in any organization who are political and administrative at the same time, that is, the executives. In the next chapter when we study the administrative establishment as a whole, we will focus on the majority of administrative officers whose work is more regularized by procedures.

Executives may be elected, appointed by elected officials, or appointed under the conditions of a permanent civil service. It is not the manner of selection for office that distinguishes the executive but the kind of work he does. (The manner of selection, however, does affect the kind of work he does, as we shall see.) Thus the American national executives include the President, several hundred important appointees of the president to cabinet, commissions, and departments, and perhaps, say, the four hundred civil servants who in 1950 were credited by the President and the Civil Service Commission with having the most important positions warranting the most pay. Almost, but not quite, Congress qualifies as a group of executives, for its members are often concerned with the general course of administration.

UNIVERSAL TASKS OF AN EXECUTIVE

All executives perform broadly similar functions. The President of the United States, like the governors of the states or the Prime Minister of England, or the dictator of the Soviet Union, does many things in common with his subordinate executives and with all men who have headed large organizations. Luther Gulick has classified these common tasks of the executive, and his categories of important executive functions may be presented here:

What is the work of the chief executive? What does he do?
The answer is POSDCORB.
POSDCORB is, of course, a made-up word designed to call attention to the various functional elements of the work of a chief executive because

'administration' and 'management' have lost all specific content. POSD-CORB is made up of the initials of and stands for the following activities:

PLANNING, that is working out in broad outline the things that need to be done and the methods for doing them to accomplish the purpose set for the enterprise;

ORGANIZING, that is the establishment of the formal structure of authority through which work subdivisions are arranged, defined and co-ordinated for the defined objective;

STAFFING, that is the whole personnel function of bringing in and training the staff and maintaining favorable conditions of work;

DIRECTING, that is the continuous task of making decisions and embodying them in specific and general orders and instructions and serving as the leader of the enterprise;

CO-ORDINATING, that is the all-important duty of interrelating the various parts of the work;

REPORTING, that is keeping those to whom the executive is responsible informed as to what is going on, which thus includes keeping himself and his subordinates informed through records, research and inspections;

BUDGETING, with all that goes with budgeting in the form of fiscal planning, accounting and control.*

THE PLACE OF SUBJECT-MATTER KNOWLEDGE

Dr. Gulick asserted that this pattern of work covered "each of the major activities and duties of any chief executive." His classification, however, brought this rueful complaint from Dr. Lewis Meriam: "The most important thing that has been omitted from that fascinating word POSDCORB is knowledge of a subject matter. You have to plan something, you have to organize something, you have to direct something. . . . Intimate knowledge of the subject matter with which an administrative agency is primarily concerned is indispensable to the effective, intelligent administration of that agency."

Therefore, we may add to the formula of POSDCORB the requirement of skill in the particular work being done. To the principles of administration, a man must join the principles of whatever applied science underlies his special work. The chief of a highway department, for example, should be well qualified in both administrative science and engineering. To use another example: in selecting a postmaster, there may be a choice between two men who have like qualifications (including their training in POSDCORB) except for their work experience. If the work experience of one of the men is more related to the work of postmaster (for instance, he may already have done responsible

* Quoted, with permission, from Luther Gulick and L. Urwick, eds., *Papers on the Science of Administration* (New York: Institute of Public Administration, 1937), p. 13.

work in the post office or in traffic management), it would be advisable to select him.

Unfortunately, reality is never so simple. At the very least, we might find that the work experience of both men has been equally related to the position. At the most (and this is true of most high appointments) we might find that the number of men in question is a dozen rather than two, the men have little in common to compare, the qualifications for the job are not precise, no applicant has had experience related to the job, and many motives other than the efficient performance of this particular job affect the final choice among the candidates.

We may be more specific on some of these points that so well reflect the character of political work. For every major appointment that a president, premier, governor, mayor, or agency head must make, a number of candidates appear with all sorts of credentials. If one of them happened to have had lengthy experience leading directly to the position at issue, the others are quick to indicate that he is probably narrow-minded about the role of that agency in the whole governmental picture. Routine experience ill befits the top executives, they would argue. And the science of vocational placement cannot answer their arguments in many cases, for, while it is possible to give the appropriate weight to technical experience in lower and middle managerial work, it is most difficult to do so in the top levels of management.

THE DEMANDS OF POLITICS AGAINST ADMINISTRATIVE SKILL

Furthermore, political power, as has been previously explained, is most often the result of a precarious balancing of numerous and opposing cliques. The appointment of chiefs to departments, bureaus, and other positions resembles the process by which some primitive tribes select their war leaders—the heads of families and clans are consulted beforehand. Often the most important consideration is not technical efficiency, but rather the cementing of a clique or faction to the ruling confederation. It would be ludicrous to attempt to explain the odd assortment of persons that became chiefs of departments under Abraham Lincoln, Franklin D. Roosevelt, or other Presidents by reference solely to the occupational fitness of the appointees according to the Gulick-plus-Meriam formula.

His secretaries said of Lincoln that his first cabinet appointments sought to "combine the experience of Seward, the integrity of Chase, the popularity of Cameron; to hold the West with Bates, attract New England with Wells, please the Whigs through Smith and convince the Democrats through Blair." From such examples, it may be surmised that, if the sole determinants in selecting executives are to be a man's ability to fill Gulick's and Meriam's specifications, the whole political system of any country must undergo the most profound modifications. If a standard of specialized competence were used to measure the personnel at the head of the administrative establishment of any country, no government that could be called efficient would exist.

We conclude that "subject-matter knowledge" among top executives is whatever unique qualities are demanded of the occupant of a given position at a given time and is not defined according to any set professional specialization. We further conclude that high political executives may fit their positions well without being highly qualified in the functions of POSDCORB. We refer back finally to our theory of leadership, where the work group as a whole provides a sum total of leadership and where the individual leader himself may have few fixed qualities. Judging the fitness of the leader should involve judging how the leader fits his group, not whether he attains a certain score on a given number of qualities.

U.S.S.R. HIERARCHY FAVORS POLITICS OVER SPECIALIZED SKILL

The general political problems or crises that disturb the top of the government also affect the executives farther down. The Soviet government might be expected to emphasize subject-matter specialization, at least for the second-level executives, since everyone is supposed to agree on politics. Yet Russia is no exception—the rule applies to socialist and capitalist countries alike. The second-level Soviet officials must be faithful and proven Communist Party members before all else. Dr. Louis Nemzer quotes a Party directive demanding that the party personnel officers (who control the high government executives) place "in the leading governmental, economic, co-operative and every other kind of post, those persons who understand the meaning and significance of Party directives, who in Comrade Stalin's words 'are able honorably and conscientiously to execute these directives.' " The "apolitical careless approach" in selecting men for promotion is attacked; the question to be asked is whether "in the first place, by political standards, they deserve responsibility, and in the second place, by working standards, they are suitable for this kind of concrete work." Thus, in 1947, M. A. Suslov, for twenty years a Party official, but without any training in a field related to culture or communications, was appointed Director of the Department for Propaganda and Agitation. The strict control over subordinates by the chief executive (Stalin) seems to prevent the placement of subject-matter experts in top posts.

DISCIPLINE AMONG TOP EXECUTIVES

In fact, we might say that subject-matter specialists get closer to the top of the executive hierarchy the less stable the chief executive and his top executive team are. Under the pre-Hitlerian German Republic, high-ranking government officials below the cabinet level had been primarily subject-matter specialists and did not play a very active role in politics; under Hitler, they became Nazis or were removed. The British Prime Minister has a much more tenacious grip over his policy-making executives, appointive and elective alike, than does the French Premier. But neither the British nor the French executive is as stable at the top as the Nazi and Soviet executive chiefs. Furthermore, neither the British nor the French high bureaucracy is as partisan or active as the totalitarian high officialdom; they are often specialists promoted through the ranks of their agencies.

In the United States, both the politically appointed (for example, a cabinet member) and the permanent executives (such as many bureau chiefs) are often inclined towards pursuing their own beliefs about government policy. Henry Morgenthau once remarked that the President was "as much a prisoner of his administration as he is master." Against the President's paramount role in foreign policy and in spite of having been appointed by the President, Secretary of the Navy Matthews in 1950 advocated the waging of a preventive war against Russia under certain conditions—a proposal basically in conflict with the administration's foreign policy at the time. Almost at the same time, General MacArthur was barely checked from voicing publicly a policy on Formosa differing from that of the President. Only months later, after several new incidents occurred, did the President, with the support of high-ranking appointed and career officials, Acheson, Marshall, Bradley, and Collins, relieve MacArthur of his commands.

Hostility among cabinet members has been common in American presidential administrations. Washington's first term of office saw the epic feud of Hamilton and Jefferson. Truman's administration was marked by another struggle of two secretaries, Johnson and Acheson. Internal bickerings are typical of all American jurisdictions from the township to the federal government. Cities and counties directed by political bosses provide exceptions, but who will say that they are salutary ones?

A brief comparison of four countries named above, then, shows the following general facts. In Russia, the chief executive is almost absolute, and the executives are primarily political, secondarily subject-matter specialists. In England, the Prime Minister is very strong, and the executives are partly political and partly expert, with the influence of the political executives the stronger one. The American chief executive is less strong but otherwise resembles the British Prime Minister. In France, the Premier is weak, lacking control over his subexecutives to a marked extent, and the subexecutives are partly political and partly permanent, with the latter being more influential. One hesitates to make these statements, but our repertoire of concepts and comparative studies in political science grants us no more succinct and accurate statements, short of full-length case studies of each executive organization in turn.

Nor can one generalize about the consequences of each condition stated above. Under certain specified circumstances, too many and too complicated for treatment here, each works efficiently or inefficiently to produce certain desired consequences. But it is presently impossible to separate the structural features of the executive arrangement (mode of selection, tenure of office, and so on) from the personality of the incumbents, or from all the other social, technical, economic, and incidental factors that bring success to one national executive policy at one time and failure at another, or success to one government and the collapse of another government. Thus, commenting on the failure of both British and French policy to stop Hitler before 1939, Winston Churchill wrote: "The French Government, which was in ceaseless flux in the fascinating game of party politics, and the British Government, which aimed at the same vices by the opposite process of general agreement to keep things quiet, were equally incapable of any drastic or clear-cut action."

The Presidency: A Case Study

REPRESENTATIVE, LEADER, AND ADMINISTRATOR

The intermingling of political and administrative tasks that characterizes the work of all high executives is particularly manifested in the case of a chief of state, who may be a president, a premier, or a strong king. Perhaps the clearest way to bring out initially the unique character of each office of chief of state is by examining intensively a single case. The American Presidency can be chosen. It has been the object of debate and dispassionate study for over a century and a half and therefore provides American political science its most complete case study of the chief executive. A brief discussion of the Presidency here will introduce its main features and illuminate the controversies surrounding it. We may see the President's role as having a triple task: expressive representation of the national community; political and legislative leadership; and administrative responsibility.

It should be understood clearly, throughout the discussion of the

American Presidency and in the discussion of any high executive office, that the executive includes a man, an office, and a corps of assistants. The budget for the White House in 1951 provided for 293 office employees, apart from 71 housekeeping personnel and numerous personnel borrowed from other agencies. A large part of all the actions performed by the President are in reality prepared for him by his advisors; we speak of the President's budget, for example, meaning by this the product of scores of men who spend all their time preparing this massive and all-embracing fiscal document that will be presented to Congress as the President's responsibility. By forgetting sometimes that the Presidency includes hundreds of men, many of whom are of high rank and independent ideas, some people are likely to look upon the President as a completely free agent with fantastic powers of intervention in thousands of matters.

THE PRESIDENT EXPRESSES NATIONAL SENTIMENTS

The authors of the American Constitution were aware that, no matter what the single national executive's powers might be, he would stand for the nation as a whole and attract more attention than any other politician in the land. They were substantially correct. Even Presidents like Jefferson and Jackson, who championed state and sectional interests, found that their very attacks against nationalists strengthened their own office of President and made it a symbol of popular protest. The symbol itself was "nationalist" and contributed to the growth of presidential influence.

The dullest President becomes a universal spectacle and commands the attention of the press, radio, television, and newsreels without effort. The health of the President is the subject of gossip and magazine articles. His private life and family are matters of public concern and controversy. The Vice President, whose very name is unknown to many Americans, becomes overnight a national figure upon the death of the President. Even the greatest Congressman has a shorter mourner's bench than the weakest President. Schoolboys learn American history by relating events to the administrations of the presidents, even though Congress might have been much stronger at certain times and although the Speaker of the House of Representatives might have been the more powerful officer for decades. They are told that they may grow up to be President, not a member of Congress or the Speaker of the House.

The President, therefore, like the commanding general of an army, the head of a church, or the president of a corporation, has a tremendous latent power. His smallest deed may be magnified in importance. Every slight legal authority granted him under the original Constitution has grown to vast proportions. Each slight increment of power newly granted him is likely to shoot up like Iowa corn in July.

THE PRESIDENT AS POLICY LEADER

Although a presidential candidate is often relatively unknown before becoming a candidate, once nominated he becomes the party leader and director of party strategy. As the leader of a party organization, even though it is rather undisciplined, he can publicize his ideas of government and influence party leaders.

Once elected, he acquires even more power within his party. He approves official statements of party policy and appoints (with the consent of the Senate) a large number of important officials. He commands a host of offices and favors; he can reward his friends and punish his political enemies by abetting or restraining their political and personal ambitions.

He lacks complete control over legislation and offices, however, because of the strength and independence of the Congress and courts. Unlike the British Prime Minister, he cannot force the legislators to stand for a new election if a majority of them reject one of his important policies.

The legislative powers of the President, although they derive much of their strength from the psychological and party position of the Chief Executive, emanate mostly from original grants under the Constitution. These powers have grown with the political successes of certain presidents, with the help of interpretations of the Constitution by the courts, and with unforeseen changes in social conditions that required greater activity on the part of the executive branch of the government.

RECOMMENDING LEGISLATION

The Constitution gives the President the power to recommend to Congress "such measures as he shall judge necessary and expedient." It is now definitely recognized that the power to recommend measures to the Congress includes the power to recommend drafted bills and to request insistently that they be enacted into law with little change. Woodrow Wilson was astute in developing this specific, rather than general, approach to the power of recommendation. Franklin D. Roosevelt employed the same technique, and Harry S. Truman followed suit.

Thus we find, in Truman's State of the Union Message for 1950, a series of points on which he desired action. Their number and variety gives some indication of how the interests of the President as chief legislator have expanded. He asked Congress to:

Maintain strong national defenses

Continue selective service

Continue the Marshall Plan for aid to Europe

Close loopholes in the Clayton Act against monopolies

Assist small business

Encourage the development of new enterprises

Repeal the Taft-Hartley Act on labor-management relations

Create an extension service for labor education and services

Provide public housing for middle-income families

Continue rent controls for another year

Provide mandatory price supports for farm commodities previously uncovered

Increase development of natural resources

Increase public power development

Authorize the St. Lawrence Seaway project

Create a Columbia Valley Authority

Establish a National Science Foundation

Develop atomic power

Enact a civil rights program against discrimination

Liberalize displaced persons law

Continue the international effort against communism

Increase old-age insurance benefits

Strengthen the unemployment compensation laws

Broaden the coverage of social security laws

Provide a system of medical insurance

Remedy the shortage of doctors, nurses, and health services

Provide federal aid to education throughout the country

Revise the tax structure.

Here were twenty-seven major recommendations on which the President asked action. As was to be expected, however, action was impossible on that many points, and he had to be content with approval of a half dozen or so of the policies. This did not prevent him, of course, from praising the record of the Congress concerned. It happened to be a Congress dominated by Democrats, and that was one reason for his post-session kindness. Harry Truman was also an optimistic man and that trait helped him view the record generously. But again, the formal message is propaganda as well as serious program, and it should be viewed in that light.

VETO POWER

A second specific power granted the President is the veto power. The President may refuse to sign a bill, sending it back to Congress with a notice of disapproval. Then two-thirds of each house is required to override the veto. Or the President may give a bill a "pocket veto" by not acting on it if it comes to his desk during the last ten days of a Congressional session. The veto has changed from a mere constitutional check in the system of checks and balances to a positive agency of legislation. Probably the veto was not regarded generally as a legislative power in the beginning. The Constitution states that legislative power shall be vested in the Congress, and, as Jefferson stated, the negative of the President is the shield provided by the Constitution for the President to protect himself against invasion by the legislature. Furthermore, Washington declared, "From motives of respect to the legislature, I give my signature to many bills with which my judgment is at variance."

Jackson was the first President to advance the theory that the President, as a representative of the whole people, could intervene positively in the legislative process through the veto to further his ideas of good and bad legislation. Even though the veto had been used only ten times before, he inflicted twelve resounding vetoes on Congress and aroused a furious controversy. The Jacksonian usage continued, however. Cleveland was responsible for 584 vetoes, Theodore Roosevelt 82, Woodrow Wilson 44, Calvin Coolidge 50, and Franklin Roosevelt 631.

Thus the veto is now commonly used in a positive way. Presidents use it to express their opinion that a bill is unconstitutional and to protect the executive branch from the legislature's "encroachment." In addition, it is used to oppose Congressional action that is against Presidential policy. Bills disagreeable to the President are often vetoed. The veto is threatened sometimes and then employed when Congress refuses to add "proper" amendments to a bill or to pass it in the form approved by the President. The veto usually ends a bill's chance of success. Two-thirds of both houses are necessary to override a veto, and, of the 1835 regular and pocket vetoes that occurred from 1789 to 1946, only 59 have been passed over by Congress.

FOREIGN RELATIONS

A third sphere of legislative power available to the President arises out of his role in foreign relations. The Constitution specifically gives the President power, "by and with the advice and consent of the Senate, to make treaties." This ostensibly legislative power was recognized as a break in the principle of the separation of powers, but it was justified because of the delicate and dangerous nature of foreign negotiations. Congress, with its many members, was thought to be too publicly exposed, to subject to local interests, and too little respected by foreign governments to be qualified for the task of treaty-making.

Even so, the Senate was to participate to some extent, and Washington tried to use the Senate as a sort of council on foreign affairs. He found that the practice inconvenienced him, and succeeding presidents took the initiative in foreign affairs, approaching the Senate only when there was a document to be ratified. In many cases, the debate over ratification gave vent to much heated advice that had been repressed.

However, beginning with Franklin D. Roosevelt, Presidents have tended to consult the Senate or its leaders in advance about final negotiations on a treaty. The sad experience of Woodrow Wilson with certain recalcitrant Senators on the issue of the League of Nations had shown the advisability of this procedure. By calling in leading Senators, a President may foresee the fate of a proposed treaty or of a foreign policy before he has committed his country to a bargain with another nation. Since two-thirds of the Senate must approve a treaty and since the President's political party often lacks such a large majority, the new form of consultation has been associated with the development of the idea of a bipartisan foreign policy. Scarcely any treaty can be ratified unless a considerable number of Senators from both parties agree to it.

With the expanded role of the President in foreign affairs has come an increasing use of the executive agreement. The executive agreement is an arrangement between the President and a foreign state. If it does not conflict with other laws, it becomes the law of the land, enforceable in the courts, even though the Senate has not debated or approved it. It sometimes substitutes for a treaty when the ratification process would be fraught with difficulties or when some temporary arrangement with another country is desired. This is one of the wide "resulting" powers that the President has by virtue of his prominent role in foreign affairs. Neither the Constitution nor Congress may grant it explicitly, but it is upheld in practice by the belief of the courts that the President needs it to accomplish his broad mission in foreign affairs. And, in general, the courts construe the President's powers in foreign affairs liberally. Declared the Supreme Court in the case of *United States v. Curtiss-Wright Export Corporation*, the President's power in international relations is "very delicate, plenary, and exclusive—a power which does not require as a basis for its exercise an act of Congress."

Associated with his power in foreign affairs are the President's war powers. The President is Commander-in-Chief of the armed forces. He has the final responsibility for grand strategy. He disposes of all the military forces of the nation. The entire power of government in any occupied territory is legally subject to his command, though Congress may affect his control by refusing appropriations and in other ways. Furthermore, although Congress has the power to declare war, the President has the greater power to make war. Lincoln, Polk, McKinley, Cleveland, Theodore Roosevelt, Franklin D. Roosevelt, and Harry S. Truman all committed acts as Presidents that required Congress to declare or otherwise to approve a war. In emergencies occurring in foreign relations, the President is never stronger, Congress never weaker.

EXECUTION OF THE LAWS

The President's role in foreign affairs may be distinguished from his domestic role. Congress is stronger in domestic affairs than in foreign affairs, although a Congress may from time to time modify the President's foreign program or even guide it. In both foreign and domestic affairs, the President has a general authority over what is usually thought of as the execution of the laws.

This general authority, however, is not easily definable in constitutional law or practice. For example, Congress determines within limits how the administrative establishment shall be organized, what functions shall be undertaken by the executive agencies, how much money shall be spent by each agency, and how funds are to be raised and disbursed. The legislative branch of the government, one can see, is the source of a great deal of administrative activity and may rule by indirection, so to speak.

However, when Congress attempts to tighten its hold on the administrative establishment, it can go only a limited distance in cutting down the President's request for money or the number of bureaus, in restricting the kind of personnel the President may hire, and in making agencies independent of the President. In part, Congress is restrained by the Constitution from interfering with the execution of the laws. It is restrained also by the hold that the President has over almost all individual executives and administrators. And, since the President has great political power, he seldom lacks friends in Congress to restrain that body from applying its fullest power against him. The President must, if he is to act at all freely, prevent Congress from uniting against him.

The American system of separation of powers, to the dismay of those who would have a neat allocation of powers, operates as a continual, shifting process in which no man or agency can hope for absolute victory or a completely reliable basis of support. Each day brings a new alignment, new bargains to be made, the need for fresh support from somewhere—in short, a search for temporary relief and alliances. We conclude, therefore, that the President as an executive acts with one eye cocked on Congressional reaction.

EXECUTIVE DISCRETION

Despite the limitations that the Congress may seek to place upon his authority, the President's control over the executive establishment is impressive in scope and depth. He has much discretion in administering existing statutes. When especially concerned that a particular statute be enforced with rigor, the President, employing his numerous assistants and staff, will "ride herd" on the agency entrusted with the administration of the statute.

In other cases, the President may act to change the policies of the administrative establishment under powers granted him by the Constitution, rather than by Congress. Thus, President Truman pressed for a quickening of the pace at which the segregation of whites and Negroes was being abandoned by the armed forces; this he could do under his powers as Commander-in-Chief of the armed forces.

The Congress has continually added to the Presidential discretion by statutes that delegate important powers to the President. Especially in legislation on economic matters, the public affairs to be regulated are often of a kind that prevents precise wording and timing. The President is authorized to perform such actions as to put controls into effect or withdraw them from effect, to include certain businesses or foreign countries within the scope of an act or to exclude them, or otherwise to act with considerable freedom over an extensive area and period of time.

EXECUTIVE COMMANDS

Ordinarily, the President exercises his political and administrative influence as any important executive would. He issues verbal orders over the phone and in conference with his subordinates. He dictates memos and signs statements of policy or letters of command. Less frequent than the foregoing means of transmitting his will is the executive order. The executive order is a more formal type of command. Usually, the conditions under which an executive order must be issued are stated by the Congress in statutes. The number of executive orders has increased sharply over the past fifty years. Cleveland and McKinley issued about one a month, Hoover about twenty-one a month, and Franklin D. Roosevelt about twenty-four.

APPOINTMENT AND REMOVAL POWER

The President maintains control over the administrative establishment partly by virtue of his power of appointment and removal.

Legislation has been passed forbidding the appointment and removal of most federal employees for political reasons. By law federal employees are appointed by examination and removed for reasons of inefficiency and immorality. Lacking the right to disturb the civil service for political reasons, the executive has little reason to introduce wholesale appointments and removals for any other reasons. Most administrators hold secure appointments, and the intermittent struggle between the President and Congress over appointment and removal centers about the higher executives who are not under civil service. Here Congress has had only limited success in preventing the President's free use of the removal power, although the Constitution gave the Senate some say over appointments. These higher executives whom the President appoints, including especially his cabinet members, extend his range of influence over the government enormously. By the single act of appointing a loyal and sympathetic cabinet member, the President can extend his policies and desires to many important events that he could never become involved with in person.

THE EXECUTIVE BUDGET

Among the developments that increased the powers of the American Presidency in the last fifty years has been the Executive Budget. This type of budget is enacted by the Congress. But, under its terms, the President, rather than the legislature, prepares a single, annual statement of the proposed expenditures of the government and of the sources of revenue to meet the costs of government (see Figure 29). He submits it to the legislature, which consigns it to committee for discussion and proposals of changes. The committees and subcommittees make important suggestions. Congress then debates and changes the contents of the budget. The legislature finally passes the budget as a series of bills and sends them to the President for his signature.

The executive branches of many states and localities follow generally the form of the American executive branch, but some follow budgetary methods more typical of the past, when the legislatures, city councils, and county boards prepared budgets as they pleased, regardless of executive desires. In England, by contrast with America, the budget is almost entirely controlled by the cabinet and Treasury, that is, by the executive. Rarely will an estimate be changed by individual members or blocs of members; the price of any significant change may well be that the Prime Minister will ask for the dissolution of Parliament and the holding of new elections. The Commons' role is thus only that of a critic.

The American Congress is much more powerful on fiscal matters

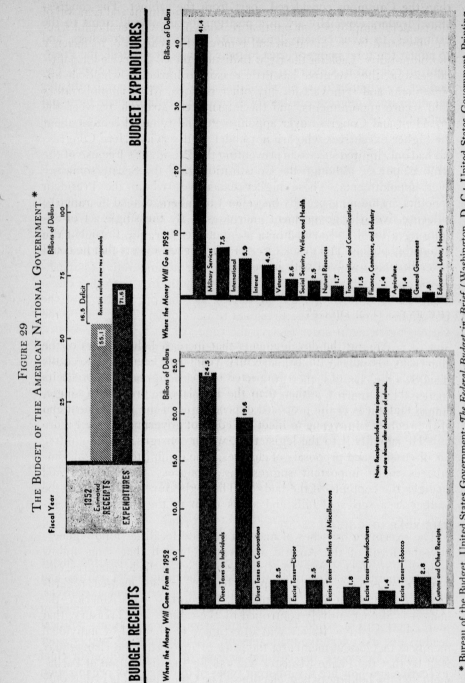

FIGURE 29

THE BUDGET OF THE AMERICAN NATIONAL GOVERNMENT *

* Bureau of the Budget, United States Government: *The Federal Budget in Brief* (Washington, D. C.: United States Government Printing Office, 1950), pp. *5, 7, 9.*

than the Commons considered apart from the cabinet. The congressional leaders especially are in a position to cut or add items to the estimates, to favor certain departments or bureaus over others, and to adjust the total budget closer to their own policies. Still, the President, in relation to Congress, is much stronger than he once was. The budget is a gigantic mass of calculations and figures. His subordinates set them up. Congress can hardly destroy the bulk of their form and content.

NEW FORMS OF DISCRETION

A new kind of important instrument—derived from the executive order idea and just now coming into some prominence—is the executive order founded on a legislative declaration and subject to a legislative veto. The new kind of executive order and legislative veto power has been employed in reorganizing the administrative establishment, and has also been used partially or wholly in a few other cases. Congress sets forth general principles for the organization of the government and allows the President to issue orders reorganizing the various agencies in order to save the time and energies of Congress, and to prevent all administrative reorganization from foundering on the rocks of political obstinacy. Then unless Congress specifically disallows the changes, they go into effect. Although used primarily to increase the internal efficiency of the government, the same scheme might be used in the future to deal with many governmental activities that regulate industry or provide services.

Top Executive Structures

THE ROLE OF CHIEF EXECUTIVES IN A CULTURE

The first section of this chapter has described the major typical functions of executives, illustrating the mingling of political and administrative purposes in the operations of government executives. The second section showed how the American President, as a chief of state, performs a triple task of expressive representation, political leadership, and executive management. We may now ask two broader questions: What are the cultural origins of the institution of chief executive and how are the different types of top executive organization shaped by the political conditions of a society?

SIGNIFICANCE OF SINGLE EXECUTIVES

Chief executives of large organizations are almost always single, rather than a group of men. The fact is so commonly known that its massive significance is often ignored. Not only armies and business enterprises, but almost all the governments of history, have been headed by individual men. Forms of government that were called or could be classified as oligarchies or democracies have been exceptional in number and duration, and a great many, even of these, possessed chief executives. Thus the Roman Republic, though sometimes an oligarchy and sometimes a democracy, had consuls and dictators as symbols of central authority much of the time.

One must conclude that two principal reasons lie behind the constant figure of the chief of state in history. The office of a chief executive has great psychological appeal; he is a symbol of national unity. In addition, a single-headed organization tends to increase the possibility of controlling the organization from the top and so tends to increase the efficiency of the organization in implementing the policies of the ultimate leaders or the chief himself.

The psychological position of a chief executive is stronger than that of a council of executives, under most conditions, because a single chief seems to represent more adequately the sought-for unity and the total group interest among members of an organization. The chief provides, more than a council could, the impression of strength and single-mindedness that many people in an organization desire. He furnishes the mass of members in an organization with a target for blame and affection—arousing in some of them a feeling of relationship like that between the father and children in a family. Some people feel more secure, more at home in the larger world of their occupation, church, or government, when they can perceive a single object of responsibility for political affairs that is reminiscent of their dependent relationship in their childhood family group.

Probably more important than the psychological strength of the single chief executive is the controlling strength that the use of a single executive fosters. The chain of control, command, and responsibility is sharper and more understandable between a single chief executive and single subordinate executives at the head of each suborganization than it is among councils of executives from top to bottom. Therefore, whenever in the history of an organization stronger controls over, and greater productive pressures on, the whole group are desired, the single executive is given greater powers or single executives are substituted in various ways for executive councils, commissions, or boards.

ADMINISTRATION HAS DEVELOPED FROM PERSONAL RULE

It is noteworthy that the apparatus of public administration has developed from the person of kings, rather than from legislatures or assemblies. In a remarkable study, *Kings and Councillors*, Professor A. M. Hocart has pointed out that primitive kings had councillors and servants who performed personal services for them. When the functions of a kingdom were expanded by war, the increased wealth of the community, or peaceable growth, the king's servitors added new jobs to their previous, traditional ones. While continuing to groom the king's horse, manage his household, transport and guard his wardrobe, and attend him at meals, they also began to collect regular taxes, maintain roads, supply armies, and perform other broad administrative functions that would be recognizable as such today.

Thus administration in early kingships grew out of the tasks of personal servants of the king. T. F. Tout, in a scholarly, matter-of-fact study, *Chapters in the Administrative History of Medieval England*, relates the story of the gradual development of the "King's Wardrobe" from a valued privilege of serving the king's person, to the provisioner of armies and custodian of royal domains. In England, says Hocart, the origin of the great administrative establishments of today may be perceived on certain ceremonial occasions in archaic names, quaint customs, and unusual duties incumbent upon certain ancient offices. British administration is still performed in the name of the Crown, although it is controlled by the *active* executive, the Prime Minister, rather than the *expressive* or titular executive, the king.

EFFECTS OF THE REVOLUTIONARY PERIOD

But one may ask: Were not all these magical factors and historical anachronisms swept away by the great revolutions of the last two centuries? The answer is that the historical continuity of administrative development was broken, but not the principle of the single-headed executive. Revolutions—American, French, Russian, Nazi—did not destroy the inherent strength of the principle of the single-headed executive in providing psychological unity and ease of control over the administrative establishment. The revolutions in question, with the exception of the Nazi, did *attempt* to destroy the single executive. But after the "directorate" periods, lasting a few years in each case, the position of the chief executive was reinforced. If we could reduce such events to a graph, they would perhaps appear as in Figure 30. The psychological forces that support the executive in American state and national governments, for example, have persisted and increased, overcoming the revolutionary antipathies. Napoleon Bonaparte replaced the French Directorate, and Joseph-Barthélemy has written that "the outlines of French administration are still those of Napoleon. The Emperor fashioned his institution in

FIGURE 30

RELATIONS BETWEEN THE POWER OF LEGISLATURES AND EXECUTIVES IN RECENT WESTERN HISTORY (HIGHLY SIMPLIFIED)

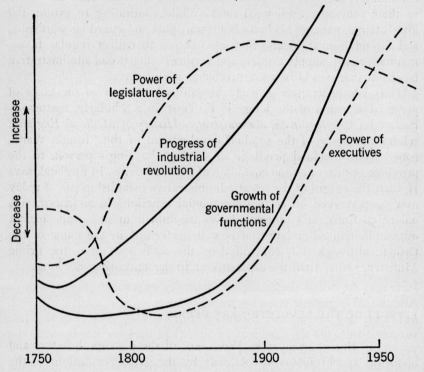

such a way that his sovereign will should be felt without delay or hindrance at every point of France, and in 1875 this edifice was crowned by parliamentary democracy." Lenin became the master of the top executive councils of the Communist Party and the Soviet Government; the executive organs remained plural-headed in form rather than in fact.

The particular organization of the executive changed from monarchy to dictatorship or republic. The new revolutionary institutions simply lost a large part of their direct and obvious connections with the past institutions. They seemed to be of a different "qualitative" order, as the modern "thinking machines" seem to be of a different order than the ancient abacus counters. A word on the Fascist and Nazi revolutions, that constituted exceptions to the temporary "directorate" period noted above, may be in order. Both these revolutions were regarded as "conservative" revolutions, not as "liberal" or "radical" revolutions. They promised greater order, greater stability, greater leadership—in short, executive supremacy—from the very start.

AMERICAN TRIALS OF EXECUTIVE ARRANGEMENTS

Several major types of organization of the chief executive of a government have been devised. The most significant of them have been employed in America, as that country has sought to "democratize" the executive. We may discuss briefly American experience with various executive structures and illustrate them by diagrams. The first diagram (Figure 31a) represents the type of executive most disliked by American and French revolutionaries. It is the *autocracy*. Commands emanate from the top of the pyramid and move downwards. As the unelected, uninfluenced executive moves, so moves the whole organization. The more complex and numerous the tasks of such a government, the larger the pyramid might be drawn (Figure 31b, *the unlimited autocracy*.)

A second variety of executive arrangement experienced by the American colonists was the constituency-controlled executive (Figure 31c). The governor was elected instead of being appointed by the Crown. Still another arrangement known to the colonists was one in which the elected legislature supervised and controlled the executive (this may be called the *legislature-controlled* executive [Figure 31d]). And the arrangement was also known whereby the executive was both *legislature and constituency controlled* (Figure 31e). But even this last variant displeased the colonists, so bitter had they become towards the very idea of a single executive.

All the new state constitutions drastically reduced the powers of the chief executive. (There had been many proposals to abolish the governorship entirely.) In several cases, the states strengthened the control of the legislature by allowing it (for the first time) to elect the governor. The United States during the Revolution and under the Articles of Confederation had no central executive figure. Committees of Congress were charged with overseeing the work of particular departments and acted as the executive chiefs. There occurred a kind of *legislature-controlled* pluralism in which the departments of the government operated independently under their executive committees. This type of executive arrangement is diagrammed in Figure 31f. Here the total executive authority is broken down and its fragments are entrusted to multiple executive direction in order to avoid the dangers of concen-

FIGURE 31
TYPES OF EXECUTIVE STRUCTURE

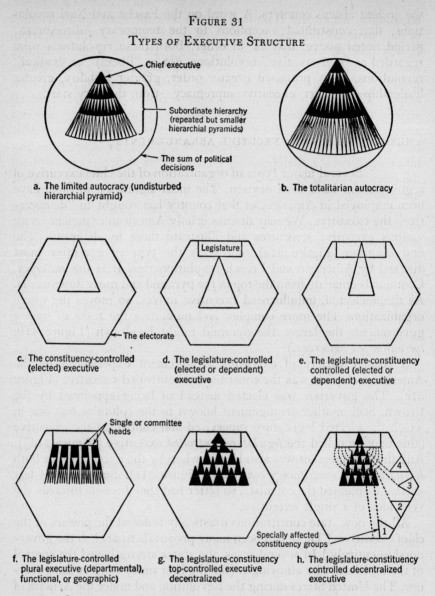

a. The limited autocracy (undisturbed hierarchial pyramid)

Chief executive

Subordinate hierarchy (repeated but smaller hierarchial pyramids)

The sum of political decisions

b. The totalitarian autocracy

Legislature

The electorate

c. The constituency-controlled (elected) executive

d. The legislature-controlled (elected or dependent) executive

e. The legislature-constituency controlled (elected or dependent) executive

Single or committee heads

Specially affected constituency groups

f. The legislature-controlled plural executive (departmental), functional, or geographic)

g. The legislature-constituency top-controlled executive decentralized

h. The legislature-constituency controlled decentralized executive

trated authority over the government as a whole and over the individual departments.

A few years later, in 1787, the Constitutional Convention met in Philadelphia and a great deal of discontent was expressed with the confederation type of executive management. Several members complained about its inefficiency. Others wanted more stability and direction. Gouverneur Morris thought that a President might represent better the whole nation than would any combination of local legislators. Alexander Hamilton emphasized the need for a custodian of the "national interest," and for greater efficiency in administration. It was pointed out that for foreign negotiations a single executive was an excellent symbol of the nation, far better than a little-known group of local legislators. But since nearly everyone feared or at least respected the tradition of fear of an "irresponsible" executive, a special election was provided for the President. Consequently, America acquired the legislature-constituency controlled executive. The constituency was at first the electoral college, but quickly developed in effect into a constituency of all qualified electors. This arrangement (without the electoral college, see Figure 31e) spread quickly among the state governments.

As the government acquired new functions and as the executive establishment expanded, controversy arose over the staffing of the subexecutive. Some, like Andrew Jackson, thought that the principle of constituency control of the executive was being evaded because the subexecutives, that is, the administrators, were becoming permanent officials. The Jacksonians proposed a periodic turnover of almost all officers. Others thought it was less important to have the constituents control the less responsible officials than to insure the efficiency of such officials. They demanded a permanent bureaucracy based on merit, and wanted presidential influence to be stronger than legislative influence in the operation of the bureaucracy.

In defense of their position, the advocates of civil service reform who opposed Jacksonianism sometimes claimed that the dangers of autocracy might be better prevented by decentralizing the executive branch in the manner of Figure 31g. The chief executive, they said, might choose to arrange his subordinate offices so as to allow plenty of initiative to them. Thus the departments and bureaus might be freed of stringent executive autocracy. However, the problem of controlling these decentralized fragments was left unsettled.

THE LEGISLATURE- AND CONSTITUENCY-INFLUENCED DECENTRALIZED EXECUTIVE

To this day, none of these theories have satisfied the advocates of a unified general executive establishment under definite legislative and public control. Another theory exists, however, that, although it is not defended strongly in the literature, conceivably might be an answer to the question: What is the structure of democratic administration? This theory is presented in the formula (Figure 31h) that the executive establishment is to be decentralized; that it shall be controlled in part by the legislature with reference both to its chief and to its important decentralized fragments; and that it shall be controlled with reference to its chief by the general public and to its major fragments by the general and special publics concerned with or affected by them.

This last situation, as can be seen by an examination of the diagram, is a complex one. It requires a science of politics with great foresight and controls, a science that has never before been available. There exists a strong possibility that the techniques for making such an arrangement work to the general satisfaction of most political groups are not now available. But political theory can go so far as to say that this arrangement is a feasible way of conducting the public business; it is not a utopian scheme, its implementation would not be impossible.

In fact, studies by John Gaus, Herbert Simon, Charles Hardin, and E. Pendleton Herring show that the theory behind Figure 31h matches better than the theory behind Figure 31e the actual condition of administration in some American federal and many state agencies, although the law still holds to the latter theory. Our discussion of the participation of special interest groups in politics and administration, contained in the last section of Chapter Seven, has also shown how the persons and groups regulated by legislation and administration often help set the rules by which they are governed. The next chapter, on administration, presents further data on such consultation as we explore the total internal environment of large-scale organizations.

Questions and Problems

1. Distinguish between executives and administrators.

2. Why is it risky to make too sharp a distinction between politics and administration?

3. List and define the general functions of the executive according to Dr. Gulick.

4. Explain as precisely as possible to what extent the President or other top executives can demand subject-matter knowledge and POSDCORB abilities in filling top appointive offices.

5. Interview one executive, preferably one controlling an establishment or suboffice of at least fifty persons. He may be in the university, in business anywhere, or in government. Ask him to verify or correct the theory that POSDCORB activities occupy a great part of his working time and that proficiency in these activities is required to him to do his work well.

6. Go through the columns of a daily newspaper for one week, picking out references to any action of executives of all kinds. Analyze them according to POSDCORB and report the results in 250 words.

7. In what ways does a legislature often do executive work?

8. Describe the wide variations in kinds of executive leadership that exist among different nations.

9. Explain the expressive role of the American Presidency in your own words.

10. List the various ways in which the President takes a directing hand in the formation of public policy.

11. Explain the different ways in which the veto power is used.

12. How does the President control his subordinate executives and the administrative establishment and how does he fail to control them? (350 words)

13. Discuss the basic sources of strength in the principle of the single-headed executive.

14. What has been the attitude of different revolutionary movements towards the single executive?

15. List and describe briefly the major forms of executive structures.

16. Examine your town or city charter and your county charter and diagram the type of executive structure in each case, following the diagrams used in this chapter.

17. Diagram the executive structure of your state government.

18. Taking any organized group to which you may now belong or have once belonged, depict its executive structure. State whether it worked well and explain why. State whether you would prefer another type and why.

Longer Study and Research
Problems Suitable for Term Papers

1. Read and write a review of ten pages on one of the following books:

Wilfred E. Binkley: *President and Congress*

Commission on Organization of the Executive Branch of the Government: *The Office of the President*

H. J. Laski: *The American Presidency*

Leslie Lipson: *The American Governor: From Figurehead to Leader*

L. D. White: *The Federalists*

Marshall E. Dimock: *The Executive in Action*

Chester I. Bernard: *Functions of the Executive*

2. Interview two executives, preferably controlling establishments or suboffices of at least fifty persons. They may be in the university, in business anywhere, or in government. Ask them to verify or correct the theory that POSDCORB activities occupy a great part of their working time and that proficiency in these activities is required of them to do their work well. Secondly, as tactfully as possible, ask them or attempt to gain elsewhere information on the proportion of their time they devote to each major function. (Sometimes their secretaries can provide the material needed for this second part of the study.)

3. Using library materials and interviews, describe and analyze in ten pages the office and powers of the chief executive(s) in your town or city, county, or state.

4. With the help of Amos J. Peaslee's *Constitutions of the Nations* or other sources, write a fifteen-page report on the methods by which the executives of all nations are selected and the formal qualifications that they must possess.

12

PUBLIC ADMINISTRATION

ADMINISTRATION, as we have set the distinction in the last chapter, may be thought of as what executives do a good part of the time and administrators most of the time. Therefore, this chapter will be, for the most part, less concerned with the policies and organization of the top executives and politicians and more concerned with the large body of "less important" appointive and civil serivce officials. "Less important," of course, does not mean less good, nor even less important in determining the course of history, for great bureaucracies in the mass have often outweighed the political officials on the scales of historical forces. We mean merely that such officials are concerned with carrying out policies that are fairly definite, in ways that are formal and circumscribed.

Public administration is the organization and activity of an agency of government that is charged with carrying out public policy. Public administration occurs today on a large scale in every country that has a considerable technological development and its concomitant division of labor. The tasks set by the laws mount into the hundreds in modern times. They develop by a process as complicated as the historical origins of a piece of legislation such as the Employment Act of 1946, discussed in Chapter Ten.

For example, earlier generations of Americans fought fires by forming volunteer fire companies, organized as clubs or governed by township and other local rules. The understandable policy of wanting to put out fires was implemented by nonprofessional personnel using primitive equipment. Then large-scale social changes occurred. The industrial revolution produced congested urban areas whose peoples worked in factories. A specific effect of these changes was the danger of destructive fires. The technological revolution also provided means of fighting large fires by devising better fire-fighting equipment. More complex equipment demanded professional mechanics, constant care, and large expenditures. The bigger communities provided themselves with the equipment and the personnel. A body of civil servants was created. Smaller communities pooled resources, jointly hired professional help, and ended up with arrangements far more complicated than their previous ones because they could not provide their services alone; but they, too, had entered upon the problems of public administration. When modern cities are threatened by fire-bomb raids in war, the central government takes over much of the responsibility and expense of fire protection and a large part of the population is assigned tasks to perform in an emergency.

A glance back at the chart of the functions of American governments (Figure 5) allows one to visualize easily the extent of public administration in modern states. The variety of special skills that are required for the performance of all the tasks is great and increasing. We obviously can say nothing here about what it takes to be a fireman, a government light-house keeper, a forest ranger, a research chemist on plant diseases, a punch-press operator, or a platoon sergeant. Special occupations must be studied in themselves.

Nor can we begin to describe the differences among the thousands of statutes and regulations that prescribe the structure and procedures of hundreds of administrative agencies of countries such as France, Russia, England, and America. The army is not organized like the treasury or the budget bureau or the power projects or even like the navy. Each agency has its own special character just as each tree in the forest is a little different from every other tree. But still there is an applied science of forestry that is based on general biology, and there is also an applied science of administration that is based on general social science. The fact that there are great foresters who have never read a book on forestry is matched by the fact that many great administrators never studied the subject in school, and neither fact is here nor there. As was stated in the first chapter, only the most highly developed sciences require some special training as an absolute necessity for high accomplishments in the appropriate art of the science. Neither public administration nor political science, its more generalized parent, has that character.

The Goals of Administration

FUNCTIONAL GOALS

Both administrators and students of administration, in drawing from the administrative world certain principles of behavior, cannot help but observe that public administration is always conducted towards some goal—winning a war, building a bridge, delivering the mail, reducing the public debt, and so on. Such goals are the *functional objectives* of government administration and their number and variety depends on historical and political factors that cause the increase or decrease, the traditionalism or the novelties of state activities.

In a society like America, general agreement is possible on specific government functions and much less possible on wholesale objectives that would permanently transform the society. American politists and public can agree on *a* dam, *a* pension plan, or *an* annual appropriation, but on no grand over-all scheme. By contrast, the functional goals of the Soviet Union are extremely broad, and they are proclaimed at every opportunity. The private sector of the state is all but eliminated in Russia today since the governmental sector encompasses industry and agriculture as well as the "normal" functions all governments carry carry out. A few of the explicitly stated goals of the government are a classless society, the withering away of the state, world communism, and the transformation of the psychology of the people so that it will be possible for each to work according to his ability and receive according to his need. This last goal is supposed to produce the "new man" and this goal assumes the possibility of fundamentally remaking the whole people. Below this highest level of Soviet goals comes the level of practical functional goals, the great plans for specific production quotas in all major industries according to established time schedules. These functional goals, though often serving the same needs—such as the development of power plants, irrigation systems, and transportation systems—as the American functional goals, are deliberately co-ordinated and viewed together as a whole. In America, most functional goals, as we have already stated, are set up to fulfill specific purposes without reference to any grand plan.

INSTRUMENTAL GOALS

Besides these functional objectives, there are *instrumental objectives* that come more properly within the scope of this chapter. Functional objectives of administration are the ends, the goals, the things that are to be completed. The instrumental objectives are the goals that evolve as the functional objectives are being sought. Thus, "efficiency" is an instrumental objective to most people. They want an agency to be efficient in order to achieve the functional objective of the agency as quickly and inexpensively as possible.

We can distinguish five such instrumental goals that pervade the whole of administrative activity. What political science can say about the general nature of man's search for these objectives forms the core of the science of administration. Three instrumental objectives are *stipulated*; two are *intrusive*. That is to say that three are often openly

espoused as instrumental goals by most people, including the lawmakers, while two are commonly observed to exist, but are less
commonly and overtly supported.

STIPULATED GOALS

The three stipulated, instrumental goals of administration
are:

1. Maximum productivity and maximum utilization of the available
human and material resources in ways reputed by experts to be most
effective and most sparing.

2. A minimum of material and psychological disturbance of the
population that is affected by the activities inherent in the functional
goal and induced by the instrumental goal.

3. A maximum of consultation with the population that is affected
by the activities inherent in the functional goal and induced by the
instrumental goal.

INTRUSIVE GOALS

The two intrusive goals are:

1. A maximum of personal and party advancement.

2. Operating procedures attuned to the personal habits and qualities
of the official class.

A discussion of the meaning, implications, and effects of these five
goals will carry out the design of this chapter.

Productivity and Utilization of Resources

THE USE OF POSDCORB IN HIERARCHICAL PYRAMIDS

The general form of public administration has been strongly
influenced by the very important objective of achieving tasks with a
most efficient utilization of the means available. In outlining the general
position of the executive in society, we pointed out that the hierarchical
pyramid, headed by a single executive chief, was the most nearly
universal form of organizing men to carry out functional tasks. The
single executive is well adapted to overseeing (POSDCORB) a few subordinates, who in turn oversee their chief subordinates, who in turn
oversee their subordinates and so on until ultimately the whole of a
vast organization may be knittted together and focused on the

FIGURE 32

ORGANIZATION OF MAJOR UNITS FOR EFFICIENCY *

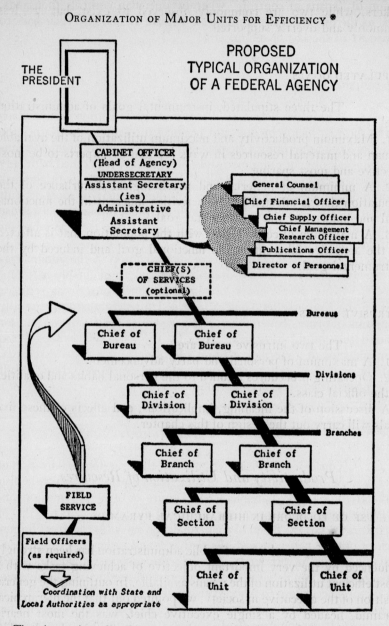

THE
PRESIDENT

PROPOSED
TYPICAL ORGANIZATION
OF A FEDERAL AGENCY

CABINET OFFICER
(Head of Agency)
UNDERSECRETARY
Assistant Secretary
(ies)
Administrative
Assistant
Secretary

General Counsel
Chief Financial Officer
Chief Supply Officer
Chief Management
Research Officer
Publications Officer
Director of Personnel

CHIEF(S)
OF SERVICES
(optional)

Bureaus

Chief of
Bureau

Chief of
Bureau

Divisions

Chief of
Division

Chief of
Division

Branches

Chief of
Branch

Chief of
Branch

FIELD
SERVICE

Chief of
Section

Chief of
Section

Field Officers
(as required)

Chief of
Unit

Chief of
Unit

Coordination with State and
Local Authorities as appropriate

There is a tendency for all large-scale organizations to assume this structural pattern, which the Hoover Commission recommended for Federal agencies in 1949.

* Commission on Organization of the Executive Branch of the Government: *General Management of the Executive Branch* (Washington, D. C.: United States Government Printing Office, 1949), p. 9.

specialized and co-ordinated parts of a much larger task. This succession of "spans of control," whereby one man controls thousands, gives us the hierarchical pyramid (see Figure 32 and also refer back to Figure 31 in the last chapter).

THE DIVISION OF LABOR

Within the hierarchical pyramid specialization occurs. Each man in the vast hierarchy does not perform the same tasks. Rather the total job, say of operating a fleet of ships, is broken down into a number of special jobs, the administrators of which are concerned with only their narrow range of tasks and who are vital links in a giant network of communications and performance. Although it may be most difficult to impart to the personnel charged with the most minute tasks a sense of their importance, it is nevertheless true that the total accomplishment does depend upon them.

Sometimes the results of extreme specialization in the administrative agencies produce strange situations that occasion outside criticism. Thus, for many years, every tiny postal money order was sent for audit to the Comptroller General of the United States until literally mountains of orders covered acres of warehouse space, all waiting for an audit that might have been made by the local post offices. From other agencies of government came additional acres of fiscal records, until the auditing agency was overwhelmed by this extreme result of the principle of special responsibility.

LONG TENURE OF OFFICE AND "PAPER MEMORY"

To the hierarchical pyramid and the minute specialization of tasks may be added the feature of long tenure of office, which is also characteristic of great bureaucracies. Tenure of office provides opportunity for mastering the required skills and the necessary teamwork of a large organization. When to these qualities one adds the great framework of precise paper procedures that is found in large-scale governmental agencies of all kinds, one has the essence of bureaucracy's response to the stipulated instrumental goal of productivity. This general picture, according to Max Weber, who has so well described it, is the most efficient of all known ways of organizing human energies for large tasks. If we compare the factory system with the domestic work system, the disciplined army with the armed horde, or the development of the huge Tennessee Valley Authority with the unco-ordinated development of other river valleys it would seem that, for great endeavors of a technological kind, the bureaucratic form of organization moves irresistibly, through perhaps slowly, towards its objectives.

ORGANIZATION OF A GOVERNMENTAL FUNCTION

In the United States, the total job of government—the carrying of the mails, the running of the army and navy, the regulation of the railroads, the manufacture of atomic materials, the arbitration of labor disputes, the construction of highways—is usually assigned to agencies according to function. The fragments of the total task are usually called departments, but may be called independent regulatory establishments, government corporations, mixed authorities of private and governmental groups, or something else. The most important fragments on the national level are organized into departments and their chiefs are given cabinet rank. Each level of government has its own major fragments. Thus the national Department of Agriculture is paralleled on the state level by the State Department of Agriculture. The county will have a health unit, the city will have a police department.

Each major department has under it a number of operating units which, since they each have separate tasks to perform, also become separately organized. The police department has its detective bureau, identification bureau, traffic bureau, and so forth. The Department of Interior has its Bureau of Mines and other subagencies.

The *bureaus* break down into even smaller operating units performing minor specialized functions. Thus the Bureau of Internal Revenue of the Treasury Department breaks down into the Accounts and Collections *Unit*, the Income Tax *Unit*, the Miscellaneous Tax *Unit* and the Alcohol Tax *Unit*.

Finally beneath the units come the *individual positions*. And all organizational patterns build on top of the individual positions, just as the army builds up to general from the private. This completes the most simple presentation of the administrative structure or hierarchy: It ascends from the position to the department. Few departments have exactly the same internal organization. The tendency seems to be toward a pattern like the one the Hoover Commission recommended (see Figure 32).

LINE, AUXILIARY, AND STAFF AGENCIES

The departments that perform major functional operations or groups of functional operations are called *line* departments. The line departments are dedicated to carrying out the functional goals of administration. They collect money, preserve the peace, fight fires, conserve the forests, operate industries, and the like. In addition, because there are some functions common to all operations—whether the object is to collect taxes, build roads, or maintain the police—special agencies have grown up whose principal tasks are to carry on work that is common to a number of agencies and can be more efficiently and cheaply conducted if concentrated in one agency. Such agencies are called *auxiliary*, *housekeeping*, or *service* agencies. Examples would be central purchasing offices, central personnel agencies, central disbursing offices, and so forth. They usually are independent of the major departments and work directly under officers appointed by the chief executive. Auxiliary or housekeeping agencies are in principle occupied exclusively with instrumental objectives, when those objectives are best accomplished by co-ordination on a wide scale among the line offices of an agency.

The other principal type of agency is the *staff* agency. A staff is an organ that advises the executive but does not have operating responsibilities. The staff is the eyes and ears and brain of the executive. The executive depends on his staff in making his decisions, because he cannot personally inform himself on all the details of vast enterprises. The division commander in the army may give all the major commands, but he is advised constantly by his personnel, intelligence, operations, and supply staff officers (G1, G2, G3, G4). The functions of a civil staff are to study administrative problems, to plan future actions, to observe and report, and to advise the executive, but not to act itself. An example of an important staff agency of the national government is the Bureau of the Budget. Through its financial surveys and planning, it can furnish a wide variety of information to the President, make suggestions, study the efficiency of administration, check deficits, and foresee probable future problems. Since the staff group occupies itself with extending the intelligence and control of the executive, it may be concerned both with functional goals and with instrumental goals.

Usually only large organizations can justify specialized staffs. The army and other agencies of the national government certainly can, as can some of the larger corporations. After a fashion, even very small units of government and business have staffs, whether formal or not. In some cases, individuals are simply called into conference to give their specialized opinion on particular problems.

EFFICIENCY CONTROLS IN THE U.S.S.R.

The leaders of the Soviet Union, probably more than any ruling group on earth have made efficiency a fetish. They have experimented with various methods of organizing and controlling their vast enterprises efficiently. They have rejected humanitarianism and consultation with the affected population. They have converted these motives in administration into remote goals which, they say, will some day characterize their administration. The Soviet leaders have bitterly rejected the intrusive motives of personal advancement and the customs of offices. At the same time, by identifying the cause of the Communist Party with the very heart of the state, they have been able to avoid viewing the advancement of the party as an intrusive goal. Inefficiency—a practice that is very difficult to define—was made a crime in the Soviet Union.

The organization of the Russian administrative establishment shows that there are few remarkable innovations today. Once, the leaders experimented with plural executives as the top managers of schools, stores, and factories. In 1934, the use of plural-headed executives was abandoned for single chief executives, in the interest of efficiency. Furthermore, at one time Soviet agencies were divided internally into separately organized and autonomous units. These units were what we should call auxiliary; finance, personnel, raw materials, planning, and other functions within the same agency were administered by individuals who were accountable to higher authorities *outside* the agency. Samuel N. Harper cites a Soviet leader's judgment that this type of organization meant "one authority when a hand was to lift food to the mouth, another when it was to write a report and still another when it had to hit somebody in the face, and thus for all hands everywhere." In 1934, this novel kind of structure, the origins of which go back to the theories of F. W. Taylor, was abandoned. Today Russian enterprises are organized along the pattern of the integrated agency, whose chief is responsible for all its functions and operations.

Finally, the Russians have installed central efficiency control machinery corresponding to American staff agencies. A Ministry of State Control and the Party Control Commission are two organizations to promote efficiency. In addition, each individual ministry has its own inspection system. Lastly there is "control by the ruble." This device is carried out through the banks and the Central Planning Organization and consists of inspecting the work of enterprises to determine whether an enterprise is making its "planned" profits, that is, the margin of income over costs expected of it according to its planning directives.

JOB CLASSIFICATION

One of the methods used in large agencies to assist in efficient selection and assignment of employees is job classification, in which the thousands of positions in a large organization are grouped according to the kinds of duties that their occupants are expected to perform and the level of responsibility required of their occupants. The qualifications that its occupants are supposed to possess, and the rate of pay that the job is supposed to require are, consequently, closely related to the classification the job possesses. Nearly 10,000 job classifications may be found among the two million positions in the federal civil service. The grand purpose of classifying the levels and branches of the hierarchical pyramid is to minimize for the controlling executive the confusion and difficulties of managing, transferring, paying, and promoting large numbers of employees.

Legislators, too, have found that classification is required if they are to maintain control and supervision over the administration. The classification system "rationalizes" the whole public employment system by relating one job to any other job. This facilitates control by the legislature as well as by executives. Although legislators could work their will more freely on individuals in the absence of a classification system, they would practically lose control over the administration as a whole. They would, furthermore, be so preoccupied with small matters as to neglect important problems. Consequently, the legislators found a classification system absolutely necessary as the number of public employees increased.

While a classification system introduces stability into administration and reduces confusion, it also produces inevitable inflexibilities. *Classes* of positions are set up and described in the classification *scheme*. *Individual* positions are then placed in a class that best describes their function and level of responsibility. Over the long run, this is done without reference to the *particular people* who will fill them. A position exists before it has an incumbent.

When there is an incumbent, he either has the qualifications and does the work required or else he does less or more than is required. If he is doing more than is required, the classification becomes less meaningful; one cannot look at the description of the position and tell what its occupant is doing. The formal way provided by all civil service systems for solving this common problem is to redescribe the position and reclassify it. The incumbent is then assigned the changed classification in order that he be given all the prerequisites and responsibilities of the actual work he is doing.

Reclassification of positions is a major task of classification officers. They try constantly, often on the request of line officers, to fit the actual work going on in a position to an appropriate class in the classification scheme. Thus change is adjusted to the central and durable scheme. The greater the lag between the change and the adjustment, the less meaningful and useful the classification scheme and system. Even in the best of classification systems, there will often be considerable variation in the way the incumbent of one position in a class operates and the way the person in another position of the same class functions. In other words a position in an excellent classification system is typical of its class, but the incumbent may not be typical of the incumbents of the position and hence not typical of the incumbents of the class of positions.

A classification system must, if it is to mean anything, be *essentially* stable, yet not so stable as to preclude necessary adjustments for the sake of efficiency and morale. However, continuous wholesale change in positions would lead to confusion as the grade and responsibilities of office-holders kept fluctuating.

FORMAL AND INFORMAL ORGANIZATION

This key problem of stability versus change in the classification system of the bureaucracy, together with several other conditions that are often present owing to factors that we shall presently discuss, leads to a situation that is most important in the study of administration. This situation is the presence of informal organization alongside the formal organization in administrative groups. Formal organization in the stipulated organization of lines of authority, and of responsibility, and of work in an office. Informal organization is the deviation from this stipulated organization. How formal and informal organization often do not coincide well may be seen in Figure 33.

For example, let us suppose that a certain girl occupies a position as secretary to a unit chief, and, in that capacity, is expected to type many letters, answer all phone calls, record all appointments and messages, and keep a set of files on the unit. That is her stipulated work budget. In fact she types many letters, but composes many of them herself; the chief likes to answer the phone himself very often; she speaks to many people and prevents them from speaking to the chief. Because of the importance of these tasks, she has managed to have the filing job delegated to a man who is filling the position of a field worker, but who, since the chief likes to be outdoors, is not in the field as much as the classification required.

This is a mild and common case, involving a contradiction between the expected and the actual performance of tasks in the office. The informal organization involves some deviation from the formal picture. Assuming that the work coming out of such an office was good or bad, an outside student could not then generalize that the formal organization of offices of such a type was good or bad, without getting a picture of the informal organization in each of the several offices. That is, he could not take the stipulated organization of lines of authority, responsibility, and work as the *real* conditions that are producing good or bad results. He might well profit from the skepticism often observed among old hands in an office with reference to the organization chart. The chart is often the dusty relic of outmoded procedures and of dead or promoted officials.

FIGURE 33

FORMAL AND INFORMAL ORGANIZATION *

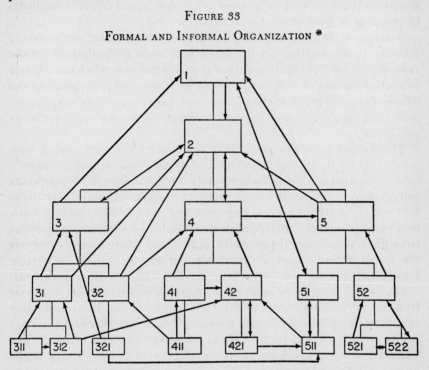

In studying the organization structure, the official organization chart is obtained. Sociometric ratings based on with whom most time is spent in getting work done are superimposed over the formal organization chart. In all samples, there are noticeable deviations between the formal organization and the informal organization as revealed by the sociometric ratings. An index of deviation to show in statistical terms the amount of deviation is in process of development.

In this figure, the formal organization chart is shown in solid lines with the pattern of interpersonal relationships in checked lines. The checked lines show the first two choices; that is, the two persons within the group with whom most time is spent. The arrow points in the direction of the person named. Thus, number 51 named number 1 and number 511, and number 1 named number 2 and number 51. One can see what are sometimes called "violations" of the organization chart. The studies of various staffs suggest that "violations" are a normal activity. The informal or interpersonal work structure represents day-to-day relationships. Staffs are usually fairly familiar with the organization chart, but little has been done to acquaint staff members with an understanding of the "interpersonal chart."

The informal structure is one index of the dynamics of getting work done, and it appears that for efficiency it will necessarily deviate from the formal structure. Extreme deviations, however, may hamper rather than promote efficiency.

* Carroll L. Shartle, "Leadership and Executive Performance," *Personnel* (1949), reprinted and copyrighted, 1949, by the American Management Association. Reproduced with the permission of the American Management Association.

DISCIPLINE AND INTERNAL CONTROLS

A contrast between the formal prescription and the real condition is also found in matters of discipline and internal controls. Depending on its degree of crystallization, the bureaucracy will have a painstaking code for disciplining infractions of the moral and technical rules of administration. The penalties will begin typically with provisions for an official reprimand that goes on the personnel record, and extend to the loss of seniority, in somewhat more serious cases. As the offense becomes greater, the penalty increases; temporary suspension, demotion, discharge, and judicial prosecution are the most rigorous punishments.

The formal penalties just listed are more often surrounded with safeguards for the disciplined employee in government business than in private business. This is owing partly to the influence of politicians and employee organizations and partly to the less "nervous" and "willful" milieu in which bureaucracy operates. By contrast, private business managers need not fear political reprisals in disciplining employees (though unions sometimes cause difficulty). Moreover, businesses often operate in an unstable market situation and respond to outside losses with drastic and immediate reactions against their personnel.

Soviet administrators seem to be more subject to outside sanctions than are the administrators in Western countries. Sanctions in Russian offices and factories are harsh. Criminal law in the Soviet Union has been extended to new areas by the creation of "economic crimes." The law aims to protect socialist property, to prevent and punish the negligence or willful misconduct of the managers of state enterprises, and to deter workers from tardiness and absenteeism. The sanctions against officials and administrators willfully or negligently breaching planning discipline are new "crimes of officials" and "crimes against the administrative order." These crimes are considered crimes against the whole community and are severely punished.

INFORMAL PENALTIES USED MORE THAN FORMAL

But just as force is rarely needed to keep peace and order in the society as a whole, in the working organization the formal penalties are imposed only rarely, usually after the failure of other controls. The right to fire, like the right of the state to imprison, is infrequently exercised because informal social pressures manage most people almost all the time. Controls exist that are almost unconscious—the office *esprit de corps*, the enthusiasm of the group for its job, the joy of work (as Henri de Man wrote of it), and the hiring only of personnel that can be expected to fit into the work group. The negative aspects of these phenomena of group life include, many times, effective punishments—ostracism by the group, loss of friendships, loss of respect.

Discipline may be maintained by the leader through a soft word or a stern one, by tightening up supervision, by making an offender's work life less pleasant by small actions such as scheduling his vacation at an inconvenient or unsatisfactory time. It may be hinted that a resignation would be a good thing for all parties, though the resignation be without dishonor; or when the budget of the agency is cut, the least desirable members may be let out, with honor, to be sure, but, informally speaking, a disciplinary measure has been taken.

Therefore, the study of discipline and internal controls, like the study of work being done, has an informal as well as a formal side. And, as with the classification process, it is unlikely that any formal system of penalties can so regulate the behavior of personnel that an informal system will not grow up alongside it. In both cases, the formal system cannot be dispensed with and the informal system is inevitable.

The formal prescriptions of organizations encompass the external directives and the best available description of the manner of utilizing resources for their accomplishment. The informal organization bespeaks the conflict of external with internal forces, and the injection of unforeseen work processes into the foreseen routines.

Effects on the Administered Population

MINIMIZING THE DISTURBANCES CAUSED BY POLICIES

Pursuit of the first stipulated goal—high productivity and maximum utilization of resources—is conditioned by the second stipulated goal of administration. It is generally agreed, even where such agreement does not find expression in the language of statutes, that the means of administration ought to be such as to minimize the material and psychological disturbances of a new policy on the people who are affected by it.

Almost every administrative policy must interfere to some extent with the habits and attitudes of some people. This is so even when the policy being carried out is one that provides universally desired services or that gives benefits to millions of people. For example, the post office delivers mail and performs other services for millions of people every day. Also, the system of social security in the United States provides a means by which millions of people save money for their old age. But, in the pursuit of these functional objectives of delivering the mail and providing for the old, the administrators must to some extent order, discipline, encourage, punish, and otherwise affect a multitude of human actions. In performing these functions administrators are often as much concerned with selecting methods that will minimize the unpleasant effects on people of having their lives reordered as they are with methods that will increase the efficiency of their operation. For example, the Veterans Administration sends each month to those who hold National Service Life Insurance policies a self-addressed envelope stating the amount due and the name of the policy holder. This practice induces more policyholders to pay premiums promptly and standardizes the handling of a large volume of mail returns. The V. A. might instead have adopted the view that premiums that are not paid promptly will cause the policy to be defaulted and leave to the policyholders the responsibility for remembering always to pay premiums promptly.

ADMINISTRATIVE POWERS OVER PEOPLE

The formal science of administration teaches human engineering according to a standard of efficiency but it does not teach, in any formal way, human engineering according to a principle of minimum distress. The principle is assumed in the sense that "no one wants to hurt anyone else if he can help it." Unfortunately, this easygoing way of treating a perennial problem of administration does not provide us with a method of describing systematically the operations of the minimum distress motive. Therefore, we must use indirect means to examine the expression of this motive in administration.

Following Dr. Leonard D. White's analysis, we will list the forms of action that administrators often have within their power in the various nations of the world. *In the case of each form of action, it may be perceived that lesser or greater pressure may be brought to bear, lesser or greater sanctions inflicted upon people, depending not only upon the desire for efficient execution of the task at hand but also upon the desire to cause as little damage as may be possible to the interests involved. Furthermore, the decision to use one form of action rather than another in any certain case is a judgment based not only on efficiency but on humaneness.*

We should remember, in examining this list, that administrators rarely have free choice of these various forms of action, and that the legislature and the political executive determine the general conditions under which they may be employed.

1. Declarations of public policy: perhaps the "softest" form of action to obtain disciplined conduct among the population concerned. The promulgator of a policy merely states that it is best for the country if a particular line of conduct is avoided or observed. Thus, the Ameri-

can government declared during the Italo-Ethiopian War of 1936 that
it was the policy of the government not to ship munitions and arms to
the warring nations. Breaches of the policy by exporters, however,
were not punishable. Policy declarations are also a common practice
among executives taking office for the first time; they state what the
policies of their offices will be, even though the laws they administer
are unchanged and their statements are mere appeals for co-operation
with government policy.

2. Declaration of legal obligation without sanctions for disobedience. Such would be a declaration of legal holidays, without penalties
against those who insisted upon working on holidays. Again, some
early factory legislation declared that the working day would be 10
hours, but no authority was charged with enforcing such a law.

3. The establishment of voluntary commercial standards. Faced
with a plethora of practices in a trade or market, the administration
determines that it would be more convenient, more efficient, and fairer
if all firms and individuals involved would use the same language,
weights, and categories in describing their products. The National
Bureau of Standards of the United States is active in promulgating
such standards. Cotton, grain, and other agricultural products have
been graded according to general standards by departments of agriculture. While no physical coercion is used to enforce these standards,
the standards enforce themselves, so to speak, because it is easier for
an individual or firm to do business with people who have accepted the
standards than with those who have avoided the standards. Furthermore, if standards are falsified, the offending party may be punished
and sued for damages.

4. The government sometimes uses its own purchasing power to
induce compliance with certain high standards of accomplishing work.
If individuals and firms wish to sell to the government, they must
follow government-established standards. Thus, the Walsh-Healy Act
of 1936 denied contracts to any firm that did not maintain certain work
and pay standards among their employees. Naturally, many firms
adopted the standards rather than lose their contracts.

5. Educational campaigns directed at the general public or affected
portions thereof. Often a sum of money spent on informing the public
will produce greater compliance with a policy than an equal sum spent
in prosecuting a few offenders under punitive clauses in the law. Examples of educational actions known to many are the savings bonds
sales drives, the dissemination of information on rights under the Social Security laws, and the exposure of grave social conditions (for
example, soil erosion) in order to obtain co-operation for the administration of a soil erosion law. One might also cite the act of Congress
ordering that all administrative rules and orders be published in the
Federal Register in order to take effect. This was done in part because

Congressmen felt that greater conformity to the law could be obtained if businessmen had surer ways of knowing what the law was, and in part as a means of reducing the insecurities of affected individuals.

6. Conferences among individuals and firms of an industry to discuss and settle points relating to trade practices are devices sometimes used by agencies like the Federal Trade Commission. This is a way of obtaining standardization through the group itself as opposed to obtaining standardization by the unilateral action of the agency. The trade conference, it ought to be noted, can develop very easily into a device for restricting competition in an industry, hiking prices to the public, and fighting off new inventions that would require great change but would also lower costs and prices to the public.

7. Mediation and conciliation. Most national and state governments have agencies for conciliating opposing parties in a labor dispute and mediating the dispute in accordance with public policy, if the parties are so minded. Here it is attempted to expedite the settlement of disputes damaging to the public without directing the course of events outright.

8. The purchase of consent. Where private rights are involved, and strong pressures arbitrate against the use of law backed by physical coercion, administrative agencies may be authorized to buy up private rights in order to go ahead with a government policy. Thus the national government has bought many thousands of acres of eroded land from its owners in order to plant trees and prevent further erosion or floods. The Agricultural Adjustment Administration, in pursuing a policy of controlling excess agricultural production, is authorized to purchase the individual farmer's abstinence from production rather than to forbid production under the threat of prosecution. Powerful farmers' pressure groups had much to do with this mild administrative form of action. Payments for damages inflicted by government officers in pursuance of their legitimate activities, and payments for land or buildings taken over by government agencies, are other forms of the purchase of consent. In these cases, however, unlike the preceding ones, the action is mandatory, and the money is used to mollify the individuals who have been disturbed economically or materially.

9. Publicity. The use of public opinion rather than force to back up recommendations based on the findings of conditions detrimental to public policy is often very effective in certain areas of the economy. The exposure, through government-sponsored publicity, of "unhealthy" conditions of work, of "shady" practices in business, of inferior and maladvertised products can induce conformity to standards. A variant of this form of action is the so-called "yardstick" enterprise whereby the government performs some operation as it "should" be performed, in order that the public, viewing the difference between

government enterprise and private enterprise, may be incited to demand new standards of private enterprise. An argument often advanced for ameliorating the working conditions of government employment is that the government should be a "model employer."

10. Individual inspection, aid, and advice. Possessed often of highly qualified experts in certain areas, the government may offer its services freely or even compel the use of this consultation. Private firms will sometimes use government advisors on public contracts, even where such advice need not be taken. They do this in order to avoid later damaging reactions to the way in which the work was performed. The advice of government tax experts is sometimes asked when a firm sets up an accounting system so that there will be less likelihood later on of having expensive investigations and a reworking of the records regarding the payment of income, surplus profits, unemployment, or social security taxes.

11. Licensing. The ancient administrative action of licensing allows persons to engage in certain activities otherwise prohibited by law, provided they demonstrate their ability to perform these activities to the satisfaction of the licensing law and of the administrators of the law. Licenses may be so unimportant as dog licenses or so important as radio broadcasting licenses. To have a dog without a license and to broadcast without a license are equally prohibited. Administrative inspectors discover both the absence of licenses and the violation of conditions under which the licenses were granted.

The care and formality with which licenses are granted and revoked depends to a large extent on the kind of property rights and human rights affected. The suspension of a license to sell milk upon the discovery of unsanitary conditions in the bottling plant is not likely to be accompanied by the same mountain of litigation as is the suspension of the broadcasting privileges of a metropolitan radio station because of alleged failure to keep "indecent" programs off the air.

12. The order of individual applicability. Where legislation of a general nature and administrative rules of general applicability cannot conveniently or justly cover the type of action desired, agencies may be authorized to promulgate special orders affecting individuals or single firms. For example, the Hepburn Act of 1906 gave the Interstate Commerce Commission the legal right to fix the freight rates of an individual railroad carrier at a "just and reasonable" level. The National Labor Relations Board similarly may order a company or a union to "cease and desist" from an action that the law declares generally to be an unfair practice. The agency, after a process that is sometimes simple and sometimes very complex, declares what shall be the behavior of the regulated private party in a particular respect. Various national agencies—the Federal Trade Commission, the Securities Ex-

change Commission, and the Federal Communications Commission, among others—and many state agencies have authority to issue orders that apply to individuals.

13. Orders of general applicability. This form of action is closest of all to legislation and is often called quasi-legislation. The chief difference between orders of general applicability and legislation is that the general order depends on a grant of authority from the principal law-making organ, and the grant of authority is almost always accompanied by conditions regarding the manner of its exercise that the legislature itself is not bound to follow in making general legislation. This power of agencies to issue general orders has grown greatly in recent times and its spread is one of the best indices of the advent of administrative authority. Over a thousand statutes give rule-making powers to over a hundred national agencies. The state governments are far behind in this development, but state agencies, also, are making rules in increasing number.

The process by which most orders of general applicability are drafted, discussed, and promulgated is almost as complicated as the legislative process itself. To be sure, the administrative rule-making process is more sharply focused on its special sphere of interest (railroads, for example), while the legislature, when it talks about railroads, talks and thinks about everything else on the agenda of the legislature and on the minds of politicians. This is a crucial difference: legislation is everything political taken together; a vote on one issue is commonly a number of votes wrapped up together and taking cognizance of many matters "irrelevant" to the issue.

On the other hand, stringent controls have been put on rule-making because legislators have been reluctant to concede to anyone else the right to make anything resembling law. The consequence, remarkably enough, is that administrative agencies go through a regimen of investigating facts, weighing merits and demerits, hearing viewpoints, and drafting orders that is hardly to be seen in any but the most exceptional legislatures when they pass the most carefully considered bills.

14. Finally, administrative adjudication should be mentioned. Administrative adjudication is the settlement of a dispute between private parties or a private party and the government on the basis of law and fact by an administrative agency. Just as orders of general applicability give to administrative agencies the character of legislatures, the rendering of judgments in legal contests gives them the character of courts. The cases falling within the quasi-judicial competence of administrative tribunals come out of controversial behavior concerning agency orders of individual and general applicability. Some fifty federal agencies have quasi-judicial powers. Like the legislatures, the regular courts are jealous of their authority and responsibilities. The courts,

consequently, take cases out of the hands of administrative tribunals whenever it seems that there has been an error of law or procedure, an important error in fact, a lack of jurisdiction, or an abuse of political discretion in the agency's conduct of a particular quasi-judicial proceeding against a private party.

These, then, are the fourteen principal forms of actions that the administration can take against private deviants. Often the forms are hedged in by the legislatures and the courts. Often two or more forms of action may be used in the case of a single party: that is, he may be cajoled, pressured by members of his profession, publicly attacked by the administration, inspected, warned, subjected to a special order, made subject to a general order against the practice in question, or prosecuted in the tribunal of the agency. Often the same law allows the use of a combination of forms of action in inducing or forcing conformity with established public policy. Several of the forms of action are designed specifically to reduce the hardships inflicted by public policy. Such would be inspection warnings, adequate notice, hearings, mediation, and education.

IMPORTANCE OF AGGRESSIVE-DEFENSIVE PATTERN OF AGENCY ACTIONS

As we have just seen, a surprising amount of the expenditures and time-budget of many agencies go towards satisfying the general goal of administration of minimizing the material and psychological effects of the policy it must execute and the means it must take to execute it. It is strange that textbooks have been written and studies designed as if the only factor in explaining administration were the "productivity" factor. In reality we can find much evidence of legal and moral restraints in an administrator's conduct towards affected individuals.

The following hypotheses suggest themselves from experience and deserve testing. Perhaps if we had more studies exploring such hypotheses, we might know a good deal more about the motives found in administrative behavior.

a. Administrative agencies may be graded according to the amount of money and time of the total budget that are devoted to the juridical, material, and psychological defense of the affected populations.

   a1. In certain cases, the "defense budget" exceeds the "offense budget." That is, the total costs of "going easy" on the people affected and of providing a rule of law exceeds the costs of carrying out the law.

b. Agencies affecting persons outside their own organizations may be graded according to their degree of intimacy with the affected population.

b1. In certain cases, agencies are the "mouthpieces" rather than the "oppressors" of the affected populations. For example, the Federal Trade Commission was at one time completely sympathetic with the desires of the industries it was supposed to regulate (1925–35). At other times (1914–25, 1935–   ), it has been expansive and desirous of more "police action."

b2. There is no positive relationship between the severity of discipline exercised on the affected population and the fact that the agency is classified as a "mouthpiece" or "oppressor" type. (That is, "mouthpiece" agencies are often goaded into more severe forms of action by the regulated and affected parties themselves.) What occurs is akin to the behavior of "student courts" that are often sterner disciplinarians than are the teachers themselves.

CONFLICTS BETWEEN "EFFICIENCY" AND "HUMAN RESISTANCES"

The goal of minimizing discomfort or distress among the affected population, despite varying intensities of effort in that direction, is often not achieved. Implicit in the preceding discussion is the fact that *the desire for efficiency or productivity may interfere frequently with the desire for "soft" administration.* The paramount objective of administration is to accomplish the goals of the agency (the functional goals that give a directive to the agency) with a maximum of efficiency. There must be some limit to the second goal of gentleness if the goal of efficiency is to mean anything. The legends of public administration contain many versions of a common plot: the private citizen who is deep in personal troubles is told by the impassive and ruthless bureaucrat that he must fulfill some obligation ("Rules must be obeyed, you know!") and is left to languish in broken health amidst the ruins of his fortune. It would be nice if political science might present some strict formula for the determination of the point of exact confluence of efficiency and humanity, but of course it cannot. There is a whole world of decisions wavering on the extreme edge of either quality, susceptible to intelligent approach only after careful individual studies.

On the other hand, efficiency is universally tempered by humanitarian resistances. *Never does efficiency alone rule the road to a functional goal.* In most cases, it is easy to see how a pure motive of efficiency is subjected to attrition by other motives. If the threat of capital punishment were to be imposed on tax evaders (not an uncommon punishment in the annals of history), tax collecting would be probably easier and the budget of the revenue-collecting agencies of government somewhat reduced. But only a few people would regard such increased efficiency as worth the human cost; human life is not to be sold so cheaply, in Western societies at any rate.

The fact is that the actual behavior of most administrative bodies, like the actual internal discipline of the agency, lags behind formal prescription of penalties. Rather than setting the formal machinery of administrative authority into action to prevent or punish an offense, the agency usually essays informal methods of relieving the undesirable situation. It down-grades, so to speak, the appropriate penalty for a particular action. Culprits are allowed to repent on the promise of good behavior, following discussions and informal pressures.

Not only American society but most other societies regard the zealous insistence upon the letter of the regulation as "persecution," so habitual is the down-grading of penalties in relation to sanctions. Such a conclusion is often borne out in fact when notoriously unlawful characters are punished by being forced to conform to the exact provisions of the law. It is common knowledge in the United States that administrative and judicial authorities use the penalties for misconduct in declaring and paying income taxes to their full extent in punishing men widely believed to be guilty of other offenses for which they cannot be so easily called to account.

WHEN FORCE ENCOUNTERS RESISTANCES, PSYCHOLOGICAL METHODS ARE FOSTERED

Sometimes in order to minimize the effects of a policy on the population, administrators use to induce conformity methods that cause psychological distress. These methods seem to be chosen because of the common belief that psychological discomforts cause less pain than material discomforts. Therefore, rather than use methods employing material sanctions and subjecting the nonconformers to material discomfort, administrators often prefer to induce the total population concerned with a given policy to conform to it out of fear or anxiety. Thus, if a wide educational net is flipped over the entire population, telling them that their futures are insecure and that they had better invest in government bonds, the buyers of bonds who are found are considered to have been induced more easily than if they had been compelled directly to invest money in government bonds. Or, to use another example, if a few infected persons in the population are uncovered by reducing the total population to anxiety over venereal diseases, the result is considered superior to a systematic singling out of vulnerable individuals. Again, a *U. S. News and World Report's* "Newsgram" reported on November 3, 1950: "Builders, often, are going to get hurt. Cutbacks, uncertainties, stop orders intentionally are somewhat obscure. Idea is to induce people to put off as much construction as possible out of fear of what might happen."

Administrators often seem to regard the minds of the population as if they were like the waters of the oceans or like the vast atmosphere, capable of being used by everybody, for all things, over and over again. This attitude, we hasten to say, does not characterize administrators alone; it represents a whole culture that has discovered how minds can be influenced but has little conception of what indirect effects such mental influence may have on the minds of the people and on the culture as a whole.

This exploitation of psychological principles to minimize the disturbance of the population by administrators seems to be used even more in the Soviet Union than in Western countries. Exasperated citizens are given a psychological lift by seeing some bureau criticized even though it may be receiving unfair criticism. For example, a newspaper takes housing administrators to task for not providing sufficient new dwellings when in fact the scarcity of housing is due to a shortage of materials. Soviet administrators frequently claim that they use irate letters to the editors of newspapers as the basis for taking action on various matters. Wall newspapers in factories also serve to soften the blow of rigid or unpopular administration by presenting people with a limited opportunity to criticize the administration. Besides the severe physical sanctions at their command, Soviet administrators are adept at so-called "socialist engineering," that is, educating the masses to accept new measures by newspapers, radio, schools, mass meetings, and even by the courts. The Party propaganda apparatus is to a large extent directed toward making Marxists of the people and toward keeping them abreast of current developments.

HOW TO DETERMINE DISTRESS AMONG THE ADMINISTERED

We are now ready to ask: What can science do to determine the conditions of material and psychological distress? Can distress, like efficiency, be measured, and accommodated? Can the administrator use the results of scientific study of these matters? Some ideas on these questions can be gained by referring to other chapters. In Chapter One we described the process of correct thinking about political matters: this characterizes correct thinking among administrators as well as scientists and laymen. In Chapter Four, on public opinion, we described some of the methods for investigating the sources of popular customs and beliefs and the configuration of public opinion on various issues. These principles of study may again be employed by administrators to good effect. In the chapters on pressure groups (Seven) and on civil conflict (Eight) were materials on special interests and sources of group conflict that can be converted to the study of the effects of administrative policies. The study, then, of political behavior is highly relevant to administration, and is to be taken, along with public law, economics, and technical (mechanical) efficiency, as the prerequisites of astute administration.

Of course, every administrator has his own hunches and ways of knowing about the effects of policies. He has close friends who give him their opinions, he hears from legislators and reads letters of complaint about the practices of his agency. He reads the newspapers, and he projects his own feelings into the minds of the population he is dealing with. Often these methods work satisfactorily, especially since there are few people around to show him better methods. But there is little reason for doubting that, in general, administrative agencies today are as backward in applying scientific methods to the determination of the effects of administrative actions, as legislators are in using such methods in their work.

THE SAMPLE SURVEY

The sample survey, based on extensive and intensive interviewing, is perhaps the best developed tool that exists for examining the impact of policies on the public. Yet few agencies employ surveys systematically. Rensis Likert, Director of the Institute for Social Research, suggests a number of questions pertinent to scientific administration that survey methods may answer in good part. He believes that top executives, given very general delegations of power by legislatures, can obtain by surveys answers to these questions: What understanding does the public have of the problem concerning which a policy must be set? How does this understanding vary in various parts of the public? What degree of support can alternative policies and programs expect to obtain?

And once the general policy is set, continues Dr. Likert, surveys can continue to answer important questions: How effectively is the program working in the judgment of the public generally? What support does it have? What segments of the population feel that the program is working well? What segments feel that it is working poorly? Why? How well informed are people about the program and its objectives? What groups are uninformed or misinformed? How can they most readily be informed? If the program involves participation on the part of people generally, what kinds of people are participating? What segments of the public are refusing to participate? Why?

We should note that survey methods can answer questions as to the external efficiency of some administrative programs and also can answer questions as to the external, material, and psychological effects of a program. They furnish contributions to both these primary goals of administration. In addition, the survey can be used to realize a third stipulated goal of administration, that of consultation with the affected population.

Consultation with Administered Populations

CONSULTATION MEANS COADMINISTRATION

Consultation is a word that needs definition. If it meant only finding out what people think, then, obviously, it would not deserve separate presentation as a goal of administration. We would have included it in our discussion of the second goal. Consultation is often confused with discovering the *reactions* of people to the *unilateral* actions of administrators. In that case, the administered population is like the defendant in court when the judge asks: "Does the accused wish to say anything to the court before sentence is pronounced?"

But consultation can be defined and is defined here as *using the affected population as co-administrators*. Consultation, as here employed, means the determination of administrative actions by collaboration between the affected population and the agency. Historically, this condition often existed in American local government when the voters elected all officers at short intervals of time. The use of the subjects of administration as co-operators is, however, a new theoretical motive in modern legislation and large-scale administration. It has been found to exist (by accident) in some agencies that have grown very close to the groups they are authorized to regulate and in some agencies that have been co-governed by those groups. Examples can be found in the Federal Trade Commission under Commissioner Humphrey, the county agent system of the Department of Agriculture at times, and the Interstate Commerce Commission (which was accused by motor carriers some time ago of being dominated by the rail carrier viewpoint). But, as the last section of the chapter on pressure groups revealed, this administrative lobbying represents something of a tendency in this generation, and, given certain modifications introduced by legislatures and agencies, some form of interest representation can be expected to develop. This would not be an open conquest of the agency, but on the other hand, neither would it be a unilateral form of administering the affairs of industries and groups. Interest representation, therefore, is one form of consultation.

Other forms of consultation are the *surveys*, provided they are made with an active intent to carry out the viewpoints of the people interrogated; a complete provision for contesting the actions of administrative agencies by allowing public hearings of contemplated actions; and the conduct of elections on specific administrative policies among the groups affected by the policies. This last form of consultation was attempted for two years under the National Industrial Recovery Administration in the United States, and is still being used by the National Labor Relations Board to ascertain union sentiment in a shop and by the Department of Agriculture to determine whether crop controls should be applied to certain crops in oversupply.

DIFFICULTIES OF CONSULTATION

Needless to say, the objective of consultation is likely in most cases to conflict immediately and sharply with the objectives of the productivity of the agency and the efficient utilization of agency resources. Consultation takes time and money. It is contrary to the tradition of administration and violates the hierarchical pyramid. Administrators at present are neither inclined nor trained to regard others as competent to judge the requirements of "good" administration. Even a legislature is often not friendly to the practice of consultation in administrative activities because such consultation implies that legislators' policies have to be checked and aided by specialists. Like some general practitioners of medicine who dislike specialists, many legislators prefer to believe that general wisdom is sufficient to solve technical problems of the body politic.

The Soviet ruling group, despite a conscious commitment to consult with the masses, has made little real headway in that respect. What one does hear about are artificial stimulations of mass response, hardly different from "socialist engineering." The irresistible efficiency obsession has crippled any real motive for consultation that may have remained from the humanitarian and egalitarian heritage left by Marx and Engels. The chief method by which the Soviets claim to consult the people is "democratic centralism." This phenomenon was defined succinctly by Lenin as "freedom in discussion—unity in action," or, in other words, a combination of democracy (mass participation) and centralism (leadership). Democratic centralism is accomplished by the application of the elective principle, a limited amount of discussion, periodical accountability of lower to higher organs, strict subordination of the minority to the majority, and the binding character of decisions of higher bodies upon lower bodies.

Mass participation in administration and in determining the rules to be administered was originally a favored principle of the Soviets. There was mass participation, for instance, in the case of the 1936 Constitution. An estimated 500,000 meetings were held, with an aggregate attendance of 36,000,000 people, to discuss the draft of the

Constitution. Some changes may actually have been adopted in the final draft as a result of these meetings. Since 1936, however, there have been no examples of mass participation in legislation.

Mass participation in administration has declined from the early days of worker control of industry but still is present to a limited extent in some production conferences in industry. Also, in industry, workers are encouraged to volunteer for special administrative work in connection with the official tasks of the local soviets or workers' councils and labor unions. And it has been estimated that some eight per cent of all rural voters perform volunteer tasks in connection with farm and village administration. In the administration of the agricultural sector of the economy the farmers still participate through the meetings of the *kolkhoz* (collective farm) membership that makes decisions regarding crops to be planted, the allocation of labor to different tasks, and other matters. These decisions, however, must be within the limits of the general plan as laid down from above and in practice are frequently taken out of the hands of the membership by the chairman of the *kolkhoz*.

The soviets or councils were developed, according to Soviet writers, as barometers to check variations in public sentiment and reactions to changing programs and events. Originally the soviets had some slight influence on governmental acts but in recent times they have been assembled, at least on the higher levels of the hierarchy, merely to put the stamp of approval on the administration. The Communist Party is the greatest limitation on the soviets as exponents of popular demands. Since the collectivization of agriculture was completed in the 1930's there has been no evidence of opposition by the soviets to top-level policy. From time to time the local soviets are "activated" or stimulated from the top to criticize the administration of policy but not the policies themselves. Administrative officers undergo some embarrassing questioning and heckling from the deputies, and this procedure helps to relieve popular discontent.

Personal Careers and Partisanship

INTRUSIVE OBJECTIVES OF ADMINISTRATION

While the three goals of administration, hitherto discussed, are displayed eagerly before the public eye and applauded generously by the large body of people, even when they are not wholly understood, two additional general objectives of administration seem to be unpopular. They are intrusive; they are inevitably present, as we shall see, but they are not the occasions for general enthusiasm. Well-received or not, the motives of personal and party advancement, and the motives of inbred habit are as much a part of administration as the motives of efficiency and humanitarianism.

PRIVATE MOTIVES FOR PUBLIC SERVICE

We will discuss first the subject of personal advancement in the public service. It is obvious that a public servant has private desires. He wants to get a good job, keep it, support a family, and advance himself in responsibility, prestige, and salary. Some administrators have additional or different motives. They may want, whatever they may say, routine, routine, and more routine. They may desire, whatever their rationalizations, nothing more than the right to inflict hardships on the administered population. They may be guided by an inner compulsion to forever process business that efficiency would dictate should be dispatched. In a satirical vein, describing such inefficiency in a fictitious government agency, Charles Dickens once wrote: "If another Gunpowder Plot had been discovered half an hour before the lighting of the match, nobody would have been justified in saving the Parliament until there had been half a score of boards, half a bushel of minutes, several sacks of official memoranda, and a family-vault full of ungrammatical correspondence, on the part of the Circumlocution Office."

Furthermore, the ordinary private motives of public servants are sometimes present in great intensity and outweigh or exclude motives which are more related to the work. The desire *for* a good job is unrelated to the desire to *do* a good job; the desire to *keep* a job has nothing to do with *taking responsibility*. Also, a man may become so entranced by his prestige or so enraged by his lack of prestige that nothing else about the job matters; and, although it may seem surprising in view of the fact that public servants are paid relatively little in many lands, even such comparatively low salaries may afford witless and aimless people their only enthusiasm.

PRIVATE MOTIVES TAMED BY THE SERVICE

Now, of course, neither the ordinary personal motives of public servants nor the abnormal motives of a few control the organization and functions of public agencies. These motives are constantly tamed and directed towards the stipulated instrumental goals of efficiency, consideration, and consultation.

The taming and directing principles are *selective recruitment, merit examinations, merit promotions,* and *pay scales adjusted to skills.* The result of the application of such principles is a career service. A career service was defined by the Commission of Inquiry on Public Service Personnel (1935) in the following words: "Steps shall be taken to make public employment a worth-while life work, with entrance to the service open and attractive to young men and women of capacity and character, and with opportunity of advancement through service and growth to posts of distinction and honor." Notice that the ordinary personal motives are generally included here, but certain vague value-words are employed to indicate that a good deal of taming and direction will occur during the process: "worth-while," "attractive," "capacity," "character," "service," "growth." Each word implies that the whole process will be governed by values external to the values of the personal advancement of the individual, even though the individual is promised a pleasant career.

Since there is no universal agreement on the precise meaning of these value-words, the whole process of recruitment, examination, pay, advancement, and secure achievement is affected by the several conflicting motives of efficiency, humanitarianism, reactions from the affected populations, partisanship, and the clique tendencies of the people already in the agencies. We can illustrate this statement by sketching the formal personnel process in administration, and giving at the same time illustrations of the interference of the external motives mentioned.

1. *Recruitment* is the process of advertising among all conceivably interested and broadly qualified persons and allowing them to apply for civil service posts. The American post offices in cities and villages carry bulletins of forthcoming opportunities for public employment, giving directions about how to apply and qualify for such posts. At this point, even the most *open* system of recruitment begins to narrow in response to the efficiency motive: the completely uneducated are ruled out of many applications; applicants for many positions must have specified experience and education; in some cases, only holders of advanced degrees or persons of great experience are allowed to take examinations.

In America, the insistent pressure of the administered population, evidenced in the form of slogans like "Government business is everyone's business" or "Everyone has a right to government jobs," checks the extent to which the interested applicants are reduced in number in the name of efficiency. In other countries, pre-World War II Germany, for example, the original applicants must already be possessed of scarce qualities of experience and education; a drastic reduction in eligibles occurs in the name of efficiency.

Although the efficiency principle is the implacable foe of the party principle, having the "right" political views can sometimes help one who applies for a job with the government. Thus, in many American civil service systems, a note from a politician or verbal "clearance" is required in the very first stage of the personnel process in order to have one's application seriously considered. Where the jobs in question are not under a civil service system, political "pull" is often quite open in its effects. Census enumerators of the United States, for example, must obtain political clearance in most localities before they can be seriously considered or examined for their meagerly-paid jobs.

The incumbent bureaucracy has a hand in determining who shall be considered as an applicant for posts in the service. The prolonged debate between those who believe general education is the best qualification for government employment and those who believe special vocational skills should be sought is in part a contest between "cultured" officials and "practical" officials: each wants more of his own kind in his office.

2. *Examination* of the eligible applicants is conducted in several ways. They may be *assembled* at one place and required to undergo intelligence testing, characterological testing, general aptitude testing, or special skill testing, and often a combination of these. Or the applicants may take an *unassembled* examination; the applicant submits personal records of his background, educational qualifications, employment record, and sometimes samples of his past work. An oral interview by the representatives of the hiring agency often completes both types of examinations, but owing to the expensive nature of oral testing, only the most likely candidates for a position are usually chosen for this stage of examination.

The examining stage of the personnel process shapes the future character of an agency to some extent, and there is a continual controversy over the kind of examination employed. Both the hiring agency and the central personnel office, if there is one, attempt to make up the examination in harmony with their own ideas. They often disagree on what will indicate future efficiency in the offices, what type of interrogations will reveal the character of the candidate, what type of character is most desirable, and how much reliance should be placed on the oral interview.

Written examinations have the merit that they may be made part of the public or government record, so that any interested person may try to discover what motives intruded into the examination from political, official, or other sources. The oral examination, although no doubt it allows some insight into fitness for a position—through the observance of appearance, address, quickness of mind, behavior in tense interpersonal situations—is peculiarly susceptible to the intrusion of personal, political, and cliquish judgments.

3. *Pay scales* require only brief mention here. The great bulk of administrators in most countries are paid salaries of a modest, lower middle-class and middle-income level. Since salary levels in civil serv-

ices are relatively inflexible, the individual administrator is economically best situated when the cost of living is constant or declining and most poorly situated when an inflation is occurring. It is frequently believed that his level of pay greatly influences the behavior of the bureaucrat, but this is not entirely true. Pay has been constantly exaggerated as a determinant of moral and prestige, as a number of studies have shown in the past two decades. While it is true that a laborer's income or a millionaire's income would distort the class position of the bureaucracy, such incomes are rare in civil service systems. And in the great belt of income levels between the rich and the poor, the pay level has little to do with the efficiency, morale, or prestige of employees.

4. *Security* and *promotion* are much more important than salary in determining the general atmosphere of public employment. To the extent that public employment is secure, the public service tends almost to become a class by itself. For, in a secure public service many conditions of employment remain stable over a long period of time and tend to produce a similar stability in standards of behavior and attitudes toward life. This situation contrasts with the relatively free condition of private employment, where a wide variety of chances to change one's social character present themselves. The opportunities for acquiring a crystallized character-type are more present in government: over a generation, the employee can look out the same window on life. Furthermore, with security, work activity adjusts to a regular pace. A routine is established that becomes venerable, sometimes sacred. Those who expect to be promoted think to do something new, but newness is not highly valued. Better to try doing the old things well. And, those who have been in an office a long time are often best at doing the old tasks without complaint. So the seniority principle, seeded, it is true, by the nature of the *pater familias* and the accumulated wisdom of aging, bursts into flower in the formal hothouse of the office. While the principle of merit, espoused by the fanatics of efficiency, restrains the principle of political preference, the principle of seniority calmly prevails in the administrative kingdom.

Now it would be ridiculous to evaluate public administration by a lofty standard while praising private administration according to a modest one. Many private companies promote by seniority or by nepotism; they also promote by mistake. In private business, nepotism is often the stipulated motive for building an enterprise "so that my son shall have something to carry on." Nepotism sometimes occurs in the civil service, but it is intrusive. John Adams once wrote, scandalized, about Thomas Hutchinson's many relatives on the payroll of the government of Massachusetts. The federal government, and many city and state governments in America evidence nepotism. But the oppor-

tunities for material advancement in America are so many as to make
nepotism a relatively minor problem.

PROMOTION BY MERIT NO SIMPLE MATTER

In addition to promoting employees by seniority and nepotism, both private and public business often promote by mistake. We
mean the belief that a "merit promotion" is being made does not
guarantee the fact. Utilizing the best known techniques and the best
available judgment in the selection of leaders is not sufficient to take
the element of risk from promotions; it can be said without fear of
denial that, with the efficiency idea in mind, seniority, nepotism, and
party affiliation are *not* adequate criteria for promoting. From this
point, we wander into a wilderness of criteria that are sometimes valid,
sometimes dangerous, for deciding on the qualities that earn a man his
promotion.

Research on criteria for promotion is presently being conducted in
several quarters. Carroll Shartle, William Henry, Rensis Likert, Angus
Campbell, Dorwin Cartwright, and a number of government and private groups are among those studying the methods of selecting leaders.
The conscientious promoting official has available today much more
in the way of objective evidence on past and potential performance
to guide his promotional decisions than he could find a generation
ago. Furthermore, there seems to be some tendency in a number of
government agencies to utilize such guiding materials.

Still, no student should retain the illusion that promotion is a simple
matter of advancing the man who is putting out the greatest tangible
product (if ever there is a tangible product); or that popularity indicates managerial skill; or that the man with whom a chief can work
well while the man holds one position can continue to work well with
the chief in a higher position, or take the chief's place when the chief
is retired, transferred, or promoted.

PARTISANSHIP AND ADMINISTRATION

Political parties in modern states, and political factions in
other periods of history, often bring their own special interests to bear
on the selection of public officials and the control of the administrative
process. Two main subtypes of motives underlie the general desire to
convert the administration to the will of the party. One is the feeling
that, if politics is to rule administration (an assumption of some important democratic theorists), then the party leaders must have ways

of carrying out their will. This means that they must be able to appoint the chief executive-administrators. An American President does not take office and set out alone to order changes in the administration. If he did, he would be swamped by the task of ordering hundreds of men to do thousands of things. He must have the power to appoint his partisans to the chief administrative posts. The limit to the number of appointments can be found empirically: it is that number of appointments that can maximize his control. It may be ten in a highly integrated, centralized administrative system with a habit of discipline. It may be hundreds in an unintegrated, decentralized administration. The most efficient number is the number that satisfies the case; then the chief executive can infuse his own policies throughout the hierarchical pyramid.

A second submotive of partisanship in administration is to seize a large number of positions and to convert them to political warfare. This is the well-known Jacksonian idea. It is sometimes rationalized by the first submotive; that is, men who want to take over civil service posts for the perquisites of the posts and in order to finance and man the party machine justify their position by saying that even the lowliest of civil service employees is an "executive," in our sense of the term, that is, political. But there is no point in wasting time on this argument; it would be pathological to see in every clerkship a saboteur of the Presidency, as pathological as to demand the confiscation of all rock and sand because *some* uranium can be found almost anywhere.

CAN PARTIES DO WITHOUT PATRONAGE?

The use of appointments for political warfare, however, still demands respectful attention, even though it is generally disliked. Political machines must be supported; support comes from money, workers, communication media, and can and has come from government employees. Before one makes the drastic recommendation, in the name of efficiency, that partisanship be eliminated in selecting administrative personnel, he must ask himself this question: Are the remaining sources of party organization strength, that will be enhanced in importance by such elimination, superior in their effects on the political party system? One can readily see that much more than efficiency is at stake here; the various administrative posts are involved in the whole party system. Might the European parties have created more stable governments if they had been based on patronage rather than class? Would the American parties, especially the Democratic, come to be more influenced by the labor unions, if patronage were abandoned? There is evidence to the affirmative on both questions. But the all-important question—*how much* difference does this factor cause—is not known.

In America, following most western European countries, the tendency has been to eliminate the political participation of the vast majority of administrators. The merit systems of the federal government and of various state and local governments have made deep inroads into the patronage system. In an attempt to reconcile efficiency with partisanship, some men have proposed two shifts of administrators, both appointed under a merit system, both partisan, each taking office when its party is in power, the other retired, temporarily, on partial pay. This would take care of the top posts but could not be applied to hundreds of thousands of less important posts. For that problem, some have hesitantly suggested an external solution: to support the political parties outright from public funds. Then they presumably would not be too dependent either on patronage or on special organized groups.

The Customs of Administrative Offices

AGENCIES EXIST FOR THEIR OWN SAKE

As we have just seen, the first intrusive goal of governmental administration is personal and party advancement. The second intrusive goal is the pursuit of customary administration for its own sake.

One might visit the offices of an agency and see how the agency is organized to accomplish its tasks, how it is concerned about the popular response to its regulatory activities, how it consults with its administered population, how its officials are plotting their careers, and yet not sense the organization fully until he had learned something of its special habits, its folklore, its group "personality."

Of course, all organizations differ in function. But what we wish to point out here is that they possess a motive that may be called their own. They exist for their own sake as well as being vehicles for expressing the other motives that have been discussed. A large-scale organization has a "will" to survive and grow very often, and may have its own distinctive habits of work.

STRUGGLE FOR SURVIVAL AND EMPIRE-BUILDING

A certain amount of organizational energy is devoted to competing with other agencies for funds and respect. If an agency is to survive amidst the welter of agencies found on all levels of modern governments, the agency's leaders have to campaign continuously for laws giving it sharper powers and more money. The agency cannot remain isolated; it must establish friendly connections among the politists who are related to it—the top executives, the legislature, the press, public opinion, the people it affects in its daily work (its clientele), and the pressure groups that make demands of it. When cordially regarded by a preponderance of influential persons and groups, the agency can regard its survival as assured. The agency whose functions are subject to bitter dispute faces the possibility of sudden or slow death; and the agency whose actions arouse no controversy may, without the "right" kind of friends, be the first to be sacrificed when the cry for economies is raised.

Many agency executives are empire-builders. Just as politicians strive for mastery of the political party and for control of legislation, agency chiefs measure their own success by the number of new functions they are enabled to undertake, the number of personnel they are allowed to hire, the amount of funds allocated to them each year, and the amount of respect and personal regard that they elicit from politicians and other public officials. Most agencies are difficult to extinguish. Like old soldiers, they never die; they simply fade away. And when the end comes, there are always a few survivors, capable still of sounding the call to arms and proclaiming the benightedness of their enemies.

"OCCUPATIONAL PERSONALITY"

Americans do not have in their minds so sharp a picture of the "bureaucratic personality" as do Europeans. To most Americans, officials seem like caricatures of the efficiency expert or the spoils politician. They imagine an efficient office where all human and material resources are combined ruthlessly towards getting a job done. Or they picture city halls where everyone, from the janitor to the mayor, smokes cigars, uses spitoons, is corpulent, and votes the same ticket. If they are more experienced than most they can remember offices they have seen like the War Production Board that, as one wag put it, looked like the central clearing house of the forty giant corporations. Or they may have heard hair-raising tales of emergency agencies like the Office of War Information where untold energies were spent in empire-building and personal interest maneuvers.

One would have to go to countries like France and Germany for a sharp sense of the bureaucratic personality whose traits come from the intrinsic character of traditional office work. There they meet Monsieur le Bureau, who does not look quite human, or the uniformed Prussian official, who is a social class unto himself and wishes always to make that point quite clear.

It seems that a stable agency, over a long period of time, and especially when buttressed by a social class system, acquires speech, methods of work, and an outlook on the outside world that distinguish it from other political associations. In America, the language of civil servants is called "gobbledygook" by critics; a large number of words, especially concepts, acquire special meanings to insiders; many abbreviations and modes of expression, liberally interspersed with numerals, find their way into the customary documentation and reports of activities, until even legal language seems more intelligible than administrative language.

Work takes on an orderly pace, not to be disturbed by crises of any kind, and reports and carbon copies of reports abound. Every step must be according to regulations; under the looming shadow of the pyramid, one cannot simply step sidewise but must first go up and then come down before one is permitted to step sidewise. There is a strong sense of superordination and subordination; the image of authority is everywhere on the premises. The outside world appears to be anarchic; work coming in from the outside world is regarded as an intrusion, probably unwarranted. Karl Mannheim describes this tendency of stable bureaucracy well:

> Every bureaucracy, therefore, in accord with the peculiar emphasis on its own position, tends to generalize its own experience and to overlook the fact that the realm of administration and of smoothly functioning order represents only a part of the total political reality. Bureaucratic thought does not deny the possibility of the science of politics, but regards it as identical with the science of administration. Thus irrational factors are overlooked, and when these nevertheless force themselves to the fore, they are treated as "routine matters of state." *

AMERICAN BUREAUCRACY NOT RIGID

American experience, unlike the German experience that so impressed Karl Mannheim, has been barren of rigid bureaucracies. American administrative agencies have been too much in flux, too newly organized, too overcast with politics to acquire all the garments of the bureaucratic personality.

Certain American agencies, however, like the Department of State, do exhibit some rigidity. They seem to have wills of their own; they cannot understand political forces; they are peculiarly immune to "efficiency" reorganizations and recruit men of a common stamp. Since the Department of State is a *rara avis* among American agencies, many Americans erroneously explain the evidences of bureaucratic personal-

* Quoted with the permission of Harcourt, Brace and Company, Inc. from Karl Mannheim, *Ideology and Utopia*, translated by Louis Wirth and Edward Shils, 1936, p. 106.

ity in the agency as a willful conspiracy, a degenerate conservatism, or some other political vice; they do not understand that most of these features, described more accurately, are typical of a matured bureaucracy.

In the Soviet Union there is more consciousness of problems of bureaucratic ingrowth than there is in America. The Soviet Union is far advanced towards being an *administrative* state in which all political problems are treated as administrative problems. Problems only now coming to be of interest to Americans are considered worthy of the intervention of the highest Russian leaders. Stalin himself commented acidly on the situation in which "instead of a leading group of responsible workers, a family group, a closed circle, is formed, the members of which try to live on peaceful terms, not to offend each other, not to wash their dirty linen in public, to eulogize each other, and from time to time to send inane and nauseating reports to the center about their successes."

HOW BUREAUCRATIC PERSONALITY IS BORN

The process by which an organization builds its bureaucratic personality is a circular one—a vicious circle, some would say. The persons who organize an agency usually volunteer to do so: therefore they are likely to have some affinity for the work of the agency. The functional affinity of the organizers for their work will be reinforced by their actual work in establishing the agency and assuring its continuous operation. When called upon to recruit new workers in the agency, they will tend to solicit types somewhat like their own, with the same training and the same interests.

The recruits will, of course, imitate the modal conduct of their superiors and will develop new operations along the lines of traditional patterns. The main characteristics of bureaucratic work—the legalism, careful documentation, slow and sure movement, conscientiousness, fear of politics, and *sacro egoismo*—will develop gradually as work habits affect character, character affects values, values affect recruitment, and recruitment re-enters the circle to reinforce the process anew.

It would be most unscientific to apply this generalized inward-growing motive of agencies as the only criterion for describing public administration, but that it exists, in embryonic or matured form, as one of the major classes of motives determining the character of public administration cannot be denied.

This chapter has sought to outline the various forces operating on public administration, and to show how these forces combine and influence each other. As with all the previous subjects in this work, and with the courts and other general subjects to come, the phenomena of general public administration cannot be rigidly classified as only administrative in character. Our mental categories hold them momentarily, until we have used them; then they run off to combine again under some other meaning, becoming events of concern to court systems, local governments, and other subjects.

Questions and Problems

1. Define "public administration" and explain how its importance to political science has increased in modern times. (Go back to Chapter Two for help in this task.)

2. Distinguish between and give examples of functional goals and instrumental goals in public administration.

3. Using the materials of this chapter and materials found elsewhere in this book, describe and explain the differences between the functional goal of administration in America and in the Soviet Union.

4. By the same process used in question 3, describe and explain the difference in the emphases that American and Soviet Russian administration place on each of the stipulated and intrusive goals of administration.

5. Explain why three goals of administration are called stipulated and two goals intrusive.

6. What are the major ways in which public administration is organized to maximize the productivity and the utilization of resources? (Also use materials from Chapter Eleven for this purpose.)

7. Write to three different agencies in a town or city, a state, and the nation, asking for their organization chart, or, using the library, find three examples of such charts. In what ways do the three charts show general similarities of formal organization and in what ways do they differ?

8. Define and describe the differences between formal and informal organization.

9. From your own experience or by asking friends, describe how a course which has been in the college catalog consistently one way has in fact been taught differently by two different professors. Describe how two club or fraternity presidents, operating under the same rules, behave differently. Do your findings have any significance for the study of formal and informal organization?

10. Describe the sanctions and pressures that produce internal control in a shop or office. Why is there a tendency for the formal sanctions to be less frequently applied than the informal?

11. What are various ways in which the goal of maximum productivity is accompanied by or modified by methods of minimizing the disturbances of carrying out policies?

12. List the fourteen principal forms of administrative action and give an example of each.

13. What procedures may be used to determine whether a program will be accepted or rejected and how much distress it will cause?

14. Define administrative consultation with the administered population and contrast it with "socialist engineering" or psychological engineering.

15. Describe the operation of private or personal motives in public administration.

16. Describe the operation of party or partisan motives in public administration.

17. How are private goals in public administration tamed and adjusted to the productivity goal? To the customs of administrative offices?

18. How does the partisan goal operate in public administration to affect the goals of productivity and of personal advancement?

19. What causes agencies to exist for their own sake? Describe an imaginary office where the predominant motive operating is the endeavor to maximize the customs of the agency.

20. Most universities today have a considerable number of administrative employees who direct student life, manage university property and finances, and prepare the curriculum. Obtain from upperclassmen or others any examples they can give of the five goals operating within the university administration and report them in 300 words.

Longer Study and Research
Problems Suitable for Term Papers

1. Write a *critical* ten-page book review on one of the following works, with special reference to what they have to say about public administration:
H. G. Wells: *The Shape of Things to Come*
Edward Bellamy: *Looking Backward, 2000–1887*
Aldous Huxley: *Brave New World*
Franz Kafka: *The Castle*
George Orwell: *1984*
Honoré de Balzac: *Bureaucracy: or a Civil Service Reformer*

2. Using library materials, write an historical essay on the "Successful Movement for a Merit System Civil Service in the American National Government." If you prefer, substitute England, France, or Germany for the United States.

3. Prepare and write a ten-page article describing the organization of administration in your town, city, or state. Call attention to any features of its administrative organization that depart from the typical features of administration described in this chapter.

4. Interrogate five classmates or other students on what they believe are the four outstanding satisfactions and four outstanding dissatisfactions of employment by a federal agency. Then interview two federal employees in your area on the same subject. Report all seven interviews, describe what differences exist between the two sets of replies, and state how you explain the differences. (The length should be eight pages of interviews, two of comment.)

13

THE COURTS

A COURT is the seat of judgment on the law. Questions of law come before the court in the form of contests or actions between two private parties or between private parties and the government of which the court forms part. In judging the law, the court decides the fate of the parties with interests at stake in the point of law at issue. This essential function of judging the law has not always been consigned to the kind of court that we know today. Legislatures, executives, and administrators have often declared that a particular act of a person was an offense and decreed punishment against the offender. But the law of a society has more frequently conceded this function to the specialized bodies that we call courts, and it is with these courts that this chapter is concerned.

As specialized parts of the apparatus of the state, the courts have usually acquired procedures and methods of thought distinguishing them from other political institutions. And their essential function of judgment, of course, always has an important influence on the political structure of a society. Sometimes the courts of a society have grown into the most powerful institutions, overshadowing other political institutions and making the juridical method of solving political disputes the characteristic mode of the culture. This chapter will call attention to several kinds of court systems, discuss the occasional triumph of courts over the other branches of the government as illustrated in the American doctrine of judicial review, and explain the ways in which courts carry out the judicial process.

The Rise and Power of Court Systems

SELF-HELP IN LAW ENFORCEMENT

In an earlier chapter on law and constitutionalism, law was defined, its sanctions were described, and various classes of law were presented. One should know that in many primitive communities the enforcement of "law" was and is left to individuals. Self-help—"taking the law into one's own hands"—was the way justice was enforced. But in complex communities self-help is outmoded.

However, there are still three areas of life in which self-help is a lawful method of carrying out the "law." In international affairs, nations have accepted no superior authority that brings alleged offenders to trial and punishment. The United Nations machinery operates with some effect, but it has not produced a world legal order. Self-help is also authorized, although to a diminishing extent, in the field of labor relations: a union or an employer may institute economic reprisals such as strikes or lockouts for breaches of agreement or to establish a more powerful position with relation to the other party. And in the area of individual relations, one may administer the "law" himself in several ways. He may resort to force in self-defense; he may protect his property, personal or real, by force. He may pursue a thief and inflict on him whatever damage may be reasonable in order to recapture his possessions.

DEVELOPMENT OF ROMAN AND ENGLISH LAW SYSTEMS

For the most part, however, in any complex social order that is not in the throes of revolution, the administration of justice has been consigned to special organs of the government. The study of the historical development of these special courts for the interpretation of the law is a fascinating phase of political science. They existed in the ancient Near East, in Greece, and elsewhere.

Two systems of law, the Roman and the English, have so greatly influenced the modern state that they deserve special mention. The Roman law developed over a thousand years; it provided the basis for canon or church law; it also strongly influenced the secular medieval law; and it was used by the early modern monarchies of western Europe to give a uniform law to their many local provinces. Ultimately, as reframed by French jurists into the Code Napoleon, Roman law came to form the core of legal systems in much of Europe, in South and Central America, and in many colonial areas of the world. We shall call those legal systems springing in large part from Roman jurisprudence "Roman law" systems.

The English system of law was able to develop continuously from native and Teutonic origins, despite periodic attempts to establish the Roman law in England. The English juridical system has provided basis for the administration of justice in the United States and in the English-speaking countries abroad.

ROMAN LAW MORE SYSTEMATIC

It is generally true that the Roman law is systematic, the English law unsystematic; the former is usually codified according to consistent and logical categories, whereas English law is a loose body of principles that are brought up individually in the solution of a single case. The English law has been identified particularly with the common law and with precedents established by the various courts; the Roman law has been developed to a far greater extent by scholars and legislators.

The use of precedent—the court's ruling in the last case that most closely resembles the case at issue—tends to *determine* the judgment of courts of the English type while it tends only to *influence* the judgment of a court of the Roman type. Judges in the English systems are recruited from lawyers; they are not specially trained to be judges, as in the Roman system.

Courts of the English type give considerable privileges to the legal parties and in that way are less controlled by the judges than are the Roman law courts. (American courts are even more loosely managed than most of the courts of the English type.) While the student preparing for the English type of court gains most of his knowledge from law cases of the past, the student who aims to practice before Roman law courts concentrates more on codes, statutes, philosophy, and logic.

ENGLISH-TYPE COURTS MORE HOSTILE TO LEGISLATION

Some writers have exclaimed that the English law is barbaric, one step beyond the principle of self-help, while other writers have accused the Roman law of being the perfect tool of despotism, since it is so coldly logical and all-embracing. Both groups grossly exaggerate the grain of truth that may be involved in their own view. Although the Roman law, like the common law, claims to rest on the "will of the people," it is much more like a positive enactment, and jurists of Roman law countries are not likely to be so antagonistic to the work of the executive and legislative departments. Judges everywhere are in large measure conservative, whether they are in Roman or English courts; the different legal systems cause them to defend their conservatism with different philosophies and arguments.

The English type of court, especially in America, was independent for so long and came to rely so completely on a massive body of case precedents, that it was hostile to the legislative process. New statutes, it felt, could hardly improve the accumulated wisdom of the ages as embodied in thousands of cases judged by learned men. "Almost," writes Herman Finer, "the Common Law was born to resist; in the U. S. A. it was deliberately set above the Congress and Executive to resist; it still resists. That is precisely why it now meets with the favour of the groups who wish to be defended from the hand of the government." *

The-use of juries to determine the facts of a case in a civil suit or criminal prosecution is found more generally in the English type of court than in the courts descended from Roman law. The grand jury, for bringing indictments that force cases to trial, is found in both English and Roman law countries. Figure 34 describes how effective a grand jury can be.

These general differences just cited can be traced through many procedures and substantive statements of rights and duties. Perhaps the greatest hold that either system has on its supporters is that they are accustomed to it. Personalities and interests have grown adjusted to procedures and dogmas, advantageous or not from some other point of view, and both would be upset by attempts to graft other systems onto them.

ROMAN AND TEUTONIC LAW SIDE BY SIDE FOR CENTURIES

Sometimes custom has established two types of law. For example, in the period following the barbarian invasions, tribal law was applied to the Germans, Roman law to the original inhabitants. Early German monarchs caused both the barbarian law and the Roman law to be drawn up, crudely, of course, until the great Code of Justinian was made generally available in the eleventh and twelfth centuries. The kings did this to prevent tribal law from being submerged into the Roman law and to prevent the knowledge of Roman law from disappearing. Courts existed in large numbers but means of enforcing their decisions was often wanting. A gentleman of the Middle Ages might become involved in Manorial Courts, Borough Courts, Pie-Powder Courts (commercial law), the Court Christian (canon or church law) or the King's Court. Roman Law was gradually introduced into the King's Court by the king's jurists and judges in preference to the customary law, as a means of systematizing and making secure the royal territorial jurisdiction. The Roman law, with its emphasis on the abstract rights of jurisdiction, the "imperial right," proved to be effective in squeezing out the elements in Teutonic tribal law that made jurisdiction personal, that is, each man being subject only to his tribal or provincial law, no matter where he happened to be.

* *The Theory and Practice of Modern Government* (New York: Dial Press, 1934), p. 106.

FIGURE 34
ARE GRAND JURIES USEFUL? *

Thurman W. Arnold, Assistant Attorney-General in charge of anti-trust enforcement, had just testified that there were evidences of price increases, artificial shortages, and foreign control in certain industries producing vital war materials. He declared that he wished to call four grand juries in New York, Chicago, Detroit, and Los Angeles. The exchange of remarks reprinted below occurred, and Mr. Arnold declared, at the end of this excerpt, that innocent men's reputations are preserved by the secrecy of the grand-jury method.

with the special duty of investigating restraints of trade in the production of war materials.

The CHAIRMAN. Is the grand jury an effective instrument, still, for investigations of this kind?

Mr. ARNOLD. I think that all you need to stop artificial price increases or restrictions of production is to empanel a grand jury, provided the defendants have a guilty conscience.

The CHAIRMAN. What is the composition of the ordinary grand jury?

Mr. ARNOLD. The ordinary grand jury varies, but on the whole it is a very intelligent body. The grand jury in New York on war materials had as its members executives of insurance companies, executives of mercantile establishments, businessmen of high standing and high intelligence.

The CHAIRMAN. In other words, these indictments were not found by juries the members of which might be regarded as prejudiced in advance?

Mr. ARNOLD. I am glad you brought that out, Senator, because grand juries in this country are one of our most effective and intelligent instruments in law enforcement. They take a great deal of pride in the work. It is a duty which can be undertaken, since they only sit a couple of hours a day, while we prepare the evidence. Jury duty can be undertaken without a man dropping his business. We find intelligent, high-grade citizens, skilled in business problems, willing to sit on them. Of course, they are selected differently in different parts of the country, they are not all of the high order that we get, for instance, in New York and San Francisco, but in general, I wish to pay a tribute to the intelligence and interest of our grand juries.

The CHAIRMAN. Would it be possible to suggest that—I mean with any factual basis—the problems which are presented in modern industry under the Antitrust Law are of such a complex nature, such a technical nature, that an ordinary grand jury couldn't understand those problems?

Mr. ARNOLD. I don't think they are too complex at all, Senator. Let's take the charges in the magnesium indictment. There we allege a contract to restrict production. A man simply needs the intelligence to have a business set-up explained to him, and the problem is really very simple. The evidence is ordinarily circumstantial; sometimes we have direct evidence. It is voluminous, but the problems are not at all difficult.

The CHAIRMAN. In other words, the central question is whether or not there is a combination or an agreement to restrict production or raise prices?

Mr. ARNOLD. That is all.

The CHAIRMAN. And any intelligent person can pass on that.

Mr. ARNOLD. Anyone.

Representative WILLIAMS. Well, after all, the effective part of it results from the efficiency in which the investigation has been made and the manner in which it has been presented to the grand jury.

Mr. ARNOLD. Yes; that is true, and yet it also rests on the grand jury itself if the grand jury becomes interested, asks questions. Another effective thing about the grand jury is that it is secret. Therefore, a man whom we suspect of price-fixing or of restrictive practice

We see here illustrated the uses of the congressional hearing, which is a source of information on many subjects. We can see how legislators work and how facts and values are brought together in arriving at public policy.

* A page from hearings before the Temporary National Economic Committee, Feb. 12, 1941, "Investigation of Concentration of Economic Power," Sen. Doc. 35, 77th Cong., 1st Sess., p. 105.

NEITHER SYSTEM IDENTIFIED WITH "LIBERTY"

What can be said in brief about the political effects of the two major legal systems, the Roman and the English? Both systems have developed in touch with each other for many centuries; both have changed considerably over the centuries; both have been employed in governments that might be called despotic or individualistic. While it is true that liberal America has used the English system, liberal Switzerland, Holland, Belgium, and Scandinavia have used the Roman system. Neither the English nor the Roman law could rescue prisoners from the Tower of London or the Bastille. One cannot subscribe to a glib division that would identify tyranny or liberty with a great legal system. The administration of justice, like the other general subjects of political science, is subjected to a great many social and political influences; none of these influences can be singled out as absolutely decisive. The two principal systems have undergone great change; they have greatly influenced each other; and they have been so much a prey to the whole political process, that distinctions between them with reference to such broad subjects as tyranny and liberty can hardly be made.

THE GROWTH OF JUDICIAL INDEPENDENCE

The tradition of independent and powerful judges is ancient. Certainly the Greeks and Romans had well-developed views on the subject of the impartiality of judges. The *praetors* and the senate of Rome were for several generations perhaps as systematic and impartial as the foremost judges that the world has known since. The Middle Ages did not lose the ideal of the integrity of justice, and, certainly, it was to some of the late medieval kings that modern times owes the beginning of a tradition of judicial impartiality. For these monarchs, bent upon tightening their controls over the local nobility and towns, called in many jurists to consolidate and expand the royal law. Central courts developed in France, in England, and elsewhere; they removed cases from local and inferior tribunals "on writ of error," and they heard cases over an increasing area of the law, passing judgment on them according to a new version of the law common to the whole realm.

ENGLISH COURTS AND THE SEPARATION OF POWERS

In England, the strength of the courts did not cease to grow when the king became unchallenged master of his realm. The King's

Bench, the highest English central court, came, under Edward Coke
in the early seventeenth century, to claim independence of the king
himself, and of the Parliament as well. Coke declared that the king
was under the law. He also said that the common law, as declared by
the courts, often "will control acts of Parliament." Here were strong
beginnings of the theory of the separation of powers and of an independent judiciary.

When Montesquieu wrote of English government in the mid-eight-
eenth century, he emphasized that the judiciary in England was independent of the Crown and of Parliament, and urged the emulation of
this example upon the continent. Principally because the age of liberalism and middle-class government was near at hand, and, not because
Montesquieu urged the separation, European courts did acquire in the
nineteenth century a considerable degree of independence of the executive and Parliament. Indefinite tenure upon good behavior came to
be the common condition of appointment to judgeships.

ENGLISH COURT SYSTEM

At the top of the court hierarchy in England today, one
finds the House of Lords, which hears some of the most important
cases on appeal and a few special classes of cases as a court of original
jursidiction. Its judicial functions, one hastens to add, are not performed by the whole motley body of its members, but by a small,
select group of judges who are appointed to the House to act in this
capacity.

The cases heard by the Lords on appeal come from the Court of
Criminal Appeals and the Court of Appeal for civil cases, which in
turn hear cases appealed from the various divisions of the High Court
of Justice. The High Court of Justice has general jurisdiction over a
great variety of cases. Below it are found many county courts and
justices of the peace.

FRENCH COURT SYSTEM AND THE ADMINISTRATIVE COURTS

The French court system is as independent and impartial
as the English. The French judicial pyramid for criminal cases and
suits involving private parties is formed by the *Cour de Cassation*,
which hears appeals from Courts of Appeals, which in turn hear appeals from the various Tribunals of First Instance. The vast business
of dealing with petty offenses begins and usually ends with the several
thousand justices of the peace.

Unlike the English and American court systems, however, the

French have a separate system of courts for trying civil cases to which the state is a party. A judicial panel of the Council of State is the highest authority on administrative law. It hears appeals of cases on administrative law from a number of *Conseils de préfecture interdéparte-mentaux*—regional councils handling the judicial business of one or more prefectures. The French system of coping with cases involving injuries to citizens by officials is thus simpler and more direct than the American system, which, as was indicated in Chapter Twelve, is scarcely a system at all. It is, rather, a network of special jurisdictions among a large number of agencies; and any court of general jurisdiction may decide cases on administrative law.

APPOINTMENT AND ELECTION OF JUDGES IN AMERICA

American governments provided both extremes of independence in the judiciary. More than any other country, the judiciary was separated from the other branches of the government. This independence was written into all the constitutions. Moreover, the courts were empowered (partly, it is true, through their own efforts) to pass judgment on whether the acts of executives or legislatures were in accord with the constitutions. This was the power of judicial review.

A second current of politics, reaching peak strength a little later than the movement toward judicial review, brought most state court justices to the bar of popular election, so that although the justices could be independent of the executive and legislature, they had to pay attention to the shifting trends of public opinion. As the political party, with its control over masses of voters, developed, judges came to occupy places on party lists, just like other candidates for public offices. The courts came to be influenced by almost the same political considerations as other branches of government, although the tradition of "impartial justice" and the greater degree of professional organization among lawyers reduced somewhat the extent to which courts responded to political pressures and issues.

Judicial Review and the American Courts

JUDICIAL REVIEW NOT A RADICAL STEP

Since American judges, whether elected or appointed with indefinite tenure, were given or allowed the right to strike down contested legislation if they deemed it unconstitutional, they became involved in political controversy continuously. There are some who believe that American courts were never meant to have this right of judicial review of legislation, but most historians of the early republic are agreed that the right was so close to acknowledgement that the final "seizure" of power was no more daring than a man's leap into the water when he is pushed from the diving board.

MARBURY V. MADISON

The immediate occasion for the leap was the case of *Marbury v. Madison*. This case is the cornerstone of the so-called judicial supremacy principle. By the right conferred on them as a result of the case, subsequent Supreme Court Justices have declared about *a hundred federal laws* and *many more state laws* (some 200 between 1865 and 1935 alone) void because they violated principles set forth in the federal Constitution.

The facts of the case are somewhat amusing. When the Federalists under Adams were defeated in the election of 1800 by Jefferson's party, they tried at the last minute to place some of their followers in the judicial branch of the government. They passed an act reorganizing and enlarging the judiciary and appointed a number of Federalists to the new positions. John Marshall had been Secretary of State under Adams and had just been appointed Chief Justice of the Supreme Court. In the confusion of changing offices and presidential administrations, he failed to deliver the commissions of these new judicial appointees to the persons designated. When Jefferson became President on March 4, 1801, he told Madison, who became his Secretary of State, not to deliver the commissions.

William Marbury, who had been one of those to be appointed, brought an action in the Supreme Court for a *mandamus*, a court order directing Madison to give Marbury his commission. The immediate issue was not important, for the new Jeffersonian Congress repealed the Federalist Judiciary Act of 1801, and that meant that Marbury, even if he had won his case, would not be able to serve very long in his post. But the indirect effect of the case was of transcendent importance.

Marshall, speaking for the Court, declared that Marbury was entitled to his commission and that Madison had no right to withhold it. But thereupon Marshall discomfited his friends and wrote the whole Federalist opinion of the judicial power into law. He did this double trick by declaring that the Supreme Court had no right to force Madison to deliver to Marbury his commission, for, he said, the original jurisdiction of the Supreme Court is stated in the Constitution. Congress cannot add to that original jurisdiction. Therefore, the provision of the Judiciary Act of 1789, which had tried to place additional original jurisdiction in the Supreme Court to issue writs of mandamus was a violation of the Constitution and consequently invalid.

The whole incident was complicated. First of all, some men claim on the basis of historical research that the clause in the Judiciary Act did *not* attempt to expand the original jurisdiction of the Supreme Court. Secondly, even if it did try to do so, the clause might be upheld because the Constitution did not state explicitly that the Supreme Court shall have original jurisdiction in certain stated cases and in *no other* cases. The Constitution might have been read to state that "in at least the following cases," the Supreme Court shall have original jurisdiction.

On the other hand, colonial customs, debates in the Convention, the practice of the state courts, and the opinions of many leading thinkers of the time all indicate that the doctrine of judicial review of the constitutionality of statutes was generally held and considered right. It is probably true, then, that the courts were supposed to have the power to declare laws unconstitutional if the laws were found to violate the Constitution. So Marshall was able to state that the courts in exercising their judicial powers were duty-bound, by oath of the Constitution, to enforce only those statutes passed by Congress that were in harmony with the Constitution. Statutes must conform to the Constitution, which is the supreme law. Statutes deemed by the courts not to conform to the Constitution are not law and cannot be enforced. Very soon thereafter the Supreme Court also assumed the right to declare unconstitutional state laws that it believed to be inconsistent with the federal Constitution.

CONFLICT OVER THE DECISION

Great excitement arose over *Marbury v. Madison* and similar "usurpations" of political power by the American courts. The situation might have been dangerous to civil peace if the issue could have been driven home to the mass of Jeffersonians. But the fact that the Federalist, Marbury, had been denied his commission was a tangible victory, and often a tangible gain, no matter how slight, will nullify a great but abstract loss. Some important issues would have turned out differently in history if the Supreme Court had not taken upon itself this power to declare laws of Congress unconstitutional.

It is true that Justice Oliver Wendell Holmes wrote once: "I do not think the United States would come to an end if we lost our power to declare an act of Congress void. I do not think the union would be imperiled if we could not make that declaration as to the laws of the several states." Yet this Olympian view would, if pursued to its ultimate, reduce a great many historical events to trivial importance. Passing judgments on the "importance" of events is an intense value itself. Certainly the statement, "Life is of no importance," is hotly contestable. While one may agree with Justice Holmes that the existence of the United States and the Union are desirable, one may also be quite concerned about the kind of United States and the kind of Union that exist.

THE RESULTS OF JUDICIAL REVIEW CONSIDERABLE

Taking an "if" position, if judicial review had been absent, the following social conditions might have resulted. The states would probably be much more active in social and economic spheres (adverse court decisions voided much state legislation aimed at regulating labor, commerce, and industry). The states would differ from each other much more than they do (extremes of economic regulation and civil rights legislation have been tempered by court decisions). The national government would be much closer today to owning, operating, and regulating many industries (railroads, mines, warehouses, shipping, airlines, grain elevators, lumbering, food processing, and other industries have been regulated and, in a few instances, owned and operated by the national government, but the Supreme Court has caused the government to make such moves with caution and deference to private enterprise). The national government would be doing by itself many things that now are accomplished in co-operation with the states (co-operation, especially through grants-in-aid, has come about partly because of fear, warranted or unwarranted, of the Supreme Court).

The executive branch of the government and the administrative agencies would be stronger and more free to do many things in the name of efficiency (for example, adverse decisions of courts on measures to control business and commerce have often compelled roundabout administrative procedures to gain such control). The legislature would be more attuned to the major currents of public opinion on economic legislation, civil rights, and other matters (the Supreme Court has sometimes tempered the quickness of legislative response to popular moods). The legal profession would not have been so universal a feature of American politics, legislation, and administration (the prestige and power of the high courts have flowed over into social life generally). Many other historical alterations might have occurred if the doctrine of judicial review had not been the law of the land.

In short, the supreme courts of the states and nation have used their power to review legislation to form a great institutional blockade. Everything that passes through has been changed to some degree.

By-passing the barrier has required shifts in administrative and political organization. And many strong and radical ideas have disappeared because of the blockade, or at least they have been modified and their attainment delayed.

THE FEDERAL COURT SYSTEM BASED ON CONSTITUTION

The whole court system of the federal government arises from the constitutional clause that provides: "The judicial power of the United States shall be vested in one Supreme Court and in such inferior courts as the Congress may from time to time ordain and establish. The judges of both the Supreme and inferior courts shall hold their offices during good behavior and shall, at stated times, receive for their services a compensation which shall not be diminished during their continuance in office."

The Constitution makes no provision as to the number of judges, the amounts of their salaries, or the terms or sessions of the courts. All of these matters were left to the discretion of Congress. Only tradition may prevent Congress from making the Court one of five members, seven members, nine members, eleven or fifteen members— that is, whatever Congress thinks fitting.

The basic statutory definition of the federal court system has come down from the famous Judiciary Act of 1789. This act set up and organized the Supreme Court, providing a chief justice and five associate justices. Today there are nine justices. The act also set up inferior courts, there were three circuit courts and thirteen district courts, and the act defined the respective jurisdictions of these courts. Today, the three types of constitutional courts still exist—the Supreme Court, the Circuit Court of Appeals (now eleven in number with three to seven judges for each circuit), and the District Courts of the United States, which are today the principal courts for the first trial of cases arising under the national Constitution, statutes, and treaties.

The district courts dispose of about 100,000 cases a year, of which some 95 per cent are settled without appeal to the Circuit Court of Appeals or the Supreme Court. There are eighty-five judicial districts, each containing one or more judges who hold court separately. In addition, each district possesses several federal officers who work closely with the court—the United States District Attorney, the United States Marshal, a clerk of the district court, and a United States Commissioner. Thus far, all judges and judicial officers have been appointed by the President with the advice and consent of the Senate. It would be possible, however, if the Congress thought it desirable, to vest the appointment of the justices of inferior courts in the Supreme Court.

INDEPENDENT STATE COURT SYSTEMS

Each of the forty-eight states has its own scheme of courts, organized under the state constitution and statutes. State courts range from justices of the peace and municipal courts up to supreme courts. Only a few judges throughout the state systems are not subject to popular election. Between the national and the state courts, separate and autonomous as they are, a considerable overlapping of jurisdiction exists. Some cases may be introduced originally either in state courts or in federal courts. The fact that a case is initiated in a state court originally does not mean that the party to the suit may not have the case transferred from a state court to a parallel or higher federal court if a constitutional or a federal issue is involved.

FEDERAL COURTS SIT IN EQUITY

The federal courts, in addition to interpreting the federal statutes and the Constitution, and besides deciding questions of admiralty and maritime law and international law, can sit as courts in equity; that is, operating without juries, they can give extraordinary aid, usually through *injunction* proceedings, to *prevent* certain wrongs from being done that could not be remedied by ordinary court action *following* the wrong.

THE COMMON LAW

The vast bulk of *common law* in America belongs, since 1938, solely to the states. From 1842 to 1938, the national courts tried to build up a body of common law that would be universally applied in the federal courts in all the states—a sort of federal common law. The decision of *Erie Railroad Company v. Tompkins* reversed this development, and the federal court now applies the common law of the state in which a case is being adjudicated.

The Judicial Process

JUDICIAL PROCESS AND CONSTITUTIONALISM

Wherever there are courts there is a judicial process, for the judicial process is simply a name for the procedures that are observed when any given court system hears and judges the cases before it. However, one country's judicial process may be quite different from another's. The way the judiciary operates in any given country is the most accurate index that we have of the state of constitutionalism in the country. The judicial process is determined by the basic conditions that determine constitutionalism; these conditions, as we know from earlier study in Chapter Nine, consist of such matters as the degree to which the written constitution is actually observed, the degree to which political power and wealth are not monopolized, the extent to which the civilian power controls the armies, and so on. We certainly know something of the court system of a country, therefore, when we know the extent to which it maintains a constitutional order; conversely if we know only the judicial system of a country we can judge the degree of constitutionalism of that country.

The judicial process itself, like the party system or the legislatures or many other institutions we study in political science, is both an effect and *a cause*. Changes directly introduced into the judicial process affect the constitutional order sooner or later. How much of an effect such changes may have, of course, depends on the particular change. For example, the appointment of a single judge who decides cases on partisan and prejudiced grounds will have much less effect on the judicial process, and thence on the constitutional order, than the general abolition of the right of a defendant in a criminal case to have a lawyer in his defense.

THE IMPORTANT ELEMENTS OF JUDICIAL PROCESS

Viewing the judicial process, therefore, as both cause and effect in relation to the larger constitutional order, we are interested in several components in the process that vary with different conditions, and, by so varying, are important both to the court system and to the larger problem of constitutionalism. These components are the importance of the case and the courts under consideration, the rights available to parties in the judicial process generally, the social and political pressures operating on the courts, the selection and personality of the judges, the kind of judicial argument used, and the degree to which there is belief in judicial neutrality and objectivity.

WIDE VARIETY OF PROCEDURES AMONG VARIOUS LEVELS OF COURTS

We may consider first, then, the effect which the importance of cases and courts has on judicial process. Litigation is heavy and the courts are diversified in the complex communities of today. Dr.

Albert Lepawsky estimated that in 1931 the metropolitan area of
Chicago, with somewhat less than five million inhabitants, presented
the court system with some 738,000 cases. Five hundred and fifty-six
courts shared this load of work (see Figure 35). The materials for
adjudication ranged from prosecutions for speeding to grave questions
of the constitutionality of legislation.

The judicial process employed by a justice of the peace in a case of
speeding cannot well be compared with the judicial process of a federal
district court in its formality. *Granted a constitutional order*, such as
exists in America, as the court is higher in the judicial hierarchy and as

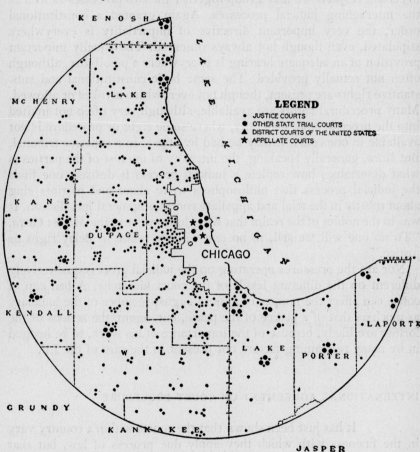

FIGURE 35

THE JUDICIAL SYSTEM OF METROPOLITAN CHICAGO *

LEGEND

● JUSTICE COURTS
● OTHER STATE TRIAL COURTS
▲ DISTRICT COURTS OF THE UNITED STATES
★ APPELLATE COURTS

* Reproduced with permission from Albert Lepawsky: *The Judicial System of Metropolitan Chicago* (Chicago: University of Chicago Press, 1932), p. iv.

the cases coming before it involve important economic and social interests, the various and numerous elements of judicial process that are *formal* become more pronounced and evident. The importance of the law at issue and the anxious and powerful interests of the litigants combine to squeeze out any apparent intrusion of arbitrary, hasty, and partisan elements.

CERTAIN RIGHTS PRESENT GENERALLY

The judicial process available on the premises of a justice of the peace, many disconsolate victims of speed traps will assure you, is a far cry from that available in the marble halls of a high court. However, in certain respects we may group together the two processes as well as the intervening judicial processes. Again granted a constitutional order, the very important directive of impartiality is everywhere stipulated, even though not always observed. The equally important provision of an adequate hearing is everywhere a possibility, although often not actually provided. The same basic constitutional and substantive rights are present, though not everywhere invoked or allowed. Many procedural rights are available, although very often not invited into the process. And, generally, where some right or procedure is not available in one court, it may be had by appeal to a superior tribunal. But since, generally speaking, the intensity of interest of the parties is what determines how replete a judicial process is desired, one finds the judicial process that philosophers write about and patriots sing about mostly in the trial and appellate courts of general jurisdiction. It was to the nobles of the realm that King John swore in the *Magna Carta*, "To no one will we sell, to no one will we refuse or delay right or justice."

Nor are the pressures operating on the judicial process qualitatively different on the different levels of the court hierarchy. A bad cup of coffee can affect the temper of a more august member of the judiciary as much as that of a justice of the peace, but, again, the actions of the former are likely, because of the importance of his work, to be hedged in by many restraining factors not present in the case of the J.P.

INTERNATIONAL AGREEMENT ON COURT PROCEDURE

It has just been shown that the courts within a country vary in the fineness with which they apply due process of law, but that certain rights may be universally stipulated within a nation like the United States. Comparing the court systems of different nations also reveals differences in court procedures, and, one should note, even where two nations have similar court procedures that the two court systems may not possess the same independence and impartiality. Independence and impartiality are much more connected with the degree of constitutionalism in a country than they are with the written rules of procedure.

How nations can agree on what constitutes a fair trial may be shown by examining a trial conducted jointly by several nations. An example was the famous Nuremberg trial of Nazi leaders after World War II. The Charter of the International Military Tribunal for the trial was drawn by representatives of the United States, Great Britain, France, and the Soviet Union.

We are not concerned here with one part of the Charter, namely the statement of the "laws" that were alleged to exist and to have been violated. Whether they were "laws," of course, was the crux of the debate over the larger question of having the trial at all. Those who supported the trials held that the "laws" were widely known when the alleged criminal acts were performed. Others held that the "laws" were coined for the purposes of the trial and were not ethical directives enforced by a body of officials before the time of the alleged violation.

When we turn from this highly important debate to the matter of interest here, that is, the agreement on how a court should conduct a trial, we find a surprising conformity among the different national law systems. The system of procedures outlined for the guidance of the tribunal was not strikingly different from ordinary court procedure in America. It is worthwhile to quote Articles 16 and 24 in entirety.

IV. Fair Trial for Defendants

Article 16. In order to ensure fair trial for the defendants, the following procedure shall be followed:

(a) The Indictment shall include full particulars specifying in detail the charges against the defendants. A copy of the Indictment and of all the documents lodged with the Indictment, translated into a language which he understands, shall be furnished to the defendant at a reasonable time before the Trial.

(b) During any preliminary examination or trial of a defendant he shall have the right to give any explanation relevant to the charges made against him.

(c) A preliminary examination of a defendant and his trial shall be conducted in, or translated into, a language which the defendant understands.

(d) A defendant shall have the right to conduct his own defense before the Tribunal or to have the assistance of counsel.

(e) A defendent shall have the right through himself or through his counsel to present evidence at the Trial in support of his defense, and to cross-examine any witness called by the Prosecution.

V. Powers of the Tribunal and Conduct of the Trial

. . .

Article 24. The proceedings at the Trial shall take the following course:

(a) The Indictment shall be read in court.

(b) The Tribunal shall ask each defendant whether he pleads "guilty" or "not guilty."

(c) The Prosecution shall make an opening statement.

(d) The Tribunal shall ask the Prosecution and the Defense what evidence (if any) they wish to submit to the Tribunal, and the Tribunal shall rule upon the admissibility of any such evidence.

(e) The witnesses for the Prosecution shall be examined and after that the witnesses for the Defense. Thereafter such rebutting evidence as may be held by the Tribunal to be admissible shall be called by either the Prosecution or the Defense.

(f) The Tribunal may put any question to any witness and to any defendant, at any time.

(g) The Prosecution and the Defense shall interrogate and may cross-examine any witnesses and any defendant who gives testimony.

(h) The Defense shall address the Court.

(i) The Prosecution shall address the Court.

(j) Each Defendant may make a statement to the Tribunal.

(k) The Tribunal shall deliver judgment and pronounce sentence.

Justice Robert H. Jackson of the United States Supreme Court, Chief of Counsel of the United States at the trials, explained the importance of the agreements on procedure in a report in 1947. He wrote:

The significance of the charter's procedural provisions is emphasized by the fact that they represent the first tried and successful effort by lawyers from nations having profoundly different legal systems, philosophies, and traditions to amalgamate their ideas of fair procedure so as to permit a joint inquiry of judicial character into criminal charges. . . .

While it obviously was indispensable to provide for an expeditious hearing of the issues, for prevention of all attempts at unreasonable delay and for elimination of every kind of irrelevancy, these necessary measures were balanced by other provisions which assured to the defendants the fundamentals of procedural "due process of law." Although this famous phrase of the American Constitution bears an occasionally unfamiliar implication abroad, the Continental countries joined us in enacting its essence—guaranties securing the defendants every reasonable opportunity to make a full and free defense. Thus the charter gives the defendant the right to counsel, to present evidence, and to cross-examine prosecution witnesses. It requires the indictment to include full particulars specifying the charges in detail—more fully than in our own practice. It gives the defendant the right to make any explanation relevant to the charge against him and to have all proceedings conducted in or translated into his own language.

JUSTICE METED OUT IS INFLUENCED BY SOCIETY

Variations in the historical development of the court systems of the different nations help to account for the differences among those systems. Certainly the history of a particular nation's court system or of particular courts in that system influences the courts' work. A court system or court with a lengthy record of incorruptibility is not likely to become venal overnight, nor is a corrupt court likely to acquire quickly an impartial and competent character. Such extended clinical records, so to speak, remind us that courts are imbedded in a matrix of institutions that forms a culture. The administration of justice is not likely to be an island either of probity or deviltry in a sea of contrary conduct.

Another way of putting this would be to declare that the influence of bribes upon judges would equal roughly over an extended period of time the influence of money upon politicians. A class system that colors the wisdom of politicians and diplomats with tints of class privilege will probably affect similarly the personnel of the bench.

SOCIAL AND POLITICAL PRESSURES

Influences more immediate than a court's tradition and class status sometimes affect the result of litigation. Threats of mob violence and other intense political and personal pressures cannot be shaken off easily by any court system. That such circumstances can bias a court's decision seems to be realized generally; almost all jurisdictions have procedures for transferring cases from one place to another to avoid intimidation, for changing the judges under the same conditions, and for converting the court proceedings from public hearings to closed ones. There are frequent examples of how political pressure can change a decision or relieve its severity. One may think readily of Franklin Roosevelt's proposal to increase the number of justices of the Supreme Court in order to get favorable majorities for his policies on the bench, and of how, without saying so in so many words, the Court adjusted its decisions on several cases to ward off the political assault.

One may recall also the many instances in which, for political reasons, pardons and leniency have been granted convicts, so as not to give cause for unruly demonstrations, or the many circumstances under which the judgments descending upon the rich and well-placed are somewhat less severe than those inflicted upon the poor and unconnected. Nor can the logic of the law or of lawyers on the bench be excepted from that sociology of law that says: every man must watch his actions and thought to see that they are not impeded by his restricted knowledge, his acquaintances, his love of the old ways and hatred of the new.

EFFECT OF MODE OF SELECTION

The mode of selection of judges, their tenure, their pay to a lesser extent—these conditions of the judiciary play a role in determining how the "law" shall be intrepreted. A bench that has been elected by popular vote will tend to reflect opinions that control the public at a given time. The same sensitivity is unlikely to be felt by appointed judges of indefinite tenure; they will certainly reflect opinions that are in a sense political, but they will be the opinions of bygone days, or of certain minorities, or of a certain legal faculty in a university.

PERSONALITY OF JUDGES A FACTOR

The personality structure of judges sometimes adds to the foregoing considerations another problem. Certain judges are known to have reasonable judicial habits except for some distortion in certain spheres. Minnesota lawyers will tell of one judge who is very biased for the defendant in hearing trials involving crimes of passion. Another judge, in Chicago, is most severe towards parties who seek a divorce. One Minneapolis judge will punish reckless drivers severely; another will punish them lightly; the "law" depends on which judge hears the case. Lasswell writes of the involved personal history of a judge who is ever so gentle with women who appear before his court. And Supreme Court Justice Frank Murphy could be expected to decide against any infringement of civil liberties whatsoever.

As Lasswell points out, these anomalies in the judgments of particular men do not always represent a superficial fallacy; their meaning may lie deep in the personality of the judge, not to be rooted out by mere exposure. The compulsive type of personality is not rare among judges and administrators; this is the characterological bent that causes a man to cling to a rigid formula for deciding all human affairs, or to employ one steadfast interpretation of a constitutional phrase in the face of all mitigating circumstances, or to insist on applying the "letter of the law."

A mediating type may also be found among many judges and politicians; this type tends to seek, in arriving at a decision, not "what the law is" but "what would make both parties least unhappy." Or exhibitionists are to be seen on the bench as they are everywhere else: men who like to perform before an audience and monopolize the stage, and who award what they can to the best listeners and the most appreciative claque.

JUDICIAL LOGIC NOT A CLOSED SYSTEM

In the actual process of law, judicial logic itself, then, is modified by the human reactions of the judge, who himself is a part of a historical and cultural environment that operate through him, the court officials, and the clients of the court. Moreover, judicial logic is often frustrated by its own nature. A case before the court, like a social fact of any kind, has many meanings and can be viewed in different ways. Courts do not "solve" a case by putting it in the legal category in which the case naturally fits. They have to force the case to fit into a relatively closed category. Social science and legal logic cannot describe any class of events such as "homicide," "the general welfare," or "interstate commerce," so exactly as to make it possible to neglect the individuality of the case at hand. No real case can be exactly fitted into one of those general categories of which the law is composed.

THE IMPOSSIBILITY OF PURELY "DEDUCTIVE" LAW

The legal mind, working at its best, without the intrusion of any motives but the stipulated motive of impartiality, can only *partially* relate *most* of the essential facts of a given case to the *relevant* meaning of the general principle of law that relates to the case. For example, consider an incident in which the elevator operators of a building, used completely by a firm engaged in interstate commerce, demand recognition of their union under the national labor relations laws. The issue is whether such workers perform tasks that affect interstate commerce. They work entirely within one state. The judge may decide that since their employers engage in interstate commerce, these employees affect interstate commerce or the judge may decide that because they are employed within the state the employees do not affect interstate commerce. Decisions in two similar cases of this general type were contrary and show that the judges were influenced by all the social facts in each case that described the exact situation of the workers' environment. In our example, whichever way the judges decided to move, they would change the meaning of the words "interstate commerce," as those words are given in the Constitution or in the statutes. As it happened, the court broadened the idea of interstate commerce with one decision, hedged it a bit in another, and ended up slightly on the "progressive side." That is, more workers were included under the congressional enactment than before. No logical ingenuity could have deduced exactly the court's conclusion, no matter what the conclusion was, from some general statement of "legal principle."

THE "LAW" AS "PROPHECY"

Conditions like the foregoing, abounding in the judicial profession, have produced a feeling of hopelessness among those who see the law only as stringent logic. Apparently the law does not exist before the case is decided. The fate of the dearest wishes of the contestants before the court cannot possibly be predetermined by logic but is determined by the court's decision. As Justice Holmes once wrote: "The prophecies of what the courts will do in fact, and nothing more pretentious, are what I mean by the law." He goes on to say that "the notion that the only force at work in the development of the law is logic" is fallacious. All the forces that play upon the court system and the judges, then, including the exercise of legal logic, are the law.

Now, if we compare this idea of the law with the more extended definition that we gave earlier in this book (p. 295), we find a difference, and we can best avoid argument by saying that what Justice Holmes is talking about is the "court law." Court law is what the courts will decide. And to predict what the courts will decide is, like every other prediction of social science, difficult, probable at best, and capable of being studied by a number of different techniques, of which only one is the tracing of the habitual logic of jurists in other cases and estimating how that logic will be applied in this case. The "case study method," so popular in American law schools, does not adequately train students for "court law" or in law.

THE FALLACIOUS IDEA OF "NO RULES IN LAW"

A final very important point must be made. To say that so far as the interests immediately affected are concerned, the "law" is only a probable prediction of what the courts will decide may invite another fallacy. Because a number of factors shape the final judgment, and because the law cannot be known before it is declared *does not mean* that there are "no rules to the law" or "no justice in the world." Many people, greatly disillusioned upon encountering for the first time this fact about law (in terms of which all clearheaded lawyers operate), flee from a belief in a mysterious logic of the law to an equally fallacious disbelief in the motives of all courts. They take up positions that court judgments are pure whimsy, or are pure politics, or, as Marx and Engels put it in the *Communist Manifesto*, "Your jurisprudence is but the will of your class made into a law for all." They are quite wrong.

FICTION OF "COURT NEUTRALITY" A BULWARK AGAINST POLITICAL COURTS

The very modesty, the very naiveté of the courts that try not to be and claim not to be political should be accepted as evidence that there is an element in "law" that is not political, an element that is not venal. No court can refrain from making law, if only a little law, but the court that makes only a "little law" is a political institution that is quite distinct from the court that operates as the active supporter of a political regime or the active servitor of rich clients.

The hypocrisy, to put it bluntly, of acting as if a law exists while knowing that it is being made, is one of the most useful inventions of mankind. It has proven historically to be the essential feature in establishing a rule of law and of juridical defense. It has moderated the acts of courts and made them much more than the puppets of political factions. Without this fiction, this enormously useful contradiction, one may wander into the camp of the one time Nazi Commissar for the Reorganization of German Jurisprudence, who declared in a speech before the German jurists:

> The maxim, "Right is whatever profits a nation; wrong is whatever harms it," marked the beginning of our legal work. . . . Pale phantoms of objective justice do not exist for us any more. We have only one aim: to prevent for all the future every subversion of our ideals and every class delusion.

The various communist governments of eastern Europe also hold "pale phantoms" in contempt. In the Soviet Union itself, according to Harold J. Berman, "Party directives may tell judges to 'intensify the struggle against thefts in the factories,' or to make examples of managers who have tampered with the books, or to bear down on some other activity which the Party is seeking to 'liquidate.' In addition, legislation may be enacted without difficulty or delay. As a result, case law loses something of its importance, and historical growth is swamped under by rapid shifts in policy." The courts are expected to reflect the sentiments of the regime on all cases believed by the regime to possess political implications. In one after another of the countries in which the communists assumed control after World War II, People's

Tribunals were set up. These courts were specifically designated as instruments of the revolution and were directed to subordinate the judicial process to the grander purpose of carrying out the laws of the government with the greatest efficiency. Thus could realism— wrenched from its proper moorings in science—batter idealism and crush it, and, in destroying it, undercut judicial independence and objectivity.

The insecure position in which courts are placed by the political struggles of the present is one shared by other institutions, too, as we have noted. Legislatures, parties, pressure groups, and other groupings of the political process are similarly affected by the intensity of politics in a transforming world. Nor do we find stability and surcease from strife and change among local governments, federal systems and the international organizations which we are now about to study. Federalism and international organization, especially, live from hand to mouth, so great is the pressure towards centralization and nationalism in contemporary times.

Questions and Problems

1. What is "self-help" in law enforcement and in what areas of human behavior does it persist?

2. Describe the principal differences between the Roman and English law systems.

3. With the aid of Bouvier's or Black's law dictionary, or an unabridged dictionary or a good encyclopedia, define "civil law," the "Civil Law" (Roman), "common law," "perjury," "grand jury," "indictment," "due process of law," "injunction," and "writ of error."

4. Describe briefly the confluence of law systems in the Middle Ages.

5. What are the essential parts of the modern English court system?

6. Describe briefly the structure of the French court system.

7. How are judges in America selected and what are the consequences to their behavior of the mode of selection?

8. Define judicial review of the constitutionality of legislation. Was it known to Americans before *Marbury v. Madison*?

9. Give the facts and the decision of the court in the case of *Marbury v. Madison*. What were the unusual external aspects of the case and how did they affect the decision and its consequences?

10. What have been the effects of the doctrine of judicial review on American government?

11. Describe briefly the American state and federal court systems.

12. Using library materials or interviews, prepare a 400 word report describing the court system of your state.

13. Summarize the facts and decision of the court in one of the following cases. Use a standard casebook on constitutional law or consult the reports

of the Supreme Court: *Marbury v. Madison*, 1 Cranch 137, 2 L. Ed. 60 (1803), *McCulloch v. Maryland*, 4 Wheat. 316, 4 L. Ed. 579, (1819), *Martin v. Hunter's Lessee*, 1 Wheat. 304, 4 L. Ed. 97, (1816), *Gibbons v. Ogden*, 9 Wheat. 1, 6 L. Ed. 23, (1824), *McGrain v. Daugherty*, 273 U. S. 135 (1927), *Near v. Minnesota*, 283 U. S. 697 (1931), *Principality of Monaco v. Mississippi*, 292 U. S. 313 (1934).

14. What is judicial process and how does it differ from court to court in a country?

15. What did the four nations concerned agree would constitute a fair trial for the defendants at the Nuremberg trial?

16. How does the meaning of court procedures depend upon the presence or absence of constitutionalism?

17. Describe how social and political pressures may affect the judgment of a court.

18. How may the personality of a judge affect his handling of cases before his court?

19. Why is purely deductive law impossible?

20. What is the practical significance of the belief that the "law" exists? Why is the theory that the law is something judges make liable to have serious consequences?

Longer Study and Research
Problems Suitable for Term Papers

1. Using the pertinent cases contained in a standard casebook in constitutional law, qualify and explain the legal meaning of the tenth amendment to the American federal Constitution.

2. Read the report of the Commission on Freedom of the Press entitled *A Free and Responsible Press* and describe the interpretation of the constitutional guarantee of freedom of the press found therein. How does the study reveal the way the meaning of the Constitution changes?

3. Read and review in ten pages one of the following works:

Edward Jenks: *Law and Politics in the Middle Ages*

Henry Maine: *Ancient Law*

Raymond Moley: *Tribunes of the People*

William Seagle: *The Quest for Law*

R. K. Carr: *The Supreme Court and Judicial Review*

W. W. Buckland and A. D. McNair: *Roman Law and the Common Law*

4. Write a fifteen page essay on the subject: "The influence of the doctrine of judicial review on constitutionalism in America." (Use Chapter Nine for your criteria of constitutionalism and a work on judicial review to see how certain cases have affected those criteria.)

14

LOCAL INSTITUTIONS

T HE PRESENT chapter is the first of three that divide the materials of political science according to *levels of government*.
The progression will be from *local* governments to *federated* states to
international organization. There is a fourth most important level, of
course, the national one, but we have tended to draw many illustrations
from national government throughout this work and, in fact, Chapter
Two, "The State and Authority," was devoted principally to introducing the study of national political organization.

How does the study of levels of government relate to the study of
political behavior and of the internal branches of the government?
First, it adds a new dimension, a new and important viewpoint to the
study of political materials; it is a new way of cross-sectioning political
events. Second, it introduces a whole new group of generalizations or
principles that pertain to political organization on a given level—local,
federal, or international.

We should emphasize, however, that the study of the *levels* of
government derives a great many principles of value from the study of
political behavior and of the *internal political organization* of governments. The elements of political behavior may be found throughout
political events. We have not hesitated, for example, to observe city
bosses as well as presidents in our study of leadership. Also we have
considered the main levels of government in our study of the legislative, executive, administrative, and judicial processes and have found
similarities in these processes on all levels of government. For example, we have found that the legislative process of the state legislatures and city councils has much in common with that of the national
Congress, and the judicial process operates in many ways the same
whether we scrutinize it in the commune, in the highest national court,
or in an international tribunal.

By our plan, then, the subject of this chapter is the government and
politics of the locality. We shall ask what are the problems especially

pertinent to the government of men in cities, towns, villages, and their surrounding countryside. In the first section, we shall be concerned with the history of the local community and with the social problems connected with the large-scale movement of people into cities in modern times. Simultaneously, we shall describe the many varieties of local jurisdictions that can be found and show how many people give their primary loyalties to their local communities.

The second part of the chapter will treat largely of the different forms and structures of local government and of the common features they possess. The third section will be concerned with the political struggle within cities, with who runs the local government, and with the movement for greater efficiency in the administration of local government. Finally, certain outstanding problems of local government will receive consideration, among them the problems of conflicting jurisdictions, centralized administration, and home rule.

From Tribe to Metropolis

UNIVERSAL NATURE OF LOCAL GOVERNMENT

Man is bound to the earth, to geography, and from birth is with few exceptions part of a territorial organization covering not more than a few miles. Whether or not the locality in which one is born maintains its primacy among his loyalties or influences exclusively his thoughts, it is rarely deserted completely by him in favor of competing political organizations. It is rarely forgotten, and always leaves an imprint on his character. A man is marked by "where he comes from." Furthermore, wherever he goes, he finds a new locality and a new local political organization about him. The national government or international order under which he lives may remain the same throughout his movements from one locality to another; Cass County, Peoria, and New York City all fly the same flag. But even if there were no national or international order, there would be a local order, as centuries of history have demonstrated. The past is laden with the importance of local government. The typical organization of mankind before the era of writing was the tribe. The first empires of the Near East and China sprang from aggressive and expanding cities. The climax of ancient history, from one point of view, was the attempt of the Persian Empire to destroy the city-states of the Greeks. The medieval cities nurtured the commerce and arts of the Western world for centuries and the folk of the country were attached firmly to small principalities, highly organized and isolated from the larger world.

THE SUBJECTION OF INDEPENDENT CITIES TO NATIONS

National government is the dominant form of the organization of political power in modern times. Sometimes this condition is laid to the development of wider markets, the increased movement of individuals, greater efficiency of government, and other reasons that assume that local sovereignty is incompatible with material progress. The fact is, however, that the unification of peoples into large nations that ushered in the modern period of Western history was not accomplished solely in the service of material progress. Venice, Florence, Genoa, Cologne, Amsterdam, Hamburg, and other medieval city-states lost their independence to greater states, not because of their poverty, their restriction of trade, or their incompetence, but, to the contrary, *because* they were tempting targets of aggrandizement to the most powerful nobles and kings. Hence we conclude that no "natural law" of efficiency directed the process by which cities became subordinate to nations.

More likely, the source of the pressure towards national unity in the nations of Europe, and thence America and Asia, came from an effective organization of rural localities. That is, as rural governments became well organized, their chiefs compelled the cities to form part of a national unity. When the kings improved the administrative and mechanical means of integrating and ruling large tracts of land, they could easily assemble the means to influence or conquer the independent cities.

The loss of local sovereignty to the nation frequently does not signify a great loss of power. This is especially true after the initial period in which a city-state becomes part of a large empire or national domain. Athens lost its sovereignty to the Roman Republic towards the end of the pagan era, but many Athenians became powerful Romans. Dutch cities lost their sovereignty to Spain in the sixteenth century, but economically they flourished and therefore constituted within the greater empire a political aggregate of considerable scope and influence. The same process occurred in the nineteenth century when the free city of Frankfort was joined to Prussia. Hence, we conclude that localities may lose sovereignty (symbolic and ultimate power) but increase their scope of power and retain many powers previously possessed.

REGIONALISM AND LOCALISM REMAIN STRONG

These glimpses of the colorful history of local government should prevent an exaggerated notion of how all-embracing nationalism has been or can be. It should also inform us that history does not move uniformly and that at any period of history, one can find tribes, city-states, and empires or other colossal human aggregations existing side by side. Among the cities and within the empires and nations one finds many differences of organization and varying degrees of independence of outside authority. The study of local government among contemporary political scientists is confined principally to localities that subsist under the aegis of a national government. This practice is in accord with the important facts of politics, for no great city or important local organization today is "free" in the sense that ancient Athens, Sparta, or Rome were free.

Yet national boundaries obscure many important internal differences and many examples of the great power of cities. For example, nationalism is weak in China where the village is the true community and strong in Germany where the Reich is the true community. But even this statement must be carefully guarded. The Chinese are not all localistic; many are Westernized or Sovietized nationalists; and some Barvarians, for instance, have always resisted German nationalism.

Also we include in localism attachments to territorial divisions larger than cities or rural neighborhoods. Many Americans are first Californians, first New Yorkers, first Texans. Italians and French are strong in regional sentiments; very often the Sicilian and the Florentine, the Breton and the Marseillais feel that national policy does not solve many regional issues. But under modern conditions, the tendency of politics seems to be to reinforce the national state and the first order or first level local government as centers of community sentiment. Internal political regionalism, be it in China or in the American South, seem to be declining as a source of political energy, and as a basis for political movements.

ADMINISTRATIVE REGIONALISM VERSUS POLITICAL REGIONALISM

However, like the receding tides, political regionalism leaves behind a clutter composed of remaining sentiments, surviving structures of governments, and vested interests of people in jobs and status. Meanwhile, a new kind of regionalism—administrative in nature, technological in origin, and efficient in motive—is developing, and this new kind of regionalism cannot move far in the direction of governmental reorganization because it is blocked by the remains of the older regionalism, among other things.

Let us glance at the central concerns of the new regionalism and appraise briefly its prospects. Giant states like China and the Soviet Union have within them many divisions which may be called regions whether one defines the term for political, economic, physiographic, or

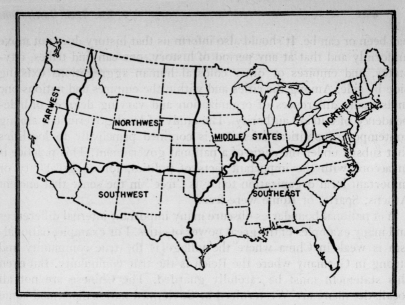

REGIONS OF SOCIO-ECONOMIC HOMOGENEITY
Showing the boundaries as they would probably be if state lines were disregarded

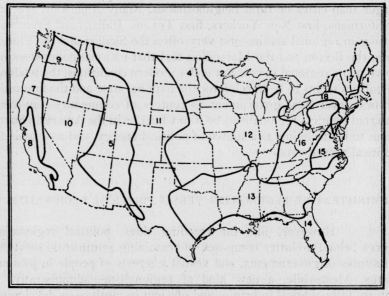

MAJOR GEOGRAPHIC REGIONS OF THE UNITED STATES
(after M. C. Stark and D. S. Whittlesey)

1. Maritime Canadian Region
2. Region of Extractive Industries
4. Spring Wheat Region
5. Region of Rocky Mts. and Plateau
7. Pacific Cordilleran Region
8. California Region
9. Columbia Plateau Wheat Region
10. Arid Region

11. Semi-Arid Region
12. Interior Mixed Farming Region
13. Cotton Region
14. Southern Coastal Region
15. Chesapeake Mixed Farming Region
16. Appalachian Upland Region
17. New England Upland Region
18. Eastern Urban Region

FIGURE 36

REGIONS OF THE UNITED STATES *

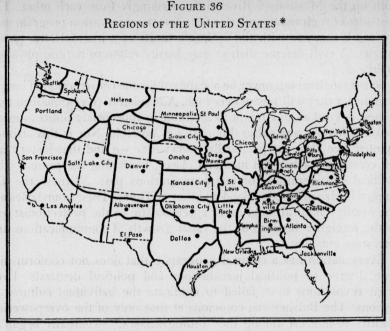

METROPOLITAN REGIONS IN THE UNITED STATES AS DEFINED BY DAILY NEWSPAPER CIRCULATION, 1929 (*after R. D. McKenzie*)

Each heavy line encloses all cities or towns receiving 50 per cent or more of their metropolitan circulation from the given center. Note: The morning daily having the most extensive circulation was chosen for each center.

* National Resources Planning Committee, *Regional Factors in National Planning and Development* (Washington, D. C.: United States Government Printing Office, 1935), pp. 174, 177. Note: two regions (3 and 6) are omitted from the map as developed by the N.R.P.C.

cultural purposes. Even small nations like England and Belgium have within them surprising diversity in all these respects. A regional map of the United States can be constructed from different physiographic, economic, and social viewpoints. Figure 36 presents three types of such regions.

But politics cannot coincide with any regional boundaries save in a general way. For one thing, regionalism, like the principle of self-determination, if pressed to its ultimate conclusions would result in dozens of unmanageable tiny areas in even a modestly sized country. The American South is a "natural" region and many political consequences emanate from that condition; yet, for example, Virginia differs in many significant ways from Texas or Arkansas. Then too, regions overlap. A region may be "natural" for one purpose but not for another. The inhabitants on one bank of a river may present a different culture from those on the opposite bank, although both share important common problems. So too may be the case with an upriver and downriver region; for example, Minnesota and Louisiana that are both on the Mississippi River differ strikingly from each other. The best sort of regional boundaries for a forest conservation program may not at all coincide with the optimum limits of a hydroelectric power district. A civil defense district may hardly relate to natural physiography.

So regionalism can never be a standard for the construction of human boundaries that will please everyone. Administrative regionalism may be best defined as an attempt to assemble in appropriate limits as many common natural and cultural qualities as possible. Nor is this attitude granted free play, for practically everywhere we find that history has left eccentric tracings on men and places, burdening the present with political considerations of many generations past. Witness the difference in size of Rhode Island and that of Texas. Their boundaries are not wholly "natural" and seem anachronistic to the perfectionist and to the foreigner because of the rapid growth of communications and interstate industry.

Every nation has a cultural geography that does not conform in a high degree to political jurisdictions and political demands. Even great revolutions have failed to eradicate the individual cultures of regions. The Bolshevists, conscious at first only of the overpowering identity of interest among the "toiling masses," eventually began to encourage regional diversities of a cultural sort. So also did the French revolutionaries who thought initially only of the equality of all men and who sought mathematically to delimit provincial boundaries. Reacting to such excessive zeal for conformity and uniformity, an influential "regionalist" movement grew up in France in the nineteenth and twentieth centuries.

Still we find, in America and in most countries of western Europe that have been reorganized politically over the last century and a half, that present political and administrative boundaries have tended to replace the customary boundaries. The French provinces of the *ancien régime* were replaced after the Revolution of 1789 by *départements* (for administration and elections) and *arrondissements* (chiefly for electoral purposes). The historic English counties (52 in number) have lost heavily in functions to the new administrative counties (62). The Italian republic of 1870–1922 created a number of administrative provinces out of the fewer historic regions of Italy, and the Fascist State carried farther the process of disregarding historic conditions by erecting a structure of *corporazione* for representing occupations regardless of their geographic location.

ADMINISTRATIVE DISTRICTS

In all countries, modern administration has by-passed traditional boundaries, including political ones, in performing its new functions. Certain of these new districts are created for ease and convenience of administration alone. Such would be election districts, judicial districts, tax collection districts, police precincts, fire protection districts, and school districts. Other kinds of districts are of far-reaching importance, for they perform tasks of great complexity and influence. Examples would be the districts formed in the United States by the Interstate Commerce Commission, or the Tennessee Valley Authority region that is almost a socio-economic world in itself and yet spreads over several "sovereign" state boundaries, making and carrying out policies that affect all the people in those states. The Port of London Authority and the Port of New York Authority are other examples of governmental bodies set up to determine and administer policy affecting the lives and fortunes of people governed by different local governments.

UNITS OF GOVERNMENT

The districts we have just described are purely administrative in the sense that their officers are selected for the performance of particular tasks and are not chosen by elections. The number of such districts is great. The United States alone may have a million such districts; and we may define units of government more strictly and still reach, according to the calculations of William Anderson and the Bureau of the Census, a total of 155,067 in 1942. Anderson defines a *unit of government* as "a resident population occupying a defined area that has a legally authorized organization and governing body, a separate legal identity, the power to provide certain public or governmental services, and a substantial degree of autonomy including legal and actual power to raise at least a part of its own revenues." (See Figure 37.)

In the metropolitan region of Chicago alone, Albert Lepawsky, using a slightly different definition, found 1673 governments. In 1942, the Bureau of Census, following Anderson's definition closely, counted 821 units in the Chicago region, 1039 in the New York region, and 353 in the Los Angeles one. Lepawsky discovered a great many overlapping police, fire, and other political jurisdictions in the Chicago area. Extensive duplications of budgets, expenditures, and revenue collections occurred. The complexity and prolixity of governing units together with the grave social problems of the rapidly growing cities have produced political problems of the first magnitude.

URBANIZATION

Indeed we might say that the great complexity of governmental units has been at least partially due to rapid urbanization. For

FIGURE 37

UNITS OF LOCAL GOVERNMENT IN THE UNITED STATES, 1942 *

Type	Number	
Nation	1	
States	48	
Counties	3,050	
Incorporated Places	16,220	(including cities, villages, and so on
Towns of the New		and the District of Columbia)
England Type and		
Organized Townships	18,919	
School Districts	108,579	
Other Units	8,299	
Total	155,067	

* Source: Bureau of the Census: *Governmental Units in the United States, 1942* (Washington: U. S. Government Printing Office, 1944).

example, the United States began as a preponderantly rural country: in 1790, only about five per cent of the population of four millions lived in what might be termed urban centers. The important forms of local government in those days were the county and the town, both essentially rural forms of government that have left their impression on local government to this day. Today 94,092,000 persons live in places of 2500 or more inhabitants or in the immediate shadow of metropolitan centers, while 53,453,000 individuals live in rural places. Thus, the urban population is almost twice the size of the rural. The same process of urbanization has occurred in the countries of western Europe and, to a smaller extent, in other parts of the world. The proportion of people living in the cities is still increasing throughout the world, though in Europe the rate of increase is not so rapid as it was during the late nineteenth and early twentieth centuries. The Soviet Union, which has undergone its period of rapid industrialization later than the western European countries is an exception; its rate of urbanization is still high.

URBAN AND RURAL SOCIETIES

The differences between the city and country as centers of human activity give rise to important differences in the government and politics of the two types of human environment. The city presents a great problem of engineering; its public works, huge private buildings, great streams of traffic, ceaseless flow of production, commerce, and consumption bewilder the mind and demand ingenious and complex economic and physical arrangements. Its large expenditures and revenues present political and administrative difficulties of the first order. The wide range of needs, demands, and expectations of its heterogeneous population gives urban politics a color and complexity that does not occur in most rural communities.

From a sociological viewpoint, there is also a great contrast between urban and rural life. The farmer in his work does not deal with men so much as with the land and its products. The city worker constantly encounters other people and works in close association and competition with them. Life in the village and country is "close" and "familiar," and the human contacts are informal and "primary," as the sociologists say. City life is "distant" and "strange," and the human contacts are formal and "secondary."

As Park and Burgess have described the contrast:

> The neighborhood or the village is the natural area of primary contacts. In primary association individuals are in contact with each other at practically all points of their lives. In the village "everyone knows everything about everyone else." Canons of conduct are absolute, social control is omnipotent, the status of the family and individuals are fixed. In secondary associations individuals are in contact with each other at only one or two points in their lives. In the city, the individual becomes anonymous; at best he is generally known in only one or two aspects of his life. Standards of behavior are relative; the old primary controls have disappeared; the new secondary instruments of discipline, necessarily formal, are for the most part crude and inefficient; the standing of the family and of the individual is uncertain and subject to abrupt changes upward or downward in the social scale.*

To say that this contrast is evident at all times and in all places would be incorrect. For instance, the rapid electrification of rural communities in America, the coming of the radio, motion pictures, and automobiles, the always restless mobility of the American people ("the frontier spirit") make the contrast at times dim. In Europe, Latin America, and Asia, the contrast between countryman and city man is more striking, often showing itself in at least apparent differences in physical stature and other features.

Political problems arising from these various differences are profound and sometimes direct. The urban-rural debates over apportionment of representation in American state legislature are full of invective against one or the other mode of life. Hitler and the Nazis, mentally recoiling from modern urban sophistication and "strangeness," wished to remake Germany into a "folk state" in which everyone could feel that he "knew" everyone else and that all were "blood brothers."

THE INTERNAL COMPLICATIONS OF LOCAL SOCIETY

Beyond the differences normally occurring in urban as against rural societies, are significant internal social differences found

* Quoted with permission from Robert E. Park and Ernest W. Burgess: *Introduction to the Science of Sociology*, 2nd ed. (Chicago: University of Chicago Press, 1924), pp. 285–6.

in both kinds of localities. Whether we study the aborigines of Australia or the inhabitants of a New England town, citizens of old Athens or those of New York City, we find that the social structures of the societies account for numerous political situations.

Looking at a modern city, for example, one perceives two general configurations of the population, one geographical and based on the neighborhood, another social and based on social class. The significant social-geographical configurations found in the city may be called its ecology. Professor Park discovered that most cities grew up similarly in recent times. The center of the city contains its main business district, communication centers, large offices, hotels, and railroad terminals. The next belt or circle around the "downtown" area holds the poor, shifting population, the factories, and newly arrived workers from the country or abroad. Next comes the area of workers' homes, and then the belt of middle class residences of clerks, more skilled workers, and older immigrant groups. Finally one reaches groups having higher incomes and more education, including the bulk of professional and managerial personnel and the oldest residents of the community. An increasing number of the last category commute long distances to work and live in suburbs outside the legal jurisdiction of the city government.

The different sociological areas of the city produce different demands on government. For example, certain wards of Chicago contain a high proportion of all Chicagoans who receive direct public assistance to relieve the effects of poverty. Other wards contain a high proportion of people who are well-to-do. Each kind of area produces different kinds of voting behavior, different types of leaders, and generally a different political process.

Linked with the ecological divisions of the city and their political consequences may be the composition of the social classes within the city. A number of sociologists and cultural anthropologists have given us detailed studies of the social structure of various cities and rural communities. Among such writers, one may name especially Robert and Helen Lynd, Lloyd Warner, Paul S. Lunt, John Dollard, Clyde Kluckhohn, George P. Murdock, James West, and Alison Davis. Lloyd Warner and his associates, for example, studied a town of 17,000 in New England over a period of years and were able to show that in a number of ways the political attitudes and political associations of an individual varied in kind and extent with his position in the class structure of the town.

Also, the studies indicated a point that the authors did not fully develop, but which had previously been developed by Roberto Michels: in a representative government with universal suffrage, *politics is one of the most important points of contact between the various social classes.* Thus, James West made a study of "Plainville," a farm village nestled between North and South in the central part of the United States. In describing the social classes that existed in this rural area, he recited the exceptional case of a man who rose in class position quickly. "Ora Bell, who died recently, was the son of 'one of the biggest and worst and most ignorant families in town.' He was 'bright in high school,' 'worked every chance he got,' 'showed himself to be absolutely reliable,' 'kept away from all bad company except his family,' married a 'good, moral girl' (from the upper edge of the lower class), bought a home, saved his money, made many friends and finally ran for one of the county offices and won. ('People give Ory lots of credit for what he done, and they helped him. He showed what anybody can do what'll try.')"

The preceding remarks suggest that the study of local government is only half-done when the formal structure of government is mastered. The social organization and the political behavior of the population must also be studied. A striking fact (encountered rather early in a political career) is that city and country government are always meshed with the social structure of the locality at many points. If one studies the old English shire without understanding the connection between the local gentry and the public officers, if one studies modern Swiss cities without realizing the importance of the ancient and haughty families of the community, if one is concerned with the American scene and misunderstands the extent to which economic power and social prestige enter into the relations among citizens and politicians, one performs purely formal exercises and starves his own cause.

Scrutiny of the accompanying chart (Figure 38), borrowed from Warner and Lunt, *The Social Life of a Modern Community*, reveals that the formal officeholders of an old New England city of 17,000 people are drawn disproportionately from the higher social classes. By a class, the authors mean "two or more orders of people who are believed to be, and are accordingly ranked by the members of the community, in socially superior and inferior positions." It will be recalled from our earlier discussion in Chapter Three, that Dr. Warner concluded that six social classes existed in the communities he studied. In "Yankee City" as the town under discussion was termed, the authors examined the social position of the 136 officeholders in 1930–1 and concluded:

> Although the voters among the three lower classes far outnumbered those in the three higher, they had a disproportionately small percentage of officers in the political hierarchy. . . . Indeed, as the importance of the political offices increased, the proportion of upper-class office-holders increased.

However, as we read the conclusion of Warner and Lunt about class, we should warn ourselves against overstating the meaning of the findings. Larger cities, rural communities, and especially localities in the

FIGURE 38

THE CLASS COMPOSITION OF VOTERS AND OFFICEHOLDERS IN "YANKEE CITY"

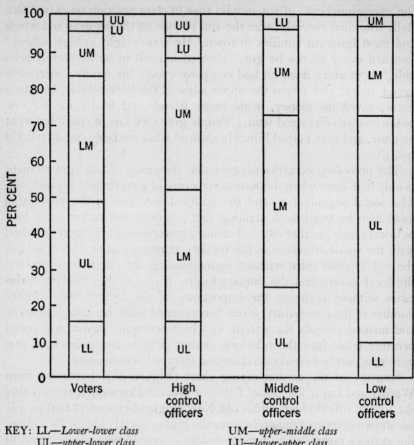

KEY: LL—*Lower-lower class*   UM—*upper-middle class*
      UL—*upper-lower class*   LU—*lower-upper class*
      LM—*lower-middle class*   UU—*upper-upper class*

"Voters" means those satisfying age, residence, citizenship, and registration requirements. "High control officers" means incumbents of officers where there are final authority and broad supervision (that is, the mayor, the city council, and the several boards). "Middle control officers" means the same, where authority and supervision are limited (that is, auxiliary executive offices, heads of departments, and agents of the several boards). "Low control officers" means administrative subordinates who are the employees of the various departments.

Reproduced from W. Lloyd Warner and Paul S. Lunt, *The Social Life of a Modern Community*, p. 370. Copyright 1941 by and reproduced with the permission of the Yale University Press.

Midwest and West may display significantly different conditions. Furthermore, we refer back to our remarks in Chapter Three about the many limitations to the concept of "class" as used in America.

Stuart Chase was so impressed by studies such as those of Warner that he urged their consideration by all who work with local government. He wrote:

The information already available . . . in these books and monographs cannot fail, as Wissler said, to be helpful to all who direct the affairs of American towns—mayors, selectmen, city managers, chiefs of police, welfare commissioners, housing authorities, city planners, social workers, police court judges, traffic officials, school boards.*

LOCAL ATTACHMENTS VARY AMONG INDIVIDUALS

While it is true that everyone in a local community is affected directly or indirectly by the government, the politics, and the social conditions of the locality, it is patent that individuals vary greatly in the extent to which they *feel involved* in the events of the locality. It will be remembered that we defined "community" in an earlier chapter as the habitual relations or communications among people reaching a stipulated scope and degree of intensity. We left it up to each student to declare what particular community he was referring to in any particular case. Now so complex is modern society that, while one person may be obviously part of a national community in a psychological sense, a neighboring individual may be psychologically part of a local community only. Psychologically, the latter is more involved in immediate local affairs; his perspective is local; his interests are viewed locally; he becomes excited mostly about local questions.

We have already commented on the fact that a world community hardly can be said to exist save by the Hydrogen Bomb test: everyone may be blown up together. So far as identifications and psychological involvements go, the overwhelming majority of men and women are not members of such a community. What is not so often appreciated perhaps is that, in many countries, most people are first members of local communities and only secondarily, if at all, members of the national community—again speaking psychologically rather than physically. Furthermore, a considerable number of individuals identify most strongly with the smallest city precinct or unit of government—if they may be said to have any political identifications at all.

LOCAL PROXIMITY GROUPS

Such "proximity-bound" individuals form a myriad of little communication pools or interaction clusters. They constitute informal political action-reaction units. These groups may be compared with the "work group" found in large-scale functional organizations. The members of such work groups are tied to one another technologically by the task to be done and psychologically by the social relations

* Quoted with permission from Stuart Chase: *The Proper Study of Mankind* (New York: Harper and Brothers, 1948), p. 135.

arising from the contacts of their personalities and their operations. Proximity-bound individuals may also be compared with the army squad that has its own perspectives, morale, and group purposes, and that has only a rough and somewhat unconscious understanding of the vast plans of the army. But, unlike the work group and the squad, the proximity-bound political group is normally purposeless with relation to any great plan of the nation, party, or even the formal side of local government. Also, its communications are voluntaristic, sporadic, and not geared to any significant extent, by consciously designed machinery, to the grand issues of local—much less national and international —politics.

Too rarely does the observer of national and international issues turn to contemplate the politics of an urban or rural neighborhood. When he does he must perceive that the problems he regards as important are as nothing to a good part of the people he encounters. Many of the cultural practices of the people are bound up with decisions in the local sphere that directly affect them. A good part of the vote in elections everywhere is motivated by local interests, the voters in no lively sense being impelled by international, national, state, or even city-wide interests. The present writer's own experience would indicate that the vast majority of all contacts between people and government occur on neighborhood matters—matters concerning streets and alleys, schools and playgrounds, disputes over minor property rights, zoning and housing regulations, jobs and contracts, personal friendships and political grudges, and other concerns directly interesting to a handful of people. In certain nations, England and the Soviet Union for example, neighborhood matters may be of less importance in government than in the American republics or in France or Italy, but they are always of momentous consideration in the study and practice of politics.

It is also interesting to note that a larger proportion of people are closer in the sense just described to their local governments than to their governments at a higher level, *even though they may trust* the officials of the higher government to a greater degree. Closeness is a product of frequency of interaction and the intensity of interest with which the interaction takes place. The teachers a child has, the policemen he observes going about their work, the cleanliness of the streets and alleys, the ordering of traffic, the removal of snow and debris, the inspection of facilities, the guidance of his recreation, and many other influences help to account for his political actions as an adult. The manner in which the most august political leaders debate in the United Nations Security Council and on the floor of Congress, and the manner in which such leaders operate the agencies of the administrative establishment invariably reflect their childhood experiences with local government.

HIGH PHYSICAL MOBILITY IN AMERICA

Moreover, in America at least, much of this local interest is not directed at the general problems of local government, but at immediate personal needs alone. To cite the complaint of many reformers, this great localism is directed at the wrong objects and therefore does not profit the locality as a whole. Local government in America would undoubtedly be the focus of more conscious and informed attention than at present, if it were not for two phenomena of modern life.

The first cause of "wrong" focusing is the high physical mobility of Americans. The census of 1950 disclosed that only 81.1 per cent of the total population of the United States lived in the same house in 1950 as in 1949. Between April 1949 and April 1950, 17.3 per cent of the population, or 25,531,000 people, were reported as having moved from one house to another. Many of these, 6.2 per cent of the whole population to be exact, had previously lived in a different county or abroad. These figures from a one-year period illuminate the fact that a large part of the urban population of the United States has come from the country and many from states other than the one in which they presently live. Thus, Detroit, with its automotive industry, has attracted thousands of workers from the South, both white and Negro. It is difficult for a mobile population to immerse itself immediately in the interests and needs of its new urban home. The same is true of many of the immigrants who came to America throughout its history. They could hardly become involved immediately in the affairs of the strange cities into which they moved. And groups with more education and higher incomes are almost as mobile; an upper-income family may dwell in three or four cities during one generation.

THE SUBURBAN PROBLEM

A second phenomenon that reduces the involvement of Americans with their local governments is the suburbs of the twentieth century. Whereas until World War I, by far the greater part of those who worked in a city lived in it, by 1940 one out of every six Americans resided in a suburb. Consequently, millions of Americans with high incomes and high education are involved neither in the civic life of the suburb, which is their dormitory, nor in the city itself, which is their place of work.

The suburban problem, unlike the first factor of long-distance physical mobility, produces many problems in addition to the highly important fact of a low degree of psychological involvement and participation. For the suburbanites, who have much of the personal wealth of the metropolitan area, cannot be taxed as easily by the city as those who live within the city boundaries. Yet the city must continue to provide the suburbanite with water, fire protection, paved streets, police protection, traffic control, and other expensive services while he is in the city. And, as the tax burden on those who remain in the city becomes higher in order to support the services to nonpaying suburbanites, more people move from the city to the suburbs and the problems become progressively more grave.

To a lesser extent, the great European cities are faced by the same problem of suburbanism. European cities, however, are not so grossly unplanned as American cities. (Sinclair Lewis once said the latter were so unplanned that they appear to have been planned that way.) Within the limits of the European standards of living, their cities are relatively "livable." Furthermore, European cities, for many reasons, are less subject to exploitation by private political interests than American cities. Their need for expansion and special governing institutions has been more favored by the governing legislature or executive.

SUMMARY OF SECTION

The preceding pages have demonstrated that local governments have varying amounts of power in different societies, and the loyalties of men to their local governments change, too, from time to time. Furthermore, the number of social and economic regions, administrative districts, and units of government is always large and frequently causes complicated problems to pile upon one another. Finally, the relation of any particular feature of governmental structure to the behavior of the population varies within and among localities; we may not expect, for example, to produce the same effect by the use of primary elections in one ward of Los Angeles as we may expect to produce in another ward of the same city; nor may we expect to produce the same effects by employing the same device in an English city and an American city.

In short, one must not hold fast to any oversimple image of local government and institutions, knowing how the "true" image must change over time and space. Rather we should remember always the great diversity of practices and laws governing local political behavior. We should recollect how several local governments will occupy several overlapping layers of territory and how the people of a locality differ remarkably in their degree of participation and interest in politics. Only with these guard-rails to our thoughts, can we use intelligently the general statements about the forms of local government that follow hereafter.

Patterns of Local Political Institutions

COMMON FEATURES OF LOCAL GOVERNMENT

Local institutions, like national institutions, differ from country to country, and yet they share several broad features almost everywhere. These common institutions may be listed, preliminary to further discussion. Concentrated town or city populations get special attention everywhere; they do not have the same form of government as rural populations. Local governments everywhere are subordinate to higher governmental authority. Local governments are operated by political officers and function within a political milieu that is separate in important ways from the political environment of national or international politics. The local institutions of modern society are acquiring an increasing number of administrative officers and are beset by the problems of public administration perhaps as much as are national governments. All local governments perform services for their people and the number of such services is constantly increasing, though the distribution of responsibility for such services is often in process of being shifted from one unit of local government to another within the same area. (Refer to Figure 5 for a list of local government functions in America.) Local governments everywhere levy and collect taxes from their people and collect payments for various services that they render the inhabitants. On the other hand, all modern local governments depend on subventions or grants from superior levels of government to make up the total income they need to provide services. These common features of local institutions will be elaborated in the paragraphs to follow.

LEGISLATION REGULATING LOCAL GOVERNMENT COMES FROM ABOVE

The various levels of local government in ten countries are listed in Figure 39. The general methods by which the structure, functions, and powers of local governments are established formally are by (1) *special charters* to particular local governments, (2) *general codes* regulating all localities, (3) *constitutional provisions*, and (4) *general legislation* or statutes.

Taking England as our first example, we find that a system of counties existed from early times, ordered by custom and by strong local independence into a pattern of which the chief characteristics were rule by local landlords and nobles and homage to distant kings. The Norman sheriffs carried the king's ordinances into the counties after

1066 and, much later on, the counties were dominated by justices of the peace representing combinations of the local gentry and nobility. Urban places were chartered specially by the crown. In the nineteenth century, the English county government was reorganized by parliamentary statute and the Local Government Act of 1933 systematized the internal organization of the transformed counties, known as *administrative counties* by contrast with the older *historic counties* (shires). Each administrative county was divided into *urban districts, rural districts,* and *municipal boroughs.* The larger urban centers became *county boroughs* (London itself is an administrative county with many metropolitan boroughs similar to municipal boroughs). Thus, Parliament has provided for general local government, covering both rural and urban areas.

The French system of local governments obtains its structure from a municipal code that owes much to the French Revolution and to Napoleon I. The country is divided into *départements* (headed by appointed prefects and watched by general councils), *arrondissements* and *cantons* (mostly judicial, electoral, and administrative districts), and nearly 40,000 *communes* that include rural, urban, and metropolitan governments.

Figure 39

Local Units of Government in Ten Countries *

NATION	PRINCIPAL LEGAL AUTHORITY	GENERAL LOCAL DIVISION	INTERMEDIATE LOCAL DIVISION	URBAN GOVERNMENT	RURAL GOVERNMENT
United States	State	County and/or Township	Often township	City, Town, Village	County or Township
China	Nation	Province	Prefecture (fu)	Hsien	Hsien
England	Nation	Administrative County	—	Municipal Borough and Urban District	Rural District
France	Nation	Département	Arrondissement and Canton	Commune	Commune
Germany	Nation and State	Gemeinde	Landkreis	Gemeinde, Stadt and Stadtkreis	Landkreis
India	Nation	Province	District	City	District
Italy	Nation	Provincia	Commune	Commune	Commune
Japan	Nation	Prefecture	—	Municipality	Rural District
Switzerland	Canton	District	—	Commune	Commune
Soviet Union	Nation (Union) and Republic	Oblast	Raion	City	Settlement

* Sources: *Encyclopedia of the Social Sciences; Encyclopedia Britannica;* W. Anderson (ed.): *Local Government in Europe;* the *Statesman's Year-Book* (1950)

In America, local governments have been organized by the grant of special charters, by constitutional provisions, and by general legislation. Today, twenty-four states have constitutions that forbid special laws granting charters of incorporation to municipalities. In these states, and also in other states without such prohibitions, either the constitution of the state may prescribe the conditions under which a local area may become a municipality or else the general statutes applying to all conditions or classes of conditions prescribes the legal route to municipal incorporation. On the whole, in practically every state of the union, the counties, townships, and urban places find their legal origins in a combination of all three methods of ordering local forms—the constitution begins the task of evolving the permissible forms, the general statutes of the state legislatures continue the process and add details, and finally special laws, granting rights or changing conditions, occur with great frequency, even where the constitution may frown on such practices.

In all local governments, rural and urban populations have, roughly speaking, the same rights to vote and participate in the government. This contrasts with the condition often found at an earlier period, when cities were able to preserve certain rights of self-government from the kings and maintain them for centuries, while the rural areas remained under the domination of a few local nobles and king's appointees.

STRUCTURE OF CONTROL FROM ABOVE

The subordination of localities to nations or states is accomplished in different ways, as Figure 40 shows. The figure presents in highly simplified fashion several kinds of central-local relationships. The state legislature in America, the departments of the national government in England, the prefects of France and Italy, and the federal executive committees and the Communist Party in the Soviet Union are the active agents in causing local policies to conform to national policies. They co-ordinate the resources of localities and central governments for distribution according to central policies. Thus, an American legislature may forbid the cities of the state to levy a sales tax. Or it may require them to own their water supply systems rather than contract with private firms for water. Or it may declare that the cities will observe certain holidays. Or the state constitution may even allow the governor, as in the case of New York, to remove local officials who are apparently quite incompetent or dishonest.

ADMINISTRATIVE RULE IN FRANCE

Control of local governments in France, unlike the United States, is partially in the hands of executives of the central administra-

FIGURE 40

FORMAL STRUCTURES OF LOCAL GOVERNMENT (GREATLY SIMPLIFIED)

I. American Forms *

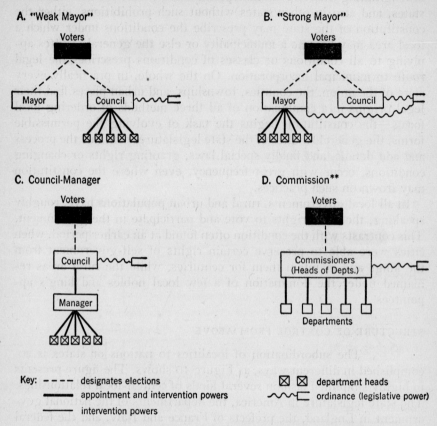

* The American forms, unlike the European, do not envision continuing intervention of higher authorities (for example, state officials or state legislatures) in the process of local administration. But such controls are increasing.

** The structure of American county government (county boards) and township government (selectmen) follows this pattern on the whole.

tion. The French prefect heads one of the ninety *départements* into which France is divided. He is a career official, appointed by the Minister of Interior. He may be transferred from one prefecture to another during his incumbency. He appoints subordinate personnel, supervises national welfare, construction, and educational activities within his area, has important public security functions, and also has crucial powers over local government. He may revoke mayoral elections, suspend temporarily the mayor or council, and insist that the council vote various mandatory expenditures. His powers to some extent are confined by the powers of a general council elected by the voters of the *départe-*

Figure 40

Formal Structures of Local Government (greatly simplified)

II. Local Government Forms Abroad

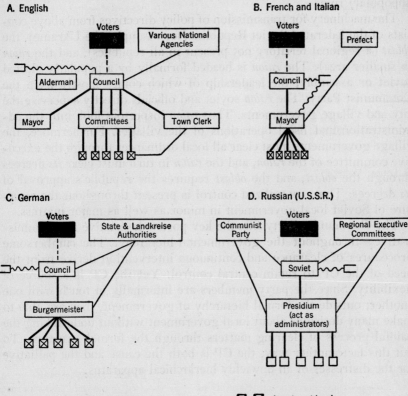

A. English

Voters

Various National Agencies

Alderman | Council

Mayor | Committees | Town Clerk

B. French and Italian

Voters

Prefect

Council

Mayor

C. German

Voters

State & Landkreise Authorities

Council

Burgermeister

D. Russian (U.S.S.R.)

Communist Party | Voters | Regional Executive Committees

Soviet

Presidium (act as administrators)

Key: ----- designates elections

⸺ appointment and intervention powers

⸺ intervention powers

⊠ ⊠ department heads

ordinance (legislative power)

ment. But this council does not at all have the powers of the American state legislature with regard to the local governments.

THE COMMUNIST PARTY AS SUPERVISOR OF SOVIET LOCALITIES

Lenin's doctrine of "centralized supervision and decentralized activity" applies well to central-local relations in the Soviet Union. For example, the national planning authority, Gosplan, sends its proposed objectives to each community, which then discusses its share of the total operation, makes recommendations, and reports back to Gosplan. Gosplan accepts, rejects, or modifies the local proposals. To take another example, the village soviets have been charged by the central authorities with the duty of carrying out the collectivization of agriculture. Since the collectivization idea was a national one, not local in origin, the local government assumed an administrative (and often unpopular) role.

The machinery for transmission of policy directives from above consists of the federated Soviet Republics (for example, the Ukraine), the *oblast* (a regional territory not present in all republics), and the *raion* (a smaller area). The *raion* is headed formally by a popularly elected soviet or assembly, the leadership of which comes mostly from the Communist Party. The *raion* soviet and officials directly supervise the city and village governments. Thus *raion* inspectors look into the administration and fiscal operations of the villages. Furthermore, the village governments must clear all local ordinances through the executive committee of the *raion*, and the *raion* in turn must clear *its* decrees through the *oblast*, and the *oblast* requires the republic's approval of *its* decrees. Thus, centralized control is present throughout the structure of Soviet local government in minor as well as major matters.

The Communist Party fills the key posts—legislative and administrative—throughout the governmental hierarchy. The cumbersome procedures of clearance and continuous intervention derive from the need of the CP to retain central control. Yet the CP is a source of flexibility. Since the party members are informally in touch with one another, outside the formal hierarchy of government, they are able to make many decisions about local government without undertaking the painful process of clearing matters through the formal structure. To put this fact another way, the CP is both the cause and the palliative for the distresses of an unwieldy hierarchical apparatus.

LOCAL POLITICAL OFFICERS

Knowing some part of the controls exercised over localities from above, we may now devote our attention to the internal structure of local governments. Political officers, we said, are elected men and executives who strongly influence policies. Practically without exception, the local citizens of the world possess the formal power of choosing important local officials. The important officials often consist of a single chief or multiple chiefs of the political and administrative structure, the councilmen, and frequently also certain independent officials charged with duties concerning finance or other special tasks. The main deviation from the pattern occurs in the manner of choosing the chief executive(s). As Figure 40 shows, in Britain, France, Germany, the Soviet Union, and in parts of the United States, the popularly elected council, rather than the voters, chooses the mayor or chief executive group.

FUNCTIONS OF LOCAL OFFICERS ANALAGOUS TO NATIONAL ONES

The local councils operate according to a legislative procedure much like that of their national legislature. Bicameralism, it is true, is rare among local governments, but the single-chambered town or city council takes up proposals, considers them in committee, debates them, and votes on them in a manner similar to the procedure followed in the national legislature. The chief officer, when popularly elected, also behaves in many ways like a president or premier, and he and the other top executives of the locality perform functions of planning, organizing, recruiting, directing, budgeting, and so forth that resemble in important respects the functions performed by the analagous officers on a higher level.

THE STRUCTURE OF AMERICAN CITY GOVERNMENT

The chief forms of American city government are the mayor-council form (weak or strong), the commission form, the council-manager form, and a small number that may be called "town-meeting" in form. The *Municipal Year Book* for 1950 reports the distribution of these forms among the 2,033 cities in America with over 5,000 inhabitants as follows:

	NUMBER OF CITIES WITH FORM	PERCENTAGE OF CITIES WITH FORM
Mayor-Council	1,163	57.2
Commission	302	14.9
Council-Manager	495	24.3
Representative Town Meeting	26	1.3
Town Meeting	47	2.3

As the table reveals, most American cities of over 5,000 inhabitants have the mayor-council form of government. Under the so-called "strong-mayor" form, the city council and mayor are each elected directly by the voters. The mayor exercises strong control over the top executives of the city administration and often has the responsibility of preparing the annual budget. Within the "weak-mayor" category, one finds much variation among cities. Most often the "weak" mayor lacks the authority to appoint and remove the most important executive officers. In these cases, the council may appoint officials or the officials may be popularly elected. At other times the mayor is denied a veto power over council ordinances. The mayors of some 21 per cent of the cities over 5,000 population do not have the right to veto enactments. Of all cities over 10,000 population (943 reporting), 58.5 per cent do not give their mayors the veto power. However, the mayors of 12.6 per cent of these cities with 10,000 population possess the most powerful veto, the item veto that may be cast against particular parts of a financial proposal without destroying the proposal as a whole.

CITY COUNCILS

The "legislative" branch of American city governments may be small or very large. Chicago has 50 aldermen, Detroit has 9, for example. As the result of past reform movements hostile to party machines, most cities have laws requiring that councils be "nonpartisan." That is, the council members do not have their party affiliations marked on the ballot. Sometimes this fact means that the men are really not affiliated with a party organization; more likely, they are informally or extralegally affiliated with a party. Of 2,023 (out of 2,033) cities over 5,000 population, 57.4 per cent have "nonpartisan" councils. The balance, 42.6 per cent, have councils the members of which are openly identified with a political party.

Most cities, especially the small ones, are not divided into electoral and administrative districts (wards). In fact, 55.4 per cent of all cities over 5,000 population (2,023 reporting) conduct elections at large for council members, while 27.3 per cent divide their electorates into wards. In 17.3 per cent of the cases, some council members are elected at large and others by wards. Most of these cities (57 per cent) stagger the terms of office of councilmen so that all are not up for election at the same time.

Continuing in many cases the old practice of electing many public officials, about half of the 2,033 American cities with over 5,000 inhabitants elect special officers other than mayor and council. Thus, 39.3 per cent elect the treasurer, 26.4 per cent elect the clerk, 16.6 elect the assessor, 13.8 elect the auditor, and 10.7 elect the city attorney. In some cases the controller, the police chief, the welfare director, the public works director, and even the city engineer are elected. The tendency in recent years has been to reduce the number of officials to be chosen by the voters, in part because most voters cannot know much about many candidates and also because a lack of co-ordination in the administration is often experienced where the mayor or council does not have the power to hire, discipline, or remove executive officials.

COUNCIL-MANAGER FORM STRESSES EFFICIENCY

Alongside the movement to reduce the number of elected officials so as to increase their control by the voter and to procure greater economy, a movement to transform the position of mayor occurred in American municipal politics. From its first success in America in 1908, the so-called "city manager" movement gained speed until about 500 cities of over 5,000 population and an equal number of smaller cities acquired managers by the end of 1950. The plan is especially popular in cities between 50,000 and 100,000 inhabitants, one third of such cities having adopted this form. Under its provisions, the council, which is elected by districts or at large, appoints a professional manager who is charged with almost all administrative powers belonging to the locality. He is responsible to the council for the results of his work and may be dismissed by the council or be released at the termination of his contract if his work is unsatisfactory.

It is understood that the manager will not engage in *partisan* politics; however, only the most naive persons will insist that the city manager can be nonpolitical. Even if he tried to avoid controversy by simply carrying out the orders given him by the council, he would be sure to offend certain council members or local interests; most of the time, a city manager has his own ideas, derived from his professional training and personal values, and will inject those ideas into the city government, perhaps going so far as to influence directly the council members in order to accomplish his goals.

Nevertheless politics in council-manager cities differs from that of mayor-council cities. The issues of municipal politics in a council-manager city are more often relevant to city problems than are the issues in a mayor-council city because the manager, unlike the mayor, usually does not have direct connections with a political organization. Differences of opinion may be heated in a council-manager city, but they tend more frequently to occur over questions of municipal services rather than the Chinese question or the question of communists in Washington jobs. Furthermore, the manager is a politist trained in administration and other skills allied to those required in operating a city, so that the day-to-day tasks of local administration are more likely to be done with a maximum utilization of the available resources than would be the case under a mayor-council system.

Complaints have been lodged against city managers from time to time to the effect that they are so devoted to the efficiency principle in administration that they are prone to neglect the other "human" aspects of local government. To a certain extent, this narrowness, when it exists, is owing to a kind of professional training that mayors usually do not possess. Consequently, the city manager form of government is not to be regarded as a panacea for every city. It may mean an actual retrogression, from the viewpoint of the majority of inhabitants, in certain cities whose mayors are experienced executives, devoted to the culture of the city, and adept at adjusting and compromising conflicts in a manner congenial to the habits of the population.

COMMISSION AND TOWN-MEETING FORMS

The two remaining, minor forms of city government in America are the commission plan and the town-meeting types. The commission plan, devised in Galveston, Texas, in 1900 and spreading rapidly over several hundred localities before 1917, has since the latter date acquired few new adoptions and lost a few of the old adherents. It calls for the election by the voters at large usually of five commissioners, who then constitute the general city government. The commission legislates as a body, but, for purposes of administering the various departments of the city, divides up into its individual members, each one of whom is charged with the supervision of a particular branch of the administration, such as parks, public safety, legal affairs, streets and improvement, and finances.

The commission plan is somewhat analagous to the county board and the selectmen of the town-meeting type of government. The first New England towns adopted the practice of conducting government local affairs through the agency of periodic meetings of the qualified voters. Later on, as the population increased, the government assumed continuing functions, and as the number of eligible voters increased owing to the liberalization of the franchise, the town meetings became relatively inefficient and cumbersome agencies of government. Nor were town meetings, close as they might be to complete "self-government," ever free of allegations of minority control and oligarchic or caucus management. As a result, the town meetings were abandoned in many towns of considerable population and often replaced by representative town meetings. These latter governing bodies were composed of representatives of the electorate, elected by the voters of districts, and they held meetings modeled after the older form. Both the older and newer forms of town meetings are supplemented by popularly elected selectmen who manage the continuous business of the towns as "boards of directors" and administrators.

AMERICAN TOWNSHIP AND COUNTY GOVERNMENT

Besides continuing as a form of urban government, the New England town became the pattern for rural government over a large part of the United States. As the New Englanders moved West, they carried with them their forms of government and established them in the newer regions of the country. Meanwhile, the original Southern states were sending settlers into the Western regions also, and their favorite unit of local government was the county. Certain areas of the West chiefly adopted the township form, other areas chose mainly the county form, and in some states both forms overlap. In Illinois, to illustrate the conflict that sometimes arose, northeastern Americans settled northern Illinois and southerners from the Border States settled the southern part of the state. The Illinois Constitution of 1818, strongly influenced by southerners, provided the county government everywhere in the state. After much political strife, the Constitution of 1848 allowed each county an option on the form of local government it wished to be dominant. The northern counties accordingly emphasized the township, while the southern counties made the county the most powerful unit.

At present six states in the New England group retain the township type (these are called "towns" in New England and are incorporated like cities); six states in the north-central part of the United States combine an important township with a county board of supervisors; eleven states of the south-central group employ an important county and a township form of small importance. Twenty-five states in the South and Far West interpose only the county form of local government between the incorporated city, urban town, or village, and the state government.

The township and the county, where either is the more important unit, perform similar tasks. They usually are charged by the state constitution and laws with the maintenance of peace (save within the boundaries of the incorporated places contained by them), with the administration of justice, the administration of probate matters (settlement of estates of deceased), assistance to the poor, maintenance of a school system, tax assessment and collection, administration of elections, administration as agent for the state government, and other (minor) functions.

As a large proportion of the population of the country has come to be enclosed within the boundaries of incorporated urban places, the township and county governments have become less important to a great number of people. Often, a great metropolitan area will include a number of skeleton townships and overlap more than one county. These remnants of a bygone day are then neglected by the public and are dominated, to the extent of their reduced powers, by a handful of petty officials. The general view of students of such areas is that the townships might best be abolished and their territory and functions taken over by the incorporated places which overlap them, and they also propose that the county, which is often much larger in area than the township, be consolidated with the metropolitan community into a single government. San Francisco and several other large cities satisfy this latter condition, since their governments do not overlap with county jurisdictions and do perform county functions. In most metropolitan communities, political agitation for such reforms has always fallen short of the goal, and state legislatures, influenced by the decadent interests of the old units of government, have failed to grant the powers necessary to accomplish the transformation. It should be remembered too that the suburbs of a large city will frequently side with the county and township interests in order to maintain their legal independence of the city upon which they depend economically.

Neither the township nor county has a uniform set of elective officers. The New England towns (townships) frequently are governed by popularly elected councils or selectmen; the townships of the Middle West, with lesser functions than those of the New England towns, are headed by a number of individually elected officers who may include supervisors (trustees), clerks, assessors, tax collectors, justices of the peace, and constables. Forty-seven states have county governing bodies (Rhode Island has county boundaries but no purely county officers). Twenty-seven different names are given to the county governing bodies, the most common among them being "Board of Commissioners," "Board of Supervisors," and "County Court." While the number of officers on the governing body is usually three or five, the smallest one has one member and the largest has ninety-nine. The members of 29 per cent of the governing bodies are elected on the district system of apportionment; 21 per cent are elected at large with the candidates required to be residents of the various districts; 21 per cent are elected part by district and part at large; and 18 per cent are elected township supervisors. The most common term of office is a four-year term, and the terms of the members commonly overlap.

GOVERNMENTAL FORMS MORE UNIFORM ABROAD

Not even England, with its penchant for retaining ancient institutions of government, has more variety in its local offices and functions than the American local governments. This fact is not only true of local government in rural areas but also of city government. It is easier to make general structural statements about English, French, German, Italian, and Soviet local governments, both urban and rural, than about American local governments. In those countries, and most others outside America, the central government has laid down a general pattern of all essential features of local government.

England, which once had a bewildering complex of local institutions in its boroughs, has standardized its forms within the last century.

Thus the English town clerk, probably the most important single official of the English urban government, is provided for by parliamentary statute. Responsible to and appointed by the council, he is the executive secretary and the principal administrative co-ordinator of the town administration.

In France, we find everywhere the pattern of the mayor who is elected by the council and controlled somewhat by the departmental prefect, and who is thus a dual agent of local and central interests.

In Germany, we find the famous *burgermeister*, heir to the tradition of the medieval Italian *podestá*, and forerunner of the American city manager. He is trained in the administration of city affairs, is appointed by the council, and has strong powers in the area of policy making and policy execution.

In the Soviet Union, we are struck by the great size of all councils (soviets), the practice of administering local affairs by committees, the use of local governments as administrators of the policies of the higher authorities, and the presence in key chairmanships and committee (presidium) posts of members of the Communist Party.

In the Far East, the form of local government in China has remained little changed by countless revolutions and constitutions, although the Communist Party threatened to accomplish a greater degree of integration than experts on Chinese history deemed possible. The Chinese villagers for many centuries were governed by councils of the elders of the village families; the elders designated customarily a village representative, the *tipao*, to treat with the district (*hsien*) officials and other authorities that might interest themselves in obtaining supplies, taxes, and manpower from the villages.

In India, the ancient forms of local government were shaken up by the British occupation of the subcontinent during the nineteenth and early twentieth century. For example, the *nagarattar*, or city assembly, that had immemorially been composed of gild and caste representatives was reorganized according to Western ideas of individual representation and balloting. Also, the *panchayat*, or village meeting (with the elders dominating), declined in prestige and powers under the British, who placed greater reliance upon the more controllable and efficient district officers of their own choosing. Late in the British occupation, there began a movement, encouraged by the British, to restore to the *panchayat* some of its old functions and authority.

SEPARATION OF POWERS WEAK IN LOCAL GOVERNMENT

City councils and rural bodies everywhere act in an administrative capacity with much greater frequency than do national legislatures. It may be noted in Figure 40 that America, England, and the

Soviet Union provide examples of active participation of local legislative officers in the general administration in government. Even in other types of structures—the French and German, for example—the councilmen have executive responsibilities that national legislators hardly ever possess.

This "violation" of the principle of separation of powers hardly ever carries over to the judiciary. Almost nowhere do urban or rural political officers have judicial functions. More often the local judiciary has political and executive functions. An outstanding case in point is the old English justice of the peace and his American derivative, called by the same name. Both officers have taken part in local politics and often have been the most important general political figure in county government. Several of the Southern states have made the justice of the peace the chief administrative officer of local government. During the nineteenth century in America, many executive duties were placed in the regular courts out of distrust of purely political officers. The county probate judge has been a favorite target for administrative assignments.

Politics, Patronage, and Administration

"COURTHOUSE GANG" AND CITY HALL

The formal structures of local institutions, such as have just been described, provide the channels for political struggle. Writing of the county boards of America, Lane Lancaster declares that "county boards do not exist in a vacuum and it will not do to treat them as if they did. A more realistic picture of such bodies is gained if we try to see them as a part of the unofficial, 'invisible' government that on every level in the United States makes 'the wheels go round.' It is safe to say that in nine-tenths of the counties in the United States public affairs are in the hands of what the irreverent call the 'courthouse gang.' This 'gang' may be described as a more or less permanent group of elective and appointive officeholders together with private individuals whose business normally brings them into contact with public officials." *

Corresponding to this politist group in the rural government of America and in other countries is the "city hall gang," as it is called, in urban government. Again we find a more or less permanent group of elective and appointive officeholders together with personally interested private individuals.

---

* Quoted with permission from Lane Lancaster: *Government in Rural America* (New York: D. Van Nostrand Co., Inc., 1937), p. 311.

It takes no transcendent public issue to keep up the interest of these individuals in local politics. They have made politics and politically affected business part of their lives, and they run local government most of the time while the vast majority of people stand by. Reconciling the private interests of individuals who are active in government with the need for adequate administration of the functions of local government is most difficult. One school of thought has directed its energies at taking the "political out of local politics." Another has aimed at improving the administration of local government. We will examine these points of view.

LOCAL GOVERNMENT WITHOUT POLITICS IMPOSSIBLE

Political parties are solidly entrenched in local governments everywhere. National parties, of course, must have national issues, but their local branches must have local issues. Frequently, the two sets of issues are scarcely related. But since parties are the operators of government as well as the coiners of issues, this discrepancy between national and local issues is not all-important. Local political organizations are the cells of the national organizations. Some of their members are inclined toward local issues; others incline toward state, national, or international interests. Amid a great jostling of interests and aspirations, the local peculiarities of the party are manifested in local political struggle.

As we have seen, many American localities do not allow local politicians to be carried on the ballots as the representatives of a particular party. But in fact, the politicians are stamped as members of one or another party, and nonpartisanship is mainly a formal requirement. Local parties do not disappear simply because they may not be called by name, any more than they disappear because many people do not believe that there is a Republican or Democratic way to clean streets, run the police department, or put out fires. While it may be true that such functions are not matters of general principle on which parties may be permanently aligned against one another, nevertheless parties may, by becoming critics of the existing administration, play dynamic roles in urban politics.

STREAMLINING LOCAL ADMINISTRATION

Simple communities, such as the thousands of villages in India and China, need hardly any staff to work continuously on communal problems. A large number of European and American communities are so small and so conservative that they too possess no permanent staff. All governmental functions are taken care of by committees of citizens, contracts with private groups, and by part-time elective officers. As we move however from the governments of rural villages, small towns, and open country into governments on a higher level—counties, *départements*, *raions*, cities, and so on—we find an increased load of work that demands constant attention, a fiscal capacity that can support certain public services, and, of course, a small or large group of appointive public who perform special tasks like the paving of roads, the administration of schools, the investigation of crimes, and the collection of taxes.

LOCAL MERIT SYSTEMS

A small community undertakes many functions without a permanent civil service establishment because no great capital investments are required. The maintenance of wagon roads, for example, is not on the same financial scale as the maintenance of paved highways. Once a community is committed to expensive functions, it usually demands regularized ways of performing them; personnel must be available constantly and be qualified to handle expensive equipment. In historical terms, this fact may be put thus: functions that are complex, expensive, and on a large scale accrue in rough relation to the rate of growth of a community, and there is almost always a lag between the complexity of the administrative establishment and the adequacy or ability of the available personnel to cope with the new administrative problems. In Britain, in France, in the United States, in the Soviet Union, and elsewhere, a period of rapid development of local large-scale functions has been accompanied by at least an initial period of incompetency and political corruption. The problem and the felt need expanded before the organization changed to cope with the problem and need.

It was many years after the advent of the Industrial Revolution in England that the English localities acquired the first essentials of efficient administration. The dirt, debris, misery, and disorganization of local life accumulated undisturbed until a small group of local reformers pushed a number of governments and Parliament itself into a reorganization of local administrative machinery. Soviet rulers strived mightly to establish local governments that would be adequate to manage the tasks imposed by a "planned" society, but no will of a few men could "plan" in a few years the birth of a great class of administrators. Soviet local government has stumbled consistently over routine administration for lack of skills, apart from questions of *formal* malorganization.

In the United States, local governments had to undertake numerous functions because of great social changes in the early nineteenth century. Many present-day techniques and practices of local administration developed according to the incompetent, haphazard standards of that period. The practices and offices of local sheriffs and constables of rural communities have been roundly denounced by a generation of expert reformers. While criminals have employed to the fullest extent the techniques presented them by the technological revolution in communication and transport, many local police officers remain rank amateurs in the face of new administrative procedures for dealing with crime.

When rural governments realize a need for expert help, they may call on outsiders or pool resources with other local governments to "rationalize," that is, increase the efficiency of, their activities. Thus, the incorporated town of Middletown, Rhode Island, contemplating the advantages of zoning the township, hired expert advice on zoning to advise its council and population. (It so happened then that the town rejected zoning on financial grounds.) On the other hand, a city like Chicago has zoning experts permanently on the city pay rolls. In another case, the town of Portland, Maine, faced with an "alarming" amount of citizen apathy towards its city-manager government, hired a social scientist to diagnose the trouble. He found that most people felt no sympathy with the "business-managed" government and the government began to conduct many local citizen meetings to correct this "illusion."

Lane W. Lancaster, in his *Government in Rural America*, illustrates by the case of the Virginia almshouses, how rural governments may apply new co-operative techniques for solving problems. He writes:

In 1918 the legislature of that state enacted a law—opposed to be sure, by many of the county political "rings"—permitting the consolidation of county almshouses, of which there were at that time about a hundred. Under this act arrangements had been made by several groups of neighboring counties to unite in maintaining district almshouses. These agreements had met with such success that in 1934 the total number of almshouses in the state had been reduced to thirty-two, and projects were under consideration which, if carried through, will eliminate fourteen more.

On the basis of experience to date there is every reason to believe that this enlarging of the area of administration will result in great improvement in institutional care of dependents. In the first place, the new districts almshouses are modern, sanitary structures as compared with the down-at-the-heel, rickety, vermin-infested county "homes." In the second place, the large number of inmates makes feasible the organization of adequate medical and nursing and social service agencies, the keeping of better records, and the adoption of a program looking toward the rehabilitation of those committed. The Virginia experience would also indicate that the district system will be considerably more economical than the old system normally is.*

These examples of how rural communities may follow the trail of professional administration indicate that the role of the expert in American government does not stop with large-scale municipal or federal agencies that hire thousands of people. Within practically any set of personal values, there is some place for the use of scienific and expert personnel in government. Therefore, the rural governments in America and abroad are as fit subjects for the employment of "rationalizing" procedures as are the great cities.

LOCAL POLITICAL MACHINES AND ADMINISTRATION

Political machines, rural or urban, have a great private investment in the game of local politics. Although local politicians, like most people, are men of many motives, a long-standing motive for participation in public affairs has been that of getting jobs for one's dependents, relatives, and friends. In practically every local government, no matter how "pure," this motive is likely to intrude to some extent upon the desire to maximize the efficiency of governmental functions. In large cities and in populous counties, the influence of this motive, representing the collectivity of private demands of many politicians, ends in a veritable army of patronage appointments. Not unexpectedly, the efficiency of administration of a local government varies inversely with the extent of such practices. Frequently, the local public pay rolls are padded with the names of "employees" who rarely report for work in the position assigned them. They do "other" political work or else do no work at all.

The jobs held by practicing politicians are not purely the "spoils of office," however. In the first place, many political appointees are competent for their jobs. Secondly, "spoils" appointees very often have a higher degree of communion with "public opinion" than do career appointees; the former certainly cannot very well be cloistered from public life, especially when their party may be defeated at the next election. Finally, the operation of most American local governments as *self-governing* units presupposes a considerable amount of activity of the voters. The patronage system encourages political activity (whether bad or good is another matter) among a portion of the population. Haphazard and inefficient though the patronage system be in most American local communities and in many localities abroad,

* Quoted with permission from Lane Lancaster: *Government in Rural America* (New York: D. Van Nostrand Co., Inc., 1937), p. 66.

it nevertheless ensures the spread of governmental experience among more people than would receive such experience under a career system of administration.

LOCAL CAREER ADMINISTRATORS

In a number of countries outside the United States—for example, France, England, Germany, the Soviet Union—men can be trained for a career in municipal administration and spend their lives at such work. In America, the possiblity of careers in local administration is increasing. The largest cities like New York, Philadelphia, Chicago, Los Angeles, Cleveland, and Boston have thousands of employees who are trained to their jobs and are secure in the possession of them, although alongside these same employees work other thousands who are political appointees, who have party work they are expected to perform, and who have relatively short terms of office.

In the rural areas of America the same situation prevails, though on a much reduced scale. In the least populous places, the few appointive employees are most frequently politically affiliated but not grossly negligent. Too often, critics demand unusual standards of efficiency of the most humble township clerk or county registrar, evidently expecting some magic of "public affairs" to transform a lowly administrative clerk into a high-powered executive with an evangelical mission; the performance of such jobs should be compared, more realistically, with the performance of a small shop-keeper, of a railway clerk in a sleepy town, or of an average farmer.

But, shifting to local governments that employ hundreds of people, perform dozens of complicated functions, and expend many millions of dollars, we naturally find a greater demand for efficiency in government. The progress of administrative reforms in such governments over the last fifty years is impressive. Most large cities and many medium-sized ones have enacted systems of recruiting, retaining, and promoting municipal employees. The existing plans are in many cases adequate in form, though more often deficient in practice. This trend towards reducing the number of public offices accessible to political influences may be expected to continue indefinitely into the future. Even counties are operating under merit systems to an increasing degree. And, as we indicated above, the use of expert consultation is becoming increasingly frequent in smaller localities as well as larger ones. To illustrate this point in another way, a number of state universities have bureaus of local government that train local officeholders, no matter how they may be selected, and that advise local officials about many local problems.

Outstanding Local Problems

STATE-LOCAL CO-OPERATION

Home-rule is the outstanding problem of local government. Although touched upon in the preceding sections, it deserves more systematic attention in connection with its principal facets—the fiscal dependence of localities, consolidation of units of government, and central interference in local affairs. Over the last fifty years, state and local governments in America have markedly increased their functions and expenditures. The states, however, have been in a better position to finance their functions. Spreading over a greater area, and possessed of legal powers greater than those of cities, the states are able to use their flexible strength to bolster the finances of cities whenever conditions so require. Local revenues are derived principally from property taxes whereas states have other major sources of revenue, including sales taxes (gasoline taxes, tobacco taxes, liquor taxes, and so on) and motor vehicle taxes. While local tax collections have increased generally by about 20 per cent over the level of collections in 1926, state collections have soared to 150 per cent over their level in 1926. The amounts of money owed by state governments to holders of their securities have consistently been less than the amounts owed by the localities. In 1945, for example, the debts of the states amounted to less than one-sixth of those of the localities. As a result of these factors, the localities consistently require help from the states in the form of grants of money. Both the states, in federal systems such as exists in the United States and Canada, and the central governments elsewhere assume part of the costs of local governments by giving grants-in-aid.

It is difficult to generalize about the extent to which the higher level governments must aid the localities. This problem is part of the general problem of assigning duties and responsibilities among the levels of government—local, intermediate, national, and international. The political activities of government cannot be completely localized or nationalized. Street cleaning may be a local function, defense a national one. But these are not purely so, even though they are selected as extremes. Should nationally owned buildings pay for services to the city or should the nation compel the localities to give free services to national property? Can civil defense be considered only a national military function? In our age, everyone is dependent to a startling extent on everyone else's work and no one can absolutely and for all time define the boundaries between the local and upper level activities of government. When a central government increases its tax rates, it makes the task of finding taxable resources more difficult and the task of collecting taxes more unpopular for local government. More than ever before, the levels of government today may be visualized as belonging to a giant trunk-line into which functions and resources may enter at many points from the smallest to the largest unit of government, may be transformed or modified at any point in the system, and may emerge at any point.

CONSOLIDATION OF UNITS OF GOVERNMENT

There are more units of government in many American localities than can reasonably be regarded as required to perform the functions of local government in a given area. A confusion of governing structures produces indirect political disadvantages in addition to fiscal disadvantages. Conflicts among personnel of overlapping units like the township and county, or county and city, or city and suburb occur almost daily in many localities. Even the few voters who are interested in local government cannot attend to the complexities of many special governments. Other voters are discouraged from taking any interest in local government at all. While it is difficult to be precise and conclusive about such matters, it would seem often that the *consolidation* of various separate units of government in the same area *might indirectly create greater efficiency and incite greater citizen participation than would a structural change in the form of government itself.* Consolidation seems especially promising as a method of reform in the metropolitan areas, where independent suburbs create problems that the large city population is rapidly finding insupportable financially, physically, and psychologically. No other factor so frustrates the self-governing aspirations of American cities of 250,000 or more as does the presence of unassimilable suburbs.

HOME-RULE MOVEMENTS

Indeed, the greatest step towards "home rule" in the general and most meaningful sense of the term would be to consolidate large urban governments into one central government and no more for an area with a radius of from fifteen to fifty miles. Even a paternalistic and interloping state legislature could not nullify the tremendous effect of such consolidation. "Home rule," in its narrower sense, is the right of a city to draft its own charter. This right is important to localities. But giving a city jurisdiction over the source of its most profound woes is much more important. Consolidation of units of government can do this.

Home rule, however, in the sense of almost complete freedom from state intervention is less and less possible as the localities become more dependent upon financial subventions from higher levels of government. Localities are also becoming dependent on the upper levels of government for technical assistance. Whatever the localities lack, by reason of their small populations and resources, may come from the central governments.

To the extent that the home-rule movement has sought complete freedom from external intervention it has been directed at abuses of the past and present rather than aimed at intergovernmental co-operation. In this way, it resembles somewhat the "states' rights" movement in America that sought to solve the problems of a centralized economy by a rigid formula of independence, and then failed, as the next chapter will show, because co-operation with the national government in many matters proved essential if state governments were to act effectively in many fields of public works, health, education, and welfare.

It would seem that home rule among today's complex and interdependent localities must arise from a combination of *adequate jurisdiction in each locality* and of *skillful consultation among the communities and between the local and central levels.* We leave out of consideration, of course, the vitally important requirements that the voters of localities choose the kind of officers who rule them "well." Concerning the jurisdictional side of home rule, the previous discussion of consolidation provides a view of the technique by which adequate jurisdiction may be attained.

DISTINCTION BETWEEN ADMINISTRATIVE AND POLITICAL CONTROLS

Much anger and little precision usually accompany judgments about the capacity of central governments for ruling the localities. Often, adequate local powers are unavailable because the American legislatures (and in Europe other central authorities) have no desire nor compulsion to discriminate between what is *necessary* for them to decide regarding the cities and what *may be decided by the cities in their own political processes.* That is, administration is confused with politics to an unwarranted and exaggerated degree.

In Germany, where the failure to distinguish between *administration* and *politics* might be called a national disease (Karl Mannheim calls it the bureaucratic ideology), there is a constant tendency even to deny the value of elections in local politics. A common attitude of Germans is expressed in their criticism of attempts by Allied occupation authorities to extend home rule to German localities. Hans Steinmetz, a German expert, refers in the following quotation specially to the *Landrat*, who is a combination county mayor, county manager, and state official, elected by the *Kreistag* (county council), which is itself elected by all voters. This statement is, however, an indication of a general viewpoint, found not only in Germany but also in America and elsewhere.

> On the basis of experience in many places during the last two years, there is a danger that the *Landrat* will become a football of changing party majorities, and that he will have difficulty in protecting himself from being a mere representative of the interests of the party or parties which elected him. With respect to changing questions of daily politics, it is desirable and indeed high time to safeguard the independence of the *Landrat* from the struggle of interests and thereby insure impartial administration. In my opinion, such independence and impartiality are less guaranteed by election than they would be if the state cabinet appointed the *Landrat*, but with confirmation by the *Kreistag*. The short term of office which the *Landrat* has (the term is now six years in the American zone) is likewise a matter of concern. Long experience indicates that an official cannot develop his full potentialities in office unless from the first he has a sufficiently lengthy tenure. I consider six years to be too short.*

A contrary general impression of various British local government experts is worth noting, as it is reported by Alderman J. W. F. Hill. A British team visited Germany, consulted with German officials, and officers of the occupying power. Though loath to generalize after a brief study, they nevertheless unanimously concluded that unless certain principles were laid down in the basic law, the German authorities would revert with little change to their previous centralized control over local government. The principles they urged upon official quarters were "that effective control of policy must remain in the hands of elected representatives; . . . that the servant of the local authority must not also be a servant of the state; and perhaps . . . that the chief executive officer should not be given security for a term longer than that of the elected councillors."

The lesson of Allied experience in Germany, then, is that there is a tendency there for local government to be regarded purely as the administrative arm of the central government and a tendency to disregard the importance of local political struggles. In the United States there is the same difficulty of distinguishing between the intervention of the state into the locality for *administrative co-ordination* and the intervention of the state *to destroy the political life of the locality*. The first type of intervention is inevitable and increasing, but can occur without destroying localism in a political and social sense.

It is perhaps impossible to devise any specific formal structure that will prevent state or national legislatures from interfering with local governments in elections, appointments, budgets, functions, finances,

---

* Quoted with permission from "The Problems of the Landrat," trans. by Roger H. Wells, *Journal of Politics*, Vol. II, no. 2 (1949), p. 333.

and otherwise, and at the same time allow the legislatures to help the localities in the same respects. There is no single structure or legal relationship that will forbid "bad" intervention and foster "good" intervention. Charges of legislative "despotism" and local "irresponsibility" will continue to be made indefinitely. First one body of opinion will be offended and then another. In order to have a maximum of home rule, moral principles, not structures, must be changed. The legislators and officers of the state body must be compelled by political pressures to act as if, or must believe that, local self-determination is one of the grand moral principles of political action.

Previous portions of this chapter have indicated the strength of local attachments, described the creative impulses that stir in localities and ultimately influence the whole society, and listed the forms and functions that furnish the media for public expression in local life. We would emphasize that the city and other local governments are the expressions of the total direct political activity of the vast majority of individuals. When legislators on a higher level of authority deny the general importance of local controversy, on the grounds that it is trivial or superfluous, they are undertaking to deprive many men and women of the only meaning politics holds for them. When men on a higher level of government interfere continually with local processes of government, they are in effect adopting an aristocratic viewpoint—even if the results are pleasing to everyone concerned. Such attitudes and actions would undoubtedly arouse even greater hostility than they now occasion if these hidden principles could be clearly revealed and their enormous consequences set forth in detail.

Questions and Problems

1. What have been some of the various roles that cities have played in history, culturally and politically?

2. Describe and distinguish between sentimental (cultural) and administrative regionalism.

3. What are the major units of government in America and what problems arise from their large number and manner of organization?

4. From library sources and interrogation of public officials, determine the number of units of government in your state. Are you satisfied that the number is appropriate to the tasks to be performed?

5. Describe the general differences between urban and rural communities and add examples from your own experience, wherever possible. (For example, if your family was once rural and is now urban, how has its life and viewpoint changed?)

6. Describe the major *internal* social complications of cities.

7. To what extent may individuals be involved physically and psychologically to different degrees in their local or national communities?

8. In what ways are local governments established by a higher level? Give examples from various countries of each method.

9. Compare the method by which American localities are controlled regularly from above and that by which French localities are governed.

10. Compare the "strong-mayor" and council-manager forms of American city government.

11. Describe the "weak-mayor" and commission forms of American city government.

12. How are rural localities governed formally in America? What is the "courthouse gang"?

13. List two important features characterizing local government in England, Germany, Italy, U.S.S.R., China, and India.

14. Comment on the statement that "local government without politics is impossible" (250 words).

15. Name and illustrate some of the ways that a merit system principle may be employed in rural and urban localities.

16. In what ways is the intervention of superior levels of government in local affairs inevitable?

17. What is local home rule? In what way is local home rule dependent upon a city's having adequate territorial and functional jurisdiction?

18. Distinguish between the administrative and political intervention of state legislatures in local government.

19. Describe the form of local government of your home locality, and tell how it differs from the typical form of its kind in Figure 40.

Longer Study and Research
Problems Suitable for Term Papers

1. Make a list of all principles of leadership contained in Chapter III, and illustrate as many of these principles as possible using Lincoln Steffens' *Autobiography* (1931), as source material.

2. Interview four politists who have *local* interests. From their accounts of local affairs, prepare a general statement of the major problems of the particular locality. What solutions do they propose for the problems? Do you believe that the problems are as important as the politists do? Do you agree that their solutions are practical and desirable?

3. Write a review of one of the following works (ten pages), outlining its contents and its methods of study.

United States National Resources Committee: *Regional Factors in National Planning and Development*

Arthur C. Millspaugh: *Local Democracy and Crime Control* (1936)

St. Clair Drake and Horace Cayton: *Black Metropolis*

H. S. Churchill: *The City is the People*

Henri Pirenne: *Medieval Cities*

R. S. Allen (ed.): *Our Fair City*

4. Prepare an introductory history of your local government (15 pages), noting especially the adoption of new political institutions, the local reform movements, and the growth of new functions of government.

15

FEDERALISM

M os t nations are *unitary* in organization. The *national* government exercises all final power and sovereignty. By contrast, federalism may be defined as a structure of government that divides final power and sovereignty between a central government and local geographic units. Independent legislative, judicial, and executive organs are often found on each level. Federalism may be distinguished usually from *confederation* by its allocation to the central government of *final authority on important matters affecting all the individuals* of the federal union. Not unexpectedly, there have been many more cases of confederation than of federation. For independent states have often banded together out of convenience and necessity, thus forming confederations, without relinquishing their final powers on any important questions.

As it operates, federalism decentralizes and limits the central governing authority in certain ways. A division of labor is worked out which gives local areas substantial autonomy. It is a form of geographic pluralism, for involved in all federal states is the idea that local values must be preserved by being given a secure place in the total political structure.

The Varieties of Federalism

LOCAL AND CENTRAL BODIES MAY BE DISSIMILAR

Whatever may be the historical, legal, or political origins of a particular federal state, within it there exist units smaller than the whole which possess such a large degree of survival ability and power of decision that they appear and act in many important ways as if they were separate governments. In the American federal union, we are especially impressed by the resemblance between the state governments and the national government. This resemblance occurred because the national Constitution imitated some features of the eixsting state constitutions, and thereafter the new states imitated closely the structure of the national government. But experience elsewhere provides many cases of federalism in which the central and local bodies hardly resemble each other in structure.

FEDERALISM A LOCAL-CENTRAL COMPROMISE

A glance at the table of federations adjoining this page (Figure 41) will show the bewildering variety of historical circumstances out of which federations arose. The table points up one of the essential conditions in the origins of federations: federalism is a compromise between two conflicting yet desirable sets of values, one local, the other central. The bonds that tie the smaller units to the larger unit may be purely spiritual and sentimental. This was the case of the Amphictyonic Council, the religious league of the ancient Greek cities. At another extreme, the bonds of unity may be strong controls such as those embodied in the economic and nationalistic program that occasioned the German federation under Bismarck. Although reasons and circumstances may vary, federalism, to be genuine, can never be completely one-sided. A balance of functions and authority, always precarious, must be maintained by the central and local authorities.

THE STRENGTH OF LOCAL VALUES

Whence comes the strength of the localities? It comes first of all from the strength of community ties, as we have shown in the preceding chapter. In the age of the city states in the ancient Mediterranean, the center of politics, trade, and culture rested in a locality containing some thousands of persons surrounded by an agricultural hinterland. In the late Middle Ages, the Italian and German cities waxed rich in trade and culture at the expense of nationalism. They conquered surrounding areas, often in league with other cities. But neither they nor the Greek cities relaxed their local independence or pride. Federalism for them was a minor convenience of an economic, religious, or cultural sort. So it was too with the feudal baronies of the Middle Ages. They fought bitterly and in the end vainly against monarchical centralization. The results of the struggle in several cases took the form of federalism—for neither the king nor the nobles (the cities were often a third force) could achieve immediate supremacy. In Spain, the kings convoked the Cortes in the early thirteenth century in order to get from the nobles and townsfolk by influence what they could not get by sovereign command. And in France the Estates-General, and in England the Parliament, served the same purposes at first.

FIGURE 41

CONFEDERATIONS AND FEDERATIONS

ANCIENT

Amphictyonic Council	Boetian League
Delian League	Lycian Confederation
Achaean League	Etruscan Confederation
Aetolian League	Roman Confederation

MEDIEVAL

Lombard League	Hanseatic League
Ghibelline League	Cinque Ports
Rhenish Confederation	Holy Roman Empire
Suabian Confederation	

EARLY MODERN AND MODERN

Swiss Confederation	German Republic
United Netherlands	Iroquois Federation
German Confederation	New England Confederation
German Zollverein	Continental Congress and Articles of Confederation
German Empire	Confederate States of America
	League of Nations

CURRENT

Switzerland	United States of Brazil
Union of Soviet Socialist Republics	Republic of Mexico
British Commonwealth of Nations	United States of Venezuela
Australia	United Nations
Canada	Organization of American States
Union of South Africa	Republic of Indonesia
United States of America	West Germany
Argentine Republic	

PROPOSED

Western European Union	Scandinavian Federation
European Union	Democratic Union
Balkan Federation	World Federation
East African Federation	Arab League
Central African Federation	

In breaking up feudalism—which we must remember represented centuries of tradition and law—the kings had to crack through the same barriers that defend the localities in modern systems of federalism. They had to break the system of local armies, of local judiciaries and law, and of local fiscal independence (see Figure 42). By the fifteenth century, their success in western Europe was assured.

It is notable that the period of the destruction and disintegration of feudalism was accompanied by the eclipse of flourishing parliaments in the principal countries involved. There exists a definite connection between early modern federalism and early representative government. Representative government is peculiarly suited to federalism for the latter requires local autonomy at the same time as it requires a central

FIGURE 42

TYPES OF FEDERAL ARRANGEMENTS

Late Feudal

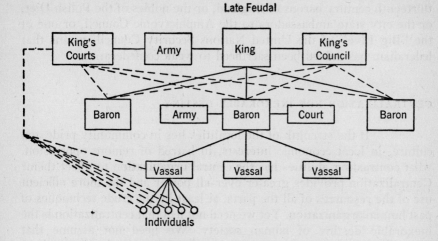

Confederation and State-to-State Federalism

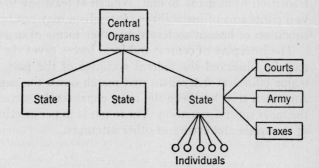

Federalism: State-to-Individual

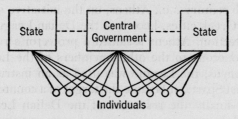

———— Main line of command

- - - - Institutional line of command

body. In fact, the more power the individual representative to an assembly has, the more truly federal a state. An extreme of such power, for example the free veto (*liberum veto*) of any law, as possessed by the thirteenth century barons of England, or the nobles of the Polish Diet, or the city state ambassadors to the Amphictyonic Council, or one of the "Big Five" of the United Nations Security Council, means that federalism has indeed been sacrificed to weak confederation.

CENTRALIZATION NOT INEXORABLE DESTINY

If the strength of the localities lies in community pride and culture, in local economic interests, in hatred of remote oppression, what contrasting abilities has the central organization to offset them? Centralization provides greater over-all power and the more efficient use of the resources of all the parts, at least by the crude techniques of past human organization. Yet we need not feel that centralization is the inexorable destiny of human society. We need not assume that federalism—for being a condition of contrasting and balancing authorities—must be a transient phenomenon, useful only in manipulating a transition from many to one. We can at least say that, history being a vast panorama of instabilities, federalism may not be a less permanent condition of human society than other forms of organization.

The interplay of central and local forces gives the angle from which may be observed the federal societies of the past. Of the forty-odd major efforts at federalism that march down the pages of history, the American trial has been the most consistently successful and deserves the most careful attention. Yet to put it in perspective, one must know of the trials and errors of other attempts.

THE DELIAN LEAGUE

Following up her leadership in the wars against the Persians in the fourth century B.C., Athens, on the initiative of Pericles, formed a league of Greek cities, known as the Delian League, for purposes of mutual protection. Athens assumed a protector's role, which became ever more onerous to the other members of the League. Policy was made by Athens, the League was used as an instrument of Athenian policy against Sparta, it became the target of a counterleague formed by Sparta, and finally the resources of the Delian League were appropriated by Athens.

The sentiments of Greek unity were cultural; beyond them the Greek community did not exist. The state is a vital far-reaching community, wrote Aristotle some years afterwards; if men "have nothing in common but exchange, alliance, and the like, that would not constitute a state." The Delian League did not grow into a fraternity but into a group of reluctant servitors of Athens. Aristophanes implored the gods for unity:

> *Put an end to our fights and our feuds and division,*
> *Till all men shall hail Thee, our Lady of Peace,*
> *Put an end to the whispers of cunning suspicion,*
> *And mingle all Greece*
> *In a cup of good fellowship. Teach us at last*
> *To forgive one another forgetting the past.*

But he prayed in vain.

The failure of co-operative federation from within brought intervention from without. Philip of Macedonia conquered the Greek cities of Europe. And after his line expired, the Romans, having gone through a period of confederation themselves, mastered the essentials of organizing divergent peoples and conquered the Greek cities.

THE GERMAN EMPIRE, 1870–1918

From 1815 to 1866, the German states were grouped loosely into a German Confederation of which the ruler of Austria was president. Prussia took the lead in demanding closer union and, after successively defeating Austria and France in war, joined with the rest of Germany (save Austria) in the German Empire. The new states was federal in structure, combining four kingdoms, six grand-duchies, five duchies, seven principalities, three free cities, and Alsace-Lorraine, all under the hereditary "presidency" of the king of Prussia. Sovereignty was declared to reside in the union of the federal princes and free cities.

But Prussia had more population and area than the rest of the union; its king was now emperor or president of Germany and controlled the imperial administrative machinery. He was able to convoke sessions of the legislature, composed of the Bundesrat and Reichstag. He might appoint and remove the powerful imperial chancellor. He controlled foreign affairs and the armed forces. Nor were the legislative powers of the empire limited nearly so much as in other federal states. Soon after the federation was formed, the will of Prussia became quite apparently the will of the empire. The autonomy of the local units was largely administrative. Taxes were collected by the states according to the demands of the imperial administration. State courts were retained but subjected to the uniting influence of a supreme court of appeal. After World War I, the German Republic accelerated the process of nationalization and Hitler completed it. Owing largely to American influence, the West German "Bonn" Constitution of 1949 revived a stronger federalism.

THE SWISS CONFEDERACY

Since 1409, a working confederation has been part of the Swiss tradition. The constitution of 1848, as modified in 1874, made Switzerland a federal state. It possesses a bicameral legislature of which the National Council represents the people directly and the Council of States the constituent members as entities. The constitution plainly limits the powers of the union and gives all others to the cantons. The federal government's powers have increased during the last fifty years. All communications, the army, and the social security system are nationalized. Unlike America, a uniform code of civil law exists for the whole land. The executive branch (Bundesrat) is a commission elected by the two houses of the federal legislature in joint session. Since 1874, a federal supreme court has handed down opinions on matters affecting cantonal and federal relations.

THE REPUBLIC OF ARGENTINA

Operating since 1853 under a constitution modeled after that of the United States, Argentina is composed of fourteen provinces possessing general grants of home rule. The provinces elect their own governors and legislatures. The central government is headed by a president and a bicameral legislature, with a supreme court having powers of judicial review of provincial legislation. A succession of revolts, however, prevented Argentina from undergoing any lengthy period of stable federal development. Provincial autonomy has afforded the leaders of factions occasion for organizing resistance to the central government in the relative isolation of provincial politics. On the other hand, neither local autonomy, nor a clearly drawn federal constitution, nor a supreme court has prevented the central government from regimenting the population, and at present the provinces are *de facto* subordinates of the national government on all important questions.

THE BRITISH COMMONWEALTH OF NATIONS

In 1926 an imperial conference gave to the British Empire the name of The British Commonwealth of Nations. In 1930, the Statute of Westminster gave equality with England to the self-governing dominions of the Empire. This was the culmination of a growth in independence on the part of not only the populations of British descent in Canada, New Zealand, Australia, and South Africa, but also on the part of foreign states such as India and Burma. Ties of blood and culture make the British components of the Commonwealth a true federation, especially in wartime. Fealty to the British crown is sworn by the member governments, but few compulsive powers are possessed by the crown or its dominion representatives.

In recent years, economic and foreign policy differences have grown stronger among the Commonwealth associates. When India, Pakistan, and Burma received grants of independence following World War II, they were invited to remain as equal members of The Commonwealth of Nations. However in their case, and to a large extent in the case of the other members, the Commonwealth tie is confederational and lacks all sanction save that of friendship and voluntary cooperation.

THE UNION OF SOVIET SOCIALIST REPUBLICS

That the U.S.S.R. is federal in formal structure cannot be doubted. In the Soviet constitution of 1936, there are clear grants of extensive authority, including even the right of withdrawal, to the sixteen republics. Thus, Article 17: "To every Union Republic is reserved the right freely to secede from the U.S.S.R." The "right" is, of course, meaningless, save to indicate that the communist leaders have always been concerned with propitiating claims for cultural autonomy.

Many federal provisions were contained in Stalin's plan for a constitution in 1922 which formed the basis for the constitution of 1924. Under the new constitution of 1936, the union government received full control of foreign trade; transport; communications; finance; concessions; currency; domestic trade; use of land, labor, and resources; the all-union budget and the individual union republics' budgets; all taxes and revenues; and citizenship. The "republics" were permitted constitutions, given educational functions, courts (with supposed autonomy), agricultural functions, and health and social welfare activities. Amendments of 1944 to all constitutions granted the republics the right to conduct foreign relations and to maintain military establishments. The republics have all the trappings of statehood but little of the powers. Their rights are primarily cultural, although they have some important powers over local government. All economic, police, and military authority is concentrated in the national government that operates directly on the people.

The union republics are represented in the central government on the Soviet Council of Nationalities with eleven representatives each. In addition to the monopoly of economic affairs and force that the central government holds, the position of the Russian Soviet Federated Republic, controlling over half the territory and population of the whole, gives it a commanding role such as that possessed by Prussia in the German Federation before World War I.

Finally, to complete the task of qualifying the federal status of the U.S.S.R., we must consider that the Communist Party is the only recognized party in the whole country and that it exercises strict discipline over all of its members whether they are in the local republican governments or in the central political and administrative organization. There seems little reason to dispute P. Gronski's thesis that the Soviet Union is an administrative dictatorship masquerading as a federation.

CONFEDERATION IN THE UNITED STATES

We need not go beyond American experience to compare the conditions of confederation and those of federation. The United States began as individual states, living in some isolation and drawing their feelings of unity partially from their common problems and their common allegiance to a distant crown and parliament. Some daring men, notable among them Benjamin Franklin (in 1754 and 1775), proposed continuing co-operation among the colonies in a permanent organization. The Revolution brought confederational union, which was formalized and cemented by the Articles of Confederation of 1781. Thereafter, until the adoption of the Constitution of the United States of America in 1789, the American states struggled to reconcile their common needs with their sovereign pretensions.

Under the Articles, central-state relations were primarily political. Congress was a unicameral assembly of ambassadors from the several states, each possessing a single vote and the undisputed power (though not the right) to dissociate itself from a collective decision of the central government. No national organ like a central executive existed to focus universal attention on common goals. For carrying out its decisions, the Confederation government relied principally on the congressmen of the various states, who were, however, dependent upon state interests and subject to the states' will. A federal administration scarcely existed and, in any event, was controlled directly by committees of Congress.

One must not imagine that the problems of such a system were so evident in those days as they would be now with our complex national economy. Actually, common interests were not important enough in many sections of the land to make haphazard co-operation the peril it would be today. The principal difficulties confronting the Confederation affected directly the more cosmopolitan and commercial groups and only indirectly or potentially the mass of the population. Decline of the credit of the central government, the presence of trade barriers among the states, depreciation of both state and confederation currency, the fear of Spanish, English, and Indian aggressions on the frontiers—these were major problems that the Confederation lacked the power to solve and that worked hardships on many people.

Federalism in America

THE SOLUTION OF THE CONSTITUTION

The solution to the conflict between nationalists and statists was a compromise between confederation, with its weak central government and strong states, and centralization, wherein the independence of each state would be curtailed completely by vesting the federal government-to-be with all final authority. Months of labor produced an intricate constitution, beautifully drawn, with several key principles establishing a division of labor between the whole and its parts.

DIVISION OF FUNCTIONS AND AUTHORITY

Functions: Certain activities that concerned the whole people were delegated to the federal government (for example, conduct of foreign relations and war, the regulation of interstate commerce and foreign trade). Certain other functions were delegated to the national government but were to be shared also by the states. The balance of functions not delegated to the central government explicitly or by implication and result of the delegated functions were to be managed by the states. Yet this simple classification could not be easily observed in practice, and controversy began immediately over the division of functions.

Structure: The states retained much of their political independence despite the powers given the national government. There were two bodies of political officers, independent of one another in most important respects. There were two systems of courts and two systems of taxation. Most important of all, loyalties were divided and these divided loyalties, although at one time polarized into warfare, served often to mitigate extreme nationalism or statism and to render the division of labor between nation and state continuously possible. But, as in the case of the assignment of functions, the structural distinctions of the federation did not prevent extensive conflicts over the legal jurisdiction of state and federal officers and over their powers with respect to one another.

Although put together bit by bit in the Constitutional Convention, the Constitution represented a whole frame of federal government. Its "rationality" came not from remote logic but from a political process that, despite the desires of many individual delegates, eventuated in a solution that was all things to all men—whether states' rights advocates or nationalists. The federalism that ensued after ratification was prevented functionally and structurally from falling prey either to the national or to the state authorities.

INTERLOCKING RELATIONSHIPS

The interrelations of state and nation in the Constitution were many. They were not those of superiority or subordination, either, when taken as a whole. The modes of electing the President, the Senate, and the House of Representatives involved the states. The federal government guaranteed the states a republican form of government and the states might call on the national government for help in repelling invasion or suppressing insurrection. The participation of the states was necessary in the amendment process, and state officers were required to take an oath to support the Constitution. Interstate agreements required congressional sanction. An independent chief executive was established to represent the nation, even though the states figured in his election through the Electoral College. The state militias might become federal troops in a national emergency. Thus the more simple organization of the Confederation was transformed. Driven on by their logic, their interests and their self-generating enthusiasm, the delegates at Philadelphia locked nation and states together almost beyond the possibility of dissolution.

Throughout the whole 160 years of American history, there were several constant factors whose stability and importance kept the federal government from rapidly developing into confederation or unitary government. These were the structural elements: political, judicial, fiscal, and protective. No power in the Constitution conceivably allows the destruction of this basic core of state autonomy.

THE POLITICAL POWER

The American states possessed working governments and administrations before the Union was formed. In many ways, they were incorporated as states in the new Constitution although new channels were provided for national intervention into the lives of all citizens without the mediation of the states. The rapid cutting of these latter channels evidences the great need that soon existed for them. Although John C. Calhoun and other states' rights advocates condemned as too rapid the shifting of authority from the confederation organization of nation-state-individual to the federal organization of nation-individual, it is questionable whether, in the face of pressing needs for national unity, the former organization would have survived at all. It might have been too feeble to harness the new national forces. If the attempt had been made to carry out all national policy through the agency of the states, the result might well have brought, in James Madison's words, "equal calamities to the innocent and the guilty, the necessity of a military force, both obnoxious and dangerous, and, in general, a scene resembling much more a civil war than the administration of a regular government. Hence was embraced the alternative of a government which, instead of operating on the states, should operate without their intervention on the individuals composing them."

Thereupon, state political machinery developed somewhat independently of the national. The United States in due course became the only large nation in the world in which strong and quasi-independent local parties prevailed throughout the land. American parties are founded to a large extent on local needs and their members are loyal to their local organizations. It is most difficult to organize the forty-eight quasi-independent political organizations into a disciplined national party.

Weaving the states as units into the federal structure re-enforces these tendencies. The states are represented equally in the Senate. They vote as units in the House when the Electoral College cannot give a majority for a presidential candidate. They set up congressional districts. Most important of all, they have almost complete control of state and local election systems, machinery and administration. And they are entrusted with the conduct of elections of federal officers, although since the Civil War there has been an increase in congressional legislation and judicial decision imposing federal controls on that part of the election machinery which affects federal officers.

THE JUDICIAL POWER

A stable federal system, one that is not a mere truce of arms between local force and national force, relies heavily on the judiciary. Dependence on a judiciary to settle federal conflicts is especially great in the formative stages of a federal government. The American Constitution insists that federal law is supreme on all matters entrusted to the competence of the federal government and that the Constitution takes precedence over state constitutions and laws. The Supreme Court is given jurisdiction over all disputes between two states or between a state and the central government. Accordingly, the Court has, with few objections, reviewed state laws and the decisions of state courts to determine whether they conformed to the federal Constitution. In important instances, the Court has used its discretion to enlarge or diminish the area of state autonomy.

The legal right of federal courts to move into state affairs is limited generally by the Constitution and specifically by the views of the Supreme Court. Wherever not authorized to intervene by the Constitution, or by federal laws passed in pursuance thereof, they must stop short; in such cases the jurisdiction of state courts is supreme. State courts exist independently, by right, with the tenure, privileges, jurisdiction, salaries, and personnel provided them by state constitutions and state laws.

THE TAXING POWER

Both state and national governments may levy taxes widely and intensively in the same area and on largely the same objects. Considerable confusion and conflict results from this practice. It is as if federal and state courts would hear the same case twice—worse, for the incentive to tax is stronger than the urge to hear a case. The states are free to levy any tax they please, except imports or duties on imports or exports, duties on tonnage, or taxes that burden the stream of interstate commerce passing through the state or stopping within the state. The national government has wide tax freedoms now, too, since it acquired the right to tax personal incomes by constitutional amendment in 1913.

Until World War I, the states depended primarily on property taxes and licenses for their income, while the federal government gathered the bulk of its funds from alcohol and tobacco taxes and tariff duties. Between 1905 and 1915, practically all states imposed motor vehicle taxes and all of them developed the motor fuel tax between 1917 and 1929. New functions more than kept pace with new taxes, however, and the states reached for even more taxes in new directions—the corporation income tax, individual income tax, more tobacco taxes, and a variety of direct consumer excise or sales taxes.

These more recent taxes caused difficulty. Sales taxes were unpopular. Income taxes benefited mainly the industrialized states like New York and Pennsylvania, and tended even there to encourage industry and individuals to move to other states. On the whole, the states were less successful than the federal government in tapping sources of revenue. Their finances suffered badly during the Great Depression of the "Thirties" and they sought and obtained federal emergency aid. Federal grants of money because an increasing proportion of their total revenue. All attempts at gaining unhampered funds or persuading the federal government to relinquish tax-rich resources like the tobacco tax failed.

Still the states might borrow money on the open market up to the limit of their credit; they might tax their citizens to their full capacity; they had full control over the collection procedures; and they could dispose of the money as they pleased. These were not small powers at all, despite difficulties on the fringes of financing, and they constitute a notable feature of state autonomy.

THE PROTECTIVE POWER

Protection means both army and police. The Constitution dictates that the state militias be jointly governed by state and nation. The states man and train their militias or "national guards" according to uniform standards of organization, armaments and discipline set down by the federal Congress. Congress may provide for calling forth the militias and incorporating them into the army of the United States. Almost from the beginning of the Union, Congress provided military funds for the states, but not until 1886 did it begin to attach meaningful conditions to their expenditure. The active intervention of the United States in world affairs caused many men to fear the inefficiency of the state forces. Furthermore, as the machinery of warfare became complicated and expensive, the militias could hardly be equipped by the individual state treasuries. New conditions were attached to the grants of federal aid in an effort to maintain the old balance between the federal standing army and the state guards without the loss of fighting preparedness. Although the possibility exists of wiping out most of the militias by federal nonfinancing, the states are entitled constitutionally to maintain whatever reserve military forces they may desire and can afford.

State and local police forces retain most of the authority and functions originally possessed, but the growth of rapid communications and a high mobility of population has necessitated in recent years a development of federal-state police co-operation. Federal facilities were employed to standardize methods of criminal identification and crime reporting among the states, to provide information and service to local authorities, and in a growing number of cases actively to aid local authorities in search and seizure. When certain problems became significantly interstate in character—among them car thefts, kidnapping, and white slavery—federal law took an active and often guiding hand.

SEPARATIST FEDERALISM

Two major theories of federalism have influenced American government since the beginning. One may be called "separatist federalism" because it visualizes a maximum separation and isolation of state and nation. The other may be called "co-operative federalism" because it seeks a solution of many social problems by joint nation-state action.

The nineteenth century had hardly begun before the Jeffersonians and Jacksonians took up an extreme separatist-federalist position. Their views dominated American legal and political thought, despite the effects of the Civil War, until World War I. In *Tarble's Case* (1871) the Supreme Court declared "there are within the territorial limits of each State two governments, restricted in their spheres of action, but independent of each other, and supreme within their respective sphere. Each has its separate departments; each has its distinct laws, and each has its own tribunals for their enforcement. Neither government can intrude within the jurisdiction, or authorize any interference therein by its judicial officers with the action of the other."

This judicially expressed separatist theory helped to limit functions of the state and nation because certain problems—such as child labor, wages and hours limits, and regulation of industry and commerce—required a flexible and sometimes co-operative solution not feasible in isolation. In the case of *Hammer v. Dagenhart* (1918), for example, the Supreme Court, in voiding a congressional act prohibiting the interstate transportation of goods in the manufacture of which child labor had been employed, declared that "the grant of authority over a purely federal matter was not intended to destroy the local power always existing and carefully reserved to the States in the Tenth Amendment to the Constitution." But a single state could not very well eliminate child labor in its industries; if it did so, the price of various products would go up, and it could not compete with similar products coming from states where child labor was still permitted.

In 1941, the Court in the case of *United States v. Darby*, reversed its position and declared that Congress "may choose the means reasonably adapted to the attainment of the permitted end, even though they involve control of intrastate activities." As a result the doctrine of separatist federalism was no longer the exclusive interpretation of the American federal system.

This great change toward increased federal control was reflected in purely intrastate matters as well. For example, in 1854, President Pierce, true to the established principles of Madison, Jackson, Monroe, and Polk had vetoed a bill granting federal lands to the states for the benefit of the insane, fearing that "the dignity of the states shall bow to the dictation of Congress by conforming their legislation thereto" and therefore cause "the beginning of the end" of federalism. Yet not quite a century later, the Supreme Court in reviewing an act of Alabama accepting federal money with many conditions attached, upheld its constitutionality, declaring: "Together the two statutes now before us embody a co-operative legislative effort by state and national governments, for carrying out a public purpose common to both, which neither could fully achieve without the co-operation of the other. The Constitution does not prohibit such co-operation."

CO-OPERATIVE FEDERALISM

The new attitude toward American federalism has been called "co-operative." It regards federal relations as an area of dynamic operations, of interchange of ideas, functions, aid, and personnel to serve mutual needs more effectively. It rejects on the one hand extreme separatist federalism and on the other hand full centralization.

The origin of co-operative federalism goes back to the government of the Articles of Confederation that set aside land in the Northwest Territory for the development of education by the territories and states to come. It goes back also to a wide variety of co-operative activities among federal and state officials in the early years of the federal republic. Submerged for long by a prevailing mood of federal-state conflict, co-operative federalism only took hold firmly in the early twentieth century.

Two far-reaching events ushered in the new period. In 1913, the federal government received the power to tax incomes and thus gained a continuing, highly productive source of funds. In 1914, the Smith-Lever Act gave half a million dollars to the Department of Agriculture to join with states and counties in a program of farm education and service. The amount of aid increased rapidly, and new programs were brought in following the success of the first program. Public opinion and officials seized on the idea of conditional grants as a needed compromise between centralization and local inadequacy. The grant system was well under way when America entered World War I, and continued to develop rapidly thereafter (see Figures 43 and 44).

GRANTS

Although at various times, central governments have granted aid to localities or states in personnel, land, and materials, the most important form of grants today is money. Central governments only infrequently give money grants to localities or states with-

FIGURE 43

THE NEW FEDERALISM: AN ADMINISTRATIVE PROBLEM

(*The American Case*)

FEDERAL-STATE ACTIVITIES INVOLVING DIVISION OF LABOR ON SAME FUNCTIONS	FEDERAL-STATE ACTIVITIES INVOLVING CONCURRENT PERFORMANCE OF SIMILAR FUNCTIONS *
Social Welfare, Health and Security Old-age assistance Aid to dependent children Aid to the blind General assistance Child welfare services Unemployment compensation Employment services Health programs	*Public Safety* Police protection Record and statistics Crime control Detention and custody of prisoners *Taxation* *Courts*
Education Land-grant colleges Vocational education Vocational rehabilitation	*Commerce, Industry, and Utilities* Maintenance of fair competition Regulation of securities and security exchanges
Veterans' Services and Benefits	
Agriculture Experiment stations Extension education Soil conservation and erosion Forestry School lunch Surplus food	*Transportation* Railroads Motor vehicles Water carriers Air carriers *Transmission and Sale of Electricity and* *Gas*
Public Works Highways Airports Public works planning	*Communications* Telephone and telegraph Radio broadcasting *Petroleum Industry*
Natural Resources Flood control and prevention Reclamation	*Rent Control* *Labor-Management Relations*
Public Housing	*Elections* (consigned almost wholly to
National Guard	states)

* The extent of co-operation between state and federal agencies varies widely but is present in each case.

out attaching conditions as to expenditure. Such unconditional grants are called "block grants." More commonly central governments give conditional grants. In some cases both types of grants are given; Canada, for example, provided subsidies to the provinces in addition to conditional grants. The relative fiscal weakness of local tax units and the strong temptation to guard scrupulously the spending of grants

FIGURE 44

FEDERAL GRANTS-IN-AID TO STATE AND LOCAL GOVERNMENTS*

ESTIMATED EXPENDITURES FISCAL YEAR 1951

Veterans' services and benefits	12,301,641
Social security, welfare, and health	1,594,133,375
Housing and community development	10,674,628
Education and general research	70,934,883
Agriculture and agricultural resources	182,739,135
Natural resources	18,595,624
Transportation and communication	459,440,062
Labor	159,362,276
District of Columbia	10,800,000
Total grants-in-aid	$2,518,981,624

* Source: *The Budget of the United States Government for the Fiscal Year ending June 30, 1952* (Washington, D. C.; Government Printing Office, 1951).

tend to make the size of grants ever larger and their conditions ever more stringent.

CONDITIONAL GRANTS

A wide variety of stipulations is imposed on the expenditure of conditional grants. The conditions range from the very broad but important statement of the general purposes for which money may be spent (for example, to establish agricultural and mechanical colleges) to minute stipulations regarding each small expenditure. We can list conditions that have been encountered:

1. Granted funds must be spent only on a stipulated program.
2. Programs must be planned in co-operation with the federal government.
3. The central, national agency has authority to review state operations and inspect progress "on the job" in fulfilling the purposes of the grant.
4. Statistical and financial records and reports must conform to federal standards.
5. State expenditures of grants are audited by the federal government.
6. The states are required to match all or part of the federal funds.
7. Federal agencies are authorized to discontinue grants to the states not fulfilling the conditions of the grants.
8. States are required to hire all personnel paid from grant funds according to merit and without reference to their political affiliations.

Conditional grants may cover the whole cost of a state-accepted and state-administered program; or, more usually, they will amount to a stated part of the total program cost and the states will be required by law to provide the balance. Such "matching grants" vary in how much they demand from the states—sometimes it is dollar for dollar, that is, 50–50, although at other times it may be 60–40, 75–25, and so forth.

Conditional grants are made according to some criterion of need; a formula is devised that adjusts the amount that the federal treasury will provide to the amount of need in a particular state. For example, given the desire to establish a good, uniform highway network throughout the United States it would be a mistake to grant equal sums to all states, large and small, urban or rural. Even granting funds according to population alone would not be desirable, because some states, New Mexico, for example, through which lengthy and vital highways pass, are sparsely populated. Therefore the federal law provided a formula that gave equal weight to population, area, and rural postal delivery route mileage in determining any single state's share of the total federal appropriation. Similarly, vocational education programs, agricultural programs, aid to the blind, and most other recent programs assist the various states according to some formula of need.

The principle of equalization is behind several programs; their aim is to counteract the centralization of wealth and resources in the United States in order to maintain or lift standards of well-being in poorer parts of the nation. Equalization, of course, is the objective of most centrally-administered social welfare programs and lies behind the principle of progressive taxation, as, for example, the income tax. Some states like some individuals are thought to need more help than others. Hence a grant program may provide more federal money to Mississippi than to Ohio in proportion to population. Since the states themselves administer grant programs, the grant system is a way of equalizing without centralizing. In a number of cases, the populous industrial states resent the equalizing process that takes money away from them through progressive taxation and gives it to other sections of the country. A survey of the vote in Congress on the early Federal Aid Road Bill of 1916, for example, shows that urban congressmen were lined up solidly against the bill. Sectional divisions have often been noted since then.

CO-OPERATION WITHOUT A FINANCIAL NEXUS

The American federal union, as well as other federations that we have noted, required federal-state co-operation to exist and operate effectively. In America such co-operation has gone beyond the basic necessities of organizing the government, even into areas not financed by grants to the states (see Figure 43). Grants stimulate co-operation, but several federal commissions and departments work actively with state agencies without an exchange of funds. The Interstate Commerce Commission and the Department of Agriculture are examples. The pattern of collaboration is usually designated by federal law and state laws and is worked out in detail by federal and state administrators. Joint federal-state conferences, joint hearings on matters of industrial and commercial regulation, exchange of information, loans of personnel, standardization of records, and co-ordination in operations commonly emerge from mutual needs. Difficulties have arisen from the lack of such co-operation and from inevitable clashes of local and national interests. But the co-operative trend has been growing stronger.

INTERSTATE RELATIONS

Another recent trend, paralleling co-operative federal-state activities in the fields of joint and concurrent administration, has been the increasing collaboration among states with or without federal participation. Often this collaboration has sprung from the fears of state leaders that the federal government might solve by itself some bothersome problem unless the states solved it themselves. Interstate relations have used four common procedures for acting in concert: interstate compacts and agreements, uniform state laws, reciprocal or contingent legislation, and administrative co-operation.

Between 1934 and 1947, thirty-seven compacts between two or more states were signed (and approved by Congress), more than the total number of such compacts from 1789 to 1913. Boundary disputes, public works, tax procedures, and natural resources were the most common subjects of compacts. The Port of New York Authority was a momentous result of the compact procedure.

Uniform state laws and reciprocal or contingent legislation are methods of adapting the internal laws of one state to that of other states with a view towards eliminating inconvenient, costly, and unnecessary conflicts of laws. The former are laws with nearly identical provisions passed by several states to regulate a problem common to all the states involved. Reciprocal or contingent legislation extends the privileges of one state to another provided the second state returns the privileges to citizens of the first state. Administrative co-operation between two or more state agencies has often accomplished the same purposes by informal agreements and procedural rules. The Council of State Governments, acting as a general secretariat for many interstate activities and as a clearing house for information, has helped accelerate the trend towards interstate co-operation.

Modern Federalism in the Balance

FEDERALISM OPERATING UNDER ADVERSE CONDITIONS

But despite the trend toward federal-state and interstate co-operation, federal systems, like most political institutions of the contemporary world, are under enormous pressures. The last century has seen increases in central power everywhere. Whatever its ultimate fate, federalism as a principle must operate more and more under conditions hitherto thought to be conclusively destructive of it.

SOCIAL AND ECONOMIC CENTRALIZATION

Foremost of these conditions is the centralization of population and industry that has occurred in all federal states. In America, a nation originally quite rural, some 20 per cent of the people today pursue agricultural occupations. The people of the rapidly growing cities, coming from many states, were inclined to be indifferent towards the state governments and to be relatively optimistic about the advantages of national regulation and administration. And many of those pursuing agricultural occupations became acutely aware that only the national government could reach out and control fully the frequently erratic markets for agricultural products.

Many Americans became aware of the fact that large-scale industry, although concentrated in a few localities, affected the whole country. Interstate commerce, which was expanding greatly, could only be regulated by the federal government. The states, indeed, were presumed to be harming the national economy when they attempted to regulate business and commerce. And increasing state interference with interstate commerce, cloaked under the police and health powers of the state, tended to bring on the states more opprobrium in the long run than it brought short-term benefits.

ECONOMIC AND EXTERNAL CRISIS

Economic depressions also had marked effects on federalism. With an imbalance of fiscal capacity between nation and state, the downward movement of the business cycle after 1929 brought fiscal poverty to the states and many demands for federal action. But the deep roots of federalism in American thought and in the federal political structure prevented the wholesale centralization of governmental functions. Instead, the conditional grant idea received wide support.

Also, to ameliorate crises in the international sphere the national government spent huge sums for foreign and military programs that overshadowed and caused the curtailment of state activities. Although temporary surpluses accumulated in many state treasuries during the war, afterward they were soon dissipated on programs that had been postponed.

INEQUALITIES AND DEPENDENCY OF LOCALITIES

The poverty of some of the states has been another condition adverse to federalism. The states have always differed among one another economically, but the difference has grown more pronounced in recent times. Per capita income in Mississippi in 1949 was $634; in California it was $1,665, almost three times as large. With such diversity, slogans about "the American standard of living" or "equality of opportunity" were challenged by scattered individuals, and the claim was put forth that only the direct intervention of the federal government through a number of important social service programs could help put matters to right. Furthermore, it could be shown that the equalization principle was not working properly through the grant system—California received $7.09 per capita in federal aid in 1947 while Mississippi received a mere $4.19. The states were conceived to be withering away from loss of functions and from incapacity to act when action was vitally necessary.

Opponents of centralization declared that the temporary success of centralization would soon be matched by a loss of initiative at the grass roots. They transferred John Stuart Mill's statement from individual to state: "A government cannot have too much of the kind of activity which does not impede, but aids and stimulates individual exertion and development. The mischief begins when, instead of calling forth the activity and powers of individuals and bodies, it substitutes its own activity for theirs; when, instead of informing, devising, and upon occasion denouncing, it makes them work in fetters, or bids them stand aside and does their work instead of them." Although grants could be admitted as better than outright centralization from the top down, the conditions attached to grants could lead ultimately to the mastery of the central government. "Block grants," with only the most general conditions, and distributed according to a simple formula of need, were proposed as an alternative.

Other federal nations felt the same struggle between central and local feeling, the same remorseless pressure of national defense, national standards, and national fiscal ability. Russia alone denies any economic localism and defends cultural federalism. But that a rigid separation of economic and cultural interests is maintainable is doubted by most social scientists. The two interact and modify each other. Therefore, under the Soviet system cultural diversity is likely to become economic apostasy and economic unity is likely to force cultural change.

ENTHUSIASM FOR UNIFORMITY

The desire for uniformity on the part of many people also works against federalism. The belief in "one right answer to every problem" affects thought about political affairs from the most important political matters to the smallest administrative matters. Certainly whether or not a case may be made for uniformity in the most important political matters, the case for uniformity in minor administrative matters is more in doubt. Since most of the force away from federalism is today a force exercised in the shadowland of administration, the dispersion of such force among many state agencies, with only an ultimate check on their behavior, may well help to preserve values more precious to a society than the values inherent in the punctilious execution of uniform detail.

THE FAILURE OF WILL

A remarkable feature, indeed, of the trend towards centralization and away from meaningful federalism is the inattention of the spokesmen for federalism to the consequences of their actions. They not only fail "to keep their houses in order," to quote one of their leaders, but in order to engage in national "logrolling," "horse-trading," and earn national publicity, they unconsciously betray the basic, local values in the name of which they call themselves Jeffersonians or states' rightists.

Woodrow Wilson inscribed the goals of balanced government in an essay that he once wrote: "Our duty is, to supply the best possible life to a federal organization, to systems within systems; to make town, city, county, state, and federal governments live with a like strength and an equally assured healthfulness, keeping each unquestionably its own master and yet making all interdependent and co-operative, combining independence with mutual helpfulness. The task is great and important enough to attract the best minds." To achieve it requires a great deal of courage, forbearance, and technical skill.

Questions and Problems

1. Distinguish between federation and confederation, giving three examples of each.

2. List five cultural and economic bonds that tend to unite New York and New Jersey; do the same for Maine and Mississippi. Must the same bonds unite every state or may they vary in kind and number? Explain your answer.

3. What are the similarities of and differences between federalism and functional representation? (For help, return to Chapters Five and Seven.)

4. How do federalism and feudalism resemble one another as *political* structures?

5. Compare and rank the strength of the chief executive in the Delian League, the German Empire, the Swiss federation, Argentina, and the United States.

6. Using the *Statesman's Year-Book* and a good encyclopedia as a supplement describe the British Commonwealth of Nations as a federation (350 words).

7. Compare with reference to their written constitutions, their distribution of powers, the role of political parties, and the strength of their national executive branch, the federalism of the Soviet Union and the United States.

8. Compare the type of union existing under the Articles of Confederation with that existing under the Constitution. Mark sharply the similarities and differences.

9. Describe how the American Constitution locks together the federal government and the state governments.

10. Explain how four structural features make the American states autonomous (350 words).

11. Describe the difference between the idea of separatist federalism and co-operative federalism. Show how both have always been present, in varying degrees, in federal-state relations.

12. Going back to the inventory of governmental activities in Chapter Two, compare it with figure 43, and estimate what proportion of the total functions of the federal government come within the scope of co-operative federalism.

13. Of the eight conditions that are sometimes exacted in conditional grant programs in America, which one do you think would arouse the most resentment among state officers? Why do you think so?

14. Define: "block grants," "matching grants," "the principle of equalization," "interstate compacts."

15. What are the conditions that at present are adversely affecting the preservation of federalism in America? Are these conditions operating only in America, do you surmise, or in Canada, the Soviet Union, and Australia as well?

16. If your goal in politics were to preserve the power of your state, what would your position be towards the Supreme Court (see Chapter Thirteen), block grants, conditional grants, co-operation without a financial nexus, interstate co-operation, and state government?

17. What is the relationship between the behavior and organization of American political parties and the organization of federalism? (Use materials from Chapter Six.)

18. Poll twenty members of the student body on the question: Which of the two governments, federal or state, is more free from political corruption, more efficient, more responsive to public opinion? Tabulate your answers and explain the results.

Longer Study and Research
Problems Suitable for Term Papers

1. Give an account in ten pages of the origin, organization, and operations of a federal state from your reading of one of the following works:
Commission on Organization of the Executive Branch of the Government, *Federal-State Relations*
James Bryce: *The Holy Roman Empire*
E. A. Freeman: *A History of Federal Government in Greece and Italy*
L. H. Morgan: *League of the Iroquois*
W. E. Rappard: *The Government of Switzerland*
W. P. M. Kennedy: *The Constitution of Canada*
A. P. Canaway: *The Failure of Federalism in Australia*
A. Kirkpatrick: *History of the Argentine Republic*

2. Write a paper of fifteen pages on the subject: "The Growth of Conditional Grants in the United States and the Methods of Administering Them."

3. Selecting a recent year, and using sources such as the *Book of the States* (published biennially) write an account of all interstate co-operative activities during the year (ten pages).

4. Compare the legal, political, cultural, and economic position of one of the American states with that of one of the Swiss cantons. Comment on their similarities and dissimilarities (ten pages).

16

INTERNATIONAL ORGANIZATION

T HE RELATIONS among nations are scarcely those one would find in a purposeful organization. Rather, the observer is impressed by the profound lack of shared beliefs among the national governments except the essentially negative belief that each state should go its own way. Imagine the chaos that would permeate an administrative agency, a political party, or even that barely organized network called the public, if the conditions attaching to international relations were present!

The persistence of the ideal of universal brotherhood seems marvellous indeed in view of the actual state of international relations. Whole peoples are segregated from one another by iron curtains and communicate principally by mutual abuse. Dozens of different educational systems exist, the chief purpose of which is to teach children to be able to read one side of the abuse, and to master the mechanics of damaging other peoples. Then, there is the telltale fact that in all countries travel abroad is regarded as a privilege, not as a normal movement. In a host of ways, the purpose of men is to forestall international organization.

Yet there are certain stable patterns of behavior in international affairs. For example, nations conduct wars and diplomacy in similar ways. Patterns of behavior tend to become institutions or organizations such as the International Red Cross or the United Nations. So we may well study international relations with an eye towards those tendencies of behavior that have almost achieved the status of worldwide international organization. In other spheres of politics, there are so many political organizations to study that we can afford to be impatient with mere tendencies. The international sphere, however, to most people's views, desperately needs organization, and the problem is too important to be dismissed, no matter how meager the materials of history.

Three principal modes of organizing international relations provide us with the general divisions of this chapter. The first is the imperial method, illustrated differently by the Roman Empire and the Medieval Church. The second is the shared beliefs in the balance of power and international law. The third method of organizing international relations is by international organs with federal or confederational authority, such as the League of Nations.

Roman World Order and Its Medieval Myth

ANCIENT GREEKS FAILED TO ORGANIZE PEACE

As we have seen in the chapter on federalism, the ancient Greeks failed to achieve international peace despite their wonderfully cultured city-states. They organized several voluntary associations or leagues, none of which developed into a true federal state or brought peace by voluntary co-operation. Although the Greek cities managed together to fight off conquest by the oriental empires, they finally succumbed to Alexander of Macedon and then to the Roman Republic.

TECHNIQUES OF ROMAN EXPANSION

The empire of the Roman Republic and the later Roman Empire were not established from a desire to co-operate with other nationalities, but were the result of conquest. In conquering the civilized world of the West and Middle East, however, the Romans had occasion to supplement their effective military might by arrangements of civil government that gave rights to the conquered. The Romans, after the fashion of their times, were not prey to torment and guilt of soul when they moved into conquered lands. No Roman consul is known to have beseeched the Almighty, as President McKinley did on the question of governing the Philippines, for advice on the disposal of new lands. The Romans occupied foreign lands, imposed Roman governors, destroyed their principal individual enemies, instituted an orderly military or civil administration, left the inhabitants with their local institutions, and diverted a not too great amount of local treasures to Rome.

Occasionally revolts of nationalities flared up, but most of the time the many groups forming the Empire felt that they could prosper and be free within the Empire at least as well as they could without. Individuals from all parts of the Empire moved at will from province to province. In Rome itself, long before the Christian era, grumpy, old politicians spoke angrily of the babel of tongues and characters that inhabited the Eternal City.

"E PLURIBUS UNUM"

The fact is that the Romans, with no great love or hatred of other people, earned universal admiration for their administrative system. By tolerating strange cultures within their empire and by allowing other people sooner or later to share their own political institutions, they caused a great imperial loyalty to arise. As the centuries passed, one could hardly say when Rome as the mistress of colonies died and the Roman Empire as an international unity began. Sufficient to say that for many generations Italians, Gauls, Greeks, Spaniards, Egyptians, Mesopotamians and many other local groups accorded sovereign legitimacy to the Roman Empire. And the legitimacy that was granted the imperial rule (*imperium*) seriously hampered the efforts of hundreds of medieval kings to establish their own legitimacy, save on the basis of charisma (Charlemagne), or on some accredited claim of being Roman Emperor (Charlemagne, later on).

"JUS GENTIUM"

A striking development during Roman times was the development of a body of international law called the *jus gentium*. This "law of the peoples" was an extraction and compilation from the analogous and common elements of the laws found among the peoples of the Empire and the fringes beyond the boundaries of the Empire. A "foreigners' judge," *praetor peregrinus*, applied and developed this law in the many disputes that arose among individuals travelling to Rome and other parts of the Empire. Similar in important respects to modern international law, the *jus gentium* had the most important quality of being enforced by an adequate administrative machinery.

Gradually, the *jus gentium* was infiltrated by elements of a theory of natural law. As the Empire was integrated, the *jus gentium* became part of the civil law, and, finally, its elements are to be found in the great Code of Justinian. It must be admitted that this is an ideal course for international law to run, and modern international jurists have such a career in mind for their rather ineffectual counterpart.

THE PSYCHOLOGICAL HERITAGE OF ROME

Medieval politists held fast to the ideal of universal empire, but demanded, as the credentials for establishing such an empire, that authority be descended from Rome. Rome, of course, was no longer in a situation where it might export legitimate force. It could only exert spiritual power. The new age had two such psychological instruments, the idea of a grand unity just referred to and the spiritual authority of the Roman Catholic Church. The idea of unity was perhaps a hindrance, except as it worked through the Church, because it was practically impossible to realize. While their fields rotted, and their peoples starved and fell prey to brigands, the medieval princes competed for the elusive imperial honors. Here was the earthly Holy Grail, sought for through great misery but never found.

The Church did better than the temporal rulers, granted that no absolute supremacy could be achieved. It was an age when violence was so customary and important as a means that few could see anything practical in peace. Yet some mitigation of warfare was accomplished by recurrent Church movements to establish the "Peace of God." At the end of the eleventh century, a "Truce of God" was declared. It aimed with some success at confining private warfare to certain periods of the year only.

Subsequently, peace leagues were formed by the Church to propagandize for peace and, in a few cases, to impose punishment on transgressors. The weak and spasmodic machinery of enforcement, it may be imagined, had to rely on motives other than dislike of aggression in order to strengthen itself. When several motives, including the dislike of aggression, were joined, punitive action sometimes resulted. "Transgressors," then as in recent times, very often happened to be principalities without powerful friends, but with temporal and religious enemies that had been nursing old grudges.

The Equilibrium of Nations and International Law

FORMATION OF THE MODERN STATE SYSTEM

The Treaty of Westphalia (1648), ending the Thirty Years' War, marked the beginning of the modern system of national states. It "recognized" the "equality" and "independence" of all the states of Europe. Now, of course, this agreement did not change much the character of the players in the game of international politics; it merely changed the conditions of play from poker to bridge. The ghost of the Roman Empire was banished from the scene; no group now claimed a right to omnipotence. Religion was put aside as the stipulated object of conflict. Each nation was given a new deal; its internal affairs were not supposed to be the business of other nations; only its external moves and motives could legitimately provoke the other governments into warlike acts towards it.

Two major developments followed the new nationalistic kind of international relations. One was the growth of the "balance-of-power" idea. The other was the growth of "international law." We may discuss them in turn, realizing always that international conflict, whatever the changes in its mode or rationalization, played the paramount role in international life.

BALANCE OF POWER DISTINGUISHED

The balance of power is the name given to a prevailing system of international relations in which peaceful and bellicose national actions are dominated by a strategy of preventing any single power from achieving a monopoly of strength (see Figure 45). It is to be distinguished from the *imperial* system, where the predominant motives for action are to maintain an existing monopoly (Roman) or recapture a vanished monopoly (medieval).

The balance-of-power system is also to be distinguished from the *imperialist* system, in which the predominant motives are revolutionary in nature, as, for example, to establish the rights of man everywhere (French Republican and Napoleonic Wars), to spread the gospel

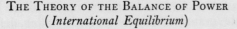

FIGURE 45

THE THEORY OF THE BALANCE OF POWER
(*International Equilibrium*)

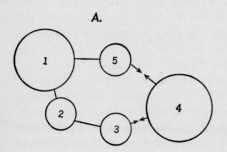
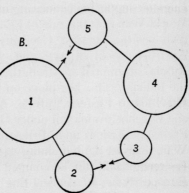

A. Equilibrium in which nation "4" is very strong. (Example: France under Napoleon is nation "4.")

B. Equilibrium in which nation "1" has accumulated strength in relation to nation "4." (Example: Germany under William II is nation "1.")

1. each nation within the balance of power network is a circle
2. size of circle represents strength
3. lines represent alliances; arrows represent direction of force

The "ideal" situation: A disposition of international means fixed to immediately repel any disturbance of the equilibrium. This disposition requires, in theory, the constant equating (through frequent jiggling) of the opposing forces at any possible rupture point.

(Christian crusades, Mohammedan expansion), to achieve world communism (Soviet imperialism), to exploit the riches of the world (Spanish imperialism of the sixteenth century, English imperialism of the eighteenth century).

No age is free of the balance-of-power motive. Soviet imperialism today is complemented by a balance-of-power motive aimed at containing the power of the United States in western Europe and elsewhere. Many medieval men fought to maintain an equilibrium, even though the shadow of the Holy Roman Empire overcast the proceedings.

HISTORICAL EXAMPLES

The strategy of the balance of power has as its major aim this situation: that no nation shall be in a position to destroy the power of a combination of other nations, that can be expected to join together to prevent monopoly. The classic illustration of this condition is English foreign policy from the seventeenth to the twentieth centuries. In the eighteenth century and part of the nineteenth century, England intervened on the continent by policy and by arms to prevent the Bourbon kings and Napoleon Bonaparte from destroying the Hapsburg regime based on Austria-Hungary and its allies.

When Prussia united Germany in 1870, after defeating France, England supported France against German power, ultimately entering World War I on the side of France. France, meanwhile, supported her own position against Germany by allying with Russia against the Austro-German alliance, and, when the Bolshevists seized power in Russia, attempted to strengthen her position in Eastern Europe and the Balkans. This last move on France's part failed in the face of Nazi activities in Eastern Europe. Austria, Hungary, Bulgaria, Rumania, and Czechoslovakia fell under German influence in the 1930's, leaving France dependent upon Britain and upon Russia.

The Soviet Union, however, ideologically hostile to France and England, could not be counted on to support France against Hitler, especially after France and England refused Russian aid in settling the demands of Hitler in Czechoslovakia at Munich in 1938. On the other hand, the Soviet Union could not enter the lists on the side of Germany. In August, 1939, the Soviet Union and Germany signed a non-aggression pact. The Soviet Union first waited out the German war against the West and then was forced to fight against Germany. Hitler had no intention of allowing Soviet Russia to amass strength while Germany languished in the West. As matters turned out, Hitler acted precipitously and foolishly. He recklessly invited enemies of great strength while gaining allies of modest strength in Japan and Italy. Like Napoleon, he acquired enemies who were joined together not out of mutual esteem but to fight a threat to the existing order.

Not only the great states but also the smaller states played the strategy of the balance of power over the last several centuries. Countries like Venice, Hungary, Savoy, Spain, Poland, and Czechoslovakia tried to achieve security and maintain their independence by allying themselves now with one, now with another, of the great powers. Their continued existence or their aspirations to independence (if they were not already states) were fostered by the reluctance of the great powers to see them assimilated into or destroyed by some threatening nation. In his *Politics among Nations*, Dr. Hans Morgenthau quotes a letter by Queen Mary of Hungary, written in 1553, in which she writes of the Venetians: "You know how they fear the power of the one and of the other of the two princes [Charles V of Austria and Francis I of France] and how they are concerned to balance their power."

THE STRATEGY OF THE BALANCE

The balance of power, says Dr. Morgenthau, is achieved by four general methods: the principle of "divide and rule"; compensations in the form of territorial grants, colonial and trading concessions (and, we may add, outright subsidies); armaments; and alliances and counteralliances.

The first method—divide and rule—has been consistently used by Germany to fight Russian attempts to unite eastern Europe in a pan-Slavic federation, for fear that Slavic power would be massed on the edge of Germany.

The Treaty of Utrecht of 1713, which ended the War of the Spanish Succession, exhibits the use of compensations to maintain the balance; the French Bourbons and Austrian Hapsburgs divided Spanish territorial possessions among them in a manner calculated to conserve the European equilibrium. Other illustrations of the use of compensation are the French post-World War I policy by which France tried to keep its eastern European allies out of the arms of Germany by means of loans, among other things, and the Marshall Plan by which America has tried to keep western Europe from allying with the Soviet Union.

The armament race is another common symptom of the jiggling of the equilibrium. A territorial conquest (like that of the Nazis in Austria, for example) will cause a nation to expand its munitions production and strengthen its frontier forces (as did France after the Austrian Putsch).

Mutual-aid alliances, by which one nation agrees to go to the aid of another nation in the event of war, are also common; they seek to establish a condition under which attempts to expand are frustrated by a forceful counterpoise to expansion. The French-Eastern European agreements, alluded to previously, exemplify this practice.

PREMISES OF BALANCE-OF-POWER POLITICS

The balance of power as the basis for international relations rests on some premises that must be made clear. A nation's leaders may dream of empire; but no nation may believe in imperium or imperialism as a practical way of settling permanently the sphere of the equilibrium. Thus, Italy could manage to take part in the balance-of-power arena quite well until Mussolini went beyond the point of dreaming of imperium to the point of believing a restoration of the Roman imperium a practical idea. However, a nation may strive for the balance of power in one sphere while being imperialistic in another sphere. For example, England in the eighteenth century sought a balance in Europe and empire overseas.

Another premise of the balance-of-power principle is that the participants in the equilibrium do not believe a legal order founded either on international co-operation or on international authority is a practical solution. Nations operating according to the balance-of-power principle may join organizations like the League of Nations but they continue to practice "secret diplomacy" according to the balance-of-power principle.

In addition, the balance-of-power principle assumes that nations are free to shift as necessity demands they shift—almost automatically, by the pure principle. Otherwise, the situation will develop into one resembling a retail trading market when a single concern owns a number of stores that are supposed to be free to set their own prices but in fact are not. It is most unlikely that Soviet Russia today will let Poland ally itself with France in order to get more French goods and perhaps, later on, better concessions from the Russians. It is even unlikely that a nation in western Europe will be allowed by the United States to ally itself with Russia.

From these examples we can see that the balance of power, which is premised on flexibility of maneuvers and diplomacy of the traditional, amoral type, now faces extreme rigidity in international affairs. If an allied nation has any choice at all, it can jump the scale once and no more. It is then transfixed by all political instruments to its new polar position, either for or against one of the superpowers, America or Russia. Both in England and France, and in South America as well, there has been talk of independence, of a third force to enter and give meaning to the equilibrium idea. But it has come to naught and is unlikely to capture the leadership and resources at this point in time that would be required to influence decisively the policies of the superpowers.

THE DECLINE OF DIPLOMACY

So it seems that the age of balanced power is passing, and with it, some of its most noted paraphernalia. Time was when a new treaty caused the greatest excitement among connoisseurs of international affairs. It would be scrutinized meticulously for its meaning to the existing equilibrium. Men would ask: Who has sold out to whom? Who is aiming at an advantage? What effects will this have on our allies, and can we use this treaty to cause jealousy and disaffection among the opposing coalition's allies? And so on. Today a treaty is often administrative in nature—that is, it presents a way of handling a technical problem or of solving a problem of minor jurisdiction within the larger system. Or it is often the publicized part of a well-known fact that A consistently dominates B and leads B by the hand, economically, socially, and politically.

Diplomacy adorned the age of the balance of power as chivalrous knights and scholarly clerics adorned the late middle ages. The individual diplomats were as necessary to kings and republican committees as agents on the stock exchange are for investment bankers. The shrewdness, deftness, and facility of diplomats for arranging affairs often brought great gain to their countries. International conferences, at which their talents were arrayed in free-for-all competition, made decisions of great moment to the *status quo*.

Today, the conditions for the effective functioning of diplomacy and conferences are absent. Diplomats with nothing to give sit at tables where there is nothing to take. Their governments, if they are the two or three most powerful of all, have locked up everything at home. The agents of the smaller states come to get inside information on events, not to make history.

THE CAREER OF INTERNATIONAL LAW

Of all the institutions that have suffered from the decline of balance-of-power politics, perhaps the most noteworthy victim is international law. If we were to trace the importance of international law in the history of international affairs, we should describe it as a lusty infant in the seventeenth century, a promising child in the eighteenth century, a young adult with a disturbing muscular weakness in the nineteenth century, and a helpless cripple in the present.

The career of international law was importantly related to that of the balance of power. The politics of balanced power required a corresponding quasi-legal order. Both processes—the balancing of power and the development of international law—were based on the ultimate premises of equality of nations and self-help. These processes could not settle with finality the question of peace and war. They might only moderate that question, substituting conditional warfare for totalitarian warfare, and substituting a fair degree of observance of common rules for a disregard of international bonds. Consequently, the history of international law has never satisfied those who seek a legal system as effective as the legal systems that regulate the domestic affairs of a nation.

In the sixteenth and seventeenth centuries, Vittoria, Suarez, Gentili, and Grotius wrote treatises on the "laws" of war, with some reference to peace. Taking the several nations of the world as equal in world affairs and all-powerful within their domestic spheres, they describe some of the uniformities observable among the nations in their relations with one another. Thus, the practice of exchanging prisoners of war was accepted, rather than the practices of making them into slaves or of killing them. Save Gentili, they believed that there was a universal law of nature which could be discovered by reason and good faith, and that nations "should" obey that law.

Of course, what nations "should" do and what they "would" do are quite different matters. Diplomats and politicians might read Grotius and approve of his ethics, but, when called to their desks, they could hardly behave as he wished them to. "Treaties must be obeyed," wrote international lawyers. But the practical politician, in order to survive, said: "Treaties must be obeyed unless the national interest demands the contrary." "Neutrals must be allowed the freedom of the seas by belligerents," wrote the jurists. It was a dictum that pleased the Americans in the last years of the eighteenth century, but Britain paid scant heed to it. Then came the Civil War, and Britain claimed the doctrine strongly, while the Union cause avoided it like the plague.

Still, it is foolish to be cynical. The fact is that there was something to international law over two centuries and more. It can be stated best in Montesquieu's terms: the Law of Nations requires nations to help each other as much as possible in time of peace and to injure each other only so much as is necessary in time of war. In an age of total war, this principle, once so trite and so vague, now appears to have been a great accomplishment. From it sprang practices that at times threatened to harry the dogs of war from earth.

METHODS OF SETTLING INTERNATIONAL DIFFERENCES

Mediation—the friendly intercession of a third party in a dispute—stopped wars like the Russo-Japanese War of 1905, prevented armed conflicts, and helped to settle conflicting claims of nations that

FIGURE 46
THE LAWS OF WAR

WAS *KAPITULATION* BEDEUTET:

TRANSLATION OF ZG. 123

WHAT *CAPITULATION* MEANS:

im Kleinen:

Kapitulation bedeutet, dass die Hoffnungslosigkeit der örtlichen Lage anerkannt wird. Alliierte Kommandeure mussten in diesem Krieg in Singapur und auf Corregidor selbst kapitulieren. Deutsche Kapitulationen erfolgten während des vergangenen Sommers örtlich an mehreren Stellen im Osten und Westen, wo rein militärisch erkannt wurde, dass weiteres Blutvergiessen nicht mehr gerechtfertigt war. In allen Fällen wurde die Übergabe korrekt und mit vollen Ehren vorgenommen.

im Grossen:

Kapitulation bedeutet, dass die Hoffnungslosigkeit der Gesamtlage anerkannt wird. Die Alliierten sind der Ansicht, dass man mit dem Nationalsozialismus nicht verhandeln kann, und dass die Kapitulation bedingungslos sein muss, damit nicht noch einmal (wie nach dem letzten Krieg) behauptet werden kann, Deutschland sei auf feindliche Versprechungen „hineingefallen". Deshalb sagen die Alliierten: Keine Versprechungen und keine Verhandlungen mit den Nazis!

On a small scale:

Capitulation means that the hopelessness of the local situation is being recognised. In this war, Allied commanders capitulated in Singapore, Tobruk and on Corregidor. German surrenders took place last summer locally at several places in the East and West where it was recognised, strictly for military reasons, that further loss of lives was no longer justified. In all these instances, the surrender took place in good order and with full honors.

On a large scale:

Capitulation means that the hopelessness of the overall situation is being recognised. The Allies hold that there can be no dealing with National Socialism and that the surrender must be unconditional, so no one can say (as after the last war) that Germany has been "tricked" by enemy promises. That is why the Allies say: No promises and no dealings with the Nazis!

WAS KAPITULATION *NICHT* BEDEUTET:

WHAT CAPITULATION *DOES NOT* MEAN:

im Kleinen: Kapitulation bedeutet *nicht*, dass der einzelne Soldat jemals der Willkür eines Feindes ausgesetzt ist. Als Kriegsgefangener untersteht er dem Schutz der Genfer Konvention, welche genaue Bestimmungen über seine Behandlung, Verpflegung, Unterbringung, usw. enthält und welche vorsieht (Artikel 75, Vertrag vom 27.VII.1929), dass Kriegsgefangene so bald wie möglich nach Friedensschluss nach Hause zurückzuschicken sind.

im Grossen: Kapitulation bedeutet *nicht*, dass der einzelne an Kriegsverbrechen unbeteiligte Deutsche von den Alliierten zur Verantwortung gezogen wird. Massenvergeltung gehört zu den Dingen, gegen welche die Alliierten kämpfen. Präsident Roosevelt hat erklärt: „Die Vereinten Nationen haben nicht die Absicht, das deutsche Volk zu versklaven. Es ist unser Wunsch, dem deutschen Volk die Möglichkeit zu normaler, friedlicher Entwicklung als nützliche und geachtete Glieder der europäischen Völkerfamilie zu geben."

ZG 123

On a small scale: capitulation does *not* mean that the soldier at any time will be subjected to the enemy's whim. As a prisoner of war he is protected by the Geneva Convention which contains detailed instructions regarding his treatment, food, shelter etc. and provided (article 75, Treaty of July 27, 1929) that prisoners of war must be returned home as soon as possible after the peace has been signed.

On a large scale: capitulation does *not* mean that the individual German who has taken no active part in war crimes, will be held responsible by the Allies. Mass retaliation belongs to the things which the Allies are fighting against. President Roosevelt declared, "The United Nations do not intend to enslave the German people. It is our desire to give the German people an opportunity to become useful, and respected members of the European community of nations."

Under some conditions, international law has meant the difference between life and death to soldiers at the front. This leaflet and others like it were fired or dropped by air over the German lines in World War II by the millions.

were out of touch with one another. Arbitration—the adjudication of a dispute between two parties by a third party or a panel of dis-interested persons, taking into account principles acceptable to both parties— settled some significant disputes in the late nineteenth and early twentieth centuries. Large numbers of states declared their adherence to treaties that laid down codified rules for the conduct of war (see Figure 46).

Dozens of international organizations dealing with special problems got under way in the late nineteenth and early twentieth centuries. Among the earliest of these were the Universal Telegraph Union (1865), the Universal Postal Union (1874), and the European Union of

Railway Freight Transportation (1890). The names of these organizations and of the others that followed signify that, in important practical matters, the national states had decided that efficiency, cultural interchange, and economic progress did not have to wait for a world state.

Finally, we may mention the efforts to establish true international law, with adjudication of disputes. At The Hague, later at the League of Nations, and ultimately at the United Nations, a panel of judges was established by election of the participating nations. This International Court of Justice, as it came to be called, was to interpret international law when pronouncing judgment on facts and law in cases involving member nations.

SOURCES AND SANCTIONS OF INTERNATIONAL LAW

Now the inquiring reader may ask what was this international law that these bodies were supposed to apply. The question should not be particularly bothersome, because it is a rare jurist who, given the right to declare the law, cannot find a law to declare. Common law courts never had serious trouble with this problem. And the judges of some Roman law countries adhere to the doctrine that there is a law to cover every case that comes before them.

More particularly, however, the international law that these international tribunals expected to apply came from four sources: (1) conventions and treaties to which the parties involved in a suit are parties; (2) international custom (the modal practices of nations in their dealings with one another); (3) general principles of public law accepted in the domestic legal systems of states; (4) the writings of jurists and the precedents set by previous court decisions on points of international law.

This richness of sources prevented, and will continue to prevent, an international court from begging leave of a case for lack of law. However, the ineffectiveness of international law as compared with the law as we defined it earlier stands out when we realize that there are no police officers and legal officers to prosecute "criminal" cases under the law of nations. Furthermore, there are no executive officers of the court. Finally, individual damage must be converted into a national claim before it can be taken up in the court, and even then, the defendant must be another nation, not the individual culprit.

Before the 1930's there seemed to be a trend towards granting international courts more and more jurisdiction, just as there seemed to be a trend towards employing international organizations for doing a number of other tasks of a legislative (multilateral treaty) and administrative (of the Postal Union type) kind. But since that time, the trend of international affairs, both major and minor in importance, has been diverted by the politics of the great issues of totalitarian war and cold war.

The success of the law and the courts, in the last analysis, whether we be discussing domestic or international affairs, depends on the power of the supporting authorities in the realm that courts and law profess to cover. International courts depend on some international authority in the realm of international affairs. Otherwise at best, they illuminate with lawfulness only those crevices of international conflict that the forces of independent nationalism find too trivial to darken.

Peace and Law by Co-operative Force

THE VARIETY OF PLANS

What has been the nature of attempts to organize a jural order of the world in which the law will be declared and enforced as a matter of course? Political writers have sometimes dedicated themselves to proposing ideal schemes for the organization of mankind. Dante Alighieri, the great medieval poet, proposed a universal empire, jointly commanded by a temporal and a spiritual state. Later examples of the same ideal of an international authority are to be found in the writings of the Abbé St. Pierre, of Jean-Jacques Rousseau, and of Immanuel Kant.

Recent times have seen any number of detailed proposals for world organization, ranging from the wildest imperial dreams of international revolutionary associations composed of Fascist or workers' spokesmen to the scholarly, technically elegant compositions of the famous card-playing expert, Ely Culbertson, or of the Committee to Frame a World Constitution, sponsored by the University of Chicago.

RELATION OF BALANCE OF POWER TO A WORLD ORDER

In describing the two modern attempts at putting into practice the ideals of world organization, we must be cautious about exaggerating the differences between the balance of power and a world order. The balance of power, we have said, no longer can govern with moderate success the relations among nations. But certain aspects of the balance of power are perennial companions of any political and legal order. The devoted advocates of world order often believe that conflicts will be reduced to near zero by the magic of universal organization. But, recalling that the national political organization has not eliminated conflict in the internal affairs of nations, one cannot take such beliefs seriously. Under any conceivable world order, nations will wrangle, men will differ bitterly, selfish interests will prosper, and honest men will be bedeviled and frustrated. Combinations will form and blocs will seek control of the international machinery. The balance-of-power idea and practice will no longer *monopolize* the policies of nations and peoples, but they will continue to operate within the world order.

Nevertheless, the world order that may be postulated realistically is one which will box in the politics of nations and interests on four sides: First, legitimacy will be accorded the world order; a dominant ideology of allegiance to the world will prevade the minds of a significant number of politists. Second, a consensus will develop, forming a basis for collective action; beliefs shared by a vast majority of the world's people will dominate the words and actions of the new order's officers and institutions. In addition, a nearly universal area of free communication will embarrass special interests and prevent men who covertly espouse the principles of the balance of power or other "antisocial" principles from overtly conspiring on their behalf in some isolated corner of the world. And, last, the world order will require large-scale administration that will have several effects: politists who are loyal to the world order will increase proportionately to sectional or nationalistic politists; administration will bring home to peoples everywhere the functional, workaday meaning of a world order; and the institutions of the world order will become sufficiently durable and massive to resist destruction. Even a relatively ineffective world organization, the League of Nations, showed some durability—writing of the administrators of the League before World War II, E. F. Ranshofen-Wertheimer declared: "The Secretariat commanded its own loyalties, it had its own corporate reaction, its own psychology. This basic unity survived even the outbreak of the war. . . ."

ORIGINS OF THE LEAGUE OF NATIONS

We will now analyze the two great operating international organizations of modern times, the League of Nations and the United Nations and try to understand why neither achieved the conditions of a world order.

The League of Nations, of course, came first; its Covenant was drafted by a special commission of the Peace Conference after World War I, under the leadership of President Woodrow Wilson of the United States. It was approved by a Plenary Conference of the victorious powers in 1919, and the League came into being on January 10, 1920. The League's subsequent career demonstrated the difficulties besetting any project for a world order by co-operative force.

Twenty-nine states formed the initial membership, thirteen neutrals joined in 1920, and the addition of further subscriptions, including those of ex-enemy nations like Germany, brought the total membership to fifty-four by 1928. The United States, whose President inspired the organization of the League, never became a member. A dislike of becoming involved in commitments to other nations, quite widespread at that time in America, combined with a violent dispute between President Wilson and a group of senators to block America's affiliation.

It is difficult at present to assess exactly the results of America's alienation from her brain child. Certainly the beginnings of the League were auspicious enough, and it is possible that American adherence to the Covenant might ultimately have made the difference between life and death for the League. America would have supplied, without doubt, a greater degree of nonpartisanship than the ultimate French and British leadership provided for the League.

Without the United States, the more disinterested motives behind the formation of the League lost a powerful spokesman, and the League became, in the opinion of many observers, an instrument for the preservation of the power position of victorious England and France. The general motivation behind the League—the growing sense of world community, the desire to provide machinery for keeping the peace and for punishing breakers of the peace, the need for positive administration of the world's resources to benefit both countries that were well off and those poorly off—these general purposes were often afterwards subordinated to the purpose of preserving the *status quo*.

COMPLEX ORGANIZATION OF THE LEAGUE

The structure of the League was formidable. Nothing like it had ever existed before. There was an assembly of all the member nations, *acting through agents of their governments*. There was a Council on which the "Great Powers" were permanently represented and to which, ultimately, ten nonpermanent members were elected by the Assembly for three-year terms. The Great Powers, primarily France and England, dominated the Council and, in turn, the Council came to dominate the League. The assembly in time confined itself mostly to declaring general policies and to acting as a sounding board for international official opinion.

A Secretariat administered the affairs of the League without much executive authority. A number of specialized agencies, such as the International Labor Organization, were attached to the League and many of these had effective economic and humanitarian programs. Thus, the League, through such agencies, helped to resettle hundreds of thousands of displaced persons. It gave loans to hard-pressed nations of eastern Europe. It fought disease throughout the world and came to grips with the problems of narcotic rings and white slavery. It hastened the freeing of certain waterways to international commerce. It gave to technically backward areas a great deal of information and technical assistance.

Yet the League failed to achieve peaceful solutions of the most important problems—aggressive nationalism and international economic maladjustments. True, the Covenant had foreseen both of these problems. In Article 12 of the Covenant, there was a provision requiring that any dispute that might lead to war be submitted to peaceful settlement. The League was to inquire, when negotiations seemed to be bogging down, into the circumstances of the conflict between two powers. Members agreed not to engage in warfare while the League was investigating. The League might then recommend adjudication or arbitration of the dispute by the Permanent Court of International Justice, or the Council itself might arrange for the settlement of the dispute in consultation with the interested parties.

If these remedies failed, or if one party defied the League, Article 16 authorized the League to inflict financial and economic penalties—such as embargoes—on the offending member, or, if deemed desirable, the League might ask its members to take up arms against the convicted aggressor.

Also, on the question of international economic maladjustments, Article 19 of the Covenant, providing for treaty revisions when deemed necessary, authorized the reform of international arrangements so that poorer powers would not be deprived of markets and raw materials.

THE FAILURE OF THE MAJOR GOALS

However, the League did not employ in a determined fashion either of these two provisions for attacking the most important problems of international politics. British policy tended to regard the League as a means of preserving the balance of power. French political leaders tended to regard the League as a means of encircling Germany and preventing the rise of new powers. The Soviet Union, belatedly a member of the League, treated it for many years as a hostile capitalist coalition.

Italy, chagrined at its poor winnings in the World War I, saw the League as a conspiracy of the wealthy powers to prevent the expansion and growth of the poorer powers. Germany, although it joined the League after a time, disliked many features of the organization that seemed to have been formed mostly to enforce the punitive terms of the Treaty of Versailles against that country. The small nations, disappointed at the abstinence of the United States, came to look with

cynical eyes upon the League; to them it was often only a new version
of the old balance-of-power politics.

The League, in retrospect, was a sacrifice to national interests, faint
hearts, and missed opportunities. Although it could stop disputes between Sweden and Finland, Germany and Poland (when Germany was
weak), Turkey and Iraq, Greece and Bulgaria, Peru and Columbia,
Poland and Czechoslovakia, and even could stop minor disputes of
great powers like Britain, it failed miserably over the gigantic issues of
Japan in China, Italy in Ethiopia, Germany in the Rhineland and
Czechoslovakia, foreign intervention in the Spanish Civil War, and
Russia in Finland.

These great failures decreed the doom of the League, for the League
was founded mostly to ensure peace by mutual aid or collective security. The League's failures in these matters overshadowed its bright
successes in less important areas. As the final crises of World War II
approached, the League was already discounted, and the failures of the
final days of those crises go to the debit of the old-fashioned diplomacy
of the balance of power.

THE UNITED NATIONS TRIES AGAIN: THE SECURITY COUNCIL

The United Nations attempted to apply the lessons learned
from the failures and successes of the League of Nations and of traditional diplomacy to a new international consolidation following World
War II. Whether the most important applications were made is at this
point questionable. Whether the total problem of international peace
can be solved even on paper is also questionable. And certainly one
cannot expect a single institution to solve handily the most lamented
problem in the history of mankind. In the heat of World War II, while
all peoples were flushed with determination to end war, Mortimer
Adler wrote that wars most probably would be with us for several
centuries. It was an unpopular prediction, but many honest predictions
of social science, of all degrees of substantiation, are bound to be unpopular. Fortunetellers have customers because they predict wealth and
romantic encounters, not because they foretell sordidness and hum-
drum marriage.

The structure of the United Nations (Figure 47) promised little
more than the League's structure did. The Great Powers were again
entrenched in a Security Council with permanent seats. A Military
Staff Committee was provided for the Council to expedite the use of
force if ever the Council were to resort to force to preserve the peace
and punish aggression. But each of the "Great Powers" was to have a
veto over all substantive decisions of the Council, unless the power
was a party to the dispute under consideration; however, if a vote was

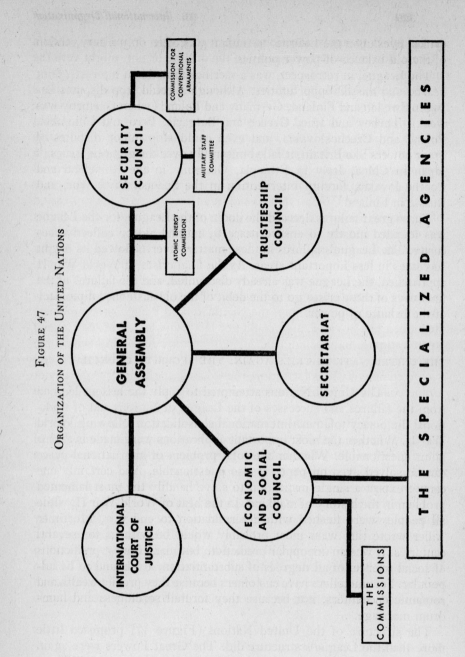

FIGURE 47

ORGANIZATION OF THE UNITED NATIONS

SECURITY COUNCIL

COMMISSION FOR CONVENTIONAL ARMAMENTS

MILITARY STAFF COMMITTEE

ATOMIC ENERGY COMMISSION

TRUSTEESHIP COUNCIL

GENERAL ASSEMBLY

SECRETARIAT

INTERNATIONAL COURT OF JUSTICE

ECONOMIC AND SOCIAL COUNCIL

THE COMMISSIONS

THE SPECIALIZED AGENCIES

to be taken to apply sanctions, either economic or military, then a
"Great Power," whether a party to the dispute or not, might veto the
measure.

This means that the Security Council might not apply sanctions
against any one of the "Big Five" that committed an act of aggression.
The "Big Five" included the United States, the Soviet Union, Great
Britain, France, and China. However a combination of powerful states
could in the past practically always exert sufficient pressure on a
weaker state to cause it to desist from some generally disapproved
course of action, and it is at least questionable whether the elaborate
machinery of the UN has not missed its main objective, the repression
of aggressive behavior among the *greater* powers. The United States
government and the Soviet dictatorship, it seems, had dealt everybody
a hand in the United Nations, but reserved the privilege of saying
"Count me out."

Thus, to take an example, the Soviet Union might veto any action,
including the application of sanctions, with respect to any of its satel-
lites, including, for example, the North Korean People's (communist)
Republic. The Soviet Union could not block any action of the Council
to investigate and recommend actions on any dispute to which the
Soviet Union was itself a party. But, beyond such an investigation and
such recommendations for action, the Council might not go; the Soviet
Union could veto punitive measures voted by the Council against the
U.S.S.R.

So the Security Council of the United Nations, like the Council of
the League, could take few actions to which a permanent member of
the Council might take umbrage. Exceptions might occur only on
those matters bearing on the investigation of disputes and the suggestion of remedies short of sanctions *when a great power is a party*.

There was provision for an international army to enforce UN decisions, but this international army could only be called into being by
the good will of the members of the United Nations. Every member
had a "hidden veto" in its willingness to respond or not to respond to
the command of the United Nations to furnish troops. In the Korean
war, few members who voted police action against the North Korean
communists sent troops to fight there under the United Nations banner.

THE GENERAL ASSEMBLY AND MINOR BODIES

The General Assembly under the United Nations was hardly
stronger than was the Assembly of the League. Again each state government appointed and controlled its delegation and each delegation
had an equal vote on all matters. The Assembly could make recommendations to its member nations and could call the attention of the

Security Council to situations that might be endangering the peace. It might not interfere in the "internal affairs" of its members. It was granted a number of other powers, all of which, however, were subject to the checks and control of the Security Council. The Assembly could not govern the behavior of the Council or even of one permanent member of the Council except in the unlikely event that the mass of Assembly members were to rise up and waive the letter of the Charter. The Assembly was the voice of many opinions from all the world, but those opinions were prevented by censorship from affecting the peoples of communist countries and the several other nations where censorship exists.

Both the Security Council and the Assembly created special committees to deal with a variety of special issues that have come up. The United Nations Atomic Energy Commission, under the direction of the Security Council, was voted into existence by the General Assembly, and thus was a kind of joint committee of the two bodies. Most of the committees of the United Nations, however, were separately created by each body or were already provided for in the original Charter of the United Nations.

The Economic and Social Council, elected for three-year terms by the General Assembly, did represent a difference in formal organization from the League. The Council was concerned with furthering the economic and social development of member states; it was a positive organization, dedicated to the solution of such problems as unemployment, submarginal standards of living, illiteracy, and the repression of political and civil rights. The Council held conferences, provided technical assistance, investigated conditions, and made various recommendations for action to the United Nations Assembly. Note again that it could operate only on an administrative level. A century of peace or so might result in these administrative operations accumulating to a point where they might influence the total behavior of the great powers.

There existed a number of international organizations affiliated with the United Nations like the International Labor Organization, the International Civil Aviation Organization, and the United Nations Educational, Scientific, and Cultural Organization (UNESCO). They continued along the League of Nations pattern. They performed useful administrative work and in many cases constituted international discussion groups on technical and scholarly matters.

Two more branches of the United Nations deserve mention. One is the Secretariat, headed by a Secretary-General, who received appointment by the General Assembly upon the recommendation of the Security Council. Although primarily an administrator of the many offices and thousands of personnel of the United Nations, the Secretary-General, unlike his predecessor of the League, was given the power to bring to the attention of the Security Council any situation which seems to threaten the peace. Inherent in this right was the germ of real executive authority, but the Secretary-General, unlike the American executive, was given very few major "laws" to administer. Consequently, he lacked a lever by which to expand his power.

The International Court of Justice, located at The Hague, Netherlands, was inherited from the League of Nations. It received its cases from those states that had signed blanket subscriptions to submit on many matters to its compulsory jurisdiction and from the voluntary agreement by two states to submit a case arising out of a particular dispute.

Even the brief description of the United Nations just given indicates the close resemblance between it and the League of Nations. One of the outstanding authorities on international organization, Dr. Leland M. Goodrich, concluded a study of the two instruments of international collaboration by writing:

> The student of international organization must recognize the United Nations for what it quite properly is, a revised League, no doubt improved in some respects, possibly weaker in others, but nonetheless a League, a voluntary association of nations, carrying on largely in the League tradition and by the League methods. Important changes have occurred in the world distribution of power, in the world's economic and political structure, in the world's ideological atmosphere. These changes create new problems and modify the chances of success or failure in meeting them, but the mechanics remain much the same.*

THE PRESENT AGE STILL FORMLESS

We may conclude, then, that so far as formal structure has anything to do with political successes, the chances of realizing a jural order of the world were not substantially changed from the time of the League to the time of the United Nations. Different results could be expected to flow from international contacts only if political, economic, and ideological changes would force their way into the structure of international organization or work their will outside of any formally organized structure.

The crisis of international relations in the mid-twentieth century took, therefore, no historical shape except that of the most troublous eras. There was no imperium, no *Pax Romana*. Imperialism was universally denounced, but worked with unknown strength beneath the surface of world affairs. The balance of power, always precarious under the best of conditions, was now more uncertain, unreal, and in-

* Quoted, with permission, from Leland M. Goodrich: "From League of Nations to United Nations," *International Organization*, Vol. I (1947), p. 21.

adequate than ever, as Dr. Morgenthau pointed out. And the co-operative organization among nations, although efficient on many small matters, was too limited and too incompetent to settle great problems—and hence was ineffective in establishing a rule of law among nations.

Questions and Problems

1. Describe the origins and characteristics of the *jus gentium*.

2. Compare the Roman and Medieval Church modes of organizing international affairs with reference to their relative possibilities of establishing peace, the techniques used in each period, the location of legitimate authority, and their relative success.

3. State the essential characteristics and conditions of the balance of power.

4. Describe the general methods by which the balance of power is achieved and give examples of each method.

5. How is international law related historically to the balance of power?

6. What were the methods of settling international differences during the period of traditional international law?

7. Describe the sources and sanctions of international law.

8. How does the principle of the balance of power operate when it is subordinated to a world order?

9. Find and describe four statements or actions reported in the international news of the past month in which the authors or participants seem to be motivated by balance-of-power ideas.

10. Obtain from the library a copy of the Covenant of the League of Nations and draw an organizational chart, showing the relationships of the main branches of the League.

11. Describe five cases in which the League of Nations successfully coped with international problems and five cases in which the League failed to do so. State whether the successes equaled in importance the failures, giving your reasons.

12. Name, inquire into, and describe in 350 words one club or group on campus or off campus that is devoted to the study of international affairs. Would you classify the group as a propaganda group or a scientific group? Explain your answer.

13. Compare the organization of the United Nations with that of the League of Nations.

14. Peruse the columns of a daily newspaper for two weeks or a weekly news magazine for four issues. Report on what organs of the United Nations are receiving the most publicity. Why is this the case? Do you believe certain other organs or offices of the United Nations are being slighted? Explain your answer.

15. Obtain access to a file of daily newspapers covering two weeks *or* a file of news magazines covering four issues. Analyze that part of its

contents that is devoted to international affairs and describe its policies on international affairs (400 words) giving quotations or examples.

16. What is the degree of independence possessed by the United States in the organization and operations of the United Nations? Give evidence for your statement.

17. What has the greatest possibilities of being realized in the near future: 1) continual cold and hot war; 2) a strong United Nations world order; 3) domination of the world by one nation. Explain your answer or describe a fourth condition that you think may be more probable.

Longer Study and Research
Problems Suitable for Term Papers

1. From the *New York Times*, the publications of the United Nations, or other sources, prepare an account of the activities of the United Nations over the period of the last year ending December 31 (ten pages).

2. Read one of the following books and write a fifteen page report on it, with special reference to the tactics of one of the principal characters in getting what he wanted:

T. Dennett: *John Hay*
Winston Churchill: *The Hinge of Fate*
Thomas A. Bailey: *Woodrow Wilson and the Great Betrayal*
J. W. Headlam: *Bismarck and the Foundation of the German Empire*
Lord Halifax: *Failure of a Mission*
James F. Byrnes: *Speaking Frankly*
John R. Deane: *The Strange Alliance*
F. de Callieres: *On the Manner of Negotiating with Princes*
Basil Rauch: *Roosevelt; From Munich to Pearl Harbor*
Joseph E. Davies: *Mission to Moscow*
Robert Lansing: *The Big Four and Others of the Peace Conference*

3. Read Gabriel Almond's *American Opinion and Foreign Affairs* and Alex Inkeles, *Public Opinion in Soviet Russia*. Contrast the role of public opinion in the two countries (ten pages).

4. By library research, interrogation of informed people, examination of newspapers files, or direct correspondence, assemble the voting record on all issues pertaining to international affairs of your congressman or any other congressman. Write a ten-page account of the position and policies of the congressman on world affairs.

IV

DEMOCRACY AND POLICY

THINKING ABOUT DEMOCRACY

Two of the most complex topics of political science have
been postponed until the last so that we might be better
prepared for them. We have studied political behavior and political organization; we have seen how politics centers about the
struggle of men to gain priority for certain of their values, and
to ensure by the appropriate machinery that the values will be
achieved. We need no longer postpone, therefore, a more specific
inquiry into those human values called "democracy" and that
collective, purposive behavior for achieving values called "public policy."

In these fields of values and policy, we shall have to renew our
caution about the meanings of words. "Liberty," "rights,"
"restraints," "rational policy," and "planning" are several of
the key words of these chapters and of political discussion in
general. But such words, and others like "democracy," in the
minds of most people, have so little precise meaning as to be
quite useless and often dangerous unless carefully defined.
Consider how silly men can be about words. "Democracy" in our
age is advocated everywhere, from the Kremlin to Washington.
By that token, it means everything and nothing. To some, a
"planned society" is a method of granting everyone's desires,
although to others it connotes the systematic annihilation of
everything anyone might want. However, if we exercise patience
and achieve a consistent, clear understanding of such concepts,
we shall find our accomplishment of great utility, not only for
understanding these chapters and this book, but also for evaluating soberly the contents of the political discussions that we shall
be hearing for the rest of our lives.

17

THINKING ABOUT DEMOCRACY

A STRIKING feature of life in a democracy is that so many people in it suspect their fellow citizens of undermining democracy. *Every imaginable value is proposed* and attacked; every group has its own platform of values. It seems obvious that no one's claim to know democracy can be considered valid. All the more reason, therefore, that one should be astonished at another feature of life in a democracy —the fact that most people, unperturbed by the implication of their suspicions, believe democracy to be *a single set of beliefs* with which everyone in the society agrees or ought to agree.

This remarkable contradiction in attitudes gives us a clue on how to proceed with the discussion of democracy. First, we shall elaborate upon the inconsistencies of political theorists, showing that great philosophers have differed about what is good for man and about what human nature is like. We shall show furthermore how a horde of propagandists continually obscures the proper study of democracy. These steps, constituting the first section of this chapter, should establish how the wish almost always hovers in the thought. They should also prepare us to expect close relationships between what men *believe* are the important *facts* of life and what they believe are the important *moral* principles of life.

The second section of the chapter will describe the social and economic conditions that prevail generally in democracies. No attempt will be made to find a consistent set of moral principles that explain the conduct of the people in such societies. Rather the actual social setting of such societies will be described.

In the third section of the chapter we shall ask whether there is a consistent ethical system of democracy. We shall find that instead of there being one absolute democracy, there are four major moral positions of democracy that, although they are in some ways mutually antagonistic, do provide the basis for thought and action in democratic societies.

Finally, an eclectic theory that considers democracy as an equilibrium of the four moral positions will be presented. When all these tasks are completed, we shall be able to understand the problem of democracy better, and, as a token of this understanding, we should be able to explain the riddle of why men dwelling in a democratic state hold the democracy of their fellows in distrust and yet claim democracy to be a single belief system.

Basic Questions of Values

GREAT MORALISTS DIFFER OVER THE "GOOD"

Whose values *ought* to prevail? Whose liberties and whose policies are the best? Whose liberties and policies shall be frustrated? Political theory, in so far as it discusses what is good or bad about human conduct, gives many answers. One may follow the advice of Aristotle, Plato, Aquinas, Spinoza, Locke, Adam Smith, John Stuart Mill, or some other philosopher, or even the exhortations of a Hitler or Stalin. These men, and many others, do not agree on what is good for man. Plato, for example, believed the community ought to assign each person his life work and train him for it. Contrariwise, Adam Smith thought that the individual is best assigned to his life work through satisfying whatever happens to be the market demand for his skill at a point in time. Smith would forbid the community from ruling the division of labor by legislation.

Though writers differ on what is good for men, there are schools or species of morality, the members of which agree more with each other than with those outside their group. Thus Plato and T. H. Green subscribe to a different moral order than that of Machiavelli and Hobbes or that of Aristotle and Locke. One of the major tasks of political scientists specializing in the history of ideas and theory is to discover these major species and explain their similarities and differences. This task forms a great branch of political theory.

GREAT SCIENTISTS DIFFER OVER HUMAN NATURE

Another great branch of political theory is devoted to a description of *what men are like, what they want, what is possible*. These theorists do not ask moral questions. They ask what are the facts of political life? Whose liberties *can* prevail? To whom might liberty possibly be consigned, and whose interests could possibly be defeated? We do not know now, nor will we know for some time to come, the answer to these factual questions.

Nor have political scientists of the past been in agreement on the answer to these questions. John Locke and Thomas Hobbes, for example, wrote their masterpieces about the same time, the middle and later seventeenth century. In the realm of morality, the two men differed greatly. Locke declared himself in favor of private, individual freedom, Hobbes in favor of authoritative control over many individual actions. The two men also put forward antagonistic theories to explain human nature. Locke thought men were naturally co-operative, social, and reasonable. Hobbes thought men were naturally in a state of conflict that made their lives "nasty, brutish, and short" until the coming of governmental authority. On the basis of his theory, Locke believed certain rights could be maintained without the intervention of government; such rights were life, liberty, and property. On the other hand, Hobbes was convinced that, so far as liberty was possible, it was only possible in a regime with enough authority and power to keep order.

There was not enough evidence then, and there seems not to be enough today, to declare that either position is correct or incorrect. We are entitled to be suspicious, under such circumstances, of both men, for, where the facts are not agreed upon, often the *partial* facts that support our own deep desires (frequently hidden from ourselves) are emphasized to bolster our own moral beliefs.

To put the case in other terms, so long as Chinese, Africans, Russians, Europeans, and Americans do not agree that the same "facts" .exist, we must view through narrowed eyes any theory purportedly based on "human nature." There is no agreement either on what is good for man or on what man is like. So human discourse on either level is likely to be treacherous.

MORAL PROPAGANDISTS OFTEN MASQUERADE AS POLITICAL SCIENTISTS

Unfortunately for the student of democratic theory, most writers on democracy muff the opportunity to set forth those facts about political behavior and political values which history and other social sciences have handed down to us. Most writers, it seems, join unrestrainedly the ranks of propagandists as soon as they begin to discuss political values. The vast literature on democracy, consequently, is filled with slapdash logic and incredible contradictions.

If we read for logic and evidence, rather than for fervid agreement, we observe that an extraordinary process occurs repeatedly. For example, a writer is moved to broadcast his democratic sentiments and writes a book or article to commemorate the urge. He declares in the text that individual rights are sacred, persuading his readers that his "principle" is correct by citing some individual "right" with which the readers agree enthusiastically. Thus, he might write: "A man has the right to the privacy of his home against pilfering officials and snooping police."

Soon afterwards, he declaims on the rights of minorities, holding that "men must be allowed to speak openly and freely against the government." Again the reading audience applauds. Then in another place, the writer will soar high in praise of the virtues of the common man and of the majority of men. He will cite the London cockney in the air raids, and the popular majorities of Fiorello La Guardia, the scourge of Tammany Hall. At this, his readers give rousing cheers.

Democracy, for them, is now complete: it gives complete freedom to the individual to work out his life plans; it allows the minority to have its liberties; and it permits the majority of commen men to govern.

But what we have in this type of argumentation is not a proof that principles of democracy may be discovered, or that these principles are consistent, or that such principles are practical. The argument relies mostly on simple emotional agreement on particular sentiments, masquerading as principles.

To show this fact, let us suppose that our writer is slightly mad and out of touch with his audience. Each time he states a "principle," he gives a different example. When he lauds individual rights, he says, by way of illustration, that "every man has a right to enslave his family and conceal stolen property in the privacy of his home." This would make his audience fidget, of course. Ignoring their reactions, however, he goes on to state the next "principle," the rights of minorities. He proclaims that unions have the right to choose the people with whom they must work; they ought to be able to discriminate against unskilled persons, persons of different race, sex, or nationality, and people who disagree with the union leadership's policies. His audience now reads his words in ominous calm.

Then he states his third principle, having to do with the great virtue of the common man and with the rightness of the majority. He cites the American Colonial mobs that rioted against smallpox vaccination, the great repute of Napoleon among the mass of Frenchmen, and the fact that the enlightened Swiss voters chose to inflict penalties, in a referendum many years ago, on persons practicing Judaism. Practically his whole audience deserts him at this point, regarding his sentiments, if not his principles, as abominable.

These examples are by way of saying that the vast bulk of writings and other expressions on the subject of democracy (and anti-democracy) are propaganda, and might be praised or attacked for being good or bad propaganda for achieving the goals of the writer or speaker. There is little science in them. By using examples that please the audience as *proof* of certain principles, the writers are able to acquire a reputation for profound thought, logical method, and scholarship. All particular likes, although one like may contradict a hundred different likes in practice, are collected and called democracy. All particular dislikes, whether they belong together or not, are heaped up and called by a horrid word.

In all humility, and realizing that it is impossible not to be sometimes a sinner, we must recognize the problem for what it is. If nonscientific thoughts and words about democracy and anti-democracy were stilled by some mighty and just hand, a vast silence would settle over the universe of politics. Hardly a pen would be put to hand, hardly a word spoken, so little have 2,500 years of logic and scientific method affected the social ideas and political practices of mankind.

SCIENCE CANNOT SAY WHAT DEMOCRACY "OUGHT TO BE"

This indictment that history reads to politics must not be understood to mean that logic and scientific procedures can tell what "democracy" really ought to be. Nor does the presence of logic and scientific method mean that democracy is also present. Men may be dominated, propagandized, coerced, and manipulated by the use of scientific procedures into subscribing to authority of many kinds. *An increased use of science will only clarify the values that men hold, reduce the confusions of thought that emerge in politics, and decrease the waste in energies and resources as men move from their present position to the liberties they visualize.*

YET THEORIES OF ETHICS AND SCIENCE ARE BASICALLY RELATED

Far below the everyday use of science as the slave of man's will, lies the problem of the relation between what knowledge man is capable of and what he wants. Some problems of science are so much a part of man's basic thought processes that they have the effect of turning men's desires in certain directions. Conversely, men's basic desires condition these root problems of science. The study of this relationship is one of the most profound problems of philosophy.

Our glimpse of past thinking has shown two general ways in which scientific and ethical problems are related. In one way, men most often assert as fact what they want to believe wherever the evidence on the point at issue is inconclusive. The wish is father to the "fact." In another way, the facts that are universally agreed to will be used by men to support their own temperament and values. An optimist will find that the incomplete facts in a situation bear out his theory about mankind's eternal progress. A pessimist will fit the same facts into a theory of man's approaching doom.

Consequently, we may expect arguments about what is good to be closely associated with arguments about what is true in fact. Indeed, no two political writers ever pursued the same method, agreed on the same facts, and then disagreed radically on what was the good life.

The Social Setting of Democracy

THE SEARCH FOR DEMOCRATIC SOCIETIES

The preceding discussion permits us, for the time being, to put aside the search for a systematic set of moral principles that may be called the democratic belief-system, and to turn our attention to another approach to the study of democracy. Democracy may be studied as a distinctive social setting. Under certain conditions, there have come into being governments that have been called democratic either because the societies termed themselves democracies or because their actions conformed to a given definition of democracy. Several of the candidates for these honors would be ancient Athens, late republican Rome, medieval Florence, Switzerland over several centuries, France and England over most of the last century and a half, and the United States.

It is not easy to discover what is common to these societies. Not only do several of them differ in many of their institutions, but the members within any one of them also differ in many ways. Certainly Socrates, Plato, Aristotle, Pericles, and Aristides held strikingly different moral principles in democratic Athens. And so did Sulla, Cicero, Catiline, Pompey, and Julius Caesar in Rome. Nor need we more than mention the differences among Franklin D. Roosevelt, Herbert Hoover, John L. Lewis, James Farley, and Huey Long. Probably all of these men, though controversial figures, have either regarded themselves as democrats or have been regarded by thousands of fellow citizens as democrats. Yet there probably exists no single, debatable issue in relation to which all of them would hold to the same position.

On the other hand, the societies in which these men lived or live would qualify for the title of democracy, because certain social and economic conditions prevailed in them that do not prevail in undemocratic societies. We will now enumerate and will subsequently define seven of the most significant conditions for democracy. These are (1) general freedom of action and speech; (2) strong attempts to uplift the common people; (3) constitutionalism and dispersal of political controls; (4) relatively high social and political mobility; (5) relatively high level of personal discontent; (6) underevaluation of the qualities of political leaders; (7) emphasis on education and economic measures, instead of force, as instruments of authority. There are perhaps other indices that signify the presence of democracy, but these seven indices seem most significant and most closely connected with the political process. Any state that possesses these conditions will be called democratic, according to our method of analysis. We will now discuss each of these conditions individually.

GENERAL FREEDOM OF ACTION AND SPEECH

Widespread freedom of action and speech is a primary criterion of democracy. Democracies often have punished men for their opinions and have prevented a full freedom of political action. But, on the whole, there seems to be little reason to doubt that democratic societies are more hospitable to, and give a wider scope to, criticism of the government, organization for political purposes, and the exercise of individual and group pressures on the state. Since we are dealing with a *general* freedom and believe this general criterion to be the important one, we are not impressed with particular deviations in individual cases. That is, democracies often restrict the freedoms of a few individuals to speak and act the way they desire; and one may not gainsay such persons for feeling bitter against the democratic societies in which they find themselves. But these occasional violations of the general conditions do not make democracy the same as despotism. The police, the ministers, the mob, and the politicians of nineteenth-century France often encroached upon freedom of speech and action, but, nevertheless, freedom then was a much more general condition than it was before the Revolution of 1789.

UPLIFTING THE COMMON PEOPLE

The second condition found in democracies is a strong concern for the mass of people. Democracy without the "people" is inconceivable. Both the political critics of democratic societies and the leading members of democratic societies are preoccupied with the role of the common man. The debate over bettering his standard of living and his intellectual and moral attainments consumes a large volume of political energy. We need not consider whether the common people of democratic societies are better fed or more cultured than those of other societies to agree with the fact that the common man is zealously spoken for and his support eagerly solicited in democratic societies. No one dare question that government ought to be *for* the people.

A great deal of economic, moral, and social effort is directed at increasing equalities of all kinds and inhibiting any inequalities that many people see fit to be concerned about.

We are speaking of a general condition. Numerous men disagree with this "populism" and act overtly or surreptitiously against it. But they are at least slightly out of tune with their society. No democratic society can be confused with a nondemocratic society when the relative strength of the "uplifting" force in each society is known. Even a charismatic mass movement of the Nazi type, originating as it did from several problems of the pre-existing democratic society, turned more and more away from slogans referring to the betterment of the masses and towards slogans exalting sacrifices for the nation and the leaders. In the Soviet Union, the uplift theory has been in cold storage for a generation; "appeasement" of the common man has given way continually to the demands of industrializing the country and fighting wars.

CONSTITUTIONALISM AND DISPERSAL OF CONTROLS

The third general condition of democracies concerns the way in which their institutions are related to each other. The amount of power possessed by any single institution is limited by a separation of powers, in fact, even if not in theory, and the level of juridical defense, as it has been described in Chapter Nine, is high. That "it is difficult to get things done in a democracy," is a common allegation of democracy's foes and the frequent complaint of its friends. The legislatures impede the executives; the executives intervene in the economy; the courts hinder the legislatures; the civilians prevent the free operation of the military; the parties fight one another over principles, or simply fight "on principle"; and local interests and jurisdictions have autonomy or passively resist the central authorities. Even when a separation of powers does not exist in their constitutions, democracies are famous for their turbulent politics. Athenian politics were incomprehensible to the Spartans; American politics similarly baffle the Russians, who have what is called by the communists "democratic centralism," that is, an inconsiderable separation of powers and a shadow of juridical defense.

HIGH SOCIAL AND POLITICAL MOBILITY

The fourth condition of democracy is high social and political mobility. The people who are proud of class distinctions and live by them are a minority in democracies. They establish small islands on the society pages of the newspapers and in certain professions and even in local areas. But they are a backwash to the greater flood that is composed of men and women who occupy their social and political position "on good behavior," so to speak. Class in a democracy tends to be a statistical and acquired status, much as we described the condition of the social classes in America in Chapter Three. Men move up and down the social ladder within a single generation; if they achieve high status before death, they consider themselves fortunate if their sons and daughters maintain that status; if they remain lowly or descend from previous heights of prestige, income, and opportunities, they console themselves with the thought that they have not bequeathed a severe handicap to their children.

In the sphere of politics proper, the politists in a democracy do not come from a single class or group. They are not a homogeneous body. They are subject to the same ups and downs as members of the social classes in general. *Political* status, even more than social status, is statistical and acquired. Certain types succeed more in politics than others, for example, lawyers in America and orators in France, but the characteristics of these types are not *class* characteristics. They are functional and psychological characteristics.

So, on the whole, a relatively high degree of freedom of opportunity may be said to be a condition of democratic societies. One must make an exception to this generalization in the case of revolutionary societies that are rarely democratic but usually have high social and political mobility, as in the Soviet Union. If communism continues in Russia for another generation, we may expect social mobility to decline there at a rapid rate because of other conditions there that are undemocratic.

HIGH LEVEL OF PERSONAL DISCONTENT

Intense social competition has its effects on the personality and is related to our fifth criterion of democracy, the high level of personal discontent. A kind of rootlessness is common in democratic societies. Making one's own way in society, rather than depending upon the position one has inherited, is likely to cause tension and anxiety. One often seems to be passing through life on a steep and narrow path between the pinnacle of social success and the abyss of social failure. There is a constant and direct pressure on the individual in a democratic society to "improve" himself, to "educate" himself, to acquire new wants.

In addition to these direct effects of the relatively classless society on the individual, a general sense of insecurity, coming from the whole political organization of the society, is likely to affect many individuals. Practically no institution or belief in the society is beyond attack; the comfortable sense of knowing exactly what to believe and how to act, which exists in a totalitarian society or a purely conservative society, is absent for the most part in a democracy. Sometimes the condition of rootlessness may be transformed into a moral principle, as in America, where a great many teachers believe their mission is to "shock" their students by adopting a belief-shattering position; this is called "stirring them up" or "making them think" and is based on the somewhat unreliable theory that anxiety is the parent of intelligence. The theory is not too reliable, because over-anxiety is the sire of irrationality.

Still, it is true that a certain complexity of mind and character is necessary if a person is to dwell in sympathy with democracy. Greater understanding, passive if not active, is required of a democratic citizen than of the citizen or subject of a nondemocratic state. At the same time, democratic politics with its multiple and contradictory beliefs and its changing institutions and officers demands a sturdiness of mind not required in other societies. The problem thus emerges of obtaining at the same time a higher intellectual average and a lower anxiety threshold among democratic citizens. Educational and psychological theory is presently incapable of dealing with this problem; nevertheless there is a widespread appreciation of its significance, expressed directly or indirectly in hundreds of books and lectures by commentators such as Reinhold Neibuhr, Margaret Mead, Erich Fromm, John Dewey, Harold D. Lasswell, T. S. Eliot, Elton Mayo, Sebastian de Grazia, and Nevitt Sanford. Needless to say, the problem is part of the everyday work and writings of hundreds of educational psychologists in America.

UNDEREVALUATION OF POLITICAL LEADERS

An underevaluation of leadership is our sixth condition of democracies. Leaders of democracies have always complained that they are not listened to, they are not followed, they are not credited with intelligence, and they are not trusted. They might quote with some bitterness the witticism that "a statesman is a dead politician." A large part of the public, on the other hand, assails the alleged double-dealing, hypocrisy, demagoguery, and incompetence of their leaders. Because of this condition, as well as others, democracy presents a spectacle that is often held in contempt by foreign societies and even by many of its own people. The derision with which the politics of a democracy are received abroad is only exceeded by the laughter constantly accorded them at home. Yet it is probable that this condition is an inescapable one; a democracy in which the political leadership is regarded with profound respect, is harkened to, and is obeyed with great confidence is unthinkable.

Whether this condition is a grave weakness or indirectly a source of some greater strength depends on the circumstances in a particular case; in some ways it causes errors and defeats; in others it prevents blunders and disasters. Such a discussion is not the task of this section, but we may indicate that here too, as with personal discontent, there often arises a competition for influence between two subfactors in a general criterion of democracy. Is the decline in morale, occasioned by mutual recriminations, of greater effect and importance than the exaggerations in thought and action committed by leaders that are insensitive to public opinion?

EMPHASIS ON EDUCATION AND ECONOMIC MEASURES

Our seventh condition of the democratic way of life is the emphasis on education and economic measures as instruments of authority and the diminished belief in, or use of, force. The tendency of a democratic government is to exhaust psychological and economic pressures before resorting to force to carry out its policies. Punishment by "re-education" and economic deprivations is favored over corporal punishment.

This reluctance to use force where force may be used legitimately is another occasion for the critics of democracy, inside and outside the country, to cry that democracy is weak. To such men it appears that force ought to be invoked whenever the government is obviously "right" and wherever force is likely to be "efficient." But these words "right" and "efficient" are deceptive. The government may have such a "right" in one sense, since it is empowered to use force. But a large part of the population may be against force and may dislike its use even where it would bring prompt and "efficient" results. Breaking an illegal strike by force may be "efficient," then, only in the sense that the strike will be broken; to the strikers and to a good part of the population, strikebreaking is not "efficient" because no act is efficient that violates their expectations of what the government ought to do in such circumstances. This part of the people put force down as a technique of last resort and are badly disappointed when the government reverses the order of expectations by skipping persuasion and economic measures and moving directly into the use of force. The illegal strike of railroad yard workers in the United States in the weeks before Christmas, 1950, illustrates perfectly these points. The government could legally have employed force. Instead, speeding up the usual process, because war shipments to Korea and Christmas shipments were being held up, the government pushed its intervention for an economic settlement and privately and publicly exhorted the workers "to do their patriotic duty." The strikers returned to work, as could have been expected, just before force was due to be employed.

Other consequences of a more fundamental sort follow the affinity of democracies for education and propaganda. The naked use of force and economic pressures leave little room for scientific thought to develop. A society that seeks peaceful psychological adjustments of human relations may invite the most absurd waste of time and energy in propaganda; but it does keep the door to factual investigation open. It allows man to introduce some rational demonstration into political conflict; and if rational demonstration may stifle or settle conflict to everyone's satisfaction, this condition of a democracy seems important. Democratic societies, through their emphasis on discussion, can maximize whatever abilities men may have to find and achieve common aims. Even though most citizens of democracy may be incapable of using, or unwilling to use, the delicate instruments of communications for anything but the mastery or destruction of their fellows, yet, once engrossed in the democratic process, they must be subjected to at least some element of scientific or rational communication.

IS DEMOCRACY ULTIMATELY DEPENDENT ON WELL-BEING?

The seven criteria of the social setting of democracy have been described and several absentees may be noted. The first absentee is a systematic set of beliefs adhered to by all; we have already explained why we do not consider it among the most important criteria and we shall have more to say about it later on in the chapter. Also absent are the many criteria of any social order—as we have described them throughout this book—the community, the public, politists, leaders, "good" men, "bad" men, government functions, legislatures, political parties, courts, and so on. These criteria are not unique to democracies. Therefore they will not help us discriminate between democratic and undemocratic societies.

But one criterion, often employed by writers, deserves special attention; that is the criterion of economic well-being. It is asserted frequently that unless a country is well-to-do, it cannot afford to be democratic. That is, it cannot be poor and at the same time support our seven conditions of democracy. This theory depends on the theory of economic determinism, which in its most strict and proper sense says that the struggle for bare subsistence will influence politics.

To take an example of this theory at work, we may inquire what happens when a country has a great excess of population to the extent that some of its people are starving at all times. Overpopulation in proportion to available resources causes great insecurity, physical and psychological, among the people of a country. These conditions may affect adversely several of the conditions for democracy in the following ways. The intended beneficial results of free speech and free action are deprived of meaning. Hopelessness about uplifting the mass of people occurs. The complex institutions of democratic government appear a useless luxury to people who are obsessed with their basic needs. Social mobility is reduced as the masses go hungry and a privileged few live in social isolation. The level of personal anxiety is increased far beyond the normal level. The dislike of politicians reaches hysterical proportions. And, finally, accumulated anxieties and hatreds are vented on domestic and foreign enemies with force and violence. In other words, economic distress of wide scope and deep impact tends to disable the conditions of democracy all along the line. Undemocratic conditions begin to be substituted for democratic ones. Ultimately the whole structure of democracy may collapse. That these events occur cannot be denied.

Does this lengthy illustration of how national poverty affects democracy mean that the seven conditions of democracy are ultimately determined by the *subsistence* level of economic well-being? In a broad and indirect sense, yes.

For our purposes here, however, in telling how to identify a democracy, poverty and wealth will not discriminate ordinarily between despotisms and democracies. The poor Scots of the sixteenth century were as democratic as the wealthier English. The poor American frontiersmen were more democratic than the wealthier Americans of the Eastern seaboard. The French under the democratic Third Republic were poorer than the Germans under the Kaiser. *It would therefore be imprudent to assert that anything but the most extreme poverty prohibits a democratic society.* A dish of hot oatmeal is enough to start a democrat on his way. Thereafter, increases in material wants are combinations of economic, political, and social motives that occur under any form of government.

Economic determinism is most clearly and convincingly at work when severe and widespread economic distress afflicts a community. So-called "economic determinants," as the Marxists habitually use the phrase, most often include not only economic motives, but also motives of social status, if they are ends, and of the struggle for power, if they are means. In these respects, the theory of economic determinism might be better understood as "the theory of invidious comparisons." Thus, the fight for gold or the ambitious drive to own and operate a business are types of competition for a higher status or more power in the community relative to the other members of the community. It is a mistake to accept the verbal rationalization that one strives for status or power only in order to have champagne and breast of guinea hen under glass on the table. It would seem that we have here a "social determinant (status)" and a "political determinant proper (power)" that are at least as influential as the pure economic determinant in molding the form of any society. And, in fact, if one re-examines the seven conditions of democracy described above, one will find these motives more actively displayed than the economic. In any event, all these motives are found in all societies. Only in impoverished and wretched societies, does economic need determine that democracy cannot exist.

We conclude, then, that for the purpose of identifying the democratic condition of life we need not go beyond the second-level symptoms incorporated in the seven stated conditions. If we go too far into the levels of causality, we should have a massive job of tracing the infinite roots of society. They would ramify intricately through human motives of all kinds. That task is certainly an important one, and our chapters on political behavior have been dedicated in part to it.

The Four Moral Positions in Democracy

THE FOUR MORAL POSITIONS OF THOUGHT AND ACTION

Thus far, this chapter has made two chief points. The first was that no clear agreement on what is good or what is true can be found among writers or men at large. The second point was that several criteria can nevertheless be employed to distinguish societies that are democratic from societies that are not. We will now see whether we can abstract from the mass of thoughts and actions relevant to the subject of democracy one or more consistent viewpoints.

It seems that we can demonstrate that four such viewpoints exist. In exploring each of them we shall learn why there is no general agreement on a pure democratic belief-system, and why, nevertheless, each one of these moral positions is essential to the democratic condition of life. These four viewpoints or moral positions of democracy occur together, plague one another, support one another, and are "undemocratic" if they occur in isolation from one another. How this mysterious equilibrium of the four moral positions is attained is described in the last section of the chapter, where it is shown that democracy is an eclectic whole rather than a unified and consistent whole. *And it is this confused and contradictory combination that provides us with the theoretical interpretation of the condition of democracy described in the section just completed.*

THE TECHNIQUE OF STUDYING MORAL POSITIONS

As we venture into the theoretical task of isolating the moral positions that are expressed in thought and action, we ought to repeat a warning advanced elsewhere in this work, notably in the discussion of legitimacy, political parties, and electoral behavior. That is, that although the concepts we are about to extract are unreal they are nevertheless useful. For instance, when we talk about the "conservative" moral position of a man, we do not mean that the man is purely conservative or always conservative, and when we talk about the conservative moral position in democracy we do not mean that there is exactly one quarter of democratic societies that is composed of purely conservative people. We have in mind rather a great number of ideas and actions that seem to have the same motivation and character (that is, *conservative*), that such ideas and actions are often concentrated in some men (*conservatives*) to the partial exclusion of opposing ideas and actions, and that the cumulative effect of these things makes the total society different (*more conservative*) from other societies.

The technique used here is somewhat akin to the theoretical technique used by a detective in hunting an unknown culprit. The detective may have a hard job ahead with few clues and an inadequate description. However he is more fortunate than we, because he is hunting a reality—an actual criminal. Our approach more closely resembles that of the bacteriologist who is studying invisible viruses. He manipulates in many ways the area in which he has reason to believe they exist and watches what happens to the things he introduces into the area. Then he constructs an "unreal" description of the viruses, which he sends off to fellow scientists elsewhere. By comparing their notes on virus areas with his he will arrive at a theory of viruses. However, his theory may conflict with that of the other scientists because the findings of all scientists do not agree and because there may be disagreements among them as to how to frame the theory. One scientist, for example, may declare that the theory of viruses should be framed in chemical terms, another may prefer biological terms. In the end, however, the findings accumulate and help enrich the theories, and the theories compete for the prize of greatest utility—utility being defined as the extent to which the theory helps find out new things about viruses, the extent to which the theory is simple, and the extent to which the theory can be used to manufacture a medicine against certain kinds of viruses. Any theory of this type is "unreal," in the natural as well as in the social sciences. To a scientist the value of a theory lies in its utility. One must ask himself, therefore, in the pages to follow, whether we have a useful theory of democracy.

THESE MORAL POSITIONS UNIVERSAL, NOT ONLY DEMOCRATIC

The four moral systems, which we are about to describe as they operate in democracies, operate in all societies. For consideraations of space and importance, however, we shall discuss the four positions principally as they function in the democratic environment. The four moral positions are the *egalitarian*, the *conservative*, the *elite*, and the *relativist*. As they function democratically, they are called: *egalitarian democracy; conservative democracy; elitist democracy;* and *relativist democracy.*

EGALITARIAN DEMOCRACY

Egalitarian democracy seeks to know what people want and to give it to them. It is called egalitarian because it does not pretend to judge the goodness or badness of individual wants; *whatever* people want *is* good, and all men's wants are to be equally valued. The big problems of politics, according to this theory, are to find out what people want and how to get those wants expressed quickly in political policy. If this theory were carried to the extreme, egalitarian democracy would have as its goal the discovery of the wishes of some 2,000,000,000 people and of the means of realizing them all on equal terms. Furthermore, we must remember that each one of these individuals has many desires, and the desires vary in intensity and change constantly.

SCIENTIFIC DIFFICULTIES OF THE EGALITARIAN POSITION

Now obviously, posing the problem of satisfying wants in this extreme form is unjust to reality, for no man is such a fool as to try to solve such a problem, granted the desirability of the egalitarian principle. If human nature were different from what it is, something like egalitarian principles could be carried out by science. That is, if all men were alike in their nature and their wants, we could at least understand the scope of the problem and have some success in saying to what extent it might be solved. Or even if all men were by nature divided into two groups, each having one end in life and no other, then we still might conceivably define the possibilities inherent in the situation, preparatory to applying the egalitarian solution of satisfying each group equally. If one group were composed of men who wanted only to extend Soviet rule over the whole world, and the other were composed of men who wanted only to see the Kremlin razed to the ground, and absolutely no other end made a particle of difference to either group, then our problem of analysis would be much simplified. We could analyze the potentialities in the situation as neatly as Dr. Neumann has depicted mathematically the complete possibilities of success for each player in a two-handed game of poker. How to explain the necessary distribution of results and satisfy the people involved would be a grave difficulty, however, for the egalitarian umpires.

About the closest that political science has come to finding a situation in which wants are simplified and hence can be interpreted with some completeness is when nationalism has run rampant, as in Nazi Germany. "Everything," Hitler scribbled once in a jail cell, "from the baby's first storybook to the last newspaper, theatre, cinema . . . will be put to this end . . . until the brain of the tiniest child is penetrated by the glowing prayer: Almighty God, bless our weapons again . . . bless our battle." And Hitler did have some success in instilling in the German people a desire for the power of the German state at home and abroad that largely superseded any other motive, although other motives were not and cannot be completely obliterated. Still, such a strong motive does permit us to analyze Nazi behavior more easily than the political behavior of a democratic society.

Another example of a simple motivation being successfully pursued is found in Machiavelli's *The Prince*. It is no coincidence that this book has long stood as a classic work in political science. For Machiavelli did something much like the process of reducing the problem we are discussing here; he assumed only one motive, the pursuit of power, and traced the way to its achievement, disregarding other conflicting motives, like the leader's desire for virtue or wealth. From his work we gain two clear conclusions: firstly, science can teach brigands as well as parsons; secondly, the simpler the value desired, the easier it is to build a science for achieving it.

But, in fact, nature is not so generous as to provide egalitarian-directed political scientists with such simple problems. The differences in the values held by human beings, and in the intensity with which they are held, are for all practical purposes infinite. Infinite difficulties face a political science that first must discover everyone's values and then calculate how they can be realized. Only by making general and imperfect categories out of a multitude of observations of human motives and behavior can we cope with the myriad human desires. The egalitarian democrats, then, must concede the minimum necessity of working only with desires that people *generally* rather than individually have. One of the grave defects of philosophers like Paine and Rousseau was that they spoke of the generality of mankind as if individuals who composed the generality were all alike.

If they admit men are different, the egalitarians must depend on social science to an undreamed of extent. Conceivably a representative sample of the whole population of the world must be studied to obtain the world's values, and then these values must be reduced to the number of individual differences that can be legislated upon. Science must resort to modes and averages in this matter as in so many others.

Modal values and average wishes must be the currency of political discourse. Legislation (and this means state intervention) is imperatively demanded because the only way the whole process of realizing egalitarian desires can be achieved is by a general statement proclaiming what must be the stipulated mode of behavior for realizing the modal value.

Yet, though the law and the science be ultra-scientific, they can never cope with the full complexity of the problem legislated upon. Every mode and average hides individual differences. And since the theory of egalitarian democracy never obtained permission to dismiss individual differences in desires, it must admit that the mode or average is a concession to practicability and will not achieve the perfect egalitarianism. And, since their individual wants will differ to a lesser or greater extent from the summary indices, most people will have to look for other ways of satisfying their desires.

MORAL DIFFICULTIES OF THE EGALITARIAN POSITION

The fact that the egalitarian position is impossible to fulfill except by using averages that most fit the population whose desires are to be followed is only one of the moral compromises egalitarians must make. In addition, the egalitarian not only must compel his supporters to accept less or more benefits than what they actually desire, but he must compel the people to accept even the solution that fits their needs exactly. This compulsion invariably introduces all the problems of political *means* to what was originally conceived of as a clear goal. That is, to compel people means domination, psychological manipulation, economic manipulation, and physical coercion in varying amounts. The choice and extent of use of each weapon can make the policy of securing equal respect for all as disturbing morally as the pursuit of any other value. The moral position behind this policy is no easier than that involved in the pursuit of any other political value. The "voice of the people" is not only difficult to hear and interpret, but its judgments also are almost always so complex as to keep those who wish to satisfy the people in a constant moral quandary.

The "voice of the people," is likely to be a clamor for two, three, or a hundred desires that *conflict*, rather than to exist as shadings of the same desire. The politician must then decide what part of the people he wishes to follow. The "majority" has been the most popular answer to this problem. So the majority principle has come to be venerated among egalitarian spokesmen as the best index of the proper course of conduct. The majority strikes off the best mode or average; the minority must be impelled by the various political instruments to submit. Without the majority principle, or something much like it—a public opinion poll, for example—egalitarianism is lost. Yet some people will lose by the application of the majority principle, so egalitarianism is still removed from its perfect theoretical extreme, that of achieving the total collectivity of individual desires.

THE POLITICAL DEMANDS OF EGALITARIANISM

In history, the writings of Jean-Jacques Rousseau, Thomas Paine, Jeremy Bentham, Thomas Jefferson, and innumerable less admired and less important figures exemplify the egalitarian position in democratic thought and action. Some of its common beliefs may be enumerated. All men are declared to be born free and equal. All the rights of government come from the mass of people and may be taken back upon demand. Government should be so far as possible that of the people themselves. It should be as close to the town-meeting form of government as possible. The people are the best judge of what concerns them.

Universal suffrage is demanded by egalitarians as a means of expressing powerfully the desires of the collectivity. Frequent elections are favored. The majority principle is adhered to almost to the exclusion of other structural principles of government. All individuals should have the same power, offices should be open to all, representatives should be immediately responsible to the majority.

Thomas Jefferson's definition of the term "republic" gives us a general picture of this form of thought:

> Were I to assign to this term a precise and definite idea, I would say, purely and simply, it means a government by its citizens in mass, acting directly and personally, according to rules established by the majority; and that every other government is more or less republican, in proportion as it has in its composition more or less of this ingredient of the direct action of the citizens. Such a government is evidently restrained to very narrow limits of space and population. I doubt if it would be practicable beyond the extent of a New England township.
>
> The first shade from this pure element, which, like that of pure vital air, cannot sustain life of itself, would be where the powers of the government, being divided, should be exercised each by representatives chosen either *pro hac vice*, or for such short terms as should render secure the duty of expressing the will of their constitutents. This I should consider as the nearest approach to a pure republic, which is practicable on a large scale of county or population. And we have examples of it in some of our state constitutions, which, if not poisoned by priest-craft, would prove its excellence over all mixtures with other elements; and, with only equal doses of poison, would still be the best.

Other shades of republicanism may be found in other forms of government, where the executive, judiciary and legislative functions, and the different branches of the latter, are chosen by the people more or less directly, for longer terms of years, or for life, or made hereditary; or where there are mixtures of authorities, some dependent on, and others independent of the people. The further the departure from direct and constant control by the citizens, the less has the government of the ingredient of republicanism. . . .*

This very important side of Thomas Jefferson, illustrated in the preceding passage, made his name renowned among the advocates of the equality of all men. He had, however, many ideas inconsistent with these principles and often acted, as all men do, contrary to them, but, in general, he earned his fame by his persistent search for the beliefs of the masses and his endeavors to devise a scheme of government that would embody those beliefs.

CONSERVATIVE DEMOCRACY

The second moral position found in a democracy may be termed "conservative democracy." Its origins were hinted at in the previous discussion. There it was stated that science had little possibility of discovering or fulfilling mankind's many desires. While the egalitarian democrats remain optimistic in the face of this condition, the conservative democrats assume a pessimistic role. They are inclined to preserve what is desirable about their present lot and not to risk their present situation for a future one. To them it seems that there exist always far more varied and excessive wants than can possibly be satisfied. The task of government is to reduce wants, rather than to uncover and exalt them. If the people want bathtubs and books and cannot have both, they must be convinced that either baths or books are harmful.

SCIENTIFIC ASPECTS OF CONSERVATISM

The utility of social science, then, to the conservative, is to provide ways of repressing the exuberant growth of new desires and of eliminating demands already present among the population. Again social policy, this time conservative policy, has problems in common with social science. In many kinds of problems studied by social scientists, the solution can only be obtained if the number of demands

---

* Quoted, with permission, from Saul K. Padover (ed.): *Thomas Jefferson on Democracy*, pp. 39–40, Mentor Books Edition. Copyright, 1939, by D. Appleton-Century Company, Inc.

in the situation being studied are kept to a minimum or if the number of demands are reduced. Thus the social scientist will try to limit his subject of study at any one time to one of manageable proportions—a small group rather than a large, a simple group rather than a complex one, a static situation rather than a changing situation, and so forth— all in the interests of science. But his motives are the same as those of the conservative who, in the realm of social policy, feels incompetent to handle the needs of a human group in which everyone wants a variety of things at the same time but in which social policy is too haphazard a skill to satisfy all the demands.

Both social scientists and conservatives, however, find the problem of reducing wants to manageable proportions a difficult one. It is quite a trick to stem a flood of wants or to reduce existing wants. Many features of society, completely beyond our control at the present time, contribute to an increase in wants. In consequence, they contribute also to the complexity of the total problem of satisfying wants. Social change has some of the qualities of a self-agitator: change creates demands or needs for even more change. Anyone who wishes to turn back the clock of technology encounters great resistance. Thus the Amishmen of Ohio, a conservative and tightly-knit religious sect, are strongly opposed to automobiles and similar "gadgets," but they could not force a member to use a horse and buggy when he required a car periodically to drive his ailing child to a doctor situated some distance away from his farm. In George Orwell's novel, *1984*, the conservative one-party state had to rewrite history constantly, at extravagant expense, to reconcile its people to a retrograde material standard of living.

Still, severe repression, especially when conducted in the name of some nationalistic frenzy, can reduce and stop the accumulation of wants of a people, as the experience of some European countries in this century evidences. Whole nations have to a large extent forgotten, and hardly miss, the advantages and goods of an earlier period. Nazi Germany threw all the machinery of the totalitarian state into such a campaign to reduce and concentrate the values of its people and achieved considerable success. The Germans were forced in a hundred ways to forget the abundant days before World War I and even the relative abundance of the republican period from 1919 to 1932.

CONSERVATIVE IDEA ESSENTIAL TO SCIENCE AND MORALITY

These examples have been presented to show how fundamental and universal is the conservative position. It is safe to say that anybody who has ever had experience in politics or human relations in general has had to employ the conservative idea at some point in his activities. Like the egalitarian idea, which is always present, both as a method in the study of human relations and as an ethical demand, but which is especially and predominantly present among certain men, the conservative idea must be present everywhere, but yet can be strong and even predominant among certain men and societies.

As it enters the field of practical political issues, the conservative idea often takes the form of a demand for preserving tradition, seeking to prevent the present from divorcing itself from the past. It affirms that some of the most pressing problems of a democracy emerge from the difficulty of adjusting a society to continuous change. The conservatives look beyond the immediate satisfaction of a want and ask wearily whether this satisfaction will not produce in turn a number of new wants, few of which can be satisfied by the machinery of government.

Among the illustrious advocates of such a position are Edmund Burke, the great conservative politician and orator of eighteenth-century England, and Henry Adams of the United States. Others are Brooks Adams, Ortega y Gassett, and Roberto Michels. A number of recent psychologists, especially those inclined toward psychoanalysis, dwell on this "reactionary" method of handling the problems of democracy. Thus, William James (not at all a psychoanalytic psychologist) defines contentment as the ratio of aspirations to achievement; when aspirations got out of hand no achievement could satisfy the individual. And Erich Fromm, psychoanalytically trained, wrote a book called *Escape From Freedom*, the theme of which has to do with man's liberties outstripping his psychological capacity for using his liberties.

BURKE'S CONSERVATISM

The works of Edmund Burke paint an authentic portrait of conservatism. In one place, Burke sets up a doctrine of the "prescriptive" constitution, the government of law that is so good because it has *grown*, rather than been rashly *created*; it is the work of many generations, each one of which added something to it. He is always wary of social reform, fearing that it will aggravate the conditions that it is supposed to correct. He is suspicious of the effects of reason in overturning custom and precedent, holding true "reason" to be the proven good effects of past generations. He warns that a concession to reformers often paves the way for increasing and incessant demands for more reform, and holds that the end result of reform is naked egalitarianism ("plain French democracy," he calls it), subject to the most extreme palpitations at the slightest fever of the popular imagination.

More precisely, Burke objects to the demand that representatives be closely controlled by their constituents, maintaining that true representation is a sympathetic independence; it is often better without actual election, for "it possesses most of its advantages, and is free from many of its inconveniences; it corrects the irregularities in the literal representation, when the shifting current of human affairs, or the acting of public interests in different ways, carry it obliquely from its first line of direction." Only so much popular control and expression is desired, he declares, as will prevent the government becoming a *complete* oligarchy or a ruthless despotism.

Caution should be the watchword of policy, he believes; political plans rarely produce the effects intended. Furthermore, the analysis of political evils is often unscientific, for people demand more elections to prevent evils caused by elections; they demand equality to remedy problems caused by the demand for equality; they demand controls over representatives when they cannot show that the evils they attack are caused by the lack of controlled representatives. Thus Burke assumes a position congenial to conservative democratic thought and action—reducing, on the scientific side, the hopelessly complex welter of demands to manageable proportions, and, on the ethical side, affirming the great good of what has been attained, the great good of the *status quo*, the great good of the objectives that can be *certainly attained*.

ELITIST DEMOCRACY

In order to understand the third moral position of democracy let us suppose that, instead of concerning ourselves exclusively with what people wanted, we decided that certain things were best for them. The "best values" would be the criteria for setting up a society, and the function of social science would be to provide the means for introducing a maximum of these best values to the people for whom they are intended. Legislation would be then, as Aristotle, St. Thomas Aquinas, and others declared it ought to be, for the "common good" and the "best interests" of people, as the common good and best interests appeared to the leaders of the community. The common good might be also what people wanted, but it might be *not* so, either; the criterion is what they "ought to have."

This moral position rests on the aristocratic or elite principle, for only the smaller part of the population can be conceivably in a position to bear such beneficent principles; otherwise if everyone shared them, we would have simple egalitarianism, with all men seeing their version of the good, seeking it, and finding it.

ELITISM INESCAPABLE IN SCIENCE

Elitism, to a certain degree, like egalitarianism and conservatism, is an inescapable attitude in science. At the same time, it is a paramount desire among many men, a guiding motive in their lives. Let us see how these two things come about.

First, one may turn to the inescapable presence of elitism in science. Science must have problems for study. Problems for study are infinite in number, save as men select only certain problems as worthy of study. In this selection both the natural scientist and the social scientist are conditioned by all the influences that make up a culture. The scientist's problems are *set for him by his culture*. The solutions that emerge from his work will project and emphasize some trend of the culture already present to greater or less degree. He will be a contributor to a current. His answers will be partial (both literally a "portion" and broadly "biased") to the culture. In that sense he is expounding limited values, not purely "objective" reality. In an egalitarian society, science will tend to study problems of universal wants (but it will be forced to select modal wants); in a conservative society science will tend to study problems of minimum needs and social controls; and in an elitist or aristocratic society science will tend to study how to foster ideas and practices conforming to the predominant beliefs as to what is good *for* the society.

A PRIMITIVE SOCIAL SCIENCE FAVORS ELITISM

Other concomitants of the scientific process increase the elitism of science. A hypothesis may be both an ethical one and a factual one: that is, the scientist, in setting up his problem may study how a certain situation is developing or he may study how to bring about a future desired situation. He may be seeking, for example, what will be the distribution of wealth ten years hence, or he may be seeking how to bring about a particular desired distribution of wealth ten years hence. It is a reputable, though not completely established, axiom of scientific method that the man who knows what he wants to learn will have a better chance of finding it out than the man who is just puttering with his data in the hope of turning something up. Similarly the man who posits specific goals is likely to come up with a formula for achieving those goals while a man who has no idea of a future desirable situation will fail to depict with any reliability any future situations at all.

HOW ELITISTS ARE FAVORED

This thought process also favors the man of few and simple objectives in politics—it is a blessing to the elitist (he who is clear about what is good for other people) and is something of a handicap to the man who would like to take into consideration not only what he himself thinks is good for others but also what other people think is good for themselves.

It has often been remarked that aristocracies have filled the pages of history. Individuals and groups of men, knowing what they wanted, have been able to achieve their goals. Men who have tried to know what everyone wanted and have endeavored to accomplish those things, tripped over their own inadequacies. So rule on behalf of the few has prospered historically because it has been more possible than rule on behalf of the many.

BUT ELITES HAVE NEVER BEEN SECURE

Of course, most of the values exalted in governments by the few have been nothing that most men would boast about; the lions and the foxes, Pareto tells us in hundreds of pages, succeeded in filling history with the triumphs of selfish violence and selfish cunning. The humanitarians and moral philosophers have been ineffectual, bogged down by their preoccupations with the needs of others and the absence of any plausible, scientific schemes for fulfilling those needs. Furthermore, the elites of history, while pursuing their own principle, have also employed the conservative principle, consigning to the masses a minimum of food, shelter, and peace; by stupefaction from abuse and by deliberate policies, the masses learned to expect little and demand less.

But even the implacable pursuit of the elite principle guarantees nothing. Human engineering, even aimed at the simple domination of a few, has never been fully a science. Certainly one elite can be more skillful than another. The inefficiency of the despotic Austro-Hungarian Empire pales besides the competence of the Hungarian Communists of today. The Nazis showed the Kaiser some undreamed of ways of employing social science to regiment the population. The most fanatic religious inquisitors of the reformation period might marvel at how the Russians use psychology in extracting confessions from opponents of their regime. Nevertheless, social science is still a babe in arms, no matter who is suckling it. History, as Pareto also said, is a "graveyard of aristocracies." What can be done by one group of leaders can also be done by a group of rebels. Changing conditions produce internal revolution. One ruling group is carried away and another replaces it. If the masses are apathetic at the bottom, they do not care who is at the top. So, at the top, the "law" of the jungle prevails. Attention to one's own demands or to those of a small group diverts attention from maintaining the support of other parts of the population. This causes the regime to become vulnerable and hastens its downfall.

DEMOCRATIC ELITISTS

Oligarchies, aristocracies, and elites—vast in number— have not always produced the same consequences. Many men, of elitist bent, have been concerned primarily with the well-being of the masses. They may have been convinced of the uselessness of finding out what the masses desire, because they regard the values of the chosen few as most worthwhile; they would rather know what "are" the highest ends of man and seek to create a state that might embrace them; but it is unlikely that they would be complete oligarchs or tyrants so long as their definition of the good of the whole people was something more than a rationalization of their personal wants. If Plato had been Thrasymachus, who believed "might was right," he would have written his *Republic* as Machiavelli wrote *The Prince*. But he refused to accept Thrasymachus' declarations about right being whatever the powerful said it was, and went to great pains to distribute justice in his ideal society according to what was fitting and best for each individual, from the most humble worker to the philosopher kings.

Other elitists are Aristotle, Aquinas, Calvin, the American Puritans, T. H. Green of the English idealist philosophers, and John Stuart Mill, an apostate from the egalitarianism of Jeremy Bentham. Of these thinkers, John Stuart Mill is especially interesting because, although his writings differ both in method and detail from those of Plato, he too is essentially concerned with getting the right kind of leadership, the kind that knows how to use intelligence and science to distribute the results of just legislation throughout the population. Mill's great contributions to political science developed by way of his inquiry into how governmental institutions could be based on reasoned and im- partial judgment of the national interest. He was intensely concerned with the mechanics of governing according to the knowledge and ideals of an enlightened few. But the values he sought to inculcate by his methods were not the same as those springing from the egoistic assumptions about politics that fostered the ideas of Thrasymachus and Machiavelli.

RELATIVIST DEMOCRACY

The fourth moral position, commonly found in democracy, produces democrats whom we may call relativists. The relativists say that it is quite impossible to determine now or in the foreseeable future either what men want or what is good for men. Furthermore, by negative implication, they foresee no possibility of controlling the increase of demands in a culture. They are sceptics about human effort and the knowledge on which such effort is allegedly based. They are somewhat in the position of the Greek cynic, Gorgias, who claimed that nothing existed, if it did exist we could not know it, and if we knew it we could not communicate it to others. The result of true cynicism, as we observe it among the Greek Sophists or in the Venetian gentleman of Voltaire's *Candide* or among one's cynical friends, is a *disinterested tolerance in questions of values*.

RELATIVISM CONNECTED WITH A MONEY SOCIETY

A bit of history can shed light on the connection between cynical tolerance and democratic relativism. Mercantile and trading societies that depend on money have been especially productive of both cynical tolerance and democratic relativism. Money, we readily observe in our own times, "can buy anything." It is a neutral intermediary among individuals; it serves any master; it reflects no history and promises nothing specific for the future. People of all beliefs, occupations, and statuses thrive in a society dominated by a money economy. The culture of a money society is suffused with variegated purposes and private affairs. None of these culture traits can be true to a significant extent of a society dominated by the egalitarian, conservative, or elitist principle. It is no accident that the most extreme proponents of the use of the money nexus as the only regulator of human relations were practically anarchists in their political views. Such were Adam Smith, Herbert Spencer, and William Graham Sumner.

MADISON'S VIEW OF SOCIETY

The most prominent advocates of the relativist position have historically been identified with the interests of the commercial classes. Witness the view of society held by James Madison (one of the most brilliant exponents of the theory of relativist democracy):

> A landed interest, a manufacturing interest, a mercantile interest, a ·
> moneyed interest, with many lesser interests, grow up of necessity in
> civilized nations, and divide them into different classes, actuated by
> different sentiments and views. The regulation of these various and inter-
> fering interest forms the principal task of modern legislation, and in-
> volves the spirit of party and faction in the necessary and ordinary
> operations of government.

The only remedy is to enlarge the sphere, and thereby divide the community into so great a number of interests and parties, that in the first place a majority will not be likely at the same moment to have a common interest, separate from that of the whole or of the minority; and in the second place, that in case they should have such an interest, they may not be able to unite in the pursuit of it.

Thus, the Madisonians saw the political process as a vacillating, bargaining arrangement, now giving a little here and there, but never succumbing conclusively to one faction or majority. As Madison would have it, no part of society, minor or major, can claim to know the good of the whole—democracy is an end result of conflict. In fact, Madison comes closer than any other democratic theorist to that eclectic theory which we shall use later on to describe democracy as a whole. He falls short in two respects: first, he tends towards elitism and sometimes tries to declare what is absolutely good for the country—something his theory of factionalism would contradict; second, he does not realize the *essential* role of conservative, elitist, and egalitarian beliefs in making up the total democratic equilibrium, because he believes democracy could exist without "fanaticism," without people who are sure of their convictions.

Holding that society is composed of diverse and conflicting elements and that men seek their own interests (the political version of Adam Smith's economic theory), the relativist position then maintains that the task of the politician is to adjust one interest or party to the others. He is a compromiser, a broker whose commission is the preservation of the peace and the public applause proceeding therefrom.

The theory seeks to cripple the majority, to render it incapable of drastic action. It approves the separation of powers. It does not consider men rational in political matters. In the words of its foremost protagonist in contemporary writing, T. V. Smith: "Legislatures are the readiest exemplars of the process of compromise. This is a humble but honorable view of the democratic process. Nothing is to be gained by not being realistic. . . . Legislation is, as William James suggested of democracy as such, a business in which you do something, then wait to see who hollers, and then relieve the hollering as best you can to see who else hollers." Obviously, following the instructions of the constituency becomes impossible: in the first place, majorities seldom occur; in the second place, carrying out the will of the majority would destroy representative government by goading minorities to open conflict.

THE "OPEN SOCIETY" VERSUS PLANNING

In addition, to the relativists political planning on a large scale seems too risky, because political behavior is unpredictable, and because such planning implies a stability at the basis of government that is presumptuous. The facts, according to the relativists, show that politics is a flux of competition and change. Since the interests and wishes of any large number of people are imponderable, and since no elite can judge the good of others, egalitarianism and elitism alike are impossible. That impossibility alone would make them unjust to the relativists. But they are also temperamentally averse to subjecting themselves or others to fixed beliefs.

Democracy as a Whole

VARIETIES OF DEMOCRATIC THOUGHT ARE INTERDEPENDENT

These four strains of democratic thought, when they operate in a democratic way, *are in no way self-sufficient. Each leans on the others for intellectual and political sustenance.* For example, thoughts very much like those of Burke have been presented by anti-democrats, pure oligarchs. But Burke himself said that his ideas must be rooted in an appreciation of the need for representing all of the people and for thinking of the future of the national interest in legislating. Jefferson's egalitarian thinking was conditioned by a delicate respect for minority rights which inclined his egalitarianism towards what we shall call the democratic complex. On the other hand, Marx wrote in isolation from the democratic complex, except that he derived from the Rousseau tradition some of the egalitarian democratic ideas. Lacking connections with democratic supports, his ideas were loosed onto the revolutionary currents of nineteenth-century Europe. The ideas of Madison and T. V. Smith, hollow vessels of tolerance by themselves, rely very strongly on filling that is provided by other democratic sources. It is notable how Italian fascist theory cited American pragmatism in its support, alleging that "whatever works is good." Thus did relativism abet anti-democracy when it was isolated from the plural democratic equilibrium.

And the elitist democrats speak often of responsibility—responsible power, responsible administration, and responsible leadership. They are obsessed, one might gather, with the necessity for tying the acts of the elite with the needs of the masses. It is remarkable that English Fabian Socialism, which on paper seems perhaps less egalitarian than Russian communism, appears more generally democratic than communism as it operates through the Labour Party government of England. One may surmise that the Fabians, whose egalitarian ideals were suffused by the reformist idealism of Mill and other nineteenth-century elite thinkers, grew accordingly different from the revolutionary brand of Marxism. Egalitarian democracy, never a pure form of thought or action anywhere, was embraced in Russia by doctrines of despotism and other descendants of Czarist institutions.

DEMOCRACY AN EQUILIBRIUM COMPOSED OF CONTRADICTIONS

The delineation of these four moral positions that operate in a democracy tells us other facts, not ordinarily associated with the philosophical position of democracy. We have an inkling now of why democracy is so often thought to be a confused philosophy, even by its supporters. Democracy is, indeed, confused. It is indeterminate. It leads to all sorts of compromises, hypocrisies, and double talk, essentially because the democratic complex as a whole is based on contradictory premises and interests. It is a balance of forces, any one of which alone would tear it apart if the others were greatly weakened. It is like the atom, an equilibrium of great forces that display none of their potential destructiveness so long as they are held together. Other forms of society, based on a clearer principle, say of pure oligarchy, or of pure equality, can be more clearly understood and can produce more startling and clear results. But no one who is our kind of eclectic democrat could call such societies democracies.

APPLIED DEMOCRACY MOST DIFFICULT OF ALL SCIENCES

From this apparent confusion, which we prefer to call an equilibrium of contradictory forces, come other interesting results. Applied democracy is the most difficult of all sciences. Since no factor in the problem of value analysis, as related above, is excluded from consideration, democratic theory must consider the consequences of any particular social action to each and every value. Again we recall Machiavelli in illustrating this point. It is significant that his book, *The Prince*, is far better known than his *Discourses*. *The Prince* was political science treating primarily of the dependencies of the egocentric variable—the desire of one man for mastery of the state, for power. The *Discourses* were political science dealing with the dependencies of the several major satisfactions sought in a republic. When the number of independent but interdependent variables is increased in a complex problem, the problem is much more difficult to solve (see pp. 555-8). So *The Prince* was an astonishing success at subjecting human behavior to the one independent variable of the prince's power drive, while the *Discourses* did not achieve the same success with the varied needs of the people.

DEMOCRACY AND SCIENCE INTERDEPENDENT

This vast difficulty in building a science of and for a democracy has a paradoxical effect: it stimulates science, especially social science. America today leads the world in public opinion research, attitude testing, mental measurement, and human engineering in general. More empirical work in social science has been done in America than in all the rest of the world before the twentieth century—even though the logic, purpose, meaning, and success of a good part of it may be seriously challenged. But apart from this country, we see in Athens, in the Renaissance Italian cities, in western Europe of the nineteenth and twentieth centuries much the same flowering of social science. We may conjecture that the complex equilibrium of democracy, especially as it is preoccupied with the individual needs of masses of people, fosters the development of the scientific method in human relations. This thesis remains to be explored and developed by the historians of science, who have concerned themselves more with the origins of natural science and not enough with the origins of social science.

DEMOCRACY NOT A UNITARY WHOLE

We can conclude, if we accept the foregoing as the most likely interpretation of democracy and its effects, that in a sense democracy is a whole. It is not a unitary whole. *It is an eclectic whole composed of a complex of ideas and practices that attempt to say what people want and to give it to them, to say what is good for people and to give that to them, to restrain the tendency of unforeseen wants and effects from unbalancing the equilibrium, and to allow the various ideas free play.*

The varieties of democracy are the true foundation of a separation of powers. Polybius long ago thought that the reason for the success of the Roman Republic was its balance. This balance, he theorized, emerged from certain institutions of the Romans—Senate, consuls, and plebian assemblies, Subsequent political scientists identified the "separation of powers" with certain institutions—bicameralism, an independent judiciary, town meetings, a separate executive branch, and so on. By our theory, the separation of powers rests on ideological conditions that are deeper than the aforesaid formal institutions. The separation of powers is an expression of the existence of an equilibrium of psychological forces, represented in the ideologies and actions of men, each force depending on the position and existence of the other forces. None would produce the same society at all, if it operated by itself.

With this theory of the nature of democracy in mind, we may go on to discuss in the concluding chapter the nature and possibilities of political policy. The science of achieving values, it will be recalled, was the second of the two grave problems requiring attention in the field of democracy and policy. The first question, whose plans ought to prevail, we have now discussed. In the final chapter, we shall discuss the procedures by which governments attempt to achieve human ends and to point out the weaknesses and strength of political policy.

Questions and Problems

1. Describe how Hobbes and Locke disagreed both on moral principles and questions of fact. (Add to your facts on both men with the aid of *The Encyclopaedia of Social Sciences*.)

2. From section one of the chapter, compose an imaginary letter of warning to a friend who says he is reading a good book on democracy, telling your friend what to watch for in the author's logic and how to avoid being fooled.

3. Ask any five persons to define democracy. Record their answers faithfully. Analyze their answers with reference to the extent to which they confuse values and facts, the extent to which they differ from one another.

4. Why cannot science tell us what democracy ought to be? (Use Chapter One in framing your reply as well as this chapter.)

5. How are facts and values basically related in thinking about sceintific problems? Is political science then very difficult or quite impossible?

6. What are the seven conditions that form the social setting of democracy?

7. Suppose a man is jailed for several days without due process of law because he spoke against a political boss. To what extent can that incident be used in determining whether the society in which he lived was democratic?

8. Suppose a king spends two-thirds of his working hours thinking and acting on affairs designed to better the living standards of his subjects. In what respects may he be called democratic? In what respects may his society be called democratic—employing only this bit of evidence?

9. Write a summary of the theory of economic determinism, using materials from this chapter and from Chapter Five on voting behavior.

10. Can the seven conditions of the democratic social setting be fitted into any one of the consistent moral positions of democracy? Explain your answer methodically, that is, step by step.

11. Why is it "unreal" to speak of an elitist moral position except as a way of studying a moral problem? In what way does such a moral position exist, however?

12. Describe briefly the four moral positions with respect to democracy.

13. What do you believe would be the moral attitude of egalitarian, elitist, conservative, and relativist democrats with respect to the "uplifting" impulse in democratic societies?

14. What do you believe would be the attitude of each moral position to the social class situation that is found in democracy?

15. What do you believe would be the attitude of each moral position to the high level of personal discontent found in democracy?

16. How do you think those who partake strongly of each of the four moral positions of democracy would regard the condition of constitutionalism and separation of powers found in a democracy?

17. What scientific interests would incline persons to be egalitarian; conservative; elitist; relativist?

18. What scientific problems would egalitarian democrats be likely to study with special interest? Conservative democrats? Elitist democrats? Relativist democrats?

19. How are elitists, conservatives, and relativists favored by the primitive condition of social science?

20. Why are elites often insecure?

21. How is relativism connected with a money society?

22. Describe the moral equilibrium of democratic theories.

Longer Study and Research
Problems Suitable for Term Papers

1. Read one of the following works and analyze the author's ideas con-concerning the problems of democracy, the conditions of democracy, and the moral positions of democracy:

Aristotle: *Ethics* or *Politics*
Plato: *The Republic* or *The Laws*
Thomas Hobbes: *Leviathan*
John Locke: *Of Civil Government* (Book II)
Sir Thomas More: *Utopia*
Henry Adams: *The Education of Henry Adams*
Theodore Roosevelt: *Autobiography*
Thomas Paine: *The Age of Reason*
Adolf Hitler: *Mein Kampf*
Edmund Burke: *Reflections on the Revolution in France*
Walter Lippmann: *The Good Society*
T. V. Smith: *The Promise of American Politics*
Charles E. Merriam: *The New Democracy and the New Despotism*

2. Extract from the editorial columns of a daily newspaper every statement about democracy over a period of six months. Does the paper expound a theory of democracy? If so, identify and describe it. If not, describe the contradictions.

3. Select any well known political leader of a democratic country, gather his speeches and writings, and write a fifteen page essay on his moral position with respect to democracy.

4. Using as a framework of analysis the seven conditions of democracy,

read one of the following works and write a ten-page report on the relative presence or absence of those conditions in the society treated:

Machiavelli: *Discourses* (on Rome)
Alexis de Tocqueville: *Democracy in America*
D. W. Brogan: *France under the Republic*
André Siegfried: *Democracy Comes of Age*
Robert S. and H. M. Lynd: *Middletown*
F. F. Abbott: *Roman Politics*
Terrot R. Glover: *Democracy in the Ancient World*
Thucydides: *History of the Peloponnesian War*

18

LIBERTY AND PUBLIC POLICY

DEMOCRACY, according to the theory just stated, is a social condition in which contrasting values are maintained in an equilibrium. It is an eclectic whole that does not take a definite position on any group of issues, although the component strains of democracy may take such a position. It is a *condition*, but not a *position*. This theory puts one in an awkward predicament when he is asked "What is the program of democracy?" The eclectic democrat must reply that there is no *program* of democracy. To advocate a conservative program would eliminate, for example, the influence of democrats like the relativist jurist, Oliver Wendell Holmes, who wanted to let people go to the devil in their own way. To advocate an elitist program would do an injustice to someone like Dr. George Gallup who would prefer to have his polls of what people want used as guides to what government ought to do. And so on.

Therefore, democratic society has no end save that of being an eternal equilibrium under which all four strains of democracy may continue to exist and to prosper. *There is no single view on any issue that so well suits democracy that every democrat must in principle agree with it.* (This statement is one of fact, not of ethics. Indeed this very statement itself must be bitterly opposed *as a moral principle* by strong groups in the community, if the democratic condition is to survive. For this statement must be distinguished from the *moral belief* of the relativist democrats, who would desire a society in which *everyone* believes that it takes all sorts of people to make a democracy. If everyone believed this or too many people believed this, the sense of community, the beliefs that men need to carry on a vigorous life, would wither away. If this scientific fact becomes the moral belief of the community as a whole, it will destroy the basis for the democratic operation of the community. Again we must warn ourselves not to look for our values in scientific theory.)

If democracy is a social condition, how can it act? Democracy does not act. The government acts. Public officials act to carry out policies that are agreed upon, for various reasons, by a good part of those who hold to any one or a mixture of the democratic strains we have described. In this case, a variety of motives is being statisfied. The government acts also to carry out functions that one of the general democratic strains, through its sponsors, has succeeded in foisting upon the community as a whole. In this second case, there is only temporary ascendancy. These two kinds of matters form the settled objectives of the government. In addition a continuing dispute over the execution of policy occurs in the political arena. Thus, legislation to control floods in the Missouri Valley may be passed for a variety of motives and, later on, questions may arise about the efficiency of the authorized public officials in controlling floods.

All the disputed problems of democracy do not have to be solved before the government can act. Moreover the government can act in many ways without proving any component strain of democracy right or wrong. The government can carry the mails, wage a war, build dams, provide pensions, and perform a hundred other functions, choosing any one of many methods, without taking a philosophical stand on the egalitarian, elitist, conservative, or relativist position. We must be clear, however, on the point that the government is not carrying out *the* policies of democracy as an eclectic whole.

Since this book, with its eclectic theory of democracy, is not intended to provide practical advice to people of any special viewpoint to the exclusion of others, we cannot favor our elitist friends, nor our egalitarian friends, nor the others, with special formulae. They will have to work out their own methods of political action. We do, however, propose to help them all together during the balance of this book, by showing them how to think and speak clearly about liberty, rights, and public policies. Then they can examine their own personal condition and human conditions generally with respect to the character of their liberties and can recognize and evaluate the effects of political policies.

Therefore, this chapter seeks to give the practical philosopher an understanding of the nature of individual liberty and rights and of rational public policy. The climax of the political struggle occurs here. All that one knows about political science in general, and all that one thinks the government ought to be, come together in the controversies over freedom and controls, and over the problem of making politics a rational form of human behavior.

In achieving this general objective, we will, in this last chapter, undertake the following specific tasks. In the first section, we will define and describe individual liberty and rights. We will show how liberties often are changed and restrained. We will discuss collective or public policy, showing how political policies develop and relate to individual liberties, and also how the process of restraint works in and out of the process of achieving individual liberties and public policies.

Then we will analyze policy, asking: What is a "rational" policy? What private and public groups make policy? How can one determine the goals of public policy? What parts of the governmental apparatus specialize in policy making? And finally, we ask: How can the rational planning of public policy be increased?

Rights, Liberty, Restraints, and Plans

A RIGHT IS PROTECTED BY LAW

A person's right is his ability to pursue a course of behavior under the protection of the law. The law is often based on community customs. It is formally defined by legislatures, courts, and other official bodies. It is enforced by courts, executive officials, and administrative officers. Therefore the protection afforded by law to a right may spring from activities of the courts or the officials of the government. Different times and places may display different institutions that assist one's rights.

SOMETIMES COMMUNITY CUSTOMS MODIFY A RIGHT

The customs of a community may provide a liberty that is otherwise unrecognized. For example, men wanted for political crimes have often found refuge among the common people. The practice has been encountered so frequently in historical annals to warrant its mention as a guarantor of liberty alongside the courts and legislatures. Tocqueville wrote of early nineteenth-century Europe that neither monarchy nor the majority of people ruled absolutely. The executive and the community each protected certain liberties from abuse by the other.

In any constitutional state in Europe, every sort of religious and political theory may be freely preached and disseminated; for there is no country in Europe so subdued by any single authority as not to protect the man who raises his voice in the cause of truth from the consequences of his hardihood. If he is unfortunate enough to live under an absolute government, the people are often on his side; if he inhabits a free country, he can, if necessary, find a shelter behind the throne.*

This opposition of political forces, we believe, is an important portection of liberty, despite the absence of official organs of government obligated to protect it. Still, it is best not to call an activity protected by the force of community sentiment a right, but to reserve the use of the word right only for the actual ability of a person to pursue a course of behavior under the protection of law, that is, under the protection of ethical directives enforced by public officers.

THE COURTS MORE FREQUENTLY ACT AS GUARANTORS

We know already that courts work continuously to protect the rights of individuals. We need say little more about how the courts perform this task. The subject of civil and political rights is often taught in America by means of the decisions of the Supreme Court. These decisions, protecting individuals in their opinions on heated questions, or in their unpopular agitation, or in their free worship, grant rights on the basis of constitutional law, statutory law, and judge-made law.

An overwhelming number of the world's constitutions declare the existence of a variety of rights respecting conscience, equality, free religion, a free press, free labor unions, social security, and other matters (see Figure 48). Many of the rights contained in the written constitutions, of course, have no reference to reality; the stipulated protection is simply not to be had by any means—popular, legislative, or judicial.

Whether rights exist can be known by examining the past behavior of the public, the executive and legislative officials, and the courts. It would be naive to take the few words of a constitutional phrase as more than a moral affirmation of unknown strength and meaning. One has to do legal and social research, for example, before he can predict that the banning of a street meeting will be prohibited by the Supreme Court as a violation of the first amendment to the Constitution. Also, the legal doctrine of the legal omnipotence of the British Parliament does not mean that the Parliament has the right to do anything, in our usage of the word "right." Parliament is bound to act in consideration of the threat of resistances from the public and the courts, and in accord with the ingrained habits and viewpoints of its elected members.

* Quoted, with permission, from Alexis de Tocqueville, *Democracy in America*, the Henry Reeves text as Revised by Francis Bowen, further corrected and edited with introduction, editorial notes, and bibliographies by Phillips Bradley (New York: Alfred A. Knopf, Inc., 1945), Vol. I, p. 263.

FIGURE 48

THE RIGHTS OF MEN AS PROCLAIMED BY THE SEVENTY-FIVE WRITTEN CON-
STITUTIONS OF THE WORLD *

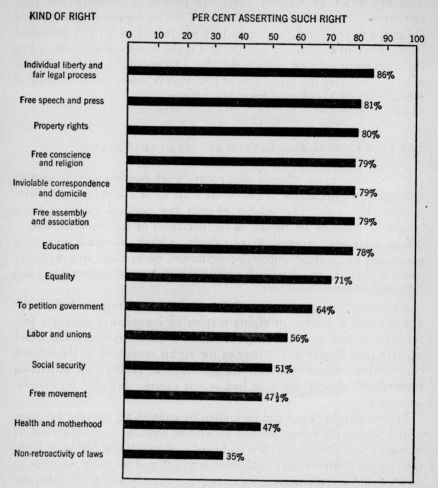

KIND OF RIGHT   PER CENT ASSERTING SUCH RIGHT

Kind of Right	Per Cent
Individual liberty and fair legal process	86%
Free speech and press	81%
Property rights	80%
Free conscience and religion	79%
Inviolable correspondence and domicile	79%
Free assembly and association	79%
Education	78%
Equality	71%
To petition government	64%
Labor and unions	56%
Social security	51%
Free movement	47½%
Health and motherhood	47%
Non-retroactivity of laws	35%

* Based on Amos J. Peaslee: *Constitutions of Nations* (1950), p. 9, with the permission of Mr. Peaslee.

A LIBERTY OR FREEDOM IS BROADER THAN A RIGHT

Disregarding the presence or absence of protection in law, we can also talk about the ability of people to do as they wish. This ability is defined as a liberty or freedom. Possessed of a liberty or freedom, a man will (1) visualize a desirable future situation (value) and resolve to achieve it (valve-*goal*); (2) take means to achieve it; and, (3) be as able as any man in similar circumstances to achieve it.

FIGURE 49

FROM LIBERTY TO PUBLIC POLICY

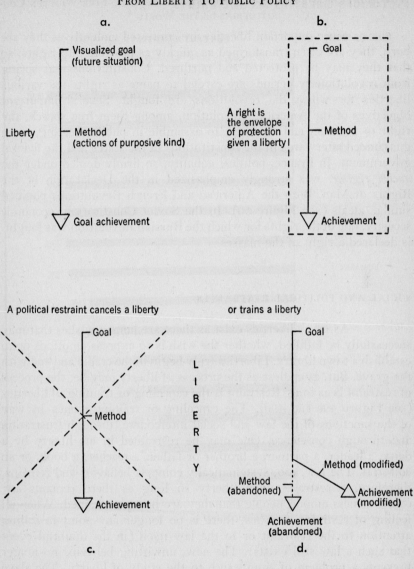

a.

Visualized goal
(future situation)

Liberty — Method
(actions of purposive kind)

Goal achievement

b.

Goal

A right is
the envelope
of protection
given a liberty

Method

Achievement

A political restraint cancels a liberty   or trains a liberty

Goal

Method

Achievement

c.

L
I
B
E
R
T
Y

Goal

Method
(abandoned)

Achievement
(abandoned)

Method (modified)

Achievement
(modified)

d.

These are the three essential elements of liberty (see Figure 49a). A liberty that is protected by law is a right (see Figure 49b); a liberty that is pursued in defiance of law is a wrong. Liberties that are in the process of being achieved for the first time by pioneering individuals usually hover in the shadows between a right and a wrong. If they are important in effect—like free speech is—their first appearance is likely to be associated with political turmoil and even revolution.

VICTORIOUS LIBERTIES BECOME RIGHTS

Since important liberties are contested violently as they are born, they are often transformed as quickly as possible into rights, so that they may be protected and nurtured. Constitutions that spring from revolutionary periods are careful to name as rights the various liberties for which the revolutions are fought. Several important objectives of the American Revolution, among them free speech, the right to petition, and the right to assemble in public meeting, were guaranteed afterwards in the constitutions of the states and the federal government. In France, political equality, so firmly denied under the *ancien régime*, was strongly emphasized in the Declaration of the Rights of Man. Both the American and French Revolutions pursued similar ideals (see Figure 50). In the Soviet Constitution, economic security, one of the rights for which the Russian Revolution was fought, is declared a right of the masses.

SOCIAL AND POLITICAL RESTRAINTS

As many liberties exist as there are human wishes that may successfully be fulfilled, whether the wish is to express emotions or to establish a town library. Liberties truly begin in the cradle and end with the grave. But, as endless as the process of liberty may be, the process of restraint is as long. Restraint is the canceling or training of liberties (see Figure 49c and 49d). The canceling or training comes by way of the sanctions of the law and social intercourse, through frustration and through conscience. One may be restrained in his liberty by a deity, a leader, a partner, a brother or father, a teacher, a book, or an editorial. The law, too, systematically compels behavior and remains, therefore, a restraint upon liberty so long as there remains any consciousness among people that they are being restrained. When all feeling of restraint vanishes, there is no longer any point in calling attention to the restraint or to the law itself (in the doubtful event that such a law still exists). The new, unwitting behavior no longer presents a problem of significance to the study of liberty. The slave who does not know he is a slave is not concerned with liberty, although an outsider may, from a different point of view, demand a change in the condition of slaves.

Examining in this light the course of a man's existence, one can picture it as an endless series of liberties and restraints. In political terms, the "life" of a society is this endless series multiplied by all the members of the community.

FIGURE 50   THE AMERICAN AND FRENCH REVOLUTIONS RELATED *

CHAPTER V.

COMPARISON OF THE FRENCH AND AMERICAN DECLARATIONS.

DÉCLARATION DES DROITS DE L'HOMME ET DU CITOYEN.	AMERICAN BILLS OF RIGHTS.
ART. 1. *Les hommes naissent et de-meurent libres et égaux en droits. Les distinctions sociales ne peuvent être fondées que sur l'utilité commune.* 2. *Le but de toute association politique est la conservation des droits naturels et imprescriptibles de l'homme. Ces droits sont la liberté, la propriété, la sûreté et*	VIRGINIA, I. That all men are by nature equally free and in-dependent, and have certain inherent rights, of which, when they enter into a state of society, they cannot, by any compact, deprive or divest their posterity; namely, the enjoy-ment of life and lib-erty, with the means of acquiring and pos-sessing property, and

27

CHAPTER VI.

THE CONTRAST BETWEEN THE AMERICAN AND ENGLISH DECLARATIONS OF RIGHTS.

THE comparison of the American and French declarations shows at once that the setting forth of principles abstract, and there-fore ambiguous, is common to both, as is also the pathos with which they are recited. The French have not only adopted the American ideas, but even the form they received on the other side of the ocean. But in contrast to the diffuseness of the Ameri-cans the French are distinguished by a brevity characteristic of their language. Articles 4–6 of the Declaration have the most specific French additions in the super-fluous and meaningless definitions of liberty [1]

[1] It harks back finally to the old definition of Florentinus L. 4 D. 1, 5: "Libertas est naturalis facultas eius, quod cuique facere libet, nisi si quid vi aut jure prohibetur."

43

Here we have illustrated the use of the comparative method in the analysis of historic documents. On the left is the beginning of the two examples, on the right, the beginning of the discussion of the comparison.

* Georg Jellinek: *The Declaration of the Rights of Man and of Citizens* (New York: Henry Holt and Company, Inc., 1901). Reproduced with the permission of Henry Holt and Company, Inc.

FIGURE 51

PUBLIC POLICY AND PLANNING

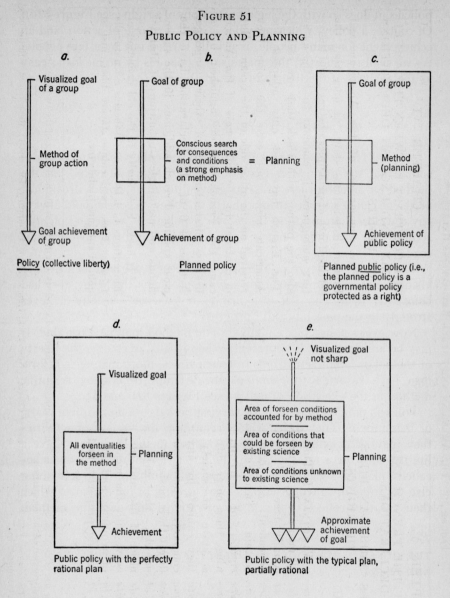

a.

Visualized goal
of a group

Method of
group action

Goal achievement
of group

Policy (collective liberty)

b.

Goal of group

Conscious search
for consequences
and conditions
(a strong emphasis = Planning
on method)

Achievement of group

Planned policy

c.

Goal of group

Method
(planning)

Achievement of
public policy

Planned public policy (i.e.,
the planned policy is a
governmental policy
protected as a right)

d.

Visualized goal

All eventualities
forseen in   Planning
the method

Achievement

Public policy with the perfectly
rational plan

e.

Visualized goal
not sharp

Area of forseen conditions
accounted for by method

Area of conditions that
could be forseen by
existing science

Area of conditions unknown
to existing science

Planning

Approximate
achievement
of goal

Public policy with the typical plan,
partially rational

A POLICY IS A COLLECTIVE LIBERTY

Our distinction between individual liberty and policy will
perhaps be clearer if we think of a policy as a collective liberty (see
Figure 51a). Any group that has a goal and can succeed in various
ways in achieving it has a collective liberty or a policy. When the
government has such a policy, it may be called a public or a political
policy, and, since the government has the authority to carry out its

policies, it does so with the legal protections of a right (see Figure 51c). Of course, a policy, which provides a goal, a course of action, and an achievement for many people, is usually carried out by a few people. As we shall see shortly, the analysis of a policy is by no means as easy as the analysis of the liberty of a single person.

RELATIONS OF PLANNING TO POLICY

The crucial aspect of a liberty or policy is the process of actualizing the goal. It is easy to visualize future heavens, but the method for arriving there presents grave difficulties. Such a dream had better be called a utopia than a liberty or policy. So one should always pay the closest attention to the *means*. A policy of "peace and plenty" sounds well to the ears but is only the beginning of a most arduous road.

The advent of science on the historical scene has given men greater visions of practical methods for solving problems than they ever had before. A man who believes firmly in "science" usually believes strongly in the possibility of "progress."

Now every policy has a method. The method may be execrable. It may be hopeless. But it is present. When it fails, of course, the liberty or the policy is not actualized. In recent times, more than ever before, men have resorted to *planning*—the attempt to employ scientific method in the execution of policy (see Figures 51b and 51c.)

Political policies may plan for varying periods—a month, five years, or indefinitely. They differ widely regarding the variety of activities they may affect and how much they affect them. Plans may have a limited effect or a total effect, in the latter case bringing about a so-called "planned society"—socialist, fascist, communist, or something else yet to be invented. And plans vary greatly in the extent to which their creation reflects a maximum of rational and scientific method.

THE GENERAL RELATIONS OF LIBERTY, RESTRAINTS, POLICIES, AND PLANS

To summarize the foregoing remarks may be helpful, for their implications are important. Everyone has liberties and restraints. Every liberty involves a method, conscious or unconscious. Political policies are collective liberties. Most policies inflict restraints on some people. Only careful studies of past policies and projected policies will disclose who will *probably* be affected by the expected operations of the policy. Only factual studies of each policy in operation will reveal who is affected and how much he is affected. When the method of a policy is carried out with conscious attempts at a scientific method, that method may be called a plan.

It follows, furthermore, that the desire for liberty and the plan emerging from that desire may *not* produce the desired liberty—the plan may be scientific in intent but unscientific in fact. (Of course, the desired liberty may itself be impossible to obtain, but to pass such a judgment also requires scientific evidence.) Also, more than one plan may be feasible and it need not necessarily be an extensive plan.

An example, in tabular form, may aid in the comprehension of the relationships among liberty, rights, restraints, policies, and plans:

1. A goal is possessed	1. A pioneer desires to build a cabin.
2. A liberty is predicted	2. He assumes or believes that no obstacle need intervene to prevent his building a home for his family.
3. Past restraints are present liberties	3. While at one time, he saw no need for a home, now, in order to be a respected member of the community, he must provide a permanent abode for his family. He has, however, become so conditioned and convinced of the value of settling down and building a home, that what were once restraints are now regarded by him as positive liberties.
4. Unconscious method	4. He builds a cabin like his father and neighbors built, employing techniques the origin of which and the meanings of which are mostly unknown to him.
5. Scientific observation	5. A visiting scientist observes that certain structural principles of physics and human principles of use-value are being used well, others badly, in implementing the conscious or latent desires of the pioneer and his family.
6. Conscious planning	6. A later home builder profits from newly available plans for building homes and adapts his plans to these specifications.
7. Scientific observation	7. Again the scientist observes that certain structural and human principles, consciously employed, are

	being used well, but that others are not well used in implementing the conscious or latent desires of the pioneer and his family.
8. Restraints	8. The builder is restrained by the availability of certain materials only, by his personal resources, by family pressures, and by the specifications of the particular plan he chose to follow.
9. Alternative plan	9. The builder might choose a different style of construction.
10. New protected liberties or rights are acquired	10. Builder acquires a legal residence, a status as home owner, sometimes the right to vote or run for office (if a property qualification is demanded). He and others elect governing officials.
11. The officials organize some liberties into rights	11. While no one may have disputed his original liberty to build, he now has additional court and legislative protection for his property holdings.
12. A private threat to his rights	12. A tannery wishes to build a factory next to his house, reducing its value.
13. Protection by right is sought for the original liberty	13. The home owner seeks to establish his liberty and right to be free of a nuisance by appealing to the courts for an injunction against the tannery.
14. One liberty prevails over another	14. The court holds the tannery is not prohibited by the common law or statutes. No right to be free of such a nuisance exists.
15. An individual liberty is transformed into a collective liberty or right	15. The home owner unites with others to demand zoning legislation prohibiting manufacturing industry in the community.
16. Political or public policy results	16. The village council reserves the area in question for residential purposes only.
17. The policy is only partly scientific	17. While taking into account the desires of most members of the community for relief from industrial

nuisances, the council fails to zone against another common disintegrator of property values and optimum family living, the use of residential dwellings as rooming houses.

18. The partly scientific character of the policy takes organized protection as a right from certain desires, and allows free play to the liberties of others

18. Rooming-house keepers buy homes in the area for business purposes.

19. The original liberty and right conflict with new restraints

19. The home owner, confounded now by his involvement in the property and the property's depreciation, must either evolve a new liberty or cut down his expectations from his old one.

20. New liberty evolves from old restraints

20. He is taken with the idea of turning his home into a rooming house and using the payments received therefrom to help build a new home in a better area.

21. Broader political planning is demanded

21. This time he examines carefully the restrictions present in his new neighborhood to see whether he will avoid all harmful possibilities.

Thus is life an endless series of liberties and restraints; it is interspersed with rights and fraught with individual and political plans that distribute and redistribute, efficiently and inefficiently, a multitude of liberties and restraints. When restraints are imposed overwhelmingly on one group, the process may be called persecution (see Figure 52). Political policies weave in and out of the fabric of existence, now clearly designed and then again confused in purpose and effect. It is useless to assign the words "democratic" or "undemocratic," or the words "bad" or "good" to the meaning of liberty, restraint, plans, or policies. Such superfluous meanings only encumber clear analysis. Water is not inherently good, inasmuch as people may sometimes drown in it or fields be flooded with it; nor is water bad, for people must have it or die of thirst. Such usages may be emotionally impressive, just as we are impressed with the imprecations addressed by a character of Eugene O'Neill to the "she-devil" sea, but they bode only danger for sanity and order in the world of fact. Depending on the values held by the one who makes the statement, our key words may be sometimes called "good" and sometimes called "bad."

FIGURE 52

CHANGES IN RESTRAINTS AND FREEDOMS DURING A SOCIAL REVOLUTION

What 92 anti-Nazis, in their own life stories, report to have occurred to them under the Nazis. The table gives percentage of subjects reporting restriction and expansion of freedom in various spheres of activity.*

SPHERE OF LIFE	% OF CASES REPORTING CONSTRICTION OF FREEDOM	% OF CASES REPORTING EXPANSION OF FREEDOM
Family	42	4
Friends	55	4
Occupation	84	2
Recreation	44	1
Religion	22	6
Politics	24	3

* Source: With permission, from G. W. Allport, J. S. Bruner, and E. M. Jandorf, "Personality under Social Catastrophe," p. 357 in Clyde Kluckhohn and Henry A. Murray, *Personality in Nature, Society, and Culture* (New York: Alfred A. Knopf, 1949).

Rational and Irrational Policies

DIFFERENCE HINGES ON FOREKNOWLEDGE OF CONSEQUENCES

An important problem of individual liberty and public policy is whether enough is known about the behavior affected by the liberty or policy to make them *rational*, that is, *productive of the intended effects.* Liberty and policy, therefore, are defined as rational in so far as they take into account all foreseeable things that lie between their goal and its achievement. Liberty and policy are irrational whenever their results are in any considerable part in excess of, in addition to, or insufficient to their goals, and these occurrences might have been foreseen. Where conscious scientific method is being used, a rational liberty or policy has a perfect plan and an irrational liberty or policy has an imperfect plan (see Figures 51d and e).

A liberty or policy is rational, we have said, in so far as it maximizes its foresight of consequences, irrational in so far as it is ignorant of known consequences. The consequences themselves may be good or bad, desirable or undesirable. Thus, if one plans a vacation to the seashore for a rest and swim, he is rational in believing that the seashore can provide both things, rational in bringing oil and umbrellas to protect himself from the burning sun that he foresees to be there, rational in knowing that a crowded beach will disturb him some of the time. He is irrational if he does not look into weather reports that predict two weeks of cold and stormy weather.

One may be irrational about both desirable and undesirable consequences. He may further be irrational about things that he might know and predict but does not know and predict, and also about things he cannot possibly know and predict—that is, it is to a degree irrational to lack complete foreknowledge of all contingencies.

Similarly, a legislature may declare that within three years there will be a power shortage in a community and order the construction of dams and new powerhouses. The legislature is rational in so far as it uses the best that science can offer in predicting the power shortage correctly. It is rational also if it realized that the power system will drain the treasury of resources—an undesirable, but a foreseen, consequence of its policy. The legislature, however, is neither rational nor irrational if it develops that, against scientific expectations, the cost of the power system does not drain the treasury. It is just lucky.

RATIONALITY IS WITH REFERENCE TO THE DESIRES OF THE ACTOR

But now let us be clear about rationality and values. If the legislature foresees correctly that the treasury will be drained, and goes ahead anyway, because it prefers public power to financial security, it is rational. It is so, *even if a majority of people disagree.* If a commander were to sacrifice a thousand troops to win a medal, his plan would be rational if he got the medal, even though the results might be most undesirable to practically everyone. We are not entitled to call some value that we do not share irrational, except for purposes of propaganda. We can only call irrational those decisions that do not take known consequences into account.

OMNISCIENT PLANS DO NOT EXIST

It must be admitted that our use of the word "rational" makes it difficult to tell in advance whether many policies are rational. But we cannot expect lawmakers to be omniscient, that is, aware of consequences not even the greatest minds can foresee. To call a policy rational because it foresees everything that men know can happen but overlooks a great deal that is known later or is not to be known at all requires that we prove that knowledge *was* or *was not* available before calling any policy rational. We must warn ourselves *not to demand omniscience from either individual liberty or political policy in practical affairs.* Else few purposive actions would survive the gauntlet. In a world of profound mysteries, we are entitled to applaud heartily the men who are relatively rational.

The Social Organization of Policy

MANY JURISDICTIONS MAKE POLICIES

There is no single rational way of organizing human behavior to make or execute policy. Under different circumstances, men organize in different ways to create liberty and policy. Human activities may take the form of individual liberties, the policies of business corporations, or the policies of political reformers. At other times, human activities may result in planning boards, pension plans, political movements and, finally, the formal activities of government agencies on a high level of authority.

INDIVIDUAL LIBERTY ON POLITICALLY RELEVANT MATTERS

At the height of the popularity of classical economics during the last century, it was believed widely that the most efficacious method of achieving social goals was by individual liberty. To Adam Smith, Herbert Spencer, and Charles Sumner it seemed that a maximum of well being in the population could be achieved if individuals were allowed to plan their own activities as they wished and could, without any positive direction. By the laws of unorganized human behavior, these writers thought, each man had automatically to work towards the good of the whole population. A kind of "invisible hand," wrote Adam Smith, operated to transform each man's self-interest into the general good. The effects, for example, of a man's desire for profit, would be the manufacture of a better product to outstrip his competitors. This would be a material gain for the rest of society.

True, such influences by a single individual would be imperceptible from an over-all view but just as one vote out of forty millions helps to elect a president, one slight influence helps to maintain a condition whereby the whole of society increases its material well-being. Individual abilities and the tastes of the massed individual consumers provide the conditions for a "greater," "natural" plan to work. No group policy is necessary; the state's only policy must be to protect this normal social condition.

This explanation of society has come to be called a defense of planlessness. Strictly speaking, however, it declares that, for certain material values which everyone presumably shares, individual planning is most effective. The theory argues that the conditions of political planning introduce some necessary accompaniments that may be rational (that is, foreseen) but undesirable, as well as some accompaniments that are irrational and mostly undesirable, that together far outweigh the possible rational advantages of political planning.

PRIVATE GROUP POLICY

A second mode of organization of policy holds that *private* groupings may by co-operation produce policies that possess rational advantages unknown to *public* policy. The theory is derived partly from the Smithian view, and partly from a belief in the value of voluntary social organization. A group of firms, for example, may "govern" a segment of the economy within limits. They may set wages and hours for the industry, adjust prices to their own views, and enforce fair trades practices. Or, in the noneconomic sphere, religious groups may pursue common goals co-operatively rather than under the direction of public authority. Or recreational, fraternal, and educational groups may establish the conditions for their own operations independently of a general directive from the state.

Policies of this kind have a limited influence on the behavior of the people concerned: adherence to the group policy is voluntary; the behavior that can be controlled is limited in scope; the instruments available for maintaining the organized movement are economic and social, rather than political. Thus an organization of religious groups to govern the preaching of the gospel cannot force all groups to agree; it can possibly affect the preaching but not the practice. It can only accomplish its goals by persuasion and propaganda and by successfully competing with outsiders in organizing the total number of souls available.

POLICY BY PUBLIC JURISDICTIONS

Another type of policy authority is the local jurisdiction. Towns, cities, states and mixed authorities of private and public interests furnish a variety of schemes for focusing group values on specific functional tasks. Cities and towns operate a number of industries—sewage disposal, water supply protective services, housing developments, parks, and many others. Just about everything that the federal government in America is doing was done initially by some state government. And, in many cases, state governments now perform functions once done by cities and towns. Certain electric power systems, water supply systems, port facilities, and other enterprises are controlled and operated by *mixed authorities*, in which political jurisdictions and private enterprise join. Both may furnish capital, ideas, and direction to the task at hand.

Many of these local authorities are quite intimately connected with the affected populations. Sewage disposal and water supply for example, are particular enterprises in which the goals are fairly clear, the need very general, and the means not very debatable. In certain types of activities, the interests directly concerned, although a minority of the total population of the jurisdiction, do not run into heavy opposition and public activities on their behalf are generally countenanced. The Port of New York Authority, for example, has many problems of detailed planning of facilities in the New York area, but its over-all purpose is clear. The interests involved—shippers, local officials, workers—are agreed in principle and the operations are tangible and observable.

On other matters, however, opposing values clash and the policy operates in a completely political milieu, that is, subject to struggle from beginning to end. Public housing developments in most American communities typify this kind of public policy activity.

There is little difference, indeed, between the nature of the political battle over controversial policy in such localities and in the national and international spheres of interest. Thus, the American states, after some controversy, regulated private grain elevators and erected public ones as a matter of course. Later efforts to bring the national government into the field also was the cue for a renewal of controversy over the legitimacy of such regulation by national agencies.

One reason why national rather than local governments have engaged in large-scale projects is that the *instruments* of national policy are more varied and strong than those of any other authority. The national government has access to the total resources of a community; adequate financing and information may be obtained; and the enforcement of policy is likely to be relatively unhindered by problems of competing jurisdictions and limited police power.

WHAT JURISDICTION SHALL MAKE POLICY?

It is no more than fair to say that all attempts at setting up some principle whereby policy making can be organized most efficiently in one or another type of jurisdiction have failed. This failure has occurred not only because *special interests tend to advocate that kind of policy organization that will give them the most favorable treatment*. Many neutral observers have striven for such a principle. Thus in the field of state-federal relations, certain business interests in richer states prefer leaving expensive social legislation to the states, feeling that their tax rates will be raised if the federal government assumes such functions. But more neutral bodies, such as the Council of State Governments, have been unable to extract a principle for assigning one function to the federal government and another to the states.

Perhaps the major reason for this failure to establish a principle by which policy making will be organized under one jurisdiction rather than another is the weakness of political science to foretell sufficiently the consequences, direct and indirect, of any *species* of policy organization. This same inherent complexity produces disagreement about the relative merits of assigning decisions mostly to individuals (the Adam Smith idea) or to private groups. It may well be that there is no such thing as a "general principle" for assigning policy making to various levels. Perhaps the individual merits of assigning a task like policy to a local level or a national level may vary from time to time. Similarly, with road building, at one time the localities may be assigned the task because the national government may have "too many" things to do, although at another time the national government may build roads because the localities where roads are needed for national travel are too poor to build them.

The nearest approach to such a principle is the "scope of interdependence" idea. According to this theory, the policy of maximum effectiveness can be obtained in an organization whose scope includes all persons or events directly connected with the plan. Thus a railroad that operates only within one state or a sewage system that serves only one city should be controlled respectively by that state and that city. Similarly, a transcontinental railroad ought to be governed, if it cannot be left entirely to a private group, only by the national government.

The scope of interdependence is not, however, always a clear idea. Before it can be considered appropriate to a particular situation, one must have rejected the possiblities inherent in "natural" adjustments through the medium of supply and demand. The stated idea, that is, assumes that some political plan is necessary. Some matters, like the distribution of magazines and books, occur through many individual and private group plans with results considered generally to be satisfactory. Government intervention is not considered necessary for their adequate operation.

Moreover, the idea, when applied without foresight to a situation, may ignore considerations other than efficiency taken in a rather narrow sense. Assuming, for example, that a network of government restaurants throughout the land would provide everyone with cheaper meals, such a policy is not necessarily in order. Multitudes of people like to own restaurants or eat in quaint places. To take a more realistic example, many people would rather preserve the habit of doing business in the same county seat that served their grandfathers than to consolidate two counties into a single unit with a different county seat.

They would prefer tradition to efficiency and they are not impressed by the scope of interdependence idea.

The Goals of Policy

Whatever the group or jurisdiction that adopts a policy, the policy cannot be evaluated apart from its goals. If there is no goal, there is no achievement; if there is no goal, there can be no plan. If a government has no idea what it will spend its money for, its tax system can hardly be called a policy; it is merely an unplanned fiscal habit. We need to know the objectives behind political policy not only to talk sensibly about the means taken to achieve policy, but also in order to separate purposeful action from the medley of random and purely habitual action occurring in the political process at all times.

The chief methods of understanding the goals of public policy, the form of action that concerns us mainly here, are the statements of written law, the study of the legislative process, the study of the administrative process, and the reactive formations that arise to encounter any plan. In addition, nothing prevents us from hypothesizing goals for policies, based on our own values. Thus if we believe that, whatever they may state, policies must agree with public opinion, then we may interpret the goals of a policy in the light of what we know to be the public's views about the policy.

One must be careful in all cases, however, to state clearly the position he is taking in declaring what are the goals of a policy. Only terrible confusion can arise if one applies a mixture of motives and values to appraising the goals of a policy. He can, if he is unscrupulous or ignorant, assert that any policy is impractical by defining the terms of the goal to suit himself. For example, if one says that the negotiations in 1944 and 1945 that gave the occupation of Eastern Germany to Russia were intended to provide the United States with a predominant military position in Europe, then the means taken can easily be proved ineffective. But that would be falsifying the goals of the American representatives. In fact, military strength was only one motive; others included the desire to be friendly with the Soviet Union and the desire to end hostilities quickly and demobilize the American economy and armies. The rationality of the policy makers cannot be properly judged by ignoring their motives or imputing motives that are not present.

Another common example of this inversion of goal and plan is the kind of propaganda that says a goal is achieved no matter how far the plan has progressed. There is some reason to believe that the goals of the various four-year and five-year plans of totalitarian states have been redefined in view of what has been accomplished so as to cover the fact that the original goals were not met.

COMPLEXITY OF MOTIVES

Returning to the methods of studying goals, we should be most happy to be able to say that the face of a law gives its goals without doubt. Unfortunately this cannot be said. In the *Discourse on the Understanding of Statutes*, written during the reign of Queen Elizabeth, Egerton assures us how elusive is the intent of a statute: "So manie hedes as there were, so manie wittes; so manie statute makers, so manie minds." And we may quote two renowned latter-day legislators to show the doubts among the legislators themselves. Declared T. V. Smith: "The predicament of the legislator is that every vote is a dozen votes upon as many issues wrapped up together, tied in a verbal package, and given a single number of this bill or that. To decide what issue of the many hidden in each bill one wants to vote upon is delicate, but to make certain that the vote will be actually on that rather than upon another issue is indelicate presumption."

Paul H. Douglas, Senator from Illinois, expressed almost the same sentiments when he wrote of the roll calls of a session of the Senate: "As the clerk called our names, those of us on the Senate floor had to answer either 'aye' or 'no.' Many times we wished an issue had never arisen. Many times the issue itself is not clear. Many times we felt that the truest answer was neither 'aye' nor 'no' but 'maybe.' "

"LEGISLATIVE WILL" A USEFUL FICTION

In most cases, the interpretation of legislative will is not complete nor accurate in details. It must remain a general interpretation. As Paul Douglas stated: "In each vote on a particular measure the Senators also vote on a general principle. Indeed, it is the operation of the general principle on their thoughts which gives a discernible unity to most of their decisions." In the case of each legislator, so to speak, the whole is greater than the sum of its parts.

And so also are the goals of the corporate legislature more than the sum of goals of the individual legislators. The idea that there is a "legislative will" that can be found in a law is a fiction. Also it is a *necessary* fiction. The signed bill is like a bulkhead slammed against complexity and confusion. A new start is made; *the goal* is now set.

The bulkhead, however, is defective. Almost all public bills use general terms to describe general situations and to describe general methods and general ends. In order to summarize its prescription, the bill must distort the summed-up goals. Since a summary often lacks precision and requires interpretation, this distortion may occasion controversy later on, requiring the reopening of inquiry into the original motives.

From this inescapable condition of the legislative process, we are led to conclude that *any directive put forth by many minds* and *any general directive put forth by a single mind* will lack complete clarity, and that greater clarity can only come from the minds through which the directive filters—the administrators, judges, and the affected or interested

FIGURE 53. THE FATE OF THE GOALS OF PUBLIC POLICY

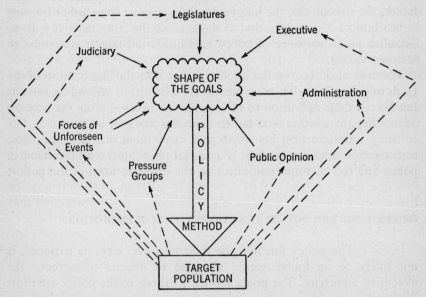

The policy method is conditioned by the shape of the goals; its effects are conditioned by the reactions of the target population, which (1) resist and/or modify the policy method and (2) send signals to the forces that shape the goals.

population. We may thence conclude that the goals of policy are conditioned by all influential elements in the political process (see Figure 53). *What exists as the central core of the goals of policy is a ponderable motive, a generalized and often high-powered surge in a given direction.*

PROPAGANDA STRUGGLES REGARDING GOALS

One can foresee how, under such conditions, an undiminished, though more limited, struggle will accompany the policy process. There is little possibility that goals will be so precisely drawn as to make their execution purely a question of administrative efficiency. All the forces that originally lock in struggle over the first statement of a goal return to the struggle to interpret the goal. For example, the original and subsequent federal legislation regulating the operation of radio stations left to the Radio Commission and, later on, the Federal Communications Commission, the task of seeing that radio broadcasting was conducted according to the "public interest." The struggle among many groups to define the "public interest" has raged undiminished for twenty-five years. In general, this process of interpreting the goal continues over a long period of time—one might say until the policy is functioning smoothly—but it is really longer than that—until the policy becomes habitual behavior on the part of the affected population. In this struggle, every participant—the legislators, the executives, the judges, the lobbyists or some other interest —proclaims his interpretation of the goal as the true one and tries to establish an atmosphere of policy administration that is congenial to his own values.

We may also observe the important fact that the clarification of the goals of policy is itself a great power. He who utters general commands but leaves their definition to others may be revered after the manner of prophets or soothsayers, but he concedes much of his power in fact to those who interpret his words and carry them out in action. The organization of policy method is a crucial phase in the achievement of policy and has an important effect on the ultimate form of the policy.

ORGANIZING THE POLICY FUNCTION WITHIN JURISDICTIONS

The policy function, be it corporative, city, or national, is not likely to be found evenly assigned to officers throughout the executive hierarchy. The goals and the methods of the policy are most likely to be set in the offices where the most important decisions are made. This would be in the legislature and in the offices of the top executives. Thus the most important policy makers in the American federal government are to be found in the congressional committees and their staffs, in the offices of the President and his cabinet members, and in the offices of several major quasi-independent regulatory agencies like the Federal Communications Commission. One finds the same situation prevailing in other countries.

LEGISLATURES INDIFFERENT TO PLANNING

Legislatures have maintained an increasingly anachronous position with respect to the "knowing" and "planning" functions of government. Blessed with the collegiate spirit, they have neglected to ask themselves whether a group of amateurs might know everything about everything until the last great day. By contrast with the executive arm of the government, they have failed conspicuously in reinforcing their judgments and prescriptions with scientific planning aids. Old remedies for a lack of omniscience are available and are used. These are the committee sessions, the committee hearings, the committee reports—all ways of adjusting goals to realities and predicting the consequences of legislative policies.

But most observers are impressed rather by the febrility of the scientific legislation movement than by its slow growth in the twentieth century. Legislative drafting aids, reference services such as those the Library of Congress provides to Congressmen, the information granted freely by pressure groups, the help afforded by administrative agencies—all of these are embryos of planning agencies present in slowly developing form as adjuncts to legislatures. Legislators, on the whole, however, are slow to appreciate the instrumentalities of social science. They tend to regard streamlined legislative techniques that employ experts on social consequences (which, after all, is another name for social scientists) like people regarded the first automobiles— with suspicion, with awe colored by fear, and with uncertainty regarding the role that the new gadgets might play in their lives.

EXECUTIVE POLICY METHODS MORE PLANNED

In the executive branch of government, the situation has been different. We find important planning agencies in every department of the federal government and in the President's office. The agencies are quite confident of their ability to draw up the blueprints of political policy. One may mention, in the United States, the defunct National Resources Planning Board that, given the assignment to evaluate national human and material resources and the means to their full realization and utilization, strove mightily to furnish a grand scheme for the total organization of the American economy. Its career, ended by Congressional opposition, left an example that was not forgotten. Many of the interests, techniques, and even personnel of that older organization may be discovered in continuing staff agencies of the executive branch. Among them are the Bureau of the Budget, the Council of Economic Advisors, the National Security Council, and the National Security Resources Board. On a slightly lower level in the Security Establishment alone, one finds the Research and Development Board, the Munitions Board, the Joint Chiefs of Staff, and the Central Intelligence Agency.

As we can see from their titles, most staff planning agencies are preoccupied with national defense. In matters of war, few dispute the efficacy of planning (see Figure 54). On social and economic matters in peacetime, Congress lacks faith in over-all planning. The plans are made, nevertheless, but almost in private chambers, one might say.

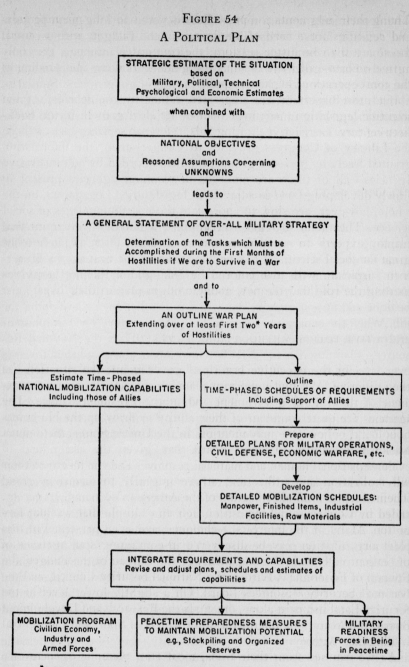

FIGURE 54

A POLITICAL PLAN

STRATEGIC ESTIMATE OF THE SITUATION
based on
Military, Political, Technical
Psychological and Economic Estimates

when combined with

NATIONAL OBJECTIVES
and
Reasoned Assumptions Concerning
UNKNOWNS

leads to

A GENERAL STATEMENT OF OVER-ALL MILITARY STRATEGY
and
Determination of the Tasks which Must be
Accomplished during the First Months of
Hostilities if We are to Survive in a War

and to

AN OUTLINE WAR PLAN
Extending over at least First Two* Years
of Hostilities

Estimate Time-Phased
NATIONAL MOBILIZATION CAPABILITIES
Including those of Allies

Outline
TIME-PHASED SCHEDULES OF REQUIREMENTS
Including Support of Allies

Prepare
DETAILED PLANS FOR MILITARY OPERATIONS,
CIVIL DEFENSE, ECONOMIC WARFARE, etc.

Develop
DETAILED MOBILIZATION SCHEDULES:
Manpower, Finished Items, Industrial
Facilities, Raw Materials

INTEGRATE REQUIREMENTS AND CAPABILITIES
Revise and adjust plans, schedules and estimates of
capabilities

MOBILIZATION PROGRAM
Civilian Economy,
Industry and
Armed Forces

PEACETIME PREPAREDNESS MEASURES
TO MAINTAIN MOBILIZATION POTENTIAL
e.g., Stockpiling and Organized
Reserves

MILITARY
READINESS
Forces in Being
in Peacetime

* In later chapters, there will be discussion indicating that U.S. industry probably requires one to two years to
reach peak war production, even with major peacetime measures of industrial preparedness.

Planning for military security as pictured by three West Point social scientists. Reproduced
with the permission of the publishers from G. A. Lincoln, W. S. Stone, and T. H. Harvey
(eds.): *Economics of National Security* (New York: Prentice-Hall, Inc., 1950), p. 73.

The departments contain many offices devoted to long-term projects and defining future needs. The Bureau of the Budget, with a central function not to be dismissed lightly—for fiscal planning is generally agreed to have good effects—has taken under its wing the planning of the total operations of the executive branch of government. Similarly, abroad, the British Treasury has played a staff planning role of great importance, owing in part to the preferred position its historical book-keeping function gave it.

RELATION OF STAFF PLANS TO OPERATIONS

A major problem faced by every authority in its internal planning is how to mesh plans into operations. There is likely to be great conflict between "thinking" and "acting" divisions of a department. Separating the planning into "thinking" and "acting" activities means in effect that you give to one office the right to say what must be done and how it must be done, and to another the task of doing the job. When the separation is great, the plans are developed in too general a form and operations remain anarchic. Thus the National Resources Planning Board (NRPB), mentioned above, tended towards ever broader reaches of ideas and projects. The actual power-drive of the executive branch was out of touch with the NRPB plans and went ahead little concerned with them. On the other hand, when policy method is left to the operating officers it often depends on mere lunch-hour hunches, or it is molded in the heat of solving immediate operational problems.

Perhaps both these extreme situations allow one to understand better why bookkeeping agencies tend to become effective planning agencies. Their work is intimately geared to operations. By handling the detailed transactions of all the offices, agencies like the British Treasury or the American Bureau of the Budget become acquainted with the total picture of agency operations. Yet the primary focus of attention of budget and financial officers on spending and saving inclines them towards a material evaluation of all problems. "Feasible" plans then become plans whereby the least is spent, everything can be accounted for in dollars and cents, and a maximum of standardized practice and central authority is maintained.

Planning within the organized authority, therefore, is systematic and effective in proportion to both its close sympathy with operations and its everyday aloofness from operations. It is also conditioned according to the motives that form the guiding influences within the planning agency—broad if the agency is top level, broad if the agency is not preoccupied with simple accounting.

WHEN A POLICY METHOD BECOMES A PLAN

In these last few pages, we have used the word "planning" with greater frequency. It seems to have been used as a synonym for "policy method." In fact, we have used "planning" to refer to one kind of policy method. As we have talked more and more about the large-scale agencies of governments and the huge and enduring projects in which they are engaged, we have gradually slipped into the use of the word *plan*, meaning by it *the conscious application of scientific method to assist in achieving the goals of policy*.

There is no need to define the term "political planning" too tightly. The line between the method a skillful executive uses to achieve his policy and the method a special staff of administrators and engineers uses to control the development of an atomic energy center is set by degrees according to four criteria: complexity of the goal, complexity of the method, size of the task, and duration of the task. When these four factors are considerable in a policy situation, what we call a *plan* is likely to emerge—that is, a complicated end result, the requirement of different special skills, an undertaking affecting millions of people, and an enduring operation combine to give an advantage to that organization of policy method called planning.

Reviewing again these factors that precipitate planning, we find that they are present in *all modern governments*. All governments today undertake numerous and complicated functions affecting the whole population over long periods of time. We should be very much surprised, therefore, if we heard nothing about planning in political discussion. The contrary, of course, is true; political planning is a most popular topic of political argumentation. It seems, however, if we listen carefully to the debate, that there is little disagreement over the question whether policy method should incorporate planning. Almost offhand, it is granted that if government is to undertake functions of great complexity and duration, political planning, as we use the term, should be substituted for haphazard and unscientific policy method.

The popular debate, however, has little to do with political planning versus hunch methods of carrying through policies. The real argument is whether or not the government *should or should not* undertake large-scale functions like regulating factories, operating mines and mills, or providing medical care to the whole population. We are tempted to ignore here this debate, having treated it briefly in Chapter Two and elsewhere, if it were not for one consideration. We must continue to insist that planning according to scientific methods is inevitable and necessary to maximize the rationality of public policy. This must be done as much for the benefit of those who are in favor of many government functions as for those who favor few public functions. Political planning is only partially understood when it is viewed as a way of streamlining the policy methods of government. Political planning is fully understood when it is viewed as a completely objective means of exposing the full consequences of policy. Many architects of planning today—be they executives or legislators—are like the magicians of early times, primitive scientists possessed of a few techniques and a dreadful role, unable themselves to see where their science ends and their quackery begins. This is said with malice towards no one but in an effort to emphasize the limitations of rationality in public policy today.

COMMON NEGLECT OF CONSEQUENCES IN POLICY AND PLANNING

It is rare indeed that a political policy or plan carries with it a full recognition of its political implications. A noteworthy historical exception that most countries have encountered is the attempt to keep military affairs under the control of civilians. An army is felt necessary but its potential political power is feared. Thus, although it made an exception in the case of General George C. Marshall, American law forbids a military man being chosen Secretery of Defense. But very often foresight is not part of the plan. For example, we have affirmation by the pens of writers like Robert Brady and Bruce Catton that many business leaders, faced with the inevitability of political planning, venture into the government to reconcile their own and the public interest to their own tastes, both in peace and war. It can be said that this phenomenon was scarcely predicted in the establishment of the Federal Trade Commission in 1914 but was better foreseen in the creation of the War Production Board in World War II. One also wonders, on this question of politization, how many civil service reformers realized that when they were taking appointive officeholders out of party politics, they were introducing a new kind of "administrative" politics among career officials. Or, when a new governmental function is established, how many realize that the prestige of politics tends to be enhanced and that of private business diminished?

Nor is it always foreseen how a new pattern of political planning will introduce a bureaucratic form of organization. So much is attention concentrated on the job to be done and whether it ought to be done that the inevitable machinery that follows is forgotten. No one has the remotest idea of the total impact of a given number of departments, bureaus, divisions, and positions on the economy. Rather, those who are "against bureaucracy" struggle against those who are "for bureaucracy" as if each new issue were the one that would make or destroy the social structure.

Sometimes the method used for the enforcement of public policy is deliberately inadequate. The American national minimum wages and hours legislation and civil rights legislation are only two examples of programs that were handicapped by insufficient staff and appropriations. More commonly, the goal of a policy is accompanied by a naive policy method. Wrote Thurman Arnold of the various attempts to restrain monopolies in America: "The actual result of the antitrust laws was to promote the growth of great industrial organizations by deflecting the attack on them into purely moral and ceremonial channels."

When political policy turns to the values of the people to be affected, it rarely considers the question of the varying particular demands, for the applied science of administration in its present state is secure only when it limits demands. It abhors complex or increasingly varied demands. We may illustrate how political policy in fulfilling one demand sometimes ignores equally meritorious demands. When the American federal government decided to grant money to the states for old-age assistance, aid to the blind, and aid to dependent children, most members of the government did not mean to "deprive" poor people of ordinary relief or foresee that such would occur. Yet, because the states had to match federal funds with their own money, the states tended to allocate their resources to the programs for which they would get equivalent federal money rather than to programs that they would support entirely by themselves. This and other cases showed that federal matching grants tended to "starve" nongrant programs of the states.

Controversy over the increased productivity that may or may not be induced by political planning is often confused—which means that it is often prey to decisions by political force and propaganda, rather than by true planning in a scientific spirit. If each new policy were assessed as to the necessary frustration it inflicts on some individual liberties, the indirect effects it has on the total redistribution of social resources, the necessary sacrifice of long-run technological improvements to the policy of supplying all needs, and the negative and positive effects on the workers involved, it might be better judged as a contribution or a handicap to a society.

IMPROVED SCIENCE OF PLANNING A VITAL NEED

The conclusion one comes to, after surveying contemporary experience, is that political policy and planning today tend to be most rational when their effects are most immediately perceived and most isolated from other social events. This experience indicates therefore that *political policy and planning can be rational at least to the extent of taking in all known and operating factors*. But political activity of this sort has been very rare in human history. Most existing legislation, examined in the light of what might have been known and foreseen but was not so known and foreseen because of various reasons, would be judged irrational. And if society has not collapsed under this burden of irrationality, it is because mankind is very durable and tough and because irrational policies and plans, like a defective slot machine, hand out lucky advantages as well as unlucky disadvantages.

As we know it today, the "planned society," in the last analysis, is itself unplanned. Special parts of it are rationally planned. The rest of it, product of despair in private planning and faith in public planning, moves on, an inexorable kismet. The only remedy for its planlessness —in local, national, and international affairs—is, strangely enough, faith in the idea of rational planning. If a science is so good as to explain beyond cavil some of what lies in store for mankind, it can command attention to desirable alternatives. In other words, liberty is as much fit subject for planning as regimentation.

That many social scientists have not realized this fact is apparent. In the Congressional hearings of 1947, relating to the proposed establishment of a National Science Foundation, Representative Harris Ellsworth expressed not only a prevailing worry among legislators but a grave weakness of past social science when he asked Dr. Robert M. Yerkes: "Would our further delving into this realm of social science that you have discussed have as its end product, or at least a tendency toward an end product, further regulation and restriction and possibly the ultimate limitation of human freedom?"

And Dr. Yerkes replied: "On the contrary. I should hope, and I would be willing to predict, that if the study of social problems is carried on intelligently and without bias it will increase freedom. The chances are that as we increase our knowledge and understanding of social behavior the individual will have larger freedom."

Mr. Ellsworth: "As we increase our knowledge of government it seems to me we pass more laws and further restrict our individual freedom."

Mr. Chairman: "I do not wish to prolong the discussion. I thank you very much for the answers, Dr. Yerkes."

Taking a cue from Mr. Chairman, we too may conclude. So long as political science trails behind events, speaking feebly in the terms of its past failures, it cannot hope to proclaim what is possible. Not in the past but in the program of a future science shall we be able to realize a political policy that says: "I give you what you need and more liberty too."

Questions and Problems

1. Define: "a liberty," "a right," "a social or political restraint," "a policy," "planning," "public policy."

2. Describe the different kinds of "rights" that are asserted in the constitutions of the world.

3. Examine the Constitution of the United States and of your state. List those rights that are explicitly asserted by each document. How do they compare with the world picture (Figure 48) as a whole? Do Americans have all the rights stated in other constitutions, even though they are not written into the American constitutions?

4. Following the form used on pages 584–6, which shows the process of liberty and restraints on housing, present another imagined situation from one of these areas: wages and hours of work; recreation; operating a shop or business; family relations; transportation; commercial fishing; civilian defense; or any other area with which you may be familiar.

5. In Figure 52, how do you explain the "Expansions of Freedom" reported in a small minority of cases in each sphere of life by men who are generally suffering a great constriction of freedom?

6. Define in detail the term "rational policy."

7. Why is it impossible to demand full rationality in public policy planning?

8. What are the principal ways of understanding the goals of policy?

9. What is meant by the useful fiction of "legislative will"? Is this the same kind of fiction as the fiction that "the law exists," described in Chapter Thirteen?

10. Why do policy goals always lack complete clarity?

11. How are policy goals continually reshaped by the political process?

12. Enumerate the ways in which liberty and policy may be organized.

13. Describe the Adam Smith theory of the substitution of liberty for public policy.

14. What are some of the characteristics of private group policy?

15. Name and describe briefly several ways of organizing public policy.

16. What is the theory of "scope of interdependence"? How might it be applied to the allocation of functions to state and federal authorities under federalism?

17. Describe how the policy function and planning are organized within the policy agencies of government (350 words).

18. When may a policy method be called a plan?

19. What are some of the common neglects of consequences in public policy planning today?

20. How can an improved social science contribute to liberty and public policy?

Longer Study and Research
Problems Suitable for Term Papers

1. Drawing together materials from various chapters in this book, prepare a memorandum for a United States Senator on how an improved social science can contribute to rational public policy, including more scientific ways of organizing liberty (15 pages).

2. Ask two people what five things they most dislike about the behavior of the government. Select the three dislikes that you understand most clearly and prepare a report on each, (1) analyzing the causes of such behavior by the government, (2) stating whether it is a condition capable of change in the foreseeable future, (3) stating what changes would be necessary in order to bring the stipulated change in the disliked behavior, and (4) presenting a practical program of action for accomplishing the required changes that would bring the stipulated change.

3. Prepare a co-operative, comparative report with another member of the class presenting your joint views on one of the following pairs of books (20 pages)

Barbara Wooten: *Freedom under Planning* and Ludwig von Mises: *Bureaucracy*

F. A. von Hayek: *Road to Serfdom* and Herman Finer: *Road to Reaction*

Frank J. Goodnow: *Politics and Administration* and Dwight Waldo, *The Administrative State*

Ordway Tead: *New Adventures in Democracy* and James D. Mooney: *The Principles of Organization*

Henri de Man: *Joy in Work* and J. A. Hobson: *Incentives in the New Order*

4. Keep a "Liberty and Policy Diary" for two weeks, recording scrupulously therein your daily activities of all kinds. At the end of the period, analyze the contents according to how many actions were "liberties," "politically restrained," "directed by public policies or other policies," and "planned." Summarize your findings under the title: "A case study on the effects of public policy on a college student." (Remember that the same action can have several motives.)

NOTES ON BIBLIOGRAPHY

CHAPTER 1

Thinking About Politics

I N T H I S N O T E on books and articles that relate to the first chapter, and in all the notes on the chapters to follow, only a small part of the published materials can be mentioned. The principles used in selecting the works cited are: importance to the field of political science, relevance to the text, readability for students, and availability in the college library. The student should know, first of all, that several general works contain understandable comments on many of the words and ideas of the present book. These are: The *Encyclopaedia of the Social Sciences;* *Encyclopaedia Britannica;* and *The Statesman's Year-Book.* On current affairs, *The New York Times, The Christian Science Monitor,* and *U. S. News and World Report* are good sources. The annual *Index* to the *New York Times* enables the student to find readily articles on the subject in which he is interested. In searching for articles on any subject, the student should go first to the *International Index to Periodicals* and then to the *Public Affairs Information Service,* which is a more specialized bibliography in the field of social science. On all general subjects of political science, one may well look into Laverne Burchfield's *Guide to Materials in Political Science* (1935). Many of the titles on political subjects appearing after the publication of Miss Burchfield's book have been listed in *The American Political Science Review* (hereafter cited as *A.P.S.R.*) in a special section on bibliography. Other important American periodicals dealing with political science are *The Political Science Quarterly* (hereafter cited as *P.S.Q.*), *The Journal of Politics, The Review of Politics, The Western Political Quarterly,* and *The Annals of the American Academy of Political and Social Science* (hereafter cited as *Annals*).

Turning to the contents of the first chapter, we can recommend a number of worthwhile works on the scope and method of political science. A careful reading of Aristotle's *Politics* and *Ethics* and Plato's *Republic* provide many rewarding insights into how a theory of political science as a whole may be constructed. By contrast, Niccolò Machiavelli's *The Prince* (1514) uses a hard, realistic approach to political science. Another, different approach to science than that of Plato and Aristotle may be had in John Dewey's *Logic: The Theory of Inquiry* (1938), which gives the "pragmatic" theory of science. James Bryant Conant's *Science and Common Sense* (1951) interprets the scope and method of science for laymen. A standard work of recent authorship is Morris Cohen's and Ernest Nagel's *Introduction to Logic and Scientific Method* (1934). It covers a very broad scope, ranging from formal logic to problems of using scientific methods in the study of social science. On things to come, read Paul H. Appleby, "Political Science, The Next Twenty-Five Years," *A.P.S.R.,* Vol. 44 (1950), p. 924. A report of the Committee for the Advancement of Teaching, American Political Science Association, presents lively discussions, for professor and student alike, on the contents and curriculum of political science. It is called *Goals for Political Science* (1951).

On the relationship between human science and natural science, several of the works just cited have pertinent materials. J. B. S. Haldane's *Human Biology and Politics* (1934) explores an interesting area of hereditary and environmental relationships. Caryl P. Haskins' *Of Societies and Men* compares animal and human groups. Morris Cohen writes understandably on "The Social Sciences and the Natural Sciences," in W. F. Ogburn and A. Goldenweiser (eds.), *The Social Sciences and Their Interrelations* (1927). Stuart Chase, in *The Proper Study of Mankind* (1948), directs his crusading pen to proclaiming the possibilities of new approaches to the study of human behavior that have produced successful results in industrial and governmental matters.

The members of the social science family are treated one by one in Ogburn and Goldenweiser, just cited. This collection of essays is perhaps the best available introduction to the ways in which the particular social sciences like Sociology, History, Psychology, Anthropology, and so on go about their work. For the impact of the other social sciences on political science one might turn to Charles E. Merriam's *New Aspects of Politics* (1931). In addition, the famous work by Langlois and Seignobos entitled *Introduction to the Study of History* (1909) presents in a remarkably easy style the methods and techniques of good historians. Equally rewarding is Louis Gottschalk's *Understanding History* (1950). Richard Hartshorne's article in *A.P.S.R.*, Vol. 29 (1935), pp. 785–804, 943–66, describes "Recent Developments in Political Geography." Slanted more towards research than Ogburn and Goldenweiser, but of great value in understanding the peculiarities of the various social sciences, is the Brookings Institution collection *Essays on Research in the Social Sciences* (1931).

A general work particularly devoted to political science is C. E. G. Catlin's *The Science and Method of Politics* (1930). The best compendium of definitions and the most systematic statement of important propositions in political science is Harold D. Lasswell and Abraham Kaplan, *Power and Society* (1950); the book is too difficult for introductory reading, however. Some of the particular techniques used by political scientists and their allies in social science are described in Marie Jahoda and others, *Research Methods in Social Relations* (2 vols., 1951); George A. Lundberg, *Social Research: A Study in Methods of Gathering Data* (1942); Pauline V. Young and Calvin F. Schmid, *Scientific Social Surveys and Research* (1939); John M. Pfiffner, *Research Methods in Public Administration* (1940); United Nations Educational, Scientific and Cultural Organization (U.N.E.S.C.O.), *Contemporary Political Science* (1950); and Ernest S. Griffith (ed.), *Research in Political Science* (1948). Specifically on the opinion polls, which get so much attention today, is Mildred Parten's *Surveys, Polls and Samples* (1950). Several cogent warnings about polls are contained in Lindsay Roger's short and readable book, *The Pollsters* (1949). An excellent report on interviewing techniques is Alexander Heard's "Interviewing Southern Politicians," *A.P.S.R.*, Vol. 44 (1950), p. 886.

Correct thinking on political subjects is of course discussed in all of the preceding works. Still, students will benefit especially from a consideration of Robert S. Lynd's *Knowledge for What?* (1939), which shows how the goals of modern man dictate much of the means and contents of modern science. On the conditions that influence the development of political science, it will be fruitful to read John Stuart Mill's *Essay on Liberty* (1859), especially Chapter Two on the liberty of thought and discussion, together with Charles A. Beard's statement of the "Conditions Favorable to Creative Work in Political Science," in the Supplement to *A.P.S.R.*, Vol. 24 (1930), pp. 25–32. We may mention finally a witty and instructive little book on correct thinking, Robert H. Thouless' *Straight and Crooked Thinking* (1932).

CHAPTER 2

The State and Authority

THE nineteenth century exhibited strong nationalism in Europe and the beginnings of nationalism in America and elsewhere. Understandably then, political scientists wrote many works describing the legal powers of the state. J. K. Bluntschli's *Theory of the State*, a German work translated into English in 1901, was one of the best and most influential of these, although it is not read much any more. The same may be said of the writings on the state of G. W. F. Hegel and Treitschke, both of whom exalted the state as the source of right and power. Alongside these nationalistic German writers may be placed the Marxian writers on the state. Perhaps the best short presentation of the ideas of Karl Marx and his immediate followers on the origin and nature of the state is to be found in Friedrich Engels, *The Origin of the Family, Private Property, and The State* (1888). Further understanding of the later Bolshevist phase of Marxism may come from reading Lenin's brief but influential work entitled *The State and Revolution* (1918). Influenced strongly by Marxist theory was Franz Oppenheimer's *The State* (first English translation, 1901), which set itself to disclose the origins of the state in conquest and slavery. A recent anthropological analysis of the state is contained in R. H. Lowie's *Social Organization* (1948), Chap. 14.

Democratic idealism, with a strong emphasis on the positive character of the state, is to be found in England in the work of T. H. Green, *Principles of Political Obligation* (1895), in France in the work of B. Bosanquet, *Philosophical Theory of the State* (trans., 1910), and in America in the book by Elijah Mulford entitled *The Nation* (1887). Herbert Spencer's *The Man versus the State* (1884) goes completely against idealistic and nationalistic beliefs by rejecting all but a bare minimum of activity on the part of the state.

More recently, H. J. Laski, in *The Problem of Sovereignty* (1917) and *Grammar of Politics* (1925), sought to destroy the theory of absolute sovereignty and recommended a decentralized and unintegrated state organization. An American, Mary P. Follett, in her *New State* (1918) also urges this "pluralistic" form of government. Materials on federalism are contained in the bibliographic note to Chapter Fifteen.

H. Krabbe's work on *The Modern Idea of the State* (1922) and R. M. McIver's *The Modern State* (1926) are two of the most prominent of recent treatises on the state. Carl J. Friedrich's *Constitutional Government and Democracy* (1950) is a general treatise on political science that, although somewhat difficult for beginning students, is well worth knowing for supplementary purposes now and for careful study in the future. In connection with the theory of sovereignty presented in this chapter, the student might well read John Dickinson's "A Working Theory of Sovereignty," *P.S.Q.*, Vol. 42 (1927), p. 542 and Vol. 43 (1928), p. 32. For a summary of much of the literature cited above, the student is referred to the series of essays on *History of Political Theories: Recent Times*, edited by C. E. Merriam and H. E. Barnes (1924).

The most striking theories of the social contract are to be found in Thomas Hobbes' *Leviathan* (1651), John Locke's *Second Treatise of Civil Government* (1690), and Jean-Jacques Rousseau's *Social Contract* (1762). For the social contract idea in America, see A. C. McLaughlin's "Social Compact and Constitutional Construction," *American Historical Review*, Vol. 5 (1900), p. 467.

Although much of the preceding literature deals broadly with the problem of authority, the chapter derives its discussion of legitimate authority principally from Max Weber's work, especially his *Theory of Social and Economic Organization* (trans., 1947), and his *Essays in Sociology* (trans., 1946). Sebastian de Grazia's *The Political Community* (1948) gives an extensive treatment of the psychological origins of authority. Charles E. Merriam's book on *Political Power* (1934) also goes into the subject of authority at some length.

On the weapons of power—magic, education, force, and economic measures with their nonlegitimate counterparts—Merriam's *Political Power* is again useful. Also useful are Bertrand Russell's *Power* (1938); Merriam's *The Making of Citizens* (1931); Bertrand de Jouvenel's *On Power* (trans., 1949); Georges Sorel's *Reflections on Violence* (trans., 1912); and Harold D. Lasswell's *Politics: Who Gets What, When, How* (1936). Special mention for its readability and shrewdness goes to Ignazio Silone's fictional dialogue with a would-be American dictator, entitled *School for Dictators* (1938). Many books on the political party are pertinent here, such as that of Frank Kent on *The Great Game of Politics* (1935). Other thought-provoking books on the way power is gained and held are G. Mosca's *The Ruling Class* (trans., 1939), and Roberto Michels's *First Lectures in Political Sociology* (trans., 1949).

All of the titles in this note necessarily treat of the extent and kind of state intervention in social relationships. To them may be added several others: W. W. Willoughby, *The Ethical Basis of Political Authority* (1930); Woodrow Wilson, *The State* (1903), Chaps. 15 and 16; G. D. H. Cole, *Social Theory* (1920); and J. O. Hertzler, *History of Utopian Thought* (1923). A student could compare Fascist Italy [Herman Finer's *Mussolini's Italy*, (1935)], Nazi Germany [Franz Neumann, *Behemoth* (1942)], Soviet Russia [Samuel N. Harper and Ronald Thompson, *Government of the Soviet Union* (1949)], Socialist England [B. de Jouvenel, *Problems of Socialist England* (1949)], and Capitalist America [A. N. Christensen and E. Kirkpatrick (eds.), *People, Politics and The Politician* (1950)]. The problem of the limits of intervention is ancient, it is sometimes necessary to note. Compare Plato's *Republic* and Aristotle's *Politics* for examples and early controversy on this point.

CHAPTER 3

Leaders and Followers

THOMAS CARLYLE's *On Heroes, Hero-Worship and the Heroic in History* (1888) and Leo Tolstoi's *War and Peace* (1864–9) (especially the last section of the novel) furnish an excellent introduction to the long-enduring controversy over the question of the leader's powers and limitations. General chapters on leadership, containing good summaries of the literature and something extraordinary in the way of analysis, are to be found in Gaetano Mosca's *The Ruling Class* (1939); H. D. Lasswell's *Politics: Who Gets What, When and How* (1936); Roberto Michels's *Political Parties* (1915) and his *First Lectures in Political Sociology* (trans., 1949); Chester Barnard, *The Functions of the Executive* (1938); Sidney Hook, *The Hero in History* (1945); Max Eastman, *Heroes I Have Known* (1942); and Niccolò Machiavelli, *The Prince* (1513). *Studies in Leadership* (1951), edited by Alvin Gouldner, contains many studies of different kinds of leadership.

The study of "Personal Factors Associated with Leadership," *Journal of Psychology*, Vol. 25 (1948), pp. 35–71, by Ralph M. Stogdill, referred to in the text, is first reading for anyone interested in the traits of leaders. His bibliography introduces some of the best literature on leadership in psychology. Also cited in the text is J. B. McConaughy, "Certain Personality Factors of State Legislators in South Carolina," *A.P.S.R.*, Vol. 44 (1950), p. 897.

More intensive studies of the development of individual leaders are to be found in: H. D. Lasswell, *Psychopathology and Politics* (1930); Max Nomad (pseud.), *Rebels and Renegades* (1932) and *Apostles of Revolution* (1939); C. E. Merriam, *Four American Party Leaders* (1926); J. T. Salter (ed.), *The American Politician* (1938); W. L. Riordan, *Plunkitt of Tammany Hall* (1905); Robert Sherwood, *Roosevelt and Hopkins* (1948); Harold Zink, *City Bosses in the United States* (1930); and Harold F. Gosnell, *Boss Platt and His New York Machine* (1924). John Dollard has furnished us with an analysis of valuable techniques for studying developing leadership in his work, *Criteria for the Life History, with Analyses of Six Notable Documents* (1935).

For material on the general functional skills of politics, the reader is referred to the works cited in the first paragraph of this note. But see also Harold D. Lasswell's *Power and Personality* (1949) and Chester Barnard's *Dilemmas of Leadership in the Democratic Process* (1939). The general functional role of politicians is a central subject in T. V. Smith's *Legislative Way of Life* (1940); L. D. White and T. V. Smith's, *Politics and Public Service* (1939); "The Army Challenge in South America," *Foreign Policy Reports*, Vol. XXV, No. 14 (Dec. 1, 1949); and H. D. Lasswell and Renzo Sereno's article entitled "Governmental and Party Leaders in Fascist Italy," *A.P.S.R.*, Vol. 31 (1937), p. 914.

On charismatic leadership, Max Weber's *Theory of Social and Economic Organization* (1947), pp. 324–8, 358 ff., and in other places, is difficult but rewarding. Sebastian de Grazia's *Political Community* goes into the early social environment from which people's attitudes towards top leadership emerges. See also E. H. Erikson, "Hitler's Imagery and German Youth," *Psychiatry*, Vol. 5 (1942), p. 475; and Jerome S. Bruner and S. J. Korchin, "The Boss and the Vote," *Public Opinion Quarterly*, Vol. 10 (1946), p. 1.

A number of articles have been written on the skill and class characteristics of corporate bodies such as legislatures and cabinets. The article by Lasswell and Sereno just referred to is pertinent here, as are also the following: On the United States, Madge McKinney, "The Personnel of the Seventy-Seventh Congress," *A.P.S.R.*, Vol. 36 (1942), p. 67; Charles Hyneman, "Who Makes Our Laws," *P.S.Q.*, Vol. 55 (1940), p. 556; W. B. Graves (ed.), "State Legislators," *Annals*, Vol. 195 (1938), 252 pp.: H. F. Gosnell, *Democracy: Threshold of Freedom* (1948), Chap. 12; C. Wright Mills and H. Schneider, *The New Men of Power* (1948), on labor leaders. On England, consult J. F. S. Ross, *Parliamentary Representation* (1943), which is a description and quantitative analysis of the ages, educations, occupations, hereditary titles, and party ties of 1,823 members of the House of Commons from 1918 to 1936; Simon Haxey (pseud.), *Tory M. P.* (1939), a survey of interlocking family and corporate relationships among Conservative M. P.'s; Harold J. Laski, *Studies in Law and Politics* (1932), pp. 181–201 on cabinet officers from 1801 to 1924. On France, see J. G. Heinberg, "The Personnel of French Cabinets," *A.P.S.R.*, Vol. 25 (1931), p. 389 and Vol. 33 (1939), p. 267, and D. W. Brogan, *French Personalities and Problems* (1946). On Germany, see Hans Gerth, "The Nazi Party: Its Leadership and Social Composition," *American Journal of Sociology*, Vol. 45 (1940) p. 517. On Soviet Russia, see Barrington Moore, jr., *Soviet Politics—the Dilemma of Power* (1950).

The literature on social class and political mobility is extensive but not too often rewarding. Among the more significant materials would be: Roberto Michels's *First Lectures on Political Sociology* (trans., 1949); John Dollard's *Caste and Class in a Southern Town* (1937); Richard Centers's *Psychology of Social Classes* (1949); Karl Marx and Friedrich Engels's *Communist Manifesto* (1848); A. N. Holcombe's *The New Party Politics* (1933); W. L. Warner and Associates'

Social Class in America (1949); Charles A. Beard's *The Economic Basis of Politics* (1945); G. Simpson's article, "Class Analysis: What Class is Not," in *American Sociological Review*, Vol. 4 (1939); and August B. Hollingshead, *Elmtown's Youth* (1949).

On the politists, that is, the politically active group in every society, Michels and Mosca, who have been cited previously, furnish much material. James Burnham's *The Machiavellians* (1943) presents the ideas of these men in a readable style. David Spitz attacks Burnham's views in *Patterns of Anti-Democratic Thought* (1949). George Seldes' *One Thousand Americans* (1947) gives a distorted opinion on the "real" sources of political decisions in America. André Siegfried's *America Comes of Age* (1927) and Ferdinand Lundberg's *America's Sixty Families* (1937) are somewhat outdated but pertinent to this subject. V. O. Key's *Southern Politics* (1949) is sound and revealing on the sources of political decision in the South.

Systematic investigations of leadership by procedures consonant with the theory presented in the last part of this chapter are becoming more frequent. The so-called "sociometric" technique is admirably displayed by Helen Hall Jennings in *Leadership and Isolation* (1947). I. Knickerbocker's article on "Leadership: A Conception and Some Implications," *Journal of Social Issues*, Vol. 4 (1948), p. 5, is worth careful reading. See also Ronald Lippett and R. K. White, "An Experimental Study of Leadership and Group Life," in T. M. Newcomb and E. L. Hartley (eds.), *Readings in Social Psychology* (1947), pp. 315–29; and Cecil A. Gibb, "The Principles and Traits of Leadership," *Journal of Abnormal and Social Psychology*, Vol. 42 (1947), p. 267.

CHAPTER 4

The Public and the Majority

SINCE, as has been shown, the public is part of the community, writings on the latter topic are most helpful in studying the public. Robert MacIver's work on the *Community* (1917) should be cited; it is readable, as are his first two parts in *The Web of Government* (1947). John Dewey's *Public and Its Problems* (1946), abstract though it is, is perhaps the best grounding a student may receive in the ideas of this chapter. Émile Durkheim's *Division of Labor* (reprinted 1947) is another basic sociological work demonstrating the conflicts, and yet the interdependence, between the community and the special interests of society. For a brilliant study, exploring the nature of the community that the ancient Mediterranean city-state produced, see Fustel de Coulanges, *The Ancient City* (1874). Community loyalties are closely related to nationalism and patriotism. For pertinent readings, see the note on bibliography to Chapter Eight, below.

The works already cited have much to say about the informal sanctions imposed by the community. See also William G. Sumner's *Folkways* (1907); Edward Jenk's *Law and Politics in the Middle Ages* (1898); B. Malinowski's *Crime and Custom in Savage Society* (1926); and R. H. Lowie's *Primitive Society* (1920). On collective behavior in general, Gustave Le Bon's *The Crowd* (1896), once influential but certainly exaggerated, set the stage for a number of later works. Sigmund Freud's *Group Psychology and the Analysis of the Ego* (1922) still is important, but is best read with some previous understanding of Freudian theory of individual psychology. Hadley Cantril in *The Psychology of Social Movements* (1941) uses the concepts of social psychology to account for various specific situations in history—lynching mobs, Father Divine, the Oxford Group, the Townsend Plan, and the Nazi Party.

More directly on the social, economic, and psychological transformations occurring in the modern community, one may consult the massive work of the President's Committee on Social Trends, entitled *Recent Social Trends* (1933), or the more recent work by Harry Elmer Barnes on modern *Society in Transition* (1939). A striking and significant early study of the trend from individualism to collectivism in political action is A. V. Dicey's *Lectures on the Relation between Law and Public Opinion in England in the Nineteenth Century* (1905). An understandable commentary on the mental difficulties facing many individuals who cannot adjust to the conditions of the great society is Karen Horney's *The Neurotic Personality of Our Times* (1937). Taking much of his theory from psychoanalytic psychology (as does Miss Horney), Erich Fromm, in his book *Escape from Freedom* (1941) describes how insupportable feelings of insecurity send many modern individuals in the directions of adulation of authority, destructiveness, and apathetic conformity. Graham Wallas' *The Great Society* (1914) and Sebastian de Grazia's *Political Community* (1948) are a rich mine of ideas on the kinds of interdependence that exist in modern communities compared with other societies. The nature of consensus is first stated and well defined by Walter Bagehot in his book, *The English Constitution* (1882). Several of the works above contain commentaries on the startling events that occurred in Germany between the two World Wars. To them may be added Frederick Schuman's book *The Nazi Dictatorship* (1935); Franz L. Neumann's *Behemoth: The Structure and Practice of National Socialism* (1944); and finally, for its jumble of mysticism and sharp insights into the psychological needs of masses of people, Adolf Hitler's *Mein Kampf* (unabridged ed., Reynal and Hitchcock, 1939). The story of Huey Long's Louisiana is to be found in Chapter Eight of H. F. Gosnell's *Grass Roots Politics* (1942), and the general political situation in Louisiana is analyzed in V. O. Key's *Southern Politics* (1949).

The Gosnell and Key books just cited contain excellent material on political separatism and voting behavior. *Political Behavior* (1928), by Frank R. Kent, is a general description of American politics that is readable and still true in many respects. Louis H. Bean's book *How to Predict Elections* (1948) is excellent on the distribution of basic party strength in the United States and the general factors conditioning shifts in the national vote. Cortez A. M. Ewing's books *Presidential Elections* (1940) and *Congressional Elections* (1947) are in the same field. Both works, as well as Bean's book, use extensively quantitative methods of presenting and analyzing data. Harold F. Gosnell has contributed other excellent works: *Voting and Non-Voting* (1924) with Charles E. Merriam; *Getting Out the Vote* (1927); *Why Europe Votes* (1930); *Machine Politics: Chicago Model* (1937), which is perhaps the most advanced book in the literature of voting behavior; and *Grass Roots Politics* (1942). Electoral behavior in Michigan is studied by James K. Pollock in *Voting Behavior: A Case Study* (1940); in urban centers by Samuel Eldersveld in the article "The Influence of Metropolitan Party Pluralities in Presidential Elections since 1920," *A.P.S.R.*, Vol. 43 (1949), p. 1189; in Ohio by Paul F. Lazarsfeld and others in *The People's Choice* (1948); and for much of western and northern Europe, and elsewhere, by H. Tingsten in *Political Behavior* (1937). All textbooks on political parties, such as those of V. O. Key, Peter H. Odegard and E. Allen Helms, and Dayton McKean, have sections dealing with electoral behavior.

In the specific field of public opinion, it is recommended that a student look first into Walter Lippmann's book *Public Opinion* (1922) and then perhaps into one of the standard textbooks such as that of Leonard Doob, *Public Opinion and Propaganda* (1948), Frederick C. Irion, *Public Opinion and Propaganda* (1950), or J. W. Albig, *Public Opinion* (1939). F. C. Bartlett's little book on *Propaganda* (1940) is easy to read and provides a good introduction to the subject. A fundamental distinction between community customs and public opinion is made by Ferdinand Tönnies in a work that was made available in English as *Fundamental Concepts of Sociology* (1940). Special problems of public opinion are studied in Max Lerner's *Ideas Are Weapons: The History and Uses of Ideas* (1939); Leo Rosten's *Washington Correspondents* (1940); Alex Inkeles' *Public Opinion in Soviet Russia* (1950); and Gabriel Almond's *The American People and Foreign Policy* (1950).

The literature on opinion polling has become vast. An easy introduction to the subject is provided by George H. Gallup and Saul F. Rae in *The Pulse of Democracy: The Public Opinion Poll and How It Works* (1940). Better, but more difficult, is Hadley Cantril and associates, *Gauging Public Opinion* (1944). A counterattack against some of the more grandiose claims of certain pollers is the book of Lindsay Rogers, *The Pollsters* (1949). H. F. Gosnell and Moyca C. David describe how polls and surveys of opinion have been used by the government in their article "Public Opinion Research in Government," *A.P.S.R.*, Vol. 43 (1949), p. 564. The opinion-survey organizations themselves publish many materials. Chief among such groups are the Institute for Social Research at the University of Michigan, directed by Rensis Likert, the National Opinion Research Center, directed by Clyde Hart, the Fortune Poll, directed by Elmo Roper, and the American Institute of Public Opinion Research, directed by George Gallup.

There is an excellent annotated bibliography on public opinion by B. L. Smith, H. D. Lasswell, and Ralph D. Casey, *Propaganda, Communication, and Public Opinion* (1946). Robin M. Williams, Jr., in a research memorandum entitled *The Reduction of Intergroup Tensions* (1947), comments on many specific proposals and efforts to ease racial and religious conflicts by the use of education and propaganda. He discusses the limitations of words in changing attitudes and conduct.

On the idea of the majority, consult the classic work of John Locke, *Second Treatise of Government* (1690) and of Jean-Jacques Rousseau, *The Social Contract* (1762). Willmoore Kendall's book, *John Locke and the Doctrine of Majority Rule* (1941) is a trenchant analysis of the meaning of the majority idea. J. G. Heinberg's article "History of the Majority Principle," *A.P.S.R.*, Vol. 20 (1926), p. 52, is also recommended.

CHAPTER 5

Representation and Elections

ON THE definition of representation, see the present author's *Public and Republic* (1951), Chap. 1 and H. F. Gosnell's *Democracy: Threshold of Freedom* (1948), Chap. 8. Robert Luce's *Legislative Principles* (1930) and John Fairlie's articles, "The Nature of Political Representation," *A.P.S.R.*, Vol. 34 (1940), pp. 236, 456, contain a number of meanings given the term "representation" by various writers. Charles A. Beard and J. D. Lewis are the authors of two stimulating articles on representation: "The Teutonic Origins of Representative Government," *A.P.S.R.* Vol. 26 (1932), p. 28; and "Representative Government in Evolution," *A.P.S.R.*, Vol. 26 (1932), p. 223. C. J. Friedrich has excellent chapters on representation in his *Constitutional Government and Democracy* (1950), Chaps. 14–17.

The historical career of the ideas of representation and representative government is treated to some extent in every standard textbook on English constitutional history. The best references are specialized works. See Maude V. Clarke's *Medieval Representation and Consent* (1936); May McKisack's *Parliamentary Representation of the English Boroughs during the Middle Ages* (1932); Ludwig Riess' *The History of the English Electoral Law in the Middle Ages* (Eng. trans., 1940); W. C. MacLeod's *Origin and History of Politics* (1931); Charles H. McIlwain's "Medieval Estates," *Cambridge Medieval History*, Vol. VII, p. 664; F. P. G. Guizot's *The History of the Origins of Representative Government in Europe* (Eng. trans., 1861); Charles H. McIlwain's *The High Court of Parliament* (1910); Edward and Anne Porritt's *The Unreformed House of Commons* (1903), Vol. I; and the present author's *Public and Republic* (1951), Chap. 2.

The American story of representation is contained in the present author's *Public and Republic* (1951); Kirk Porter's *History of Suffrage in the United States* (1918); indirectly, in various places, in Vernon Parrington's *Main Currents in American Thought* (1930); and in G. H. Hallett, Jr.'s and C. G. Hoag's *Proportional Representation* (1940). Experience with systems of representation here and elsewhere in the world is dealt with in John Stuart Mill's *Representative Government* (1861); F. A. Hermens' *Democracy or Anarchy?* (1941); J. Hogan, *Election and Representation* (1945); H. F. Gosnell's *Democracy: Threshold of Freedom* (1948) and in his *Why Europe Votes* (1930).

On modern problems of representation, in addition to the foregoing works there may be recommended: Charles Beard, *The Economic Basis of Politics* (1945); D. C. Blaisdell, *Economic Power and Political Pressures* (1941); Robert Brady, *Business as a System of Power* (1943); Mary P. Follett, *The New State* (1918); Pope Pius XI, *On Reconstructing the Social Order* (1931); Avery Leiserson, *Interest Representation in Administrative Regulation* (1942); and Belle Zeller and H. Bone, "The Repeal of PR in New York City," *A.P.S.R.*, Vol. 42 (1948), p. 1127.

The relations between constituents and representatives, besides being treated at length in several of the works cited in this note, are dealt with by T. V. Smith in *The Legislative Way of Life* (1940); W. Bagehot, *The English Constitution* (1867); S. and B. Webb, *Industrial Democracy* (1908), Chaps. 1–2; E. J. Flynn, *You're the Boss* (1947); G. W. Hartmann, "Judgments of State Legislators Concerning Public Opinion," *Journal of Social Psychology*, Vol. 21 (1945), p. 105; Roberto Michels, *Political Parties* (1915); and J. P. Chamberlain, *Legislative Processes, National and State* (1936), Chap. 4.

On party primaries, consult C. E. Merriam and Louise Overacker, *Primary Elections* (1928), and the election laws of the state in which one is interested. Such materials may usually be obtained from the Secretary of State. On the initiative and referendum, see Joseph G. La Palombara and Charles B. Hagan, "Direct Legislation: An Appraisal and a Suggestion," *A.P.S.R.*, Vol. 45 (1951), p. 400. The Southern primaries are discussed in V. O. Key's *Southern Politics* (1949) and textbooks on political parties contain chapters on nominating elections and other means of selecting nominees.

CHAPTER 6

Political Parties

POLITICAL parties are discussed in a large number of works dealing with government as a whole. Among them are: F. A. Ogg and Harold Zink, *Modern Foreign Governments* (1949); Herman Finer, *Theory and Practice of Modern Government* (1949); John C. Ranney and Gwendolen M. Carter, *The Major Foreign*

Powers: The Governments of Great Britain, France, The Soviet Union, and China (1949); Fritz Morstein Marx and others, *Foreign Governments* (1949); M. Oakeshott, *Social and Political Doctrines of Contemporary Europe* (1939); and *The Statesman's Year-Book* (annual). Only a few works treat of parties comparatively with reference to specific party problems. Such would be James K. Pollock's *Money and Politics Abroad* (1932); Louise Overacker's *Money in Elections* (1932); and H. F. Gosnell's *Why Europe Votes* (1930).

Turning to the American scene, one finds many books specifically about parties, and most textbooks on American government contain a small amount of party materials. Among the best are V. O. Key, *Politics, Parties and Pressure Groups* (1947); Peter Odegard and E. Allen Helms, *American Politics* (1947); Dayton McKean, *Party and Pressure Politics* (1949); H. F. Gosnell and C. E. Merriam, *The American Party System* (1949); E. M. Sait, *American Parties and Elections* (1942); E. E. Schattschneider, *The Struggle for Party Government* (1948); Hugh A. Bone, *American Politics and the Party System* (1949); and E. Pendleton Herring, *The Politics of Democracy* (1940); The *Journal of Politics* for May, 1948 is devoted to "The Southern Political Scene, 1938–1948," and the *Annals* of September, 1948, to "Parties and Politics: 1948." See also two sectional studies, V. O. Key, *Southern Politics* (1949) and T. C. Donnelly (ed.), *Rocky Mountain Politics* (1940).

Most general works on American parties contain sections on party history. The best general history of political parties in America is W. E. Binkley's *American Political Parties: Their Natural History* (1943). Other works describing party history are: F. R. Kent, *The Democratic Party* (1928); W. S. Myers, *The Republican Party: A History* (1928); C. A. Beard, *The American Party Battle* (1928); David Loth, *Public Plunder* (1938). On third parties, see S. J. Buck, *The Agrarian Crusade* (1921); J. D. Hicks, *The Populist Revolt* (1931); and Murray S. and Susan W. Stedman, *Discontent at the Polls*, (1950). James Bryce's *American Commonwealth* (1891) stands as an impressive commentary on American parties at an important phase of their development.

M. Ostrogorski, in *Democracy and the Party Systems* (2 vols., 1902), deals with the history both of American parties and of English and Continental parties. In addition, he wrote a lasting analysis of the social composition and internal organization of modern political parties. At this point, Roberto Michels's *Political Parties* (1915) should again be mentioned for its historical materials on European parties and for its acute analysis of the inner workings of parties. Chapter Seven of Michels's *First Lectures on Political Sociology* (1949) summarizes various plans to classify parties and discusses Max Weber's definition of the party. For those interested in analogies from ancient history, Lily Ross Taylor's *Party Politics in the Age of Caesar* (1949) will prove interesting. Seymour Martin Lipset has given us a remarkable study of a regional Canadian party in *Agrarian Socialism* (1950).

Returning to the American scene, one finds a number of special works, ranging from detailed studies of a certain party phenomenon to commentaries on the problems of the party system as a whole. Intimate glimpses of the party organization at work are found in F. R. Kent's *The Great Game of Politics* (1935); J. T. Salter's *The Pattern of Politics* (1940); Roy Peel's *The Political Clubs of New York City* (1935); E. E. Schattschneider's *Politics, Pressures, and the Tariff* (1935); Raymond Moley's *After Seven Years* (1939); Edward J. Flynn's *You're the Boss* (1947); James A. Farley's *Behind the Ballots* (1938); H. F. Gosnell's *Machine Politics: Chicago Model* (1937); and the two books of R. V. Peel and Donnelly on *The 1928 Presidential Campaign* and *The 1932 Presidential Campaign*.

On the subject of the English Labour Party and the English party system, see Dean McHenry, *The Labour Party in Transition, 1931–1938* (1938); G. M. Trevelyan, *The Two-Party System in English Political History* (1926); Eric Willenz,

"The Conservative Party in Britain Since 1945," *Social Research* (March, 1949); E. Wertheimer, *A Portrait of the Labour Party* (1929); H. Fyfe, *The British Liberal Party: An Historical Sketch* (1928); Max Beer, *A History of British Socialism* (1940); G. D. H. Cole, *A History of the Labour Party from 1914* (1948); and R. A. Dahl, "Workers' Control of Industry and the British Labour Party," *A.P.S.R.* (October, 1947); and J. M. Burns, "The Parliamentary Labour Party in Great Britain," *A.P.S.R.*, Vol. 44 (1950), p. 855.

The French party system is treated in W. R. Sharp, *The Government of the French Republic* (1938); G. Wright, *The Reshaping of French Democracy* (1948); and André Malraux and James Burnham, *The Case for De Gaulle* (1948). Certain aspects of the French and Italian party systems, and others of western Europe as well, are discussed by Gabriel Almond in "The Christian Parties of Western Europe," *World Politics* Vol. 1 (1948) p. 130; by A. T. Bouscaren in "The European Christian Democrats," *Western Political Quarterly* Vol. 2 (1949), p. 59; and by M. Einaudi, "Christian Democracy in Italy," *Review of Politics*, Vol. 8 (1947), p. 16. The onetime Fascist Party of Italy is adequately treated in Herman Finer's *Mussolini's Italy* (1935) and G. A. Borgese's *Goliath: The March of Fascism* (1937).

On the Russian Communist Party, a number of works are available, among them Samuel N. Harper and Ronald Thompson, *The Government of the Soviet Union* (1949); Sidney and Beatrice Webb's *Soviet Communism* (2 vols., 1936), Vol. II, pp. 529–601. Leon Trotsky's *The Revolution Betrayed* (1937) has important material on the great internal schism in the party during the twenties. Merle Fainsod brings the Communist Party up to date in his article "The Postwar Role of the Communist Party," pp. 20–32 in P. E. Mosely (ed.), "The Soviet Union Since World War II," *Annals*, Vol. 263 (May, 1949). See also Julian Towster, *Political Power in the U.S.S.R., 1917–1947* (1948); Barrington Moore, Jr., *Soviet Politics* (1950); and Philip Selznick, *The Organizational Weapon* (1952).

The bibliography on the other party systems of the world cannot be dealt with here. Current bibliographies, of the type mentioned in Chapter One, can furnish leads. Generally, any book treating of the government of a country will have a section on its political parties. Discussions of party trends and tendencies are scattered throughout the literature on political parties.

CHAPTER 7

Pressure Groups

MOST of the textbooks on political parties listed in the bibliographic note to Chapter Six, "Political Parties," have sections dealing with pressure groups, since such groups both work by themselves and through the political parties. The annotated bibliography by B. L. Smith, H. D. Lasswell, and R. D. Casey, called *Propaganda, Communication, and Public Opinion* (1946), is useful for many titles on promotional and pressure groups. E. P. Herring's *The Politics of Democracy* (1940); T. V. Smith's *The Legislative Way of Life* (1930); A. F. Bentley's *The Process of Government* (1908); James Madison's article No. 10 in *The Federalist Papers* (1788); and David B. Truman's *The Governmental Process* (1951) give general ways of looking at the role of pressure politics in political science. H. D. Lasswell and A. Kaplan, *Power and Society* (1950) presents a difficult and comprehensive scheme for analyzing human values.

On the operations of individuals in pressure politics, the following works contain interesting materials: Louise Overacker, *Money in Elections* (1932); Ida M. Tarbell, *The History of the Standard Oil Company* (1904); David Loth, *Public*

Plunder (1938); V. O. Key, *The Techniques of Political Graft* (1936); Eugene Staley, *War and the Private Investor* (1935); K. W. Swart, *Sale of Offices in the Seventeenth Century* (1949); John T. Flynn, *Graft in Business* (1931); Raymond Moley, *Politics and Criminal Prosecution* (1929); Fritz Thyssen, *I Paid Hitler* (1941); H. M. Bratter, "Committee for the Nation: A Case History in Monetary Propaganda," *Journal of Political Economy*, Vol. 49 (1941), p. 531; and H. H. Wilson, *Congress: Corruption and Compromise* (1951).

Various general works on lobbying include the following: Stuart Chase, *Democracy under Pressure* (1944); L. H. Chamberlain, *The President, Congress and Legislation* (1946); H. L. Childs (ed.), "Pressure Groups and Propaganda," *Annals*, Vol. 179 (May, 1935); R. S. Allen (ed.), *Our Sovereign State* (1949); Gunnar Heckscher, "Group Organization in Sweden," *Public Opinion Quarterly*, Vol. 3 (1939), p. 130; Dayton D. McKean, *Pressures on the Legislature of New Jersey* (1938); M. M. Grodzins, *Americans Betrayed* (1949); Madge M. McKinney, "Constitutional Amendment in New York State," *Public Opinion Quarterly*, Vol. 3 (1939), p. 635; Belle Zeller, *Pressure Politics in New York* (1937); and E. E. Schattschneider, *Politics, Pressures, and the Tariff* (1935).

On the lobbying of business groups, the following titles may be added: George L. Ridgeway, *Merchants of Peace: Twenty Years of Business Diplomacy through the International Chamber of Commerce, 1919–1938* (1938); R. C. Hall, "Representation of Big Business in The House of Commons," *Public Opinion Quarterly*, Vol. 2 (1938), p. 473; Robert A. Brady, *Business as a System of Power* (1943); Oland D. Russell, *The House of Mitsui* (1939); Richard Sasuly, *I. G. Farben* (1947); W. O. Douglas, *Democracy and Finance* (1940); Ernest Davies, *"National Capitalism": The Government's Record as Protector of Private Monopoly* (1939); The United States Temporary National Economic Committee, *Hearings* (30 vols., 1939–41), especially monograph No. 26 by D. C. Blaisdell, entitled *Economic Power and Political Pressures*; Jack Levin, *Power Ethics* (1931); and Charles S. Campbell, Jr., *Special Business Interests and the Open Door Policy* (1951).

On farmer pressures, see D. C. Blaisdell, *Government and Agriculture* (1940); J. E. Dalton, *Sugar, A Case Study of Government Control* (1937); J. M. Gaus and Leon D. Wolcott, *Public Administration and the United States Department of Agriculture* (1940); B. J. Hibbard, "Legislative Pressure Groups Among Farmers," *Annals*, Vol. 179 (1935), p. 7.

Labor union activity is dealt with in Louise Overacker's article "Labor's Political Contributions," *P.S.Q.*, Vol. 54 (1939), p. 56. The organization and techniques of political action from the point of view of the C.I.O. are incorporated in a *Manual of Practical Political Action*, published by the National Citizens Political Action Committee (1946, looseleaf binder with supplements). Frank Tannenbaum's *A Philosophy of Labor* (1951); C. Wright Mills and Helen Schneider, *The New Men of Power* (1948); H. L. Childs' *Labor and Capital in National Politics* (1930); L. L. Lorwin's *Labor and Internationalism* (1929); H. A. Marquand's *Organized Labor in Four Continents* (1939); J. B. S. Hardman and M. F. Neufeld (eds.), *The House of Labor* (1951); and W. H. Crook's *The General Strike* (1931) treat generally of the role of labor in politics.

Various additional studies of other kinds of pressure groups ought to be mentioned. Among them are: Oliver Garceau, *The Public Library in the Political Process* (1949); Arthur Maass, *Muddy Waters: The Army Engineers and the Nation's Rivers* (1951); L. C. Kesselman, *The Social Politics of FEPC* (1949); parts of Stephen K. Bailey, *Congress Makes a Law* (1950); Peter Odegard, *Pressure Politics: The Story of the Anti-Saloon League* (1928); Martin P. Harney, *The Jesuits in History* (1941); Luke Eugenie Ebersole, *Church Lobbying in the Nation's Capital* (1951); J. A. Hutchison, *We Are Not Divided: A Critical and Historical*

Study of the Federal Council of the Churches of Christ in America (1941); C. J. Child,
The German-Americans in Politics, 1914–1917 (1939); R. L. Jack, *History of the
National Association for the Advancement of Colored People* (1943); and Helen
Cam's enlightening essay on "The Legislators of Medieval England," *Proceedings of the British Academy* (1945), p. 127.

For an introduction to the problems of interest representation, the reader may
be referred to F. W. Coker's article "The Technique of the Pluralistic State,"
A.P.S.R., Vol. 15 (1921), p. 186; Mary P. Follett's *The New State* (1918);
Pope Pius XI's encyclical, *On Reconstructing the Social Order* (1931); G. D. H.
Cole's *Guild Socialism Restated* (1921); J. A. Hobson's *National Guilds and the
State* (1920); the preface to the second edition of Émile Durkheim's *The Division
of Labor in Society* (English trans., 1947); Alfred de Grazia's *Public and Republic*
(1951); Niles Carpenter's criticisms of pluralism in *Guild Socialism* (1922); and
Ralph H. Bowen's *German Theories of the Corporative State* (1947). The United
States National Resources Committee's report, *The Structure of the American
Economy: Part I, Basic Characteristics* (1939), presents some of the social elements on which the theory of interest representation must rest.

Special aspects of interest representation are treated in these works: G. L.
Field, *The Syndical and Corporative Institutions of Italian Fascism* (1938); L. S.
Lyon and others, *The National Recovery Administration* (1935); C. H. Monsees,
Industry-Government Co-operation (1944); A. N. Holcombe, *Government in a
Planned Democracy* (1934); E. P. Herring, *Public Administration and the Public
Interest* (1936); Oliver Garceau, *The Political Life of the American Medical Association* (1941); Carl D. Thompson, *Confessions of the Power Trust* (1932), esp.
Chap. 65; M. Louise Rutherford, *The Influence of the American Bar Association on
Public Opinion and Legislation* (1937); Nathan Reich, *Labour Relations in Republican Germany: An Experiment in Industrial Democracy, 1918–1933* (1938);
Georges Sorel, *Reflections on Violence* (1912); Avery Leiserson, *Interest Representation in Administrative Regulation* (1942); and J. A. C. Grant, "The Gild Returns to America," *Journal of Politics*, Vol. 4 (1942), pp. 303, 458.

CHAPTER 8

Civil Conflict and War

DEFINITIONS and theories of force and violence may be found in Charles E.
Merriam's *Political Power* (1934) and *Systematic Politics* (1947); in Bertrand
Russell's *Power* (1938); and in H. D. Lasswell's *Politics: Who Gets What, When,
How?* (1936); Hans Morgenthau treats international power systematically in his
Politics Among Nations (1949). Readable historical materials are to be found in
Frederick Schuman's *International Politics* (1949). Lyman Bryson and others contribute a noteworthy symposium on *Conflicts of Power in Modern Culture* (1947).

For the economic objectives of force and violence, see Lionel Robbins, *The
Economic Causes of War* (1939); Jacob Viner, "Power versus Plenty as Objectives
of Foreign Policy in the Seventeenth and Eighteenth Centuries," *World Politics*,
Vol. 1 (1948), p. 1. P. T. Moon, *Imperialism and World Politics* (1926); C. A.
Beard, *The Devil Theory of War* (1936); V. I. Lenin, *Imperialism: The Highest
Stage of Capitalism* (1933); and Francis Delaisi, *Political Myths and Economic
Realities* (1927). Students of American history will find of interest L. D. Baldwin's book, *Whiskey Rebels: The Story of a Frontier Uprising* (1939), and Avery
Craven's *The Repressible Conflict, 1830–1861* (1939). The prestige factor is the
subject of Harold Nicolson's lecture on *The Meaning of Prestige* (1947). The

Freudian theory of destructiveness is discussed in J. F. Brown's readable article "The Theory of the Aggressive Urges and War-Time Behavior," *Journal of Social Psychology*, Vol. 15 (1942), pp. 355–380; in E. Glover's *War, Sadism, and Pacifism* (1933); and in Ranyard West's *Conscience and Society* (1945). Other psychological analyses of the impulses to violence are: William James, *The Moral Equivalent of War* (1926); John Dollard and others, *Frustration and Aggression* (1939); John Cohen, *Human Nature, War, and Society* (1946); Edward C. Tolman, *Drives Toward War* (1942); E. R. Guthrie, *The Psychology of Human Conflict* (1938); E. F. M. Durbin and J. Bowlby, *Personal Aggressiveness and War* (1938); and Otto Klineberg, *Tensions Affecting International Understanding* (1950). On destructiveness as a feature of Nazism, F. Schuman's *The Nazi Dictatorship* (1935) and H. Rauschning's *The Revolution of Nihilism* (1939) are pertinent.

For general treatments of war through the ages, the reader may turn to Quincy Wright, *A Study of War* (2 vols., 1942); P. Sorokin's *Social and Cultural Dynamics* (4 vols., 1937–41), Vol. III; and Alfred Vagts, *A History of Militarism* (1937). The *coup d'etat* is clearly treated in Curzio Malaparte's *Coup d'état: The Technique of Revolution* (1932); Gaetano Mosca's *The Ruling Class* (1939), Chap. 8; and Aristotle's *Politics*, Book V. Those and the following works deal with the general subject of revolutions: Crane Brinton, *The Anatomy of Revolution* (1938); Jakob C. Burckhardt, *Force and Freedom* (1943); W. R. Hunter, *Revolution, Why, How, When?* (1940); V. I. Lenin, *The State and Revolution* (1917); G. Sorel, *Reflections on Violence* (1914); E. H. Carr, *Studies in Revolution* (1950); G. S. Pettee, *The Process of Revolution* (1938); and Bertram Wolfe, *Three Who Made a Revolution*, on the Russian Revolution (1948).

On national minorities, consult C. A. Macartney, *National States and National Minorities* (1934); Alfred Cobban, *National Self-Determination* (1948); and O. I. Janowsky, *Nationalities and National Minorities* (1945). On the subject of national character and nationality, see Ruth Benedict, *The Chrysanthemum and the Sword* (1946); D. W. Brogan, *The American Character* (1944); Frederick Hertz, *Nationality in History and Politics: A Study of the Psychology and Sociology of National Sentiment and Character* (1944); R. Michels, *First Lectures in Political Sociology* (1949) Chap. 8; Lyman Bryson, L. Finkelstein and R. M. MacIver, *Approaches to National Unity* (1945); and Ernest Barker, *Christianity and Nationality* (1927). Books and articles on nationalism are numerous. Among the best are: C. J. Hayes, *The Historical Evolution of Modern Nationalism* (1931); Hans Kohn, *The Idea of Nationalism: A Study of Its Origin and Background* (1944); E. H. Carr, *Nationalism and After* (1945); the Royal Institute of International Affairs, *Nationalism* (1946); and Luigi Sturzo, *Nationalism and Internationalism* (1946). On communism, see M. Einaudi and others, *Communism in Western Europe* (1951), and M. Ebon, *World Communism Today* (1948). On American foreign policies, see Samuel Flagg Bemis, "The Shifting Strategy of American Defense and Diplomacy," *Virginia Quarterly Review*, Vol. 24 (1948), p. 321.

On the decisions to make war and the reactions of men to international violence, consult the following: Homer, *The Iliad*; August C. Krey, *The First Crusade: The Accounts of Eye-Witnesses and Participants* (1921); Hugh E. Egerton, *Causes and Character of the American Revolution* (1923); Leo Tolstoi, *War and Peace*; Sidney B. Fay, *The Origins of the World War* (1930); Frederick L. Schuman, *Night over Europe* (1941); Winston Churchill, *The Gathering Storm* (1948); and Robert Sherwood, *Roosevelt and Hopkins* (1948).

On modern warfare, some of the better titles available are B. H. Liddell Hart, *The Revolution in Warfare* (1946); Bernard Brodie (ed.), *The Absolute Weapon: Atomic Power and World Order* (1946); Quincy Wright, *The Causes of War and the Conditions of Peace* (1935); and Hans Speier and Alfred Kahler (eds.), *War in*

Our Time (1939). The preceding works and the following analyze the elements of national military might: Hanson W. Baldwin, *The Price of Power* (1948); Robert Strausz-Hupé, *The Balance of Tomorrow* (1945); Nicholas J. Spykman, *The Geography of the Peace* (1944); Bertrand de Jouvenel, *On Power* (1949); Harold and Margaret Sprout, *Foundations of National Power* (1945); Étienne Dennery, "Democracy and The French Army," *Military Affairs*, Vol. 5 (1941), p. 233; H. D. Lasswell, "The Garrison State," *The American Journal of Sociology*, Vol. 46 (1941), p. 455, and Paul Linebarger, *Psychological Warfare* (1948).

A number of interesting works deal with the effects and limits of violence, unfortunately too many of them on international violence. Aldous Huxley's *Ends and Means* (1937) may be supplemented by Machiavelli's *Prince*; C. M. Case's *Non-Violent Coercion* (1923); R. B. Gregg's *The Power of Non-Violence* (1934); Reinhold Niebuhr's *Moral Man and Immoral Society* (1932), *Christianity and Power Politics* (1940), and *The Nature and Destiny of Man* (1943); M. J. Bonn's *Wealth, Welfare, or War* (1939); John Dewey's "Force and Coercion," *Ethics*, Vol. 26 (1916), pp. 359–67; Frederick S. Dunn's, *Peaceful Change* (1937). See also George B. de Huszar (ed.), *New Perspectives on Peace* (1944); and Gardner Murphy (ed.), *Human Nature and Enduring Peace* (1945).

CHAPTER 9

Law and Constitutionalism

DISCUSSIONS of what law is tend to be complicated and abstruse. The works of St. Thomas Aquinas and Max Weber referred to in the text are not suitable for introducing one to the law, nor are other important works such as Hans Kelsen's *General Theory of Law and State* (1945) or Roscoe Pound's "The Scope and Progress of Sociological Jurisprudence," *Harvard Law Review*, Vol. XXIV (1911), p. 591; XXV (1911–12), pp. 140, 489. Perhaps it is best to begin one's acquaintance with the nature of law by means of a book like William A. Robson's *Civilization and the Growth of Law* (1945), or Max Radin's *The Law and You* (1948), or Carleton K. Allen's *Law in the Making* (1939), or selections from Sidney Post and Julius Stone's *Cases and Readings in Law and Society* (1950).

Several good works explain the origins and nature of constitutions and constitutionalism: Charles H. McIlwain, *Constitutionalism Ancient and Modern* (1940) and *Constitutionalism and the Changing World* (1939); H. M. Clokie, *The Origin and Nature of Constitutional Government* (1936); and Francis D. Wormuth, *The Origins of Modern Constitutionalism* (1949). More specifically on American experience are Carl Van Doren's description of the writing of the American Constitution, *The Great Rehearsal* (1948) and the treatises of J. M. Mathews, *The American Constitutional System* (1940) and of Carl B. Swisher, *American Constitutional Development* (1943). Edward S. Corwin's *The Constitution and What It Means Today* (1948) is a readable and reliable interpretation of the American Constitution.

The subjects of the rule of law and juridical defense are treated in two books by A. V. Dicey on the *Introduction to the Study of the Law of the Constitution* (1926) and *Lectures on the Relation between Law and Public Opinion in Nineteenth Century England* (1924), and in Gaetano Mosca's *The Ruling Class* (trans., 1939). On the British constitution today, one may read W. Ivor Jenning's *The British Constitution* (1947), which is concise and clear, or H. R. G. Greaves' *The British Constitution* (1938). The constitutions of other governments of today are treated to some extent in the works on comparative government cited in the note to

Chapter Six. Additional works that may be cited are: Mario Einaudi, "The Constitution of the Italian Republic," *A.P.S.R.*, Vol. 42 (1948), p. 661 and R. G. Newman, "New Constitutions in Germany," *A.P.S.R.*, Vol. 42 (1948), p. 448. Carl J. Friedrich, in his *Constitutional Government and Democracy* (1950), especially Chaps. 1, 6–10, and 26, has perhaps the best general treatment of constitutional practice that is available.

Some of the preceding works are certainly useful in tracing the several essential elements of constitutionalism listed in this chapter. Striking more sharply at special points are: Benjamin N. Cardozo, *The Nature of the Judicial Process* (1925); John Dickinson, *Administrative Justice and the Supremacy of Law in the United States* (1927), on administrative powers over justice; Walton Hamilton and Douglas Adair, *The Power to Govern; The Constitution Then and Now* (1937), on economic concentrations; Emil Brunner, *Justice and the Social Order* (1945); and Charles A. Beard, *The Republic* (1943). On the subject of the separation of powers one may wish to look into Polybius' *History*, Book VI, the defense of the separation of powers in *The Federalist*, and the attack on the separation in J. Allen Smith's *Growth and Decadence of Constitutional Government* (1930). Clinton L. Rossiter's *Constitutional Dictatorship* (1948) is a study of crises of constitutionalism in Rome, France, Britain, Germany, and the United States. Recent works on civil-military relations are Harold D. Lasswell, *National Security and Individual Freedom* (1950); Silas Bent McKinley, *Democracy and Military Power* (1934); Jere Clemens King, *Generals and Politicians* (1951), and Jerome G. Kerwin (ed.), *Civil-Military Relationships in American Life* (1948). On church-state relations one may turn first to John N. Figgis' *Churches in the Modern State* (1913), and then perhaps to Alvin W. Johnson and Frank H. Yost, *Separation of Church and State in the United States* (1948).

The laws and constitutions in many ways cannot be separated from the operation of court systems and one will find references pertinent to the topics of this chapter in the bibliographic note to Chapter Thirteen.

CHAPTER 10

Legislatures

ADVANCED and general discussions of legislatures are to be found in Charles E. Merriam's *Systematic Politics* (1945), Gaetano Mosca's *The Ruling Class* (trans., 1939), and Carl J. Friedrich's *Constitutional Government and Democracy* (1950). Several historical studies depict the evolution of government by legislature: Edward and Annie Porritt, *The Unreformed House of Commons*, Vol. I (1903); A. F. Pollard, *The Evolution of Parliament* (1926); J. A. Thomas, *The House of Commons, 1832–1901* (1939); and D. W. Brogan, *The Development of Modern France* (1940). Williard Hurst, in *The Growth of American Law: The Law Makers* (1950), outlines the growth in legal functions from 1790–1940.

Bicameralism is the special subject of H. W. V. Temperley's *Senates and Upper Chambers* (1910); J. A. R. Marriott's *Second Chambers* (1927); and H. B. Lees-Smith's *Second Chambers in Theory and Practice* (1923). The bicameral problem is treated incidentally in two authoritative studies of the American Senate, Lindsay Rogers', *The Senate* (1926) and G. H. Haynes', *The Senate of the United States; Its History and Practice* (1938).

Among the many studies of the procedure and process of The American Congress may be mentioned: F. H. Riddick, *Congressional Procedure* (1941); Roland Young, *This is Congress* (1946); and George Galloway, *Congress at the Cross-*

roads (1946). Too formidable for quick reading but useful for reference and systematic study is Harvey Walker's *The Legislative Process* (1948). On England, one may turn to Harold J. Laski's *Parliamentary Government in England* (1938) and W. Ivor Jennings's *Parliament* (1940). For other nations one should consult one of the works on comparative government referred to in the notes on the chapters on political parties and on law and constitutionalism. One may select for special mention Herman Finer's *Theory and Practice of Modern Government* (1949), and, although they are preponderantly American in emphasis, Robert Luce's several works, *Legislative Procedures* (1922), *Legislative Assemblies* (1924), and *Legislative Principles* (1930). These last works, however, are much too massive to be digested as supplementary reading.

The book *Congress Makes a Law* (1950) by Stephen K. Bailey is one of the best of works that trace special enactments through the legislative process. The story of a legislative failure is contained in L. C. Kesselman's *The Social Politics of FEPC* (1949). Briefer histories of a number of enactments are presented in L. H. Chamberlain's *The President, Congress, and Legislation* (1946).

Grave forebodings about the future of legislatures are found in many quarters today. Gaetano Mosca's analysis of the decline of legislatures has been influential. H. J. Laski presents his own general viewpoint in "The Present Position of Representative Democracy," *A.P.S.R.*, Vol. 26 (1932), p. 629. There and in *Parliamentary Government in England* (1938) and in *The Rise of Liberalism* (1936), he felt legislatures too closely identified with the propertied interests to be adjustable to "inevitable" socialism. Lindsay Rogers, in *Crisis Government* (1934), and Harold Lasswell, in "The Garrison State," *American Journal of Sociology*, Vol. 46 (1941), p. 455, write convincingly of the difficult predicament of legislatures in modern times. James M. Burns in *Congress on Trial* (1950) elaborates on the political and structural handicaps that faced congressional leadership. A more optimistic view of the confusing ways of American legislatures is to be found in T. V. Smith's admirable recapitulation of the philosophy of the practical politician (if the latter could express it), *The Legislative Way of Life* (1940). Harold F. Gosnell, in *Democracy: Threshold of Freedom* (1947), contributes valuable materials to the understanding of why legislators must behave as they do. For a more intensive analysis of the problem of legislative leadership P. D. Hasbrouck's *Party Government in the House of Representatives* (1927) is useful.

The American executive rarely has excellent relationships with the legislature. The Burns, Galloway, Rogers, and Young books cited above are pertinent to this problem and so is W. E. Binkley's *The President and Congress* (1947). The strength of the legislature's power of granting funds is demonstrated for the American Congress in Arthur MacMahon's systematic and scholarly articles "Congressional Oversight of Administration," *P.S.Q.*, Vol. 58 (1943), pp. 161–90, 380–414. L. D. White makes several strong points about the ways in which Congress uses its powers to balk the executive establishment in his article "Congressional Control of the Public Service," *A.P.S.R.*, Vol. 39 (1945), p. 1. One who is specially interested in problems of appropriations may read Lucius Wilmerding, *The Spending Power* (1943), and Elias Huzar, *The Purse and the Sword* (1950).

The subject of the legislature's attempt to act in an informed fashion is treated in W. Brooke Graves, "The Legislative Reference Service for the Congress of the United States," *A.P.S.R.*, Vol. 41 (1947), p. 289; V. O. Key, "Legislative Control," in Fritz Morstein Marx, *Elements of Public Administration* (1946); "Congressional Investigations," *The University of Chicago Law Review*, Vol. 18 (1951), No. 3; and J. E. Johnson, *The Investigating Powers of Congress* (1951). On the subject of attempts at technical improvement of the legislative process the Council of State Governments' booklet, *Our State Legislatures* (1948) is especially recommended.

CHAPTER 11

The Chief Executive

POLITICAL science lacks an authoritative, broad study of the executive in society that would combine historical and social-psychological materials. One of the best ways to appreciate this need is to browse among the biographies of different historical figures like Julius Caesar, Edward III of England, Louis XIV of France, Frederick the Great of Prussia, Napoleon Bonaparte, Winston Churchill, Franklin Roosevelt, Andrew Carnegie, Henry Ford, Alexander Hamilton, and so on, looking for common ways in which policies are decided and carried out on a high level. Perhaps a good combination for an introduction to the study of executives would be afforded by the following works: Marshall E. Dimock, *The Executive in Action* (1945); T. N. Whitehead, *Leadership in a Free Society* (1936); Chester I. Barnard, *Functions of the Executive* (1938); Alexander H. Leighton, *The Governing of Men* (1945); and Roberto Michels, *First Lectures in Political Sociology* (1949). In addition, one should consult the titles on general administration contained in the bibliographic note to Chapter Twelve. The passages from Luther Gulick presented in the chapter come from Luther Gulick and Lyndall Urwick (eds.), *Papers on the Science of Administration* (1937).

The development of the American executive is treated in L. D. White's *The Federalists* (1948); George F. Milton's *The Use of Presidential Power, 1789–1943* (1944); Leslie Lipson's, *The American Governor: From Figurehead to Leader* (1938); and C. Perry Patterson's *Presidential Government in the United States* (1947). On the Presidency today, many studies exist, among them E. P. Herring, *Presidential Leadership* (1940); Harold J. Laski, *The American Presidency* (1940); E. S. Corwin, *The President: Office and Powers* (1948); Fritz Morstein Marx, *The President and His Staff Advisors* (1947); and Lindsay Rogers, "The American Presidential System," *Political Quarterly*, Vol. 8 (1937), p. 517. See also R. Bendix, *Higher Civil Servants in American Society* (1949). The executive's relations with the legislature are a favorite subject of comment by writers on the executive; to the studies cited above, however, may be added several works emphasizing the relationship: Wilfred E. Binkley, *The President and Congress* (1947); C. A. Beard, *The Republic* (1943), especially Chaps. 13, 15, and 18; George B. Galloway, *Congress at the Crossroads* (1946), especially Chap. 7; Ernest S. Griffith, "The Changing Pattern of Public Policy Formation," *A.P.S.R.*, Vol. 38 (1944), p. 445; W. Y. Elliott, *The Need for Constitutional Reform* (1935); and John D. Millett and Lindsay Rogers, "The Legislative Veto and the Reorganization Act of 1939," *Public Administration Review*, Vol. 1 (1941), p. 176.

With reference to the executive institutions of other lands, again, one may suggest one of the works on comparative government cited in the note to Chapter Six. Also refer to the last three paragraphs of the note to Chapter Ten. Karl Loewenstein, "The Presidency Outside the United States," *Journal of Politics*, Vol. 11 (1949), p. 447, presents a unique and succinct survey of the main presidencies of the world. The British executive is amply discussed in W. Ivor Jennings, *Cabinet Government* (1936). Franz Neumann makes important theoretical contributions to the study of the executive in his work on the German Nazi movement, *Behemoth* (1944). Barrington Moore, Jr.'s *Soviet Politics: The Dilemma of Power* (1950) or Samuel N. Harper and Ronald Thompson's *The Government of the Soviet Union* (1949) will provide one with a good understanding of the executive structure and system of controls in the Soviet Union.

CHAPTER 12

Public Administration

THE study of public administration is a well-established field. Two works, George A. Graham, *Education for Public Administration* (1941) and Joseph E. McLean (ed.), *The Public Service and University Education* (1949) show the extent to which specialized training in administration is provided by American universities. The literature on public administration is correspondingly abundant. Several textbooks describe the scope and principles of public administration, among them L. D. White, *Introduction to the Study of Public Administration* (1948); Herbert Simon, D. Smithburg, and V. Thompson, *Public Administration* (1950); Harvey Walker, *Administration in the United States* (1937); John M. Pfiffner, *Public Administration* (1946); Fritz Morstein Marx (ed.), *Elements of Public Administration* (1946); and W. Brooke Graves, *Public Administration in a Democratic Society* (1950).

General works emphasizing public administration elsewhere than the United States are: L. D. White and others, *Civil Service Abroad: Great Britain, Canada, France, Germany* (1935); Ernest Davies, *National Enterprise* (1946), on England; and C. J. Friedrich and Taylor Cole, *Responsible Bureaucracy: A Study in the Swiss Civil Service* (1932).

An important sociological analysis of administration is contained in Max Weber's *Essays in Sociology* (1946) and *The Theory of Social and Economic Organization* (trans., 1947). Gaetano Mosca's *Ruling Class* (trans., 1939) has a striking theory of the coming of bureaucratic society and Carl J. Friedrich's *Constitutional Government and Democracy* (1950) has a learned discussion of the problems of administration in a constitutional order.

The general works cited above provide material on the various categories of the chapter. In addition, on the objective of productivity and utilization of resources, we may recommend: Luther Gulick and Lyndall Urwick (eds.), *Papers on the Science of Administration* (1937); Herbert Emmerich, *Essays on Federal Reorganization* (1950); G. Bienstock, S. M. Schwarz, and A. Yugow, *Management in Russian Industry and Agriculture* (1944); S. D. Hoslett (ed.), *Human Factors in Management* (1946); Henri de Man, *Joy in Work* (trans., 1929); J. A. Hobson, *Incentives in the New Industrial Order* (1922); and Ludwig von Mises, *Bureaucracy* (1944).

The subject of minimizing the impact of administration on the affected population is nowhere treated systematically. Rather there is an abundant literature on forms of actions in the textbooks cited previously, with a considerable side-discussion of the problem of choosing the proper action at the right time. Most works on efficiency and productivity similarly develop this motive in administration as a by-product of efficient administration. Additional insights into the special problems of this objective of administration can be obtained from the following studies: J. M. Gaus, L. D. White, and M. E. Dimock, *The Frontiers of Public Administration* (1936); J. M. Gaus, *Reflections on Public Administration* (1947); and Gladys Baker, *The County Agent* (1939). The relation of administrators to public opinion is dealt with in J. L. McCamy, *Government Publicity* (1939); H. W. Stoke, "Executive Leadership and the Growth of Propaganda," *A.P.S.R.*, Vol. 35 (1941), p. 490; V. M. Sims, "Factors Influencing Attitudes towards the TVA," *Journal of Abnormal and Social Psychology*, Vol. 33 (1938), p. 34; Rensis Likert, "Opinion Studies and Government Policy," in *Research Frontiers in Human Relations*, Proceedings of the American Philosophical Society, Vol. 92, No. 5

(Nov. 12, 1948); J. L. Woodward, "Making Government Opinion Research Bear upon Operations," *American Sociological Review*, Vol. 9 (1944), p. 670; and Alex Inkeles, *Public Opinion in Soviet Russia* (1950). For titles pertinent to the subject of consultation with the affected population, one should refer back to the part of the bibliographic note to Chapter Seven on interest representation. Also consult Philip Selznick, *TVA and the Grass Roots* (1949) and J. W. Fesler (ed.), "Government and Water Resources," *A.P.S.R.*, Vol. 44 (1950), p. 575.

On the motive of personal advancement, an excellent introduction is L. D. White's *Government Career Service* (1935). A standard textbook on public personnel practices is W. E. Mosher and J. D. Kingsley's *Public Personnel Administration* (1941). On party politics and administration, the dialogue by L. D. White and T. V. Smith entitled *Politics and Public Service* (1939) is easily the best general work. Earl R. Fish's book, *Civil Service and Patronage* (1905) gives the history of spoils and reform in the civil service, but many important, related events have since occurred. Paul Appleby's *Big Democracy* (1945) provides fascinating reading on the informal side of administration in general and an intimate view of the connections between politics and administration. Textbooks on political parties, specially those of Merriam and Gosnell, and V. O. Key, cited in the bibliography to Chapter Six, discuss the relations between the patronage system and the civil service.

The customs of office, more formidably expressed as the problem of the bureaucratic personality, receive an excellent theoretical formulation by Max Weber in his works cited above. Other works on this subject are Roberto Michels, *Political Parties* (with reference to party organization); J. D. Kingsley, *Representative Bureaucracy* (1944, on England); Marshall Dimock, "Bureaucracy Self-Examined," *Public Administration Review*, Vol. 4 (1944), p. 197; Philip Selznick, "An Approach to a Theory of Bureaucracy," *American Sociological Review*, Vol. 8 (1943), p. 47; and Goodwin Watson, "Bureaucracy in the Federal Government," *Journal of Social Issues*, Vol. 1 (1945), p. 14. If the *Journal of Public Administration* is accessible, one may be entertained and instructed by reading Humbert Wolfe's article, "Some Public Servants in Fiction," Vol. 2 (1924), p. 39. Charles S. Hyneman, *Bureaucracy in a Democracy* (1950) has striking passages on the customs of office and in general supplements formal administrative analysis with poignant realism.

CHAPTER 13

The Courts

ONE may be introduced into the legal and judicial systems discussed in this chapter by way of the books by Post and Stone, Radin, and Allen, cited in the note to Chapter Nine, and by several others that we list here. Edmund M. Morgan and Francis X. Dwyer, *Introduction to the Study of Law* (1948) is an introduction to law put in the layman's language. John C. Gray's *The Nature and Sources of Law* (1924) covers well the law as enunciated by American courts. Ernest Mortenson's *You Be the Judge* is a practical and understandable inside view of the forms that trials, procedure, and judgments take in America.

Sir Henry Maine's *Ancient Law* (1887) is a hardy classic of research into the relations between law and politics and is clearly and interestingly written. Greek and early Roman law is discussed in Fustel de Coulanges, *The Ancient City: A Study on the Religion, Laws, and Institutions of Greece and Rome* (1874). For a comparison of the two great legal systems emphasized in this chapter, refer to

W. W. Buckland and A. D. McNair, *Roman Law and the Common Law* (1936). Fritz Schultz' *Principles of Roman Law* (1936) and W. S. Holdsworth's *A History of English Law* (1922) are two outstanding works from which comparisons can be made between Roman and English systems. The vital concept of precedent is the subject of an important comparative study by A. L. Goodhart called *Precedent in English and Continental Law* (1934). One should not overlook the excellent work of Charles H. McIlwain, *The High Court of Parliament and Its Supremacy* (1910), which relates law to representative institutions from their early origins. Many biographies of great jurists exist and constitute for some a pleasant method of immersion in legal materials; we may suggest here only *Edward Coke, Oracle of the Law* (1929), by H. Lyon and H. Block.

Existing judicial practice and court systems are treated in most works on comparative government. We recommend R. M. Jackson's *The Machinery of Justice in England* (1940). Broader in scope is the work of R. C. K. Ensor, *Courts and Judges in France, Germany, and England* (1933). Also of interest is Harold J. Berman's *Justice in Russia: An Interpretation of Soviet Law* (1950); (the quotation used at the conclusion of the chapter was borrowed from p. 194). On American courts and law, Roscoe Pound's two books are authoritative and not too difficult for persons without legal training: *The Formative Era of American Law* (1939) covers the interesting developments in American practice during the nineteenth century; *The Organization of Courts* (1940) is a contemporary survey. Evan Haynes' *The Selection and Tenure of Judges* (1944) deals with two subjects of constant concern to American politics.

The subject of judicial review is usually treated in works on the development of and changes in the American constitutional system. We refer the reader, therefore, to the books by Mathews, Swisher, and McBain cited in Chapter Nine. An additional work that may be specially recommended is R. K. Carr's *The Supreme Court and Judicial Review* (1942). Brief introductions to the subject of judicial review are to be found also in textbooks on American government, and in the legal dictionaries of Black and Bouvier.

When we turn to the judicial process and the political and social conditions that modify its operations, we are again reminded of Cardozo's influential book on *The Nature of the Judicial Process* (1925), which, beneath its even style and moderation of thought, contains a dynamic and enlightened scientific approach. The two books from which quotations were taken to illustrate common beliefs in fair procedure among different court systems are: Robert H. Jackson's report *International Conference on Military Trials* (1945) and his *Trial of the Major War Criminals before the International Military Tribunal*, Vol. 1 (1947).

E. S. Robinson, in *Law and the Lawyers* (1935), takes the legal profession to task for its lack of "responsibility" and "insight" into its habits and biases. This reorientation is again recommended by Harold D. Lasswell in an article titled "Self-analysis and Judicial Thinking," *Ethics*, Vol. 40 (1930), p. 354, and in a difficult article by Lasswell and M. S. McDougal on "Legal Education and Public Policy," reprinted in Harold D. Lasswell, *The Analysis of Political Behavior* (1948). *The Personality of the Judge* (1944), by Bernard L. Shientage and Jerome Frank's *Law and the Modern Mind* (1931) and *Courts on Trial* (1949) are works in the same tradition, striving to make judges and law more "objective" and scientific.

Studies in public opinion cited in the note to Chapter Four provide ample material on the pressure exercised by public opinion on the operation of the courts. One may also refer to Frank Shay, *Judge Lynch, His First Hundred Years* (1938). The consequences of a union between party politics and judicial process are revealed in sordid detail in Raymond Moley's *Politics and Criminal Prosecution* (1929). The career of the United States Department of Justice is traced in a clear but pedestrian manner in Homer Cummings and Carl McFarland, *Federal Justice* (1937). Someone someday ought to investigate the world's legal history to discover whether any court and judicial system in the world has ever given the poor equal treatment with the rich. One may start his reflections on this subject by reading Reginald H. Smith's *Justice and the Poor* (1919), unless he has previously read novels like Victor Hugo's *Les Misérables.*

The final question of the chapter: to what extent courts can become political ideologists and maintain due process, is a principal topic of Brooks Adams' *The Theory of Social Revolutions* (1913), in which Adams deplored the courts of the French Revolution and the increasingly overt biases of American courts on political issues. The changed character of the American Supreme Court after 1935 is the subject of a shrewd and relatively objective analysis by Arthur Schlesinger, Jr. in *Fortune* magazine (January, 1947), p. 202; it is called "The Supreme Court, 1947." Much of the change in court thinking in America has occurred in accord with the legal philosophy of Justice Brandeis, and one will read with profit the biography of this remarkable man by A. T. Mason, *Brandeis: A Free Man's Life* (1946). John B. Mason, in "The Judicial System of the Nazi Party," *A.P.S.R.*, Vol. 38 (1944), p. 96, discusses the changes introduced by the Nazi Revolution in Germany.

CHAPTER 14

Local Institutions

BEFORE mentioning works particularly devoted to local institutions, we should remind ourselves of the materials on local government that are readily accessible in many textbooks on general American government, on political parties and on comparative government and the state (see especially the bibliographic notes to Chapters Two and Six). Year-to-year developments in city government, together with much statistical data, may be found in the annual *Municipal Year-Book.* The history of local government is treated in W. B. Munro, *The Government of European Cities*, Chaps. 1, 11, 19, and 21; in Austin F. MacDonald, *American City Government and Administration* (1946), Chaps. 2–4; and in E. S. Griffith, *The History of American City Government* (1938). Many famous old cities like Athens, Rome, Florence, Venice, Genoa, Cologne, London, and Paris are the subjects of marvellous histories. Such works are too numerous to list here, but can be found in any good library. We might emphasize Fustel de Coulanges' *Ancient City* (1874), H. Pirenne's *Medieval Cities* (1925), and, for fascinating essays on the modern metropolis, Lewis Mumford's *The Culture of Cities* (1938) and *Technics and Civilization* (1934). H. S. Churchill, *The City is the People* (1945) and E. Saarinen, *The City: Its Growth, Its Decay, Its Future* (1943) are general discussions of urban physical planning in relation to urban culture.

A valuable collection of materials on regionalism is Merrill Jensen's *Regionalism in America* (1951); it contains historical, aesthetic, and political studies. On units of government, see William Anderson, *Units of Local Government in the United States* (1941) and Bureau of the Census, *Governmental Units in the United States, 1942* (1944).

The political and economic problems of urban civilization may be studied in Carroll H. Wooddy's chapter, "The Growth of Governmental Functions," Charles E. Merriam's chapter, "Government and Society," and other chapters in *Recent Social Trends in the United States*, 2 vols. (1936). Also consult the *Reader in Urban Sociology* (1951), edited by P. K. Hatt and A. J. Reiss, Jr. Two books on metropolitan functional problems are C. E. Merriam, Spencer Parratt, and Albert Lepawsky, *The Government of the Metropolitan Region of Chicago* (1933) and Victor Jones, *Metropolitan Government* (1942).

Other works on the political sociology of cities are R. E. Park and E. W. Burgess, *The City* (1921); R. D. McKenzie, *The Metropolitan Community* (1933); Ernest W. Burgess (ed.), *The Urban Community* (1926); and St. Clair Drake and Horace R. Cayton, *Black Metropolis* (1945). The last named work, incidentally to its important task of describing Negro urban society, summarizes a good deal of the literature of urban sociology. The James West study, quoted in the chapter, is *Plainville, U. S. A.* (1945). Besides the work by Warner cited in Figure 39, one may well look into his *Democracy in Jonesville* (1949), which is a study of the social structure of a Midwestern town.

Granville Hicks' *Small Town* (1946) is readable and full of insights into the political and social climate of semiurban America. The studies of a small Midwestern city by Robert and Helen Lynd, *Middletown* (1929) and *Middletown in Transition* (1937), deserve mention again in connection with this chapter. A book of articles by many journalists on their own cities, called *Our Fair City* (1949), of which R. S. Allen is the editor, provides enlightening glimpses into the politics, culture and economy of important American cities. C. E. Merriam, *Chicago: A More Intimate View of Urban Politics* (1929) contains the reminiscences of a political scientist on politics; V. O. Key, Jr., *Southern Politics* (1949) conveys a profound impression of the integration of political with social and economic cultures in Southern communities. Also see the works cited in the bibliographic notes to Chapters Six and Seven.

The study of local government, of course, centers on governmental institutions. On American local government, see Charles M. Kneier, *City Government in the United States* (1947); A. W. Bromage, *Introduction to Municipal Government and Administration* (1950); William Anderson and Edward Weidner, *American City Government* (1951); Roger H. Wells, *American Local Government* (1939); S. A. MacCorkle, *American Municipal Government and Administration*; C. F. Snider, *American State and Local Government* (1950); P. W. Wager (ed.), *County Government Across the Nation* (1950); L. W. Lancaster, *Government in Rural America* (1937); and T. B. Manny, *Rural Municipalities: A Sociological Study of Local Government in the United States* (1932). Specifically devoted to the city-manager plan are C. E. Ridley and O. F. Nolting, *The City Manager Profession* (1934) and Harold A. Stone, D. K. Price, and K. H. Stone, *City Manager Government in the United States* (1940). For information on the techniques of evaluating the performance of various city functions, consult Clarence E. Ridley and H. A. Simon, *Measuring Municipal Activities* (1943). William Anderson (ed.), *Local Government in Europe* (1939) has essays and documents on local government in England, France, Italy, Germany, and the Soviet Union. See also G. Montagu Harris, *Comparative Local Government* (1949). For more detailed studies of English Local institutions, see Herman Finer, *English Local Government* (1945) and W. E. Jackson, *Local Government in England* (1945).

The subject of state-local relations is an invariable part of any general work on local government. The best special work on the subject is the Council of State Government's *State-Local Relations* (1946).

A number of diagnoses of the ills of municipal government and of suggested cures are contained in R. V. Peel (ed.), "Better City Government," *Annals*, Vol. 199 (Sept. 1938). The articles cited in the text on the problem of local democracy in Germany are Hans Steinmetz, "The Problems of the Landrat: A Study of County Government in the United States Zone of Germany," *Journal of Politics*, Vol. 11 (1949), p. 318, and J. W. F. Hill, "Local Government in Western Germany," *Political Quarterly*, Vol. 20 (1949), p. 256. Monica Felton in "Democracy in Town and County Planning," *Political Quarterly*, Vol. 20 (1949), p. 74, writes perceptively and sharply of the differences between central government planning *for* localities and planning *in consultation with* localities. Herman Finer presents a concise summary of "The Case for Local Self-Government" in *Public Administration*, Vol. 3 (1943), p. 51. Finally, the reader may be referred to Rodney L. Mott's *Home Rule for America's Cities* (1949).

CHAPTER 15

Federalism

PROBABLY the broadest and most understandable introduction to the meaning of federalism is contained in Roscoe Pound *et al, Federalism as a Democratic Process* (1942). See especially the paper by C. H. McIlwain, "The Historical Background of Federal Government," contained therein. K. C. Wheare's *Federal Government* (1946) is the best comprehensive survey of federalism, although it has a somewhat distant and legalistic air about it which makes it difficult for beginning students. Sobei Mogi's *The Problem of Federalism* (2 vols., 1931) summarizes many historical treatises on and claims about sovereignty federation, and confederation.

Several interesting and competent works have been written on the varieties of federalism through time. Edward A. Freeman's *History of Federal Government in Greece and Italy* (1893) treats at great length certain ancient Greek and medieval Italian experiments in federalism. Arnold Brecht writes authoritatively of *Federalism and Regionalism in Germany* (1945) but his writing will probably be found more difficult for the student than the broader treatise of Rudolf Schlesinger, *Federalism in Central and Eastern Europe* (1946). On Australia, one may refer to A. P. Canaway, *The Failure of Federalism in Australia* (1930); on Argentina, to Frederick A. Kirkpatrick, *History of the Argentine Republic* (1931); on the British Commonwealth of Nations, to G. E. Elton, *Imperial Commonwealth* (1946) and to an article by K. C. Wheare, "Is the British Commonwealth Withering Away," *A.P.S.R.*, Vol. 44 (1950), p. 545; on Switzerland, to W. E. Rappard, *The Government of Switzerland* (1936); and on the Soviet Union, to P. Gronski, "The Soviet System of Federation," *A.P.S.R.*, Vol. 23 (1929), p. 159 and to Julian Towster, *Political Power in the U.S.S.R.* (1948). The problem of the movement for a union of western Europe after World War II is discussed in an article by Paul-Henry Spaak, "The Integration of Europe: Dreams and Realities," *Foreign Affairs* (October 1950), and in A. K. H. Boyd's *Western Union* (1948), and may be pursued in the current files of the newspapers. Other problems of international federalism are explored in various works on the League of Nations and the United Nations, to be cited in the note on the next chapter, and in H. A. Freeman and T. Paulling, *Coercion of States in Federal Unions* (1943) and J. A. R. Marriott, *Federalism and the Problem of the Small State* (1943).

The Federalist Papers (1788) are a good introduction to the essential structure of federalism in America. The latest and most comprehensive study of federalism in operation was made for the Commission on Organization of the Executive Branch of the Government and was published by the United States Government Printing Office as Senate Document No. 81, 81st Congress, 1st Session, under the title *Federal-State Relations* (1949). Jane P. Clark has given us an instructive and entertaining study of co-operative federalism in her *Rise of a New Federalism* (1938). Three works dealing with special aspects of American federalism that are important are: Louis W. Koenig, "Federal and State Cooperation under the

Constitution," *Michigan Law Review*, Vol. 30 (1938), p. 752; and Arnold Brecht, "Federalism and Business Regulation," *Social Research*, Vol. 2 (1935), p. 352. Finally, George Benson has written a book entitled *The New Centralization: A Study of Intergovernmental Relationships in the United States* (1941), which depicts the effects of technology and crisis on federal relations of the nineteenth-century kind in America.

CHAPTER 16

International Organization

AMONG the general works dealing with international organization and relations are: Robert Strausz-Hupé and Stefan T. Possony, *International Relations* (1950); Hans J. Morgenthau, *Politics Among Nations* (1949), which is somewhat difficult to read but contains excellent analytic thinking; and Frederick L. Schuman, *International Politics* (1949). All three works have different viewpoints and methods. Schuman has the easiest style. A shorter book, more suitable for supplementary reading, is *Persistent International Issues* (1947), edited by George B. de Huszar; it gives a broad view of several crucial problems by various experts. One should also refer back to the note to Chapter Eight for readings on war, power politics, and nationalism that are relevant to the topics of this chapter.

On international relations in the ancient world, we recommend several works. W. E. Caldwell's *Hellenic Conceptions of Peace* (1919) is interesting and useful on Greek ideas. Edward K. Rand, *The Building of Eternal Rome* (1943) discusses the ancient international community built up under Roman influence. On medieval times, we recommend G. G. Walsh's *Medieval Humanism* (1942). Dante Alighieri's *De Monarchia* (several translations available) is well worth the student's energies. The Austro-Hungarian Empire as an international holding company is described in R. A. Kann's *The Multinational Empire* (1950). Finally, we recommend S. J. Hemleben's *Plans for World Peace Through Six Centuries* (1943).

Discussions of the balance-of-power mode of organizing international relations are to be found in the general works initially suggested in this note, especially in Morgenthau's study. Nicholas Spykman's *America's Strategy in World Politics* (1942) is excellent on the general subject of the geography of international relations as well as the equilibrium. Frank Tannenbaum's article "The Balance of Power in Society," *P.S.Q.*, Vol. 61 (1946), p. 481, presents an abstract, broad analysis of the concept. Alfred Vagts relates the concept to America in his article "The United States and the Balance of Power," *Journal of Politics*, Vol. III (1941), p. 401. Martin Wight's *Power Politics* (1946) is also generally relevant.

On diplomacy, H. G. Nicolson's *Diplomacy* (1937) is outstanding and J. W. Thompson and S. K. Padover's *Secret Diplomacy* (1937) is exciting and perhaps a little exaggerated. J. Rives Childs' *American Foreign Service* (1948) is a description of American diplomatic work that may be compared with an ancient analogue, F. de Callières' *On the Manner of Negotiating with Princes* (1716, trans., 1919). William L. Langer's *The Diplomacy of Imperialism* (1935) covers authoritatively an important phase of modern diplomacy. Elmer Plischke's *Conduct of American Diplomacy* (1950) is a manual of diplomatic procedures and machinery. Good histories of American diplomacy exist, among them Samuel F. Bemis, *A Diplomatic History of the United States* (1950) and Thomas A. Bailey, *A Diplomatic History of the American People* (1950).

Three fine books can help one to understand international law: Arthur Nussbaum, *A Concise History of the Law of Nations* (1947); John L. Brierly, *The Law of*

Nations (1949); and Gerhart Niemeyer, *Law without Force* (1941), a sceptical examination of the pretensions of international law held by many people.

On the failure of the balanced-world idea today, we may recommend: Emery Reves, *The Anatomy of Peace* (1945), for a statement of the situation; W. T. R. Fox (ed.), *United States Policy in a Two-Power World* (1947); and William B. Ziff, *Two Worlds* (1947). The world order versus the world of independent powers is the theme of *The World Community* (1948), edited by Quincy Wright, and of Reinhold Niebuhr's *Christianity and Power Politics* (1940). The technological background of the world society is the subject of W. F. Ogburn's *Technology and International Relations* (1949).

Changes in international affairs are not always produced by war and unseen forces. It would be enlightening to examine one of these works on peaceful change: C. A. W. Manning (ed.), *Peaceful Change: An International Problem* (1937); Frederick S. Dunn, *Peaceful Change* (1947), and C. R. M. F. Cruttwell, *A History of Peaceful Change in the Modern World* (1937). A good formulation of the requirements that must precede a world legal order is Crane Brinton's *From Many One: The Process of Political Integration* (1948). For comment on the League of Nations, one may go to the general works cited in the first paragraph, and to Harriet E. David (ed.), *Pioneers of World Order: An American Appraisal of the League of Nations* (1944). On the administration of League affairs, Egon F. Ranshofen-Wertheimer, *The International Secretariat* (1945) is recommended. (The quotation in the chapter is from page xiii.) Herbert Vere Evatt's *United Nations* (1948) and Eugene Parker Chase's *The United Nations in Action* (1950) can supplement the general texts' discussion of the United Nations and one's reading of newspapers and periodicals. Werner Levi's *Fundamentals of World Organization* (1950) is an admirable broad discussion of the common bonds and basic conflicts underlying the movements for international organization. Alan de Rusett's *Strengthening the Framework of Peace* (1950) is a comprehensive and scholarly account of proposals to change or replace present international institutions designed to preserve peace.

CHAPTER 17

Thinking About Democracy

Some of the best books with which to begin one's thinking about democracy are famous classics. Most of them contain descriptions of democratic social settings as well as extensive and systematic analyses of questions of democratic theory. Among such books would be: Thucydides, *History of the Peloponnesian War*; Aristotle, *Politics*; Plato, *The Republic* and *The Laws*; Niccolò Machiavelli, *Discourses*; John Locke, *Of Civil Government* Pt. II; and Thomas Hobbes, *Leviathan*. These works and others, which are especially relevant to our statements about the disagreements among philosophers, are also pertinent to our inquiry into the different strains of democracy.

On modern democracy and its enemies, one may refer to Reinhold Niebuhr, *The Children of Light and the Children of Darkness* (1944); Charles E. Merriam, *The New Democracy and the New Despotism* (1939); Edward Heimann, *Communism, Fascism, or Democracy* (1938); and J. Roland Pennock, *Liberal Democracy; Its Merits and Prospects* (1950). A little book that progresses easily and clearly is George de Huszar's *Practical Applications of Democracy* (1945).

The number of works devoted to the general subject of democracy is legion. Mention of new ones and reprints of old ones appear in almost every issue of the

Book Review Section of the Sunday *New York Times*. Selecting the right ones to read should be done with the help of the instructor, for no subject is so likely to waste the time of the innocent reader as this one. One can, of course, rely on an excellent collection like that of W. Y. Elliott and N. A. McDonald, called *Western Political Heritage* (1949), for selections from a number of influential discussions of democratic theory and the democratic social setting, and one can trust the bibliography provided in such a work.

A number of readings on the subject of the social setting of democracy are available. First, we should call attention to the readings on constitutionalism listed in the note to Chapter Nine. Then we should point out that one of the best ways to steep oneself in the conditions of democracy is to read various plays and social novels by writers like Aristophanes, Molière, Voltaire, Stendhal, Manzoni, Dickens, Hugo, Mann, Forster, Steinbeck, and Huxley. To these we may add the descriptive writings of sociologists and anthropologists like the Lynds, the Kluckhohns, and William Whyte, and also the contents of newspapers, films, magazines, political speeches, and the endless variety of precise and objective studies in the journals of opinion and psychology. One man's experience is not enough to allow him to think fruitfully about democracy; he should achieve a great sympathy with all conditions and facts of social life.

A few books have described rather directly the political setting of democracy. Thucydides' history is one of them. Others are Henry J. Haskell's *The New Deal in Old Rome* (1947); Alexis de Tocqueville's *Democracy in America*, 2 vols. (1835 and 1840, trans., 1945); André Siegfried's books on England, France, and the United States—the last called *America Comes of Age* (trans., 1927); Fustel de Coulanges, *The Ancient City* (1874); Mary P. Follett, *The New State* (1926); C. L. Becker, *Modern Democracy* (1941); R. W. Davenport (ed.), *U. S. A. The Permanent Revolution* (1951); Alfred M. Bingham, *The Techniques of Democracy* (1942); Hans Kohn, *Force or Reason* (1937); Frank Tannenbaum, "On Certain Characteristics of American Democracy," *P.S.Q.*, Vol. 60 (1945), p. 343; D. W. Brogan, *The American Character* (1944); A. D. Lindsay, *The Modern Democratic State* (1943), Vol. I; Richard Carlton Snyder and Hubert Wilson (eds.), *Roots of Political Behavior* (1949), Chaps. 11–12. The cool and systematic analysis contained in *American Society* (1951), by Robin M. Williams, Jr., deserves attention and applause.

It is not surprising that many of the works already listed should also concern themselves with what democracy ought to provide. But we may add other studies that are especially pertinent to each of the four strains of democracy. For studying egalitarian democracy, *The Leveller Manifestoes of the Puritan Revolution* (1944), collected and edited by Don M. Wolfe, are useful; so are the following works: Alfred Cobban, *Rousseau and the Modern State* (1934); Thomas Paine, *The Age of Reason* and *The Rights of Man* (both contained in *Works*, Foner (ed.), 1945); Vernon Parrington, *Main Currents in American Thought* (1930); Alfred de Grazia, *Public and Republic* (1951); John Dewey, *Freedom and Culture* (1939); Émile Faguet, *The Cult of Incompetence* (trans., 1912); H. S. Commager, *Majority Rule and Minority Rights* (1943); and E. F. M. Durbin, *The Politics of Democratic Socialism* (1940).

On conservative democracy, one may turn to Edmund Burke, *Burke's Politics: Selected Writings and Speeches*, edited by R. J. S. Hoffman and Paul Senack (1949); R. White (ed.), *The Conservative Reaction* (1950), a collection of famous conservative writings; R. B. Perry, *Puritanism and Democracy* (1944); the difficult but masterful study of Perry Miller, *The New England Mind* (1939); Walter Bagehot, *The English Constitution* (1867); Quintin Hogg, *The Case for Conservatism* (1947) which is a plea in contemporary terms for the British Conservative Party; and Peter Viereck, Jr., *Conservatism Revisited* (1948).

For light on elitist democracy, one may refer to several widely differing works. W. A. Orton writes understandably in *The Liberal Tradition* (1945), explaining many of the ideas that dominated nineteenth-century humanitarian and liberal thought and action. John Stuart Mill's *Representative Government* (1861) is a most subtle combination of factual observations about politics and defense of "rational and enlightened" leadership. J. Ortega y Gasset's *Revolt of the Masses* (trans., 1932) is a remarkably prescient book about contemporary mass movements and cherishes an established, legal, and cultural order against the onslaughts of egalitarianism. Benedetto Croce's *History as the Story of Liberty* (trans., 1941) presents an idealistic and liberal interpretation of history. Walter Lippmann, in *An Inquiry into the Principles of the Good Society* (1937), proposes leadership by a politically skilled, informed, and active public opinion. T. S. Eliot, in his *Notes towards a Definition of Culture* (1949), suggests that there are grave disadvantages to a culture that is not led by a social class. Finally, Jacques Maritain interprets the teachings of St. Thomas Aquinas for modern society in his *Freedom in the Modern World* (1935).

Relativist democratic thought can be drawn from the writings of James Madison (see, for example, some of his selections in the *Federalist*); A. F. Bentley, *The Process of Government* (1908); C. W. Morris, *Pragmatism and the Crisis of Democracy* (1934); T. V. Smith, *The Promise of American Politics* (1936); and E. Pendleton Herring, *The Politics of Democracy* (1940). The relation of capitalism to relativist democracy is implied by many economists such as Von Hayek, but is more clearly realized by Harold J. Laski in his *Rise of Liberalism* (1936) and by Werner Sombart in his *Quintessence of Capitalism* (trans., 1915).

CHAPTER 18

Liberty and Public Policy

EXTENDED discussions of rights, liberty, and freedom will be found in many of the works cited in the note to the last chapter. These words are as broad as one wishes to make them, and they may be used as the central themes of a whole book or as incidental parts of the total work. To aid in considering the words as they are used in this chapter, one may consult, in addition to the works previously listed, John Stuart Mill's essay on *Liberty* (1859); John E. E. D. Acton's *The History of Freedom and Other Essays* (1907); Delisle Burn's *Political Ideals* (1929); and Bertrand Russell's *Proposed Roads to Freedom* (1919). Selections from American discussions on liberty and restraints may be found in Francis W. Coker's general collection, called *Democracy, Liberty and Property: Readings in the American Political Tradition* (1943). Our usages of the words liberty, restraint, rights, and policy have similarities with the usages of economists, and one might therefore wish to consult Frank Knight's *Freedom and Reform* (1947) and F. A. von Hayek's *The Road to Serfdom* (1944), although no subscription to their beliefs is intended. Frank Tannenbaum's *A Philosophy of Labor* (1951) is a perspicacious essay on the unwitting conservatism of trade unionism.

A solid foundation for reflecting on the meaning of public policy is provided by Charles A. Beard's *Public Policy and the General Welfare* (1941), by Charles E. Merriam's *On the Agenda of Democracy* (1941), by Carl J. Friedrich and E. S. Mason (eds.), *Public Policy* (1940), by E. S. Griffith, "The Changing Pattern of Public Policy Formation," *A.P.S.R.*, Vol. XXXVIII (1944), p. 445; and by Barbara Wooton's *Freedom under Planning* (1944), a small book of readability and consequence. G. D. H. Cole's *Principles of Economic Planning* (1935) is an explanation and defense, like Wooton's, of British socialist ideas. One may compare both works with Arthur N. Holcombe's short book entitled *Government in a*

Planned Democracy (1935), which does not presuppose socialism as a consequence of extensive use of government policies, but which does foresee a wider use of functional representation in the government.

Two works may be employed to introduce one to the factors explaining the increase in public policy on economic affairs. They are F. E. Lawley's *The Growth of Collective Economy* (1938) and S. Eldridge (ed.), *The Development of Collective Enterprise* (1943). H. L. Marx has edited a compilation of speeches and articles called *The Welfare State* (1950), intended for scholastic debaters. But too often we consider policy as economic only, disregarding that policies and their plans are often social and cultural more than economic and that economic policies have all kinds of social effects. It would be well, then, to read Leonard W. Doob's *The Plans of Man* (1940), or John Dewey's *The Public and Its Problems* (1946), or Graham Wallas' *The Great Society* (1914); all of these works place public policy and planning in their broad and proper settings. One may broaden his scope also by reading R. S. Lynd's "Planned Social Solidarity in the Soviet Union," *American Journal of Sociology*, Vol. 51 (1945), p. 183; or Morton Grodzins' *Americans Betrayed* (1948), which traces in great detail public policy of the different levels of government with reference to the Japanese-Americans during World War II; or by observing the social effects of government economic planning in the Tennessee Valley in Philip Selznick's *TVA and the Grass Roots* (1949); or by understanding how the military operates as described in Otto Nelson's *National Security and the General Staff* (1946); or by watching the making of foreign policy in Sumner Welles' *Seven Decisions that Shaped History* (1951).

Ludwig von Mises' *Bureaucracy* (1944) emphasizes what are generally considered to be the unfavorable and unforeseen consequences of extensive government intervention in economic matters and decrees that scientific planning is impossible. David Mitrany has written an excellent article entitled "The Political Consequences of Economic Planning," *The Sociological Review*, Vol. 26 (1934), p. 321.

When we turn to the large problem of the organization of policy determination and planning, we find that the works by Doob, Dewey, and Wallas cited above are highly relevant. Wallas' chief purpose, for example, is to determine the capabilities of political organization for making rational policies, and the last chapter of Dewey's work is a remarkable invitation to democratic societies to employ the scientific method in order to survive.

More specifically on the machinery of planning, several works may be cited: John D. Millett, *The Process and Organization of Government Planning* (1947); L. L. Lorwin, *Advisory Economic Councils* (1931); Henry Bunbury, *Governmental Planning Machinery: A Comparative Survey* (1938); and Oliver Franks, *Central Planning and Control in War and Peace* (1947). The general works on public administration cited in Chapter Twelve have sections also on planning; the Simon, Smithburg, and Thompson work has a clear chapter devoted to defining and characterizing planning in general and within agencies.

Several books and articles are addressed to the technical problems of sharpening executive policy faculties; among them are: H. M. Clokie and J. W. Robinson, *Royal Commissions of Inquiry* (1937); Fritz Morstein Marx, "Commissions of Inquiry in Germany," *A.P.S.R.*, Vol. 30 (1936), p. 1134; and Russell Sage Foundation, *Effective Use of Social Science Research in the Federal Services* (1950). See also H. B. Creighton's *Political Control of Science in the U.S.S.R.* (1950).

Finally, the role of individual social scientists in relation to policy planning is discussed in a popular article by Harold D. Laski, "Limitations of the Expert," *Harper's Magazine* (December 1930), p. 62; Peter H. Odegard, "The Political Scientist in the Democratic Service State," *Journal of Politics*, Vol. 2 (1940), p. 140; and Florian Znaniecki, *Social Role of the Man of Knowledge* (1940.)

INDEX

*Page numbers in italics refer to works
cited in the* NOTES ON BIBLIOGRAPHY.

A NOTE ON THE TYPE
IN WHICH THIS BOOK IS SET

This book is set in Monotype Bell, a copy of the English Mono-type face of the same name. The Englishman John Bell (1745–1831) was responsible for the original cutting of this design. The vocations of Bell were many—among a few might be mentioned bookseller, printer, publisher, type-founder, and journalist. His types were considerably influenced by the delicacy and beauty of the French copper-plate engravers. Monotype Bell might also be classified as a delicate and refined rendering of Scotch Roman.

Composed, printed, and bound by Kingsport Press, Inc.,
Kingsport, Tennessee
Designed by Harry Ford